Niles Public Library District
6960 Oakton Street • Niles, Illinois 60714
Phone 847-663-1234

DATE DUE	DATE DUE

DICTIONARY OF THEOLOGICAL TERMS

ALAN CAIRNS
General Editor

Belfast and Greenville

DICTIONARY OF
THEOLOGICAL TERMS

Copyright © 1998 Alan Cairns

First edition published by the Whitefield College of the Bible, 1982
Second edition published by Ambassador-Emerald International, 1998

Ambassador-Emerald International

Ambassador Productions, Ltd
Providence House
16 Hillview Avenue
Belfast, Northern Ireland BT5 6JR
United Kingdom

Emerald House Group, Inc.
1 Chick Springs Road, Suite 203
Greenville, SC 29609
USA
www.emeraldhouse.com

Published in Association with
Whitfield College of the Bible
Laurencetown, Banbridge,
Co. Down, Northern Ireland
United Kingdom

Printed in Canada

Preface

The second edition of this dictionary has been a long time coming. The first edition has been out of print for some twelve years, during which time many people have asked for it to be reprinted. I felt, however, that I needed to revise and enlarge the original work considerably, and in the midst of a busy pastorate and teaching schedule, it was not easy to find the necessary time to complete the work.

That the job has been done at all is due in no small degree to the dedicated help I have received from a number of people. To Mary Christopher and my wife, Joan, for typing the manuscript, I am deeply indebted. Dr. Michael Barrett made time in the midst of teaching summer school at Bob Jones University to read the manuscript and check my theology, logic, and use of the Biblical languages. Judy Brown and Sara Elliott were my editors, always having to work against the clock and trying to get me to write decent English—not an easy job! Debbi Spears and my wife not only helped in proofreading but checked every Bible reference in the book. Laurie Hartz spent many hours researching copyright permissions, and a volunteer army of proofreaders helped check the final proofs: Carl Abrams, Sandra Barrett, Marie Bayer, Rachel Carper, Alice Cromley, Amy Dickerson, Sara Elliott, Gene Elliott, Sue Farr, Jan Gardner, Alice Gingery, Gail Gingery, Vanessa Greeley, Christa Habegger, Randy Habegger, Jennifer Knutson, Charles Koelsch, Verta Koelsch, Grace Ludlum, Carolyn McNeely, Rosemary Nelson, Susan Peck, Mark Sidwell, Debbi Spears, and Lynn Wiser. These folk deserve a major part of the credit for getting this dictionary ready for Stephen Christopher to prepare for the press. To every one of them I offer my sincere thanks.

I am also grateful to Ambassador Publications for their patience and encouragement throughout this project, and to the Whitefield College of the Bible which initially prompted the idea that led to the publication of the first edition back in 1982.

Most of all, I am grateful to our triune God for His help and grace in the work. The study of Christian theology is a thrilling and blessed privilege. It is a labour of love to try to make the great truths of the faith accessible to God's people in a form they can readily use. I trust that the Lord will be pleased to seal the united efforts of all the people I have mentioned with His mighty blessing. No one realizes the limitations of my work better than I; nevertheless I commit it to God with the prayer I have often prayed during the preparation of the book: that He will be pleased to use it for the glory of His name and for the edification of His people.

Alan Cairns
Faith Free Presbyterian Church
Greenville, South Carolina.
August 1998

Acknowledgements

I wish to acknowledge use of the following sources:

D. R. Ap-Thomas, *A Primer of Old Testament Text Criticism* (Minneapolis: Fortress Press, 1966); Gleason L. Archer, *A Survey of Old Testament Introduction* (Chicago: Moody, 1964); L. Berkhof, *Systematic Theology* (Edinburgh: Banner of Truth Trust, 1939); G. C. Berkouwer, *The Providence of God* (Grand Rapids: Eerdmans, 1952); Loraine Boettner, *The Reformed Doctrine of Predestination* (Philadelphia: Presbyterian and Reformed, 1932); Loraine Boettner, *Roman Catholicism* (Philadelphia: Presbyterian and Reformed, 1962); Emil Brunner, *The Theology of Crisis* (New York: Scribners, 1929); E. J.Carnell, *The Case for Orthodox Theology* (Philadelphia: Westminster, 1959); E. J.Carnell, *A Philosophy of the Christian Religion* (Grand Rapids : Eerdmans, 1952); *Catechism of the Catholic Church* (Washington, D. C.: United States Catholic Conference, 1994); Stewart Custer, *The Truth about the King James Version Controversy* (Greenville, S.C.: Bob Jones University, 1981); K. R. Davis, *Anabaptism and Asceticism* (Scottsdale, Pa., 1974); C. H. Dodd, *The Parables of the Kingdom* (New York: Scribners, 1935); Sinclair B. Ferguson and David F. Wright, eds., *New Dictionary of Theology* (London: Universities and Colleges Christian Fellowship, 1988); Everett Harrison, ed. *Baker's Dictionary of Theology* (Grand Rapids: Baker Book House, 1960); R. K Harrison, B. K. Waltke, D. Guthrie, G. D. Fee, *Biblical Criticism: Historical, Literary and Textual* (Grand Rapids: Zondervan, 1978); Hank Hanegraaff, *Counter-feit Revival* (Waco, Texas: Word Publishing, 1997); C. S. Hawkins, *Goddess Worship, Witchcraft and Neo-Paganism* (Grand Rapids: Zondervan, 1998); Edward F. Hills, *Believing Bible Study*, 2d ed. (Des Moines: The Christian Research Press, 1967); Edward F. Hills, *The King James Version Defended* (Des Moines: The Christian Research Press, 1956); Paul K. Jewett, *Infant Baptism and the Covenant of Grace* (Grand Rapids: Eerdmans, 1978); Donald T. Kauffman, ed. *Baker's Pocket Dictionary of Religious Terms* (Donald T. Kauffman, 1967); Reginald Kimbro, *The Gospel According to Dispensationalism* (Toronto, Ontario: Wittenberg Publications, 1995); R. C. Lenski, *The Interpretation of St. Paul's Epistle to the Romans* (Minneapolis: Augsburg, 1936); R. C. Lenski, *The Interpretation of St. Paul's Epistles to the Galatians to the Ephesians and to the Philippians* (Minneapolis: Augsburg, 1936); Lefferts A. Loetscher, ed., *Twentieth Century Encyclopedia of Religious Knowledge* (Grand Rapids: Baker Book House, 1955); Richard P. McBrien, *Catholicism: Study Edition* (New York: Winston Press, 1981); John Warwick Mont-gomery, *The Suicide of Christian Theology* (Minneapolis: Bethany Fellowship, 1970); John Murray, *Collected Works* (Edinburgh: Banner of Truth, 1976); J. Barton Payne, *The Theology of the Older Covenant* (Grand Rapids: Zondervan, 1962); Wilbur Pickering, *The Identity of the New Testament Text* (Nashville: Thomas Nelson, 1977); Ron Rhodes, *New Age Movement* (Grand Rapids: Zondervan, 1995); Rousas John Rushdoony, *Institutes of Biblical Law* (Phillipsburg, N.J.: Craig Press, 1972); Robert C. Torbet, *A History of the Baptists* (Philadelphia: Judson Press, 1950); Merrill F. Unger, *New Testament Teaching on Tongues* (Grand Rapids: Kregel Publica-tions, 1971); J. K. Van Baalen, *The Chaos of the Cults* (Grand Rapids: Eerdmans, 1938); Jakob Van Bruggen, *The Ancient Text of the New Testament* (Manitoba: Premier Printing, 1978); Cornelius Van Til, *A Survey of Christian Epistemology* (Philadelphia: den Dulk Christian Foun-dation, 1969); W. E. Vine, *Expository Dictionary of New Testament Words* (London: Oliphants, 1940); Geerhardus Vos, *Biblical Theology* (Grand Rapids: Eerdmans, 1948); B. B. Warfield, *Biblical Foundations* (London: Tyndale, 1958); Ernst Wurthwein, *The Text of the Old Testament* (Grand Rapids: Eerdmans, 1979); Gunther Zuntz, *The Text of the Epistles: A Disquisition upon the Corpus Paulinum* (London: Oxford University Press, 1953).

Cross Referencing System

Throughout this work an asterisk after a word or phrase denotes another entry in the dictionary. The *form* of the word so marked may not be the same as that of the title of the article referred to. For example, "Pentecostal"* directs the reader to the article on "Pentecostalism," and "antinomian"* to the article on "Antinomianism."

Major Reference Works Abbreviations
Almost all works quoted or referred to are identified by name in the text; however, the following are abbreviated throughout:

I.S.B.E. . . . . *The International Standard Bible Encyclopedia*
McClintock and Strong . . *Cyclopedia of Biblical, Theological, and Ecclesiastical Literature*
Schaff Hertzog . . . . *Twentieth Century Encyclopedia of Religious Knowledge*

References
Reference to a multi-volume work is by volume number followed by a colon and the page number(s). Thus volume two, page 248 of Charles Hodge's *Systematic Theology* would appear as "Hodge, *Systematic Theology,* 2:248."

Abbreviations of Bible Versions
All quotations in this dictionary are from the Authorized Version of the Scriptures. The following abbreviations appear:

AV	Authorized Version, often called the King James Version
GNB	Good News Bible
NASB	New American Standard Bible
NEB	New English Bible
NIV	New International Version
REB	Revised English Bible
RSV	Revised Standard Version
RV	Revised Version

General Abbreviations

cf.	*compare*
chap.	*chapter*
ca.	*about*
e.g.	*for example*
f. or ff.	*and the following* verse(s) or page(s)
ibid.	*the same work,* referring to a book named in the work last named in a quotation.
i.e.	*that is*
NT	*New Testament*
OT	*Old Testament*
sec.	*section*

A

A POSTERIORI

Latin *ab,* "from," *posterius,* "subsequent, following;" argument from effect to cause, from particulars to general principles. It is inductive as opposed to deductive. It is the mode of argument employed in empiricism.*

See **Arguments for God's Existence**.

A PRIORI

Latin, *ab,* "from," *prius,* "first"; argument from cause to effect, or from an original principle or supposition to its logical effects. It is deductive rather than inductive, from general principles to individual conclusions. The significance of the *prius* in its designation is that there are certain innate ideas that must come before, and furnish a basis for, experience.

See **Arguments for God's Existence**.

ABBA

A Palestinian Aramaic word that is found in three places in the NT to refer to God. It means "father." It is the address of a child as distinct from a slave and denotes family intimacy. In Mark 14:36 Christ uses *abba* to address God in His prayer in Gethsemane. In Rom. 8:15 and Gal. 4:6 Christians use the same form of address to God. It is used in such a way that it both emphasizes our nearness to God and inculcates respect. Each time it is used it appears with the word *pater,* giving us the title *Abba Father* for God. Christians must never confuse intimacy with God their Father with familiarity and triteness. There is no basis in the NT use of *abba* to support the almost blasphemous references some make to God as "Dad" or "Daddy." It is surely significant that the Aramaic *abba* is not translated into Greek as *papa* but is merely transliterated.

ABBOT

The head or superior of an abbey. The word comes from the Aramaic *abba,* "father." At first the title *abbot* was given to every monk, but after the sixth century it was limited to the heads of religious houses. Later it was extended to the heads of other institutions. In the Roman hierarchy, abbots are usually subject to the authority of a diocesan bishop. In Germany the title *abbot* was given to some Protestant divines, especially if they received the revenues of former abbeys.

ABECEDARIANS

1. An extreme German sect of the Reformation period, followers of Nicholas Storch, who considered that no other teaching than that of the Holy Spirit was necessary. They thus rejected all human teaching, refusing to learn to read and write. Their name originates from the *A B C D*'s which they despised.
2. As an adjective, *abecedarian* may be used to mean "alphabetically arranged," as Psalm 119.

ABILITY

Theologically, it means innate power to do the will of God. It is taught by Pelagians and denied by all Reformed creeds.

See **Inability.**

ABJURATION

1. The solemn oath by which Roman Catholics suspected or convicted of heresy deny or remove the charge.
2. In England, the Oath of Abjuration required every person who held any office, civil, military, or spiritual, to abjure the exiled James II and repudiate any right he or

1

his descendants claimed to the throne. The justices of the peace could require any citizen to take the oath. Any who refused were liable to imprisonment for as long as they continued in their refusal.

ABLUTION

From the Latin verb *abluere,* "to wash off," it signifies a ceremonial and symbolic washing. In the OT priests and Levites were required to wash prior to performing their religious duties (Lev. 8:6; Exod. 30:19-21; Num. 8:21). Various things rendered an Israelite ceremonially unclean and required an ablution: contact with a dead body (Num. 19:11-13); eating "that which died of itself or that which was torn with beasts" (Lev. 17:15); leprosy (Lev. 13:14); various skin diseases, scurf, mould in clothes, fungus in houses, discoloration of the skin, scabs, and inflammation (Lev. 14); discharges from the human body (Lev. 15); copulation (Lev. 18); menstruation (Lev. 15); and childbirth (Lev. 12).

There were special ablutions to be performed on the day of atonement (Lev. 16:24-28). Numbers 19 details the rite of the red heifer and for those rendered unclean through contact with the dead. In other cases fresh, usually running, water was sufficient for ritual purification (Lev. 15:13).

Exodus 19:10-14 records the ablutions of the children of Israel before the Lord came down to meet with them at Mt. Sinai. From 1 Sam. 16:5 we may gather that the act of ablution became accepted practice before the presentation of a sacrifice. A special ablution mentioned in Deut. 21:1-9 was the washing of hands by the elders of a village nearest to where the victim of an unknown murderer was found. The washing of hands declared, "Our hands have not shed this blood, neither have our eyes seen it" (v. 7). Pilate sought to employ this symbolic ritual to rid himself of guilt in the death of Christ (Matt. 27:24), but obviously inappropriately.

The Jews in Christ's day elevated the ritual purification produced by the washings of Judaism to ethical purification. Ablution could never remove moral defilement, but clearly the Pharisees held it in higher honour than ethical integrity (Matt. 15:1-9). Thus they multiplied their ablutions (Mark 7:3,4) and found fault with Christ's disciples for failing to observe their rituals (vv. 2, 5).

The NT epistles contain only two references to ablution, Heb. 6:2; 9:10. In 6:2 "the doctrine of baptisms" (lit. washings, ablutions) is said to be a fundamental principle of Christianity. It signifies "a statement of the nature and design of Christian baptism, as distinguished from the baptism of John and the ceremonial washings or baptisms under the law" (John Brown).

Heb 9:10 specifically names OT ablutions as "carnal ordinances," that is, ordinances that were merely of an external and symbolic nature. They served to cleanse the body from ceremonial defilement but could not cleanse the soul from moral guilt. Thus they were only a temporary institution, "imposed" (v. 10) until their shadowing forth of the truth of purification would give place to the actual substance of it in the atonement of Christ (vv. 10-14).

That emphasis on the passing of all symbolic ablutions, with the sole exception of Christian baptism, renders the reinstitution of ceremonial washings by the Greek and Roman churches all the more objectionable. In the Greek church ablution is a ceremony observed seven days after baptism. It is to wash off the unction of the chrism, or, the oil used in baptism.

The Roman Catholic church has introduced ablutions into its liturgy of the mass.* According to the Roman Missal,* the priest celebrating the mass washes his hands as an expression of his desire for inward purification. As he washes he is supposed to recite Psa. 51:2 quietly. Another ablution takes place when at the end of the mass the priest or deacon purifies the paten (shallow dish for holding the bread of the Eucharist) over the chalice, which he then washes with water or with wine and water poured over his fingers into it. Finally, he drinks this water/wine mixture. In this way Rome provides for the washing of the Eucharistic vessels while ensuring that any remains of what she holds to be the very body and blood of Christ are consumed and not flushed away, as would happen with normal washing.

ABOMINATION OF DESOLATION

In His Olivet discourse the Lord Jesus Christ said, "When ye therefore shall see the abomination of desolation, spoken of by Daniel the prophet, stand in the holy place, (whoso readeth, let him understand:) then let them which be in Judaea flee into the mountains" (Matt. 24:15, 16; see also Mark 13:14). Thus the key to understanding the term *abomination of desolation* is to be found in the prophecy of Daniel where there are three, or possibly four, references to it: Dan. 9:27; 11:31; 12:11; and possibly 8:13. The various Hebrew and Greek terms rendered *abomination* and *abominable* carry the idea of something abhorrent, detestable, disgusting, foul, horrible, and impure, and therefore repugnant and unlawful on that account.

While *abomination* may describe a merely human prejudice or convention (Gen. 43:32; 46:34), it usually refers to something deeply offensive and repugnant to the Lord. Hence the Bible labels sodomy, bestiality, sacrilege, and idolatry "abominations" (Exod. 8:26; Deut. 17:1; 7:25, 26). One of the Hebrew words translated "abomination," *shiqquts*, is most frequently used as a description of heathen gods. For example in 2 Chron. 15:8 it is translated "abominable idols," while in 2 Kings 23:13 it describes Ashtoreth "the abomination of the Zidonians," and Chemosh, "the abomination of the Moabites." Since *shiqquts* is the term Daniel uses in 9:27; 11:31; and 12:11 the strong inference is that the abomination

of desolation is an idol placed in the temple in Jerusalem.

Desolation (the word is plural in the Greek of Matt 24:15 and Mark 13:14) signifies a laying waste. Abomination always causes desolation, disaster, and judgment. The presence of an abomination, an idol or anything else the Lord has denounced as repugnant to Him, renders a place unfit for the presence and service of the Lord. Though the expression of the Lord Jesus Christ in Matt. 24 and Mark 13 is eschatological we must not overlook the timeless principle He teaches. Nowadays it is becoming increasingly prevalent in churches to accept what God has rejected as abominable. In the name of justice and love many churches have opened not only their membership but even their ministry to sodomites. The acceptance of the abomination of sodomy guarantees both the loss of the Lord's presence and the certainty of His wrath. The same may be said of those interfaith services which are so often hailed as progressive and enlightened attempts to unite a divided world. Joint worship with what God has called abominable inevitably brings dire consequences.

The entire phrase *the abomination of desolation,* then, obviously refers to an idol, or false god, and its worship, placed in the temple of God and causing desolation. Two of the four references noted in Daniel (8:13 and 11:31) are generally taken to refer to the pollution of the Temple by Antiochus Epiphanes in 168 B.C. Antiochus, with the help of some apostate Jews, set up a statue in the Temple, raised an altar to Jupiter Olympus on the altar of burnt offering, and sacrificed swine's flesh. He dedicated the Temple to his idol and rescinded the Mosaic laws. Thus was the Holy Place desolated but not destroyed.

Daniel's other two references (9:27; 12:11) clearly cannot be to Antiochus. Some commentators argue that the case of Antiochus gives us a clue to the proper understanding of Matt. 24:15. As the *Speakers Commentary* puts it, "We should naturally understand [Matt. 24:15] as implying some pollution of the Temple by the Jews, to be punished by its destruction at the hands of the Romans." Those who see "the abomination of desolation" fulfilled in the destruction of Jerusalem by the Romans appeal to Luke 21:20. They hold that the wording "when ye shall see Jerusalem compassed with armies, then know that the desolation thereof is nigh" explains the desolation of Matt. 24:15.

However, this argument misses the mark. Luke 21 does not record the same discourse as Matt. 24. It precedes the Matthew account. It was given in the temple (Luke 21:1), whereas Matt. 24 was given after He "went out, and departed from the Temple" (v. 1) "as He sat upon the mount of Olives" (v. 3). The discourse in Luke 21 coincides with Matt. 24 as far as v. 11. That is, Luke 21:7-11 corresponds with Matt 24: 3-8. Then the two portions diverge. Luke 21:12 specifically states that the rest of the discourse is a retrospect—that the Lord goes back to what happens before all the things He has been speaking about. Matthew 24:9 clearly indicates that in His second discourse He continues His prophecy of future events, without any retrospect.

This yields two important conclusions.

First, in view of this, it is impossible to equate the Roman armies compassing Jerusalem to destroy it with "the abomination of desolation."

Second, the prophecy of "the abomination of desolation" remained to be fulfilled after the fall of Jerusalem to the Romans.

Some interpreters seek the prophecy's fulfilment in the rise of the papacy. Clearly the idolatry of the papal system has caused untold havoc in the visible church and is abominable, but it cannot be the fulfilment of Christ's prophecy. The local and geographical data in Matt 24:16f. forbid any interpretation that fails to place "the abomination of desolation" in the Temple in Jerusalem.

We are left, then, with a prophecy of the placing of an idol in the Temple in Jerusalem after the destruction of the city by the Romans in A.D. 70. That means the prophecy yet awaits fulfilment, for there has never been a temple in Jerusalem from then until now. The action of Antiochus foreshadowed the final abomination of which Daniel and Christ spoke. That final abomination is described by Daniel in 9:26, 27 as caused by "the prince that shall come," a man who will confirm a covenant with the Jews and then break it. This is the "little horn" of Dan. 7:8, 24-26; 8:9-12, 23-25. He is the Antichrist, the Man of Sin, and Son of Perdition (Dan. 11:36 with 2 Thess. 2:4). *The abomination of desolation,* therefore, is the final and greatest eruption of idolatry, as the Antichrist sets up his abominable worship in the Temple in Jerusalem and proclaims himself to be God. As in the case of Antiochus, the Antichrist will be welcomed by some foolish Jews into their city. They will think they are opening their doors to a saviour. In fact, he whom they welcome will be a desolator, pursuing a course of persecution, terror, and deception that will be terminated only by the second coming* of the Lord Jesus Christ.

ABORTION

From Latin *abortio,* "miscarriage," the term is used in two senses:

1. A spontaneous abortion is the act of miscarriage or producing a child before the natural time, with the loss of its life.

2. A forced abortion is the deliberate expulsion of an unborn child from the womb, thus depriving it of its life.

Despite the fact that forced abortions are now legal in almost all developed countries, they are almost always scripturally unlawful. Historically, this has been the almost uniform Christian position, based, first, on the truth that man is created in the image of God, and second, that there is plain Biblical evidence that God views the child in the womb as a full person. In earlier times, some theologians believed that some time after conception—usually 60 to 80 days into the pregnancy—*ensoulment* occurred; until that time the fetus was not yet a true person. There is no evidence for such a belief, either in Scripture or in science and the general belief of the Christian church now reflects the ancient opinion of Tertullian (*Apologia,* 9) that to terminate a pregnancy is as unlawful as the killing of a full-grown man. The word of God allows for the taking of life only under very strictly defined circumstances, such as in a just war, or as punishment for crimes such as murder. An unborn child has not done anything worthy of capital punishment. The sole exception to this general rule is the case where to continue a pregnancy would kill the mother. Because of her views on baptismal regeneration,* the Roman Catholic church usually places the life of the child above that of the mother, though church law accepts the principle of "double effect"—i.e., that if, for example, a woman with cancer of the uterus needed surgery to save her life, she may have that surgery even though it would certainly kill her unborn child. Protestantism has always accepted that in cases where it is impossible to save the life of the mother and that of the child, the life of the mother should have the first right to be protected; even an unborn child does not have an innate right to kill its parent.

To say that forced abortions—whether as a form of birth control, or for some personal, social, or economic reason invoked by the mother—is scripturally unlawful is to say that according to God's word, such abortion is murder. The popular claim that an unborn child is no more than fetal matter, without personal dignity or rights, that may be disposed of according to a woman's "right to choose what she does with her own body," is as baseless biologically as it is scripturally. The killing of an unborn child is the deliberate taking of a human life, and that is a crime which God views with abhorrence. Mark Allison, an associate of the present writer, presented the case for the protection of the lives of the unborn as follows:

"The Biblical arguments against abortion are very straightforward. First, God requires the same punishment for killing a child in the womb as He does for killing a man. In Exodus 21:22-23 we read, 'If men strive, and hurt a woman with child, so that her fruit depart from her, and yet no mischief follow: he shall be surely punished, according as the woman's husband will lay upon him; and he shall pay as the judges determine. And if any mischief follow, then thou shalt give life for life.' Here is a case in which a woman with child is struck in such a way that she gives birth. If the striking results in the death of the child, then the man who struck the woman is to forfeit his own life.

"Calvin comments, 'Wherefore this, in my opinion, is the meaning of the law, that it would be a crime punishable with death, not only when the mother died from the effects of the abortion, but also if the infant should be killed; whether it should die from the wound abortively, or soon after its birth." Since this punishment is the same as that for killing a full-grown man (Gen. 9:6; Exod. 21:12; Lev. 24:17), it demonstrates that God considers the child in the womb as real and as valuable a person as an adult.

"Second, there are passages throughout the Scriptures that describe the child in the womb as a person. For instance, we read concerning Rebekah that 'the children struggled together within her' (Gen. 25:22). The word for 'children' in this passage is the normal Old Testament word translated 'sons' (Gen. 5:4, 7, 10; Prov. 7:7). This is even true in the New Testament where we read concerning Elisabeth that she 'conceived a son in her old age' (Luke 1:36; compare with v. 57). Also, the word for 'babe' that is used in Luke 1:41, 44 in reference to the child in the womb is also used for newborn children (Luke 2:12; 2 Tim. 3:15; 1 Pet. 2:2). Hence, God uses the same words to describe children before and after birth. Besides these words, there is also David's description of himself in Psalm 139:1-16, where he uses first-person pronouns to describe his life as an adult (vv. 6-12) and as an unborn child (vv. 13-15). There is a personal identity between the child in the womb and the full-grown man.

"Finally, the Scriptures also portray the child in the womb as one who can move (Gen. 25:22), respond to noises from the outside (Luke 1:41, 44), and be filled with the Holy Spirit (Luke 1:15). "The weight of this Scriptural evidence indicates that God considers the unborn child a person and that therefore the child's life should be protected as other people's lives are protected. However, even an unborn child has no inherent right to kill. 'Thou shalt not kill' (Exod. 20:13) applies to it as to everyone else. Thus, historic Protestant theology recognizes that a woman may obtain an abortion only if her unborn child is actually killing her.

"When the humanistic leaders of society justify the murder of unborn children, Christians should remember the standard raised in Isaiah 8:20: 'To the law and to the testimony: if they speak not according to this word, it is because there is no light in them.' Believers must stand against those defending abortion, for Scripture makes it clear that God hates 'hands that shed innocent blood' (Prov. 6:20)" *(American Revivalist,* May 1989, pp. 2, 3).

ABSOLUTION

From the Latin word meaning "to set free," it denotes the forgiveness of sins. Roman Catholic theology uses it specifically to denote the forgiveness they claim to be given by the church.

See **Confession.**

ACCEPTANCE

The believer received as well-pleasing to God, solely in the person, and through the redeeming merit of, the Lord Jesus Christ.

See **Imputation, Justification.**

ACCEPTILATION

In Roman commercial law *acceptilatio* was a verbal discharge from obligation; an imaginary payment. "A creditor is an absolute owner of his own property, and if he pleases to discharge his debtor from his obligation to pay the debt which he owes him, he can do so by a word without any literal payment being made. He can call the debt paid, and it is paid. Or he can cancel the entire debt upon the payment of a part only. This arbitrary and optional acceptance of nothing for something, or of a part for the whole of a debt, is acceptilation" (W. G. T. Shedd, *History of Christian Doctrine,* II. 348).

In theology acceptilation was the term adopted from its place in Roman commercial law by Duns Scotus in his controversy with the followers of Thomas Aquinas. Scotus rejected their teaching that Christ's atonement* was necessary and that it rendered to God a true and sufficient satisfaction* for sin. He laid down the proposition: "Every created oblation or offering is worth what God is pleased to accept it for, and no more." From this Scotus argued that God accepts Christ's atonement as a satisfaction for sin, not because of any infinite value inherent in it, but because He is graciously willing to accept a satisfaction that is not strictly infinite in value. Thus Christ's atonement is sufficient to satisfy the law solely because God is willing to accept it as such. He accepted it as sufficient, even though it was not, just as a man may receive a portion of what is owed to him in full payment of a debt. In this view, salvation comes to us by a relaxation, not a satisfaction, of the law.

The Roman Catholic church is still divided on this question, and no pope or council has established the official position. In contrast, the Lutheran and Reformed churches have stood for the scriptural truth of the proposition that Christ offered a true and sufficient satisfaction to God for sin. They teach that the merits of Christ's atonement are real, infinite, and sufficient. Our salvation comes from the satisfaction, not the relaxation, of God's law.

ACCESS

The entrance a believer enjoys into God's presence and grace; he is brought into this position by the merits of Christ's substitutionary sufferings (Rom. 5:2; Eph. 2:18; 3:12; 1 Pet. 3:18).

ACCIDENT

A term borrowed from philosophy by the Roman Catholic church to be pressed into service in defence of its dogma of transubstantiation.*

An accident is a property or characteristic of a substance that is not essential to it. For example, the roundness and redness of an apple are properties of an apple but not essential to its being an apple. They are not essential to its substance. However, when we note the presence of all the properties of an apple—form, taste, odour, specific gravity, chemical constituents—we conclude that we have an apple. These properties cannot exist apart from it. Properties do not exist apart from a subject to which they belong. That would appear to be self-evident.

But that is exactly what the Roman Catholic church denies in its defence of transubstantiation. Rome claims that when consecrated, the Eucharistic* bread and wine become the actual body and blood of Christ. They continue to look, taste, and feel like bread and wine. If subjected to chemical analysis they have all the properties of bread and wine, and none of the properties of flesh and blood. If consumed they have all the nutritive properties of bread and wine. Yet according to Rome they are not bread and wine. They are Christ's flesh and blood, indeed His entire humanity and deity.

To deny that the consecrated bread and wine remain bread and wine is obviously absurd. Yet Rome defends the absurd by appealing to the notion that the properties of the bread and wine are mere accidents; they are not essential. The essence—the bread and wine—has been converted into a completely different essence, but the accidents of that now nonexistent essence remain. In the language of Thomas Aquinas the accidents continue to "subsist in the sacrament without a subject." They do not become the properties of the new substance (the body and blood of Christ) for as Rome admits, the same accidents cannot pass from one subject to another.

The best arguments Rome's apologists can muster to support their theory is that "transubstantiation is a real conversion of the bread and wine into the body and blood of Jesus Christ. Now, in every conversion there must be something common to both substances remaining the same after the change that it was before, else it would be simply a substitution of one thing for another" (McClintoch and Strong).

This is no answer to Rome's dilemma. It simply states what it needs to prove and cannot. Why must the properties of the bread and wine remain after conversion? Why would there not be a conversion of the properties as well as of the substance, if the bread and wine were converted? Indeed, would that not make the conversion complete? It would certainly settle the argument about transubstantiation! This notion of the continued existence of the discernible properties of a subject without the subject itself is a fallacy fabricated to support the insupportable.

ACCOMMODATION

The adjustment of language by a Biblical writer to meet the limitations of his readers, without any compromise of the truth of what is written. This has some legitimate uses (e.g., where God is described as having physical

7

parts and passions—*see Anthropomorphism*), but it has been illegitimately used by liberal scholars, who claim (1) that Christ accommodated Himself to the prejudices and errors of the Jews of His day; (2) that Scripture writers adopted pagan ideas and then, after some polishing, incorporated them into the Bible; (3) that the early church and the NT writers placed a meaning on the prophecies of the OT which they cannot properly have, thus accommodating them to their own messianic ideas.

ACCOUNTABILITY

The responsibility and liability to judgment by God of moral agents for their affections and actions. The inbred sense of accountability is a strong indication that the just Creator has written His law on the hearts of all men (Rom. 2:15).

See Arguments for God's Existence.

ACCUSER

See Satan.

ACOLYTE

From the Greek *akolouthos*, "follower." Cyprian (died A.D. 258) mentions the order of acolytes, and the Latin church made it one of the minor orders of the clergy. An acolyte, then, was a candidate for the priesthood with the task of assisting priests or bishops. His duties included such things as the lighting of candles and the preparation of the elements for use in the Eucharist.*

The Greek church never recognized the order of acolytes, and the Scriptures make no mention of it whatever. The Roman Catholic church still retains it but since 1972 has allowed lay people to become acolytes. No longer must an acolyte be a candidate for priestly orders. In reforming the order of acolyte, Pope Paul VI said he was adapting it "to present-day needs, eliminating what is obsolete, retaining what is useful and determining what is necessary" *(Ministeria Quaedam)*.

In contrast to this claimed authority to determine the ministerial offices in the church, the Reformed churches hold that Scripture sets forth the offices the Lord has established in His church. These offices never become obsolete and need no others to be added to them for the proper functioning of the church.

ADIAPHORISTS

From the Greek word meaning "indifferent," *adiaphorists* were those Protestants in Germany at the time of the Reformation, notably Philip Melanchthon and his followers, who were willing to accept a compromise confession of faith, strongly leavened with Roman superstition, on the basis that certain doctrines are of minor importance and may be taught or denied without damaging the essentials of the faith. Melanchthon, opposed by Matthias Flacius, confessed the error of his policy of deliberately veiling real difficulties by the use of vague forms of words and treating the concessions made thereby to Rome as "indifferent," *adiaphora*.

ADOPTION

"The act of God's free grace whereby believers are received into the number of, and have a right to all the privileges of, the Sons of God" *(Shorter Catechism, 34)*. *The Westminster Confession of Faith* (chap. 12) speaks of "the grace of adoption" by which the justified have God's name put upon them (2 Cor. 6:18; Rev. 3:12); receive the Spirit of adoption (Rom. 8:15); have access to the throne of grace with boldness (Rom. 5:2; Eph. 3:12); are enabled to cry, "Abba, Father" (Gal. 4:6); are pitied (Ps. 103:13); protected (Prov. 14:26); provided for (Matt. 6:30, 32; 1 Pet. 5:7); and chastened by Him as a Father (Heb. 12:6); are never cast off (Lam. 3:31); but are sealed to the day of redemption (Eph. 4:30); and inherit the promises (Heb. 6:12) as heirs of everlasting salvation (1 Pet. 1:3, 4; Heb. 1:14).

Robert Shaw in his exposition of the *Confession's* statement remarks, "Among men adoption signifies that act by which a person takes the child of another into the place, and entitles him to the privileges of his own son. Spiritual adoption is that act by which God receives sinners into His family, and gives them a right to all the privileges of His children."

The statements of Scripture on this subject show the inestimable depths of God's grace to His people. While men usually adopt to supply a deficiency, God did not, for He was fully satisfied with "His only begotten Son." Men usually adopt one or two, but God will bring "many sons unto glory" (Heb. 2:10). Men are influenced by some excellence, real or supposed, in the one they adopt, but God had no such inducement, for guilty sinners have nothing about them to merit His favour.

We may note:

1. Adoption is an *act,* not a process. It is completed at once and is conferred equally upon all believers in Christ (Gal. 3:26, 28).

2. It is a *gracious act* (Eph. 1:4, 5; 1 John 3:1), carried out on the merit of Christ's redemption (Gal. 4:4, 5).

3. It is a *forensic act,* dealing with the legal right and status of the justified (John 1:12; Rom. 8:17). It is not to be confounded with regeneration, which describes an actual moral change whereby, being born of the Spirit (John 3:3, 5), we "are made partakers of the divine nature" (2 Pet. 1:4).

4. Like justification, it is *a direct result of our union with Christ (see **Mystical Union**).*

5. It is *received by faith* (Gal. 3:26) and exalts to the highest liberty (Gal. 4:7) and dignity (Isa. 43:4; Heb. 12:23, "firstborn," Rom. 8:17).

6. It always *results in glorification* (Rom.8:16-18). "Adoption ends in coronation" (Thomas Watson).

ADOPTIONISM

An early heresy teaching that Christ was a man, who by God's decree was born of a virgin, was given supernatural powers at his baptism and, because of his character and work, was raised from the dead and adopted into the Godhead.

In 8th-century Spain, Felix, Bishop of Urgel, popularized another form of Adoptionism. Felix taught that as to His human nature, Christ was not the natural but the adopted Son of God. It appears, however, that he did not deny that in His divine nature Christ was the eternal Son of God. McClintock and Strong sum up the Spanish adoptionist views:

"By the use of the term *adoptio* this school wished to mark the distinction of proper and improper in reference to the Son. They made use of the illustration that, as a son cannot have two fathers, but may have one by birth and the other by adoption, so in Christ a distinction must be made between his proper sonship and his sonship by adoption. Still, they regarded as the important point the different relation in which Christ is called the Son of God according to his divine or his human nature. The former relation marked something founded in the nature of God, the second something that was founded not in his nature, but in a free act of the Divine will, by which God assumed human nature into connection with himself. Accordingly Felix distinguished between how far Christ was the Son of God and God according to nature, and how far he was so by virtue of grace, by an act of the Divine will, by the Divine choice and good pleasure; and the name Son of God was given to him only in consequence of his connection with God."

Thus in its Spanish form, Adoptionism may have been only a clumsy attempt at explaining how the man Christ Jesus is called the Son of God. A better solution to that problem is by a proper understanding of the *communicatio idiomatum.* *

*See **Eternal Sonship.***

ADORATION

Generally, an expression of love, admiration, or obeisance toward another; in religion, the reverence and worship* offered to God, together with appropriate physical postures, such as bowing, kneeling, prostration, etc.

"Adoration is perhaps the highest type of worship, involving the reverent and rapt contemplation of the Divine perfections and prerogatives, the acknowledgment of them in words of praise, together with the visible symbols and postures that express the adoring attitude of the creature in the presence of his Creator. It is the expression of the soul's mystical realization of God's presence in His transcendent greatness, holiness, and lovingkindness. As a form of prayer, adoration is to be distinguished from other forms, such as petition, thanksgiving, confession, and intercession....

"In the OT, the literature of adoration reaches its high-water mark in the Pss (cf. esp. the group Pss 95-100), where the ineffable majesty, power and holiness of God are set forth in lofty strains. In the NT, adoration of the Deity finds its most rapturous expression in Rev., where the vision of God calls forth a chorus of praise addressed to the thrice-holy God (4:8-11; 7:11, 12), with whom is associated the Redeemer-Lamb" (*ISBE*, 1:60, 61).

On the social level, bowing to kings and superiors is acceptable (e.g., 2 Sam. 14:4; Ruth 2:10). To bow down to any but God in religious worship is idolatry, a breach of the first and/or second commandments. Thus, Peter refused to allow Cornelius to bow to him in worship, or homage (Acts 10:25, 26), as did the angel before whom John fell (Rev. 22:8, 9). In contrast to these reactions, the Lord Jesus Christ received all expressions of worship, a clear testimony of His personal consciousness of His deity and dignity.

The Roman Catholic and the Eastern Orthodox churches practice adoration and veneration of the host,* Mary, the saints, martyrs, and angels. Canon 898 of Rome's *Code of Canon Law* states that the faithful "should reverence it [the Mass*] with the greatest adoration." The Second Vatican Council (*Dogmatic Constitution on the Church, #50*) notes that Rome "has always venerated [the martyrs] with special devotion, together with the Blessed Virgin Mary and the holy angels. The Church too has devoutly implored the aid of their intercession."

To the criticism of Protestants who object that all such adoration, veneration, and invocation is unscriptural and derogatory from Christ's right to Christians' adoration as their sole mediator with God, Rome replies as follows: when she "suppliantly invokes" saints and angels and has "recourse to their prayers, their power and help in obtaining benefits from God" it is "through His Son, Jesus Christ our Lord, who is our sole Redeemer and Saviour" (Council of Trent, Session 25). "For by its very nature every genuine testimony of love which we show to those in heaven tends toward and terminates in Christ" (Vatican II, *Dogmatic Constitution, #50*).

According to Rome, therefore, adoration of saints and angels leads Christians to Christ, though why the angel in Rev. 22:8, 9 seems to have been unaware of this neither Trent* nor Vatican II makes clear.

Rome also seeks to evade the force of Protestant criticism of her religious adoration of mere creatures by having recourse to artificially distributing adoration, or worship, into three categories: *dulia** is adoration of saints; *hyperdulia** is adoration of Mary; *latria** is adoration of God (Council of Trent, session 25).

As R. P. Blakeney long ago pointed out (*Manual of Romish Controversy*, p.185) these distinctions are baseless scripturally and useless practically. According to Matt. 6:24 *dulia* belongs to God. Blakeney's contention is confirmed by the superstitions of Roman Catholics worldwide: "No one could so nicely balance his feelings, as to give to God, the Virgin, and the saints, their exact portion.

We may go even further: in the matter of religious worship and the power to obtain heaven's blessings for us, the Virgin and the saints have no portion at all allotted to them in Scripture."

ADVENT

1. From the Latin word *adventus,* "coming"; it can be used to describe either Christ's first or second coming.

2. The season preceding Christmas. The Anglican, Lutheran, and Roman Catholic churches observe it for four weeks and the Eastern Orthodox for six weeks.

ADVERSARY

See Apollyon; Satan.

ADVOCATE

The translation of the Greek word *parakletos,* which signifies "one called alongside to help." *Parakletos* is used of the Holy Spirit* (John 14:16, 26; 15:26; 16:7), where it is translated "Comforter," with the sense that He is the believer's advocate, helper, and intercessor (see Rom. 8:26). It is also used of our Lord Jesus Christ (1 John. 2:1) and shows Him to be our intercessor, pleading the merits of His own propitiatory sacrifice on our behalf.

ADVOCATUS DEI, DIABOLI

Latin, meaning "God's Advocate" and the "Devil's Advocate" respectively; two people appointed at Rome in considering the alleged miracles of a candidate for canonization.* God's Advocate sustains the merits of the candidate while the Devil's Advocate opposes them. The entire performance is mere theatre in the superstitious preservation of a relic from paganism.

ADVOWSON

In English law, the right of a patron to appoint a vicar or rector to a vacant parish. This right is founded in the theory of the Church of England that whoever built a church had the perpetual right to choose its minister—i.e., he became its patron. This right became part of his estate to be passed on to his heirs. Soon advowsons became "saleable commodity, transferred, or sold by auction, to the highest bidder, like any other real property, and the patronage of the Church of England is consequently dispersed wherever wealth has found its way" (the words of a Church of England apologist, quoted by McClintock and Strong).

Many advowsons became the property of the crown, many more the property of bishops, cathedral chapters, the universities, and city corporations. Evangelicals set up trusts to purchase advowsons so that they could place evangelical pastors in parishes that otherwise might be left without a clear gospel ministry. They thus sought to make the best of an evil system. Under the patronage* system church members have no say in the most important decision affecting the life and witness of their church, the election of its minister.

AFFECTIONS

Theologically, some see the affections as the inclination or disposition of the will,* which is fundamentally governed by love for God or love for self. All other affections, or responses to objects that affect us, are really expressions of the basic affection or disposition of our will.

Others hold that affection is different from disposition, contending that affection can exist only after there is an opportunity to exert it on a particular object. Thus, it cannot be part of the original constitution of the will. This is very faulty logic for when God created man He set Himself before his will as the supreme good to be chosen, loved, and served, and Satan lost no time in tempting Eve to see herself as the proper object of her own affections.

Affection, therefore, is an original part of man's voluntary nature, the expression or exercise of the governing disposition of his will. Since the fall* this fundamental disposition of man's will has been selfward and not Godward, rendering all the volitions of the unregenerate inherently sinful.

AFFINITY

Relationship by marriage as distinguished from consanguinity, which is relationship by blood. The Mosaic law (Lev. 18:7-18) prohibited marriage within certain degrees of affinity and consanguinity. Though marriage had previously been permitted in some of these cases (e.g., Cain had to marry his sister and Abraham married his half-sister, Sarah), the law forbade all marriage and sexual relations between

1. Parents and their children;
2. Stepparents and their children;
3. A man and his sister, or half-sister;
4. A man and his daughter-in-law;
5. A man and his aunt;
6. A man and his sister-in-law, except in the case where his brother had died without issue. In this case under the law of Levirate marriage he was obliged to marry her and raise up children to his deceased brother;
7. A man and a woman and her daughter or granddaughter;
8. A man and two sisters.

In these last two cases many commentators take the prohibition to be restricted to polygamous marriages and hold that the law did not prohibit a man marrying the daughter, granddaughter, or sister of a deceased wife.

A good case may be made for this position in regard to marrying two sisters, but there is no good reason to apply it to the case of marrying a woman and her daughter. At least the Scripture makes no such concession in this case as it does in reference to that of marrying sisters.

Leviticus 18:18 says, "Neither shalt thou take a wife to her sister, to vex her, to uncover her nakedness, beside the other in her lifetime." This is the only case in the entire list given in this passage in which the reason for the prohibition is given as avoiding causing vexation to a wife and in which the period of the prohibition is limited to her lifetime. One would think that if Moses had intended to attach either or both of these conditions to the case of a man marrying the daughter or granddaughter of his wife, he would have said so. Given the silence of Scripture it appears that they take a great liberty who hold that the death of a wife clears the way for the husband to marry her daughter or granddaughter.

How far are these enactments binding on Christians today? Secular law recognizes some of the Mosaic code and prohibits marriage in cases of close consanguinity. Christians, however, go further and recognize that the moral imperative of God's rule on affinity and consanguinity has not changed. *The Westminster Confession of Faith* summarizes the duty of believers in this matter as follows:

"Marriage ought not to be within the degrees of consanguinity or affinity forbidden in the Word; nor can such incestuous marriages ever be made lawful by any law of man, or consent of parties, so as those persons may live together as man and wife. The man may not marry any of his wife's kindred nearer in blood than he may of his own, nor the woman of her husband's kindred nearer in blood than of her own" (chap. 24, sec. 4).

AFRICAN THEOLOGY

The attempt to marry the theology of traditional African religions with contemporary "Christian" faith; "an attempt to synthesize Christianity with African traditional religions" (Byang H. Kato, *Theological Pitfalls in Africa*, p. 55). African theology is not merely the interpretation of Christian theology by African theologians, using African thought forms. It is the exploration of what the traditional, pre-Christian, animistic religions have been saying on the presupposition that they represent authentic divine revelation. In the subsequent synthesis with Christianity the Bible's data are only accepted if they support what has already been established from the traditional religions. In itself the Bible is not the source of truth for proponents of African theology.

Though hailed by many both within and outside Africa, African theology deserves Kato's criticism: "It is a funeral march of Biblical Christianity and a heralding of syncretism and universalism. It has for its funeral directors the undiscerning theologians who fail to see the spiritual issues at stake because of their unguided enthusiasm for projecting African personality" (pp. 55-56).

See **Black Theology**, **Ethiopianist Theology**, **Liberation Theology**, **Political Theology**.

AGNOSTICISM

A term coined in 1869 by Thomas Huxley to denote his theory that no one can know whether God exists, or indeed that anything exists which cannot be empirically* investigated.

See **Atheism (Sceptical)**; **Empiricism**.

AGNUS DEI

Latin expression meaning "Lamb of God"; a medallion stamped with the figure of a lamb, blessed by the pope, and worn as a talisman to protect the wearer from disease and calamity.

AGRAPHA

Greek, "unwritten things"; sayings of Jesus not recorded in the canonical gospels, usually claimed to have been preserved by oral tradition and recorded in later documents. Some assert that the NT mentions some *agrapha,* unwritten saying of Jesus. They cite Acts 1:5; 1:7; 11:16; 20:35; and 1 Cor. 11:24f. which record words of His that are not found in the Gospels. However, it is inaccurate to make these part of the *agrapha* for the very obvious reason that they have been recorded in the inspired word, at the direction of the same Spirit who inspired the Gospels.

The *agrapha* are properly sayings attributed to Jesus in uninspired sources. Some arose out of variant readings of the text of the Gospels and appear in the Apocryphal Gospels, writings of some church fathers, the Jewish Talmud,* and the Koran. There is no way that even the most plausible of these purported sayings of our Lord can be validated—illustrating the folly of making tradition* a basis for doctrinal formulations.

Most of the *agrapha* are valueless. The difference between the canonical NT and the extra-canonical books is so clear and so great that it leaves no doubt as to the divine origin of the former and the uninspired (and poverty stricken) character of the latter.

ALBIGENSES

A widely spread group of dissenters from the medieval papal church. It flourished in southern France and northern Italy in the 12th century and remained, despite papal persecution, until the 14th century. The name *Albigenses* comes from the district of Albi in southern France where they were most numerous.

Unfortunately, most of our information about them comes from their Romish persecutors, and while some of them held unscriptural views (see below), others were probably humble believers who repudiated the errors and corruptions of medieval Romanism. They were accused of espousing dualism,* Manicheism,* and docetism.* However, Roman Catholic writers level similar accusations against the Waldenses* who were certainly innocent of them. The same is probably true of the Albigenses.

Their origin has been traced by some to the Paulicians,* and they have been given a number of names—e.g., Bulgarians, Boni Homines (Latin, "Good Men"), Petrobrusians,* Henricians, and Abelardists. They were also known as Cathars, from the Greek *katharoi,* "pure ones." This would seem to have been the title they themselves adopted.

Cathars were divided into two classes of people: Believers and The Perfect. The latter became such by spiritual asceticism and were held to be the only people who could approach God directly. Thus they were deeply venerated by the Believers.

The greatest power of the movement was smashed by a crusade of intense persecution set in motion in A.D. 1208 by Pope Innocent III. To accomplish this the papal authorities killed many thousands of people. Milman (*Latin Christianity*) describes the awful carnage caused by Innocent's crusade. The pope's legates led a military expedition against the Albigenses in 1209 and slaughtered between 20,000 and 40,000 people at Beziers. Twenty years later the Albigenses finally "were handed over to the proselytizing zeal of the order of Dominicans, and the bloody tribunals of the inquisition; and both used their utmost power to bring the recusant Albigenses to the stake, and also, by inflicting severe punishment on the penitent converts, to inspire dread of incurring the Church's displeasure" (McClintock and Strong).

ALEXANDRIAN MS

A Greek copy of the Scriptures, usually denoted as Codex A or Alexandrinus because it is supposed to have originated in Alexandria. Written in uncial script, it is on vellum and dates from the early to mid 5th century. It contains the whole Bible in Greek, including the Septuagint* version of the Old Testament. It also includes the first part of the second epistle of Clement to the Corinthians. Codex A is defective in several places. Some leaves of the Psalms are missing as are some New Testament passages: Matt. 1:1-25:5; John 6:50-8:52; 2 Cor. 4:13-12:6. Codex A is now in the British Museum.

See Textual Criticism.

ALEXANDRIAN SCHOOL

The school established in Alexandria in the late second century by Pantænus, which became the centre of one of the two opposing systems of Bible interpretation in the church (the other being the Antiochan*) until they were in effect brought together in the fourfold understanding of Scripture that governed most exposition until the Reformation.

Pantænus was followed as principal of the school by Clement, who in turn was succeeded by Origen. To Clement and Origen the school owed its widespread influence and success. It was they who effectively united Christian theology with Greek philosophy. In earlier times the Christian apologists and controversialists had used Greek philosophy to confront their heathen opponents on their own ground, but it was left to Clement and Origen to "build a bridge between the Gospel and Gentile wisdom" (G. P. Fisher). They adopted a mystical approach to Scripture and interpreted it allegorically *(see Allegory).* Philip Schaff, who praised the Alexandrian school for its "immortal service" to its own and later times—despite the charges of heresy which the orthodox later levelled against it—admitted its hermeneutical weakness:

"The Alexandrian theology is intellectual, profound, stirring, and full of fruitful germs of thought, but rather unduly idealistic and spiritualistic, and, in exegesis, loses itself in arbitrary allegorical fancies."

Without sound Bible exegesis, dogmatic theology loses its peculiarly Christian character and strength and descends to the level of philosophical speculation. While one may believe that the Alexandrian teachers had the highest motives in marrying their theology to Greek philosophy, the result was far from satisfactory and was a marked decline from the methods of the apostles. In the controversies surrounding the doctrine of Christ's theanthropic person,* while both orthodox and heterodox employed the methodolgy of both the Alexandrian and Antiochan schools, it would be fair to say that the mysticism of the Alexandrians led some in the direction of monophysitism.*

ALEXANDRIAN VERSION

Another name for the Septuagint* version of the Old Testament.

ALLEGORY

1. Greek *allos,* "other," and *agoreuein,* "to speak in the place of assembly"; a figure of speech in which a description of one thing is given under the image of another. It is usually a story to explain or expound a truth, in which people, things, and events have another meaning than the obvious or literal. Both the Old and New Testaments employ allegory—Psa. 80:8-19; Ecc. 12:3-7; John 10:1-16; Eph. 6:11-17. Many see the entire book of the Song of Solomon as an allegory, while others see it as telling an actual historical story that conveys a spiritual message.
2. Whereas *allegory* is a Scriptural genre, some employ *allegorizing* as a method of interpretation. This is the unwarrantable practice of converting what Scripture records as history into allegory and drawing all sorts of dogmatic and moral conclusions from it.

Many evangelicals, while entirely accepting the historicity of the Scripture narratives, hold that there is also a spiritual sense behind the literal. Perhaps it would be more accurate to say that they view much of the history of the Old Testament as typical as well as historical. Thus their exegesis of the history will be literal and grammatical while their application of it will be spiritual.

There is Scripture warrant for this. We have the example of Christ and His apostles. Jesus saw in the story of Moses raising up the brazen serpent the truth of His own redeeming death (John 3:15). Paul saw the story of Sarah and Hagar as an allegory of the church and its gracious liberty opposed by Judaism and its legalistic bondage (Gal. 4:24). Paul also saw the Passover as a type of Christ (1 Cor. 5:7) and treated the historical narrative of Israel's journey to Canaan as typical of Christian experience (see 1 Cor. 10:1-11). He described the Mosaic ritual as a "shadow" of which the gospel is the substance (Col. 2:16,17; Heb. 8:1-5).

While some insist that we may treat as typical and allegorical only those things the apostles actually named as such, Paul's statement in Rom. 15:4 appears to warrant our making allegorical applications of the historical narratives of the Old Testament. However, some cautions are in order.

a. We must never deny or lose sight of the historicity of the narrative;
b. We must be sober in all allegorical application and not seek to establish any doctrine that we cannot establish by plain Biblical statement. In other words, allegorical application is to be illustrative not dogmatic.

The most serious misuse of allegory is found in the use of the alleged fourfold sense of Scripture. The four senses attributed to a passage are the literal, the allegorical (or analogical), the moral, and the anagogical.* The place of each is summed up in the saying, "The literal shows things done; the allegoric, what you should believe; the moral (or topical) what you should do; and the anagogical, what you should hope (referring to eternal life)."

The first to employ this method were the Greek philosophers of Alexandria, who applied it to Greek mythology to find higher religious conceptions. They were followed by Philo and other writers of the Jewish school of philosophy in Alexandria. Then many sections of the Christian church began to follow the same method. It became the chosen mode of treating Scripture in the Romish church and played a major role in keeping the Bible a closed book to clergy and laity throughout the dark ages.

Even when the Reformation* had called men back to the plain meaning of Scripture, Rome persisted in her adherence to the fourfold sense of Scripture. This is interesting because in the classification already mentioned, the dogmatic (i.e., doctrinal, theological) meaning of Scripture lies, not in its plain sense, but in its allegorical interpretation. This, of course, left all the room in the world for Rome to cite "Biblical" authority for dogmas for which she could never hope to adduce proof from the plain words of Scripture.

ALMIGHTY
*See **Names of God**.*

ALPHA AND OMEGA
The first and last letters of the Greek alphabet, used to translate the phrase *to A kai to O* (Rev. 1:8, 11; 21:6; 22:13). It is the title of Christ, clearly identifying Him as the eternal God who spoke through Isaiah, saying, "I am the first, and I am the last; and beside me there is no God" (Isa. 44:6).

AMILLENNIALISM
The theory that there will be no thousand-year period of great spiritual blessing before the Lord Jesus returns, and no thousand-year reign of Christ on earth after His return. Thus in Revelation 20 the multiple references to the thousand years are spiritualized to convey the idea of completeness or perfection: "It expresses no period of time" (W. W. Milligan). Amillennialists view the thousand years of Rev. 20 as a spiritual description of the entire period between Christ's ascension and the end of the age. For example, John Wilmot has a chapter in his *Inspired Principles of Prophetic Interpretation* entitled, "The Millennial Administration of the Ascended Christ"—his description of this inter-adventual period. With this view, amillennialists tend to idealize not only the events detailed in the book of Revelation but most other end-time prophecies, so that their prophetic content lies more in their elucidation of spiritual principles than in any reference to time. However, some amillennialists modify this position to allow a literal fulfilment of some prophetic events before the second coming of Christ.
*See **Millennium**.*

AMYRALDISM
The theory of Moses Amyrald (1596-1664) and the theological school of Saumur* regarding the extent of Christ's atonement* and the nature of regeneration.* These views, first introduced into English theology by Scottish theologian John Cameron, are described as hypothetical universalism* and mediate regeneration.* Amyrald and Cameron professed allegiance to the statements of the Synod of Dort and a desire to return to the Calvinism of Calvin instead of what they saw as a sort of reformed scholasticism. They are not to be associated with the doctrine of mediate imputation* advocated by Saumur professor Joshua Placaeus, which is at times identified as the Saumur doctrine.

ANABAPTISTS
Meaning of the Term
Anabaptist means "Re-baptizer." In the early centuries of church history the Donatists,* and later groups such as the Novatians* and Paulicians* rebaptized some who had previously been baptized in the Catholic church.* Their reason for rebaptizing was usually their rejection of the fitness or authority of the bishop or priest who had administered the first baptism.*

The Code of Justinian* (A.D. 529) made rebaptism an offence punishable by death—a fact that produced tragic consequences in the period of the Reformation* when it was applied to those groups that repudiated infant baptism and therefore rebaptized (or, in their view, scripturally baptized) their Roman Catholic and Protestant converts. The term *Anabaptists* is usually restricted to these groups and it is to them we give attention in this article. In investigating them and their beliefs we will gratefully avail ourselves of the research done by the Rev. Myron Mooney in the unpublished thesis he completed as part of his M.Div. degree in the American branch of the Whitefield College of the Bible.

The Origin of the Anabaptists

There are three distinct claims made regarding their origin.

The Trail of Blood Theory. This is the idea that there has been a more or less continuous Baptist witness from the days of the apostles. The Anabaptists, in this view, are one of the links in this great historical chain of a pure church witness. J. M. Carroll claimed that "the name Anabaptists is the oldest denominational name in history" (*Trail of Blood,* p. 54). There is, however, no discernible historical link between the 16th-century Anabaptists and the groups Carroll claims as their spiritual forebears.

Carroll's views of church successionism lack all historical evidence and credibility. Anabaptist historians state as much. K. R. Davis (*Anabaptism and Asceticism,* pp. 295, 296) holds that there is no proven connection between the Anabaptists and medieval groups such as the Albigenses.* Indeed Arnold Snyder writing in the *Mennonite Quarterly Review* (July 1986) traced the origin of the Anabaptists to medieval mysticism. Whatever merit Snyder's argument may have, it can trace only a community of ideas between the Anabaptists and the Roman Catholic mystics. The uniform testimony of history is that the Anabaptists were Roman Catholics who left the Church of Rome at the time of the Reformation. They were initially a part of the Reformers' movement. The fact that they later broke away from the Reformers emphasizes that historically they are an offshoot of the Protestant Reformation. To postulate a pre-Reformation origin for them is to mistake opinion for history.

The Theory of a German Origin. Until recent times the received view among church historians was that the Anabaptists arose in Zwickau, Saxony, with the Zwickau Prophets, wild enthusiasts who mistook their fanatical dreams for divine revelation and correspondingly devalued Scripture. Their leader was a weaver named Nicolas Storch, who was a disciple of Thomas Müntzer. Expelled from Zwickau, the prophets went to Wittenberg and, during Luther's incarceration in the Wartburg, almost wrecked the work of reform. They found an ally in the volatile Carlstadt and their madness was repulsed only by Luther's timely reappearance to resume leadership of the work.

Thomas Müntzer left Wittenberg and ultimately settled in Muhlhausen, Thuringia. Here his views of reform became more radical than ever, and he advocated violent measures to further his cause: "We must exterminate with the sword, like Joshua, the Canaanitish nations." In Luther's words, "Müntzer is king, and emperor of the Muhlhausen, and no longer is pastor."

Anarchy prevailed. The peasants of Germany were ready to rise in rebellion against their cruel masters. Müntzer fanned the flames of their discontent. When he heard that 40,000 peasants in Franconia were arming themselves, he exhorted those of Thuringia to do the same. His letter to them was a call to war. The peasants obeyed his call and he led them on a march of mad excess and plunder. Melancthon said, "Müntzer's progress is marked by more than Scythian cruelty." Finally in May 1525 Müntzer led 8,000 insurgents against the infantry and cavalry of the princes, with fatal results. Between 5,000 and 7,000 peasants were killed. Müntzer himself was taken and executed.

Müntzer did not unilaterally cause the Peasants' War. The peasants' lot was so unjustly severe that an uprising was inevitable. The folly of the princes in failing to heed Luther's calls for justice was more to blame than Müntzer's actions. But he did call for war. He did lead the peasants to destruction. And in so doing he brought shame on generations of Anabaptists, for as noted, until recently church historians labelled his followers with that name—with how much justice we will consider below.

Along with Müntzer and the Zwickau Prophets another group of admitted

Anabaptists displayed similar fanaticism. These were the followers of John of Leyden, who set up the Kingdom of New Zion in Münster, Westphalia. McClintock and Strong outlined the character and history of this movement: "Its leaders, by their lawless fanaticism, completely separated themselves from the cause of the reformers, and with the subject of adult baptism connected principles subversive to all religious and civil order."

Despite horrible persecution, the movement gained ground and spread beyond Germany to Holland and Switzerland. John Bochhold, or Bochel, and John Matthiesen, or Matthias, subverted the work of the Reformation in Münster. Matthieson came forward as their prophet and at his instruction the people burned all their books except the Bible and gave over all their wealth and movable property for the common cause. Matthieson was killed in an attack on the forces of the Roman Catholic Bishop of Münster that were then besieging the city. Bochhold took over the prophet's office and adopted the name John of Leyden. Since the Anabaptists called Münster New Zion, he styled himself the King of New Zion and caused himself to be formally crowned as such.

"From this period (1534) Münster was a theatre of all the excesses of fanaticism, lust and cruelty. The introduction of polygamy, and the neglect of civil order, concealed from the infatuated people the avarice and madness of their young tyrant [he was about 27 years old] and the daily increase of danger from abroad. Bochhold lived in princely luxury and magnificence, he sent out seditious proclamations against neighbouring rulers—against the Pope and Luther; he threatened to destroy with his mob all who differed from him; made himself an object of terror to his subjects by frequent executions" (McClintock and Strong).

In 1535, after a brave defence, Münster was taken and the kingdom of New Zion was destroyed by the execution of the Anabaptist leaders. John of Leyden, their king, and two of his chief aides, were brutally tortured and slain. John of Leyden sent out twenty-six apostles to carry the message of the Anabaptists abroad and they met with considerable success. The societies they founded repudiated the worst excesses of the Münsterists, such as polygamy and fanatical intolerance of those opinions different from theirs. They did not, however, escape some serious doctrinal deviations which found wide acceptance among Anabaptists (see below).

Modern Anabaptist apologists deny the German origin of their movement. They hold that neither the Zwickau Prophets nor Thomas Müntzer can accurately be described as Anabaptists and that the New Zionists of Münster were a temporary aberration from Anabaptist principles and practice. At any rate, they did not originate the movement and must not be considered normative.

However, this position is not easy to maintain in the light of all the facts. The respected leaders of Swiss Anabaptism, Conrad Grebel and Felix Manz, looked on Thomas Müntzer as a "true and beloved brother," a "true proclaimer of the gospel," and "the purest proclaimer and preacher of the purest word of God" (George H. Williams, *The Radical Reformation,* pp. 73-78). Even the spiritualistic ravings of the Zwickau Prophets cannot be shrugged off as atypical of Anabaptists, for they were clearly repeated among Swiss and Dutch Anabaptists. It would appear, therefore, that Anabaptism first arose in Germany with the Lutheran Reformation.

The Theory of a Swiss Origin. Anabaptist scholars, dismissing the claim that the Zwickau Prophets or the followers of Thomas Müntzer were Anabaptists, trace the origin of their movement to Zurich, 1524-25. There it sprang up among the followers of Ulrich Zwingli. Its leaders were Conrad Grebel (died 1526), Felix Manz (executed in 1527, the first Anabaptist martyr in Switzerland), and George Blaurock (exiled from Zurich in 1527 and martyred in Tyrol in 1529). There is no doubt that Anabaptism arose in Zurich as claimed. What is not established is that the Zurich movement preceded an Anabaptist movement in Germany. It would appear that Anabaptism followed in the train of the Lutheran and Zwinglian Reformations and that neither its German nor its Swiss expression derived its existence from the other, anymore than did the Lutheran Reformation spring from the Zwinglian, or vice versa.

The Beliefs of the Anabaptists

According to Harold S. Bender *(Twentieth Century Encyclopedia of Religious Knowledge)* the Anabaptists formed a radical but Biblical branch of the Reformation. Anabaptism "conceived of itself as carrying through in a more complete and consistent fashion the original goals of the Reformation which had been abandoned by Luther and Zwingli; namely the restoration of original, unadulterated New Testament Christianity."

Bender goes on to set out the distinctive doctrines of Anabaptism:

"The distinctive Anabaptist tenets were: a voluntary church of believers only, with baptism of adults on confession of faith and commitment to discipleship; separation of church and state; full liberty of conscience; holiness of life in full obedience to Christ; nonconformity to the world; a love-ethic including nonresistance and total rejection of warfare and the use of force; a brotherhood type of church with mutual aid; non-swearing of oaths; literal obedience to the Sermon on the Mount and the other teachings of Jesus; and simplicity of life and dress. The doctrines of the historic early Christian creeds, as well as the Protestant doctrines of justification by faith, the sole authority of Scripture, and the priesthood of all believers, were fully held, though not theologically

developed. The Anabaptists emphasized an existential more than a theological Christianity. Their major break with Protestantism was on the central concept of the gathered church rather than the folk-church, and the nature of Christianity as discipleship or transformation of life rather than primarily as the enjoyment of forgiveness and salvation as status. Their rejection of war and insistence on religious liberty in an age when even the church (both Roman Catholic and Protestant) used war and force as an instrument of promotion and protection of the faith, is remarkable. They have been the almost forgotten forerunners of much that is today commonly accepted by Protestant Christendom, particularly in England and the United States."

This statement is typical of the claims made nowadays for Anabaptism, but it obscures the serious deficiencies of Anabaptist theology. To say that among Anabaptists "the Protestant doctrine of justification by faith, and the priesthood of all believers, were fully held, though not theologically developed" conceals the fact that in vital ways the Anabaptist position on justification was closer to the Council of Trent than it was to the Reformers. Bender's statements that "the Anabaptists emphasized an existential more than a theological Christianity" and that they broke with Protestantism on "the nature of Christianity as discipleship or transformation of life rather than primarily as the enjoyment of forgiveness and salvation as status," are an admission of this affinity to Rome's doctrine of justification. An "existential Christianity" in contrast to a theological Christianity is primarily subjective, with the ever-present danger of exalting personal feelings and ideas to a place of authority that is equal or superior to God's written word. And it also runs the very real risk of attributing to sanctification what belongs to justification in the plan of salvation, resulting in a species of the notion of salvation by works.

Anabaptist apologists vigorously deny these charges. However, the history and writings of the early Anabaptists supply ample testimony that they did fall into these heresies.

Not only did Thomas Müntzer and the Zwickau Prophets claim direct revelation that often relegated the Bible to the position of "a dead letter," as Nicholas Storch called it, but the same idea found acceptance among some Swiss and Dutch Anabaptists. Some of them, like Jacob Storger, set up "the inner word" as the standard for judging doctrinal truth, while others, like David Joris (who later recanted and died a Calvinist), believed they enjoyed clearer revelation than Biblical writers such as David and Paul.

On the subject of salvation, the affinity of leading Anabaptists with the Roman Catholic position may be seen from the following:

Jacob Kautz taught that walking the way which Christ blazed for us is the only payment for our sins.

Peter Walpot taught that following Christ's words and commands is alone what saves us.

Michael Sattler rejected all idea of unconditional election.

Balthasar Hubmaier denied man's total depravity because of the fall* and championed the idea of man's freedom of will* (paradoxically he claimed that in Eden man had been "forced against his will" to sin, yet somehow now enjoys a "free" will!).

These were not merely aberrant views by an Anabaptist lunatic fringe. Anabaptist theology reflected the Roman Catholic idea of synergism.* It also reflected Rome's notion of children being innocent of original sin. In Rome's case original sin is removed by baptism while the Anabaptists went one better (or worse)—rejecting infant baptism, they taught that children were born in a state somewhat like Adam's before the fall. This is pure Pelagianism.*

These anthropological and soteriological departures from the Biblical faith of the Reformers had serious consequences, chief of which was, contrary to Bender's claim, a repudiation of the Protestant doctrine of *sola fide,* justification by faith alone.

Anabaptists laid great stress on the redemptive value of personal suffering. Leonard Schiemer said, "Without my suffering God cannot save me in spite of all His power." Hans Hut taught that we can be justified only through our personal suffering. Hubmaier taught that God expects a sinner "through remorse, regret, and contrition" to "make a payment to His godly and offended righteousness."

All this is directly in line with the theology of Trent and affords faith no greater place in the scheme of salvation than Rome's soteriology* does. Anabaptists further betrayed their theological affinity with Rome by adopting the doctrine of the possibility of justified souls falling away and being eternally lost. Hans Denck taught that God may reject in damnation some whom He had received in faith, while Hubmaier taught that through perverseness truly regenerate souls could bring themselves again under condemnation.

These are serious departures from the Biblical faith of the Reformers and explain the fervency with which the Protestant leaders opposed the Anabaptists. Many of the Anabaptist characteristics enumerated by Bender evoke support from most modern Christians. Separation of church and state has become accepted dogma for most churches and in this Anabaptists blazed the way. Or did they?

According to Arnold Snyder, Swiss Anabaptism made a "serious attempt…to establish itself as a territorial church" (*Mennonite Quarterly Review,* January 1983, "The Monastic Origins of Swiss Anabaptist Sectarianism," p. 7). He points out that they temporarily succeeded in doing so in Waldshut and Hallau, while they made vigorous attempts to do the same in Schaffhausen, St.

Gall, and Grünigen. According to Zwingli, Grebel and Manz wished to reform the church in Zurich by electing a new "God-fearing" city council. And, of course, Thomas Müntzer's Peasants' War and the Münster rebellion were overt attempts to integrate church and state.

While not all Anabaptists would have agreed with these attempts, the question still remains: Were the Anabaptists proponents of separation between church and state because they failed to obtain the kind of state church they preferred? Would their doctrine have followed the same course if their claimed founders, Grebel and Manz, had been able to work through the city council to produce a church to their liking?

We cannot be sure, but we can be sure that the notion that the Anabaptist leaders saw the issue of church and state much more clearly than the Protestant Reformers and tried to take the Reformers' work to its logical and Biblical conclusion is not justified by the facts.

Many of the Anabaptists' most serious departures from the faith are entirely ignored in Bender's statement of their beliefs. Their Pelagian tendency, already noted, is emphasized by their doctrine of free will,* of original sin,* and of the relation of faith to regeneration.*

They tended also to asceticism,* Felix Manz going so far as to say that those who join themselves to the church should know themselves to be without sin (Davis, p. 70). Davis summarizes Anabaptist asceticism: "Luther's and Calvin's Reformation may be considered a Protestantization of Augustine of Hippo, so Anabaptism is a Protestantization of Francis of Assisi, Gerhard Groote, and, perhaps even more, a Protestantization of Erasmus" (p. 297).

Among serious Anabaptist doctrinal departures, perhaps none is more important than their Docetic* views of the person of Christ. Even some of the most celebrated of Anabaptist leaders held defective views of the humanity of Christ. Menno Simons denied that Christ's flesh was derived from Mary. This was the generally received Anabaptist position. Bernard Rothmann, Melchior Hoffman, Obbe Philips, and Adam Pastor all echoed Simons' belief. John S. Oyer, an Anabaptist, says that docetism was "the usual deviation from orthodox Christology in Central German Anabaptism" (*Lutheran Reformers Against Anabaptists,* pp. 98, 192).

Antitrinitarianism was also rife among 16th-century Anabaptists. Baptist historian W. J. McGlothlin wrote, "Most of the forms of Unitarianism were represented among Anabaptists" (*A Guide to the Study of Church History,* p. 231). The Italian Anabaptists and the Polish Brethren were Unitarian. Modern Anabaptists deny that these groups may properly be described as Anabaptists. But even excluding them, the stigma of Unitarianism lingers with recognized Anabaptists. Han Denck, John Companus, David Joris, Adam Pastor, Mechior Hoffman, Louis Haetzer, and Claas Epp undermined the doctrine of the Trinity.*

It would be wrong to saddle all 16th-century Anabaptists with all these heresies. But it is equally unhistorical to speak of the Anabaptist "radical Reformation" or to give the impression that the Anabaptists represented a nearer and purer return to New Testament Christianity than did the churches of the Reformation. Anabaptism at its best was doctrinally flawed on the crucial matters of the person of Christ and justification. It presented a wide spectrum of belief and practice with baptism upon profession of faith (usually by pouring or sprinkling, not by immersion) as the common doctrinal bond.

The Spread and Suffering of the Anabaptists

The Anabaptists presented a series of beliefs and practices that appeared to threaten all good government in both church and state. No doubt Roman Catholics and Protestants in both overreacted, though that is easier to see with the benefit of hindsight than it would have been amid the upheavals of the 16th century. As a result Anabaptists suffered persecution, often unto death. As we have noted, Felix Manz was executed in Zurich, a stain on the Zwinglian Reformation that time has not removed. He was followed by many more martyrs, especially in regions ruled by Roman Catholicism,* though the Protestants were not free from Anabaptist blood.

Despite all their sufferings the Anabaptists spread quickly. They were all but eradicated in Switzerland but spread through Germany, Austria, Poland, Moravia, Holland, and England. Starting in the 18th century they even penetrated into the Ukraine, Southern Russia, and Siberia. The most influential branches of the movement were the followers of Jacob Hutter (the Hutterite Brotherhood), of Balthasar Hubmaier, and of Menno Simons (the Mennonites). Simons (1496-1561) led the Dutch Anabaptists in a vigorous and extensive movement that was for some time the strongest Protestant group in Holland. From Europe the Anabaptists emigrated to North America where their influence is still strong in the Mennonite churches and among the Amish people.

In retrospect, perhaps the fairest summary we can make of the turbulent and tragic confrontations between the Anabaptists and the mainstream Reformers is that the Anabaptists as a whole were neither as pernicious as the Reformers imagined, nor as pure as their modern apologists insist—though in the ferment of the 16th-century Reformation it is understandable that the Reformers did not discriminate between the better Anabaptists and their less worthy colleagues.

ANAGOGICAL

From the Greek *anago* "to lead," or "bring up." It is one of the four senses in which Scripture was interpreted by the Alexandrian

school* of Origen and by the Roman Catholic church. "The anagogical sense is when the sacred text is explained with regard to eternal life; for example, the rest of the Sabbath, in the anagogical sense, signifies the repose of everlasting happiness" (McClintock and Strong, I.212). This example uses an interpretation which the New Testament itself appears to use. In the view of many, Hebrews 4 attaches such an eschatological significance to the sabbath. However, the anagogical meanings claimed by Romish interpreters were usually very much more imaginary. Coming from a distaste for and distrust of the literal sense of Scripture, anagogical interpretation did more to obscure God's word than to elucidate it.

See **Allegory**.

ANALOGY

1. A form of scholastic* reasoning based on the inference that an object which resembles another in a number of points will probably resemble it in others. On this basis scholasticism developed an intricate system of natural theology,* arguing from the finite to the infinite. The basic fallacy in this approach, as in so many others, is in making man's reason the starting point and ultimate reference point of knowledge, which in reality means that man is the judge of God and the determiner of what God is.

2. In the study of Christian evidences* and epistemology* analogy has a varied meaning and usage. Bishop Butler titled his famous book of Christian evidences the *Analogy of Religion Natural and Revealed to the Constitution and Courses of Nature*. Butler argued in favour of the probability of Christianity by means of analogical reasoning. That is, starting with the known "constitution and courses of nature," he proceeded to reason about unknown possibilities. The analogy (or likeness) between the natural realm and that of Scripture argues strongly for the probability that nature and Scripture have the same Author, God.

For example, on the subject of a future life, Butler argues (to quote Cornelius Van Til's summary), "Although we have in our lifetime undergone much change, we have still survived. Therefore, it is likely that we shall survive death also" (Van Til, *Christian-Theistic Evidences,* class syllabus, p. 5). Butler believed what the Bible taught about the certainty that death was not the end of man's existence. His argument from analogy was that such a revelation is not unreasonable. Van Til regarded this use of analogy as defective and ultimately unchristian and ineffective for its professed purpose, the defence of Christianity from scepticism.

Butler argued as an inconsistent empiricist,* one who believed that reason could only accept what came to it via the experience of our senses. Later empiricists, such as David Hume, rejected his use of analogy. For example, Hume rejected Butler's argument for a future life by saying that such a belief has no real point of resemblance to the changes from embryo to infant to mature age—a resemblance on which Butler had rested his case. Hume argued that human experience cannot predict the future. "Analogy cannot carry us into the unknown" (Van Til, p. 30).

Despite this it is the usual method of apologetics* to depend to some degree on a false view of analogy. "If we seek to defend the Christian religion by an 'appeal to the facts of experience' in accord with the current scientific method, we shall have to adulterate Christianity beyond recognition. The Christianity defended by Bishop Butler was not full fledged Christianity. It was Christianity neatly trimmed down to the needs of a method that was based upon non-Christian assumptions. And what was true of Butler is largely true of English-American evidences and apologetics in general" (Van Til, p. 51).

Van Til replaces Butler's notion of analogy with one that is squarely based upon the presupposition of the ontological Trinity,* self-revealed in the self-authenticating Scriptures, and fully declared in the incarnate Son, the Lord Jesus Christ. He is the Creator and upholder of all things, the One by whom all created things exist and have their meaning. Without Him nothing has any meaning.

"As Christians we hold that it is impossible to interpret any fact without a basic falsification unless it be regarded in its relation to God the Creator and Christ the Redeemer....That this implies a reversal of the method employed by Butler and the others is apparent. We do not offer Christianity to men apologetically, admitting that their interpretation of life is right as far as it goes. In particular we do not accept the 'appeal to facts' as a common meeting place between believers and unbelievers. Christianity does not thus need to take shelter under the roof of 'known facts.' It rather offers itself as a roof to facts if they would be known. Christianity does not need to take shelter under the roof of a scientific method independent of itself. It rather offers itself as a roof to methods that would be scientific" (Van Til, p. 54).

In other words, God is the "constitutive Creator and interpreter of the facts of the universe." Man can be only a re-interpreter. His highest achievement is to think God's thoughts after Him. That is the true use of analogy—to think of things as God does. As Van Til put it in his *Survey of Christian Epistemology:*

"The necessity of reasoning analogically is always implied in the theistic conception of God. If God is to be thought of at all as necessary for man's interpretation of the facts or objects of knowledge, he must be thought of as being determinative of the objects of knowledge. In other words, he must then be thought of as the only ultimate interpreter, and man must be thought of as a finite reinterpreter. Since, then, the absolute self-consciousness of God is the final interpreter of all facts, man's knowledge is analogical of God's knowledge. Since all finite facts exist by virtue of the interpretation of God, man's interpretation of the finite facts is ultimately dependent upon God's interpretation of the facts. Man cannot, except to his own hurt, look at the facts without looking at God's interpretation of the facts. Man's knowledge of the facts is then a reinterpretation of God's interpretation. It is this that is meant by saying that man's knowledge is analogical of God's knowledge" (pp. 203, 204).

See **Presupposition**.

ANAMNESIS

The Greek noun used in Luke 22:19 and 1 Cor. 11:24, 25 in the phrase *eis ten emen anamnesin,* translated "in remembrance of me," lit., "for my remembrance (or, memorial)."

The Roman Catholic church makes a lot of this term in defence of its dogma of the mass* as a sacrifice of expiation* made to God for the sins of the living and the dead: "In all the Eucharist prayers we find after the words of institution a prayer called the anamnesis or memorial. In the sense of sacred Scripture the memorial is not merely the recollection of past events but the proclamation of the mighty works wrought by God for men. In the liturgical celebration of these events, they become in a certain way present and real....In the New Testament, the memorial takes on a new meaning. When the Church celebrates the Eucharist, she commemorates Christ's Passover, and it is made present: the sacrifice Christ offered once for all on the cross remains ever present. 'As often as the sacrifice of the cross by which Christ our Pasch has been sacrificed is celebrated on the altar, the work of our redemption is carried out.' Because it is the memorial of Christ's Passover, the Eucharist is also a sacrifice" (*Catechism of the Catholic Church,* ¶ 1362–1365).

In this use of *anamnesis* it is God who is reminded; otherwise there would be a complete lack of logic in the statement, "Because it is the memorial of Christ's Passover, the Eucharist is also a sacrifice." If the bread and wine in the communion feast are designed to remind us of Christ's sacrifice at Calvary, there is no logical presumption that the reminder of the sacrifice is itself a sacrifice. In fact, the opposite is true. That which is to us a reminder of Christ's sacrifice is presumably not the very sacrifice it is designed to remind us of. If, however, the primary design of the communion service is to offer to God a reminder of Christ's sacrifice, it may be logical to look on that reminder as a sacrifice, or the same sacrifice re-presented to God, as Rome's standards like to put it (*Catechism of the Catholic Church,* ¶ 1366; Council of Trent, Session 22, chap. 1).

However, it is quite clear that Rome's liturgical use of *anamnesis* does not correspond with Christ's simple use of the term in instituting the Lord's Supper.* There He clearly intended the bread and wine to be a constant reminder to His people of His sacrifice at Calvary. There is no suggestion either of reminding God of Calvary (could He forget?) or of making physically present that which is past. Yet it is on this nonexistent usage and meaning of *anamnesis* that modern day ecumenists* largely depend to produce an accommodation between Protestant theology and the Roman dogma of the mass (e.g., the 1982 Baptism, Eucharist, and Ministry document of the World Council of Churches*).

ANATHEMA

From the Greek verb *anatithemi,* "to lay up"; *anathema* is found in the Greek NT in two forms, one with *eta* (long *e*) and the other with *epsilon* (short *e*) in the penult syllable. Originally the word denoted anything laid up, or set apart, for divine service. This meaning is reflected in Luke 21:5 where it is translated "gifts." The LXX used *anathema* to translate the Hebrew *cherem*, which the AV translates as "accursed" (Josh. 6:17, 18; 7:1, 11, 12, 13, 15; 1 Chron. 2:7); "cursed thing" (Deut. 7:26; 13:17); "curse" (Josh. 6:18; Isa. 34:5; 43:28); "utter destruction" (Zech. 14:11); "devoted" (Lev. 27:21, 28, 29; Num. 18:14) and "dedicated thing" (Ezek. 44:29).

While there appears to be a very broad scope of meaning in *cherem*, all the way from "dedicated" to "accursed," the fact is that what was dedicated or devoted to holy use was off limits for secular use. Thus it was banned. Anyone failing to observe the ban would come under appropriate condemnation; he would be accursed. That was the meaning that attached to *anathema* when the LXX translators used it to translate *cherem*.

The NT carries on this meaning. 1 Corinthians 16:22 pronounces the curse on any who love not our Lord Jesus Christ, *anathema maranatha*. Elsewhere the AV translates *anathema* "accursed" (Rom. 9:3; 1 Cor. 12:3; Gal. 1:8) and once "curse" (Acts 23:12). Thus *anathema* signifies the utter ruin of one devoted to destruction. It is significant that this is the word Paul used in Gal. 1:8, 9 to condemn anyone who would "preach any other gospel" than the gospel of free, redeeming, justifying grace received by faith without the works of the law.

ANCHORITE

An ascetic whose title indicates that he has retired from human society; from the Greek *ana,* "back," and *chorein,* "to retire." Ascetics used different appellations to express their solitary lifestyle: monk, from *monos,* "alone," signified one who dwelt alone; eremite, from *eremos,* "desert," (Anglicized as "hermit") signified a desert dweller.

In time these distinctions came to indicate the degree of austerity by which a recluse lived. The anchorites practised excessive austerity, choosing the wildest localities for their retreats. Many of them "voluntarily subjected themselves to the vicissitudes of the weather, without habita-

tion or clothing, restricted themselves to coarse and scanty fare, wore chains and iron rings, and even throughout many years maintained painful postures, such as standing on top of a pillar" (McClintock and Strong). Those pillar-dwellers were called *stylites.*

Anchorites abounded in the ancient Eastern church and were admired as men of superior holiness whose blessing or opinions were often sought. When they left their retreats to re-enter society with a message of warning, instruction, or encouragement, they were received as if they were inspired prophets of God.

ANGEL

The Hebrew *mal'ak,* and the Greek *angelos* carry the idea of "agent" or "messenger" and are used in the following ways:
1. To describe intelligent, moral, immortal, and spiritual creatures of God, higher in rank than man (Ps. 8:5).
2. As the title given in Rev. 1-3 to the messenger or ministering elder of a local church.
3. As a title of Christ as mediator, "messenger (angel) of the covenant" (Mal. 3:1; cf. Gen. 48:16, etc.). This title in no way lessens the Scripture testimony to Christ's deity, for Mal. 3:1 identifies the *angel* with *ha'adon,* "the Lord." The definite article in *ha'adon* always refers to God. Thus the use of *angel* to describe Christ does not compromise His deity but emphasizes that the Father sent Him as the only Redeemer of His elect *(see Theophany).*

Considering the normal use of the word in Scripture we may note the following data about angels.
1. Their creation (Ps. 148:2, 5; Col. 1:16; cf. 1 Kings 22:19; Ps. 103:20, 21). That this took place within the creation week of Gen. 1 is clear from Exod. 20:11.
2. They are spiritual and incorporeal (Matt. 8:16; 12:45; Luke. 7:21; 8:2, 30; 11:26; 24:39; Col. 1:16; Heb. 1:7, 14), though they may assume a bodily form for a specific service for the Lord (e.g., Gen. 19:1, etc.).

3. They are rational, moral, and immortal beings, endowed with intelligence and will (2 Sam. 14:20; Matt. 24:36; Eph. 3:10; 1 Pet. 1:12; 2 Pet. 2:11). As responsible moral agents they are rewarded for obedience and punished for disobedience.

4. Some are good and some evil. Holy angels (Matt. 25:31; Mark 8:38, etc.) are "elect" and therefore loyal (1 Tim. 5:21). Others are called the devil's angels (Matt. 25:41), those who sinned (2 Pet. 2:4) and "kept not their first estate" and are under condemnation (Jude 6, 7).

5. They have great power, but are under divine control (Ps. 103:20; Col. 1:16; Eph. 1:21; 3:10; Heb. 1:14; cf. Luke 11:20-22; 2 Thess. 2:9; 1 Pet. 5:8.)

6. They are very numerous (Deut. 33:2; Ps. 68:17; Mark 5:9, 15; Matt. 26:53; Rev. 5:11).

7. They are organized in ranks of dignity and function. *Cherubim* (Gen. 3:24; Exod. 25:18; 2 Sam. 22:11; Ezek. 1; Rev. 4) more than any other creatures reveal the power and majesty of God. *Seraphim* (Isa. 6:2, 6) are clearly prepared for the immediate execution of the Lord's commands. *Principalities, powers, thrones,* and *dominions* (Eph. 3:10; Col. 1:16; 2:10; Eph. 1:21; 1 Pet. 3:22) indicate God-ordained differences in rank or dignity.

8. Only two are actually named in Scripture. Michael (Dan. 10:13, 21; Jude 9; Rev. 12:7) is called the archangel, which would seem to place him first in rank among, or at least in the first rank of, the angels. Gabriel is the only other angel named (Dan. 8:16; 9:21; Luke 1:19, 26).

9. Their ordinary service is praising God (Job 38:7; Isa. 6:3; Rev. 5:11) and since the fall,* ministering to the heirs of salvation (Heb. 1:14; note Luke. 15:10; Ps. 34:7; 91:11; Matt. 18:10; 1 Cor. 11:10; 1 Tim. 5:21; Luke. 16:22).

10. They also perform extraordinary service. Because of the fall they have an important part in God's special revelation.* Berkhof remarks, "They often mediate the special revelations of God, communicate blessings to His people, and execute judgment upon His enemies. Their activity is most prominent in the great turning points of the economy of salvation."

See **Satan.**

ANGELUS

The thrice daily recitation of prayers and *Hail Marys** to the Virgin Mary by Roman Catholics. The hours for these prayers are marked by sounding a bell three times, three strokes each time. The Angelus was instituted by Pope John XXII in 1316. Since then several popes have granted indulgences to those who say the Angelus prayers on their knees.

The introduction of the Angelus occurred during a period of increasing devotion to Mary and the popular acceptance of such notions as her assumption,* her immaculate conception,* and her participation in procuring redemption, as co-redemptrix, and co-mediatrix with her Son. *(See* **Maryolatry.***)*

ANGLICANISM

The system of doctrine and government of the Church of England. Historically, Anglicanism embraced a variety of theological positions. The Church of England does not hold to a definite theological system but has long been divided into parties that have very little in common beyond their adherence to the church. These parties are generally known as high church *(see* **Anglo-Catholicism),** and low church (evangelical), and broad church (liberal; *see* **Latitudinarianism).**

At first, however, Anglicanism, despite its adherence to episcopacy, was clearly Protestant. For the most part, Anglicanism repudiated Rome's views on papal supremacy and sacramentalism* and strongly defended justification* by faith alone. However, the Church of England repudiated Puritanism as surely as it did Romanism. Thus in time it came to see itself as a middle way between Geneva and Rome, while remaining avowedly Protestant. Later it declined further by presenting itself as a middle way between Protestantism and Roman Catholicism, gradually losing its Protestant distinctives and leaning more openly toward Rome. This decline has accelerated as Anglican leaders have assumed a prominent role in the effort to effect union with Rome under the headship of the pope.

For a couple of centuries after the time of Elizabeth I, Anglicanism comprehended only the Church of England and Wales and the Church of Ireland. It expanded with the consecration of bishops in America and other colonies and with the absorption of the Episcopal Church of Scotland. Today it is a worldwide communion loosely held together by the Lambeth Conference, which meets every ten years.

ANGLO-CATHOLICISM

Also known as *Tractarianism** (because it was launched through a series of *Tracts for the Times* in 1833) and the *Oxford Movement* (because these tracts were produced by a group of Anglican clergymen at Oxford University). The movement wanted a return to pre-Reformation beliefs and practices in the Church of England, with all its formularies interpreted in a Roman Catholic sense.

The first leader of the movement was John Henry Newman, who joined the Church of Rome in 1845 and was made a cardinal in 1879. Another prominent figure was E. B. Pusey, whose name gave rise to the popular name by which the Anglo-Catholics were, and are, known: Puseyites.

This movement is still very active in the Church of England and has prompted the use of such Romish inventions as monasticism, the mass,* and auricular confession.*

ANIMISM

The belief that inanimate objects possess a soul or spirit or that they are indwelt by spirits. Often the indwelling spirit is thought to be that of the departed, resulting in ancestor worship. Animistic religion is a religion of fear. Some New Age* advocates view animism as a way of deifying the earth.

*See **African Theology.***

ANNIHILATION

From the Latin *nihil,* "nothing," the belief that

1. All men pass out of existence at death; or
2. While God confers the gift of immortality upon His redeemed people, He allows the rest of humanity to sink into nothingness (this is the theory of conditional immortality*); or
3. All men are created immortal, but reprobates are by the direct act of God, or through the natural effects of their sin, put out of existence.

These last two notions are usually regarded as one.

ANNUNCIATION

1. The announcement of the coming birth of Christ. While such an announcement was made both to Joseph (Matt. 1:20) and Mary (Luke 1:26-35), the usage of the word is frequently limited to the latter event.
2. The festival observed in honour of that announcement, usually March 25. Observances of the Feast of the Annunciation may be traced back to the 4th or 5th century in both the Eastern and Western church.

ANTEDELUVIAN

Descriptive of the period before the deluge, or flood, in the days of Noah (Gen. 2:6-8). The Biblical description of the period contradicts many popular opinions about early man and society. Man was not a savage a step or two away from the apes. Indeed he was not evolving biologically, morally, or socially, but was devolving. From his initial created purity man was declining to such an extent that he provoked the wrath of God upon the world.

Antedeluvian man had a knowledge of God, which he corrupted. He was endowed with great intellectual powers and artistic gifts. He was acquainted with music (Gen. 4:21) and with various branches of science (e.g., zoology, biology, botany, astronomy, mineralogy).

The most noticeable characteristics of antedeluvian man were his enjoyment of a uniform language, his longevity, and his terrible apostasy from revealed truth, the results of which were widespread moral turpitude, utter carelessness about the things of God (Matt. 24:38,39), and a ripeness for judgment that called forth the great flood.

Our knowledge of the antedeluvian earth is limited, but some have concluded that it enjoyed a uniform temperate climate, that it was enclosed in a great vapour envelope (the source of most of the enormous amounts of water that fell during the first forty days of the flood), that its geographical and topographical features were very different from the post-deluvian world (especially with regard to the great ice caps, the continents, the depths of the oceans, and the heights of the mountains), and that it supported a population of about one billion people. (J. C. Whitcomb and Henry Morris present the evidence for these views in their work *The Genesis Flood*).

ANTHROPOCENTRIC

"Man-centred," a term often used of most schemes of modern theology and philosophy.

See Consciousness Theology.

ANTHROPOLOGY

The science, or study, of man. As a section of systematic theology* it deals with man's creation, his original state, his probation and fall* into sin,* original sin* (including the nature, transmission and effects of sin), and actual transgressions.

ANTHROPOMORPHISM

1. The representation of God under a human form.

2. The figure of speech by which Scripture attributes human parts, actions, affections, and emotions to God. Thus while God as a pure spirit has no bodily parts or passions the Bible speaks of His eyes, His ears, His hands, etc. God does not actually have any bodily parts (though it should be remembered that the Son of God did take an actual human body and soul into personal union with Himself. Thus any references to the incarnate Son's physical presence and properties must be taken literally; they are not anthropomorphic).

When the Bible attributes human characteristics to God, it speaks metaphorically to enable us to understand an otherwise abstract truth. Thus God's *eye* speaks of His knowledge; His *hand* speaks of His action; His *heart* speaks of His love; His *face* speaks of His presence. Failing to understand this figurative usage, some heretics in the early church interpreted literally those Scriptures which metaphorically attributed some physical characteristic to God. They especially emphasized Gen. 1:26, 27, which they understood to teach that God had an actual physical form upon which He modelled man!

Anthropomorphists have reappeared from time to time in church history. Mormons* are anthropomorphists.

See Anthropopathy.

ANTHROPOPATHY

A form of anthropomorphism.* Anthropomorphism covers the attribution to God of anything that may properly be attributed only to man. Anthropopathy attributes human feelings or passions to God. If the Bible attributes any human passion or feeling to God that, strictly understood, conflicts with His absolute perfection, it is speaking anthropopathetically. We should see the use of this figure as a divine condescension that explains God's motives and actions in terms we can understand.

As rational, sentient, physical, and psychical beings we are limited by our own physical, intellectual, and emotional abilities to comprehend God's revelation of Himself. We need the anthropomorphic and anthropopathic language of the Bible to enable us to grasp truth that would otherwise be beyond our reach. However, we must be careful to remember that the Biblical usage of these figures is part of God's self-revelation. We should seek to understand from Scripture what He means to convey by using the figures, but we are not free to proceed to invent new anthropomorphic or anthropopathic images of Him. We have no authority to do so. It would be idolatry.

ANTIBAPTISTS

1. Those, for example the Quakers,* who deny the propriety of water baptism in the Christian church. Such people hold that water baptism has been replaced by Spirit baptism. It is interesting that early extreme dispensationalists* approximated this view, holding that water baptism belonged to the gospel of the kingdom, Spirit baptism to the gospel of the grace of God. Thus in the "church age" water baptism is not an ordinance; it will be reintroduced only after the rapture* of the church when the gospel of the kingdom is again preached.
2. Those who believe that baptism should be administered to new converts from other religions, but not to their descendants, infant or adult, who are born in Christianity. The claimed basis for this idea is twofold—the Saviour's words of commission and the practice of the apostles. Needless to say neither provides any real foundation for the theory.

ANTIBURGHERS

*See **Burghers**.*

ANTICHRIST

The Greek preposition *anti* signifies "in place of," rather than merely "against." The word *antichrist*, then, speaks of one who opposes Christ by posing as Him or usurping His place. He opposes and exalts himself above all that is called God; thus he is called "the man of sin," "the lawless one," "that wicked one," "the son of perdition" in 2 Thess. 2. The same evil person is called "the little horn" in Dan. 7:8 and the beast out of the sea in Rev. 13. 1 John 2:18 shows that while there are many antichrists, there will come one to whom the title preeminently belongs. He will be aided by the beast out of the land, the false prophet (Rev. 13:11; 16:13), and will finally be destroyed by the spirit of the Lord's mouth and the brightness of His coming (2 Thess. 2:8), being cast alive into the lake of fire (Rev. 19:20).

Many Protestants have identified the papacy as the antichrist. The *Westminster Confession of Faith* (chap. 25, sec. 5) agrees in that identification, noting his sphere of deception as being "in the church." The fact that it describes the entire papal system of Rome as anti-Christian does not necessarily preclude the idea of a future revelation of one who will merit the name *antichrist* in a preeminent degree.

ANTILEGOMENA

A term first used by Origen to denote disputed books that claimed a place in the New Testament canon. The NT books about which questions were raised were Hebrews, James, 2 Peter, 2 and 3 John, Jude, and Revelation.
*See **Homolegoumena**.*

ANTINOMIANISM
Meaning of the Term

Greek, *anti*, "against," *nomos*, "law"; a term that literally means "against the law," it is the title given to those who hold that
1. When Scripture says that believers are not under law but under grace, it means that

the moral law is not binding upon believers in any sense, even in the sense of a rule of life; and/or

2. A believer may sin with impunity because the grace of God superabounds over his sin.

In the first sense, antinomianism has attracted many Calvinistic supporters who have seen it as a bulwark of the doctrine of free grace. Many dispensationalists have also adopted it, ostensibly for the same reasons, but much more on account of their peculiar views on the relationship of the OT and NT in God's plan of salvation.

Whereas Protestant theology has been careful to note the difference between the law as a covenant and the law as a commandment or rule of life, antinomians reject such a distinction. To them there is "no Moses now," to use the words of 17th century antinomian John Saltmarsh. Saltmarsh stated his own view: "The gospel is…a perfect law of life and righteousness…and therefore I wonder at any that should contend for the ministry of the law or Ten Commandments under Moses" (*Free Grace,* p. 146, quoted, Ernest Kevan, *The Grace of Law,* p. 169). Restricted to the idea of the law as covenant, this would be a perfectly orthodox Puritan sentiment. However, Saltmarsh included every suggestion of the law as a rule or standard of obedience. This rejection of the law as a rule of life is the essence of antinomianism.

Alleged Scripture Support for Antinomianism

Antinomians claim the support of various NT texts:

Gal. 2:19, "I through the law am dead to the law, that I might live unto God";

Rom. 6:14, "Sin shall not have dominion over you: for ye are not under the law but under grace";

Rom. 7:4-6, particularly v. 6, "Now we are delivered from the law, that being dead wherein we were held; that we should serve in newness of spirit, and not in the oldness

of the letter";

1 Tim. 1:9, "The law is not made for a righteous man, but for the lawless and disobedient."

Scripture Proofs Against Antinomianism

All these Scripture texts mean nothing more than that the law is no longer a covenant of life for believers. We are not under the law of works-righteousness but under grace with its provision of the imputation of the perfect righteousness of Christ through faith without works. But that is a very long way from denying that God's law, reflecting His essential holiness, is a commandment to be obeyed by believers out love for Him. A careful reading of the very texts antinomians cite will show that they impose a meaning on the words of Scripture that the writers of Scripture never intended.

Gal. 2:19 and Rom. 7:4-6 teach that in Christ believers are legally free from the law's condemnation. In the latter passage, Paul shows that the law is not dead but satisfied.

Rom. 6:14 cannot have an antinomian meaning. It cannot mean that Christians have no obligation to obey God's law, for the very next verse says, "What then, shall we sin, because we are not under the law, but under grace? God forbid." Sin is the breach of the law (1 John 3:4). On antinomian principles, since the law has nothing to say to believers, they cannot sin whatever they do in any matter covered by it. However, Rom. 6:15 is clearly an argument for obeying the law. Its meaning is beyond dispute: "Since we are not under the law as a covenant of life but are saved by free grace, let us keep the righteous standard of the law as our rule of life."

When Paul told Timothy, "The law is not made for a righteous man, but for the lawless and disobedient" (1 Tim. 1:9), he used an interesting verb. The expression *is not made for* translates the Greek verb *keimai,* which has the force of *to lie upon.* What Paul said was that the law lies upon sinners, not justified people. The Puritan interpretation of this verse is to the point: the law was not given to condemn the righteous but sinners. Therefore to use it to bring justified people under condemnation is an unlawful use of the law.

Positive arguments in favour of the classic Protestant position are plain and persuasive.

1. According to Exod. 20:1-3 the Lord addressed the law to the Israelites as His redeemed. Redemption was all the more reason for obeying it.

2. The NT goes further and makes obedience to the rule of God's law the mark of true believers: "Hereby we do know that we know him, if we keep his commandments. He that saith, I know him, and keepeth not his commandments, is a liar, and the truth is not in him" (1 John 2:3, 4).

3. Paul gave the testimony of a justified man: "I delight in the law of God after the inward man" (Rom. 7:22).

4. In a statement that is the very opposite of both antinomianism and legalism* Paul defined the essence of the covenant of grace in such a way as to prove that it neither makes the law the way of salvation nor eradicates it as the rule of Christian living: "I will make a new covenant with the house of Israel and with the house of Judah:…this is the covenant that I will make with the house of Israel after those days, saith the Lord; I will put my laws into their mind, and write them in their hearts" (Heb. 8:8, 10).

5. According to Rom. 3:31, grace does not lessen but increase a believer's obligation to keep God's law: "Do we then make void [or, abolish, do away with] the law through faith? God forbid: yea we establish the law."

6. Perhaps 1 Cor. 9:21 sums up the believer's relation to the law as simply as any text of Scripture: "[We are] not without law to God, but under the law to Christ." The Greek for "under the law to Christ" is *ennomos Christo,* "in law to Christ." Thus believers are not without law. Neither are they

under law so that it condemns them. Rather, they are in (not outside) law to Christ, that is under its direction as a rule of life. As Puritan Thomas Taylor put it, "The liberty of a Christian man is not liberty from obedience to the law but from disobedience to it."

*See **Decalogue; Law of God.***

ANTIOCHAN SCHOOL

1. A system of Bible interpretation, centred in Antioch, which opposed the Alexandrian school* of interpretation. Whereas the Alexandrians depended on Plato's philosophy, the Antiochans embraced Aristotle's. Their method was more historical and literal and therefore avoided the wild allegorizing that the Alexandrian mysticism* foisted upon Scripture. While this was a true advance, the dependence on Greek philosophy remained a weakness. *(See **Aristotelianism; Platonism.**)*

2. The term used to describe the peculiar theological speculations of the Syrian church in the controversies surrounding the theanthropic person* of Christ. In this sense, the Antiochan school means Nestorianism,* or views tending toward it.

ANTIPOPE

A pope elected, usually by the will of a powerful sovereign, as a rival of the pope "canonically" elected. During the Middle Ages there were at times three or four competing popes. "The thirteenth and fourteenth centuries swarm with antipopes" (McClintock and Strong). For half a century from 1378, the European church was divided by the Great Schism of the West. The world was treated to the spectacle of two popes, Clement VII and Urban VI, excommunicating each other. After them, there were three competing popes until, in 1415, the Council of Constance deposed all three. The last antipope was Clement VIII, who in 1429 finally recognized the decision of the Council of Constance and resigned in favour of their nominee, Martin V.

ANTITRINITARIANS

Unitarians;* the name given to the various groups who opposed the doctrine of the Trinity,* especially in the first three centuries of the church and in the period during and after the Protestant Reformation.* In the ancient church, antitrinitarians included Monarchians,* Patripassians,* Sabellians,* and Arians.* In the 16th century, rationalistic or dynamic Monarchians came to be known as Socinians.* Socinianism and Sabellianism broke out in various parts of the Anabaptist* movement, and even Tritheism* found some supporters.

ANTITYPE

From the Greek *antitupos,* which occurs in Heb. 9:24 and 1 Pet. 3:21 where the AV translates it "figure." An antitype is the substance of which a type* is the shadow, or the fulfilment of that which the type foreshadowed.

APOCALYPSE

From the Greek word used in Rev. 1:1, it means the Revelation, while the adjective *apocalyptic* is loosely used to describe (1) anything pertaining to the end time, and (2) those cataclysmic events which precede the end.

See **Second Coming**.

APOCALYPTICISM

The style of writing in the book of the Revelation (Greek, *apokalupsis*). Scripturally, apocalypticism is the revelation or unveiling of Christ, especially in relation to His second coming,* by means of visions and symbols that demonstrate the following:
1. The power of God over heaven, earth, and hell;
2. His sovereign outworking of His purposes in the history of the world, especially in the climactic scenes of the end time; and
3. The ultimate victory of redemptive grace in and through the Lord Jesus Christ.
 More generally, *apocalypticism* is applied to

portions of Daniel and even to uninspired Jewish writings of the inter-testamental period. In the popular mind it signifies reference to any great cataclysmic events or forces that portend or threaten the destruction of the world. Christians must not allow this defective notion of apocalypticism. They remember that everything that really portends the end of the age is the outworking of the sovereign purpose of their God and leads to the revelation of their Saviour. There can be no apocalypse without Him.

APOCRYPHA

A collection of uninspired, uncanonical literature from OT and inter-testamental times, for whose inclusion in the canon arguments have been made. The Roman Catholic church calls ten of these *deuterocanonical** and accepts them as part of the Biblical canon. These books were never accepted in the Hebrew canon and were never endorsed or quoted by our Lord or His apostles.

See **Canon**.

APOKATASTASIS

Universalism;* the belief, especially as formulated by Origen, that all human souls will finally be saved—indeed that even sin and Satan would be reconciled to God through Christ. The theory as Origen formulated it was based on a misinterpretation of Peter's words in Acts 3:21.

APOLLINARIANISM

An early heresy which taught that Christ had a true body and an animal soul, but that in Him the eternal Son, or Logos, took the place of a rational spirit.

APOLOGETICS

The branch of theological science which sets out to vindicate "Christian theism against any form of non-theistic or non-Christian thought" (Cornelius Van Til, *Christian Theistic Evidences,* 1951 Class Syllabus, p. 1). It is a broader term than *Christian evidences.* Apologetics is usually said to deal with philosophy, while Christian evidences deals with facts. They are not really divisible, since the facts which Christian evidences produces in support of the claims of Christianity can have no significance apart from a system of interpretation. However, the peculiar emphasis of each is pointed up by making apologetics refer to the system of interpretation and Christian evidences to the facts adduced in that system to demonstrate the uniqueness of Christianity. Thus while apologetics defends Christianity from non-Christian philosophy, Christian evidences defends it from non-Christian science.

Basically there are two methods employed by apologists. The first, adopted by both Roman Catholic and evangelical Protestant apologists, approaches an unbeliever on the ground that we all possess a common pool of facts and that, on the basis of these facts, a reasonable use of reason will lead to the acceptance of Christianity. This, for example, is Bishop Butler's method in his famous *Analogy.*

The second method is that of consistent Calvinism,* which denies that fallen man can employ reason rightly, or that as a creature he has the right to sit in judgment upon the facts of God's revelation, or that he can rightly know any fact apart from God, since all of God's creation reveals Him.

The first approach is possible only on the basis of deficient views of revelation,* creation,* and the fall.* It accepts that man has the ability to see the truth if only he is made to look in the right direction. All he needs is a sufficient amount of information and the reasonable use of reason.

But this is false and leads to apologetic failure. "The revelation of a self-sufficient God can have no meaning for a mind that thinks of itself as ultimately autonomous" (Van Til). The best that can be expected from such an approach is a God who is most emphatically less than the God of the Scriptures.

This is vividly demonstrated by Josh McDowell's popular book *Evidence That Demands a Verdict.* McDowell sets out to show that Christianity is a factual religion solidly based on historically provable events. But his "facts" lead to a mere "historical probability." He sets out to weigh the evidence for and against the claim of Christ to be the Son of God. He reaches the conclusion that the historical probability is that Christ was the Son of God. He deliberately discounts any idea of looking for absolute truth and holds that in dealing with facts we can never ascend higher than mere probability.

With this approach, there is evidence against Christ as well as for Him. This is a retreat from real Christianity. It is a denial of any knowledge of absolute truth.

This retreat from reality is because of McDowell's basic deviation from the Bible doctrine of man and his fall. He insists on the notion of man's inherent ability to interpret the facts aright. But a man who starts by denying or questioning the self-sufficiency and ultimacy of God cannot properly understand any fact of creation, for the stamp of God is on it all. This denial renders him incapable of seeing straight and dealing honestly with the facts. The light that is in him is darkness. Any system of apologetics or evangelism that suggests that such innate darkness is sufficient to judge the facts is unfaithful to God and His revelation.

The second, or Calvinistic, method proceeds upon the teaching of Romans 1 that God has so stamped His signature on the entire creation that every man ought to recognize Him in His creation. Furthermore, on every man's heart God has stamped the revelation of Himself. If men cannot see it, it is because of wilful ignorance, a sinful suppression of the truth. The following quotations from Van Til clearly expound this Calvinistic approach. (All our quotations from him in this article are from *Apologetics,* his class syllabus of 1951).

"No man can escape knowing God. It is

indelibly involved in his awareness of anything whatsoever. Man ought, therefore, as Calvin puts it, to recognize God. There is no excuse from him if he does not. The reason for his failure to recognize God lies exclusively in him. It is due to his wilful transgression of the very law of his being" (p. 57).

"The natural man at bottom knows that he is the creature of God. He knows also that he is responsible to God. He knows that he should live to the glory of God. He knows that in all that he does he should stress that the field of reality which he investigates has the stamp of God's ownership upon it. But he suppresses his knowledge of himself as he truly is. He is the man with the iron mask. A true method of Apologetics must seek to tear off that iron mask" (p. 64).

This Calvinistic method refuses "to grant that any area or aspect of reality, any fact or any law of nature or of history, can be correctly interpreted except it be seen in the light of the main doctrines of Christianity" (p. 60).

This method recognizes something very important: that all the reasoning of finite men must be by presupposition* (see Analogy). The other method effectively presupposes that the ultimacy of God and the consequent dependence of man are false. Every method except the consistently Calvinistic one fails here, and yet such methods are presented as true inductive reasoning, free from restricting presuppositions.

A true apologetic cannot be established by a mere direct discussion of "the facts." There must be a recognition that the significance of those facts, what interprets them and gives them meaning, is their place in the creation of the self-contained God. To *this fact* men are wilfully blind, and thus they misinterpret all other facts. The Christian apologist is called upon to witness to the truth and so must witness clearly against man's sinful suppression of God's truth, remembering that God is not "discovered" by man, or found at the end of a syllogism, or

received in any merely natural way, but that He supernaturally regenerates souls unto knowledge, righteousness, and holiness (Eph. 4:24, where "in" is *eis,* meaning "in order to"; Col. 3:10).

Thus, true knowledge, righteousness, and holiness are the result, not of some naturalistic investigation by man, but of a supernatural gracious movement of the Spirit of God. In apologetics as much as in every other branch of theology, the Calvinist recognizes the supernaturalness of the work of God in enlightening the mind, renewing the will, and producing a new creation.

See **Epistemology**.

APOLOGISTS, APOLOGY

The Greek term *apologia,* translated "answer" in Acts 25:16; 1 Cor. 9:3; 2 Tim. 4:16, and 1 Pet. 3:15, means "a verbal defence" (see Acts 22:1; Phil. 1:7,17). An apology for Christianity, therefore, is a defence of it against the various arguments that have been employed to attack it *(see* **Apologetics).**

The apologists is a title usually reserved for those who in the early centuries of the church defended Christianity from the attacks mounted against it by Jewish objections or Greek philosophy. While some writers speak of the period of the apologists as lying between the apostolic fathers and the Alexandrian and anti-Gnostic fathers, there seems to be no sufficient reason for such a cut-and-dried partition of church history. Justin Martyr, Tatian, Athenagoras, Theophilus of Antioch, and Hermas fall within the narrower definition of the term *apologists,* but we would probably be better to include Origen, Tertullian, and Arnobius in their number.

Perhaps the main distinction to be observed in the writings of the apologists is that between the Greek and Latin approach. "The Greek apologies are more learned and philosophical; the Latin more practical and juridical in their matter and style. The former labour to prove the truth of Christianity, and its adaptedness to the intellectual wants of man; the latter plead for its legal right to exist, and exhibit mainly its moral excellency and salutary effect upon society. The Latins are, in general, more rigorously opposed to heathenism, while the Greeks recognize in the Grecian philosophy a certain affinity to the Christian religion" (McClintock and Strong).

APOSTASY

Greek *apostasia,* "a falling away," a revolt or defection from God's truth. 2 Thessalonians 2:3 indicates that apostates will welcome the Antichrist* when he is revealed. The use of the word in Acts 21:21 shows that it is properly used to describe a forsaking of the great truths of the written word.

Historically, the first great area of apostasy was in Christology.* Apostasy's first attack was on the incarnate Word of God *(see Gnosticism, Marcion).* The next was on the written word *(see Textual Criticism of the New Testament).* Textual corruption was often introduced into the canonical Scriptures to manufacture support for some aberrant view of a point of doctrine.

At a very early stage the scene was set for sacerdotalism* and sacramentalism.* The identification of the church with the Roman Empire was a major factor in her drift into apostasy, but undoubtedly the falling away from Biblical purity was mostly due to the erection of the monstrous system of papal tyranny that finally overran the Western church.

In modern times rationalistic criticism of Scripture, the poisoning of the seminaries of the historic Protestant denominations with infidelity, the arrival of the ecumenical movement with its agenda for a one-world church—not on the basis of Biblical truth but on the acceptance of the fundamental claims of Rome—and finally the adoption of all kinds of political theology,* have spread apostasy across the world.

According to 2 Thess. 2 the day of the Lord will follow a great apostasy. Thus the darkness of apostasy, while a cause for grief to every believer, is not a reason for defeat or despair. It reminds us that our Lord is coming again and leads us to pray with John, "Even so, come, Lord Jesus." And it stirs our souls to remain faithful until He does.

APOSTLES' CREED

A statement of faith probably put in its final form around the end of the second century. It was not written by the apostles, but is a summary of Christian doctrine. A. A. Hodge says it was "gradually formed, by common consent, out of the Confessions adopted severally by particular churches, and used in the reception of their members."

In Puritan England, the creed was appended to the Shorter Catechism, with the Lord's Prayer and the Ten Commandments by order of Parliament, "because it is a brief sum of Christian faith, agreeable to the Word of God, and anciently received in the Churches of Christ."

The text of the Apostles' Creed is:

"I believe in God the Father Almighty, Maker of heaven and earth, and in Jesus Christ his only Son our Lord, who was conceived by the Holy Ghost; born of the Virgin Mary; suffered under Pontius Pilate, was crucified, dead, and buried; he descended into hell; the third day he rose from the dead; he ascended into heaven, and sitteth on the right hand of God the Father Almighty; from thence he shall come to judge the quick and the dead. I believe in the Holy Ghost; the holy Catholic Church, the communion of saints; the forgiveness of sins; the resurrection of the body; and the life everlasting. Amen."

See Descent into Hell.

APOSTOLIC CONSTITUTIONS AND CANONS

A body of ecclesiastical law, rightly identified as not being apostolic, but which nonetheless exercised a profound influence on the Canon Law* of the medieval Western church.

APOSTOLIC FATHERS

The Christian writers who were contemporary with an apostle; those who lived and wrote before A.D. 120. Six names are usually included in the list of the apostolic fathers: Barnabas, Clement of Rome, Ignatius, Polycarp, Hermas, and Papias. Barnabas was accepted as the writer of the *Epistle of Barnabas* by many in the ancient and modern church, but it seems certain from internal evidence that the first missionary companion of the apostle Paul was not the author. However, the epistle is of early date and justifies the pseudo-Barnabas's place among the apostolic fathers.

APOSTOLIC SUCCESSION

The notion that an unbroken line of succession extends from the twelve apostles through the bishops they ordained right up to the present day, thus giving apostolic validity to the ministry of those bishops and to the ministry of those on whom they lay hands in ordination.* The theory is historically unprovable. Also, it proceeds on the assumption that the unique power of the apostles to lay hands on men that they might receive the gift of the Holy Spirit was passed on to their successors. It was not. There is no evidence that the Lord ever intended it for continual use in the church. The usual way of ordination, even in NT times, was by the laying on of hands of the presbytery, or the eldership (1 Tim. 4:14; 2 Tim. 1:6). The NT knows nothing of bishops in the sense in which proponents of apostolic succession understand them, thus destroying the very foundation of the theory of episcopal succession.

APOSTOLICITY

One of the notes or marks of the church* claimed by the Roman Catholic church as a proof of her claim to be the one true church of Christ. Rome's claim is that in both a chronological and a dynamic sense (i.e., in the sense of unbroken succession and of unfailing fidelity to apostolic teaching) she stands in the direct line of descent from Christ and His apostles.

Protestants agree that apostolicity is a necessary mark of a true church, but they define it as essential acceptance of and obedience to New Testament doctrine and instruction. William Cunningham, noting Rome's serious departure from the doctrine and practice of the apostles as set down in the New Testament, stated the essence of the Protestant position:

"No professing church…can have any claim to be regarded as possessed of sanctity or apostolicity, unless its system of doctrine be in accordance with the Word of God; and a church is apostolical just in proportion as in all its arrangements it is framed after the model, so far as the Scripture makes it known to us, of the church which the apostles established. The churches which have been most forward to assume the designation and the character of apostolical are just those which have departed furthest from what a faithful adherence to the practice of the apostles would have led them to adopt. …It is certainly marvellous that any man having access to the Scriptures should believe that the Church of Rome bears any resemblance to the church of the New Testament" (*Historical Theology*, 1:25, 26).

APOTHEOSIS

Deification; exalting a creature to the honours of deity. In the Greek church there has always been a strong taint of this in their view of salvation. For many of their theologians, salvation means ultimate deification *(see **Theosis**).* This is also the folly of Mormonism* and many New Age* cults.

The Roman Catholic church denies that she deifies the Virgin Mary, but that is the practical result of her teaching. Whatever semantic distinctions her documents may employ, by commanding belief in Mary's immaculate conception, bodily assumption into heaven, cooperation with Christ in the work of redemption so that she is co-redemptrix and co-mediatrix, and by calling for prayers and worship to be directed to her, Rome effectively exalts Mary to deity *(see Adoration).*

ARCHANGEL

Chief angel (1 Thes. 4:16; Jude 9).

"Those angels are so styled who occupy the highest rank in the celestial order of hierarchy, which consists according to the apostles, of 'thrones, dominions, principalities, and powers' (Eph. 1:21; Col 1:16; 1 Pet. 3:22). Of these there are said [i.e., by tradition] to be seven, who stand immediately before the throne of God (Luke 1:19; Rev. 8:2), who have authority over other angels, and are the patrons of particular nations (Rev. 7:7; Dan. 10:13). In Matt. 26:53; 2 Thess. 1:7, hosts of angels are spoken of in the same manner as human armies. These the Almighty is said to employ in executing his commands, or in displaying his dignity and majesty, in the manner of human princes. These armies of angels are also represented as divided into orders and classes, having each its leader, and all these are subject to one chief or archangel. The names of two only are found in the Scripture—Michael, the patron of the Jewish nation (Dan. 10:13,21; 12:1; Jude 9; Rev. 12:7); and Gabriel (Dan. 8:16; 9:21; Luke 1:19,26). The apocryphal book of Tobit (3:17; 5:4) mentions one, Raphael; and 2 Esdras (4:34) another, Uriel; while the book of Enoch names the whole seven (20:1-7)" (McClintock and Strong).

See Angel.

ARCHBISHOP

In churches which adhere to episcopacy,* the chief bishop of a province or archdiocese. In Roman Catholicism an archbishop ranks under a cardinal and patriarch, but above a bishop, and must receive the *pallium* (or pall, a scarf-like vestment to be worn only on special occasions) as a badge of his authority. Archbishops are "enthroned" and take such grandiose titles as "Your Grace" and "Most Reverend Father in God." While the title and the office were introduced early in church history (fourth century) there is absolutely no foundation for them in the NT Scriptures.

ARCHIMANDRITE

In Eastern Orthodoxy the name given to the head of a monastery; the equivalent of an abbot* in the Roman Catholic church.

ARGUMENTS FOR GOD'S EXISTENCE

The evidences produced, by the use of logic, in favour of God's existence. Some have held that by one or other of these arguments the existence of God can be demonstrated or proved. Others hold that a demonstration is not possible, but that the accumulated weight of the evidence from all the arguments confirms belief in God's existence. Still others give even less credibility to all logical arguments on the subject and hold that God's existence is a truth revealed to, and received by, faith alone.

The arguments most often used in favour of God's existence are as follows:

1. The *a priori* argument argues from cause to effect and is based on "self-evident truths," or upon essential laws of human intelligence. From these principles it labours to show that belief in God is a logical necessity.

2. The *ontological* argument of Anselm—i.e., Anselm's argument from the nature of being or existence. Recognizing the difference between absolute, perfect being, and relative, imperfect being, he argued in the form of a syllogism.

Major premise: The human mind possesses the idea of an absolutely perfect being.

Minor premise: Absolute perfection of being implies necessity of existence (for that which

37

must exist is of a higher order than that which may exist).

Conclusion: An absolutely perfect being does exist—for that which must exist, does exist.

3. The *cosmological,* or *a posteriori** argument argues from effect to cause. It proceeds: Every effect must have a cause adequate to produce it. The world, or the universe, is an effect and, therefore, must have an adequate cause. The only cause capable of producing such an effect is an all-powerful, eternal Creator, God.

4. The *teleological* argument is the argument from design. The universe bears evident marks of design or purpose; everywhere there is a wise and skilful adaptation of means to end. But design presupposes an intelligent designer, God.

5. The *moral* argument considers the phenomena of conscience in the human soul and the universal feeling of accountability and dependence in men (the religious sentiment). It is argued that this sentiment is common to the moral constitution of all men, and if God does not exist this universal conscience is a lie. Thus, the primary sources of our belief in God are built into our moral constitution.

6. The *historical* argument shows three things: (a) that the human race is not eternal—that it had a beginning, or was created; (b) that the providential presence of God is evident in human history; (c) that it has been the universal consent of all men of all races throughout all history that God exists.

7. The *Scriptural* argument uses the evident supernatural origin of the Bible, its miracles, its prophecies, and the beneficial effects it always produces wherever it is introduced as proofs that the God of the Bible does indeed exist.

In all such arguments the danger to be avoided is that of assuming man's ability to be a competent judge and interpreter of the facts. All argument starts with some presupposition. To presuppose the ultimacy of human reason and interpretation is to deny the ultimacy of God and the fallen state of man. On the presupposition of the ontological Trinity,* each form of argument has merit and appears in Scripture. But on any other presupposition, no argument can demonstrate the truth of God's existence, for truth cannot be established by presupposing a lie.

See **Analogy**; **Epistemology**; **Presuppositionalism**.

ARIANISM

Named after Arius, this heresy maintained that God the Father alone is eternal and made His Son to be the first creature He created *ex nihilo.* Some Arians went on to teach that the Holy Spirit was the first and greatest creature produced by the Son. The Council of Nicea met in A.D. 325 to deal with the subject and it firmly rejected Arianism. It held that the Son was of the same substance with the Father (*homoousion*) not merely of similar substance (*homoiousion*), pronouncing its Scriptural faith that the Son was "Son of God, light of light, very God of very God, being of one substance with the Father." The Nicene decision was upheld in A.D. 381 by the Council of Constantinople.

See **Deity of Christ**; **Eternal Sonship**; **Trinity**.

ARISTOTELIANISM

The philosophy of Aristotle (384-322 B.C.), a pupil of Plato. Whereas Plato concentrated on absolutes, Aristotle concentrated on the effects we discern around us and may examine. Whereas Plato had sought for the one God in the realm of ethics, Aristotle sought him in physics and metaphysics.* He accepted that all nature had a purpose and moved toward a goal. This is the first statement in philosophy of the "proof of the first cause" *(see* **The Five Ways)** that gained such popularity among Christian apologists.

Aristotle was preeminently a logician and classifier. His *a posteriori** reasoning was to have a profound effect on Christian theology. After centuries of the dominance of the mysticism of Neoplatonism (see **Platonism**), the philosophy of Aristotle was reintroduced by a Spanish Muslim scholar. The papal church at first banned his works but finally admitted them for study.

Thomas Aquinas adopted the method and ideas of Aristotle to produce his monumental work on natural theology and the role of reason and its relationship to faith. This became the accepted dogma of the church of Rome and remains so to this day. Aquinas even employed Aristotle's physics as well as his metaphysics,* including the idea that the sun revolved around the earth—a theory never set forth in Scripture but one which came to be looked on as the essence of Christian orthodoxy, as Galileo found out almost at the cost of his life.

In the scholastic debate between nominalism* and realism* the nominalists largely followed the method of Aristotle while the Realists found their support in Platonism. Cornelius Van Til's judgment reminds us that the overall effect of Greek philosophy on theology was not healthy: "The God of Greek philosophy is either exclusively deistic or exclusively pantheistic" (A Survey of Christian Epistemology, p. 16).

ARMINIANISM

A system of doctrine, named after a Dutch theologian Jacob Hermann Arminius, which rejects the Reformed view of God's sovereignty. It is worth noting that the position of Arminius himself was less objectionable than that of his later followers—and he certainly evidenced no animosity toward Calvin, whose writings he esteemed second only to Scripture itself. His theological position was almost the same as John Wesley's. He held proper views of man's depravity and inability, and because of this, of the need for supernatural grace to effect salvation. This contrasts with the position adopted by later Arminians (see below, points 4, 5, 6; also

The Five Points of Controversy).

It is usual, but wrong, to think of Arminianism as merely the doctrine that Christ died for all men, without distinction, or that it is possible to lose justifying grace. These are tenets of Arminianism, but there are others of great significance, as for example:

1. God's knowledge of the future acts of free agents is mediate (see **Scientia Media).**
2. The decrees of God are conditional on some thing or things not themselves absolutely decreed. Particularly it is held that election is on account of foreseen faith (see **Conditional Decrees).**
3. God created Adam merely innocent, not in holiness—i.e., his will* was in a state of balance between good and evil, not positively inclined toward good.
4. Sin consists in acts of the will (see **Pelagianism).**
5. Only the pollution, not the guilt, of Adam's sin is imputed to his descendants.
6. Man's depravity is not total. He has the ability to incline his will toward God and good.
7. The atonement,* which was not necessary but merely one way which God chose to show His love without prejudice to His righteousness, was offered equally for each and every man.
8. The atonement does not actually effect the salvation of those for whom Christ offered it but merely makes their salvation possible.
9. Salvation becomes effectual only when accepted by the penitent sinner, whose repentance and faith precede his regeneration.*
10. The human will is one of the causes of regeneration (see **Synergism).**
11. Faith is a good work and a ground of acceptance with God.
12. There is no such thing as common grace* as distinct from special grace. The external call of the gospel is accompanied by a universal sufficient grace which may enable the

sinner to repent and believe, but which may be resisted.

13. The righteousness of Christ is not imputed to the believer.

14. A believer is able to attain to perfect conformity to the divine will in this life; he may also fall from grace and be lost eternally.

Some Arminians went even further and became very rationalistic. Arminius's original views were adopted by the Dutch Remonstrants whose position was condemned by the Synod of Dort.* The Remonstrants still hold to Pelagian notions and have lax views of the doctrine of inspiration* and the Trinity.*

Wesleyan Methodism adopted Arminianism in a revised form known as Evangelical Arminianism, in which points (5) and (6) above are restated so as not to be so openly in conflict with the Reformed position.

ARTICLE OF FAITH

A dogmatic statement of a fundamental truth of the faith set forth by church authority and incumbent upon all under that authority. In Protestant churches and confessions the sole ground for promulgating articles of faith is the authority of the statements of Scripture on the subject.

ASCETICISM

The complete renunciation of the flesh. There is a good Biblical base for the practice of mortification (1 Cor. 9:27; Rom. 8:13), but the practice of asceticism in the church degenerated into making men hermits or recluses, with the idea of meriting God's favour by suffering.

See **Anchorite**.

ASEITY

The absolute self-existence of God. He has life in Himself (John. 5:26), or to use the Latin phrase, life *a se,* hence the word *a-se-ity.*

ASHERAH, ASHEROTH

Translated "grove" or "groves." Asherah was the name of the heathen goddess of Tyre, whose worship found its way into Israel (1 Kings 15:13; 2 Kings 21:7).

ASSOCIATE SYNOD

The Secession church that separated from the established church of Scotland in 1733, under the leadership of Ebenezer Erskine. The 1731 General Assembly approved an overture to give elders and heritors (landowners in a parish who had the responsibility to provide and maintain the church building, manse, and churchyard) the right to place a minister in their parish without the call of the congregation. The next year the Assembly moved to pass this as an act, despite the opposition of the majority of presbyteries. Erskine vehemently opposed the Assembly's action and was formally rebuked by the 1733 Assembly. He submitted a protest, in which he was joined by Alexander Moncrieff, James Fisher, and William Wilson. These men were suspended and removed from their charges. Refusing to accept such a sentence they seceded and on December 5, 1733, they formed the Associate Presbytery. In 1740 they were deposed by the General Assembly and so the secession was made final. In 1745 in the light of considerable growth the Associate Presbytery constituted itself into the Associate Synod, with three presbyteries. Two years later the Associate Synod split on the matter of the Burgess Oath (*see* **Burghers).**

ASSUMPTION OF THE VIRGIN MARY

The Romish dogma, promulgated on November 1, 1950, by Pope Pius XII, that the ever-virgin Mary was assumed, body and soul, into heaven. Romanists argue that the Lord Jesus would not allow the body in which He had dwelt to fall into corruption. Rome terms this dogma an apostolic tradition, but there is not the slightest trace of it in any statement or doctrinal position of an apostle.

ASSURANCE

The certainty of being "in the state of grace," is "the full assurance of faith founded upon the divine truth of the promises of salvation, the inward evidences of those graces…and the testimony of the Spirit of adoption, witnessing with our spirits that we are the children of God" (*Westminster Confession of Faith,* chap 18, sec. 1, 2). The *Confession* goes on to teach that this assurance is not of the essence of faith (i.e., not necessary to salvation; true believers may lack it, though all should labour to obtain it) and that believers may find variations in their level of enjoyment of it, though they are never left totally "destitute of that seed of God, and life of faith…by which they are supported from utter despair" (sects. 3, 4).

The Greek word for assurance means "full conviction" (see Rom. 4:21; 14:5; 1 Thess. 1:5; Col. 2:2; Heb. 6:11; 10:22), indicating that assurance is not merely a subjective feeling, but has a solid objective base in the evidence of the word and work of God.

ATHANASIAN CREED

A statement of basic Christian belief, in forty-four brief sections, which concentrate on the orthodox doctrines of the Trinity* in unity and of the unipersonality of Christ. It was thought to have been the production of Athanasius, bishop of Alexandria (*circa* A.D. 328-373), who was the leader of the orthodox Trinitarian party in opposition to the heresy of Arius. However, it is now thought that the creed came much after Athanasius' time, probably around the end of the fifth century.

The text of the Athanasian Creed is:

"Whoever will be saved, before all things it is necessary that he hold the catholic faith. Which faith, except every one do keep whole and undefiled, without doubt he shall perish everlastingly. And the catholic faith is this: that we worship one God in Trinity, and Trinity in Unity; neither confounding the persons, nor dividing the substance. For there is one person of the Father, another of the Son, and another of the Holy Ghost. But the Godhead of the Father, of the Son, and of the Holy Ghost is all one: the glory equal, the majesty coeternal. Such as the Father is, such is the Son, and such is the Holy Ghost. The Father uncreate[d], the Son uncreate[d], and the Holy Ghost uncreate[d]. The Father incomprehensible, the Son incomprehensible, and the Holy Ghost incomprehensible. The Father eternal, the Son eternal, and the Holy Ghost eternal. And yet they are not three eternals, but one eternal. As also there are not three incomprehensibles, nor three uncreated, but one uncreated, and one incomprehensible. So likewise the Father is almighty, the Son almighty , and the Holy Ghost almighty. And yet there are not three almightys, but one almighty. So the Father is God, the Son is God, and the Holy Ghost is God. And yet there are not three Gods, but one God. So likewise the Father is Lord, the Son Lord, and the Holy Ghost Lord. And yet not three Lords, but one Lord. For like as we are compelled by the Christian verity to acknowledge every person by himself to be God and Lord, so are we forbidden by the catholic religion to say there be three Gods and three Lords. The Father is made of none, neither created nor begotten. The Son is of the Father alone; not made, nor created, but begotten. The Holy Ghost is of the Father and of the Son; neither made, nor created, nor begotten, but proceeding. So there is one Father, not three Fathers; one Son, not three Sons; one Holy Ghost, not three Holy Ghosts. And in this Trinity none is afore or after other; none is greater or less than another. But the whole three persons are coeternal together, and coequal. So that in all things, as is aforesaid, the Unity in Trinity and the Trinity in Unity is to be worshipped. He therefore that will be saved must thus think of the Trinity. Furthermore, it is necessary to everlasting salvation that he also believe rightly the incarnation of our Lord Jesus Christ. For the right faith is that

41

we believe and confess that our Lord Jesus Christ, the Son of God, is God and man. God of the substance of the Father, begotten before the worlds; and man of the substance of his mother, born in the world. Perfect God and perfect man, of a reasonable soul and human flesh subsisting. Equal to the Father as touching his Godhead, and inferior to the Father as touching his manhood. Who, although he be God and man, yet he is not two, but one Christ. One, not by conversion of the Godhead into flesh, but by taking of the manhood into God. One altogether, not by confusion of substance, but by unity of person. For as the reasonable soul and flesh is one man, so God and man is one Christ. Who suffered for our salvation, descended into hell, rose again the third day from the dead. He ascended into heaven, he sitteth on the right hand of the Father, God Almighty. From whence he shall come to judge the quick and the dead. At whose coming all men shall rise again with their bodies, and shall give account for their own works. And they that have done good shall go into life everlasting, and they that have done evil into everlasting fire. This is the catholic faith which, except a man believe faithfully, he cannot be saved. Glory be to the Father, and to the Son, and to the Holy Ghost. As it was in the beginning, is now, and ever shall be, world without end. Amen."

ATHEISM

Scripturally, a term which designates those "without God" (Eph. 2:12, where the Greek is *atheos*). Broadly, however, atheism is the denial of God.

Practical atheists are simply godless persons who, whatever their theoretical beliefs, live as if there were no God, and who do not therefore reckon with Him in their manner of life.

Theoretical atheists are those who seek by rational argument to justify their assertion that there is no God. They are subdivided into three groups:

1. *Dogmatic atheists,* who flatly deny God's existence.
2. *Sceptical atheists,* who doubt the ability of the human mind to determine whether or not there is a God (*see **Agnosticism***).
3. *Critical atheists,* who hold that there is no valid proof of the existence of God.

Such distinctions, while useful, should not becloud the basic fact: all these classes of theoretical atheists wilfully delude themselves that Rom. 1:20 and 2:15 are false.

ATONEMENT

The satisfaction* of divine justice by the Lord Jesus Christ in His active and passive obedience (i.e., His life and death), which procures for His people a perfect salvation.

The Bible Terms

The OT verb *kaphar,* which is translated "to make atonement," means "to cover over"—so as not to be seen. The word *salach,* translated "to forgive," has the meaning of "lightness," "lifting up," "to be at rest or peace" (Gesenius), or "to be sent away," "to let go" (Young). Shedd says: "The connection of ideas then in the Hebrew text appears to be this: the suffering of the substitute bullock or ram has the effect to cover over the guilt of the real criminal and to make it invisible to the eyes of God...When this is done the transgressor is at rest."

In the Septuagint translation of the Hebrew Scriptures, *kaphar* was rendered by the Greek *exilaskomai,* and *salach* by *aphiemi.* The NT also makes use of these words and so stamps the added shades of meaning in them with divine authority. The NT word *hilaskomai* means "to propitiate" or "to appease." *Aphiemi* means "to release," or "to let go." Again Shedd notes: "By the suffering of the sinner's atoning substitute, the divine wrath on sin is propitiated, and as a consequence of this propitiation, the punishment due to sin is released and not inflicted upon the transgressor. This release, or non-infliction of penalty, is forgiveness in the Biblical representation."

Thus in the word of God, forgiveness is always connected with the atonement and remission or release with the propitiation, as a matter of effect to cause. The word *atonement* appears only once in our AV, in Rom. 5:11. Here the Greek *katallage* more properly signifies "reconciliation," but the thought is of reconciliation on the ground of a satisfaction having been made.

The Characteristics of the Atonement

1. It is *vicarious* or *substitutionary*. It was rendered by the Lord Jesus Christ for His people, i.e., not merely for their benefit, but "in their place" (Matt. 20:28). (*See* **Substitution**.)
2. *Suffering* is an essential element in the atonement (Luke 9:22; 24:26; Matt. 16:21). In Matt. 27:34, Christ on the cross refused to have His pain deadened. His sufferings were penal on account of His bearing our sin (1 Pet. 2:24). (*See* **Sufferings of Christ**.)
3. It is *objective*—i.e., it makes its primary impression on God, to whom it is offered.
4. It is *necessary*. God has decreed it as the only way whereby He could be just and yet save sinners. Thus the necessity of the atonement is based on God's nature and God's will. By nature He is holy, and must punish sin; by His gracious will He has decreed the salvation of His elect; Christ's work of atonement is the only way to execute that gracious purpose. "The Son of man must be lifted up," (John 3:14).
5. It is *definite* —i.e., Christ made atonement with a definite purpose in view. That purpose was to save sinners. This view is in sharp contrast with the Arminian view that Christ's death merely made salvation possible. Definite atonement emphasizes that in His death Christ was actually the substitute and surety for all for whom He died.
6. It was *particular:* it was made specifically for God's elect. Calvinists hold that Christ gave Himself for His church (Eph. 5:25) and

laid down His life for His sheep (John 10:15). Arminians and universalists hold that He offered up a sacrifice equally for each and every man. The Calvinist asks, "Why then are not all men saved?" Arminians answer, "Because of the unbelief of some." To this the Calvinist replies, "Is not unbelief a sin? Is it not therefore covered by the death of Christ? Or, did He die for all our sin, except our unbelief?"

The Calvinist position is that the blood of Christ is sufficient to save each and every man who ever lived, but is efficient to save only God's elect. John Owen's famous summary of the situation put it like this:

a. Either, Christ died for all the sins of all men—in which case all men must be saved;

b. Or, He died for some of the sins of all men, in which case none will be saved;

c. Or, He died for all the sins of some men—in which case, while some are lost, some will be saved.

We know that conclusions (a) and (b) are unscriptural, and that (c) is an accurate statement of scriptural fact. Clearly, Christ died to make atonement for all the sins of His elect, His Church, His sheep, those given to Him by His Father (John 6:37; 17:2, 6, 9, 19).

7. It is *successful*. What God aimed at in the atonement is exactly what He accomplished, and what He accomplished is exactly what He aimed at. Isaiah 53:11 tells us of the Lord's entire satisfaction with His sacrificial work. The great anthem of Rev. 5 allows no room for the thought that Jesus tried to accomplish a lot more than He actually did.

Also, the entire doctrine of gospel assurance depends on the fact that Christ's atonement cannot fail to accomplish its end. Christ did not merely attempt to bear away our sin; He did it. He did not seek to redeem us; He did it. The cause and effect inherent in the message of the Cross is clear in such texts as 2 Cor. 5:21: "He [God] hath made him to be sin for us, who knew no sin, that we might be made the righteousness of God in him." All for whom Christ was made sin must of necessity be made the righteousness of God in Him. His suffering cannot be in vain.

See **Universal Terms;** various theories of the atonement are dealt with in their alphabetical order: see **Example Theory**; **Governmental Theory**; **Hypothetical Universalism**; **Moral Influence Theory**; **Mystical Theory**; **Ransom to Satan Theory**; **Recapitulation Theory**; **Satisfaction Theory**; **Vicarious Repentance Theory**.

ATTRIBUTES OF GOD

The divine perfections; the characteristics of the Divine Being. The *Shorter Catechism* sets them out as follows: "God is a spirit infinite, eternal, and unchangeable, in His being, wisdom, power, holiness, justice, goodness and truth."

Theologians have suggested certain divisions in the classification of God's attributes:
1. *Natural and Moral Attributes,* i.e., the attributes which belong to His essence (as distinct from His will) are called natural, while those like truth, holiness, goodness, justice, etc., are called moral. The basic objection to this classification, or at least to the terms used to describe it, is that the "moral" attributes are just as essential to God, and therefore "natural," as those called "natural" attributes.
2. *Absolute and Relative Attributes.* The absolute attributes are those which belong to the essence of God considered in itself, while the relative attributes belong to His creation. Again, the objection may be raised that attributes like wisdom, power, holiness, and truth belong just as absolutely to the divine essence as, say, eternity.
3. *Immanent or Intransitive, and Emanent or Transitive Attributes.* This classification distinguishes between those attributes which do not go forth and operate outside of the divine essence (immanent), and those which

do issue forth and produce effects external to God (emanent). This is a better classification than the one above, but it has been objected to on the ground that if some attributes are purely immanent, we could have no knowledge of them. This is not a weighty objection: the power and wisdom of God, which under this classification are emanent attributes, could well impart the knowledge that God has immanent attributes like simplicity, infinity, eternity, and immutability.
4. *Incommunicable and Communicable Attributes.* This is the most common classification. The incommunicable attributes are those of which there is nothing analogous in the creature (e.g., aseity*); the communicable attributes are those to which the properties of the human spirit bear some analogy (e.g., power, knowledge). This classification also labours under a difficult objection that since in all His perfections God is infinite, He does not communicate any of them to the creature. Man's life is derived from God by creation, and therefore we say that God's aseity, His self-existence, is incommunicable. But man's power, knowledge, etc., are equally derived from God by creation and cannot be thought of in any way as being a communication of God's infinite power and knowledge. Such difficulties of classification are to be expected in any finite description of the infinite God.

ATTRITION

Imperfect contrition. The term was introduced by the schoolmen (*see* **Scholasticism**) in the 12th century after they had made penance a sacrament.* Contrition meant complete repentance, with a crushing sense of sin; attrition meant an incomplete repentance, with a lesser degree of sorrow arising chiefly from a servile fear of hell. The Council of Trent confirmed the distinction as official Roman Catholic dogma. While it does not in itself lead to justification, according to Rome, it will achieve that end by means of penance and priestly absolution.

AUCHTERARDER CREED

A statement of belief framed by the Presbytery of Auchterarder, Perthshire, Scotland, to be put to all candidates for the ministry, in addition to the questions already prescribed. Its aim was to erect safeguards for the preaching of the gospel of free grace against the prevailing ideas of the necessity of special preparation for grace. One of its propositions was, "I believe that it is not sound and orthodox to teach that we must forsake sin in order to our coming to Christ, and instating us in covenant with God."

When a student, William Craig, complained to the General Assembly of 1717, the Assembly condemned the Presbytery's proposition as "unsound and most detestable." The next year a Commission of the Assembly reported that the Presbytery was "sound and orthodox" though it had expressed its meaning in "words very unwarrantable and exceptionable."

Though it sounds strange to modern defenders of Reformed orthodoxy, the Auchterarder proposition was the production of the truly evangelical section of the Church of Scotland. The wording was clumsy and harsh and lent itself to grave misrepresentation. The framers intended to avoid the dead religion of those who made repentance a precondition of faith and thereby produced a dry, moralistic religion of works. The way they expressed themselves gave rise to the charge that they were antinomians who were enemies of all gospel holiness.

On learning of the Assembly's stand against the Auchterarder brethren, Thomas Boston introduced a friend to a little book he had discovered and which in his estimation was the best scriptural statement of the issues involved. That book, *The Marrow of Modern Divinity,* was soon republished. Its appearance and popularity led to the famous Marrow* controversy, which shook the Church of Scotland much more deeply than the Auchterarder Creed dispute had done. *The Marrow* and its supporters, the *Marrowmen,* defended the positions the Presbytery of Auchterarder had sought to establish and in the course of their defence produced one of the most powerful statements of evangelical Calvinism ever written.

AUGSBURG CONFESSION

The statement of belief drawn up by Martin Luther and Philip Melanchthon and presented to the Emperor and Imperial Diet in Augsburg on June 25, 1530. It is in two parts: the first contains twenty-one articles of faith; the second lists the leading abuses that needed reform.

AUGUSTINIANISM

The philosophical and theological system of Augustine (A.D. 354-430), Bishop of Hippo. Though deficient in his understanding of such doctrines as baptism* (he held to baptismal regeneration*) and the church* (in these particulars his teachings were taken up by others and developed into the Roman Catholic views of the church and sacraments*), Augustine taught salvation by grace alone. What is usually called Calvinism* is in the main Augustinianism.

AUTHENTICITY

A word used of a Bible book to indicate that it was written by its professed (human) author at the time and under the circumstances claimed or implied in Scripture.

See **Genuineness.**

AUTHORITY

The right to bind the conscience in matters of faith and to command the will in matters of practice. This right belongs properly to God alone. However, He has given us the declaration of His mind and will on matters of faith and practice in His word and has made that written word our sole rule of belief and behaviour. He has vested this authority in the church,* its confessions, its ministers, and its courts only so far as what they teach and command is scriptural.

"The whole counsel of God, concerning all things necessary for his own glory, man's salvation, faith, and life, is either expressly set down in Scripture, or by good and necessary consequence may be deduced from Scripture: unto which nothing at anytime is to be added whether by new revelations of the Spirit, or traditions of men" (*Westminster Confession of Faith,* chap. 1, sec. 6).

So in the two areas of faith and practice authority belongs alone to God and is vested in the Scriptures. As to matters of faith, the *Confession* says:

"God alone is Lord of the conscience, and hath left it free from the doctrines and commandments of men which are in anything contrary to his Word, or beside it, in matters of faith or worship. So that to believe such doctrines, or to obey such commandments out of conscience, is to betray true liberty of conscience: and the requiring of an implicit faith, and an absolute and blind obedience, is to destroy liberty of conscience, and reason also" (chap. 30, sec. 2).

As to practice, it goes on to state the scriptural limits of the authority of church officers to impose censures (church discipline) on members whose behaviour they condemn:

"To these officers the keys of the kingdom of heaven are committed, by virtue whereof they have power respectively to retain and remit sins, to shut the kingdom against the impenitent, both by the Word and censures; and to open it unto penitent sinners, by the ministry of the gospel and by absolution from censures, as occasion shall require" (chap. 30, sec. 2).

This power is ministerial, not priestly. That is, it lies in the application of the Scriptures to the offender and his offence. It does not lie in any authority inherent in the office of those administering the censure. The *Confession* makes this point very plainly in dealing with the proper exercise of authority by church courts. In chapter 30, sections 2 and 3 (quoting Acts 15; 16:4; Matt. 18:17–20 for section 2, and Eph. 2:20; Acts 17:11;

1 Cor. 2:5; 2 Cor. 1:24 for section 3) it states:

"It belongeth to synods and councils ministerially to determine controversies of faith and cases of conscience; to set down rules and directions for the better ordering of the public worship of God and government of his Church; to receive complaints in cases of maladministration, and authoritatively to determine the same: which decrees and determinations, if consonant to the Word of God, are to be received with reverence and submission not only for their agreement with the Word, but also for the power whereby they are made, as being an ordinance of God, appointed thereunto in his Word. All synods and councils since the apostles' times, whether general or particular, may err, and many have erred, therefore they are not to be made the rule of faith or practice, but to be used as an help in both."

This is a vital principle. It guarantees the liberty of God's people. Any attempt to usurp God's authority and vest it in any man, council of men, or office is both unscriptural and tyrannical.

Over against all this the Church of Rome has developed a theory of authority that is vested in men because of the offices they occupy. To Rome a teaching is authentic because it is taught by the authority of one who holds a canonically recognized office in the church. While the First Vatican Council (*Dogmatic Constitution of the Catholic Faith*) stated, "We believe that what God has revealed is true...because of the authority of God who reveals it," Rome has assumed a magisterial authority for her bishops, who in turn depend on the pope "for the actualization of their authority" (John A. Hardon, S.J., *The Catholic Catechism,* p. 223).

According to Rome the right to teach and govern authoritatively resides in the episcopacy. They have the right to "direct the people of God according to norms of worship and conduct that are binding on the consciences of the faithful" (Hardon, p. 222). However, this right is strictly limited to their continued union with the pope, which "determines whether and how much authority the bishops actually exercise" (Hardon, p. 223).

For his part the pope is dependent on no bishop or college of bishops: "In virtue of his office, that is, as vicar of Christ and pastor of the whole church, the Roman Pontiff has full, supreme, and universal power over the church. He is always free to exercise this power" (Vatican II, *Dogmatic Constitution on the Church,* 3.22).

Rome derives all this authority from the imagined primacy of Peter and the investment of the bishops of Rome with his pontifical position and authority. It is a baseless invention. In the NT Peter never exercised any such pontifical office, and certainly the other inspired apostles did not depend on him for their authority, which they had directly from Christ. In Acts 15, at the council of Jerusalem, it would appear that James, not Peter, was in the chair. But even if it could be shown that Peter did exercise a greater authority than the rest of the apostles, there is not the slightest suggestion that such authority was to be passed on to the bishops of Rome in all succeeding generations.

The exercise of authority outside the strict limits of Scripture is antagonistic to the liberty of Christians. It makes men the judges of Scripture, and it lends the colour of divine favour to the indefensible campaigns of persecution that have long been the favourite weapons of authoritarian churchmen to subjugate people whose only crime has been to allow no man to come between them and Christ.

AUTOGRAPHA

The original manuscripts of the Scriptures.*

AUTOSOTERISM

The doctrine that man is the author of his own salvation, or that he is saved chiefly on the ground of his own merit and obedience.

AVE MARIA

Latin for "Hail Mary," the angel Gabriel's salutation to the virgin Mary when he visited her to tell her that she would miraculously conceive a Son (Luke 1:28). The Roman Catholic church has turned an angelic salutation into an idolatrous supplication. The *Hail Mary* is:

"Hail Mary, full of grace! The Lord is with thee; blessed art thou among women, and blessed is the fruit of thy womb, Jesus. Holy Mary, Mother of God, pray for us sinners, now at the hour of our death. Amen."

The use of this prayer can be traced to the 11th century. There is no scriptural warrant whatsoever for it.

AWAKENING

This has been used in two senses in theological literature:

1. An arousal to a sense of sin and need of Christ—i.e., conviction which precedes conversion.

2. A general revival of religion.

AZAZEL

The Hebrew word *azazel* appears four times in Scripture, all in Lev. 16 (vv. 8, 10, 26). The AV rightly translates it "scapegoat." On the Day of Atonement, the high priest had to take two goats, which together made one sin offering unto the Lord (Lev. 16:5), and cast lots over them. In this way one goat was appointed to be slain and later wholly burned. The second goat was left alive and, after the high priest had laid his hands on it to confess the iniquity of Israel over it, was sent away into the wilderness. Typically, both goats, constituting one sin offering, prefigure Christ. The first prefigures Him bearing the penalty due to the sins of His people; the second prefigures Him clearing the record of His people and removing from them forever the obligation to suffer the penalty of their sin.

It is this second goat that is called *azazel.* The word is a compound of *ez,* "goat,"

47

and *azal,* "to go away, depart." It can signify nothing other than the scapegoat, or the goat that "went away" into the wilderness.

However, strange opinions have been voiced about this word, and the RV lends colour to these ideas by making it a proper name, rendering it *Azazel.* Some scholars' interpretation, avidly seized by Seventh Day Adventism,* makes Azazel a name for Satan. Seventh Day Adventist teaching goes on to say that the sins of God's people will be removed by being laid on Satan—so Satan actually bears away sin and is part of the great sin offering of Christ to His Father (for in Lev. 16 only one offering is typified by the two goats, v. 5).

The simple fact is that *azazel* is not a proper name. It does not mean Satan. There is nothing in the etymology or usage of the word to allow such an interpretation. It is part of the OT picture of Christ as the one who vicariously bore our sins.

See **Textual Criticism of the Old Testament** for further discussion of the Hebrew term.

B

BABYLONIAN CAPTIVITY OF THE CHURCH

1. The name given by the Roman Catholic church to the period 1309-1378 when, under the controlling influence of France, the papacy was removed from the Vatican to Avignon.

2. The title of Martin Luther's strong polemic (published 1520) against the Roman Catholic sacramentalism,* especially the dogma that the mass* is an expiatory sacrifice. Luther believed that such unscriptural impositions brought the people of God under bondage.

BAHA'ISM

A syncretistic religion of Persian Mohammedan origin, with its world headquarters in Haifa, Israel. It was founded by Mirza Husayn Ali (1818-92), who took the title *Baha-ullah,* "glory of God." The myth is that the last true successor of Mohammed, who disappeared in the tenth century, never died but lived on to reappear later to fill the earth with justice. Baha-ullah is the fulfilment of this purpose, the last in the line of prophets—Abraham, Moses, Christ, and Mohammed. Baha'ism takes a little from various religions, aiming at the unity of all, the elimination of war, and the evolution of man to perfect love. Love is the most frequently used word in the Bahai vocabulary. Unity based on the adoption of Hinduism, Islam, Judaism, and Christianity is its aim. Doctrine is not important. Only unity and brotherhood matter. That is its basic "theology."

As a religion, it is far removed from Biblical truth, but has much in common with Spiritism* and Theosophy.* Its prophet claimed to be God (*Star of the West,* official Bahai organ, Feb. 7, 1914) and stands condemned by the plain statements of the Scriptures, e.g., Matt. 24:24, 26; Col. 1:19; 2:3, 9.

BAPTISM
The Institution of Baptism

Christian baptism was instituted by the Lord Jesus Christ after He had finished the work of atonement* and had risen from the dead. Berkhof draws attention to the fact that the Lord Jesus prefaced the great commission, with its reference to baptism, with words, "all power [authority] is given unto me in heaven and in earth." He remarks, "Clothed with that mediatorial authority, He instituted Christian baptism and thus made it binding for all generations" (*Systematic Theology,* p. 624). Almost all Christians agree that Christ's command is binding on all succeeding generations, though some extreme dispensationalists maintain that water baptism belongs to the Kingdom Age and that only the baptism of the Spirit has any place in the church.

The Baptismal Formula

In Matt. 28:19 the Lord Jesus Christ commanded His disciples to baptize "in the name of the Father and of the Son and of the Holy Ghost." The phrase denotes more than "on the authority of," and carries in it the thought of "in relation to" or "with regard to," emphasizing that baptism signifies a new relationship, a new faith, and a new obedience.

While Matt. 28:19 is usually called the baptismal formula, it is not commanded to be used as such. The verse states as a fact that Christian baptism signifies a new relationship with the Triune God. It does not stipulate a necessary form of words, as can be seen from the apostolic emphasis on baptism "in the name of Jesus Christ." It is significant that water baptism is in the *name* of Christ; spiritual baptism (1 Cor. 12:13; *see* **Regeneration**) is "*into* Jesus Christ" (Rom. 6:3). This reminds us that water baptism signifies a profession of faith and does not in itself bring one into the reality of union with Christ. Only the Holy Spirit can do that, and water baptism is not necessary to His work.

Various prepositions are used in the phrase "in the name of." In Acts 2:38 the preposition *epi* is used and "probably refers to a baptism on the confession of Jesus as the Messiah" (Berkhof, *Systematic Theology,* p. 625). In Acts 10:48 *en* is used with the thought "on the authority of Jesus Christ." In all other references, *eis* is used, with the thought "in relation to Jesus Christ."

The Meaning of Baptism

The *Westminster Confession of Faith* teaches that baptism is more than the solemn admission of a person into the visible church. It is also "a sign and seal of the covenant of grace, of his ingrafting into Christ, of regeneration, of remission of sins, and of his giving up unto God through Jesus Christ, to walk in newness of life" (Rom. 4:11; Col. 2:11, 12; Gal. 3:27; Rom. 6:5; Titus 3:5; Acts 2:38; 22:16; Rom. 6:3, 4). The Confession holds that baptism is a sign and seal of our union with Christ, "seal" being used in the sense of a token, pledge, confirmation, or assurance.

The *Heidelberg Catechism,* Q. 69, states: "Christ has appointed the outward washing with water and added the promise that I am washed with His Blood and Spirit from the pollution of my soul, that is, from all my sins, as certainly as I am washed outwardly with water, by which the filthiness of the body is commonly washed away."

Thus, purification is essential to the symbolism of baptism (Acts 2:38; 22:16) and union with Christ is its basic significance.

The Efficacy of Baptism

Protestantism rejects all shades of baptismal regeneration and the popish notion that the sacrament operates *opus operatum.* * Baptism is not essential to salvation. In Rom. 4:9-11 Paul carefully distinguishes three things: (1) the righteousness upon which we are accepted by God; (2) faith, by which we appropriate that righteousness; and (3) the seal, which is an after-deed. "It assumes or takes for granted, the validity of the previous transaction. It proceeds upon the supposition, first, of the covenant being itself made and ratified, exclusively on the footing of the perfect righteousness of God; and, secondly, of its being made over to me, and made practically and personally mine, exclusively through faith" (R. S. Candlish, *Exposition of Genesis,* p. 176). Thus, baptism is neither the meritorious cause of our salvation, nor the instrument by which it is appropriated.

Against this view, some sects quote Acts 2:38; 22:16; and 1 Pet. 3:21. Acts 2:38 and 1 Pet. 3:21 are fully discussed under Baptismal Regeneration.*

Acts 22:16 must be understood in a sacramental or symbolic way. Paul was saved on the Damascus road, for there he acknowledged Jesus as Lord (Acts 9:5, 6), and this is proof of the regenerating grace of the Holy Spirit (1 Cor. 12:3). Thus, the baptismal washing was symbolic of the spiritual cleansing he had already received.

Were baptism necessary to salvation, what would become of all the OT saints? Or the penitent thief? Or infants who die unbaptized? It is of fundamental importance to recognize that salvation is by free grace, on the ground of Christ's righteousness, received by faith alone. However the sacraments may express and strengthen that faith, they are not the instrument of salvation.

The Modes of Baptism

Most Christians, with the notable exception of Baptists,* hold that baptism may be validly administered by immersion, pouring, or sprinkling. Baptists insist that the symbolism of burial demands immersion and furthermore that the verb *baptizo* "always signifies to dip; never expressing anything but mode" (Carson, *Baptism in its Mode and Subjects*).

NT usage does not justify such an assertion. In Mark 7:4 we read of the Pharisees washing before meals and of their ceremonial washing of various household items, the last of which is "tables" or "couches," the beds on which they reclined at meals. In both cases *baptizo* is used, and it is clear that immersion is out of the question. Furthermore, how can immersion be read into *baptizo* in Matt. 3:11; Luke 11:37, 38; 12:50; 1 Cor. 10:2; 12:13? In the OT many of the washings ("baptizings") were by sprinkling (Num. 8:7; 19:13; 19:20; Ezek. 36:25; Heb. 9:10), and there is nothing to suggest that such a mode is no longer valid. Indeed, the evidence of the *Didache** is that multiple modes of baptism were observed in the early church.

The Subjects of Baptism

Terms of the Dispute. This is the most vexed area of the baptismal controversy. Baptists, often making baptism merely a badge of profession and testimony and the door to joining the church, hold that only believers may be scripturally baptized. The Reformed churches generally—holding it to be the sign and seal of the covenant—believe that it should also be administered to the children of believers. They do not oppose adult baptism and recognize that it must be preceded by a profession of faith (Mark 16:16; Acts 2:41; 16:31-33), but they insist that the children of baptized believers should be baptized because God has included them in the covenant (Acts 2:39).

Baptists argue that the NT nowhere commands infant baptism, nor does it afford any examples of it. Both these points are admitted by paedobaptists, though they point out that in the NT we read of whole households

being baptized and hold, especially in the light of the OT and of the example of proselyte baptisms among the Jews, that there is little doubt that the children of the house were included.

Paedobaptists hold that in the missionary situation of the early church, the emphasis naturally would fall on adult baptism. But Berkhof remarks, "At the same time, the language of the NT is perfectly consistent with a continuation of the organic administration of the covenant, which required the circumcision of children, Matt. 19:14; Mark 10:13-16; Acts 2:39; 1 Cor. 7:14."

Baptism and Circumcision. The allusion to circumcision holds the key to the controversy. Baptists hold that the parallelism is invalid: "Nor does it serve to introduce the OT sign of circumcision. There is certainly a kinship between the signs. But there are also great differences. The fact that one was given to infant boys on a fixed day is no argument for giving the other to all children some time in infancy. They belong, if not to different covenants, at least to different dispensations of the one covenant: the one to a preparatory stage, when a national people was singled out and its sons belonged naturally to the people of God; the other to the fulfilment, when the Israel of God is spiritual and children are added by spiritual rather than natural regeneration. In any case, God Himself gave a clear command to circumcise the male descendants of Abraham; he has given no similar command to baptize the male and female descendants of Christians" (*Baker's Dictionary of Theology*).

Paedobaptists, however, hold that the covenant made with Abraham was essentially spiritual and circumcision was its sign and seal. NT quotations indicate the spiritual nature of the covenant (Rom. 4:16-18; Gal. 3:8, 9, 14, 16; Heb. 8:10; 11:9, 10, 13). Also, circumcision had a spiritual significance (Deut. 10:16; 30:6; Jer. 4:4; 9:25, 26; Rom. 2:26-29; 4:11). That all this cannot be divorced from the gospel is clear from Gal.

3:8, where the promise of the Abrahamic covenant is specifically termed "the gospel." Thus, the covenant made with Abraham is the same covenant which is called "the new covenant" and which Christians enjoy. We are justified on the same ground as Abraham. We are said to be "blessed with faithful Abraham" (Gal. 3:9). Justification by faith in Christ is said to be "the blessing of Abraham," which "comes on the Gentiles through Jesus Christ" (Gal. 3:14).

All this points to unity and continuity. Colossians 2:11-13 shows circumcision and baptism to have the same spiritual significance, and since circumcision was applicable to children, then "without an express intimation to the contrary, the practice of administering the initiatory seal of the covenant to infants would be kept up, as a matter of course, under the gospel. It required no formal injunction to warrant its continuance, but very explicit authority must be produced to enable the church to set it aside" (Candlish, p. 180).

Ursinus, the coauthor of the *Heidelberg Catechism,* reduced this argument to a simple syllogism: "Under the Old Testament, infants were circumcised as well as adults. Baptism occupies the place of circumcision in the New Testament and has the same use circumcision had in the Old Testament. Therefore infants are to be baptized as well as adults" (*Commentary of Ursinus*, p. 367).

Peter Edwards on Baptism. Peter Edwards, a Baptist pastor who set out to write a work to establish the Baptist position and who was convinced of paedobaptism by his research for that projected work, summed up the Baptist and paedobaptist position to support the scripturalness of the latter:

Baptist arguments are basically two:
1. Only those who are expressly given a right to the ordinance by Scripture may receive baptism. Children are not so mentioned and therefore may not be baptized. Peter Edwards replied that by the same token women would have to be debarred from the Lord's table, but Baptists admit them, rightly but inconsistently. Clearly the NT does not set out to give express rights to all who may receive a sacrament.

2. Faith and repentance are required in order to baptism. Infants cannot exercise these; therefore, infants may not be baptized.

Edwards replied that all such requirements were made of adults. Thus the argument really is this: faith and repentance are required of adults in order to be baptized, but infants cannot exercise these; therefore, infants may not be baptized. Logically, such an argument is useless, for the premise does not lead to the conclusion.

Furthermore, Edwards argued, the same logic would prove that

a. Infants may not be circumcised (Rom. 2:25; Gal. 5:3—they could not keep the law);

b. Infants cannot be saved (Mk. 16:16—if infants are imported at all into this text, it proves that an infant dying is lost);

c. Christ should not have been baptized, for He could not repent.

Edwards' case is that each conclusion is wrong because the argument which produced it is wrong.

Paedobaptist arguments are basically three:
1. Infants of believers were in the OT admitted to membership in God's visible church, and that by a religious rite.

2. Such membership has never been set aside in Scripture—Rom. 11:17, 18, 23, 24; Eph. 2:14; Mark 10:14; Luke 9:47, 48 (cf. Rom. 14:1; Matt. 10:40); Acts 2:39. All indicate the opposite.

3. Since infants must be received into the visible church (Luke 9:47, 48), it must be with or without baptism. Since Scripture warrants no reception into the visible church without baptism, the admission of infants must be with baptism.

A Covenant Theology Baptist on Paedobaptism. Paul K. Jewett, while affirming his acceptance of covenant theology,* rejected such arguments, especially the analogy of baptism to circumcision. Unlike some Baptist controversialists who reduce circumcision to being the mark of citizenship in the Jewish nation, Jewett admits, "There is a fundamental affinity of meaning between circumcision in the Old Testament and baptism in the New" (*Infant Baptism and the Covenant of Grace*, p. 87). However, in dealing with the covenant he argues that the "*affinity* of the old with the new must be counterbalanced by a proper emphasis on the diversity between the two" (Jewett, p. 90). Jewett pressed the argument as follows:

"With the advent of Messiah—the promised seed *par excellence*—and the Pentecostal effusion of the Spirit, the salvation contained in the promise to Israel was brought nigh. No longer was it a hope on the distant horizon but rather an accomplished fact in history. Then—and for our discussion, this THEN is of capital significance—the temporal, earthly, typical elements of the old dispensation were dropped from the great house of salvation as scaffolding from the finished edifice. It is our contention that the Paedobaptists, in framing their argument from circumcision, have failed to keep this significant historical development in clear focus. Proceeding from the basically correct postulate that baptism stands in the place of circumcision, they have urged this analogy to a distortion. They have so far pressed the *unity* of the covenant as to suppress the *diversity* of its administration. They have, to be specific, Christianized the Old Testament and Judaized the New.

"It is this double movement within the argument from circumcision—reading the New Testament as though it were the Old and the Old Testament as though it were the New—which makes the argument so easy to use and so difficult to criticize....It is this compounded error that makes the Reformed argument for infant baptism, apparently so plausible on a superficial level, seem utterly confused when one probes it in depth" (pp. 91, 92).

Jewett argued that while it is right for Christians to read the OT in the light of the New, it is unwarrantable to read it as if it were the New, ignoring the theological significance of the terms "Old" and "New." This, he claims, is the error paedobaptists make. He charges that they practically submerge all the ethnic and national significance of circumcision under its religious and spiritual meaning. Jewett goes on to state that there are two vital considerations that undermine the evangelical paedobaptists' contention.

1. In the OT, circumcision had two aspects: one temporal and earthly, the other eternal and heavenly.

2. Participation in the earthly aspect (i.e., being of the physical line of Abraham) was sufficient to establish a person's right to circumcision. This is where circumcision and baptism differ. Baptism has only a single significance, one that is spiritual and heavenly. "No-one in the New Testament times is born with a right to baptism apart from faith" (p. 97). Evangelical paedobaptists admit that there is no right to baptism through mere physical lineage. They admit that the only right is that of faith. But this admission highlights the clear difference between circumcision and baptism and invalidates the paedobaptist argument from the affinity of baptism with circumcision. The dilemma is not resolved by the substitution of the faith of a parent or sponsor in place of the personal faith of the child. This idea of vicarious faith "is wholly without warrant in the Scripture and repugnant to the fundamental truth that no one can receive and rest upon Christ for salvation by proxy" (p. 184).

Covenant Theology and Believer's Baptism. Jewett concludes his case against paedobaptism by arguing that covenant theology implies "believer baptism" (Jewett prefers this to the more usual "believer's baptism"):

"The troubled water of Paedobaptism can be rendered a clear and flowing stream if one recognizes that the promise of the seed made to Abraham had a twofold reference. In the age of type and anticipation, it embraced not only those who shared Abraham's faith but also the whole nation of Israel, which descended from his loins according to the flesh. In the age of fulfillment the promise embraces the true seed according to the Spirit, typified by the literal seed according to the flesh. This true seed of Abraham is 'born, not of blood, nor of the will of the flesh nor of the will of man, but of God' (John 1:13). If in the typical age of the Old Testament all the literal seed of Abraham are to be circumcised, then in the age of fulfillment all those who answer to the type as the true seed of Abraham are to be baptized. And who are they? The New Testament gives an unequivocal answer: those who are of faith are the sons of Abraham (Gal. 3:7). Therefore, those who are of faith are to be baptized—*which is precisely believer baptism"* (p. 236).

Significance of Baptism as Initiatory Rite

After all the disagreement on the subject of circumcision and its significance for baptism, it is good to be able to quote a paedobaptist on the two rites as he speaks on an aspect of the subject on which both paedobaptists and baptists entirely agree. Commenting on Gen. 17, Robert Candlish discussed the propriety of circumcision and baptism as initiatory symbolic rites:

"It [circumcision] has obvious reference to Abraham's approaching paternity, his having a son, not after the flesh but by promise; and it is the sign and symbol of something peculiar and remarkable in the manner of the birth, as well as of some special purity and holiness in what was to be born. It has respect to the seed about to be begotten. It points to the Messiah, the Saviour about to be manifested as the righteousness of God....It prefigures His assumption of humanity, in a way securing His exemption from the sinfulness of humanity;...hence, perhaps, one reason for circumcision, as the

initial or introductory seal for the covenant, being superseded and another sacrament coming in its place. Circumcision pointed to the future birth of Christ—His assumption of our nature, pure and perfect. That birth being accomplished, the propriety of circumcision as a sacrament ceases. Any corresponding rite now must be not prospective, but retrospective....Such a rite accordingly is baptism....Our baptism signifies our ingrafting into Christ, as not merely born, but buried and risen again....Abraham and the faithful of old were circumcised into His birth, the redemption being yet future; we are baptized into His death, the redemption being now past" (p. 178).

Toleration of Different Views on Baptism

The discussion of baptism is all too frequently acrimonious and has led to division among the people of God. Is there not clearly a case for holding our views in love for differing brethren, ensuring that neither adult nor paedobaptism is so exalted as to become essential to the gospel and salvation?

We must never forget the importance of baptism. As Calvin taught, the faithful preaching of the Word and the valid administration of the sacraments are essential marks of a true church. However Paul's words, "Christ sent me not to baptize, but to preach the gospel" (1 Cor. 1:17), should teach us to temper our zeal for an exclusive position on the subject. We ought not to make our own particular view of baptism an integral part of the gospel and a ground for fellowship or separation.

In this spirit, the Free Presbyterian Church of Ulster has, since its inception, practised acceptance of both baptist and paedobaptist believers in its communicant membership and ministry. *Separated unto the Gospel: The Mission and Work of the Free Presbyterian Church* quotes Article 6a of the church's Articles of Faith: "The Free Presbyterian Church of Ulster, under Christ the great King and Head of the Church, realizes that bitter controversy raging around the mode and proper subjects of the ordinance of Christian Baptism has divided the Body of Christ when that Body should have been united in Christian love and Holy Ghost power to stem the onslaughts and hell-inspired assaults of modernism, hereby affirms that each member of the Free Presbyterian Church shall have liberty to decide for himself which courses to adopt on these controversial issues, each member giving due honour in love to the views held by differing brethren, but none espousing the error of baptismal regeneration."

BAPTISM FOR THE DEAD

Vicarious baptism practised by Mormons for those who died unbaptized, based on a perversion of Paul's words in 1 Cor. 15:29. The Mormon dogma is best understood in the words of a Mormon apologist:

"Millions of earth's sons and daughters have passed out of the body without obeying the law of baptism. Many of them will gladly accept the word and law of the Lord when it is proclaimed to them in the spirit world. But they cannot there attend to ordinances that belong to the sphere which they have left. Can nothing be done in their case? Must they forever be shut out of the kingdom of heaven? Both justice and mercy join in answering 'yes' to the first 'no' to the last question. What, then, is the way of their deliverance? The living may be baptized for the dead. Other essential ordinances may be attended to vicariously. This glorious truth, hid from human knowledge for centuries, has been made known in this greatest of all divine dispensations....It gives men and women the power to become 'Saviours on Mount Zion,' Jesus being the great Captain in the army of redeemers" (C. Penrose, *Mormon Doctrine*, p. 48, quoted by J. K. Van Baalen, *Chaos of the Cults*, p. 180).

The practice of vicarious baptism for the dead was prevalent in some second-century heretical groups. Some trace the practice back to heathenism. It is possible that it had found its way into Corinth as early as the writing of Paul's first epistle.

Paul does not endorse or support the practice. Indeed his language indicates that he dissociates himself and orthodox believers from it. He asks, "What shall *they* do which are baptized for the dead?" Not "what shall *we* do." Yet he does use *we* in the next verse: "And why stand *we* in jeopardy every hour?" If he is referring to vicarious baptism at all, Paul appears to draw a clear line of demarcation between *they* and *we*.

His argument is, "The behaviour of those who are baptized in the place of their unbaptized friends proves that they believe in the resurrection of the dead." Paul is quite capable of noting beliefs and practices with which his readers are familiar to support his own argument.

Some maintain that he could not have referred to a practice like vicarious baptism without condemning it. However, a comparison between 1 Cor. 8 and 10 will show that he did at times uncritically refer to things which he actually condemned. In 1 Cor. 8 he refers to Christians sitting down to eat in a heathen temple, but he does not stop to condemn them (though he later does so, 1 Cor. 10). So his lack of condemnation may mean no more than that this subject is one of those he "will set in order when I come" (11:34). The entire disappearance of vicarious baptism from Corinth is taken by many to support this view.

Many good commentators deny that there is any reference at all to vicarious baptism in 1 Cor. 15:29. Some see in it a reference to newly baptized people taking the place in the church of those who had died. Others see it as a reference to those who had been inspired by the martyrdom of saints to receive Christ and profess Him in baptism, thus filling up their vacant places in the church.

From all this it is clear how notoriously difficult a text 1 Cor. 15:29 is. For the Mormons to construct on it a doctrine of a second chance to be saved for those who die in their sin is plainly ludicrous. It also betrays an utterly unscriptural idea of baptism and its place in the economy of grace, to say nothing of the heresy it promotes in giving "men and women the power to become 'Saviours on Mount Zion.'"

BAPTISM OF BLOOD

The doctrine of the Church of Rome that those who die for the faith being yet unbaptized are baptized by their death for and with Christ (*Catechism of the Catholic Church,* ¶1258).

BAPTISM OF DESIRE

The process by which, according to the Roman Catholic church, unbaptized people may merit eternal life. Rome's dogmas that baptism is essential to salvation and that outside the (Roman) church there is no salvation, raised questions about the destiny of people in OT times and of those since the time of Christ who have never heard the gospel. It would appear that Rome's dogmas condemn all who are not baptized into her communion.

Thomas Aquinas held that prior to Christ it was sufficient for salvation to believe in God and in providence. Such belief was equal to implicit faith in Christ. Others went further and extended this idea to those after the time of Christ who live and die without hearing and responding in baptism to the gospel. They also may be saved by implicit faith.

Vatican II (*Dogmatic Constitution on the Church,* chap. 2, ¶16) confirms this as official dogma.

BAPTISMAL REGENERATION

The theory that regeneration is effected by the means of baptism,* or that it cannot be effected without baptism. Some modify these positions to allow for exceptions in extreme cases.

Advocates of Baptismal Regeneration

Baptismal regeneration is the teaching of very diverse groups.

Roman Catholics. The Roman Catholic church teaches it, describing baptism as "the laver of regeneration" (Council of Trent, Sess. 6, chap. 4). It anathematizes any who disagree: "If any one saith, that baptism is free, that is, not necessary unto salvation: let him be anathema" (Canon V). In Rome's view baptism signifies, celebrates, and effects the new birth of the baptized, *opus operatum.* *

Eastern Orthodox. The *Orthodox Confession of the Eastern Church* takes a similar position: baptism is a regeneration by water and the Spirit which cleanses and removes original sin, and without which there is no entrance to the kingdom of God (Q. 102). "Baptism is a sacrament, in which a man who believes, having his body thrice plunged in water in the name of the Father, the Son, and the Holy Ghost, dies to the carnal life of sin, and is born again of the Holy Ghost to a life spiritual and holy" (*Larger Catechism of the Eastern Church,* Q. 288).

Lutherans. Lutheranism also teaches that baptism is necessary to salvation. Article 9 of the *Augsburg Confession* (1530) states: "By Baptism the grace of God is offered, and…children are to be baptized, who by Baptism, being offered to God, are received into God's favour." Luther in his *Small Catechism* says, "Baptism is not simply common water, but it is the water comprehended in God's command, and connected with God's Word.…It worketh forgiveness of sins, delivers from death and the devil, and gives everlasting salvation to all who believe, as the Word and promise of God declare" (Part 4, 1 and 2).

Anglicans. Anglicanism also holds to a kind of baptismal regeneration, though its articles are variously interpreted by Low and High churchmen. The *Thirty-nine Articles of the Church of England* (1571) state that baptism is "a sign of Regeneration or

New Birth, whereby, as by an instrument, they that receive Baptism rightly are grafted into the church; the promises of our adoption to be the sons of God by the Holy Ghost, are visibly signed and sealed; Faith is confirmed, and grace increased by virtue of prayer unto God" (Art. 27). The *Anglican Catechism* teaches that the "inward spiritual grace" of which baptism in water is the outward sign and form is "a death unto sin, and a new birth unto righteousness: for, being by nature born in sin, and children of wrath, we are hereby made children of grace." The *Prayer Book* uses even stronger language, teaching that the baptized are thereby born again and made inheritors of the kingdom of God.

Moravians. The Moravian church's Easter Litany (1749) says, "I believe that by holy baptism I am embodied a member of the church of Christ, which he hath loved, and for which he gave himself that he might sanctify and cleanse it with the washing of water by the word."

It should be noted that all these Protestant churches entirely reject Rome's notion that baptism works *opus operatum.* *

The Reformed View

The Reformed view is succinctly put by the *Westminster Confession of Faith:*

"Baptism is a sacrament of the New Testament, ordained by Jesus Christ, not only for the solemn admission of the party baptized into the visible Church, but also to be unto him a sign and seal of the covenant of grace, of his ingrafting into Christ, of regeneration, of remission of sins, and of his giving up unto God, through Jesus Christ, to walk in newness of life: which sacrament is, by Christ's own appointment, to be continued in his Church until the end of the world.... Although it be a great sin to condemn or neglect this ordinance, yet grace and salvation are not so inseparably annexed unto it, as that no person can be regenerated or saved without it, or that all that are

baptized are undoubtedly regenerated" (chap. 28, sec. 1, 4).

Antipaedobaptist Views

Antipaedobaptists have often set forth their own version of the concept. Allowing baptism only upon profession of faith the Campbellites* (the self-styled Disciples of Christ and Churches of Christ) have taken a strong stand for baptismal regeneration.

The *Baptist Confession* (1689) and the *New Hampshire Confession* (1833) both clearly make baptism a sign of the believer's fellowship with Christ in His death and resurrection, and of his ingrafting into Him. They say nothing of the necessity of baptism for salvation, though they recognize it as a sovereign institution of Christ that should be continued in the Church to the end of the age.

However, those who hold the Baptist successionist view of the church (see Baptist) come very near to a form of baptismal regeneration in that, logically, their position is that without valid baptism (by which they usually mean baptism by a Baptist or even a Baptist successionist) no one has a place in the church. Can a person outside the church of Christ be saved?

Connection Between Baptism and Regeneration

G. W. Bromiley *(ISBE, Revised)* holds that there is a scriptural and an unscriptural way of stating the connection between baptism and salvation. The scriptural way is to see baptism as the sign of regeneration and regeneration as true baptism—the reality of the thing signified in baptism. No one could take issue with such statements, but they do not justify the language of baptismal regeneration. To speak as Bromiley does of all who receive baptism as being "regenerate in sign, i.e., baptismally" is dangerous and unwarranted, especially in a paedobaptist setting. Bromiley rightly points out that any introduction of cause and effect into the connection between baptism and regeneration is illegitimate. That, of course, is the very sense in which Rome employs the terms: baptism is the instrument of regeneration.

Claimed Biblical Support

The Biblical evidence for baptismal regeneration is scanty. Indeed, properly understood it is nonexistent. John 3:5; Mark 16:16; Acts 2:38; Rom. 6:4-6; Titus 3:5; 1 Pet. 3:21; are the texts chiefly relied upon.

Examination of Texts

John 3:5: "Except a man be born of water and of the Spirit, he cannot enter into the kingdom of God."

Calvin rejected a reference to baptism here, and proponents of baptismal regeneration are hard put to explain a reference to Christian baptism by Christ to Nicodemus long before Pentecost and the institution of the NT church. We may understand the expression "born of water and of the spirit" as a *hendiadys.* There is no article in the Greek text which reads simply "water and spirit." *Hendiadys* is a figure of speech in which two nouns connected by *and* are used instead of one noun and an adjective. The second noun has the force of a superlative or emphatic adjective. In John 3:5 the meaning is, therefore, "spiritual water." This is essentially the same conclusion Calvin reached. He saw *water* and *spirit* as signifying the same thing.

Would "spiritual water" have conveyed anything to Nicodemus? Assuredly it would. He was well aware of the waters of separation (Num. 19) and the cleansing waters specifically associated with obtaining "a new heart" and receiving God's Spirit (Ezek. 36:25-27). The Lord Jesus was showing him that these had to be understood as references, not to sacramental ablutions, but to the activity of the Holy Spirit. Paul follows the same line of thought in Eph. 5:26, "the washing of water by the word."

Mark 16:16: "He that believeth and is baptized shall be saved; but he that believeth not shall be damned."

While the importance of baptism as the expected public acknowledgment of Christ as Saviour is clear here, it is obvious that the thing that is so essential to salvation that its absence invariably damns a man is faith. Those who trust Christ should not fail to be baptized and those who are baptized must ensure that they do indeed have saving faith. Without it their baptism can do nothing to save them.

Rom. 6:4-6: "Therefore we are buried with him by baptism into death: that like as Christ was raised up from the dead by the glory of the Father, even so we also should walk in newness of life. For if we have been planted together in the likeness of his death, we shall be also in the likeness of his resurrection: knowing this, that our old man is crucified with him, that the body of sin might be destroyed, that henceforth we should not serve sin."

There is no reference to water baptism here. The reference is to real, not professed, or sacramental incorporation into Christ. The baptism is spiritual, as in 1 Cor. 12:13. It is the action of the Holy Spirit actually putting us into saving union with Christ.

Titus 3:5: "Not by works of righteousness which we have done, but according to his mercy he saved us, by the washing of regeneration, and renewing of the Holy Ghost."

The washing of regeneration is literally "the laver of regeneration" which is explained by the following phrase, the "renewing of the Holy Ghost." There is no mention of baptism. The laver is to be spiritually understood. The OT tabernacle and temple had their lavers. Here we learn that their true import was that they pointed to the renewing work of the Holy Spirit. That is the laver of regeneration, not water baptism.

Acts 2:38: "Then Peter said unto them, Repent, and be baptized every one of you in the name of Jesus Christ for the remission of sins, and ye shall receive the gift of the Holy Ghost."

Campbellites are so confident that this text teaches their baptismal regeneration dogma that they at times style their gospel *The Acts 2:38 Gospel*. The entire argument hinges on the force of the preposition *for*. The Greek word is *eis* and it usually means "to, unto." Therefore, we are told, baptism is "unto the remission of sins." Remission follows baptism, it does not precede it.

That is the claim. But is it true? It is not. The Greek preposition *eis* has a much wider meaning than "unto" in the sense of "with a view to."

Matthew 3:11 is clearly a parallel passage. John the Baptist said, "I indeed baptize you with water unto repentance." Here again *unto* is *eis*. On the Campbellite interpretation of Acts 2:38 the repentance would have to *follow* the baptism. But did not those who came to be baptized by John receive baptism because they had *already* repented? The preposition *eis* here does not indicate the order the Campbellites infer in Acts 2:38, but the opposite.

Take another example. In Matt. 12:41 we read, "The men of Nineveh…repented at [*eis*] the preaching of Jonas." If the Campbellite interpretation of Acts 2:38 here, Matt. 12:41 would be saying that the Ninevites repented *in order to obtain* the preaching of Jonah. Clearly that was not the case. They repented because they had already received it.

And that is the force of *eis* in Acts 2:38. Baptism *for* (*eis*) the remission of sins is baptism *at,* or *in connection with* the remission received through repentance and faith.

1 Peter 3:21: "The like figure whereunto even baptism doth now save us (not the putting away of the filth of the flesh, but the answer of a good conscience toward God,) by the resurrection of Jesus Christ."

It is almost universally asserted that this text plainly attributes some saving action to baptism (even if it is only symbolic or declarative). However there are serious objections to this view.

First, the Greek text has nothing corresponding to "the like figure whereunto even baptism doth now save us."

Second, as the text now reads, baptism is the antitype of the waters of the flood. But Noah was not saved *by* water but *from* water. In what way then is his salvation from the flood typical of our salvation by Christ in baptism?

Let us consider these points.

The Greek of v. 21 reads, *ho kai hemas antitupon nun sozei.* The first question is, What is the antecedent of *ho,* "which"? Our translation practically ignores it, but really refers it to the *hudatos,* "water," of v. 20. On this basis the literal rendering would be: "Which (water) even (or also) us the antitype now saves."

Robert Nevin in *Misunderstood Scriptures* suggests that a better answer to the question of an antecedent to *which* would be "the Spirit," v. 18, by which Christ preached to the sinners of Noah's day (v. 19). That would yield the translation, "Which (or who, the Holy Spirit) now saves us, the antitype (of Noah and his family) by the resurrection of Jesus Christ."

This is the natural force of the word order of the Greek text and so far makes perfect sense. If this is the correct translation then we must start a new sentence with, "Baptism is not the putting away of the filth of the flesh (i.e., of sin's defilement) but the seeking or appeal of a good conscience toward God."

It is clear, whether we follow the common English version or this suggested translation, that baptism cannot cleanse away sin. It is a testimony or an appeal of a purified conscience to God on the merits of the work of Christ. In other words, baptism declares that our trust for salvation is not in baptism but in Christ who died and rose again.

Another possible view of 1 Pet. 3:21 makes *water* the antecedent of the relative *which.* In this view baptism is a reference to the death and judgment-bearing of Christ so that vv. 20-22 would then mean:

"The longsuffering of God waited, the ark having been prepared, in which few, that is eight souls were saved through and out of water (the instrument of God's judgment). Which (water shows us how) baptism (another emblem of the judgment of God on sin) now saves us the antitype (of those saved in the ark): it is not the putting away of the filth of the flesh (sin) but the appeal (or demand) of a good conscience (one cleared from guilt) through the resurrection of Jesus Christ, who is now at the right hand of God, angels and authorities and powers having been subjected unto Him."

If we adopt this treatment, the reference to baptism is a reminder of Christ's bearing the wrath of God against our sin just as the ark bore it in the days of the flood.

1 Peter 3:21 cannot justly be made a witness for the theory of baptismal regeneration. As Nevin long ago remarked, "The doctrine of baptismal regeneration is not of Christian but of Pagan origin. It had a prominent place in the ancient Babylonian mysteries" (Nevin, p. 227). It has no place in Christian theology.

BAPTIST

Meaning of the Term

Baptist is the designation claimed by churches that

1. Deny the validity of infant baptism;
2. Hold that baptism* may be administered only upon personal profession of faith;
3. Insist that immersion is the only acceptable mode of baptism;
4. Pursue the church polity of independency and congregationalism;*
5. Reject the idea of a territorial church,* or a mixed church, holding to the concept of the gathered church,* the local assembly constituted solely of a regenerate church membership.

Theories of Baptist Origins

While all Baptists naturally believe that the original churches of the NT were established on Baptist beliefs and principles, they have not been agreed on the historical lin-

eage of modern Baptist churches. Baptist historian Robert G. Torbet says, "There is no common agreement among Baptist historians concerning the origin of Baptists" (*History of the Baptists*, p. 159). Torbet discusses three popular theories.

The Jerusalem-Jordan-John Theory. This is the theory of the so-called *Baptist Bride* proponents. In defence of their idea that the church Christ came to save—His Bride—is the Baptist church, they hold that Baptists enjoy an apostolic succession that traces their churches back in an unbroken line through the apostles, to the ministry of Christ, or of John the Baptist. This view sees all the nonconformist groups that rebelled against Catholic institutionalism—such as the Donatists,* Novatians,* Petrobrussians,* Waldenses,* and Albigenses*—as Baptists. Whatever points of similarity they may have had, it stretches the historical data to the breaking point to make these nonconformist groups Baptist churches.

The Anabaptist Spiritual Kinship Theory. This is the theory that traces a spiritual, as distinct from an historical, connection between Baptists and the Anabaptists* and the groups mentioned above. Whatever truth there may be in this idea—and clearly there is some, though, major differences abound in doctrine, church polity, and even on the subject of baptism—it clearly supplies no information on the historical development of Baptist churches.

The English Separatist Descent Theory. This is the theory that traces the history of the Baptist churches to some English separatists who held to congregational church government and believers' baptism as their two distinctive beliefs.

This third theory provides the best way of tracing the historical development of Baptist churches.

English Baptist Roots

English General Baptists. English Baptists arose in Holland under the ministry of John

Smith, a refugee from persecution in his homeland. Smith went to Holland as a Congregationalist. In Amsterdam he became convinced of believer's baptism. Unwilling to become a Mennonite he baptized himself by pouring and then baptized as many of his congregation as desired him to do so. However, he soon came to regret this "private" baptism and with the majority of his group petitioned the Mennonites to be received into their membership.

His colleague, Thomas Helwys, led a group of about ten people in repudiating Smith's connection with the Mennonites. Helwys and his group returned to England in 1611 or 1612 as England's first Baptist church. It had about ten members, was Arminian* in its soteriology,* and practised baptism by pouring. Helwys made a powerful plea for freedom of conscience in matters of religion, "the first claim for freedom of worship to be published in the English language" (Torbet, p. 67).

By 1644 there were forty-seven General Baptist churches, "Arminian in theology, evangelistic in purpose, and dedicated to religious liberty" (Torbet, p. 69).

English Particular Baptists. Particular Baptists arose around 1640 and adopted immersion as the only scriptural mode of believers' baptism. They were Calvinistic in theology. By 1644 there were seven Particular Baptist churches that adopted the *London Confession,* a Calvinistic confession of 50 articles of faith.

In 1677, and then again in 1688 and 1689, English Particular Baptists produced *A Confession of Faith put forth by the Elders and Brethren of many Congregations of Christians, Baptized upon Profession of their Faith in London and the Country.* This *Confession* "is a slight modification of the Confession of the Westminster Assembly (1647) and the Savoy Declaration (1658), with changes to suit the Baptist views on Church polity and on the subjects and mode of baptism" (Philip Schaff, *Creeds of Christendom,* 3:738).

Growth and Division

In the century that followed the Toleration Act of 1690, English Baptists experienced growth, produced eminent leaders, scholars, and theologians, pioneered the modern missionary movement through the vision and work of William Carey, and suffered from internal divisions because of the emergence of unitarianism, mostly among the General, or Arminian, Baptists.

While the Calvinistic Baptists were only slightly bothered by Unitarianism, they were hurt by a hyper-Calvinistic theology that was unevangelistic and often antinomian.* It should be noted, however, that the great missionary impulse that so invigorated Baptist evangelism at home and abroad came from Calvinists like Carey and Andrew Fuller.

The 18th and 19th centuries saw a wide expansion of Baptist witness in England and the rest of the British Isles and then even further afield.

Welsh Baptists. Wales had enjoyed the ministry of men such as Vavasor Powell as far back as the 1640's. In the next century they experienced great growth and were blessed by the ministry of their greatest evangelist, Christmas Evans (1766-1838). By 1900 there were 835 Baptist churches in Wales. From the beginning, Welsh Baptists were Calvinistic.

Scottish Baptists. Baptists in Scotland originated with Cromwell's invasion. Many of his troops were Baptists. It was not until about 1750 that Scotland produced its first indigenous Baptist church. Scottish Baptists were Calvinistic, practised a church polity that demanded a plurality of elders, and observed close communion. At length they were largely converted to the English Baptist polity and allowed open communion.

Scottish Baptist witness was greatly enhanced by the ministry of the Haldane brothers, James and Robert. James Haldane was a noted evangelist while Robert is still widely known because of his commentary on the epistle to the Romans. Both exercised a widespread influence through their experience of revival blessing in their ministries.

Irish Baptists. Cromwell's army was also the means of bringing Baptist churches to Ireland. Some eleven churches were established between 1652 and 1654. However, over time these grew weak, and it was not until the 19th century that Baptist churches began a successful witness. One of the converts to Baptistic views was a young Presbyterian minister, Alexander Carson, whose work on baptism is still highly regarded.

Dominion Baptists. From the homeland, British Baptists spread to Britain's foreign dominions. Churches were established in Canada (starting in 1763 under the influence of American Baptists and English loyalists fleeing from the new republic), Australia (1831), and New Zealand (1851) and met with considerable success.

American Baptists. "The heritage of American Baptists is chiefly British. While it is true that in America the earliest advocates of strictly Baptist views stemmed from the little band that surrounded Roger Williams—whose expulsion from the Massachusetts Bay Colony because of his insistence upon the separation of church and state issued in the establishment of the Providence Plantation—the majority of early Baptists in the new world came from the British Isles, being English, Welsh, Scotch, and Irish....One other source of Baptists was German—a small group of Dunkards, as they were called from their practice of immersing, settled in Pennsylvania" (Torbet, p. 219).

Outside Rhode Island, New England was not at all favourable to the Baptist cause, especially its insistence on the separation of church and state, and the refusal of its members to present their children for baptism. Thus New England, whose Puritan and congregational state church practised infant baptism, presents the sorry spectacle of those who had fled religious persecution in the Old World practising it on fellow refugees for freedom in the New World.

Persecution had its predictable result of fortifying the persecuted. Baptist churches took root despite the efforts of the authorities and spread throughout the original colonies.

American Baptist Divisions

In the aftermath of the Edwards and Whitefield revivals, Baptists encountered the same division of opinion that caused rifts in the Congregational and Presbyterian churches. They divided into *Regular Baptists,* who subscribed to the *Philadelphia Confession—The English Particular Baptist Confession* of 1689—and who were Calvinistic in theology, and *Separate Baptists,* who claimed the Bible alone as their rule of faith without any human confession.

There were further differences between Arminians and Calvinists and between trinitarians and unitarian universalists. Missionary strategy caused further disputes, and the arrival of Alexander Campbell led many Baptists into his embryonic denomination *(see **Campbellites).***

Severe tensions over the issue of slavery posed an ongoing threat to Baptist unity. They finally led to a major division between northern and southern Baptists in 1845. As a result, the Southern Baptist Convention was formed in May of that year and was set up as "a firmly centralized denominational body functioning through various boards" (Torbet, p. 309).

Despite all these factional forces, Baptist expansion was little short of phenomenal. By 1844 there were almost three-quarters of a million Baptists in the United States, with over 9,000 churches and over 6,000 ministers. Despite losing thousands of members as the direct result of the Civil War, in subsequent years Baptists saw that growth continued, until today they are a major Protestant constituency in America.

Baptist Associations

One of the central tenets of Baptist churches is the principle of the autonomy of the local church. On the face of it this must ever be a deterrent to the formation of a Baptist denomination. However, Baptists have from the beginning displayed a strong attachment to the idea of Baptist associations, first in England and then in the United States, and these have often displayed a distinct denominational character.

British Associations. In the British Isles the Baptists formed national unions, notably the Baptist Union of Great Britain and Ireland. With the spread of theological liberalism within this Union the stage was set for C. H. Spurgeon's heroic stand in the Downgrade controversy of the 1880's. Spurgeon felt he had no option but to withdraw from the Union because to remain in it would demand a serious compromise with fundamental error.

In later years the Union proved the justice of Spurgeon's condemnation of its decline into infidelity as it played a full part in the developing ecumenical activities of the British Council of Churches and the World Council of Churches.*

American Associations. In America the first association was the Philadelphia Association, formed in 1707 by five small churches. It adopted the Confession of the English Particular Baptists of 1689, making it and the associations that flowed from it Calvinistic bodies.

Further associations were formed, until by 1800 there were 48 in all. The Philadelphia Association exercised a strong leadership role among them and there was even an attempt to establish something of a national Baptist Church "in one body politic, by having the Association of Philadelphia (the centre) incorporated by charter, and by taking one delegate out of each Association into the corporation," to quote the proposal of Morgan Edwards, the minister of the First Baptist Church in Philadelphia.

The role of an association was advisory but powerful. While the association was not a superior court over the local church, and each church retained its autonomy, it did exercise considerable power over its constituent members. It had the power to act as a council of ordination. It could disbar a church from its fellowship for doctrinal defection. It acted to advise churches on matters great and small, and had the disciplining of ministers in its discretion.

American Associations and Missionary Work. Baptist associations provided a powerful impetus toward missionary work at home and abroad. In 1814 all the associations gathered in Philadelphia to create a national missionary society, "The General Missionary Convention of the Baptist Denomination in the United States for Foreign Missions." One of its first missionaries was the famed Adoniram Judson who, on his way to minister as a Congregational missionary in Burma came to hold Baptist convictions, resigned from the Congregationalists and joined the Baptists.

Soon the General Missionary Convention came to be known as the Triennial Convention and, after the schism with the Southern churches, as the American Baptist Missionary Union. Ultimately, in 1908, Northern Baptists formed the Northern (later called the American) Baptist Convention so that there were two strong Baptist conventions which, though still evidencing the marks of their earlier division, yet carried on a Baptist witness in America.

Conventionism. Conventionism led to further disputes, chiefly the Landmark controversy which resulted in the separation of Landmark Baptists from the Southern Baptist Convention. Many other Baptists took similar action in protest against denominational connectionism and the emergence of liberalism,* notably the churches that seceded from the Northern Baptist Convention in 1933 to form the General Association of Regular Baptist Churches. This group adopted the *New Hampshire Confession of Faith* with a specifically premillennial interpretation of its last article.

Reaction to liberalism and conventionism has led to a strong separatist, independent, fundamental Baptist church movement that is still growing at a fast pace across America. Attitudes to bodies like the Federal (later National) Council of Churches (NCC) and the World Council of Churches (WCC) have produced deep dissention among Baptists, both in America and abroad.

The American Baptist Convention has maintained membership in the NCC and the WCC and in recent years has taken part in the dialogues on church unity sponsored by the Faith and Order movement of the WCC. Dealing with such issues as baptism, the eucharist (mass*), and the ministry (priesthood), it contributed remarkably mild, most unbaptistic, responses to the ecumenical proposals under discussion.

The Southern Baptist Convention declined membership in the NCC and WCC. However, though it cited the influence of theological liberalism as a major reason for its decision not to join the NCC, the Convention has had many bitter internal conflicts over the presence of liberalism in its seminaries, a controversy that still rages today.

An Effective Protestant Witness

From very small and persecuted beginnings Baptist churches have spread across the world and have made major contributions to the cause of missions. For many years they, with others, carried on a courageous witness in Communist countries behind the Iron Curtain, often as "underground," or unregistered, churches. Baptists now represent a major part of Protestant evangelicalism, a part in which "the vital principles of the Protestant reformation have come to full fruition" (Tolbert, p. 493).

BARTHIANISM
See Neo-Orthodoxy.

BEATIFIC VISION
A term denoting the blessed state of the glorified saints in heaven, where they behold the glory of the Lord and enjoy perfect and sinless communion with Him.

BEATIFICATION
The penultimate step in the creation of a "saint" in the Roman Catholic church. It occurs at least fifty years after the death of the candidate, allows the title *Blessed* to be prefixed to his name, and permits worship or *cultus* to be offered to him in a particular diocese or religious order. It is followed by Canonization.*

BIBLE
See Scriptures.

BIBLICAL THEOLOGY
In the general sense, this term describes a theology that draws its material from the Bible and seeks to be faithful to the divine revelation of inspired Scripture. In this sense all branches of the theological method may justly claim to be Biblical theology—e.g., systematic theology will be truly Biblical if it remains faithful to the word of God.

The term is also used in a more restricted sense. Taking theology to have four main departments—exegetical, systematic, historical, and practical—Biblical theology is a branch of exegetical theology, "that branch which deals with the process of the self-revelation of God deposited in the Bible" (Geerhardus Vos). J. Barton Payne defined it as "the Biblical history of divine redemption."

Antisupernaturalistic critics have debased the term *Biblical theology* to make it nothing more than a study of their evolutionary notions of the history of Israel's religion. Neo-orthodox theologians, such as Barth, claim to have produced a Biblical theology. This is to stretch the term too far, for to deny the true historicity of such supernatural events as the virgin birth and the resurrection of Christ, or to hold that as history they are not revelational, as Barthianism does, is plainly to deal falsely with the Biblical record, and thus is incapable of measuring up to either the general or particular use of the term *Biblical theology.*

BIBLIOLOGY

The section of systematic theology* which deals with "topics relating to the written revelation of God: namely, the inspiration, authenticity, credibility, and canonicity of the Scriptures of the Old and New Testaments" (Shedd).

BLACK THEOLOGY

A theology of black liberation that originated in the United States and gained widespread acceptance in Southern Africa. It differs from African Theology.* African Theology is primarily a theology of pre-Christian African traditional religions. Black Theology is the theology that the OT is the story of a black nation, Israel, written by black Jews as a history of their people. Jesus was a black Messiah who built upon the black OT and came on a mission to liberate His black people from the oppression of white Gentiles.

See *Ethiopianist Theology*; *Liberation Theology*; *Political Theology*; *Theology of Decolonization.*

BLASPHEMY

A word used to denote all forms of evil speaking against God or His perfections, such as slander, defamation, detraction, reproach, or cursing. While in the Greek NT such evil speaking when aimed at man is also termed *blasphemy* (Rom. 3:8; 14:16; 1 Pet. 4:4), it is usual to limit blasphemy to a crime against God.

The most serious form of blasphemy is blasphemy against the Holy Spirit (Matt. 12:31, 32; Mark 3:28, 29; Luke 12:10). From the earliest times there have been many varying explanations of this sin. The context of the words of Christ on the subject leads us to see it as the Pharisees' sin in deliberately attributing to Satan what they saw

in Christ to be a work of the Holy Spirit, and in stubbornly seeking to spread their pernicious slander to others.

Many commentators have seen the sin mentioned in Heb. 6:4-6 and 10:26-31 as a peculiar form of the blasphemy against the Holy Spirit, chiefly because these passages speak of a sin that will never be forgiven. The sin these texts describe is that of Jews who professed to be Christians, giving up Christ to return to the sacrificial system of the temple. The indications are that such people were never saved. According to Heb. 6:9, they evidently did not possess the things "having salvation," as the Greek text puts it. Once they gave up Christ's one-and-only sacrifice for sin, there remained no other and there was nothing left for them but the certainty of judgment.

The connection between the sin of Heb. 6 and that of Matt. 12 seems to be established by the description of the spiritual experiences of those Jews who apostatized. They had been "enlightened"; had "tasted of the heavenly gift and were made partakers of the Holy Ghost" (probably meaning they had experienced His supernatural power); and had "tasted the good word of God, and the powers of the world to come" (Heb. 6:4-5). Like the Pharisees of Matt. 12, they knew by abundant proof through the supernatural working of the Holy Spirit that Jesus Christ was the true and only Saviour. In such circumstances, giving Him up for animal sacrifices may aptly be termed *blasphemy* against the Holy Spirit.

Some commentators find another equivalent of the sin of Matt. 12 in John's reference to "the sin unto death" (1 John 5:16). There is no reason to identify the two sins and no evidence that John so understood the sin unto death. This is a sin Christians could commit. It is better to see it as a description of the sin Paul mentions in 1 Cor. 11:30-32. There he speaks of believers sinning and being unwilling to judge their own sin. The result is that the Lord calls them to an early death, *so that they would not be condemned with the world.* This seems to show that the sin unto death is not the blasphemy against the Holy Spirit.

BLOOD OF CHRIST

1. The actual blood of the Lord Jesus which He shed on the cross.
2. His sacrificial death. In this case blood is a metonym for *death,* as *cross* also is in Gal. 6:14. For example, in Rom. 5:9 the phrase "by his blood" is clearly equivalent to "Christ died for us" (v. 8).

Blood Not Merely a Metaphor

The fact that Christ's blood may be spoken of metaphorically for His death has led some evangelicals to downplay or even deny the redemptive virtue of the actual blood of Christ. They do not scruple to say that Christ's blood perished in the dust of Palestine. They claim to uphold the atoning death of Christ while denying His atoning blood. This is dangerous and without Biblical warrant. The equivalence of the expressions "by His blood" and "Christ died for us" does not for a moment obscure the peculiar aspect of the truth contained in each. To be atoning, Christ's death had to be a sacrificial blood-shedding, and His blood had to be shed in the death of the cross. In other words, *death* and *blood* are not mutually exclusive terms. Each supposes the other.

Biblical Emphasis on the Blood . The Bible places immense emphasis on the blood of atonement: Exod. 12:13; Lev. 16; 17:11; Matt. 26:28; John 6:53-56; 19:34; Acts 20:28; Rom. 3:25; 5:9; 1 Cor. 10:16; 11:25, 27; Eph. 1:7; 2:13; Col. 1:14, 20; Heb. 9:7, 12, 14, 22; 10:19, 29; 12:24; 13:12, 20; 1 Pet. 1:2, 19; 1 John 1:7; 5:6, 8; Rev. 1:5; 5:9; 7:14; 12:11. In light of this emphasis it is utterly foolhardy to deny the atoning virtue of the actual blood of Christ.

If such expressions as "the blood of his cross" (Col. 1:20) cannot be taken literally, we may ask what the apostle could have written that would convey the idea of the actual blood of Christ. If the contrast between animal blood and Christ's blood in the book of Hebrews cannot be understood to teach that it was by His own actual blood that Christ purged His people, how could the apostle have expressed himself to convince his readers that that was what he intended to teach?

Remembrance of the Blood in Communion. The references to the blood in the communion service strongly support the view that we are to think of the actual blood and not make it solely a metaphor for *death.* Both elements, bread and wine, denote Christ's atoning death. If we take the blood of Christ to be nothing more than a metaphor for His death it is difficult to see the need for the cup. The bread would say it all. As the bread speaks of the actual body of Christ so the cup must speak of His actual blood.

Literal Blood in Figurative Statements. It is often argued that such clearly figurative phrases as "washed in the blood of the Lamb"—which simply means "saved through His sacrificial death"—prove that we are to see all references to the saving virtue of the blood figuratively. In such references *blood* cannot be understood literally.

But this is not so. *Washed in the blood* is certainly a figure of speech, but the figure is in the *washed* not in the *blood.* It is similar to the phrase "baptized into his death" (Rom. 6:3). Baptism in its literal sense involves a washing in water, but in Rom. 6 it refers to our union with Christ in His death. The baptism is figurative, or spiritual, but the death is literal. Similarly, when John speaks of Christ's having "washed us from our sins in his own blood" (Rev. 1:5; cf. 7:14), he means that He has removed our sins by the merit of His blood. The washing is figurative, or spiritual, but the blood is literal.

Christ's Blood Human, Not Divine

The blood of Christ, then, must not be downplayed. It must not be taken solely as a figure of speech. On the other hand, it must not be deified. It belongs to Christ's humanity, not His deity. While what theologians term the *communicatio idiomatum** (or communication of characteristics) allows us to speak as Paul did of the "church of God which he hath purchased with his own blood" (Acts 20:28), we must never forget that in the incarnation there was no confusion of natures. Christ's deity was not humanized nor His humanity deified. The blood is not eternal (except in the decree of God). It had a beginning in time. It does not possess the attribute of divine necessity. That is, Christ came to shed His blood by a loving act of God's will, not by some eternal necessity inherent in His very being. To attribute eternal necessity to His humanity, even to His precious blood, would be to make man and his salvation equally eternally necessary with God. It would destroy the essential distinction between God and man.

Significance of Incorruptible Blood

However, the blood of Christ is precious, sinless, and incorruptible (1 Pet. 1:18, 19). The incorruptibility of Christ's body means that it was supernaturally raised from the dead (Acts 2:27, 31-32). There is no Biblical reason to deny that the incorruptibility of Christ's blood means that it was raised along with His body. One thing is clear. Peter's reference to the blood of Christ as incorruptible cannot be reconciled with the view that it fell to the ground at Calvary and corrupted.

Where the Blood Is Now

That helps answer a pressing question. Where is the blood of Christ now? If it did not corrupt in the ground of Palestine but was raised as His body was, the answer is clear: it is in heaven. The entire testimony of Scripture would lead us to expect this. For example, the OT Day of Atonement pictures our high priest taking the blood within the veil to sprinkle the mercy seat. Hebrews 9:12 tells us that Christ fulfilled the type:

"By his own blood he entered in once into the holy place having obtained eternal redemption for us." Hebrews 12:24 adds support to this view that the blood is where God is, where Christ is; that is, in heaven.

We may go even further. If the blood of Christ was preserved and raised incorruptible with His body we would expect it to be *in* His body. This expectation is strengthened when we remember that Christ is the antitype of the mercy seat. The blood on the mercy seat does not symbolize Christ's blood apart from His body. It shows it united with Him in one complete type. The fulfilment of the OT type of the Day of Atonement would thus be beautifully exact, down to the last particular.

To many that is a novel idea, though in fact it is far from being so. The conventional thinking has been that Christ's is a bloodless body in His glorified state. This theory rests on a misunderstanding of a few texts.

The most important of these is Luke 24:39 where Jesus, appearing to His frightened disciples, rebuked their fear and said, "Behold my hands and my feet, that it is I myself: handle me, and see; for a spirit hath not flesh and bones, as ye see me have." Frequently we hear the comment, "He said flesh and bone, not flesh and blood. Therefore there was no blood in His resurrection body." This was the view of Dean Henry Alford in his famous NT *Notes:* "Observe 'flesh and bones' but not blood. This the resurrection body probably had not—as being animal life." He refers us to his further notes on John 6:51 and 20:27. But neither place offers the slightest support for his suggestion. To assume that because Christ said "flesh and bones" not "flesh and blood" He had no blood is really an unwarranted leap. It would have been out of place for Him to speak of His blood in Luke 24:39. He was proving His corporeality to the disciples by what they could see and touch. They could see His flesh and feel His bones. Could they have seen or touched the blood in His veins?

67

Hardly. Hence there was no reason for Him to mention it. Alford's reference to the blood belonging to mere animal life is strange. In context he can only mean physical life. But was not that part of the very point Christ was demonstrating—that He was alive physically and not merely spiritually? Since "the life of the flesh is in the blood" (Lev. 17:11), we have no ground for saying that the risen Christ was physically alive but without blood in His body.

Some use 1 Cor. 15:50 to show that resurrection bodies do not have blood. "Flesh and blood cannot inherit the kingdom of God." *Flesh and blood* is a phrase that denotes human nature, or mere man, or (and this is the meaning in 1 Cor. 15:50 as the remainder of the verse shows) corrupt and unregenerate human nature (see Matt. 16:17; Gal. 1:16; Eph. 6:12; Heb. 2:14 for its NT usage).

Since there is no reason to exclude Christ's blood from His resurrected body and much to say in favour of including it, we conclude that the body and blood of Christ are equally glorified. That His blood may exist in a glorified body is clear from the fact that His disciples saw Him temporarily glorified on the Mount of Transfiguration and we may be sure that on that occasion His blood was still in His body.

The Value and Virtue of the Blood

We should ever speak well of Christ's "precious blood." It is of eternal value and infinite virtue. Every aspect of our Christian life is connected with the blood. We are redeemed (Eph. 1:7; 1 Pet. 1:18, 19), cleansed (1 John 1:7), justified (Rom. 5:9), and reconciled (Col. 1:20) by Christ's blood. By it we enjoy access to God (Heb. 10:19) and victory over Satan (Rev. 12:11). It is the basis of Christ's advocacy in heaven *(see Intercession of Christ).* The testimony of the redeemed on earth exalts the blood of Christ (Rev. 1:5). The song of the redeemed in heaven does the same (Rev. 5:9).

The Bible testimony to the blood of Christ is clear and unequivocal. One fears that it is not the demands of a serious exegesis, but the desire to avoid the attacks of liberal criticism, that leads evangelicals to relegate the blood of Christ to the status of metaphor.

BONDAGE OF THE WILL

The total depravity and inability* of man as the result of the fall,* as they affect his will.* The disposition of man's will being now firmly fixed on self, he is incapable of originating a new godly disposition. He is incapable of spiritual good, dead in trespasses and sins, and walking "according to the prince of the power of the air, the spirit that now worketh in the children of disobedience" (Eph. 2:2).

See Free Will.

BRITISH ISRAELISM

A fanciful theory which holds that Great Britain is really the Israelite tribe of Ephraim, the United States is Manasseh, and the British throne is the throne of David. British Israelism (B.I.) has constructed a theory, which it passes off as history, that makes the British and American white populations direct descendants of the Israelites from the dispersion period.

The most plausible arguments advanced for the theory are based on the similarity of a few Hebrew and English words. For example, *Saxon* is said to be really *Isaacson,* or son of Isaac; *British* is said to be two Hebrew words, *berith,* "covenant," and *ish,* "man," yielding the meaning "the men of the covenant." The *Engl* part of *England* is alleged to be the Hebrew *'egel,* "bullock," because of the widespread sacrifice of bullocks there by "Isaacsons," leading to the popular title *John Bull.*

These arguments are purely imaginary. They are based upon the similarity in sound of a few words and have no foundation in fact. B.I.'s "history" of Jeremiah's escape with Zedekiah's daughter from Egypt to Ireland, carrying the Stone of Scone, is also unattested fancy. The removal of this "stone of destiny" to Scotland and then to Westminster Abbey is all part of B.I. lore. Professor Ramsey, the London geologist, upon chemical examination of the stone pronounced it to be "calcareous sandstone of a reddish or purplish colour with heterogeneous pebbles, and of Scottish origin."

The entire theory of the ten lost tribes is a myth also. According to B.I., the ten northern tribes were lost and were not included in the regathering with Judah after the exile. But according to Luke 2:36, Anna was of the northern tribe of Asher. In Acts 26:7 Paul mentions the presence of "our twelve tribes," indicating that none of them had been "lost."

B.I. exhibits an arbitrary exegesis of Scripture married to a fairy-tale tradition posing as history and has produced "one of the most baseless and absurd varieties of Bible study that the human mind has yet produced" (A. Pieters, *The Seed of Abraham,* p. 159).

BROWNISTS

A very early group of English Independents, followers of Robert Brown. Brown was a Puritan who was violently opposed to the English national church. He established an independent congregation, which he removed to Holland because of persecution. However, once there, the Brownists splintered, and Brown returned to England, renounced his Independent views, and became a Church of England rector in Northamptonshire. By some reports, he lived a dissolute life, having a wife with whom he did not live for many years and a church in which he did not preach.

Brown died in 1630, but his principles survived him and still form the basis of independency and congregationalism,* though it is fair to say that Independents do not trace their origin to Brown but affirm that such churches as theirs predated Brown's congregation in England.

BUCHMANISM

The Moral Rearmament* movement, so called after its founder, American Lutheran minister, Frank Buchman (1878-1961). Buchman had a conversion experience at the Keswick convention in 1908 and developed a concern to reform the world. The vehicle he chose to accomplish this was the Oxford Group, founded in 1929, which in 1938 became Moral Rearmament.

BULL

Bull is the name given to an "apostolic letter" from the pope, in which—according to Roman Catholic belief—he speaks to the church *ex cathedra,* or infallibly on some matter of faith and morals. The word *bull* in this connection comes from the Latin name for the lead seal with which papal documents used to be sealed—Latin *bulla,* "seal."

BURGHERS

The original seceders from the Church of Scotland divided into two synods in 1747 over the issue of the Burgess Oath. By the Burgess Oath, every burgess in Scotland's chief towns was required to swear that he professed and allowed with all his heart "the true religion presently professed within this realm."

To some Seceders this meant approving the errors in the state church from which they had seceded. To others it merely meant approving true Presbyterianism. These latter allowed the oath and were popularly known as Burghers, while the former rejected the oath and were known as Anti-Burghers.

The Burghers, who held the name "The Associate Synod," refused to make the Burgess Oath a matter of church discipline. The Anti-Burghers took the name "The General Associate Synod." The two streams united in 1820 after both had basically amended their historic position on parts of the *Westminster Confession of*

Faith, a union repudiated by the "Old Lights," or *Auld Lichts,* as those who maintained the original principles of the Secession were known in Scotland.

BURGON

John William Burgon (1813-1888), Fellow of Oriel College, Oxford, vicar of St. Mary's (the University Church), Gresham Professor of Divinity, and for the last twelve years of his life, Dean of Chichester. Burgon was one of the most outstanding of England's textual scholars and he bent all his energies to combat the efforts of Westcott and Hort to discredit the traditional text* of the NT. An ardent defender of the truth of the inspiration* of Scripture, Burgon wholeheartedly opposed the idea of naturalistic scholars that the genuine text of the word of God may be reached through conjectural emendation, or on the ground of "probability," as Hort taught. He argued that variant readings* must be subjected to objective criteria of verifiability, and that the genuine reading must bear certain "notes of truth" *(see Textual Criticism of the New Testament).*

However, Burgon's scheme has never found favour with naturalistic scholars, because its adoption would undoubtedly establish the readings of the traditional text —which underlies our Authorized Version—and would effectively put an end to the ceaseless speculations of eclectic critics. Burgon's method allows us to *know* the text of the inspired word; his opponents' methods in many instances put certainty as to the actual words of God beyond human reach—something Satan has ever been keen to do.

BYZANTINE

From Byzantium, the former name of Constantinople, a major centre of the Eastern church. *Byzantine* when used to refer to the church means the Greek (though this title is not very appropriate) or Eastern Orthodox church.

When applied to the NT text, *Byzantine* refers to the traditional text* found in the vast majority of NT manuscripts. *See Byzantine Text.*

BYZANTINE TEXT

One name given to the text-type which is found in the vast majority of the Greek MSS* of the NT. Called after the city of Byzantium (Constantinople) which was the centre of the ancient Greek-speaking church, the name is inappropriate in that it tends to portray the traditional text* as a merely local text, or as one imposed by the authority of the Eastern church. In fact it was the text used throughout the various branches of the church for over a thousand years before the Reformation.

See Textual Criticism of the New Testament.

C

CABALA

Sometimes written *cabbala* or *kabala.* From the Hebrew *qabal,* "to receive," it is an occult system of religious philosophy developed by some medieval Jewish rabbis and based on a mystical interpretation of the Scriptures. In popular speech, *cabalistic* means occult or mysterious.

CALLING

The command or invitation of God addressed to sinners in the gospel, directing them to repent of their sins and believe on the Lord Jesus Christ for the saving of their souls. There is a general call and there is a special, or effectual, call. This effectual call is equivalent to regeneration* *(see Effectual Calling).*

The General Call

The general call is the address of the gospel to all sinners who hear it. The Scriptures clearly distinguish between the general and the effectual calling. Matt. 22:14 says, "Many are called, but few are chosen." In many cases this general call is not followed by the obedience of faith and therefore does not lead to the experience of salvation. Contrast this with Rom. 8:30, "Whom he called, them he also justified." This is an internal,* effectual call that is invariably followed by justification.

Thus, the general call of the gospel is addressed to sinners without distinction. It sets forth the truths and terms of the gospel and carries the promise that all who receive Christ by faith on the terms of the gospel will receive the gift of eternal life. But it does not effect the internal change in sinners that is necessary for them to exercise repentance and faith. That all sinners should repent and believe is beyond dispute. God condemns them for not doing so (John 16:8,9). But sinners are so depraved that without the miracle of regeneration they remain wilfully incapable of any good spiritual response to the gospel (Rom. 8:7; *see Depravity, Inability*).

The Effectual Call

The effectual call does all that the general call does and more. Addressed exclusively to God's elect, it effects what it commands by regenerating the spiritually dead sinner, enlightening his mind, renewing his will, and giving him the gifts of repentance and faith (Acts 11:18; Eph. 2:8,9; Phil. 1:29).

Opposition to Idea of General Call

Opposition to the entire idea of a general call comes from two very different theological camps: Arminian and Hyper-Calvinist.

Arminian Opposition. Arminians object that if Christ's death made atonement* only for the elect,* and if God effectually calls only the elect and enables none but the elect to repent and exercise saving faith, then the general offer of the gospel is insincere. This logic appeals to depraved human reason but is very different from the reasoning of Scripture.

First, it fails to take note of the clear distinction already referred to between Matt. 22:14 and Rom. 8:30.

Second, it fails to give due weight to the fact that the sinner's inability is a willing inability. The general call of the gospel accentuates that fact. The gospel invitation is absolutely true: "Let him that is athirst come. And whosoever will, let him take of the water of life freely" (Rev. 22:17). The fact that the will of those who hear that call is so depraved that they "will not come to me that [they] might have life" (John 5:40) in no way shows insincerity on God's part in issuing the call.

Third, we have plenty of evidence in Scripture that God issues commands and promises to people in whom He did no regenerating work to produce the needed obedience. For example, men are depraved and cannot keep His law, yet He commands them to keep it and will hold them to that standard in the judgment. Is God unjust in commanding their obedience or insincere in promising His blessing if they obey? Such an idea would destroy the entire moral foundation of God's dealings with men and would perversely make man's sinful depravity the means of escaping all moral accountability to his Creator. But if there is no insincerity on God's part in giving the commands of the law to sinners who cannot keep it, there can be no insincerity in His issuing the call of the gospel to those same sinners.

Hyper-Calvinist Opposition. Hyper-Calvinists argue that since Christ made atonement for the elect alone, the invitation and promises of the gospel should not be given indiscriminately to all sinners. In their view such a call would be untruthful. It is therefore unscriptural for preachers to issue such a general call. Often the argument is put in this form: gospel preachers have no warrant to make saving faith the duty of unregenerate sinners—faith is not a human duty but a divine gift. Those who call sinners to believe are often scornfully described as "duty faith* preachers." In this hyper-Calvinistic view a person should have clear evidences that God has awakened him (and therefore that he is one of the elect) before we give him the invitation and promise of the gospel.

The response to the Arminian objection applies here as well. In addition, we may note that the Scripture very clearly establishes the two points these objectors refuse to accept:

1. Faith in Christ is the duty of all who hear the gospel. We have the testimony of Christ Himself. He said that the Holy Spirit would "reprove the world of sin, and of righteousness, and of judgment: of sin, because they believe not on me" (John 16:8, 9). If unbelief is a sin then clearly faith in Christ is a duty.

2. Gospel preachers have a clear warrant to call every sinner to Christ with the promise that all who come will be welcomed and received. Here again we have the Saviour's personal testimony. In Matt. 22:1-10 and Luke 14:15-24, He tells two parables that symbolize the gospel feast in which the invitation was given to those who despised it and who were consequently excluded from it. Nothing could be clearer: Christ commands that the call of the gospel should be given even to those who wickedly reject. Add to this His great commission to preach the gospel to every creature (Mark 16:15, 16)—including those who believe not and are finally damned.

All Scripture bears the same testimony. Jeremiah 25:4-7 details how God sent His prophets on fruitless missions of mercy to obstinate sinners. Paul quotes Isaiah's words, "All day long have I stretched forth my hands unto a disobedient and gainsaying people" (Isa. 65:2; Rom. 10:21). In the light of this clear testimony of Christ, the prophets, and the apostles, there can be no doubt that preachers have a divine warrant to offer Christ to all who hear the gospel. It calls sinners to faith in Him and promises life to all who come to Him. This offer of gospel grace is real and sincere—just as it was when God gave it to Cain, the world's first reprobate. 1 John 3:12 assures us that "Cain was of that wicked one," that is, he was a reprobate; yet we read in Gen. 4:7 that God addressed him in terms that can be seen only as an offer of mercy if he would receive it on God's terms.

Many hyper-Calvinists look on the role of the gospel to the non-elect, not as any kind of offer but as a means of increasing the guilt of sinners—"fattening them for slaughter," as some have put it. This is false to Scripture and injurious to the character of God. The gospel preached and rejected does exacerbate the guilt of sinners (John 16:8-9), but this is a very different thing from saying that such is God's sole or central motive in proclaiming the gospel to the non-elect. "Come, for all things are now ready" (addressed to despisers who did not come) can hardly be interpreted as a mere device to make those addressed worthier of the hell they have already well deserved. Jesus said, "God sent not his Son into the world to condemn the world; but that the world through him might be saved" (John 3:17).

The gospel calls sinners to believe on Him whom it reveals as the sole Saviour of the lost. It is "worthy of all acceptation" (1 Tim. 1:15) and promises salvation to all who believe (Acts 16:31).

CALVINISM

B. B. Warfield defines Calvinism as theism and evangelicalism come to their own. That is to say, quite simply, that God saves sinners. He does not merely provide the possibility or opportunity for them to be saved. He does not "do His part" and leave man to do his part to accomplish salvation. No, God actually saves sinners, and that salvation is all of Him.

Cornelius Van Til says that Calvinism's only system is to be open to the Scriptures. He adds, "The doctrines of Calvinism are not deduced in *a priori* fashion from one major principle such as the sovereignty of God." This has been one of the most frequent arguments against Calvinism. The charge is that it fastens on to one Scripture principle, God's sovereignty, and proceeds to develop a logical system based on that principle, with little or no regard to Scripture. As Van Til indicates, such a charge is groundless.

By taking the exact opposite of the long list of doctrines taught by Arminianism* we arrive at a fair statement of the Calvinistic position. We may here note the following in particular:

1. The Five Points. What has just been said will make it clear that Calvinism is more than "five points." The five points were actually answers to five points made by Arminians. Five-point Calvinism is frequently referred to as *TULIP* theology, using the T-U-L-I-P as an acrostic: **T**otal Depravity; **U**nconditional Election; **L**imited Atonement (though Calvinists believe that Arminians, not they, limit the atonement; they prefer such terms as particular redemption or definite atonement); **I**rresistible Grace; **P**erseverance of the saints. *(See **Five Points of Controversy**.)*

2. Calvinists believe in "the unrestricted, universal offer of the gospel" (Van Til).

3. They believe in human responsibility, emphasizing that the true meaning of this term must be taken from Scripture and not from human philosophy.

4. They believe that man has a "free will," which means Scripturally that man acts according to the determination of the inclination of his own will. Thus he is a free agent. But the inclination of the human will since the fall is inveterately opposed to God (Rom. 8:7). All man's acts of will proceed freely from this self-determination to sin. Calvinists hold that fallen man cannot originate a new inclination of will. Only God can do that when He regenerates a sinner. *(See **Free Will; Will**.)*

5. Thus, as the Word of God teaches, salvation must be all of grace, originating with God in His eternal purpose and executed by Him without the merits or efforts of our fallen nature.

6. Paul's great statement in Rom. 11:36 sums up the entire outlook of the Calvinist: "of him, and through him, and to him, are all things: to whom be glory for ever. Amen."

7. Needless to say, Calvinism did not originate with Calvin but has been given his name because of his magnificent work in restating the theology of Scripture.

CAMERONIANS

Followers of Richard Cameron (*circa* 1648-1680), "the lion of the Scottish Covenant." They refused to enter the Church of Scotland after the Revolution Settlement (1689), seeking to maintain the obligations of the Covenant and refusing to go along with the practice of accepting into the church those who had been conformist during the period of royal and prelatic tyranny.

CAMPBELLITES

Followers of Alexander Campbell; also known as the Disciples of Christ and the Churches of Christ. Campbell (1788-1866) was a Presbyterian, born in Ballymena, Northern Ireland. In 1809 he joined his father in America. Both Campbells became involved in an effort to establish unity among the churches by a return to what they saw as New Testament Christianity.

In 1812 they espoused believer's baptism* and left the Presbyterian church. Until 1827 they were associated with the Baptists;* however, Alexander Campbell's view that baptism is necessary for the remission of sin estranged him from the Baptists, and his followers began to organize themselves into a separate body. In 1832 the congregations that held with him joined with those of the Christian Connection led by another ex-Presbyterian, Barton W. Stone, to form the Disciples, or Churches, of Christ.

Campbellite principles included congregational independency (with independent local churches cooperating for evangelistic purposes), weekly celebration of the Lord's Supper, believer's baptism by immersion for the forgiveness of sins, and the rejection of all human confessions of faith. Many Campbellites have called their gospel "the Acts 2:38 gospel," misinterpreting that text to be a plain scriptural proof that baptism is for the remission of sins (*see Baptismal Regeneration* for a discussion of this text).

Campbellite churches flourished in America and continue to do so. For a time they also flourished in Britain, especially in Scotland. After World War II, however, their membership declined and in 1981 the majority of the British Churches of Christ merged with the United Reformed Church.

CANON

The complete body of inspired Scripture.

Meaning of the Term

The word *canon* appears in 2 Cor. 10:13, 15, 16; Gal. 6:16; Phil. 3:16—and in all these cases is translated "rule" or "line." Thus the basic meaning of the word among the Greeks was a straight rod or rule, used as a measuring instrument. It also bore the meaning of a rod, which being straight in itself, was used to determine the straightness or otherwise of anything laid beside it. The meaning of the word developed to include not only that which measures, but that which is measured—a measured space. That appears to be the meaning of the word in 2 Cor. 10:13, 15, 16, where Paul defines his sphere or province of labour. This last meaning of the word gave rise to its use in theology to describe the entire body of inspired Scripture, as distinct from spurious or non-inspired writings.

Canonical writings are those which fall within the province of divine inspiration; non-canonical writings, whatever other merits may be claimed for them, have no place in Scripture because they are not inspired of God.

The more basic meaning of "rule" is not lost in our use of the word *canon,* for when we say a book is canonical we say, in effect, that it was written according to a special rule (i.e., that it furnishes proof of its divine authorship); and that it therefore puts forth God's rule and is to be received as authoritative in all matters of doctrine and practice. It is worth noting that here a basic division between Protestantism and Romanism surfaces: Rome is willing to accept Scripture as "written according to rule" (i.e., inspired, though she admits into the body of Scripture writings which have no proper claim to be there), but she is not willing to accept that Scripture is the sole rule of faith and practice.

The Old Testament Canon

The Jewish canon of the OT corresponds with our OT, though the Jews enumerated the books differently. They frequently referred to it as "the twenty-four books," or by the technical term *T.N.K.,* or *Torah* (the law), *Nebi'im* (the prophets) and *Kethubim* (the writings). The Lord Jesus Christ clearly endorsed this canon of the OT in Luke 24:44. It is interesting to note that an apocryphal book, 2 Esdras in chapter 14, clearly distinguishes between canonical Scripture and others, in which it places itself. Thus, to place the apocryphal writings on a par with the canonical Scriptures, as Rome does, is to fly in the face of the OT, of the Lord Jesus Christ, and of the plain evidence of the apocrypha itself.

The New Testament Canon

The canon of the NT was not settled by what Rome considers church authority. Her view virtually makes Scripture a creature of the church and dependent upon it for its authority. However, inspired Scripture has its authority inherent in itself, direct from its divine author. The NT writings, with very few exceptions, were immediately recognized as the productions of Christ's apostles or of their close collaborators. They were circulated widely during the lifetime of the apostles and were received as authoritative throughout the churches. The few disputed books were received by most Christians from the beginning, and the questions raised about them served only to confirm the evidence of their divine and human authorship, thus leading to their universal acceptance by God's people.

See Antilegomena.

CANON LAW

The body of ecclesiastical law, especially of the Roman Catholic church.

CANONIZATION

An ecclesiastical decree which purports to create a "saint," one long dead but now discovered to be worthy of public worship or cultus.

See Beatification.

CAPITATION

The poll tax ordained in the days of Moses (Exod. 30:13), set at the rate of half a shekel per head.

CASUISTRY

"That branch of Christian morals which treats of *casus conscientiae* (cases of conscience); that is to say, questions of conduct in which apparently conflicting duties seem at first to perplex and disturb the moral faculty and make it necessary to trace, with careful exclusion of everything but moral considerations, the consequences of the rules of morality. Kant calls casuistry 'the dialectics of conscience.' In this sense the word might have a good meaning; but its ordinary use is to designate sophistical perversion or evasion of the moral law" (McClintock and Strong). The word is rarely, if ever, used in a good sense. Protestant moral philosophers and theologians have written extensively on cases of conscience. Puritan writers paid careful attention to the duties of Christians in matters in which doubtful consciences needed instruction. In these cases the aim was to understand the plain revelation of the Word of God and seek to apply its requirements to matters of concern to Christians that are not explicitly mentioned in Scripture. These cases of conscience could be very difficult and divisive. The case of the Burghers* and Antiburghers* in Scotland was a painful example.

Casuistry is not the term we would now use to cover such cases of conscience, because the church of Rome developed a system of miscalled *Moral Theology* that "poisoned the very fountains of morality" (McClintock and Strong). This system dealt with the intricate system of restrictions and requirements the church laid upon the consciences of its members, with particular reference to the distinction between venial and mortal sins. Romish casuists "could easily find some excuse for what was most culpable, while they continued under the impression that they were not deviating from what, as moral beings, was incumbent upon them" (*Watsons Theological Dictionary,* quoted by McClintock and Strong). This perversion of morality was carried even further by the Jesuits.* Men such as Alphonsus Liguori (raised to sainthood by Rome) produced moral theologies that were often flagrantly immoral. Their efforts have practically limited the modern definition of casuistry to a negative sense—a subtle quibbling that seeks to provide cover for the conscience while it evades its plain duty of obedience to the law of God. Thus Liguori could argue from various points of supposed superior good (i.e., promoting the interests of the church of Rome) that Roman Catholics may lawfully practice deception and even violence on "heretic" Protestants. Thus cheating and murder became moral virtues if they served the interests of mother church—notwithstanding the fact that they broke the law of God.

CATABAPTISTS

Greek *kata,* "against," and *baptistes,* "baptist"; a term that describes all who deny the necessity of Christian baptism.

CATECHISM

Greek, *katecheo,* "to sound aloud; to sound in one's ears"; originally, an oral instruction; then the simple giving of fundamental instruction in the doctrines of the faith, especially to children. Calvin defined a catechism as "a formula of instructing children in the doctrine of Christ." The method was usually by question and answer, and the person catechized had to learn the answer given to each question. It had the advantage of

conveying the great truths of the Word of God in a memorable, concise, and simple form that was yet profound and sufficiently full in its Biblical exposition. Good catechists have never been content to have children learn the mere words of a catechism, but have been careful to explain and apply the catechism's instruction to daily life.

The Protestant Reformation produced a number of useful catechisms. The Puritan period produced many more. The most enduring of all has been the *Shorter Catechism* of the Westminster Assembly of Divines *(see* **Westminster Standards).**

CATECHUMENS

Candidates for baptism in the ancient church who were set to complete a system of religious instruction before being admitted to the church. The length of this period of instruction varied from a matter of days or weeks, to years.

CATENA

A chain of connected subjects; a synopsis of the views of various authors to form an exposition of a portion of Scripture.

CATHARI

From the Greek *katharoi,* "pure ones," a name given at various times in church history to different reformist groups that claimed or aimed at a purity of life and morals in sharp contrast with the decadence of the Catholic church, especially in her clerical classes. Thus the Cathari were always a protest movement against the corruption prevailing in the Catholic church. The name was given to the Novatians* in the third century and to the Albigenses* and Waldenses* in the twelfth century.

CATHOLIC

Catholic means "general, universal." It was used as early as the second century as a word to describe the orthodox Christian church. Subsequent to the Reformation,*

Rome claimed the title exclusively. The term Roman Catholic then arose out of a controversy between the Roman and Anglican churches, since the latter, too, laid claim to the term *catholic.*

CATHOLIC APOSTOLIC CHURCH

The London church of which Rev. Edward Irving (1792-1834) was pastor. It gained national attention first through Irving's outstanding pulpit gifts and then as a centre of a Pentecostal-type revival. Irving taught that the church is forever entitled to all the spiritual gifts of the apostolic church. In 1830, through the influence of Irving's colleague, Rev. A. J. Scott, Mary Campbell of Fernicarry (in the West of Scotland) spoke in tongues. The phenomenon spread first to Port Glasgow, where Margaret MacDonald also spoke in tongues. Through an English group that had visited Scotland, there was a manifestation of tongues in London in 1831, and Irving's congregation welcomed this as a proof of the restoration of apostolic gifts.

Healings and prophecy also appeared in his church; and under the guidance of a "prophetic message," the church proceeded to acknowledge the reinstitution of the apostolic office. Apostles were divinely appointed, as the Irvingites believed, by being named in prophetic utterances. Irving was not one of them and never personally received any supernatural spiritual gifts.

The Catholic Apostolic Church was Pentecostalist (before Pentecostalism!) and strongly millennarian. It established outposts in Scotland, Ireland, and Europe but then gradually waned.

CATHOLICITY

See **Church**.

CELIBACY

The maintenance of a state of virginity; the avoidance of all sexual relationships. The Roman Catholic church has legislated celibacy for its priests, despite the experience of centuries that grave moral excesses are the inevitable results. The Second Vatican Council admitted that the nature of the priesthood does not demand celibacy (*Decree on the Ministry and Life of the Priests,* III ¶ 16) but holds that it "accords with the priesthood on many scores."

While voluntary virginity under certain circumstances "for the kingdom of heaven's sake" is commended in Scripture (Matt. 19:9, 12; 1 Cor. 7:7, 38) there is absolutely no Biblical warrant for imposing it. Indeed, there is much to be said for the view that for Christian ministers it should be the exception, marriage being the rule (1 Tim. 3:2-5; Titus 1:6). Certainly it was not required of Christ's apostles or of the ministers of the early church.

CERINTHIANS

Followers of the heretic Cerinthus (*circa* A.D. 100) who, among other things, taught that Jesus was an ordinary mortal upon whom Christ, a divine power, came at baptism and from whom it departed before his crucifixion.

CESSATIONISM

The belief that the *charismata*—the supernatural gifts of the apostolic church—ceased with or very soon after the days of the apostles. This was the common belief of the churches of the Reformation, but in time a new theory arose. This theory postulated that the *charismata* continued in the church into the third century, until about the time of Constantine, after which they gradually dwindled. The fullest exposition of the classic Protestant position, and the most trenchant criticism of the idea of the retention of the *charismata* by the church, or of their restoration to it, was produced by B. B. Warfield in a series of lectures given at Columbia Theological Seminary, South Carolina in 1917. These were later published as *Counterfeit Miracles.*

Warfield's Argument for Cessationism

Christ exhibited a wonderful supernatural power, doing many miracles—signs that accompanied His ministry. He continued this exercise of supernatural power through His apostles who in turn, "as part of their own miracle-working and the crowning sign of their divine commission," transmitted it to others. Thus the "apostolic church was characteristically a miracle-working church."

The Argument from History. Miracle-working power did not remain in the church but passed away with the apostles and those to whom they had transmitted it. Those who received the supernatural gifts through the ministry of an apostle had no power to transmit them to others. There is a distinct lack of evidence of miraculous powers in the church in the first hundred years after the apostles. Only in the third century did miraculous claims became more abundant and they continued to increase in succeeding centuries. Warfield quotes the conclusion of Bishop Kaye on reviewing the evidence of the early centuries: "My conclusion is, that the power of working miracles was not extended beyond the disciples upon whom the apostles conferred it by the imposition of their hands."

The Argument from Scripture. This argument from history is important but the clinching proof of the cessationist position must come from Scripture itself. Two things are necessary to establish it from Scripture:
1. To show that the miracles of Christ and His apostles were exclusively confirmations of revelation—that is, that according to Scripture, they belong solely to a period of inspired revelation and are themselves revelatory phenomena;
2. To show that the NT testifies to their cessation on the completion of its revelation.

Miracles Part of Revelation. That the miracles of Christ and of His apostles were designed as divine confirmations of their peculiar ministries is beyond dispute. Mark 16:20: "They went forth, and preached every where, the Lord working with them, and confirming the word with signs following." Acts 14:3: "Long time therefore abode they speaking boldly in the Lord, which gave testimony unto the word of his grace, and granted signs and wonders to be done by their hands." Heb. 2:3, 4: "How shall we escape, if we neglect so great salvation; which at the first began to be spoken by the Lord, and was confirmed unto us by them that heard him; God also bearing them witness, both with signs and wonders, and with divers miracles, and gifts of the Holy Ghost, according to his own will?"

Cornelius Van Til argued that a miracle is one of the three modes of revelation, each of which confirms the other two: theophany—God's intervention in His own person; prophecy—God's intervention by His own word; and miracle—God's intervention by His own power.

NT Witness to Cessation of Miracles. Many deny that the NT itself testifies to the cessation of sign miracles with the completion of the Biblical revelation. However, Paul's words in 1 Cor. 13:8-13 clearly establish the point. He emphatically states that the supernatural gifts of prophecy, tongues, and knowledge will vanish away, or be abolished (v. 8). He sets the time of this in verse 10, "when that which is perfect is come."

The crucial question is, what does he mean by "that which is perfect?" Cessationists argue that he means the completion of the canon of Scripture. Others insist that cannot be the meaning because when that which is perfect is come we shall no longer know in part and prophecy in part but then we shall know even as we are known (v. 12). Thus *that which is perfect* must refer to the day of Christ, or our perfect glorification. This argument seems cogent, but on closer investigation that semblance falls away and leads us to the conclusion that Paul did indeed refer to the completion of the New Testament.

That which is perfect cannot refer to the day of Christ, for the following reasons:

1. Those who support this view quote, "Then shall I know even as also I am known," as proof that Paul must be speaking of the glorified state. This is a mistake. If this speaks of the state of glorification, then it means that Paul, when glorified, would know things as God knows him—that he would have a kind of omniscience. That is impossible, and the interpretation that produces it is therefore wrong.

2. Paul's statement in v. 13 proves he places *that which is perfect* in the present age. He argues: "Now abideth [remaineth, continueth] faith, hope, charity, these three; but the greatest of these is charity." These things remain after the passing away of the miracles he has mentioned. That he cannot be referring to the day of Christ is obvious for then hope will have given place to sight. As Paul himself said, "What a man seeth, why doth he yet hope for?" (Rom. 8:24). The significance of this is far reaching: the things that do not remain—the gifts of prophecy, tongues, and knowledge—pass away in this age, not the future one.

3. Making *that which is perfect* mean the day of Christ involves a contradiction. It teaches that supernatural knowledge will cease at Christ's coming, and yet it holds that Christians will gain a knowledge far more supernatural and full than anything they have known before (v. 12).

4. It also contradicts a great truth of Scripture. Paul clearly states: "Eye hath not seen, nor ear heard, neither have entered into the heart of man, the things which God hath prepared for them that love him. But God hath revealed them unto us by his Spirit" (1 Cor. 2:9, 10). According to this view, until the coming of Christ we see through a glass darkly, or we see everything as a *riddle* (v. 12). 1 Corinthians 2:9-10 hardly describes seeing things in a riddle! Again, Peter says: "We have also a more sure word of prophecy; whereunto

ye do well that ye take heed, as unto a light that shineth in a dark place, until the day dawn, and the day star arise in your hearts" (2 Pet. 1:19). This is not seeing everything darkly, or in a riddle.

Since *that which is perfect* cannot mean the day of Christ we are left with the historic Protestant interpretation of the passage. Paul meant that with the completion of the NT the revelation of God would be perfect and that therefore the temporary signs and supernatural gifts would be removed.

It may still fairly be asked, "What does, 'Then shall I know even as also I am known' mean?" The tense of the Greek verb *am known* signifies that the Lord knows the believer completely, without any need for added sources of information. Similarly, with the coming of the NT the believer has a complete source of spiritual knowledge without the need for added revelations.

This interpretation accords with the two reasons Paul gives for the cessation of miraculous gifts:

1. The gifts are at best fragmentary: "We know in part, and we prophesy in part" (v. 9). As a rule, the arrival of something more perfect replaces a previous inferior form. Every message the prophets at Corinth brought to the church was at best a mere fragment of the full revelation of God. The NT was as yet incomplete. We now have the complete revelation of the gospel in Scripture. God is no longer continuing to give new revelation. The NT is His final word. Thus, the NT has replaced the temporary gifts listed in 1 Corinthians.

2. The gifts belong to the early days of the church's development. "When I was a child, I spake as a child, I understood as a child, I thought as a child: but when I became a man, I put away childish things [or, the things of a child]" (v. 11). The church is more mature when it has the full and final Word of God in written form and is not dependent on partial prophecies or occasional miracles.

Cessationism Is Not the Removal of Power

Cessationism does not imply that God has removed His power and activity from the church. It teaches that he has ceased using sign miracles. But He still answers prayer. He still fills His people with the power of His Spirit to equip them for His service. He still gives them power over Satan and his devices. In the act of regeneration* He still exercises His sovereign power directly upon the soul of man, without the use of any human means in the proper sense of the word. He still sends revival. These are not merely natural events. They all depend entirely on the exercise of God's power in a direct and sovereign manner. Cessationism recognizes this. Its great concern is that we do not accept counterfeits of the NT *charismata* and fail to enjoy the real working of His power available to His church today.

CHALCEDON

A city in Bithynia, the meeting place for the fourth so-called ecumenical council of the church in 451. That council was called to deal with the Eutychian* and Nestorian* heresies. It formulated the following statement of the Scriptural doctrine of the Person of Christ, which has ever since been the standard of orthodoxy (though many Protestants reject the references to Mary as "the mother of God," even when modified by the words "according to the Manhood"):

"We, then, following the holy Fathers, all with one consent, teach men to confess one and the same Son, our Lord Jesus Christ, the same perfect in Godhead and also perfect in manhood; truly God and truly man, of a reasonable [rational] soul and body; consubstantial [coessential] with the Father according to the Godhead, and consubstantial with us according to the Manhood; in all things like unto us, without sin; begotten before all ages of the Father according to the Godhead, and in these latter days, for us and for our salvation, born of the Virgin Mary, the Mother of God, according to the Manhood; one and the same Christ, Son, Lord, Only-begotten, to be acknowledged in two natures, inconfusedly, unchangeably, indivisibly, inseparably; the distinction of natures being by no means taken away by the union, but rather the property of each nature being preserved, and concurring in one Person and one Subsistence, not parted or divided into two persons, but one and the same Son, and only begotten, God the Word, the Lord Jesus Christ, as the prophets from the beginning [have declared] concerning him, and the Lord Jesus Christ himself has taught us, and the Creed of the holy Fathers has handed down to us."

CHARACTER SACRAMENTS

The sacraments of the Roman Catholic church that have a permanent effect, and therefore, cannot be conferred more than once. They are Baptism,* Confirmation,* and Holy Orders.

CHARISMATIC MOVEMENT

Neo-Pentecostalism; the adoption of Pentecostalist views and practices by ministers and members of non-Pentecostalist denominations, especially the "Baptism in the Spirit," speaking in tongues, and healing ministries. In mainline Protestant denominations their neo-Pentecostalism is generally known as the Charismatic Movement; in the Roman Catholic church it is usually described as the Catholic Charismatic Renewal.

Protestant Neo-Pentecostalism.

In the United States. The birth of the Charismatic Movement is usually traced to the public announcement in April 1960 of Dennis Bennett, minister of St. Mark's Episcopal church, Van Nuys, California, that he had received the gift of tongues. This was the beginning of a new development, the adoption of Pentecostal belief and practice within mainline denominations. In the years that followed great numbers of church members in those denominations followed this course.

In contrast to those charismatics who remained in mainline denominations, great numbers congregated in nondenominational assemblies. These assemblies were neither classical Pentecostalist nor affiliated with the major Protestant denominations in which neo-Pentecostalism had taken root. Some of them remained entirely independent while others affiliated themselves with some association of charismatic pastors or churches.

In the estimation of many, the Charismatic Movement reached its high-water mark with the strongly supported Kansas City conference of July 1977 on the theme of the Charismatic Renewal in the Christian churches. Over 50,000 people attended what they perceived to be an important ecumenical event. The common charismatic experience of the participants overcame the divisions between Roman Catholics and Protestants (Cardinal Suenens of Belgium attended and shared the platform with the leader of the Assemblies of God and other Protestants) and between members of mainline denominations and Pentecostalists. In Kansas City, charismatic prophets castigated Christians—especially church leaders—for attachment to their own priorities and called them to mourn divisions in the body of Christ. In context, this meant that the attachment to the distinctive evangelical truths of the Reformation was now a sin to be confessed and abandoned.

This ecumenical emphasis of the Charismatic Movement was deliberate and enduring. It has become increasingly clear. In July 1987 in New Orleans, Charismatics again gathered with an even more overt emphasis on the ecumenical nature of the Charismatic Movement, with Roman Catholics making up half of the 35,000 who attended.

While the Charismatic Movement centred on Pentecostalist experiences and practices in non-Pentecostalist churches, and while it was hailed by many denominational leaders as a means of reviving their often moribund churches, it is now clear that it has actually weakened the mainline denominations. It is estimated that some 50% of denominational Charismatics have moved on to Pentecostal denominations like the Assemblies of God or to nondenominational Charismatic groups.

In Europe. European charismatism developed out of the American movement in the 1960's. American Charismatic leaders visited Europe and spread their messages, as did American charismatic literature, notably David Wilkerson's *The Cross and the Switchblade.* In England, as in America, the initial stirrings of the Charismatic Movement were in the Anglican communion. Two of the leaders of the Charismatic Movement had served as curates under John Stott in All Souls, Langham Place. Stott and other evangelicals opposed the movement, and the tension persisted until 1977 when evangelicals and charismatics published a joint statement, "Gospel and Spirit."

The Charismatic influence began to spread to other denominations. After the Anglicans, the Baptists were most affected. The Methodists also saw a rise in Charismatic interest, as did the Roman Catholic church. In Scotland and Northern Ireland the Charismatic Movement made slower progress than in England. The reason for this may be debated. A greater theological awareness among evangelical church members may well have been a barrier against the allurements of Charismatism. It is also likely that the openly ecumenical character of the Charismatic Movement would have hindered its acceptance.

In the rest of Europe, the Charismatic Movement at first flourished more in the north and only in the late 1970's in the south. As in America and Britain, the Roman Catholic church became deeply involved, without, however, any movement away from distinctive Roman Catholic dogmas or the acceptance of any of the doctrines Protestants have always held to be essential to Biblical Christianity.

In Latin America. Pentecostal experiences surfaced in all sections of the Protestant churches in South America—Baptist, Brethren, Episcopalian, Methodist, Presbyterian. This caused tensions in these various churches, but there continued to be a fairly widespread acceptance and practice of Pentecostalism* outside the Pentecostal churches. Thus far, it was still a Protestant church phenomenon. Then the Roman Catholic church became involved, and for a time the Charismatic Movement was strongly ecumenical. However, the Roman Catholic hierarchy soon came to fear the involvement of their lay leaders with Protestant Pentecostalists. The result is that Charismatism has developed more or less separately in the Protestant churches and the Roman Catholic churches of Latin America, despite the efforts of David du Plessis and others who see ecumenism as essential to the Charismatic Movement.

Roman Catholic Neo-Pentecostalism.

The Catholic Charismatic Renewal (CCR) began in Duquesne University when two young lay instructors in this Roman Catholic institution studied David Wilkerson's *The Cross and the Switchblade* and John Sherrill's *They Spake with Other Tongues.* As a result they attended a Pentecostalist prayer meeting in a Presbyterian home in Pittsburgh. On their second visit they spoke in tongues. Within a few weeks—in February 1967—they sponsored prayer meetings for interested students and CCR was born. It soon spread to Notre Dame and Michigan State universities, schools that have played a major role in the worldwide development of CCR. Notre Dame hosted an annual charismatic conference that grew year by year until, in 1976, over 30,000 people attended. CCR led to the formation of thousands of charismatic prayer groups within the Roman Catholic church. It spread to Canada, Bolivia, Mexico,

Peru, Puerto Rico, Colombia, Australia, Korea, Japan, India, and, of course, to Europe.

From the beginning of the CCR, Protestant charismatics (in the case of the instructors from Duquesene) and Pentecostalist pastors and deacons (in the case of Notre Dame) were deeply involved in leading Roman Catholics to experience a "Spirit baptism." This ecumenical aspect was maintained despite the fact that Roman Catholic charismatics openly stated that their new experience had led them to a deeper devotion than ever to such things as the Mass,* the rosary,* and praying to Mary. (Roman Catholics who found their new views incompatible with what they had traditionally been taught, generally quit their church and joined the Pentecostalist group that had influenced them.) Many Roman Catholic charismatic prayer groups precede or follow their prayer meetings with a Mass. Yet Protestant charismatics are so overwhelmed by their participation in their so-called Pentecostal experience that they either overlook or openly welcome their celebration of the Mass—despite the fact that every historic Protestant confession of faith denounces the Mass as idolatrous and as an abominable insult to Christ's once-for-all sacrifice for sin.

CCR gained enormous recognition within the Roman Catholic church through the influence of Cardinal Leon Joseph Suenens of Belgium, one of the four presidents of the Second Vatican Council. Pope Paul VI gave him pastoral supervision of CCR worldwide, and he did much to spread and consolidate the role of CCR in the Roman Catholic church. CCR is parish-based, with regional and national organizations to coordinate its efforts. It also boasts an international body, the International Catholic Charismatic Renewal Office, which, as Pope John Paul II said, "attempts to assure the pastoral and theological soundness of renewal groups everywhere," as well as fostering their ecumenical and evangelizing possibilities.

Thus, CCR is a potent and valuable asset to the Roman Catholic church. It influences vast numbers of Roman Catholics around the world and guards Vatican interests in two vital areas: first, it advances the cause of ecumenism without a critical analysis of Rome's traditional, unscriptural dogma; second, it holds many Roman Catholics in the Roman church, while satisfying their desire for a warmer, more experience-based religion than Rome had previously offered, but without allowing them to embrace the true gospel of Christ.

Essential Elements in the Charismatic Movement

Charismatics claim such things as a focus on Jesus, praise, expectation of Christ's return, awareness of evil, and evangelism as the essential elements of their movement. These elements are in evidence in the Charismatic Movement but they are not its most distinctive features. The essential elements of charismatism are:

1. Restorationism—the belief that the supernatural gifts of the apostolic church are available to the church today, especially speaking in tongues, healing, and prophecy. *(See Gifts of the Holy Spirit; Cessationism).*

2. Continuing Revelation—the belief that "God speaks to his people, corporately and personally, as directly and as regularly as in the first Christian century." That is, the Holy Ghost gives new, authoritative, extra-Biblical revelations that are binding on the consciences of those to whom they are directed. To Bible-believing Protestants this dogma is one of the most objectionable features of both charismatism and Pentecostalism, for it seriously undermines the crucial doctrine of the sufficiency of the finished revelation of Scripture.

3. Ecumenism—the pursuit of unity on the basis of a shared experience rather than on the great essential doctrines of the gospel. David du Plessis, sometimes called "Mr. Pentecost," insisted that to be truly charismatic you must be ecumenical, and to be truly

ecumenical you must be charismatic. Charismatic ecumenism mourns the breach with Rome caused by the Reformation and seeks to repair it, without seeking to turn Rome away from any of the gross apostasy that necessitated the Reformation. It elevates experience above revealed truth.

These essential elements of the Charismatic Movement—restorationism, continuing revelation, and unscriptural ecumenism—mark it as a serious threat to the purity of the gospel and to the mission of the church as it seeks to be faithful to Christ in the face of widespread apostasy.

CHERUBIM
See Angels.

CHILIASM

From the Greek word *chilioi,* "thousand," this is the view, based on Rev. 20:1-5, that Christ will reign on earth for a thousand years following His second coming.* Chiliasm can be traced through church history to the very early days of NT Christianity.
See Millennium.

CHRISM

Greek *chrisma,* translated "unction" in 1 John 2:20 and "anointing" in verse 27; the term employed in the Eastern and Roman Catholic churches to describe a so-called "holy" oil, or a mixture of olive oil and balsam used during the ceremonies of baptism,* confirmation,* extreme unction,* ordination of bishops, and the consecration of churches, altars, etc.

CHRISTADELPHIANISM

The title Christadelphians, "Brethren in Christ," was adopted in 1864 by John Thomas, M.D., as a designation of his followers in a breakaway movement from the Campbellites. Thomas (1805-71) was born in England, the son of a Dissenting minister who emigrated to the United States and laboured as a Baptist pastor. As a business venture Dr. Thomas sailed for New York in 1832. He soon associated himself with the Campbellites and began to preach and lecture among them. However, his views drove him into controversy with Alexander Campbell, though he continued to find a hearing in many Campbellite churches.

Thomas boasted a fellowship of *ecclesiae* that espoused his peculiar views in various American cities, as well as in Canada, England, and Scotland.

The organization of Christadelphian assemblies has always been simple, with no clergy and little ecclesiastical polity. In their early days, Christadelphians had a reputation of not speaking against those of different creeds, only asking for liberty to hold and express their own views. This gentle attitude appears to have been short-lived, however, as their literature exudes intolerance and bigotry against orthodox Christianity.

Christadelphianism groups its beliefs under two heads:

1. *Things Concerning the Kingdom of God.* The physical return of Christ to set up His kingdom is imminent, and Christadelphians will, if worthy, be made priests and kings to rule with Him on earth.

2. *Things Concerning the Name of Jesus Christ.* Here the cult exposes the full force of its heresy, denying the deity of Christ, the personality of the Holy Spirit, the Trinity, and the atonement of Christ to satisfy divine wrath.

From Christadelphian writings we obtain a clear view of their creed:

1. Christadelphians constitute the body of Christ.

2. There is no salvation in any other church.

3. The fundamental doctrines of Christendom are all wrong.

4. Jesus had no existence prior to His birth in Bethlehem.

5. He did not possess an immaculate nature, and His flesh was full of the same propensities and desires as ours. He rendered complete obedience and was therefore sinless, but was all the while subject to the impulses and consequences of innate sin.

6. Christadelphians do not worship the Lord Jesus Christ in the same way they do the Father.

7. The Holy Spirit is not a divine person, but merely an invisible power or energy radiating from God.

8. There is no personal devil. The term *devil* is a personification of sin in the flesh.

9. Christ made no satisfaction to God by His death and paid no debt for us. His righteousness is not imputed to believers. The orthodox doctrines of substitutionary atonement and imputed righteousness are "demoralizing" and "blighting."

10. Saints never go to heaven, either immediately after death or at any later time.

11. The immortality of the soul is a fiction.

12. There is no hell or everlasting torment for the wicked.

13. Baptism, which is essential to salvation, must follow an acknowledgment of the Christadelphian creed. No other baptism is valid.

14. The enquirer who is baptized is "born of water," and has his sins covered and his past life cancelled. He is then put on probation as a candidate for resurrection. If he attains that, he will finally be "born of the Spirit" and become a son of God. Thus Christadelphianism espouses the two heresies of Conditional Immortality* and autosoterism,* for a person's enjoyment of immortality and salvation depends on the character he develops following his baptism. If he fails, he will be annihilated.

The best Christadelphianism can offer a poor sinner is a period of probation—no certain message of salvation. Such darkness is perfectly in keeping with the character of the cult. Anything that presents a Christ denuded of His eternal deity and a prey to passion and lust as other men, can never hold out any true hope to the lost. It is perhaps for that reason that, as Oswald Sanders has charged, Christadelphians go to great lengths to make converts from other churches but show little zeal to reach outcast sinners in our society.

CHRISTIAN EVIDENCES

The branch of Apologetics* which is chiefly concerned with the factual vindication of Christianity. Since "facts" prove nothing apart from a framework of interpretation, the consistent use of Christian Evidences proceeds upon the presupposition that apart from the ontological Trinity there can be no sound methodology for the interpretation of facts, whether scientific or historical. Thus, Christian Evidences as much as Apologetics has to face the issue of philosophy, and in particular the philosophy of science. The philosophic framework of Calvinism (discussed under Apologetics) yields a sound scientific methodology for treating the factual data of nature and of history, and every fact so viewed will evidence the truth of Christianity. *See Epistemology.*

CHRISTIAN SCIENCE

In 1862 Mrs. Mary Baker Eddy (1821-1910), then Mrs. Daniel Patterson, visited P. P. Quimby for treatment of her long-standing nervous troubles. Quimby stressed the state of his patients' minds, not medicine, as the cure for their ailments, and Mrs. Patterson claimed to receive healing. She herself began to practice healing, and in 1875 she published her book *Science and Health with Key to the Scriptures.*

Mrs. Eddy taught, "God is divine Principle, supreme incorporeal Being, Mind, Spirit, Soul, Life, Truth, Love." From this she developed four "self-evident" propositions: "1. God is All-in-all. 2. God is Good, God is Mind. 3. God, Spirit, being all, nothing is matter. 4. Life, God, omnipotent good, deny death, evil, sin, disease. Disease, sin, evil, death, deny good, omnipotent God, life."

Thus matter, disease, hunger, and even death do not actually exist! They are merely the mistaken ideas of "mortal mind"! Since in the pantheistic theory of Christian Science, God is All-in-all, where does this "mortal mind" come from? Again, "has the Christian Scientist ever paused to answer the following problem: If I cannot trust my senses when they report death and pain, how can I trust them when I read the works of Mary Baker Eddy? The latter data are far less compelling than the former" (Carnell, *A Philosophy of the Christian Religion,* p. 292).

The antichristianity of this cult is seen in its heretical—and heathen—roots, as well as in its dogmatic positions. (The quotations of Mrs. Eddy are from *Science and Health* and her *Miscellaneous Writings.*)

1. It is pantheistic. It is basically Buddhist, not Christian, though it has appropriated Christian terminology. According to this system God is all and all is God.

2. It is gnostic.* It teaches salvation by esoteric knowledge. It looks on matter as an illusion—a throwback to the ancient docetic* idea.

3. It is autosoteric:* "Final deliverance from error, whereby we rejoice in immortality, boundless freedom and sinless sense, is not reached through paths of flowers nor by pinning one's faith without works to another's vicarious effort."

4. It elevates *Science and Health* to the status of divine revelation but denies the inspiration of Scripture, parts of which Mrs. Eddy labelled "a lie."

5. It repudiates the Deity of Christ. "Jesus Christ is not God as Jesus Himself declared but is the Son of God." "Jesus is the human man, and Christ is the divine idea" and the human "Jesus was the offspring of Mary's self-conscious communion with God."

6. It denies the personality of the Holy Spirit and appropriated His office to her cult: "Christian Science is the Holy Comforter." "The Holy Spirit is the Science of Christianity." "Receiving the Holy Spirit means an enlarged understanding of Christian Science."

7. It denies the Biblical doctrine of the Trinity. "Belief in the trinity is heathenish." According to Mrs. Eddy, "Jehovah was a tribal god idolatrously worshipped by Israel, ranking with Baal, Moloch, Vishnu, Aphrodite." This flies in the face of the command of both Testaments that we should love and serve Jehovah (Deut. 6:3, 4; Matt. 22:37, 38).

8. It holds that there is neither a personal deity, a personal devil, nor a personal man. "Man is not matter; he is not made up of brain, bones, and other material elements." This non-personal, this immaterial phantom is perfect and immortal, has no birth or death, and is "self-existent and eternal like God."

9. It denies the reality of sin, sickness, and death. "Man is incapable of sin, sickness or death."

10. It denies the possibility that a soul may be lost or that Christ made any atonement. "Jesus did not suffer on the cross to annul the divine sentence against sin." "Salvation is not through faith in another's vicarious sacrifice." There is no such place as hell or heaven, which is really "a state of mind."

11. It denies the reality of matter. "Matter is a human concept."

When Mrs. Eddy died, a leading Christian Scientist claimed, "The same situation exists today as when Jesus of Nazareth died and was buried. After three days He manifested Himself to prove there is life after death. Mrs. Eddy will do the same, for she occupies in the world today precisely the same position that Jesus did in His day" (J. Oswald Sanders, *Cults and Isms,* p. 51). Mrs. Eddy, of course, did not come forth from the grave. Her body slowly returned to the dust from which it was made, despite all her fulminations to the contrary.

Christian Science still follows Mrs. Eddy. Since her death the cult has been under the control of a board of directors. The mother church is located in Boston, with satellite churches worldwide. Its structure of government is rigidly and efficiently authoritarian.

It produces a highly regarded daily newspaper, *The Christian Science Monitor.*

By order of Mrs. Eddy, Christian Science meetings have no preaching (despite Mark 16:15), but rather a reading from Scripture and another from *Science and Health,* some singing and the repetition of Mrs. Eddy's perversion of the Lord's prayer, which reads, "Our Father-Mother God, all harmonious, Adorable One. Thy kingdom is come; Thou art ever-present. Enable us to know—as in heaven, so on earth,—God is omnipotent, supreme. Give us grace for today; feed the famished affections; And Love is reflected in love. And God leadeth us not into temptation, but delivereth us from sin, disease, and death. For God is infinite, all power, all Life, Truth, Love, over all, and All." It is strange that Christian Science uses this prayer, not only because of its total inconsistency with all Mrs. Eddy taught about God, man, sin, and death, but because she taught that "audible prayer leads to temptation."

That such a pantheistic, autosoteric, and hopelessly confused system should ever pass for either Christianity or science is a glaring example of the misuse of words.

CHRISTOLOGY

The department of Systematic Theology* which deals with the doctrine of the Person of Christ the Redeemer. It covers the following subjects: His Theanthropic Person;* His Deity;* His Humanity;* His Unipersonality;* His Impeccability.*

CHURCH
Definition

The word *ekklesia* is derived from the two words *ek,* "out," and *kaleo,* "to call." In its broadest and basic sense, it refers to any assembly of people (cf. Acts 19:32, 39, 41), but its usual application in the Scriptures is, of course, to Christian assemblies of the *kletoi,* "the called ones." In this second sense, the word is used in five distinct ways in the Scriptures:

1. To denote the entire body of God's people, whether in heaven or in earth, who have believed or who will believe in Christ (Matt. 16:18; Eph. 5:25-27). In keeping with this are those descriptions of the church which cannot be limited to any particular society of Christians on earth, viz., the bride of Christ (Eph. 5:31, 32); the body of Christ (Eph. 1:23; 4:12, 13); the building of the Lord (Eph. 2:21). The description of Heb. 12:23, "the general assembly and church of the firstborn," is surely of "the whole number of the elect that have been, are, or shall be gathered into one under Christ, the head thereof" (*Westminster Confession of Faith,* chap. 25, sec. 1). "The general assembly," or universal gathering, establishes this meaning of the term, a meaning which yields important consequences.

2. To denote the whole body of those throughout the world who profess the faith of Christ (Acts 2:47; 1 Cor. 12:28; Eph. 4:11, 12). The reference here is to a visible society on earth. The meaning cannot be limited to "the local church," first, because these promises are not made in terms that speak of an abstract concept, but of the church as a concrete reality; and second, because to use *church* in the singular to mean each and every local church is a usage which advocates of the local church interpretation would not want to admit, destructive as it is of the notion of independency.

3. To denote the believers in a particular place, associated for worship and service (Acts 14:23; Rom. 16:3-5; 1 Cor. 16:19; Col. 4:15; Philem. 2; 1 Thess. 1:1, etc.).

4. To denote a number of congregations, associated together. This use of the term is vehemently denied by Independents, but from what we noted under (2) above it is difficult for them to maintain their position consistently. From the texts noted there, we have the use of *church* in the singular to denote all the congregations or churches of God's people. Furthermore, considering the statement of Acts 21:20 regarding the "many

thousands" of believing Jews in Jerusalem (see Acts 2:41, 47; 4:4; 5:14 for how this vast group was formed), it is inconceivable that there should not have been a number of congregations in Jerusalem. Yet in Acts 15:4, 22, *church* in the singular is used to denote all the Christians in the city. (Some appeal to Acts 9:31, where *church,* singular, is preferred in most critical editions of the Greek text; however, the AV reading is correct, reflecting the traditional Greek text.)

5. To denote a body of believers as represented by their spiritual rulers (Matt. 18:17; cf. Heb. 13:7, 17, 24). James Bannerman remarked, "In such an injunction our Lord referred to the synagogue court known and established among the Jews, which had its elders and officers for the decision of such matters of discipline; and in the expression 'the Church' which He made use of, the Jews who heard Him must have understood the authorized rulers, as distinct from the ruled, to be the parties who were to determine in such controversies" (*Church of Christ,* 1:14). This interpretation is rejected by Independents, but remembering the circumstances of Christ's statement, it is difficult to resist Bannerman's conclusions.

Institution of Church

The church is a divine institution (Matt. 16:18), not a mere human society that owes its origin and establishment to the voluntary agreement of its members. While this agreement is not absent from the church, still the church owes its existence and continuance to the institution and power of the Lord. It enjoys His presence (Matt. 18:20), is regulated by His word and is disciplined according to laws He has fixed. Furthermore, the church is not the creature of the state (contrast Erastianism*), and it holds its powers and privileges, within its proper sphere, directly from the Lord, without the sanction of the State.

"The church actually exercised the rights resulting from its Divine institution, and conferred by Christ, both in the times of the apostles and in subsequent ages, when it received no gift from the State except the gift of persecution and blood" (Bannerman, 1:23).

The church is not only a divine institution; it is also a spiritual one. Its administration is spiritual in its nature and aims, different in kind from the kingdom of the world. The realization of this, by both church and state, would go far to resolve the repeated difficulties in reconciling the freedom of Christian conscience on the one hand and the legitimate rights of the state on the other. The Lord commands His people to render to Caesar the things which are Caesar's and to God the things which are God's. But Caesar has no legitimate control over the things of God.

Invisible and Visible

According to the first definition of *church* given above, we are warranted in speaking of "the invisible church." In this sense, every member of the church is truly elect and redeemed. That is not true of any society on earth (cf. Matt. 13:24-30, 47); and therefore, the true church is invisible in the sense that some are admitted to the society of professing Christians on earth whose names are not written in heaven. It is also invisible in the sense that never on earth have we had all the elect from all the ages gathered together in a visible society.

The reality of the distinction between the visible and invisible church is important if we are to escape the gross corruptions of Romanism's notion of the church. Maintaining this distinction, but recognizing that the visible and invisible are not two churches but one viewed in two ways, we can see that some things predicated of the one cannot be predicated of the other. Thus, to be a member of the invisible church is to be absolutely sure of heaven, as a part of the body of Christ; but to be merely in the visible church, without any vital union with Christ, is to be excluded from heaven.

Church Militant and Triumphant

These are terms frequently employed to denote the church yet on earth, still battling for God, and the church in heaven whose warfare has been accomplished.

Notes or Marks of the Church

Rome makes much of the indefectibility of the church—i.e., that it has never ceased to exist after its institution. Protestants admit this, but deny the Romish theory that "there must be at all times, in unbroken and continuous succession, an organized society publicly and palpably standing out to the eyes of men as the church of Christ" (William Cunningham, *Historical Theology* 1:10). There is no scriptural promise that such would be the case, and indeed the representation of the mustard seed in Matt. 13 is much against it. Indefectibility belongs to the church invisible, not to the church visible. Rome wants to attach it *a priori* to the earthly society and then claim that she alone can be that society.

Four other notes are claimed for the church: unity, sanctity, apostolicity, and catholicity. Understood in a scriptural sense, these may be accepted; but in the sense in which Rome holds them, they are far from scriptural. Scripturally these marks belong primarily to the invisible church, though the visible church should strive to avoid division, unholiness, and all departures from apostolic principles and practice and should ever seek to be an expression of the catholic or universal faith and practice of the people of God. That any visible society has always existed bearing all these marks without mixture of error and sin is a figment, and no society has less claim to such a distinction than the church of Rome, whose doctrines and practices are in every major area far removed from the apostolic model.

Promises to the Church

The *Westminster Confession of Faith* (chap. 25, sec. 3) states: "Unto this catholic visible church Christ hath given the ministry, oracles, and ordinances of God, for the gathering and perfecting of the saints in this life to the end of the world; and doth by His own presence and Spirit, according to His promise, make them effectual thereunto."

This is an important statement. Rome claims that where there is not a valid ministry there can be no true church. Protestants, she claims, do not have a valid ministry and therefore are not a true church. Protestants reverse the order: where there is a true church, there is or may be a valid ministry. Thus "the church of Rome makes ministry the end, and the church the means; Protestants...make the ministry the means, and the church the end" (Cunningham, 1:27, 28).

The Scripture statements are opposed to the Romish view (1 Cor. 12:28; Eph. 4:11-13). The result of the Romish position is a hierarchy that virtually takes the place of God and certainly replaces the work of the Spirit through the Word with human channels and activities that purport to bear divine grace to the faithful. If Rome's view were scriptural, the Reformers would have been in sin in separating from her; but in fact, on the clear command of the Word, they were not only entitled, but bound, to leave her communion because of the sinfulness and heresy with which she was infected. Thus, in separating from Rome, Protestants formed true, scriptural churches to which, as He promised, Christ gave a valid ministry.

To His church Christ also promised His presence and Spirit, which in Cunningham's words means "that by Christ's presence, and the operation of the Spirit, His church should enjoy and effect all that He intended it to enjoy and effect; that all who were chosen by God to eternal life should be brought to a knowledge and belief of the truth as it is in Jesus, and be trained up to a meetness for heaven; and that, therefore, all who had really entered Christ's service might boldly devote themselves to the advancement of His cause, and to the discharge of all the duties which He might impose upon them, assured that they should suffer no real loss by faithfulness to Him, but would find all things made to work together for their good" (1:33).

The Government of the Church

Extremely different views—varying from the professed absence of any form of church government among groups like the Quakers to the hierarchical notions of the church of Rome—have been voiced on this subject. Erastianism* cedes church government to the state. Episcopacy* holds that "Christ as the head of the church, has entrusted the government of the church directly and exclusively to an order of prelates or bishops, as the successors of the apostles; and that He has constituted these bishops a separate, independent, and self-perpetuating order" (Berkhof, *Systematic Theology*, p. 579). Rome carries this idea further and pretends not only successors to the apostles but, in the pope, a successor to Peter, whom it claims to have been primate among the apostles. Thus, in Romanism, there is a hierarchy ruled by an absolute monarch, under whom serve various lesser orders.

All these ideas are foreign to the Scriptures, which accord the right of governing the church to the church, not the state, and which recognize no such separate superior officers as bishops in the episcopal sense. Rome's notion of Peter's primacy finds no support in the Bible and her claim of an unbroken line of popes from him breaks down before the testimony of history. The principle in episcopacy and Romanism that the people have no say in church government is also foreign to Scripture.

The opposite to such ideas is found in independency *(see Congregationalism),* which views church officers as mere functionaries of the local congregation, in which final governmental power resides.

Presbyterianism is a scriptural mean between these two extremes, avoiding the institution of a superior class, as in episcopacy, and granting a real involvement by the people, and also avoiding the unscriptural position of congregationalism, which makes the ministry dependent upon the action of the people and allows no appeal from any decision by a local congregation. The Biblical principle of this system of government is more fully explained under **Presbyterianism**;* but we may here note that for its government, the church has been given certain officers by Christ, her great King and sole Head:

1. Apostles and prophets were extraordinary officers. Apostles were personally commissioned by Christ (Mark 3:14; Gal. 1:1), were witnesses of His resurrection (Acts 1:21, 22; 1 Cor. 9:1), had special miraculous power used to ratify their message (2 Cor. 12:12; Heb. 2:4) and were inspired in their teaching (Acts 15:28; 1 Cor. 2:13; 1 Thess. 4:8; 1 John 5:9-12). Prophets also spoke by inspiration (cf. Acts 11:28; 13:1, 2; 15:32; 1 Cor. 12:10; Eph. 2:20, etc.). Prophets clearly had a ministry of edification (Eph. 4:11, 12) and this function continues in the church, but divine inspiration has ceased with the completion of Scripture.

2. Elders (*presbuteroi*) or bishops or overseers (*episkopoi*)—cf. Acts 11:30; 20:17, 28; 1 Tim. 3:1; 4:14; Tit. 1:5, 7; 1 Pet. 5:1, 2— were the officers for church government and for teaching. Ephesians 4:11 speaks of pastors and teachers as one group. 1 Peter 5:1-2 uses all three terms (presbyters, overseers, shepherds or pastors) as descriptive of one class of church officer. From 1 Tim. 5:17 we learn that the pastors and teachers were distinguishable from other elders whose function was chiefly to rule. These officers are perpetual in the church.

3. Deacons (Acts 6:1-6; Phil. 1:1; 1 Tim. 3:8-12) were charged with the temporal affairs of the church, and the office clearly was meant to continue in the church. The Scriptures speak of the role of the people in the election of their office-bearers (Acts 1:15-26; 6:2-6) and of their ordination as

an act of the presbytery (1 Tim. 4:14; cf. Acts 14:23), an act accompanied by the laying on of hands (Acts 6:6; 1 Tim. 5:22). Ordination clearly sets a man aside for a specific function, and in apostolic times conferred some special spiritual gift. With the passing of the apostles, the act of ordination no longer conveys the miraculous power of the Spirit, but denotes the church's recognition of the Lord's calling and power upon the ordinand.

The Power of the Church

From its nature, institution, and promises the church derives the God-given power of self-propagation (by the power of the Spirit through the preaching of the gospel), self-government and self-correction, or the discipline of its members (see, for example, Matt. 18:17 and 1 Cor. 5:1-5; 6:1-4; 1 Tim. 5:17; Heb. 13:7, 17, "rule"). In all this, her business is to do God's will as expressed in Scripture, whatever the cost, remaining ever truly "the pillar and ground of truth," the support and stay (not the originator or revelator) of what God has revealed in His infallible word.

CIRCUMINCESSION

A term sometimes employed to describe the mutual indwelling of the three persons in the Godhead. The Godhead is a tri-unity. The Father, Son, and Holy Spirit are one God, indivisible in essence. There is no tension between the plurality of persons in the Godhead and the absolute unity of the divine essence. God is not one *and* three, or three *and* one. He is one *in* three, and three *in* one.

The Lord Jesus Christ referred to the mutual indwelling of the trinitarian persons in John 14:10,11: "I am in the Father, and the Father in me." Again in John 17:21 He said, "Thou, Father, art in me, and I in thee." Thus, in describing His own works, He said, "The Father that dwelleth in me, he doeth the works" (John 14:10).

Circumincession, then, denotes the absolute unity of the Godhead while safeguarding the personal distinctions of the Father, Son, and Holy Spirit. It notes, but does not seek to explain, the fact that though each trinitarian person has peculiar roles attributed to him in the works of creation, providence, and redemption, he does not—and cannot—fulfill these in isolation. There can be no isolation of persons in the Godhead. Jesus said, "The Son can do nothing of himself," or *from* himself (Greek, *apo*; John 5:19). Similarly, speaking of the ministry of the Holy Spirit, He said, "He shall not speak *of* (from, Greek *apo*) himself" (John 16:13).

By *circumincession* theologians try to do justice to these data. The term cannot explain the mystery of the Godhead. God is incomprehensible. In the end Anselm's verdict is surely to be adopted. He said that the mystery of the tri-unity of God was "so sublime," that it "transcends all the vision of the human intellect. And for that reason I think it best to refrain from the attempt to explain how this thing is."

See **Trinity**.

CIVIL LAW

One of the three major divisions of OT law—moral, ceremonial and civil. The *Westminster Confession of Faith* (chap. 19, sec. 4) states the purpose of civil law: "To them [Israel] also, as a body politic, he gave sundry judicial laws, which expired together with the state of that people, not obliging any other now, further than the general equity thereof may require."

Thus those laws that belonged peculiarly to Israel—whose blessings and penalties are couched peculiarly in terms that have meaning only in connection with the Jewish state—are civil laws. A. A. Hodge wrote, "that the judicial laws of the Jews have ceased to have binding obligation upon us follows plainly, from the fact that the peculiar relations of the people to God as theocratical King, and to one another as fellow-members of an Old

Testament church State, to which these laws were adjusted, now no longer exist" (*Commentary on Westminster Confession of Faith*, chap. 19, sec. 3-5).

CLAPHAM SECT

Not really a sect* at all "but a movement within Anglican Evangelicalism at the close of the 18th and the beginning of the 19th century. Named after Clapham, a village outside of London where John Venn (1759-1813) was rector, an intimate and influential circle of evangelicals was formed which included prominent laymen such as William Wilberforce. Wealth and public position were placed in the service of a puritanical piety which expressed itself in social reform and missions" (Schaff-Herzog).

This "puritanical piety that expressed itself in social reform and missions" was really an attempt to apply the gospel to the great vices of late 18th-century Britain. It sought to suppress the vice and immorality that were public scandals and it set out to eradicate an even greater scandal, the African slave trade. In these efforts the Anglican evangelicals, especially Wilberforce, gained some notable victories.

Venn and his colleagues also had the distinction of being an early part of the evangelical revival in the Church of England. That revival culminated in the ministry of Charles Simeon of Cambridge (1759-1836) and led to the formation of the Low Church party and its missionary arm, the Church Missionary Society.

CLERGY

The general title given to those ordained to the ministry of the Word and sacraments. The Greek word *kleros* appears, among other places, in Acts 1:17, 25 and 1 Pet. 5:3. In the Acts reference it denotes a "part of this ministry and apostleship," while in Peter's reference it denotes God's heritage, that is, His people. In this latter sense all Christians are the clergy. This agrees with the sentiment expressed in those places where *kleros* denotes an inheritance (Acts 26:18; Col. 1:12), for all God's people share that inheritance. It also accords with the idea of saints inheriting eternal life and glory, expressed in the cognate verbs *kleronomeo,* "inherit" (Matt. 19:29), and *kleroomai* (Eph. 1:11), and in the nouns *kleronomia,* "inheritance" (1 Pet. 1:4) and *kleronomos,* "heir" (Rom. 8:17). These all set forth the everlasting blessing of the gospel upon all the people of God. They are all His heritage, His clergy.

However, *kleros* also means "a lot" (Matt. 27:35; Acts 1:26) and, as noted above, the part each apostle had in the ministry of the gospel. Since this obviously came by divine appointment, declared by the casting of lots in the case of Matthias (Acts 1:26), the use of the name *kleroi* came to denote those set apart by divine appointment to the work of the ministry.

Viewed in this way, *clergy* may be accepted as a scriptural designation of Christ's ministers. However, there is a danger that must be avoided and that is the error of the Roman Catholic church which has too often tended to look on the clergy as the church and the people merely as "the faithful." When Rome defines what "the church" has enacted or delivered to the faithful, she means what the hierarchy, the superior clergy, have decreed. This sets the clergy apart from the faithful, as the very things Peter prohibits, "lords over God's heritage." Vatican II puts it bluntly: "The ministerial priest, by the sacred power he enjoys moulds and rules the priestly people [i.e., the faithful]" (*Dogmatic Constitution on the Church,* 2:10). The clergy have this power because they are "acting in the person of Christ."

Protestants contend that to claim such clerical power and position is unscriptural. To them, the clergy may rule only ministerially (Heb. 13:17), never sacerdotally. With this proviso, ministers may be termed the clergy, as those whom God has set apart for the work of the gospel. Otherwise, the designation is misleading and unacceptable.

CLINIC BAPTISM

Baptism on a sick bed (from Greek, *kline,* "bed"), allowed in the ancient church to a candidate for baptism whose life was endangered. The early infection of superstitious sacramentalism* in the church may be recognized in the solemn practice of excluding from ordination anyone who had received clinic baptism and recovered.

CODE OF HAMMURABI

An ancient Babylonian collection of legal decisions written in 300 paragraphs of Akkadian cuneiform* script. It was discovered at Susa in 1901. Hammurabi was the last king of the first Babylonian Dynasty (*circa* 1728-1676 B.C.). His legal code covers a variety of matters of a commercial, social, domestic, and moral nature. It has some interesting parallels with the Mosaic code. It appears to codify laws that were generally accepted in the pre-Mosaic period. Some of those laws are discernible in the OT account of the lives of the patriarchs, as the following examples (See *Companion Bible,* Appendix 15) will show:

1. The law of adoption made Eliezer Abraham's heir (Gen. 15, Code sec. 191).
2. The giving of Hagar to Abraham (Gen. 16) and of Bilhah and Zilpah to Jacob (Gen. 30, Code sec. 146).
3. Abraham's inability to sell Hagar (Gen. 16, Code sec. 119).
4. The manner of Abraham's purchase of Machpelah (Gen. 23, Code sec. 7).
5. Jacob's proposal of capital punishment for anyone guilty of stealing Laban's *teraphim* (Gen. 31, Code sec. 6).
6. Judah's threat to punish his daughter-in-law by burning (Gen. 38, Code sec. 110).
7. Joseph's steward's proposal that the one with whom Joseph's cup was found would die (for the crime of stealing from a palace; Gen. 48, Code sec. 6).

8. Jacob's gift of a special portion to his favourite son (Gen. 48, Code sec. 165).

9. Jacob's cutting off of Reuben for defiling his father's concubine (Gen. 49, Code sec. 158).

These examples will suffice to show that while some critics reduce the Mosaic code to the level of an uninspired composition dependent on Hammurabi's code, the real nature of their relationship is altogether different. In many particulars, Hammurabi's code displays the laws that long predated it in the ancient world. Some of those laws reflected the statutes, restrictions, and correctives that arose from God's revelation to Noah and his descendents. Not surprisingly, therefore, they coincide with what we find in the Mosaic records.

However, the similarities should not be over emphasized. There are also notable differences between Hammurabi and Moses which, on the assumption of the divine inspiration of the Mosaic code, would indicate that Hammurabi's code exemplifies a modification or corruption of the earlier divine revelation, or an uninspired response to the developing needs of human society.

CODEX

An ancient Bible manuscript with leaves bound in book form.

See MSS.

COLLECT

A short form of prayer in Roman Catholic and Anglican liturgies.

COMMON GRACE

A term used to describe the goodness of God to a sin-cursed world, not including salvation. By His common grace, God places a restraint upon sin and its natural results and upon the immediate execution of wrath against sinners.

It is not merely negative. It includes the bestowal of favour and blessing of a general nature, but not of that special kind which leads to salvation. Thus, Prof. John Murray defined common grace as "Every favour of whatsoever kind and degree, falling short of salvation, which this undeserving and sin-cursed world enjoys at the hand of God."

See Special Grace.

COMMON SENSE PHILOSOPHY

Also known as Scottish Common Sense Philosophy or Scottish Realism. The theory of Thomas Reid (1710-96) and a school of Scottish philosophers and theologians who followed him, that there are certain truths that we know intuitively, beliefs not arrived at by any process of induction, but by common sense. These intuitive beliefs are fundamental laws of thought. They are "laws, principles, or powers in the mind [that exist] anterior to any reflex observation of them" (James McCosh, *The Scottish Philosophy,* p. 7).

Reid's philosophy took shape as a reaction to the sceptical empiricism* of David Hume. Hume made experience the judge of all knowledge. To him the "laws of nature" were merely generalisations from past experience. They were not really laws at all and provided no rational grounds for predicting future events. Hume also reduced man to a "bundle of sensations," denying the reality of the soul. He attacked the teleological arguments for God's existence. He denied the validity of any appeal to miracles as proofs of the claims of Christianity. In a word, his views were rationalistic and naturalistic.

Common Sense Philosophy was for a time (until about 1850) a distinctively national philosophy. It had a great appeal to many Scottish ministers who liked its emphasis on intuitive principles and self-evident truth. Both moderates and evangelicals in the Church of Scotland readily espoused it and saw it as a powerful tool against scepticism. They held that God planted self-evident truth in man. Indeed, some went on to say that God was one of the self-evident truths. That

God exists is a self-evident truth that any rational person, not blinded by prejudice, would accept.

Therein is the weakness of the theory. Where in all the world is there an unregenerate man not blinded by his own sin? Totally depraved men have their understanding darkened. The light that is in them is darkness. The principles the Realists sought to establish were real enough, but not self-evident to the depraved and darkened mind of fallen man.

Scottish Realism exercised a powerful influence in America as well as in Scotland but fell into decline under the impact of European idealism.* It has continued to have its advocates but after the middle of the 19th century it ceased to be Scotland's distinctive philosophy.

COMMUNICATIO IDIOMATUM

Latin meaning "the communication of properties"; the doctrine that the properties of the divine and human natures in Christ are the properties of a single person and that therefore both are ascribed to that person. Thus, He can be described as "Almighty" or "a man of sorrows." This explains how Christ, spoken of under a human title, can have divine properties ascribed to Him (e.g., John 3:13), or how, when He is spoken of under His divine title, He can have human acts or properties ascribed to Him (e.g., Acts 20:28). In all this there is no confusion of the natures.

See **Theanthropic Person**; **Ubiquity**.

COMMUNION

Latin *communio,* "fellowship."
1. The word most frequently used to describe the Lord's Supper,* reflecting Paul's words in 1 Cor. 10:16.
2. A description of people in union together in a religious body with a common doctrine, worship, and discipline— e.g., The Anglican Communion, as a description of Episcopalians in union with the See of Canterbury.

COMMUNION OF SAINTS

A phrase from the Apostles' Creed, which has been variously interpreted, but has been understood by Protestants simply as the fellowship of believers. Rome stretches the idea beyond anything suggested in Scripture to support her doctrine of the church's treasury, and the bestowal of merit and blessing upon people on earth and in Purgatory* by those who have reached heaven. *(See **Indulgence.**)*

COMPARATIVE RELIGION

The study of the religions of the world that seeks to trace their similarities and dissimilarities. On the assumption that the Biblical revelation presents the only true religion, this study may be valuable in showing the points of divergence from God's truth exhibited by the world's religions. It may also be of use in preparing appropriate methods of presenting the gospel to people of various religious backgrounds.

However, all too often the study of comparative religion is rooted in a number of liberal* fallacies—e.g., that the origin of OT principles and practice is traceable to the religions of the pagan nations surrounding Israel; that all religions are expressions of the evolution of man's search for God; that all religions have a certain amount of divine light in them; and that Christianity, far from being uniquely God's saving revelation to the world, is only one of many valid ways of worshipping God acceptably.

See **World Council of Churches**.

COMPLACENCY

A word used in dealing with the goodness of God. It signifies "that approving affection with which God regards His own infinite perfections, and every image and reflection of them…in the sanctified subjects of the new creation" (A. A. Hodge).

COMPLEX PERSON

The term used to convey the fact that, though He is truly one person *(see*

Unipersonality), the Lord Jesus Christ is both perfect God and perfect man. See **Theanthropic Person**.

CONCOMITANCE

A technical term used by Roman Catholic theologians to signify the alleged presence of both the body and blood of Christ in each of the species at the Lord's Supper. On this ground, the cup was long denied to the laity (i.e., though they partook only of the bread, it was claimed on the basis of concomitance that they received both the body and blood of Christ).

CONCREATED HOLINESS

The positive holiness Adam possessed by God's creative act. At his creation, Adam was not merely innocent of sin. His will was not balanced between good and evil; it was created positively holy. Its inclination, or disposition, was holy. This is the plain testimony of Scripture.

The Biblical Teaching

A. A. Hodge summarized that testimony as follows:

"**1.** As a moral creature man was created in the image of God.—Gen. 1:27.

2. God pronounced all his works, man included, to be "very good."—Gen. 1:31. The goodness of a mechanical provision is essentially its fitness to attain its end. The 'goodness' of a moral agent can be nothing other than his conformity of will to the moral law. Moral indifference in a moral agent is itself of the nature of sin.

3. This truth is asserted.—Eccl. 7:29.

4. In regeneration, man is renewed in the image of God; in creation, man was made in the image of God; the image, in both cases, must be the same, and includes holiness.—Eph. 4:24.

5. Christ is called, 1 Cor. 15:45, *ho eschatos Adam,* and in 15:47, *deuteros anthropos.* He is recognized by friend and foe as the only perfect man in all history, the exemplar of

normal humanity. Yet his human nature was formed by the Holy Ghost, antecedently to all action of its own, absolutely holy. Luke 1:35" *(Outlines of Theology).*

The Reformed churches have laid great emphasis on this truth. Error here has grave repercussions in formulating a doctrine of sin and salvation. Indeed the peculiar errors of Pelagianism,* Arminianism,* and Romanism on these subjects have their roots in their denial of concreated holiness.

Pelagian Views

Pelagianism holds that Adam was created a moral agent, but without a positive moral character. He was created in a state of moral equilibrium between good and evil, and left free to form his own character by his own free unbiased choices. Every descendant of Adam has been born into the world in the same moral state as Adam at his creation. He is not predisposed to either good or evil, and he forms his own character by a series of personal choices. *(See **Existentialism**).* Death is not the result of sin but a natural result of man's humanity. Thus salvation, in the Biblical sense, by means of the atoning sacrifice, is impossible and unnecessary.

Arminian Views

Arminianism shares the Pelagian view of man's original moral constitution but not its doctrine of the moral state of Adam's descendants by birth. Arminians hold that if Adam had been created with an inclination to holiness he would not have been rewardable for acting according to it, since he did not originate it.

Similarly, had he been created with a bias toward evil he would not have been punishable for acting on it. He could be rewarded or punished for his own moral character only if he originated it himself.

Thus he was created in a state of moral equilibrium or indifference. He chose to sin and produced a sinful character that is bad and justly punishable. As a result his descendants are born with corrupt natures. But since this is not through any fault of their own they are not punishable for their natural corruption, only for the personal choices they make. All this makes sin merely a matter of volition or action, and nothing deeper. Man is not responsible for what he is by nature, only for what he does and what he becomes as a result.

This makes no sense. If what man is by birth (corrupt and depraved) inclines him to evil, then the Arminian doctrine would logically remove all basis for God's judging him at all. Of course, Arminians do not go this far, but they are inconsistent with their own basic premises in not doing so.

Even then the results of their rejection of concreated holiness in Adam are not finished. They touch on the Arminian view of salvation. Arminianism holds that man may originate a good disposition of will; he may freely choose to repent and believe the gospel. As a result he may be regenerated. Thus regeneration is the result of faith that man chooses to exercise while in his unregenerate state. The Arminian denies that there is any trace of salvation by works in this; but again, he is inconsistent. He is also in defiance of Scripture which says emphatically, "The carnal mind is enmity against God: for it is not subject to the law of God, neither indeed can be" (Rom. 8:7); and, "In my flesh dwelleth no good thing" (Rom. 7:18). Arminianism produces a salvation which is a joint effort between God and the sinner, a synergism;* and its error is traceable to a deficient view of Adam's creation in holiness.

Roman Catholic Views

Romanism also denies concreated holiness. Romish theology holds that God endowed Adam with the natural constitutional powers and faculties of body and soul, in perfect innocence of all sin. He had no defect in body or soul. These powers and faculties Rome terms *dona naturalia,* "natural gifts." God then tempered all these natural

powers, placing the lower in subordination to the higher. Rome calls this harmony of powers and faculties in Adam *Justitia,* "natural righteousness."

A. A. Hodge describes how Rome develops her theory:

"There was, however in the very nature of things, a natural tendency in the lower appetites and passions to rebel against the authority of the higher powers of reason and conscience. This tendency is not sin in itself, but becomes sin only when it is consented to by the will, and passes into voluntary action. This is concupiscence; not sin, but the fuel and occasion of sin.

"To prevent this natural tendency to disorder from the rebellion of the lower elements of the human constitution against the higher, God granted man the additional gift of the *dona supernaturalia,* or gifts extra-constitutional. This is original righteousness, which was a foreign gift superadded to his constitution, by means of which his natural powers duly attempted are kept in due subjection and order. Some of their theologians held that these supernatural gifts were bestowed upon man immediately upon his creation, at the same time with his natural powers. The more prevalent and consistent view, however, is that it was given subsequently as a reward for the proper use of his natural powers" (*Outlines of Theology*).

According to Rome both natural righteousness and original righteousness were superadded gifts, not of the original nature of man. By his fall, man lost these superadded gifts but his proper nature, the *dona naturalia*—i.e., man's reason, conscience, will, and moral ability—remain intact. Thus, man's fall and consequent depravity are not total. Man still has the free will with which Adam was created, and is capable of good works, while still in his unregenerate state (Council of Trent, session 6, can. 5, 7). He may dispose himself to grace; and he is not blameworthy for his mere concupiscence.* The foundation of

Rome's entire view of works in the salvation of sinners is thus laid in her view of the original constitution and fall of man.

The Reformed View

The *Westminster Confession of Faith* gives a beautiful statement of the Biblical doctrine of Adam's creation in holiness and of his fall into sin, thus laying a solid foundation for the doctrine of a salvation that is all of grace, through the atoning merits of Christ, received by faith without works:

"God…created man, male and female, with reasonable and immortal souls, endued with knowledge, righteousness, and true holiness, after his own image, having the law of God written in their hearts, and power to fulfil it; and yet under a possibility of transgressing, being left to the liberty of their own will, which was subject unto change. Besides this law written in their hearts, they received a command not to eat of the tree of the knowledge of good and evil; which while they kept, they were happy in their communion with God, and had dominion over the creatures.…By this sin they fell from their original righteousness, and communion with God, and so became dead in sin, and wholly defiled in all the faculties and parts of soul and body" (chap 4, sec. 2; chap. 6, sec. 2).

CONCUPISCENCE

Lust.

The church of Rome uses the term to speak of the natural tendency of the lower appetites in human nature to rebel against the higher powers of reason and conscience. This tendency existed even in unfallen man and still exists in fallen man. The tendency is not in itself sin and becomes sin only when the will acts upon it. Thus, in Roman Catholic theology, concupiscence is not sin, but is the fuel or occasion of sin.

Cardinal Bellamine defined Rome's rejection of the opposing Reformed doctrine: "The whole controversy is whether that corruption of nature and especially concupiscence *per se* and of its own nature, as it is found in the baptized and justified is properly original sin. This Catholics deny." Thomas Aquinas made concupiscence a consequence of original sin, not itself part of original sin. The Council of Trent taught that justification removes original sin from the baptized. It does not remove concupiscence. Therefore, concupiscence is not part of original sin.

Rome's logic is faulty here and her soteriology* even worse. How original sin can be actually removed and yet its consequences remain is something of a mystery. The root of Rome's error is her rejection of justification* as a forensic act, and her insistence on confounding it with regeneration.* Her whole scheme of salvation necessitates a view of the fall that does not leave man with an inherently depraved and sinful nature. If she accepted concreated holiness* she would have to abandon her views of sin and human ability, and the role of works in obtaining salvation.

The simple answer to Rome's theory of concupiscence is the plain teaching of Paul in Rom 7:7, 8; Col. 3:5. According to the Romans passage, sin works itself out in concupiscence; the law convicts us of the sinfulness of concupiscence. The statement to the Colossians bluntly numbers concupiscence with the other great sins of the flesh. No amount of sophistry can evade the force of this fact. According to God's law, concupiscence is sin, not merely fuel for sin.

CONCURSUS

A philosophical theory, produced by the schoolmen *(see Scholasticism),* which sought to explain the relation of God's providential operations and the activities of His creatures. *Previous concursus* was said to be the act of God exciting and determining His creatures to perform one act rather than another; *simultaneous concursus* was said to be the act of God concurring with them in the production of the act.

There is a division in Protestant thought, some accepting the idea of concurrence (e.g., Berkhof) and some rejecting it (e.g., Dabney, Hodge). The theory proceeds on the unprovable assumption that a creature cannot originate action. It is better simply to accept that God governs all His creatures and all their actions according to His purpose (Eph. 1:11), consistently with their nature and His excellence, without theorizing how He does so.

See **Providence.**

CONDIGNITY

The Roman Catholic church in its teaching on the subject of human merit* distinguishes between the merit of condignity and the merit of congruity.

The merit of condignity is the merit of works done after regeneration, by the aid of divine grace. Such works have a right to divine reward because of their intrinsic nature, not because of any promise or covenant.

The merit of congruity, on the other hand, belongs to those good works or dispositions which an unregenerate man may effect without the help of divine grace. It is said to be congruous, or fitting, for God to reward the person who exhibits such good works or dispositions, by infusing grace into his heart.

The teachings of Rome are deliberately confused and ambiguous in the exposition of this notion, but clearly the entire idea rests on a totally false and unscriptural doctrine of human merit.

CONDITIONAL DECREES

The theory that God has decreed that certain events will happen upon condition that some other events, which He foresees as possible but has not decreed, actually occur. For example, "Arminians, admitting that God certainly foreknows the acts of free agents as well as all other events, maintain that He absolutely decreed to create man; and foreseeing that man would sin, He

absolutely decreed to provide a salvation for all, and actually to save all that repent and believe; but that He conditionally decreed to save individual men, on the condition, foreseen but not foreordained, of their faith and obedience" (A. A. Hodge, *Outlines of Theology,* p. 170).

Such a theory is open to serious objections. It makes the absolute decree of God dependent upon the uncontrollable and changeable acts of His creatures. It renders the entire course of events covered by God's decree liable to change. An upholder of this theory usually replies that though God did not foreordain the free actions of His creatures, yet He infallibly foresaw them, and thus His decree is not liable to change. But "if God foresaw that a given man, in given circumstances, would act at a given juncture in a certain way, then God, in decreeing to create that very man and place him at that very juncture, did foreordain the certain futurition of that very event, and all of its consequences" (Hodge).

More simply, the theory postulates the possibility of fallen man originating faith apart from the decree and will of God (a fallacy, for faith is the gift of God, Eph. 2:8; Phil. 1:29), and altogether falls short of the Scripture declarations that God works all things according to the "good pleasure" and the "counsel of His own will" (Eph. 1:5, 11).

See **Decrees of God.**

CONDITIONAL IMMORTALITY

The belief that immortality is a gift conferred only upon believers and that the wicked are annihilated. *(See **Annihilation.**)*

CONFESSION (AURICULAR)

In Roman Catholic theology, auricular confession is a full and unreserved disclosure of sin, a self-accusation, to a human priest, who is claimed to have "the power of the keys,"* that is, the power to pardon or deny pardon for sin. If a mortal sin is not confessed it is not forgiven;

and if confession is wilfully omitted, it is sacrilege, with a consequently greater degree of guilt. The entire theory has no warrant in Scripture, which admits of no mediator between us and the "one mediator between God and men, the man Christ Jesus" (1 Tim. 2:5).

CONFESSION OF FAITH

1. Originally and basically, a public profession of a person's faith in Christ (1 Tim. 6:12).
2. A description of a formal statement of belief made by the Protestant church at or after the Reformation.

*See **Westminster Standards**.*

CONFIRMATION

The rite of full admission of baptized persons into the church by prayer and the laying on of hands. In the Greek church it is administered even to infants; in the Roman Catholic church to children usually between the ages of seven and twelve years old. In this rite a baptized person is alleged to receive confirmation of the supernatural life he received in baptism, by means of a fresh unction, or anointing, of the Holy Spirit.

The only claimed Biblical basis for the practice is found in Acts 8:12-17; 14:22; 19:5-6; 2 Cor. 1:21 and 1 John 2:20, 27. None of these has the slightest reference to anything like the rite of confirmation. In Acts 8:12-17 and 19:5-6, the reference is to the impartation of miraculous gifts by the apostles—something no one claims for confirmation. In Acts 14:22 Paul and Barnabas confirmed persecuted believers in their faith. They did so by their ministry. There is no ground for importing the innovation of late churchmen into the actions of Paul and Barnabas. The texts in 2 Cor. 1 and 1 John 2 make no reference to the rite of confirmation. They state the fact that every Christian has an anointing of the Holy Spirit and make no allusion at all to any ceremony of the church.

Though there is no support for the practice of confirmation in the New Testament church, it is widely used. Rome and the Greek churches make it a sacrament. To them a Christian is not complete until he has received confirmation. Considering it dangerous to die without it, the Greek church administers it with, or as soon as possible after, baptism. Since Rome does not usually confirm children for some years after their baptism she has a difficulty explaining how and why those who die baptized but unconfirmed are eternally saved. Her answer is that they are confirmed by death, because they cannot sin afterwards!

The Anglican church has always maintained the rite of confirmation. The early German Reformers rejected it entirely, but in the 17th century it was reintroduced into Lutheranism as a renewal of the baptismal covenant. Some Reformed churches also practise it in this way.

The danger is that the practice of confirmation tends to become part of a sacramentalist view of salvation and is injurious to a truly evangelical presentation of the way of salvation. This is clear from the language of the Church of England that a child should be confirmed "so soon as he can say the Creed, the Lord's Prayer, and the Ten Commandments in the Vulgar tongue, and is further instructed in the Church Catechism set forth for that purpose."

CONGREGATIONALISM

The theory of church government which holds that
1. Each individual congregation has a divine right to entire independence in the regulation of all its affairs;
2. The power of government and the right of regulating all the church's affairs are vested in the body of members, not in the office-bearers of the church. The former view has given rise to the term independency, while the latter has given rise to the term congregationalism, but the choice of terms is merely a matter of preference: they signify essentially the same thing.

*See **Brownists**; **Church (Government of)**.*

CONSANGUINITY

See **Affinity**.

CONSCIENCE

The faculty of discerning between right and wrong, according to the law written on the heart (Rom. 2:14, 15). It may lie latent (e.g., in cases where a sinner is given up to carnal indifference for a time), but it clearly cannot be destroyed, as evidenced by the fact that its accusations form part of the torments of the lost.

Conscience cannot act apart from the intellect, and since this is darkened in fallen and unregenerate man, it continually delivers false decisions. "Notwithstanding this, however, the normal sense of the distinction between right and wrong, as an eternal law to itself, lies indestructible even in the most depraved breasts…when aroused to action, and when not deceived, as to the true state of the case, its language is eternally the same" (A. A. Hodge).

See **Understanding**.

CONSCIOUSNESS THEOLOGY

The school of Friedrich Schleiermacher (1767-1837), "the father of modern theology," which replaced the Bible with man's religious consciousness, his feeling of dependence, as the source of the knowledge of God. Thus God's self-revelation was made to give way to man's discovery of God. The starting point in this method is anthropological, making the knowledge of God depend on the intuition of man, with the result that the truth of the transcendence of God is lost (rather, it is the mind of the creature which is viewed as transcendent, for it transcends the need for an objective revelation of God from God). The final result of the consciousness theology of Schleiermacher is a form of pantheism, in which God and the universe are confounded.

Though the term "consciousness theology" is descriptive particularly of Schleiermacher's school of thought, it is applicable also as a proper description of every theological system which makes man its starting point or elevates the consciousness of man to the role of final arbiter in arriving at theological truth. Carried to its logical conclusion, this includes the system of Karl Barth, who, though trained in the Schleiermacher school, felt he had to repudiate it. In contrast to Schleiermacher's pantheistic tendency, Barth stressed that God was "The Wholly Other." But, when all is said and done, Barth (despite his claim to hold to a theology of the Word) did not make the Bible the source of all theology. Like other neo-orthodox theologians, he held that the Bible may become the word of God to individuals, but it is not to be looked upon as the word of God in itself. This is, in reality, exalting human consciousness to the same role as Schleiermacher.

In contrast to all forms of consciousness theology, orthodox reformed theology emphasizes that the only things we can say about God are the things which God has first said about Himself. Revelation is knowledge and truth; anything else is speculation and liable to be false.

See **Neo-Orthodoxy**.

CONSENSUS THEOLOGY

The practice, prevalent in ecumenical circles, of seeking to arrive at theological conclusions by agreement reached through a dialogue between previously disagreeing churches.

The theory behind the practice is that most theological differences arise out of misunderstanding the positions of other churches. Thus, the problem with Rome's doctrine of justification* is not that it is wrong or unscriptural; it is that Protestants have not properly understood it. By dialogue old barriers may be removed and a fresh statement of doctrine that is acceptable to the parties concerned may be formulated.

The reality, as distinct from the theory, is that the ecumenical practice of consensus theology is an exercise in compromise and deliberate double talk. Deep theological differences are covered over with a form of words that the partners in dialogue interpret in their various ways. Thus, the consensus is insubstantial. It is an agreement in equivocal expression or in outright rejection of the historic Protestantism.

See **World Council of Churches**.

CONSERVATIVE

One whose political or theological bent is toward conserving or retaining the philosophy or creed which he has received. Thus, in the political sphere, a conservative in a communist country would be an extreme left winger, while in a capitalist country he would be a right winger. In theological matters, a conservative Roman Catholic is one who wishes to retain the pre-Vatican II Tridentine form of Roman Catholicism, or one who wishes to retain strict obedience to church dogma and practice. A conservative Protestant, on the other hand, is one who wishes to retain the Reformation faith in its purity with special emphasis upon the authority and sufficiency of Scripture, the sole efficacy of the merits and mediation of Christ for the salvation of His people, justification* by faith alone, and the necessity of the regenerating action of the Holy Spirit to lead each individual to personal saving faith in Christ.

CONSUBSTANTIALITY

The doctrine that the Son of God is of the same substance as the Father. This was a vital part of the doctrine of the Trinitarian party which opposed the Arian heresy (see **Arianism**). The Nicene Creed set forth the truth that the Son was *homoousion,* * of the same substance as the Father; not merely *homoiousion,* of similar substance to the Father.

See **Trinity**; **Eternal Generation**.

CONSUBSTANTIATION

The word used to describe the view of Luther and the Lutherans that the actual body and blood of Christ exist "in, with and under" the bread and wine of the Lord's supper. Luther conceived this miracle to happen by the power of the Word and not by any priestly consecration, and he was careful to maintain that there was no change in the substance of the bread and wine (see **Mass; Transubstantiation),** and no permanent association between the elements and the corporeal presence of Christ. The theory of the real, corporeal presence of the body and blood of Christ in the Supper is rejected by most Protestants, who hold that Christ's body and blood are symbolically or spiritually received by faith.

See **Ubiquity.**

CONTEXTUALIZATION

A method of literary criticism that seeks to distinguish the meaning of the text of Scripture from the cultural and historical context in which it was given. The latter is regarded as the temporary garb in which God's revelation appeared in a particular place at a particular time. The theory is that we may change the garb to suit another culture in which we are called to preach the gospel.

Those who invented the term—Shoki Coe and Aharoan Sapezian, directors of the Theological Education Fund of the World Council of Churches—in their 1972 report, Ministry and Context, stated that contextualization takes account of "the process of secularity, technology and the struggle for justice which characterized the historical moment of nations in the third world."

The announced aim of contextualization is to relate the Biblical text to the modern context; but in reality, it has become the tool of choice for ecumenists and radical critics to make the gospel present the politically correct message of today, whether it is African Theology,* Black Theology,* or Liberation Theology. Even professed evangelicals have embraced contextualization, though in a modified form. They accept that the Bible text is culturally and historically conditioned. As a result they endorse Scripture translations targeted at different people in different cultural settings (even within the same nation) using the dynamic equivalency* method of translation.

The fundamental premise of contextualization is flawed. While the Bible is culturally and historically *mediated,* which is to say that God did not simply drop it down out of heaven but gave it through a developing historical process, first in Israel, and then in the early church, it is not culturally and historically *conditioned,* or limited. In other words, the *words* of Scripture are inspired, not merely the thoughts or the message. "Every word of God is pure" (Prov. 30:5). The statement of Christ in Matt. 5:18 does not describe the words of the law of God as dispensable, or as the changeable evidence of a different time and place.

It is only as we refuse to impose the figment of contextualization on the inspired word and preach it in all the world as it stands, that we can truly relate the text of Scripture to the context of the modern world. Only in this way, can we address the problems men face with the message they really need to hear—not the politically correct perversion of that message ecumenists and radicals wish them to hear.

CONTINGENT EVENTS

These are events whose immediate causes (1)are indeterminate or uncertain to us—e.g., as the throwing of dice; or (2) may be the act of a free agent—e.g., of the men who crucified Christ.

Those under (1) are not uncertain to God; nor are those under (2), for He foreknows them as contingent in their cause, i.e., dependent upon the will of a free agent (1 Sam. 23:11, 12; Acts 2:23; 15:18; Isa. 46:9, 10). From Scripture such as Mark 14:21, 30 we learn that actions which depend upon the will of a free agent are

divinely decreed and therefore certain to come to pass.

CONVERSION

A turning to God. The word has been employed in two senses by theologians:
1. In a wide sense, to signify both the change of nature and the exercise of that nature when it is changed. This change of nature is more properly termed regeneration.
2. In a strict sense, to denote the exercise of the new nature, subsequent to and because of regeneration, in faith and repentance, the constituent parts of conversion.

Such a dual usage led to confusion, a confusion still evident today in the practice of blurring the distinctions between regeneration and conversion. Thus, Francis Turretin suggested the terms *passive conversion,* by which he understood regeneration; and *active conversion,* by which he understood conversion proper.

The distinction between regeneration and conversion needs to be kept in mind. Regeneration is the cause of conversion, or our turning to God. Regeneration is totally God's work; man is passive in it. But man is active in conversion. Regeneration is a once-for-all act; conversion is the continuing activity of turning to God.

COSMOLOGICAL ARGUMENT
See **Arguments for God's Existence**.

COSMOLOGY

The study of the universe as an ordered whole. Biblical cosmology is the Biblical doctrine of the creation of the universe.

COUNTER REFORMATION

The response of the Roman Catholic church to the Protestant Reformation in the 16th century. In this response, Rome made much use of the Inquisition,* and in the decrees of the Council of Trent, produced a theological statement anathematizing the leading doctrines of the Reformation. The names of some prominent Roman Catholic "saints" stand to the fore in Rome's attack on Protestantism: Cajetan, Ignatius Loyola, Vincent de Paul, etc. The work of the Counter Reformation was, and is, carried on mostly by the order Loyola founded, the so-called Society of Jesus, the Jesuits.

COVENANT

Both the Hebrew *berith,* and the Greek *diatheke* denote a compact or an agreement between two parties, the obligations of which are mutually binding. See *Covenant Theology.*

COVENANT THEOLOGY

The theology of the Reformed churches, or rather the rediscovery of NT theology by the Reformed churches, which represents the whole of the Scriptures as being covered by two covenants.

The Covenant of Works

Genesis 2:16, 17 describes the covenant of works. The parties to this covenant were God and Adam. The promise of the covenant was life. The proviso was Adam's perfect obedience. The penalty of disobedience was death. *(See **Probation.**)* That God placed Adam in a covenant relation with Him is clear from Hosea 6:7: "They like men (Heb. *Adam*) have transgressed the covenant."

The Covenant of Mercy

This covenant was made from all eternity, and put into operation at the fall of man to bring salvation from sin and its penalty. It is generally subdivided in theological literature into the *covenant of redemption,* made between the Father and the Son, and the *covenant of grace,* which is based on the Covenant of Redemption, and which is made between God and His elect.

Covenant of Redemption. The covenant of redemption is sometimes called the "counsel of peace" *(pactum salutis),* a term derived from Zec. 6:13, though this verse does not address the subject of the covenant of redemption. Nevertheless the Scripture warrants the idea of such a covenant, speaking freely of the eternal nature of salvation and giving prominence to the promises made from eternity by the Father to the Son. In addition, Christ repeatedly referred to the commission He had received from the Father (John 5:30, 43; 6:38-40; 17:4-12). Here then are the elements of a covenant—contracting parties, promises, and a condition. In Luke 22:29 Christ said, "I appoint unto you a kingdom, even as my Father appointed unto me." The verb here is *diatithemi* (from which *diatheke,* "covenant" is derived) and means "to give by covenant or testament." Thus, Christ Himself speaks of the covenant between His Father and Himself.

Covenant of Grace. The covenant of grace is the outworking in time of the Covenant of Redemption. They are not two covenants, but two aspects of the one evangelical covenant of mercy. In the covenant of grace, God promises life eternal to His elect, on the ground of Christ's merits, by faith in Him.

Questions Raised by Covenant Theology

Introducing the memoirs of a great covenant theologian, Thomas Boston (1676-1732), Rev. G. H. Morrison wrote: "Every theology has its point of strain. And in the covenant system, so rich in intellectual satisfaction, one point of strain must be the inter-relation of the covenants. Was the moral law in the covenant of grace? Was the covenant between God and Christ the very same as that between God and Adam? And does the believer accept the moral law out of the hand of God the Creator or God the Redeemer?...Sooner or later [these questions] must be asked and answered by every student of the covenant theology."

Answers Given by Covenant Theology

Covenant theology addresses these questions as follows:

The covenant of mercy does not ignore, relax (at least as to its right to fulfilment), or abrogate the law of God which formed the basis of the covenant of works. Rather it made provision to fulfil and completely satisfy the law with regard both to its precept and its penalty.

That provision was and remains the vicarious obedience unto death of the Lord Jesus Christ. He met His people's double obligation to the law of God. He lived and died and rose again for them. In the terms of the covenant, He and His people are one. He is the head; they are the body. He took their guilt so that they might receive His righteousness.

What is, for believers, a covenant of pure grace, is for Christ, in one respect, a covenant of works; for it depends entirely upon His perfect obedience. It is also, of course, a covenant of grace, in that only free grace could appoint and accept Christ's vicarious obedience on behalf of believers.

Covenant theology maintains that the Mosaic economy was an administration of the covenant of grace. God never intended the moral law to be a way of salvation for sinful Israelites. He did not teach or offer the Jews salvation by works. When He gave the decalogue* He also gave the ceremonial sacrificial system, which plainly pointed to "the Lamb of God" who alone could take away sin.

Thus there is a deep sense of continuity between the OT and the NT. The differences are those between types and their fulfilment, between shadows and their substance. It is a matter of historical and spiritual development. But both OT and NT present the same redemptive purpose of God, the same way of salvation, and the same great eschatological hope.

Both Testaments present these truths in terms of "the everlasting covenant." This covenant was successively proclaimed throughout the OT (Gen. 3:15; Gen. 9; Gen. 12), afterwards becoming a national covenant. According to the NT, believers are reckoned in the same covenant as OT saints

(Rom. 4; Gal. 3; Heb. 8 with Jer. 31). In all cases, salvation is only on the ground of the blood and righteousness of Christ.

Though the same covenant of mercy operates in both the OT and the NT, in the NT it is called a *new* and *better* covenant, because in the OT it was administered by Moses the servant, whereas in NT times it is administered personally by Christ the Son (Heb. 3:5, 6).

CREATION

Only God is eternal; therefore, every other being and thing had a beginning in time. The Biblical record of creation is the revealed truth of God regarding the beginning of all these temporal things. "In the beginning God created the heavens and the earth" (Gen. 1:1). In this one sentence is summed up the whole truth on the subject.

The Biblical Doctrine

1. Nothing in the material universe is eternal.
2. God created all things in heaven and earth.
3. In this creation, He brought into existence that which before had no existence.
4. Thus, *creation,* properly speaking, is the doctrine that by His own will and word, the eternal, sovereign, and almighty God called into existence such things as He pleased, without the use of preexisting materials *(see Ex Nihilo).* "Through faith we understand that the worlds were framed by the word of God, so that things which are seen were not made of things which do appear" (Heb. 11:3). From this, it is evident that the entire material universe, in all its parts, is neither uncaused, nor self-caused, nor accidentally caused. It is God-caused.

Evolutionary Theory

Such a statement at once brings us into conflict with the theory of evolution, for at the bottom of that theory lies the notion that something other than God is eternal. One eminent scientist put it this way: "In the beginning…hydrogen!" From such an inauspicious beginning, all other things are said to have evolved, following a course which was not predetermined by any rational power but which nevertheless became more and more complex.

Such, in the most basic terms, are the two views of the origin of things—though, in truth, what God reveals cannot be termed a "view," and what man proposes to replace God's revelation is hardly worthy of being called a view, since that word carries in it the idea of something seen. Obviously rebellion against God is an expression of blindness, not of sight.

On account of man's wilful blindness, the evolutionary notion has gained wide acceptance as the scientific statement of the case, while the Biblical revelation has been shrugged off as blind religious faith, unworthy of serious consideration. That this is indeed because of wilful blindness is clear. By the plain testimony of God's word and by the concrete findings of modern physics, the theory of evolution is determined to be most unscientific. Physics has taught us that everything is energy in one form or another, and that as time goes on, the amount of energy available for useful work is becoming less and less. This is devolution, the opposite of evolution. Evolution is a nonstarter.

Of course, the only way we can really know anything about the origin of things is by divine revelation. No man was there to record the event for us. Science, properly so called, can deal only with what is observable and repeatable, and so cannot make any statements on the subject of origins, a subject outside its province. In the Bible, we have the divine revelation, and it gives us God's truth about His creation.

Six-Day Creation Period

All things in heaven and earth were made by the Lord in the space of six days.

"In six days the Lord made heaven and earth, the sea and all that in them is" (Ex. 20:11).

Ponder this statement carefully. It includes the record of the creation of angels,* the creation of the material universe, the creation of the world and all in it, and the creation of man. Look again at the statement: it shows that the fossils in the earth cannot be dated before the six-day creation—for the creatures now fossilized are included in the description "all that in them is."

The Gap Theory. This fact will help us to evaluate a popular theory that there is a vast period of time between the first and second verses of Genesis chapter one, the "gap theory," as it is known. Many Christians use this supposed gap (of millions or even billions of years) as an escape route from the "findings" of modern science, especially of modern geology.

Geologists and paleontologists (fossil experts) maintain that fossils in certain strata of the earth's crust are millions of years old and certainly predate Adam. How can we explain these fossils? As noted, many Christians use the gap theory and, as one eminent Ulster preacher said, "You can stuff all the fossils you like in there!"

But can you? Are we to allow the theory of infidel scientists that there were men on the earth before Adam? To harmonise our thoughts with the ill-founded theories of unbelievers, are we to repudiate or modify the plain statement of the Scripture that Adam was the first man? And what is to become of the assertion of Exodus 20:11, which insists that all things in heaven and earth date from the same six-day creation? According to this verse, the oldest created thing can be only a maximum of five days older than Adam.

So, how do we answer the claims of geologists? Simply that they have their dates all wrong. They have adopted wrong premises, and they have made their calculations on a set of wrong (and totally unsupported) presuppositions. Every dating method of evolutionists is an exercise in circular reasoning. It says in effect, "We assume that evolution is true and we produce this assumption as proof that evolution is true!"

The Days of Creation. Were the six days of creation real days or prolonged, indefinite periods of time? Some, noting that the word *day* in Scripture does not always refer to a 24-hour day, hold that the days of Genesis chapter one are merely periods of indefinite length. To this we may briefly reply:

First, on the face of it, it must appear strange to any candid reader that the thought of millions and billions of years should be conveyed by the statement, "In six days the Lord made heaven and earth."

Second, nothing in the Scripture narrative of creation leads us to look on the days of Genesis chapter one as indefinite periods of time. The interpretation of *yom,* "day," as *aeon,* "age," is warranted by neither the plain sense of the passage nor Hebrew usage.

Third, there is plenty to suggest that the six days were just what they are called, "days." For example, they were divided into evening and morning—how may that with justice be treated in a metaphorical sense? Furthermore, it is indisputable that at least some of the six days of creation in Genesis chapter one were 24-hour periods, for after the creation of the sun, moon, and stars, the Bible explicitly states that the sun ruled the day and the moon the night—a statement that cannot refer to anything but a twenty-four hour day. Once this is admitted, the introduction of any other meaning for the days of creation is purely arbitrary.

Finally, the language of Exodus 20: 9-11 is conclusive. We are to keep one day out of seven as a day of rest from work, because that is what God did in creation. How can anyone suggest that the use of the word *day* in this text is anything less than strict? The language of Scripture could not be plainer: in six days

God made all things in heaven and in earth, the entire universe of created things.

The Creation of Man. The crown of God's earthly creation was man. He was the immediate creation of God, not the last link in an evolutionary chain. "God created man in his own image, in the image of God created he him; male and female created he them" (Genesis 1:27). From this one human pair—Adam and Eve—the entire human race is descended.

The Image of God. They were created "in the image of God." Diverse theories and extravagant notions as to the meaning of this phrase abound. The Scriptures themselves must be their own interpreter. Two NT references will throw light on the true meaning: "Be renewed in the spirit of your mind; and…put on the new man, which after God is created in righteousness and true holiness (Eph. 4:23, 24).

"And [ye] have put on the new man, which is renewed in knowledge after the image of him that created him" (Col. 3:10).

From these, along with the Genesis account, we may confidently affirm that the "image of God" means that:

1. Man was created as a rational soul. These texts emphasize man's capability of knowing God. This capability denotes that man is by creation a rational, personal, and moral spirit, capable of being subject to the moral government of his Creator.

2. Man was created as a perfect being, with knowledge (the proper understanding of revealed truth and of his own position relative to God), righteousness (a full obedience to the law of God written on his heart), and true holiness (an inclination of will towards God as his chief end; an inbuilt love of God).

3. Man was created with dignity and authority over the earthly creation (Genesis 1:28).

Viewed in this way, we can see that the "image of God" in man has been sadly marred by the fall.* Fallen man still retains the ruins of the rationality conferred on him at his creation and is still a morally responsible agent, but he no longer has a proper apprehension of truth—especially of his own relationship to God. Fallen man automatically thinks of himself as self-governing and self-contained, capable of passing judgment on what God has revealed: he is now blind (2 Cor. 4:4)—and is both ungodly and unrighteous (Rom. 1:18). His dominion over the earthly creation has also suffered. Earth is in revolt against him, and he has, in many ways, sunk lower than the brute creation (Isa. 1:3).

On the other hand, unfallen man could not look at anything within himself or in the creation around him without seeing evidence of the true God.

Unfallen Man's View of Creation. "The heavens declare the glory of God; and the firmament showeth his handiwork" (Ps. 19:1). "The invisible things of him from the creation of the world are clearly seen, being understood by the things that are made" (Rom. 1:20).

Having been created in knowledge and true holiness, unfallen man could not consider interpreting anything—either himself or any other part of creation—as fallen men do. Fallen men, vainly imagining themselves to be free and independent beings, set up their own intelligence as the final judge of what is to be believed or rejected. Thus, we have the spectacle of "intelligent" men using the facts of the very creation which declares God's glory to "prove" that there is no Creator, no God.

Unfallen man could never have attempted such an interpretation. Around him was a perfect natural revelation; within him was the law of God written on his heart, and an in-built holiness of will and enlightenment of understanding. He knew that God was his Creator. He did not merely assemble a lot of *pros* and *cons* and sit in judgment on the facts, giving it as his probable opinion that God was his Creator. No. He could no more think of himself or anything else apart from God than he could breathe without air. Adam knew himself to be God's creature,

dependent on, and subject to, Him, and that his continued happiness consisted in his continued acceptance of this fact.

This Biblical view of man's primitive state is of the utmost importance in the study of the doctrine of the fall. Too many people make the fall a mere upset of man's moral balance, whereas it was a total wrecking of a holy disposition of will and its replacement with one of rebellion and ungodliness. Following the fall, the light of God's revelation in nature continued to shine, but by wilful sin man put out his own eyes, so that ever since he has been blind to the truth—and must remain that way unless God shines in his heart (2 Cor. 4:6) with supernatural grace.

God's Covenant with Man at His Creation. God revealed Himself to unfallen man, both in the creation around him and in his own nature within him. In addition, He entered into a Covenant of Life with man *(see **Covenant Theology),** the terms of which He clearly revealed. On the basis of that revelation and that covenant, God and man held sweet communion prior to the entrance of sin. (See Genesis 2:16-19).

Man's Probation. "The Lord God commanded the man, saying, Of every tree of the garden thou mayest freely eat; but of the tree of the knowledge of good and evil, thou shalt not eat of it; for in the day that thou eatest thereof thou shalt surely die" (Genesis 2:16, 17).

Clearly, Adam's state at creation was one of probation. He was holy, but he was not unchangeably confirmed in holiness. He was given every advantage by the manner in which he was created, but he was not infallibly determined by God's sustaining power to continue holy. He was left to the freedom of his own will and was placed under the Covenant of Works, the terms of which these two verses lay before us.

The Grand Design of All Creation

God created all things for His own glory. That was the original and ongoing design of the Creator. "Thou hast created all things, and for thy pleasure they are and were created" (Rev. 4:11).

John Calvin's opening words in his *Institutes of the Christian Religion* are: "Our wisdom, in so far as it ought to be deemed true and solid wisdom, consists almost entirely of two parts; the knowledge of God and of ourselves."

We cannot truly know ourselves until we know God. The knowledge of God is twofold: as Creator, and as Redeemer in Christ. The first of these is the knowledge with which Adam was created. To recover it, his sinful posterity must first be led to the knowledge of God as Redeemer in Christ, and then, as new creatures in Christ, they experience being "renewed in knowledge after the image of him that created them" (Col. 3:10).

CREATIONISM

A word used in two entirely different senses:

1. The Biblical belief that "God created all things out of nothing, by the word of His power, in the space of six days, and all very good" (Shorter Catechism). This doctrine of creation* is often referred to as creation *ex nihilo* ("creation out of nothing").

2. A theory that seeks to explain the origin of the individual soul. According to it, God creates a new soul every time a conception takes place and immediately unites it with the body. The soul is created sinless, but it becomes immediately sinful because of its contact with the inherited pollution and guilt of the body.

This theory claims the support of some texts of Scripture (e.g., Zech. 12:1; Isa. 42:5; Num. 16:22; Heb. 12:9) and has been widely accepted among Protestants, but it labours under great difficulties. For example, it fails to explain how guilt can belong to the body apart from the soul; it fails to come to terms with the doctrine of a finished creation (i.e., in the six days of the creation period); and it fails to explain how a holy God can continu-

ally create sinless souls, by His own act unite them with sinful bodies, and then account the guilt of that sinfulness to those souls. On the basis of this last consideration, it seems to make the guilt of the human soul something less than a matter of will and self-determined choice.

See the other theories of the soul which are advanced, **Preexistence** *and* **Traducianism.** *See also* in connection with creationism, **Mediate Imputation** and **Immediate Imputation.**

CREED

From the Latin *credere,* "to believe;" a statement of faith, not necessarily comprehensive or complete, but containing articles that cover matters that are fundamental and that have been called in dispute. The reference to dispute is important. "While the doctrine of the atonement must be reckoned a fundamental part of the apostles' doctrine, it is yet not in the Apostle's Creed as a doctrine. Hence some infer that it was not believed, though the more obvious inference would be that it was not disputed" (McClintock and Strong). When reference to The Creed is made, it is usually the Apostles' Creed* that is meant. The Apostles' Creed is one of the three great creeds of the ancient church, the others being the Athanasian Creed* and the Nicene Creed.*

CREED OF PIUS IV

Also known as the Profession of the Tridentine Faith, this is one of the authorized standards of the church of Rome. It was prepared in 1564 by Pius IV (pope from 1560-1565) immediately after the rising of the Council of Trent, to embody and express the substance of that council's decisions. Rome made this creed binding on all clergymen, doctors, teachers, heads of universities, and of all monastic orders, as well as on all who joined the church from other communions.

While it is difficult to find references to the Creed of Pius IV in post-Vatican II Roman Catholic literature, the Catechism of the Catholic church (¶ 192) teaches that such creeds cannot be superseded. Indeed, in view of Rome's dogma of papal infallibility the Creed of Pius cannot be abrogated, or even treated as a mere relic of history, a witness to bygone attitudes. Pius prepared the way for his creed by issuing a papal bull* that describes the Tridentine faith as "the present, true, real, and only distinctive public and authorized creed of the holy catholic and apostolic church, the mother and mistress of churches." So, while Rome may for cosmetic, ecumenical purposes make its points less stridently nowadays, the Creed of Pius remains her unchanged and unchangeable position. She still fully espouses and teaches every one of the points of the Tridentine faith it sets forth. The Creed of Pius IV is still her "true, real, and only distinctive public and authorized creed."

CRITICISM

Lower criticism is the scholarly investigation of the text of the books of the Bible, its transmission, and its purity *(see **Textual Criticism).***

Higher criticism is the scholarly investigation of the date, authorship, place, and circumstances of composition of the books of the Bible, together with a study of their purpose and nature.

Critics frequently have not lived up to the definition of their science. Critics of the text have often added to their scholarship their own anti-scriptural prejudices, for which they can offer no sound reason. Higher critics have become synonymous with rationalists, a name given to adherents of a system of philosophy which rejects the authority of the Bible as a divine revelation, exalting human reason as the only guide into truth. Rationalism is in effect the application of the development notion of the theory of evolution to religion.

While conservative scholars reverently base their investigations on an honest recognition of the inspiration, infallibility, and authority of the Bible, higher critics have always reduced it to a merely human level—though the passage of time and patient investigation has always proved the fallacy of their notions.

Old Testament Criticism

In the criticism of the OT, "documentary analysis" long held the affection of the critics, resulting finally in the Graf-Wellhausen theory or the *J E D P* * theory—the theory that the religion of Israel was not a special revelation, but developed naturally; that the patriarchs were not historical persons, but mythological characters; and that the Pentateuch is a patchwork of documents written by unknown men whose hand can be traced by their use of the divine names and other literary marks. Thus *J* used the name Jehovah, *E* used Elohim, *D* fused their work to produce Deuteronomy, and *P* was a very late priestly writer.

This high-flown theorizing was carried right through the OT, to deny the authenticity of the Psalms of David, the prophecies of Isaiah and Daniel, and much else. Though this theory has been rendered obsolete by the patient study of the whole procedure of deducing different documents by the use of the divine names, and by the discoveries of modern archaeology, it is still taught in many theological institutions.

The destruction of the Graf-Wellhausen theory has put a brake on many aspects of critical arrogance, but it has not rendered the naturalistic critic any more hospitable to the supernatural nature of the Bible. Hatred of the supernatural lies back of all the critics' theories, and the theory currently most favoured seeks to explain the Bible books by study of the *sitz im leben,* the life situation which gave rise to each bit of OT material. Thus it starts off by accepting that the OT Scriptures are merely the product of oral traditions which were put in writing at a late date, not a direct revelation from God. *(See Form Criticism.)*

New Testament Criticism

NT criticism betrays the same bias and has generally been carried out with a view to destroy confidence in the authenticity and historicity of the NT books *(see Myth; Tübingen School).* Again, such critical attempts have ended in failure, having nothing more than conjecture as their basis, while competent scholars have vindicated the integrity of the NT. However, another theory has emerged and has been used even by "evangelicals." This is the "priority theory," the notion that Matthew and Luke borrowed from Mark in writing their gospels. Critics go on to theorize that unknown documents which they label Q* (from *Quelle,* German for "source"), M, and L were also used by Matthew and Luke to produce their gospels. Such theorizing is endless. It presents human speculation run mad, but it still passes for sober criticism.

CRUX INTERPRETUM

A text of Scripture whose proper exegesis and interpretation is crucial to a proper Biblical understanding of the subject it deals with.

CULDEES

The name given to missionaries of the ancient Irish church who, in the sixth century, took the gospel to Scotland, England, and then many European countries. The word probably means "servant of God" and describes the reputation those early missionaries established among friends and foes.

Ireland had received the gospel through Patrick's great mission (probably 405-465). The churches he founded were independent of Rome, as may be seen from the fact that when the Pope sent Palladius to bring the Irish Christians into his fold, they (and probably Patrick personally) repulsed his advances. The recorded history of the Culdees shows that they arose and flourished in the church Patrick had founded.

In 563, with twelve associates, Columba (or *Columbkille,* as he is often called), who was both a prince and a minister of Christ, went to the Scottish island of Iona (then called I, or Hy). There he founded a monastery that became a notable college and training ground for further missionary outreach. Columba and his company evangelized the Picts. Then they worked in northern England. Soon their influence and success were felt in many parts of England.

The Culdees took the gospel to Europe also, ministering to Saxons and Normans, and establishing churches in various countries, including Germany. The Culdees were often ascetic. They built monasteries, but these were not like the Roman Catholic fraternities of Reformation times whose monks were often lazy, licentious, and luxurious. Often, Culdee monks were married men. They supported themselves through their own labour. While some remained single by choice, others raised families. There was no enforced celibacy.*

Culdee churches and missionaries were a witness against the growing corruption of the papal church. Thomas Scott (*Presbyterianism,* pp. 417-419) summarized their beliefs and practices:

"They maintained the exclusive authority of Scripture as a rule of faith. They rejected the Romish doctrines, ceremonies, and traditions. They did not believe in auricular confession, neither did they do penance, receive confirmation, or admit the heresy of celibacy and the sacramental efficacy of priestly matrimony. In common with all the northern Picts and Scots, they differed from the Romish practice in the observance of Easter. Their offices [rites] were Gallican and not Roman. They rejected also authoritative absolution, and confessed to God alone, believing God alone could forgive sins. They administered baptism in any water, and without the superstitious ceremonies of the Romish order. This is confirmed by Lanfranc, archbishop of Canterbury, who says they did not use consecrated chrism. They opposed also the doctrine of the real presence. They withstood the idolatrous worship of the Romanists. Culdean churches were dedicated to the holy Trinity and not to the blessed Virgin or any other saints. They neither prayed to dead men nor for them. The Irish never practised the service for the dead, till they were obliged to do so by the Council of Cashel, convoked by order of Henry II in 1172. The Culdees were also enemies to the doctrine of works and supererogation,* and held, as Claudius teaches, to the doctrines of justification* by faith only, of predestination* and of grace.* Their whole manner of celebrating divine ordinances was peculiar and opposed to the Romish rites. Romanists despised them for the nakedness of their forms of worship. They paid no respect to holy relics or to the mass. They would not receive Romish ordination. They were more willing to sacrifice their property than to receive the 'canonical rites according to the custom of the Roman and apostolical churches.' Bede also testifies that this difference not only affected the question of Easter, but that they held 'a great many other things contrary to ecclesiastical purity and peace.' This charge is repeated in the register of St. Andrews, where it is said, 'that those called Culdees lived more according to their own opinion and tradition of men than according to the statutes of the holy fathers.' When Boniface was sent from Rome, in order, if possible, to bring the Scots to a full obedience and conformity to Rome, he was opposed by several of the Scots Culdees, namely, Clemens and Samson, who openly withstood him and his design, which was to bring men into subjection to the pope and slavery to Rome by withdrawing them from obedience unto Christ. They charged the Romanists with being corrupters of Christ's doctrine. Such being their discordant

sentiments, it may be expected that the Romanists and the Culdees regarded each other with no greater love than do their successors, the Romanists and the Protestants of the present time. The Culdees, both in Ireland and in Scotland, refused to hold any religious communion or intercourse with the Romanists. According to Bede they esteemed the Romish system 'as of no account, and held no more communication with its abettors than with the heathen.'"

The Culdees continued to flourish for centuries. Rome made every attempt to bring them into submission to the pope. At times she used force, at times she used seduction. She exerted every kind of pressure to achieve her aim. Culdees were deprived of their privileges. They were dispossessed of their property. "They were driven from one retreat after another, until at length their light was extinguished, by the wide-spreading and gross darkness which covered the nations of the earth" (Scott, p. 420).

Some Culdees existed as late as the early 14th century but they were only the isolated remains of a once great movement. In Ireland, the church which produced the Culdees remained staunchly independent of Rome until the 11th century, when it began to weaken. Pope Adrian IV (the only English man to become pope) gave Ireland to Henry II of England. Pope Alexander III, Adrian's successor, confirmed the gift. When in 1171, Henry commenced the English occupation of Ireland, the Irish bishops, assembled at Cashel, recognized him and his successors as the lawful kings of Ireland. In doing so, they acknowledged the pope's right to dispose of nations and their thrones. The subjugation of the Culdees and their long-independent church was complete.

CULT

Latin *cultus,* "worship"; etymologically, a system of religious worship, homage, or devotion. Theologically, it is used of those systems that profess to be Christian but that are antagonistic to the basic doctrines of Scripture, as for example, Mormonism, Russellism, etc.

Inherent in cult worship is the elevation of some authority to or beyond an equality with the Biblical revelation. Frequently, this takes the form of some special revelation claimed by the cult leader or some peculiar interpretation of Scripture that is binding on the adherents of the cult. The natural result is either a denial of Biblical authority, tacit or expressed, or a practical embargo on the freedom to ascertain and accept what the Bible teaches. Cults are naturally exclusive. Usually truth belongs to them alone. Salvation is found in them alone. They identify themselves as *the* church.

Thus a cult is, in effect, idolatry posing as Christianity, for, whatever protestations are made to the contrary, worship based on a repudiation of fundamental Bible truth is idolatry.

CULTURAL MANDATE

Also termed the Creation Mandate; God's original placement of Adam as ruler over all the earthly creation (Gen. 1:26-28). The creation mandate was given to unfallen Adam in the covenant of works *(see Covenant Theology),* and Adam broke that covenant by his fall.*

Some Reformed theologians argue that the covenant relationship was restored in Christ for all His elect and that the fulfilment of the covenant is their great commission—viz., to subdue all things and all nations to Christ. R. J. Rushdoony argues for this position in his *Institutes of Biblical Law.* He insists that there is no Biblical evidence that the creation mandate has ever been abrogated. By making the creation mandate the believer's and the church's cultural mandate, such theologians extend the whole idea of evangelism beyond the winning of souls to the redemption and reclamation of every part of society, even including its entertainment industry, so building the kingdom of God on earth.

See *Reconstructionism.*

CULTUS

From the Latin *cultus* meaning "worship;" veneration or worship ascribed by the Roman Catholic church to one who has been *beatified* (in this case the *cultus* is limited to a locality such as a diocese or religious order; see **Beatification**) or *canonized* (in this case the *cultus* is made public, or open, to be practised throughout the Roman Catholic church; see **Canonization**).

CUNEIFORM

From Latin *cuneus,* "wedge;" wedge-shaped lettering impressed in clay with a stylus, or cut into wood or stone with a chisel.

Cuneiform writing has been dated as far back as 3400-3200 B.C. and was the most widespread writing system in the ancient Middle East before the spread of the Phoenician alphabet. In its earliest form, the lettering was not really cuneiform, or even lettering in the strict sense. It was pictographic, i.e., each sign was a pictorial representation. In due time, the Akkadians adopted the system to represent syllables, and used it for trade, bills, receipts, etc. Ugaritic texts display a further adaptation, with the development of an alphabetic system which, though using wedge-shaped writing on clay tablets, is not related in form or vocalization to the cuneiform of Mesopotamia. The Amarna Tablets are an example of Akkadian cuneiform, and the Ras Shamrah texts of the Ugaritic.

The decipherment of cuneiform took a long time, but the work of C. F. Grotefend, Henry Rawlinson, Edward Hincks, and Felicien de Saulcy finally led to success in understanding it.

CURSIVE

The running or connected script in which later (ninth century and later) NT MSS* were copied.

D

DEAD SEA SCROLLS

While manuscripts and scrolls have been unearthed in three different locations near the Dead Sea, the name *Dead Sea Scrolls* usually refers to the more than 400 scrolls discovered since 1947 in caves at Qumran, on the northwest shores of the sea. About 100 of the scrolls are Biblical, containing all the OT books except Esther. They apparently formed part of an ancient library of a community that flourished at Qumran between 100 B.C. and A.D. 68.

One far-reaching result of the study of the scrolls is the general correspondence of their Hebrew text with the Masoretic text *(see Masora),* thus witnessing to the integrity of that text as a faithful representation of the ancient text.

*See **Textual Criticism of the Old Testament**.*

DEATH OF GOD THEOLOGY

A theory, or rather a series of theories, that gained widespread notoriety in the 1960's. It has been well named *Christian Atheism.* It is a repudiation of the Biblical representation of the transcendence* of God.

Soft Radicals

Some Death of God proponents, sometimes called "soft radicals," proceed from a neo-orthodox* Barthian position, and put quotation marks around the word *death.* Gabriel Vahanian for example, wrote, "This does not mean, obviously, that God himself no longer is, but that, regardless of whether he is or not, his reality, as the Christian tradition has presented it, has become culturally irrelevant" (Vahanian, *Wait Without Idols,* pp. 31-32).

According to Vahanian, the transcendent God has been brought down to the level of a merely immanent being—i.e., He has been reduced to a cultural idol. He argues that "God dies as soon as he becomes a cultural accessory or a human ideal." Vahanian does not respond to this by returning to the Biblical presentation of God's transcendence. Rather, he adopts the paradox theology of Barth. The transcendent God can never be "objectified" or verified. He is "wholly other." Thus, though "we can no longer assume that God is, we may once again realize that he must be. God is not necessary, but he is inevitable. He is wholly other and wholly present. Faith in him, the conversion of our human reality, both culturally and existentially, is the demand he still makes of us" (ibid., p. 46). In this "soft" radical statement of God-is-dead theology, "the word *God* has perhaps outlived its usefulness owing to its associations with old idolatries" (J. Warwick Montgomery, *The Suicide of Christian Theology,* p. 82).

Hard Radicals

Others, who are decidedly "hard radicals," plainly teach the death of God in the sense that, even if He once existed, He is no more.

William Hamilton. William Hamilton, for example, wrote, "There is no way, ontological, cultural, or psychological, to locate a part of the self or a part of human experience that needs God." According to him, "there is no God-shaped blank within man." The conclusion is obvious: "We trust the world, not God, to be our need fulfiller and problem solver" (*The Christian Scholar,* XLVIII, "The Death of God Theology," p. 40). Strangely,

Hamilton argues that God who is not, and cannot be of use to us, may be enjoyed! So despite the death of God Hamilton continues to pray!

Paul M. Van Buren. Another hard radical, Paul M. Van Buren, goes much further. According to him, there is no God. Christianity is about man, not about God. Its God-language is merely a now outdated way of saying something about human life and history. This is particularly true in the case of Jesus Christ. Van Buren wrote, "One of the ways in which the New Testament writers speak about Jesus is in divine quasi-divine terms—Son of God, and what have you.…What I'm trying to do is to understand the Bible on a naturalistic or humanistic level, to find out how the references to the absolute and supernatural are used in expressing on a human level the understanding and convictions that the New Testament writers had about their world. For by using these large cosmological terms in speaking about this particular happening, this event—the history of Jesus—they were saying the most that they could say about this man. If a man in the first century had wanted to say of a certain person that he had given him an insight into what human life was all about, he would have almost normally said, 'That man is divine'" (Interview in the *New Yorker,* Nov. 13, 1965, p. 148).

Van Buren applies this secularization of the gospel to the Biblical record of Christ's death and resurrection. In *The Secular Meaning of the Gospel* he wrote, "Jesus of Nazareth was a free man in his own life, who attracted followers and created enemies according to the dynamics of personality and in a manner comparable to the effect of other liberated persons in history upon people about them. He died as a result of the threat that such a free man poses for insecure and bound men. His disciples were left no less insecure and frightened. Two days later, Peter, and then other disciples…experienced a discernment situation in which Jesus the free man whom they had known, themselves, and indeed the whole world, were seen in a quite new way. From that moment, the disciple began to possess something of the freedom of Jesus. His freedom began to be 'contagious'" (p. 134).

J. A. T. Robinson. The most popular presentation of this God-is-dead theology came from the Anglican bishop of Woolwich, J. A. T. Robinson, in his book *Honest to God.* According to Robinson, modern man can no longer accept the outdated myth of a God who is "up there," that is the transcendent God of the Bible. He adopts the inherently confused and self-contradictory notion of Paul Tillich, that God is not a supernatural Being but the "ground" or "depth" of all being. At best, this is either pantheism or atheism. It dogmatically tells us what God is—and yet it tells us nothing, for as critical philosophers have often pointed out, "If God is simply 'being itself' or 'the depth of being,' there is no point in talking about him at all, since this tells us nothing more than we knew before, namely, that the universe exists!" (Montgomery, p. 51).

Though Robinson's work gained popular notoriety, it irritated most critics because of its confused and ambiguous character. J. I. Packer dismissed it as "a plateful of mashed-up Tillich fried in Bultmann and garnished with Bonhoeffer."

Thomas J. J. Altizer. As noted above, the common thread running through every type of God-is-dead theology is the rejection of the Biblical doctrine of the transcendence of God. During a debate between Thomas J. J. Altizer and John Warwick Montgomery at Chicago University, February 24, 1967, the moderator remarked that to Altizer "the notion of the transcendent God is such a horror."

Altizer clearly accepted the characterization and went on to state, "It's no longer possible for Western man to know the transcendent God as a source of life or joy. Instead transcendence appears either as a wholly alien oppressive realm or as a wholly abstract and empty realm....I would say that the only form of transcendence which we can actually know, which we can live, is either an alien or an empty one. It is precisely for this reason that the Christian can know the death of God as gospel, as joy, as liberation" (Montgomery, pp. 160-161).

Altizer's frank statement unmasked the real thrust of the God-is-dead theology. It is just another attempt by men who want to be autonomous, independent of the absolute God. To them, submission to the transcendent God of Scripture is "a horror." Existential theologian John MacQuarrie put the matter bluntly: "Our modern scheme of thought affords no place for another being, however exalted, in addition to the beings we encounter within the world" (*Theology Today,* July 1965, p. 200).

God-is-dead theologians have no place for a transcendent God in their thinking, so they deny His existence. If God and their scheme clash, God must die, not their scheme. Yet they obviously feel constrained to deal with the Biblical data, especially concerning the Lord Jesus Christ. Those data defeat every scheme proposed by those whom Montgomery called "morticians of the Absolute."

The modern secular "understanding" of the apostolic documents amounts to a rejection of them, not an honest or even plausible exposition of them. However, ignoring them does not remove or invalidate them. They demand to be heard, and they must be heard. Their data affirm—and the witnesses to the ministry, death, and resurrection of Jesus Christ confirm—that the transcendent "God was in Christ, reconciling the world unto himself" (2 Cor. 5:19). "The fool hath said in his heart, there is no God" (Ps. 14:1). The folly of atheism is outdone only by the folly of so-called Christian atheism.

DECALOGUE

The Ten Commandments. The Hebrew of Exod. 34:28 and Deut. 10:4 literally means "the ten words." The Greek translation was *hoi deka logoi,* which gives us our word *decalogue.* The decalogue is usually termed the *Moral Law,* as distinct from the ceremonial and the civil law of Israel. It is fully recorded in Exod. 20:3-17 and Deut. 5:7-21.

According to Exod. 20:1, 18-19 and Deut. 5:4 the Lord actually *spoke* the decalogue to the nation of Israel gathered at Mt. Sinai. Hebrews 12:19, 20 confirms this. At Sinai the Jews heard "the voice of words; which voice they that heard intreated that the word should not be spoken to them any more: (for they could not endure that which was commanded)."

After speaking it to the children of Israel, the Lord wrote the Ten Commandments on two tables of stone (Exod. 31:18). On discovering Israel's sin in making the golden calf, Moses smashed these tables (Exod. 32:19). The Lord commanded him to prepare two new tables of stone and promised "I will write upon these tables the words that were in the first tables, which thou brakest" (Exod. 34:1). In time, at God's command, these tables were placed in the Ark of the Covenant within the Holy of Holies in the tabernacle (Deut.. 10:1-2).

Some believe that each stone contained all ten commandments, but most hold that there was a division, though there have been competing views as to where the division came. Augustine held that there were three commands on the first stone and seven on the second. The Reformed churches usually speak of the first table of the law as comprising our duty to God (commandments one through four) and the second as comprising our duty to man (five through ten). This follows the view of Origen that the second commandment is, "Thou shalt not make unto thee any graven image" and the tenth is, "Thou shalt not covet thy neighbour's house...nor anything that is thy neighbour's."

Lutherans and Roman Catholics combine the second commandment with the first and make up the number ten by dividing the tenth commandment. The fact that Deut. 5:21 inverts the order of the clauses of Exod. 20:17 would seem to confirm that the commandment against covetousness is one and indivisible.

As an expression of the moral law, the Decalogue is permanently binding on all men. The moral law was evidently given to our first parents, written on their hearts at their creation. The positive command of Gen. 2:17, "Of the tree of the knowledge of good and evil, thou shalt not eat of it," would be incomprehensible if it did not rest on the basis of moral law. Adam was to love God with all his heart. This is the first and great commandment of the law because it encompasses all our duty to God required by the law. Clearly, Adam was to have no other gods before the Lord—hence the great wickedness of receiving Satan's lie, "Ye shall be as gods." He received the Sabbath at his creation, his very first day on earth being the first Sabbath. He was created "in righteousness and true holiness" (Eph. 4:24). Righteousness in man is conformity to God's law, as holiness is conformity to His nature.

The Lord maintained His moral law through the times of the patriarchs. The law of the Sabbath (Gen. 2:3), the law against idolatry (Gen. 35:3), the law of parental authority (Gen. 9:25; 18:19), the law against murder (Gen. 9:5), and the law against adultery (Gen. 12:18f; 20:3, 9), were all known before Moses.

The Lord repeated His law through His prophets (Isa. 1:10; Mal. 4:4). He established it in Christ, who called attention to its abiding force (Rom. 7:12, 22; 1 Cor. 9:21).

The Lord has written His law on the hearts of all men (Rom. 2:14, 15) and He assures us that He puts it into the minds of believers and writes it in their hearts (Heb. 8:10).

All this testifies to the permanence of the moral law. The Ten Commandments have never been abrogated. True, Christians are

no longer "under the law but under grace." But *law* here means the law as a covenant, or as a basis of justification and acceptance, not as a command to moral living that is incumbent on every Christian. To hold that He has abrogated the law as a rule of life for His people runs contrary to Christ's plain statement of purpose in Matt. 5:17. It also makes nonsense of God's own description of what He does when He saves sinners: He says He puts His laws in their minds and writes them in their hearts (Heb. 8:10).

Nevertheless, salvation is not by law or by legal obedience or observance. The law exposes sin (Rom. 3:20). It condemns sin and brings sinners under its curse (Gal. 3:10). It requires a total, positive obedience, and calls for the full infliction of punishment on all lawbreakers. At first sight, this would seem to render salvation impossible for sinners. It clearly does, if sinners must do anything to merit salvation. But they do not. That is the glory and genius of the gospel of grace. Christ, as a true man, rendered a perfect obedience to the law and so provided a perfect righteousness which God imputes to all who believe in Him (Rom. 5:18-19). Furthermore, Christ paid the penalty of the broken law for His people by His atoning death on Calvary (Gal. 3:13; 2 Cor. 5:21). In this way, the law is perfectly satisfied and honoured, both as to its precept and its penalty. This merit of the obedience and oblation of Christ becomes ours by grace through faith, without any meritorious action on our part (Rom. 3:28; 4:5; 5:1). Even the faith that receives justification is the gift of God on the merits of Christ (Phil. 1:29). It was in the light of all this that Paul could write, "Do we then make void the law through faith? God forbid: yea, we establish the law" (Rom. 3:31).

DECISIONAL REGENERATION, DECISIONISM

The Arminian belief, popular among many evangelicals and Fundamentalists,* that faith precedes regeneration and is the autonomous decision or choice of the human will. In this view it is the unregenerate man who decides to exercise faith and is regenerated only after, and as a result of, this action.

The theory is unscriptural and illogical. It is unscriptural because Rom. 8:7 clearly shows the impossibility of an unregenerate man doing anything to please God or originate good. It is unscriptural and illogical because it presumes that in his unregenerate state fallen man is not so depraved that his will is morally incapable of originating spiritual good.

The Scripture refutation is plain. Regeneration precedes faith; it does not follow it. 1 Pet. 1:2: "Elect according to the foreknowledge [i.e., predetermined counsel] of God the Father, through sanctification of the Spirit, unto obedience and sprinkling of the blood of Christ." The obedience of faith follows the work of the Spirit. While saving faith does include a decision or choice to have Christ as Saviour—a decision that is truly ours—it is the decision of the new man, not the old man. The new man is the product of the regenerating act of the Spirit.

DECLARATORY ACT

An enactment by the highest court of a Presbyterian denomination clarifying or adjusting that church's attitude to its confessional standards (see **Westminster Standards**). The impetus for such an act has usually been a desire to weaken the confessional faith in predestination* and election.*

The first declaratory act was passed by the Synod of the United Presbyterian Church in Scotland in 1879. The Free Church of Scotland passed a similar act in 1892. In both cases, ministers and elders subscribing the *Westminster Confession of Faith* received liberty of interpretation in matters that did not enter into the substance of the faith, or of the *Reformed Faith,* in the Free Church act. Critics of the acts pointed out that the attempted balance between the Calvinism of the old standards and an Arminian* or Amyraldian* description of universal love already compromised the Reformed faith. Indeed, they charged, the new formulae could not be honestly interpreted as anything other than a repudiation of the old faith of the church.

Such considerations did not appear to be of concern to the United Presbyterian Church—its decision to adopt the declaratory act was unanimous and practically undebated. By contrast, the Free Church suffered deep division, resulting in a secesssion and the founding of the Free Presbyterian Church of Scotland.

Declaratory acts have since been adopted by the Church of Scotland and the Presbyterian Church in the U.S.A. In these cases also, the purpose of the acts was to weaken the predestinarian theology of the Westminster standards.

DECREES OF GOD

"God's eternal purpose according to the counsel of His will, whereby for His own glory, He hath foreordained whatsoever comes to pass" (*Shorter Catechism,* Q. 7).

Scripture shows that God's decree (for it is better to think of one all-comprehending purpose) relates to all events: Eph. 1:10, 11; Acts 15:18, 17:26; Job 14:5; Isa. 46:10. The free acts of man (Eph. 2:10), and even their wicked actions (Acts 2:23; 4:27, 28; Ps. 76:10; Prov. 16:4) are included, as well as what men call accidental events (Prov. 16:33). In a word, God's decree comprehends all things in heaven and earth (Dan. 4:34, 35).

God's decrees are said to be

1. *Free,* because He was moved solely by his own good pleasure;

2. *Sovereign,* because, "while they determine absolutely whatever occurs without (i.e., outside of) God, their whole reason and motive is within the divine nature, and they are neither suggested nor occasioned by, nor conditional upon, anything whatsoever without him" (A. A. Hodge);

3. *Absolute,* that is, unconditional *(see Conditional Decrees),* because they are not dependent upon conditions that are not themselves determined by divine decree; and **4.** *Efficacious,* because they infallibly determine the certainty of the future events decreed. Theologians usually subdivide God's efficacious decrees into two classes:

a. Those that are efficacious in the strict sense of the word; i.e., those relating to events that God determined to effect through necessary causes or His own immediate agency;

b. Those that are permissive *(see Permissive Decree);* i.e., those relating to things that He has determined to allow created free agents to effect.

In both cases, the certain futurition of the event decreed is determined, but sinful creatures are responsible for their own sins. God is not the author of sin. The Biblical doctrine of the divine decree represents God as decreeing that sin should eventuate as the free act of man, not by any divine agency or inducement.

DECRETALS (FALSE)

Also called the *Isidorian Decretals.* These false decretals are a collection of ecclesiastical laws that, in part, profess to be the writings of ancient Bishops of Rome, in which the office and dignity of the pope are greatly exalted. Every one of the writings of the ancient bishops is a forgery, but Rome made effective use of them and the spurious Donation of Constantine* in establishing her papal claims. The forgery has long been admitted by Roman Catholic historians.

DEISM

A kind of rationalism that flourished in England from the mid 17th century until the mid 18th century. It looked upon God as the absolute, self-existent, infinite Spirit, but denied that He had ever revealed Himself to men or that He ever intervened in the natural order of things.

118

DEITY OF CHRIST

The doctrine of the person of Christ is basic to the entire revelation of Bible Christianity. Error in this department is so serious as to make the one who holds it an heretic. To go wrong here is to go wrong everywhere for every other doctrine of grace is inextricably bound up with the doctrine of Christ's person. The distinguishing mark of most false cults is their denial of Christ's essential and eternal deity. It is little wonder that the fundamental statement of the Christian faith given by the inspired Apostle Paul in 1 Tim. 3:16 commenced with, "God was manifest in the flesh."

The following four lines of argument will establish the deity of Christ as a Biblical truth:

The Divine Name Given to the Lord Jesus Christ

In reference to 1 Tim 3:16, "God was manifest in the flesh," some claim that the force of this text is diminished because the most ancient Greek manuscripts read *who* instead of *God.* In fact, evidence for *God* in the original text is overwhelming *(see Textual Criticism of the New Testament).* The testimony of 1 Tim. 3:16 to Christ's deity stands firm. He is "God manifest in the flesh."

John 1:1 says, "In the beginning was the Word, and the Word was with God, and the Word was God." In verses 14-18, the Word is identified as Jesus Christ. No testimony could be clearer to His eternal and essential deity.

In Romans 9:5 Christ is called "God over all blessed forever." Some modern translations change the punctuation of this verse and commence a new sentence to make the verse read, "Of whom as concerning the flesh Christ came. May God Who is over all be blessed for ever." Thus, what is a clear testimony to the deity of our Saviour is made into a doxology. But this is unwarranted. In the words of an eminent German scholar, "Romans 9:5 cannot according to the Greek Language be read as a doxology." Here again, Christ is called God.

In Isaiah 9:6 we have the prophecy of the Saviour's birth, and once again the name of God is given to Him. "Unto us a child is born, and unto us a son is given…and his Name shall be called…the Mighty God."

Jeremiah 23:5, 6 is a prophecy of Christ as "the righteous Branch, the King who shall reign and prosper." The name given to Him is "Jehovah our righteousness."

Revelation 1:8 reads, "I am Alpha and Omega, the beginning and the ending, saith the Lord, which is, and which was, and which is to come, The Almighty." There is no doubt that the Speaker is God Almighty. But He is further identified. The words "I am Alpha and Omega" are repeated in verse 11, and John, seeking to "see the voice that spake" (verse 12), identified the speaker as the Son of man (verse 13). To put matters beyond all doubt, the One who said, "I am the Lord Almighty" goes on to say, "I am he that liveth, and was dead, and behold, I am alive for evermore" (verse 18). It is clearly antichristian to deny the deity of Christ when the Lord Jesus Himself says, "I am the Almighty."

Jesus Christ Further Identified as Jehovah. In addition, there are frequent examples of what is said of "God" and "Jehovah" in the OT being applied directly to the Lord Jesus Christ in the NT. Consider the following:

Psalm 45:6 reads, "Thy throne, O God, is for ever and ever." Hebrews 1:8, 9 reveals that the Father addressed these words to the Son.

In Numbers 14:20-22 and Psalm 95:6-9 the Jews are said to have tempted Jehovah. In 1 Cor. 10:9 we are told that they tempted Christ.

In Psalm 102:25, 26 we are taught that Jehovah God (see vv. 1, 24) laid the foundations of the earth and that the heavens are the works of His hands. In Hebrews 1:10-12 we are told that it is the Son, the Lord Jesus, who did this.

In Joel 2:32 we read, "Whosoever shall call on the name of Jehovah shall be deliv-

ered." In Romans 10:13 this is quoted with reference to Christ (compare v. 9).

In Isaiah 6 the prophet relates his vision of the Lord Jehovah. Both *Adonai* and *Jehovah,* which are exclusive names for God *(see **Names of God),** are used (vv. 1, 3). In John 12:40 Isaiah's words from chapter 6:10 are quoted, and verse 41 adds, "These things said Esaias when he saw his [Christ's] glory and spake of him."

The Granville Sharpe Rule. Enough has been done to show that the divine name is given to the Lord Jesus, but we can go on to add a very valuable list, opening up a new and deeper line of study. This list is of texts that have such words as *Christ* and *God* joined by the word *and,* where in the Greek, the use of the definite article indicates that both refer to one and the same person. To appreciate this line of study we must first grasp a basic rule of Greek grammar, known as the Granville Sharpe Rule.* It shows that when two nouns are joined together by *and,* the first having the definite article and the second not having it, both refer to the same person or thing. Dr. William Graham says, "Let us now consider the usage of the NT in this important matter. 'God and Father' is a common phrase in Scripture, and it never signifies two persons, but only one (2 Cor. 1:3; 11:31; Eph. 1:3; 1 Thes. 1:3; Col. 1:3; Rev. 1:6). In all these passages the first noun has the article and the second has not, and they are both descriptions of the same Person."

The very same kind of word structure is used when speaking of Christ. He is referred to as "The Christ and God"—and by the same rule of grammar illustrated in the foregoing references, only one person can be in view. Ponder this argument in the following passages, in each of which the *and* has the force of *even:*

In Eph. 5:5 we read of the "kingdom of Christ and [*even*] of God," which means "the kingdom of Him who is the Christ and God." Similarly in Titus 2:13 the words "the great

God and [*even*] our Saviour" mean that our Saviour is the great God. In 2 Thes. 1:12 the English translation "the grace of our God and the Lord Jesus Christ" may leave the impression that two persons are in view. But according to the Granville Sharpe rule the meaning is "the grace of our God, *even* the Lord Jesus Christ." In Jude 4 we read of "the only Lord God and (even) our Lord Jesus Christ," an explicit testimony that our Lord Jesus is the only Lord God.

Divine Attributes Ascribed to the Lord Jesus Christ

The ascription of the attributes of God to Christ also proves that He is truly God.
1. He is *eternal* (Micah 5:2; Rev. 1:8, 11-13).
2. He is *unchangeable* (Heb. 13:8).
3. He is *infinite* (John 8:58, where "I am" describes absolute being).
4. He has *life in Himself*—aseity* (John 5:26).
5. Other divine properties are ascribed to Him: *wisdom* (1 Cor. 1:24, 30; John 21:17); *power* (1 Cor. 1:24; Matt. 28:18; John 5:19); *holiness* (Luke 1:35; Mk. 1:24; Acts 3:14); *justice* (Acts 3:14); *goodness* (John 10:32; Mark 7:37); *truth* (John 14:6). These are the attributes of God. They can be ascribed to Christ only because He is truly God.

Divine Works Ascribed to the Lord Jesus Christ

1. *Creation* (John 1:3; Col. 1:16, 17; Heb. 1:2, 10).
2. *Preservation* (Heb. 1:3; Col. 1:17).
3. *Miracles* were performed by Him (John 5:36), and by His apostles in His name (Acts 3:16). And the source of this power was in Himself (Lk. 6:19; 8:46).
4. *Salvation* in all its parts is ascribed to Christ:
   a. Redemption (Acts 20:28);
   b. Election (John 13:18; 15:16);
   c. Effectual calling (John 10:16);
   d. Sanctification (Eph. 5:26);
   e. Sending the Spirit (John 15:26; 16:7);
   f. Power to bestow eternal life (John 10:28);
   g. Resurrection of the body (John 5:21);
   h. Judgment (John 5:22; Acts 17:31).

The consistent testimony of the word of God is "Salvation is of Jehovah" (Jonah 2:9). By ascribing it in all its parts to the Lord Jesus, the NT Scriptures bear witness to His deity.

Religious Worship Rendered to Christ

Worship is due to God alone. Scripture commands it to be given to Christ (Heb. 1:6). Therefore according to Scripture Christ is truly God.
1. *Faith* is an act of religious worship directed to Christ (John 14:1; Acts 10:21; Ps. 2:12; compare Jer. 17:5).
2. *Adoration* is commanded to be given to Christ (Heb. 1:6; John 5:23; Phil. 2:9, 10).
3. *Prayer* is directed to Him (1 Cor. 1:2; Acts 7:59).

Any one of these four lines of proof would suffice to show from Scripture that Jesus Christ is truly God. Together they form an unanswerable argument against every gainsayer and provoke every humble believer to cry out with Peter, "To him be praise and dominion for ever and ever. Amen" (1 Pet. 4:11).

DEMIURGE

A name given to the creator in Platonic philosophy, and taken up by some early heretics in the church. For example, Tertullian charged the heretic Marcion with teaching that the Demiurge is a supreme being (apart from God the author of good) to whom he attributed the creation of all sin and evil.

*See **Gnosticism**.*

DEMONIAC

One possessed by a demon. Such possession was at times evidenced by dumbness (Matt. 9:32), blindness (Matt. 12:22), or by an epileptic condition (Mark 9:17-27). These conditions were not always or necessarily caused by demon possession.

The blind man in John 9 was not blind because of demonism. And Matt. 4:24 draws a clear distinction among those whom Jesus healed: some were demon possessed while others were "lunatic." *Lunatic* means "moonstruck" and some take it to refer to epilepsy, then thought to be caused by the moon. Whether we understand it of mental derangement or of epilepsy, it is clear that in this instance it stands in contrast to demon possession.

According to the NT, demonism is undoubtedly real. Rationalists have tried to explain it away as merely mythical, or symbolic, or at best an accommodation by Christ to the superstitious belief the Jews entertained of its reality.

These arguments are shallow and foolish. To adopt them would be to deny many plain statements of Scripture: demons spoke, confessed Christ, and hurled a herd of swine headlong down a hill to their death. These are hard, factual statements meant to be taken as historically accurate.

It is significant that much more widespread activity is attributed to demons in the Gospels than in the rest of the NT. This fact clearly infers that while Satan and his host were still active in apostolic times—even in demonism—the death and resurrection of Christ greatly reduced the exercise of Satanic power. Christ crushed Satan's head (Gen. 3:15). He made a show of principalities and powers and triumphed over them at the cross (Col. 2:15).

However, the book of Revelation (9:20; 16:14) shows that demonic activity will be strong in the last days before the return of Christ. We conclude from Rev. 9:20 that much of this activity will be in the religious realm (see 1 Tim. 4:1) and will further the programme of Satan described in 2 Thess. 2:9-11—viz., "the lie," deception, made attractive by the exercise of "power and signs and lying wonders." Then demonic activity will reach its climax and receive its final judgment (2 Thess. 2:8; 2 Pet. 2:4).

DEMONISM

The state of being a demoniac,* a case of demon* possession.

DEMONS

Greek *daimon, daimonion,* rendered "devil" in the AV, though the proper word for "devil" is *diabolos.* Demons are spirits (Matt. 8:16; 10:1) with intelligence and will (Mark 1:24; 5:12; James 2:19), and they exercise great power (Mark 5:2-5; Eph. 6:12). Though they are specifically termed "evil spirits" (Acts 19:12, 13), they recognise Christ as the Son of God (Matt. 8:29; Luke 4:41). They believe in God and tremble (James 2:19). They recognise the power of Jesus' name used by His appointed servants to exorcise them (Acts 19:15). They look forward in terror to the judgment of God (Matt. 8:29). Most Bible scholars believe them to be fallen angels, though some vehemently deny this. The evidence in favour of this view is summarized by McClintoch and Strong:

"As the messengers and agents of Satan...the probability seems to be that they to belong to the same class as himself. He is called the Prince of the Demons; the demons whom our Lord cast out are collectively called Satan (Matt. 12:24-29; Luke 13:16); and the phrase 'unclean spirits,' which is applied also to fallen angels (Rev. 16:13; 18:2), and even in the singular to Satan himself (Mark 3:30; comp. 22). These considerations, we think, render it probable that the *daimonia* of the NT belong to the number of those angels 'who kept not their first estate'; and we conclude probably (though attempts have been made to deny the inference) that they must be the same as 'the angels of the devil' (Matt. 25:41; Rev. 12:7, 9), 'the principalities and powers' against whom we 'wrestle' (Eph. 6:12, etc.)."

Scripture details the activities of these unclean and evil spirits (Matt. 10:1; 12:45). They may cause disease (though not all diseases, for much of it is the direct result of the entrance of sin into the world) or derangement (though, again, not all derangement is demonic).

Demons are particularly active in religious and spiritual matters. Though idols represent gods that have no objective existence, their worship is in reality the worship of demons (1 Cor. 10:19, 20). Even in the church, demons are active in drawing people away from the truth. Paul warns against "giving heed to seducing spirits, and doctrines of demons" (1 Tim. 4:1). This is perhaps the most subtle work done by demons (cf. 2 Cor. 11:14-15).

Demons are "reserved in everlasting chains under darkness unto the judgement of the great day" (Jude 6; cf. 2 Pet. 2:4).

This description of their punishment leads some to deny that demons are fallen angels. They argue that fallen angels are clearly confined in hell whereas demons are still active in the world. Were it not for the evidence in favour of identifying demons with fallen angels, and were the alternative suggestions not so incredible and in defiance of other plain Scriptures (e.g., that they are a pre-Adamic race that came under judgment and continue their rebellion against God by their activity in the world; or that they are, or include, the wicked dead of former generations), this objection would be very strong. As it is we can only conclude that Jude 6 and 2 Pet. 2:4 mean that fallen angels are now under punishment from which there is no escape and which will lead them to the final torments of everlasting fire before prepared for them (Matt. 25:41). The verb *tartaroo,* "cast into hell," in 2 Pet. 2:4 would therefore speak of their present state, rather than their location.

DEPRAVITY

By the fall,* man became guilty (liable to punishment) and polluted (without original righteousness, having a positively evil bent). This pollution is usually considered under the headings *Total Depravity* and *Total Inability.*

Total Depravity

This term denotes that inherited pollution pervades the entire human character. Louis Berkhof points out what the phrase does *not* imply.

What It Does Not Mean

1. That every man is as thoroughly depraved as he can possibly become.

2. That the sinner is without an innate knowledge of the will of God or a conscience that discriminates between good and evil.

3. That sinful man does not often admire virtuous character and actions in others, or is incapable of disinterested affections and actions in his relations with his fellow men.

4. That every unregenerate man will indulge in every form of sin (e.g., sometimes one form of sin excludes another).

What It Does Mean

1. That the inherent corruption extends to every part of man's nature, to all the faculties and powers, both of body and soul.

2. That there is no spiritual good, that is, good in relation to God, in the sinner at all, but only perversion.

Total depravity is denied by Pelagians, Socinians, and Arminians. It is upheld by all the Reformed churches and is clearly taught in the Word of God (John 5:42; Rom. 7:18, 23; 8:7; Eph. 2:1-3; 4:18; 2 Tim. 3:2-4; Tit. 1:15; Heb. 3:12; Gen. 6:5; Isa. 1:6; Jer. 17:9).

Total Inability

Total Inability is the term used to describe the effect of the pollution of sin on man's spiritual powers. Reformed theologians admit that unregenerate man is able to perform natural and civil good; but they insist that by nature no man can do anything that will either change his own basic bias of will toward self and sin, or that will meet the requirements of God's holy law and merit His favour.

The Scripture plainly teaches total inability: John 1:13, 3:5, 6:44, 8:34, 15:4, 5; Rom. 7:18, 24; 8:7, 8; 1 Cor. 2:14; 2 Cor. 3:5; Eph. 2:1, 8-10; Heb. 11:6.

See **Fall**; **Inability**; **Ungodliness**; **Will.**

DESCENT INTO HELL (DESCENSUS AD INFEROS)

The doctrine that, after His death, the Lord Jesus descended into Hades. Various reasons are suggested for this descent:

1. To lead out the OT saints who could not enter into heaven before the death and resurrection of Christ. Eph. 4:8-10 is often quoted in support of this view.

2. To announce His victory over every power of hell. 1 Pet. 3:18-20 is quoted to support this.

3. To preach the gospel and so give a "second chance" to those who died in their sins. Again 1 Pet. 3:18-20 is quoted in support.

This last idea may be easily disposed of. The Scripture does not proclaim any other day of grace and gospel opportunity than the one enjoyed before death. The passage cited simply means that Christ, by His Spirit, preached through Noah to men who were "disobedient" in Noah's day and were condemned for their sin. Those disobedient and condemned sinners were "spirits in prison" in Peter's day. The use of "sometime" clearly marks the disobedience and the preaching as contemporaneous. The longsuffering of God is shown in His waiting in the days of Noah, not in a "second chance" after death. Further, why only the disobedient of Noah's day should be said to receive the gospel from Christ in Hades, without mention of any of the rest of the wicked, is a mystery that the proponents of the "second chance" notion cannot explain.

Many conservative Protestant theologians altogether reject the idea of any descent by Christ into Hades (except in the sense that His body was buried in the grave) and hold that the texts cited prove no such doctrine. The explanation given above to 1 Pet. 3:18-20 is sufficient to undermine the entire notion of Christ going personally to Hades. Furthermore, Eph. 4:8-10 teaches the incarnation of Christ, His descent into the world, not into Hades. Isa. 44:23 uses similar terms with the evident contrast between this lower world of earth and heaven. In Rom. 10:7 Christ's descent "into the deep" is shown to refer to His burial.

Indeed, the original sense of the words of the Apostles' Creed, "He descended into Hades," was merely that He was truly buried. In its original form, the Creed had no such clause in it. It was inserted toward the end of the 4th century by the Church of Aquileia. Rufinus, the presbyter of Aquileia, equated the statements "He was crucified, dead and buried" and "He descended into Hades," Hades referring merely to the grave. For some time either one of these clauses was used in creedal statements, but in the Middle Ages both were used together in the Creed, thus aiding the belief that something more than burial is indicated.

See *Sufferings of Christ*.

DEUTERO-CANONICAL BOOKS

The name given by Roman Catholic writers to the books they include in their canon of Scripture, but which the Jewish and Protestant canons reject as apocryphal.*

DEVOTIO MODERNA

The name given to the spiritual disciplines of the Brethren of the Common Life, a reformist group that arose in the late 14th century. Thomas á Kempis's *Imitation of Christ* is the most famous example of their spirituality. While the *devotio moderna* did not come to the clear understanding of justification that the Protestant Reformers later expounded, it did lay an admirable stress on godliness of life and sought to introduce the Scripture to the people in their own language. Luther and Melancthon spoke highly of it and of the Brethren who practised it.

DIALECTICS AND DIALECTIC THEOLOGY

Dialectic is the description of a supposedly logical system of investigation in which the "truth is discovered by a process of assertion and denial. Something is asserted;

this is called the thesis. Then, its denial is stated; this is the antithesis. Then the two are reconciled by means of a synthesis." The synthesis itself becomes a new thesis, and the process is continued until a universal synthesis is found.

This method was used by the German philosopher Hegel, whose work was taken along another road by Karl Marx. Hegel taught *dialectical idealism,* while Marx proclaimed *dialectical materialism.* Both saw history as a succession of dialectical changes: i.e., a continuous series of contradictions or paradoxes, which were reconciled (the synthesis), each synthesis giving rise to a new paradox and a new reconciliation, with the result of a gradual development. Hegel's philosophy was of a development of ideas; Marx's was of a development of social changes determined by economic factors. Thus Marx set the scene for communism and the socialist revolution: capitalism (the thesis) trod upon the poor or the workers (the antithesis), a situation which could only be resolved by revolution (the synthesis). He justified revolution as the means of leading to a society without class or conflict (the ultimate synthesis). How far astray his theories were is attested by the facts of life in modern communist countries.

Theologically, the dialectical method has a long history. It was used with great skill by Thomas Aquinas (1225-74). In recent times it has re-emerged in the theology of Neo-orthodoxy. Soren Kierkegaard, Karl Barth, and Emil Brunner all laid great stress on paradox. Paradox theology holds that the revelation of the infinite God to finite man in finite history is bound to involve contradictory elements. Indeed, according to this view, divine revelation can appear to the finite man only as a series of contradictions. Neo-orthodoxy holds that no reconciliation is possible, except in faith ("man's highest emotion"), or in subjectivity (within the mind of the thinker). According to this view, man is to accept all the contradictory elements,

and such acceptance is viewed as a leap or risk—the exercise of existential faith *(see Existentialism).* Thus what is believed as a divine revelation ultimately depends upon the subjective judgment of the individual.

To the Bible believer, there is no risk in accepting all that God has revealed, even when he lacks a full understanding of that revelation in all its relations. The limitations of fallen man's perception are no ground for charging the revelation of God with contradiction.

See **Theology of Crisis**.

DIATESSARON

A harmony of the four gospels. The term is used especially in reference to the harmony composed by Tatian in the second century.

DICHOTOMY
*See **Soul**.*

DIDACHE

The Greek word for doctrine, or teaching. The word appears thirty times in the NT. The AV translates it *doctrine* in all but one place (Tit. 1:9 where the Greek, "according to the doctrine" is translated, "as he hath been taught").

The Didache is the title of an anonymous work that probably dates to the early second century. Its full title is, "The teaching of the Lord, through the Twelve Apostles, to the Gentiles" and it appears to have been an evangelistic effort to set before the nations what the apostles of Christ had personally taught the Gentiles. It commences by setting forth *The Two Ways—The Way of Life* and *The Way of Death*—and proceeds to deal with a variety of doctrinal and practical matters that demanded attention, as the early Christians sought to introduce the gospel to the Gentile nations.

The Didache seems to be of Jewish Christian origin, and therefore indicates that that section of the early church followed in the train of the apostle Paul and took the gospel to the Gentile world. It is a witness to the early distribution of the gospels, though it adds much non-canonical material.

DISCIPLES OF CHRIST
See Campbellites.

DISPENSATION, DISPENSATIONALISM

The word *dispensation* is a Scriptural term. The Greek word is *oikonomia* (see Lk. 16:2-4; 1 Cor. 9:17; Eph. 1:10; 3:2; Col. 1:25). This word is composed of *oikos,* "house," and *nomos,* "law." Etymologically it indicates "the law of the house," from which it naturally signifies the idea of "stewardship, arrangement, or administration."

Thus we may justly define a dispensation in Scripture as a divine plan or administration of the affairs of God's house, which, committed to men, becomes a stewardship which they are required to discharge faithfully. The Covenant of Grace *(see Covenant Theology)* is administered under two dispensations or modes of administration. Heb. 10:9 says, "He taketh away the first that he may establish the second," in which the shadows of the first are replaced by the substance of the second. Under the covenant of works, man was placed on probation. He fell into the ruin of sin and depravity. His probation was over, once and for all. God in grace put into operation His Covenant of Grace, which He has administered in two ways, the old and the new, or the first and the second (Heb. 10:9).

Dispensationalists are those who hold that God has tested man again and again, in respect of obedience to some specific revelation of His will. Each period of testing they call a dispensation. They normally claim that there are seven such dispensations: innocence, conscience, human government, promise, law, grace, and the Kingdom. Each of these is "regarded as a new test of the natural man, and each ends in judgment" (C. I. Scofield, *Rightly Dividing the Word of Truth,* p. 20). Dispensationalists further claim that each dispensation is distinct from all the others and cannot commingle with them. It is only by grasping this "dispensational truth" (as it is usually referred to by dispensationalists) that we can "rightly divide the word of truth" (2 Tim. 2:15).

Dispensationalism labours under very serious objections. The use of the word *dispensation* as "a period of time" (Scofield) is unscriptural. The appointment of the beginning and end of each dispensation is quite arbitrary and has led to controversy among dispensationalists, some claiming more than seven and some claiming fewer than seven. Even on the admission of some dispensationalists the periods overlap. How then are they distinct?

As Berkhof notes, "The second dispensation is called the dispensation of conscience, but according to Paul conscience was still the monitor of the Gentiles of his day, Rom. 2:14, 15. The third is known as the dispensation of human government, but the specific command in it which was disobeyed and therefore rendered man liable to judgment, was not the command to rule the world for God—of which there is no trace—but the command to replenish the earth. The fourth is designated the dispensation of promise and is supposed to terminate with the giving of the law, but Paul says that the law did not disannul the promise, and that this was still in effect in his own day, Rom. 4:13-17; Gal. 3:15-29. The so-called dispensation of the law is replete with glorious promises, and the so-called dispensation of grace did not abrogate the law as a rule of life" (*Systematic Theology,* p. 290, 291).

The most dangerous element in the dispensational scheme is that it affects the very basis of the gospel of salvation by grace alone, through faith in Christ. It posits the idea that man has been on probation all along, and that God's mercy is displayed in giving him a new trial after every failure, thus holding out the possibility of salvation by works of obedience. Rev. Reginald Kimbro, in a book that testifies of his personal journey out of dispensationalism into covenant theology, identifies the leading issues in the dispensational scheme. They are:

1. The definition of the church. Covenant theology stresses the unity of the entire body of the redeemed throughout all ages. "Dispensationalism, on the other hand, teaches that there have been at least *two* groups of men with whom God has entered into a relationship, and that these two groups of redeemed men must be viewed as totally distinct, that they have nothing to do with each other, and that God has totally different purposes in mind in calling them each out" (*The Gospel According to Dispensationalism,* p. 20).

2. The doctrine of salvation. "The fatal flaw in Dispensational theology is the effect that its dichotomy between Israel and the Church has on the doctrine of salvation" (*ibid.,* p. 93). Kimbro details how dispensationalists have taught multiple ways of salvation. C. I. Scofield, whose Reference Bible brought millions into the dispensational camp, taught that under the law God *required* righteousness while under grace He *gives* it.

Lewis Sperry Chafer taught, "There are two very different, standardized, divine provisions, whereby man, who, is utterly fallen, might stand in favour with God." He criticized covenant theology because it "engenders the notion that there is *but one soteriology"* (*ibid.,* p. 99).

Charles Ryrie, possibly the most influential modern dispensational theologian, defends these men. He insists that neither they nor dispensationalists today teach more than one way of salvation. He says, "The basis of salvation is always the death of Christ; the means is always faith" (*ibid.,* p. 121). He reconciles the apparent contradictions between their statements and his by pleading that all they intend to teach is that while sinners have always been saved through faith the *content*

of that faith differs from one dispensation to another. In other words, it was not always faith in Christ or His atonement by which sinners were saved (p. 121). If this does not teach more than one way of salvation, words are meaningless.

Because of their view of law and grace, dispensationalists often propound antinomian* sentiments. According to one dispensationalist writer, "In the Old Testament there is not one sentence that applies to the Christian as a Rule of Faith and Practice" (Cook, *God's Book Speaking for Itself,* p. 31).

This soteriological weakness is evident in dispensationalist eschatology.* The descriptions dispensationalists give of the conversion and standing of tribulation saints, and of the millennial kingdom, compel us to characterize their view of the religion then practised as revived and barely reformed Judaism, cetainly not the Christianity of the apostles of Christ.

Thankfully, there is evidence that many dispensationalists are awakening to the failures of the system. Even in moving quite radically away from its fundamental tenets they try to hold on to the name. But that name is too fraught with theological error. As Reginald Kimbro argues, dispensationalists must recognize the error, admit that it continues in the system, be clear on the soteriological effects of it, and entirely repudiate it.

DISPERSION

The scattering of the Jewish nation from their land as a result of their disobedience to the Lord, in accordance with His plainly stated word (Deut. 4:27, etc.).

DISRUPTION

The name given to the secession in 1843 from the Church of Scotland, by which the Free Church of Scotland was formed. The Law of Patronage, by which ministers were placed in churches at the behest of heritors, or patrons, without (and often in defiance of) the will of the congregation, had caused previous secessions. It was vigorously upheld by the state and the Moderate party (*see Moderatism*), but in 1834 the General Assembly passed the Veto Act, allowing the nominee or patron to be vetoed by a majority vote of the congregation. The Assembly also, under the guidance of Thomas Chalmers, launched a church extension programme, giving the ministers of the new churches the right to sit and vote in church courts. Both measures were disallowed by the Westminster Parliament, resulting in great strife in the church. The Moderates were in favour of yielding to the state, which stubbornly refused to recognize the basic liberties the Church of Scotland claimed. Thus on May 18, 1843, Dr. Chalmers walked out of the General Assembly and formed the Free Church of Scotland, claiming to carry with them the rights and privileges of the national church.

DISTINCTIONS IN THE ATTRIBUTES OF GOD
See *Attributes*.

DISTINCTIONS IN THE GODHEAD

The properties which are exclusively predicable of each person in the Trinity. *Begetting* is the distinctive property of the Father; *eternal generation* is the distinctive property of the Son; *spiration* is the distinctive property of the Spirit. These indicate that in the unity of the divine essence there are eternal, necessary distinctions, or "forms of God." This is the term Paul used in Phil. 2:6, where "being in the form of God" is, in the Greek text, "being in *a* form of God." The distinctions in the Godhead are so personalized as to demand the use of personal pronouns, "I," "Thou," "He."
See *Opera Ad Intra*.

DISTRIBUTIVE JUSTICE
See *Justice*.

DOCETISM

An early heresy about the person of Christ. The Docetae took their name from the Greek verb *dokeo*, "to seem, appear," and taught that Christ merely *seemed* to be a man. The first known advocate of Docetism was Cerinthus, who lived in the first century A.D.

DOCTRINES OF GRACE

A name given to the system usually known as Calvinism,* which emphasizes that salvation is all of grace, by the merit of Christ alone, absolutely without any addition from the works of man, either in an unregenerate state or in a regenerate state.

DOGMA

The Greek word *dogma* signifies a decree (Lk. 2:1; Acts 16:4; Eph. 2:15; Col. 2:14). It later came to signify an article of belief set forth by ecclesiastical decree, as for example, Rome's dogma of the Immaculate Conception.

The word has a wider theological use to describe a proposition of religious belief, derived from divine revelation, and set forth as part of a comprehensive doctrinal system—hence the term Dogmatic Theology.

DONATION OF CONSTANTINE

A seventh-century forgery, purporting to have come from the Roman Emperor Constantine, in which he granted the city of Rome and the entire Western Empire to the pope and set his throne above all others, even that of Constantine himself. Though Rome had to admit that the Donation of Constantine was a forgery, that admission came centuries after the forged document had done its work, that of claiming a primacy for the Bishop of Rome which received no support from Scripture or from antiquity.
See *Decretals (False)*.

DONATISTS

A schismatic movement of the fourth and fifth centuries named after Donatus, a North

127

African bishop. The Donatists had their roots in the period of persecution under the Roman Emperor Diocletian. One section of the church showed an utter disdain of suffering and death, and looked upon flight from danger, and especially the delivering up of sacred books to the persecutors, as base treachery and cowardice. Another party, one of whom was Cecilian, were of a different mind, being more discreet and conformist. When, in the reign of Constantine, Cecilian was hastily ordained bishop of Carthage, the Donatists refused to recognize him, alleging first that the North African bishops had been slighted, and that Cecilian had been a traditor, or one who had delivered up sacred books to heathen persecutors. The Donatists ordained their own bishop of Carthage, Majorinus, and he was succeeded in 315 by Donatus, who gave his name to the whole party.

The churches of North Africa were deeply divided on the issue and the Donatists made representations to the Emperor to endorse their views. These appeals were rejected and Cecilian was recognized as bishop of Carthage. Following this the Donatists argued strongly for a total separation of church and state, though they had themselves invoked the Emperor's power. They were fiercely persecuted, but they persisted until the devastation of the African church in 428 by the Arian Vandals. A remnant of the Donatists existed until the seventh century, when the Saracens wiped out all sections of the North African church.

The rationale of Donatist separation was as follows: Though they held to baptismal regeneration* and sacramentalism,* as did most of their opponents, they took the position that "unholy priests are incapable of administering the sacrament; for how can regeneration proceed from the unregenerate, or holiness from the unholy? None can give what he does not himself possess. He who would receive faith from a faithless man, receives not faith but guilt. It was on this

ground, in fact, that they rejected the election of Cecilian; that he had been ordained bishop by an unworthy person" (Schaff, *History of the Christian Church*).

The Donatists looked upon themselves as the true church, and all others as part of the system of Babylon. They looked upon themselves as pure, and held to the view of the church as a society of those already made holy, a society, moreover, which must guard its holiness by means of very rigorous discipline against all offenders within its ranks.

The leading opponent of the Donatists was Augustine (354-430), who first sought to win them by argument, and failing in that, by persecution. The parable of the tares and the wheat, and of the fish in the net (Matt. 13), became the major exegetical battleground between them. On the one hand, the Donatists wrongly claimed to be the only true church. They failed to do justice to the essential unity of the church of Christ. They were also far from apostolic purity of doctrine—what they were contending for was basically a system of sacramentalism.

On the other hand, Augustine, while emphasizing the unity of the church and setting forth the germ of the distinction between the visible and invisible church, erred when he virtually argued from numerical preponderance that the Catholic church must be adhered to. Furthermore, he was wrong in his argument from apostolic succession. He was wrong in allowing no grounds at all for separation from a system which had become doctrinally impure and was to become more and more so in the centuries which followed.

Taken to their logical conclusion, Augustine's arguments would preclude any separation and would thus militate against the Protestant Reformation. This should be faced by Protestants, especially of an evangelical persuasion, who recite Augustine's views and try to pin the label *Donatist* on those who have separated from churches which either have denied or are in the process of denying the elementary truths of the gospel and who willingly ordain ministers who have repudiated that gospel.

We do not believe in separation on sacramental grounds, or on any notion that we can erect a church of perfect purity. Ecclesiastical purity is the desire of every Christian, but it is an ideal of which every church falls short in a greater or lesser degree. While we accept the position of the Reformers that "we are not on account of every minute difference to abandon a church provided it retain sound and unimpaired the fundamental doctrine of our salvation" (Calvin), we are justified in separating from a body in which the distinguishing badge of a true church (the ministry of the word and the scriptural administration of the sacraments) no longer "exists entire and unimpaired" (Calvin). Indeed, we are obligated to separate. To quote Calvin again, "If the true Church is the 'pillar and ground of the truth' (1 Tim. 3:15), it is certain that there is no church where lying and falsehood have usurped the ascendancy."

The Reformers applied this principle, rightly, to Rome. With equal right, we apply it to those erstwhile Protestant churches that seek reunion with Rome, and which have either repudiated their ancient confessional standards, or have allowed them to be ignored, violated, or denied. Such want of truth clearly comes under Calvin's condemnation.

Donatism was a schismatic revolt, though in the ensuing debate, on some points—notably on the exegesis of Matt. 13—Donatist writers were more scriptural than their opponents. The Protestant principle of scriptural separation is not schism.* It is the repudiation of a departure from the basic doctrines of the faith, by a body which has become apostate.

See **Schism**.

DOUBLE PREDESTINATION

The theory that by predestinating some to salvation by a free and sovereign decree, God in the same way predestinated all others to be damned. It is a very deficient theory, for it makes condemnation to rest upon an arbitrary decree of God, without reference to the sinner's guilt. It therefore presents a false view of reprobation.* C. H. Spurgeon's maxim is well worth remembering: "Salvation is all of grace, damnation is all of sin." The elect receive a salvation which they have not personally merited. Their election is entirely sovereign and takes no account whatever of their personal merits.

Reprobation is partly sovereign and partly judicial. The reprobate receive a damnation which they have fully and personally merited. No man goes to hell *merely because he is not elect.* All who perish do so *because they personally deserve to perish.* God's predetermination that the reprobate should perish everlastingly takes note of their sin, and is based upon His holy hatred of it.

See **Predestination**.

DUALISM

The philosophic system which proposes two original and independent principles in the universe, one good and the other evil.

DULIA

In Roman Catholicism, the worship accorded to the saints.

See **Adoration**; **Hyperdulia**; **Latria**.

DUNKERS

Also called "Dunkards"; the German Baptist Brethren, or a German-American Anabaptist* group.

DUTCH REMONSTRANTS

The followers of Jacob Arminius whose views in opposition to the accepted Calvinism of the Reformed Church were considered by the Synod of Dort.

See **Five Points of Controversy**; **Arminianism**.

DUTY FAITH

The name given, usually by hyper-Calvinists, to describe those, usually Calvinists, who believe that in the gospel Christ is offered to all men if they will believe on Him. In this scheme, all who hear the gospel should believe on Christ in the certainty that if they do they will be saved (hence the name *duty faith* preachers).

Hyper-Calvinists reject the idea of the free offer of the gospel. They look on telling sinners that they ought to believe on Christ as inherently absurd, because sinners are dead and cannot believe until the Holy Spirit regenerates them. Here they go beyond Scripture. The sinner's inability in no way lessens his responsibility. God commands sinners to keep His law, though they cannot do it. Equally, He commands them to believe His gospel and His Son. If this were not so, how could Christ state that the Holy Spirit would reprove the world, "of sin, because they believe not on me" (John 16:8-9)? If unbelief is a sin, then faith is clearly a duty.

DYNAMIC EQUIVALENCE

A method of Bible translation that purports to reproduce the message of the text of Scripture using such expressions as will produce in the modern reader a response equivalent to that which the original would have produced in those to whom it was addressed. It aims, not at word for word, but at thought for thought, translation. The NIV has largely adopted this method. The AV adopts the method of formal equivalence.* Though neither method can be employed exclusively, the inspiration of the *words* of Scripture demand a formal equivalent approach wherever possible.

The use of dynamic equivalence has a Biblical precedent. Hebrews 10:5 quotes Ps. 40:6 from the LXX.* The Hebrew of Ps. 40:6 literally reads, "Mine ears hast thou opened," and this is the translation of the text in the AV. The LXX translation was, "A body thou hast prepared me," and this is what the NT quotes. Clearly, the LXX does not give a formal equivalence translation in this place. Nevertheless, its translation dis-

plays the real meaning of the Hebrew text, as the NT quotation assures us. It would appear that the LXX translator on this occasion grasped the meaning of the Hebrew idiom and his dynamic equivalent reveals the true meaning of the text to non-Hebrew speakers, whereas a formal, or literal, translation would fail to convey all its meaning.

Every good translation, including the AV, at times must use dynamic equivalence, or idiomatic translation. This is part of what some modern conservative linguists term "complete equivalence," to describe their attempt to capture the full meaning of the original languages of Scripture by formal equivalence where possible, and by dynamic equivalence where necessary.

DYSTELEOLOGY

An apparent absence of design or intelligent purpose in parts of the created universe or in phases of human experience. Gleason L. Archer described it as follows: "It refers to instances where something seems to have gone wrong, such as misshapen or monstrous births, or long and excruciatingly painful fatal illness by people of godly convictions and exemplary life. It may even be applied to devastating plagues like the medieval Black Death, or widely destructive floods, or earthquakes. Cases like these are very difficult to reconcile with the all-wise purpose of a loving and omnipotent God. Hence the term *dysteleology* (apparent absence of intelligent purpose)" (*A Survey of Old Testament Introduction*, p. 192, n. 11).

The "absence" of divine design is only apparent. The difficulty lies in our extremely limited knowledge and ability to comprehend God's purpose. The fact of the entrance of sin and its consequent curse upon the whole of creation goes a long way to explain why there is so much apparently useless suffering in the world.

Ultimately, Christian faith transcends the human inability to comprehend the *why* of God's providential dealings and rests in the fact that He is working all things after the counsel of His own will (Eph. 1:11), that His purpose toward His people is good and gracious (Jer. 29:11), that He has a good and gracious design even when we cannot perceive it, and that He will produce good for His people and glory to His own name through all the events of life (Rom. 8:28).

Darwin and later evolutionists have used examples of dysteleology to try to overthrow the popular appeal of the argument from design in nature. They point to such things as the vast over production of eggs by a fish (only a few ever actually mature into more fish) and of seeds by fruit-bearing trees (only a few of which become trees). Why the provision of such abundant food sources for other creatures should be imagined purposeless is difficult to see.

Evolutionists also point to such "useless" parts of the human body as the appendix, and to the almost unlimited vastness of the universe, and seek to draw a dysteleological conclusion. At best this is an argument from ignorance. It is also highly arrogant, for in effect it says, "If we cannot discern a purpose, there is none." The more we get to know of created bodies, whether human bodies or astronomical, the more we see that there is nothing purposeless in God's creation and providence.

EBIONITES

An early Jewish sect of professing Christians who denied the deity of the Lord Jesus, regarding Him as the natural son of Mary and Joseph, the last and greatest of the prophets. They held that when Jesus was baptized, Christ came upon Him in the form of a dove and departed from Him before His crucifixion. The Ebionites used only Matthew's gospel and completely repudiated Paul as an apostate from the Law.

ECCLESIOLOGY

That branch of systematic theology* that treats the church,* covering such things as the scriptural definition of its names, nature, government, and power. Some theologians (e.g., Berkhof) go on to deal with the means of grace at this point, but most treat these as a branch of soteriology.*

ECUMENICAL

Greek oik*oumene*, the "inhabited earth." The word appears 15 times in the NT and has been appropriated by various branches of Christendom to denote catholicity* or universality. The Eastern Orthodox church refers to its synods as "ecumenical synods." The Roman Catholic church calls its councils "ecumenical councils." They thereby claim that catholicity is one of the marks or notes of Christ's one true church and that it belongs to them.

ECUMENICAL MOVEMENT, ECUMENISM

The movement whose goal is to unite all the churches of Christendom, including of course, the union of Protestantism and Roman Catholicism. The World Council of Churches* (WCC) has taken the leading role in its development, and other movements, such as the Charismatic Movement,* have greatly abetted the endeavour. There is evidence that many WCC ecumenists aim to proceed beyond the unity of all the churches of Christendom to the union of all religions.

*See **Syncretism**.*

EFFECTUAL CALLING

The term used by the *Westminster Confession* and catechisms to cover the subject of regeneration.* According to the *Shorter Catechism,* "Effectual calling is the work of God's Spirit, whereby, convincing us of our sin and misery, enlightening our minds in the knowledge of Christ, and renewing our wills, he doth persuade and enable us to embrace Jesus Christ, freely offered to us in the gospel" (Q. 31).

Effectual calling denotes the internal, special, life-giving call of the Spirit, experienced only by God's elect, in contrast to the external, general call extended to all who hear the gospel. This effectual call is the "exercise of divine power upon the soul, immediate, spiritual, and supernatural, communicating a new spiritual life and thus making a new mode of spiritual activity possible" (A. A. Hodge).

The effect of this call is to persuade and enable us to receive Christ as He is freely offered in the gospel. That is, it leads us to repentance and faith. This order is important. Repentance and faith are acts of the regenerate man, whose ability to perform them is solely by virtue of the change wrought by the Holy Spirit in effectual calling.

*See **Internal Call**; **Irresistible Grace**.*

EGO

The Latin word for "I." It is used to mean the "self." In discussing the subject of personality, theologians and philosophers point out that self-consciousness implies a trinal distinction: the rational spirit (and therefore called the *subjective ego*) makes itself the object of contemplation (the *objective ego*) and knows that it has done so (the *ego percipient*).

Some theologians see this inherent trinality in the human self as a reflection of the trinality of the divine nature. That is not to say that this human trinality defines the divine. It means simply that God created man in His own likeness. The trinal distinctions in man do not mean he is three persons in one essence, but they prepare us for the Biblical revelation that the divine original on which man was fashioned exists eternally as one undivided essence in the three persons of the Trinity.

ELECT, ELECTION

The words *elect* and *election* may be taken actively to denote God's choice, or passively to denote the privilege of being chosen by Him. The verb occurs 29 times in the NT. Once it refers to Mary's choice of the better part (Luke 10:42) and once to the apostles' choice of men to go to Antioch (Acts 15:22). In every other case it refers to God's choice: of the Jewish nation (Acts 13:17), of the apostles (Luke 6:13; John 6:70), of men for special service (Acts 15:7), or (and this in the vast majority of cases) of individuals to everlasting life (e.g., 1 Cor. 1:27; Eph. 1:4).

God's election of men to salvation is His eternal and sovereign choice of them to be His adopted children (Eph. 1:4; Rom. 8:29), not because of any foreseen merit or obedience on their part. Rather, the faith and obedience by which they, in time, enter into salvation through Christ are the result of election, not the cause of it (1 Pet. 1:2; 2 Pet. 1:3; 2 Tim. 1:9).

The noun occurs seven times in the NT. It is used to signify God's choice of Paul as an apostle (Acts 9:15), but in every other case it is used to signify His purpose or act in choosing men to salvation (Rom. 9:11; 11:5, 7, 28; 1 Thess. 1:4; 2 Pet. 1:10).

As an adjective, elect refers not only to men but to Christ. He is "elect" or "chosen" in the sense that the Father appointed Him to the distinctive office of mediator (cf. 1 Pet. 2:4, 6).

ELOHIST

An imaginary character claimed by rationalistic Higher Critics *(see **Criticism)*** to be one of a number of unknown authors whose documents were welded together with others, by a later editor, and presented to the world as the work of Moses. The Elohist is supposed to be distinguished by his use of *Elohim* for the divine name, many critics holding that he was a much earlier writer than the Jehovist who used the name *Jehovah* (which, they claim, was unknown to the Elohist) and many others insisting that he wrote after the Jehovist! The entire theory is a figment and has been sufficiently refuted, but is still tenaciously adhered to by the critics. The fact is that each of the names of God has its own special meaning. Each is God's revelation of Himself in a particular manner, not man's description of God. The use of Elohim or Jehovah does not indicate different original authors who knew no other name for God; rather it signifies a particular emphasis laid by the Lord in His revelation of Himself.

EMPIRICISM

The philosophical theory that holds sense perception to be the only test of knowledge. Empirical knowledge is knowledge gained by experience, and the empirical method is the way of observation and experiment. Empiricism was largely a reaction to rationalism,* which insisted on reason as the source of knowledge.

David Hume, the most famous empiricist, divided knowledge into two classes: the knowledge of facts and the relations of ideas. The relations of ideas belong to the realm of logic and mathematics. Such truths are true by definition and of necessity. They cannot be otherwise and are known *a priori.** Matters of fact, by contrast, may only be known *a posteriori.** They arise from sense experience. Matters of fact are only contingently true. They could be other than what they are.

Hume used his empiricism to attack the Biblical record of miracles. Making our experience the standard by which to judge the record of miracles, he concluded that miracles do not happen and therefore did not happen. If the recorded events did occur, they would still not be miracles but pieces of human experience, which is by definition natural, not supernatural.

This use of empiricism makes the unjustifiable assumption that our present experience is the judge of recorded experiences of people in other times. It further assumes that it is impossible for God to act upon and within His creation in any supernatural way that is unique to particular people at particular points in time. The absence of the kinds of miracles found in the NT gives empiricists no logical reason to conclude that God could not perform them at other times for the purpose of authenticating His special revelation.

ENDLESS PUNISHMENT

The doctrine of Scripture that the finally unrepentant will be punished for their sin forever in hell. The same terminology is used to describe the everlasting duration of hell's punishments and to describe the everlasting duration of eternal life (Matt. 25:46 speaks of both). Nowhere in Scripture is there the slightest hint of a cessation or lessening of the torments and punishments of those who are condemned to the place "where their worm dieth not, and the fire is not quenched" (Mark 9:48) and from where "the smoke of their torment ascendeth up for ever and ever" (Rev. 14:11). The lake of fire cannot be construed in Scripture to be

of a temporary duration (Rev. 14:10, 11; 19:20; 20:10, 15).

See Gehenna; Wrath of God.

ENLIGHTENMENT

The title given to the development of thought in Europe and America in the late 17th and 18th centuries. Essentially, the Enlightenment was the expression of modern man's attempt to break free from the rule of dogma based on divine revelation and to exercise his own reason with complete autonomy. Hence the Enlightenment has been called "The Age of Reason." This reason is in reality rebellion against God. In Scripture we learn that the light that is in fallen men is darkness. Their understanding is darkened because of sin; enlightenment comes only by divine revelation (see Eph. 4:18; 5:8).

EPISCOPACY

The system of church government by diocesan bishops, held by Episcopalian churches to be the system laid down in the NT. Usually it is claimed that bishops are true successors of the apostles *(see Apostolic Succession)* and that they alone have the power to ordain (i.e., without their ordination there is no valid ministry).

However, in the NT, *episkopos* does not signify a bishop of a diocese, but an overseer, elder, or presbyter in the local church. *Bishop* and *elder* are never named together as being distinct offices, as *bishop* and *deacon* are (e.g., 1 Tim. 3:1, 8). The same persons are described as bishops and elders (Acts 20:17, 18; Titus. 1:5, 8). The elder's task is to do the work of a bishop. In 1 Pet. 5, the presbyters (v. 1) are told to "exercise episcopacy" over the flock of God (v. 2), and this clearly sets the Scriptural meaning of the office and function of a bishop.

EPISTEMOLOGY

The theory or science of the nature, grounds, and method of knowledge. It seeks to answer questions about the nature of knowledge and the means by which it is acquired. Despite the large number of schools of philosophy, epistemology breaks down into two categories, one consistently Christian (or theistic) and the other basically antitheistic.

Christian Epistemology

A consistently Christian epistemology recognizes the ontological Trinity* as the ultimate starting point of all knowledge. It sees all the universe as God's creation and holds that no fact of creation can be properly described without reference to God the creator. In other words, every fact must be recognized as a created fact, or it cannot be properly recognized at all.

Thus, man's thinking cannot be creative, but analogical *(see Analogy)*. If he is to speak truly, man must say what God has already said. The triune God who has given us the Bible as His infallible revelation must be the ultimate starting point of all our knowledge. That is not to say that the Bible must become our source book for the study of, say, biochemistry or physics, but it is to say that all investigation into these and all other subjects must be interpreted in the light of the Bible.

Antitheistic Epistemology

The only alternative to this consistently Christian approach to epistemology is to start with a denial of the ultimacy of the ontological Trinity. All avowedly atheistic philosophies do this. But so do many professedly theistic approaches. For example, a common view is that the Christian shares the same reservoir of "facts" with the unbeliever and that each then must proceed to "judge" from these facts such things as whether God exists. However, this makes man the judge of God. It supposes God to be one fact among many other facts. It is, therefore, a denial of the absolute, ultimate reality of God and ascribes to Him at best the possibility of His coexistence with the universe. In effect, it posits the ultimacy of the creature.

Circular Reasoning

In each of these categories man reasons in a circle. He starts off with a presupposition, either theistic or antitheistic, and argues in a circle to the conclusion that what he presupposed was right. This is an important point: circular reasoning is really the only kind of reasoning open to finite man. Cornelius Van Til remarked that the only alternative to reasoning in a circle is reasoning in a vicious circle.

God is, and everything in the universe must be interpreted as a created fact. Only the presupposition of the God of revelation can encompass all the data. Every false presupposition breaks off a fragment of those data and presses them into service as witness against their creator. But theirs is a false and forced testimony. The entire body of created facts yields a consistent testimony to truth only when their united voice is raised as a witness to their creator.

Any epistemology that fails to recognize this drifts from the consistently Christian position. And the only real alternative to a consistently Christian position is to reason in the vicious circle of creature worship (Rom. 1:25).

See Knowledge of God (Man's).

ERASTIANISM

The theory propounded by Thomas Erastus (1524-83) that the power of government and discipline in the church is entrusted by God to the civil authority. It argued as follows. The church's power is solely one of admonition. Punitive power belongs solely to the civil authority. Therefore, the exercise of punitive power belongs to the civil authority.

Though it was advocated by Selden and Whitelock, Erastianism was rejected by the Westminster Assembly *(see Westminster Standards)*. The Assembly held that church and state each have their separate spheres, with each holding supreme power in its own province; but they are to cooperate for the glory of God.

EREMITE

Greek *eremos,* "desert"; ascetics who lived in isolation in a wilderness or some other solitary place.

See **Anchorite.**

ESCHATOLOGY

Greek *eschatos,* "last"; the doctrine of last things or the part of systematic theology that deals with last things. Eschatology sets forth the truth that the history of the individual, of the race, and of the world will reach its appointed consummation.

Individual eschatology covers the subjects of physical death; the immortality* of the soul, and the intermediate state.*

General eschatology covers the subjects of the second coming* of Christ; the millennium;* the resurrection* of the dead; and heaven and hell.*

ETERNAL GENERATION, ETERNAL SONSHIP

Who is the redeemer of God's elect? The *Shorter Catechism* answers, "The only Redeemer of God's elect is the Lord Jesus Christ, Who, being the eternal Son of God, became man, and so was, and continueth to be, God and man in two distinct natures, and one person for ever."

This statement is a theological masterpiece, wonderfully brief, but full of scriptural truth. It lays down the following Biblical doctrines about Christ's person:

1. His eternal sonship.*
2. His incarnation.*
3. His theanthropic person*—He is "God and man in two distinct natures."
4. His unipersonality*—though "God and man," He is "one person."
5. His sole position as the redeemer of God's elect, a position He holds forever, both in His state of humiliation and exaltation.

Eternal sonship is vital to a scriptural view of all these aspects of Christ's person.

J. C. Philpot says, "All Trinitarians...allow the following three truths.... 1. The union

of the two natures, the human and the divine, in the Person of the Lord Jesus. 2. That the human nature of the Lord Jesus was formed of the flesh of the Virgin by the supernatural operation of the Holy Ghost. 3. That He Who was born at Bethlehem was called the Son of God."

So far so good. But did He become the Son of God by His birth in Bethlehem, or later in His life, or was He the Son of God essentially and eternally? Some contend that Christ became the Son of God by birth. Others hold that He became the Son of God by virtue of His baptism, by His resurrection, or by His exaltation. Still others make *Son of God* refer merely to the office Christ assumed as our Saviour.

Each of these positions is exclusive. Only one of them is scriptural. The fact that each of the others stands condemned by the plain statements of the Bible and by the demands of simple logic shows that the doctrine of Christ's eternal sonship is the scriptural one.

Christ did not become the Son of God by His birth in Bethlehem.

Luke 1:35 is cited to prove that He did: "The Holy Ghost shall come upon thee, and the power of the Highest shall overshadow thee; therefore also that holy thing which shall be born of thee shall be called the Son of God."

This does not say that Christ became the Son of God by His birth. A comparison with the parallel promise in Matt. 1:23 demonstrates this. Each refers to the supernatural virgin birth of Christ. Matthew 1:23 says, "They shall call His name Emmanuel, which being interpreted is, God with us." Christ did not become God by His virgin birth. He could be called God at His birth because He already was God. Similarly, in Luke 1:35, He could be called the Son of God because He already was the Son of God.

This is the consistent testimony of the Word of God, as John 1:1-14 and Rom. 1:3

make clear. From these passages we reach some important conclusions:

1. That the Word existed from all eternity, for He "was God" and "was in the beginning with God" (John 1:1, 2).

2. That the Word became flesh (John 1:14; Rom. 1:3).

3. That He who became flesh was "God's Son, Jesus Christ our Lord" (Rom. 1:3).

4. That therefore the sonship of Christ preceded His coming into the world. It is eternal sonship. The same truths can be seen in a host of other texts. For example:

John 3:16: "For God so loved the world, that he gave his only begotten Son, that whosoever believeth in him should not perish, but have everlasting life." The sonship of Christ necessarily precedes His being given as God's gift to a lost world. Even God cannot give what does not exist.

1 John 4:9: "God sent his only begotten Son into the world." The verb *sent* testifies that Christ's sonship precedes the act of sending. The words cannot mean that God sent someone who had no existence as His Son prior to the act of sending.

The word *monogenes,* "only begotten," shows that these texts speak of sonship in the strict sense of the word. It denotes that the Son is the same eternal essence as the Father. It has in it no idea of subordination or inferiority. This is an important fact. It is often glibly stated that sonship denotes subjection and therefore cannot refer to the eternal relationship of the second person of the Trinity to the first person. Hebrews 5:8 clearly shows this assertion to be baseless: "Though he were a Son, yet learned he obedience." Christ's humiliation and obedience were not because He was a Son, but in spite of the fact that He was a Son. In the Godhead, *Son* indicates equality, not inferiority or subordination, for His existence as a Son preceded His learning obedience.

The parable of the wicked husbandman settles the point once and for all: "Having yet therefore one son, his wellbeloved, he sent him also last unto them" (Mark 12:6). The reference is clearly to Christ Himself and the doctrine is plain that He was God's Son before being sent into the world.

Christ did not become the Son of God by baptism.

Those who claim that Christ's sonship began at His baptism cite Matthew 3:17. But this text merely proves that God announced the fact of Christ's sonship at His baptism, not that Christ then became His Son. The Father again proclaimed Christ's sonship on the Mount of Transfiguration (Matt. 17:5). Was He made the Son of God on two occasions? Yet if "This is my beloved Son" in Matt. 3:17 means that He became God's Son at His baptism, the same words in Matt. 17:5 must mean that He became God's Son at His transfiguration. The notion is totally absurd. Both texts mean that He who was eternally the Son of God was on these occasions declared to be such by His Father.

Christ did not become the Son of God at His resurrection.

Acts 13:33 is cited as proof that it was at the resurrection that Christ became the Son of God. The simple fact that God had publicly identified Christ as His Son both at His baptism and His transfiguration proves that this cannot possibly be the meaning of this text. Acts 13:33 means that at His resurrection Christ was manifested to be the Son of God. Romans 1:4 makes this plain. It tells us that He was then "declared to be the Son of God."

Christ did not become the Son of God by His exaltation.

Some cite Hebrews 1:4 to show that it was when He was exalted to God's right hand that Christ became the Son of God. The argument we have just employed above holds good here, too. We may also note that Heb. 1 teaches that Christ the Son of God was made heir to all things. He was appointed heir because He was the Son of God;

He was not appointed the Son of God because He was made heir. Philippians 2:7-11 teaches the same truth. Christ's exaltation did not make Him the Son of God. Rather, being the eternal Son of God, He became man, the true mediator, representative, and high priest of all His people and as such is highly exalted.

Christ is not the Son of God by being our Mediator.

Many take *Son* to be exclusively a mediatorial title. Sabellians hold this position. They deny that God exists eternally as Father, Son, and Holy Spirit. They make these names to be nothing more than official titles under which the one and the same divine person has made Himself known to men. *Father, Son,* and *Holy Spirit* do not describe anything of the essential being of God. They merely describe certain relations into which He enters with His creatures. This third century heresy has surfaced in recent "oneness" sects.

Some evangelicals who claim to be sound trinitarians also make *Son* an exclusively mediatorial title. However, both Sabellian and evangelical proponents of this idea must designate some point in time at which Christ became the Son of God. Once they try to do that their argument breaks down.

The evidence of Scripture is that Christ's sonship is eternal. We have noted the force of the term *monogenes,* "only begotten." It is a very deep term and has given rise to the theological term the *eternal generation* of the Son. *Begotten* cannot denote anything but generation. At the same time, as we have seen, Christ's sonship is eternal and has in it no idea of inferiority of essence or posteriority of time. Thus we are shut up to the term *eternal generation.* Since we are describing the eternal God, it is understandable that human intelligence fails to define the term. We are limited to saying about God that which He has already said about Himself. The nearest thing to a definition of eternal generation which finite man can come to is that it is the communication of the divine essence by the Father to the Son from all eternity.

Arguing from John 1:14 and 17:5, J. C. Philpot puts the issue as clearly as anyone. His argument is in four steps leading to an inevitable conclusion.

"Jesus is the only begotten of the Father; this is the first step. As the only begotten of the Father He has a peculiar glory; this is the second step. This glory He had with the Father before the world was; this is the third step. As He could only possess this glory in His Divine nature, for His human did not then exist, He is the only begotten Son of God as God; this is the fourth step, and establishes the conclusion that He is the eternal Son of the Father, and that by eternal generation."

ETERNITY

Popularly used to denote the never-ending existence of souls after death; often spoken of in terms that almost equate it with a place. It is also popularly used to denote either immeasurable time or timelessness. Strictly, eternity is an attribute of God. He only possesses immortality, or true eternity (1 Tim. 1:17; 6:16). In this sense eternity denotes the absolute, unconditioned, simultaneous, immutable, and successionless existence of God. He is the great "I AM" (Exod. 3:14), "the first and the last" (Isa. 44:6), the One who is free from all limitations and constraints of time. He inhabits eternity (Isa. 57:15).

Thus true eternity belongs only to God. As theologians put it, His eternity is *a parte ante* and *a parte post*—i.e., it precedes the beginning of creation, and it continues after all the ages of history have run their course. However, the gospel promises eternal life to those who believe on the Lord Jesus Christ (John 3:15, 16). This life is everlasting; it will endure forever. But the idea goes beyond mere endlessness and includes the character of the life promised. It is life in fellowship with God, indeed the life of God in the soul of man, as Henry Scougal termed it.

On the other hand, Scripture speaks of "everlasting punishment" for the wicked (Matt. 25:46). Here again, while endless duration is clearly intended, the idea of the character of the punishment is included. The peculiar nature of eternal punishment arises from its relation to the action of the eternal God. It is an existence of unrelieved endurance of His retributive justice.*

Since we are creatures of time, the idea of eternity baffles us. It stresses the utter transcendence* of God and our utter dependence upon Him. And it warns us not to commit the unspeakable folly of becoming so engrossed in the affairs of this world, which are but for a day, that we neglect the gospel warning to lay hold on eternal life.

ETHICS

The science of morals. It concerns itself with man's actions of will and purpose. "All ethics then deals with these three questions: (a) What is the motive for human action? (b) What is the standard of human action? (c) What is the end or purpose of human action?" (Cornelius Van Til). In Van Til's last question, the goal for which men should strive is raised. The goal, usually called the *summum bonum,* or "highest good," is variously defined by different ethical writers according to the system they adopt. The scriptural standard is ably summed up in the answer to the first question in the *Shorter Catechism:* "Man's chief end is to glorify God and to enjoy Him forever."

ETHIOPIANIST THEOLOGY

A concept based on Psalm 68:31, "Ethiopia shall soon stretch out her hands unto God." Dibinga Wa Said summarized it as follows:

"The slogan of Ethiopianism was and still is Africa for the Africans. This theology stands for (1) radical recapture of the lost land; (2) radical withdrawal of whitianity from all African institutions (including white God, white Jesus); (3) joint action of local African anti-colonial movements of liberation (i.e., Mau Mau); (4) unconditional recognition and radical affirmation of Blackness through Black Sainthood (i.e., Kimpa Vita in the Congo, around 1450); Black Messiahhood (i.e., Chilembwe, Kimbangu, Shembe, etc.); through Black Prophethood (i.e., Alice Lenclina); (5) pursuit of a true Biblical religion which will save man from material and spiritual bondages: Generally the idea was and still is that the Black Messiah is at the gate of heaven; and that he is the holder of the keys. Only Black can enter. But under special circumstances, a few human whites may also enter depending on the number of seats left in the Kingdom of God or the New Jerusalem" (*Harvard Theological Review,* October 1971, p. 501-524).

See African Theology; Black Theology; Liberation Theology; Theology of Decolonization.

EUCHARIST

The Greek verb *eucharisteo,* "to give thanks," is used in 1 Cor. 11:24 of Christ giving thanks for the bread in the first celebration of the Lord's Supper.* The NT does not use the noun *eucharistia* as a description of the Lord's Supper. Its adoption expressed a growing sacramental attitude toward the communion service and nowadays it is almost exclusively employed by liturgical or ecumenical churches.

EUTYCHIANISM

The heresy of Eutyches concerning the theanthropic person* of Christ. Eutyches taught that the two natures of Christ united to form one compound nature. Though condemned by the council of Chalcedon in 451, Eutychianism later emerged as the Monophysitic heresy.

See Nestorianism; Monophysitism.

EVANGELICAL

From the word *euangelion,* "gospel," *evangelical* is a description of those who maintain:

1. The inspiration and authority of the Bible as the Word of God and the only rule of faith and practice.

2. Salvation as preeminently a matter of personal relationship with God through Jesus Christ.

3. The historic doctrines of the Christian faith, with particular emphasis on those which are essential to salvation.

4. Salvation by grace through faith in the person and work of the Lord Jesus Christ, not by human merit. Justification by faith in the merits of Christ's finished work has always been the distinguishing mark of evangelicalism. Thus, evangelicals direct men not to depend on any sacramental experience to bring them into a right relationship with God, but to receive Christ by personal, appropriating faith.

As J. I. Packer makes clear in *Fundamentalism and the Word of God,* historically *evangelicalism* and *fundamentalism* were different words that described the same theological position. A softer response toward liberalism* caused many evangelicals to distance themselves from the Fundamentalists to form what has become known as New Evangelicalism.*

EVOLUTION

The theory that in the very remote past lifeless matter gave rise by the action of natural forces to one or more living organisms. These in turn have developed and diversified to produce all living and extinct plants and animals, including man. In effect, this theory implies continuous creation, postulating increasing organization and complexity in the universe. Theistic evolution is the theory that God used such an evolutionary scheme to develop His creation.

Evolution as a theory is both unbiblical and unscientific. Indeed, while its basic propositions are continuous creation and increasing levels of organization and complexity, the most basic laws of all physical science—the laws of thermodynamics—make it clear that energy is no longer being created and that there is a decreasing level of organization and complexity throughout creation. Thus, on scientific evidence, the opposite to evolution is taking place.

See **Creation**.

EX NIHILO

A Latin phrase meaning "from nothing," used to convey the truth that in creation God did not merely reorganize already existent material, but by the power of His own creative word brought into being that which had no prior existence.

EX OPERE OPERATO

Opus Operatum. *

EXALTATION OF CHRIST

"Christ's exaltation consisteth in his rising again from the dead on the third day, in ascending up into heaven, in sitting at the right hand of God the Father, and in coming to judge the world at the last day" (*Shorter Catechism,* Q. 28.).

EXAMPLE THEORY OF THE ATONEMENT

A theory propounded by Socinians *(see* **Socinianism***)* that the death of Christ could not atone for our sin or render God propitious to sinners. Rather, the atonement gives men an example of faith and obedience as the way of eternal life. The theory is based on the notion that there is no such justice in God as demands that sin be punished.

The theory is totally wrong on every point, but glaringly so in that it allows no real connection between the death of Christ and the salvation of the sinner. In an attempt to overcome this failure Socinians taught that as a reward for His obedience unto death, Christ received power to bestow eternal life upon believers. But still it establishes no real connection between Christ's work and the salvation of sinners. Nor does it account for the salvation of OT saints or of infants, neither of whom could learn from Christ's example. The truth is that Christ is set forth in Scripture as an example to those whose sins have been expiated by His blood. He is never set forth as an example for sinners to follow in order to obtain salvation.

See **Expiation**.

EXCOMMUNICATION

The strongest discipline a church can exercise toward a member in its fellowship; judicial exclusion from the fellowship and privileges of membership in the visible church. It was instituted by Christ (Matt. 18:15, 18) and practised by His apostles (1Cor. 5:11; 1 Tim. 1:20; Titus. 3:10).

An excommunicated person becomes as a publican and heathen to the church, one to be "avoided" (Rom. 16:17; 1 Tim. 6:3) and "rejected" (Titus. 3:10), though not counted as an enemy (2 Thess. 3:14, 15). Excommunication is a last resort. It should not be employed lightly. McClintock and Strong sum up the Biblical data regarding its exercise. They make the following points:
1. It is a spiritual penalty, involving no temporal punishment except accidentally.
2. It consists in separation from the communion of the church.
3. Its object is the good of the sufferer (1 Cor. 5:5) and the protection of the sound members of the church (2 Tim. 3:1-7).
4. Its subjects are those who are guilty of heresy (1 Tim. 1:20) or gross immorality (1 Cor. 5:1. [We may add other categories such as those who cause divisions, Rom. 16:17.]
5. It is inflicted by the authority of the church (Matt. 18:18).

2 Thessalonians 3:14-15 indicates that the aim of excommunication should be restoration. It would appear that the incestuous person who was excommunicated in Corinth repented and was restored to fellowship.

EXEGESIS

A Greek word meaning "explanation." Exegesis is a branch of hermeneutics,* the science of interpretation. Hermeneutics has to do with the principles and scheme of interpretation; exegesis establishes the meaning of particular statements or passages.

See **Hermeneutics**; **Scripture (Interpretation of)**.

EXILIC

Pertaining to the exile, the 70-year captivity of the Jews in Babylon.

EXISTENTIALISM

The philosophy that there are no absolute values outside of man himself. It concentrates "on the existence of the individual who, being free and responsible, develops his essence through acts of the will" (*Oxford Illustrated Dictionary*). It is the doctrine of free will taken to its ultimate absurdity. Existentialism has adopted the ancient heresy of Pelagianism,* which stated
1. That a man may rightly be held responsible only for his unbiased volitions, and
2. Consequently, moral character cannot precede moral action. That is, man must choose his own character, or he cannot be held responsible for it.

Existentialism has fastened on to this notion. It denies that there is such a thing as a nature with which we are born. To the existentialist, nature is something acquired by free will, not inherited.

It has been said that existentialists are taken up completely with man. They have certainly made man the starting point and the consummation of their theory. Since existentialism is totally subjective and rebels against all absolute values imposed on man from outside of himself, existentialists have reached widely differing conclusions. The father of existentialism, Danish philosopher Soren Kierkegaard, professed that existentialism deepened his faith in God, while Jean-Paul Sartre, a twentieth-century French existential philosopher, was an atheist.

Though Neo-Orthodoxy* professes that existential faith is belief with an inward passion, and that Kierkegaard merely rescued the church from the dead formalism which substituted the symbols of the faith (baptism, doctrine, etc.) for faith itself, the truth is that the theism of Kierkegaard and the atheism of Sartre are not so opposed as they may at first appear. Both agree that man and not God is the starting point for all epistemology,* and that human judgment and not the Word of God is the determining factor in what is to be believed. It is ultimately a blatant self-contradiction for the existentialist to say, as neo-orthodox apologists for the system do, that existential faith is an act of self-surrender. There can be no surrender to God by any man while he holds on to the notion that there is no absolute value or authority outside his own will and while he makes himself the measure of God.

EXPIATION

The removal of guilt by means of an atonement or satisfaction rendered to God. "Expiation and propitiation are correlative terms; the sinner, or his guilt, is expiated; God, or justice, is propitiated. Guilt must, from the nature of God, be visited with punishment, which is the expression of God's disapprobation of sin. Guilt is expiated, in the Scriptural representation, covered, by satisfaction, i.e., by vicarious punishment. God is thereby rendered propitious, i.e., it is now consistent with His nature to pardon and bless the sinner. Propitious and loving are not convertible terms. God is love. He loved us while sinners and before satisfaction was rendered. Satisfaction or expiation does not awaken love in the divine mind. It only renders it consistent with His justice that God should exercise His love towards transgressors of His law" (Charles Hodge).

EXTERNAL CALL
*See **Calling**.*

EXTREME UNCTION

A sacrament of the Roman Catholic church in which there is an anointing of the sick with oil consecrated by a bishop. Extreme has a double significance:

1. Primarily, this unction is administered when the patient is *in extremis,* at the point of death;

2. It is the last of the three so-called sacramental unctions, baptism and confirmation being the other two. Rome's appeal to James 5:14, 15 for Biblical authority for this practice is far from convincing. In truth, there is no Biblical basis for the sacrament of extreme unction.

F

FAITH

1. In the general sense, faith is the assent of the mind to the truth of something of which we do not have an immediate conception, whereas knowledge is the perception of the truth of something of which we have an immediate conception. And yet, as A. A. Hodge points out in his commentary on the *Westminster Confession of Faith* (chapter 14), faith demands and rests upon evidence just as much as knowledge, and "when grounded on legitimate evidence it leads to absolute assurance."

2. Saving faith, or as the *Confession of Faith* puts it, "the grace of faith," is in the view of Thomas Halyburton, one of Scotland's greatest theologians, basically a hearty approbation of God's method of saving sinners. We may define it as the work of the Holy Spirit, His gift to God's elect, enabling them to believe as true whatever God has revealed in His Word and to accept, receive, and rest upon Christ alone for justification, sanctification, and eternal life. It is never alone, being always accompanied by repentance, and producing good works (Jas. 2:17-26).

3. *The Faith* is used as a general description of the entire gospel revelation, as in 1 Tim. 4:1; 5:8; 2 Tim. 4:7; Jude 3.

FAITH AND ORDER MOVEMENT

See **World Council of Churches**.

FALL

The name given to Adam's first transgression and his immediate descent into a state of guilt and condemnation before God. In the words of the *Shorter Catechism,* "The covenant being made with Adam not only for himself, but for all his posterity; all mankind, descending from him by ordinary generation, sinned in him, and fell with him in his first transgression" (Q. 16). The fall brought mankind into a condition of sinfulness and misery. Question 18 of the *Catechism* describes the *sinfulness* of fallen man's condition as consisting in "the guilt of Adam's first sin, the want [absence] of original righteousness, and the corruption of his whole nature, which is commonly called Original Sin; together with all actual transgressions" which proceed from such a corrupt source. In Q. 19 the *Catechism* goes on to describe the *misery* of mankind because of the fall: the loss of communion with God; His wrath and curse; the liability to all miseries in this life, to death itself, and the to pains of hell forever.

See **Primitive State**.

FALSE DECRETALS

See **Decretals (False)**.

FAMA CLAMOSA

Latin, meaning in general, "a bad report." In Presbyterian church codes, it is the ground for proceeding against a minister or member on common report rather than on a charge. "If the rumour, or *fama clamosa,* be general and hurtful, the court can investigate it without any accuser, for the vindication of the character of the church and of the court, and with a view to the preservation of good morals in the community" (McClintock and Strong).

FANATICISM

From the Latin *fanaticus,* "pertaining to, or inspired from, a temple" (*fanum*); excessive and unreasonable zeal for a cause or opinion. The charge of fanaticism has often been levelled against Christians who are "zealously affected in a good thing" (Gal. 4:18), but this is unjust. There is a world of difference between Christian zeal and fanaticism. Fanaticism rejects reason and follows the fancy of the fanatic. It is usually absorbed with a single idea and lacks the balance of seeing that idea in the overall system of revealed truth. It is intolerant of investigation and of any different interpretation of its pet opinion or cause.

Fanaticism has frequently developed a persecuting spirit. It launched the crusades; it stoked the fires of the Inquisition; it sounded Pope Gregory XIII's *Te Deum* as a jubilant response to the massacre of St. Bartholomew's eve. In recent times it has unleashed the violence of the bomb and the bullet at abortion clinics.

All these examples are clear departures from Christian belief and conduct. They are far removed from the zeal of people like the early Methodists, who were nevertheless stigmatized as *enthusiasts,* the jargon of the day for fanatics. But zealous Christianity is not fanaticism. If fanaticism is "enthusiasm enflamed by hatred," it has no place in the creed or conduct of Christians. Yet Christians may be and should be militant for the truth of the gospel and should dedicate their time, talents, and resources to its propagation. The fear of the label of fanaticism must never frighten them into abandoning their zeal for the spread and defence of the gospel. Nevertheless, they must ensure that their zeal is always "according to knowledge."

FATALISM

The theory of inevitable necessity; the heathen oriental philosophy that all things are predetermined by blind, irrational forces and that therefore there is no point in human effort to change anything. It is the satanic counterfeit of the revealed truth of God's word that the all-wise God has planned all things according to His will.

*See **Predestination**.*

FEDERAL THEOLOGY

All mankind are viewed in Scripture in relation to the two Adams. The first Adam was the natural head of the entire human race. According to Rom. 5:12 we all sinned in him. We were in him, and in him were a party to the covenant of works. Thus, Adam was not merely a private person, but a public person, the real and proper head of all his posterity. He was their federal head, as well as their natural head. Therefore, legally, the guilt of his fall is righteously imputed to all his posterity.

The last Adam, the Lord Jesus Christ is, by the grace of God, placed at the head of His people. Their union with Him is spiritual, not natural, but nonetheless real. They are said to be "in Christ" just as truly as Adam's posterity is said to be "in Adam." Thus, as the disobedience of Adam was righteously imputed to all those for whom he was a federal head and representative, the obedience of Christ is righteously, legally, and effectively imputed to all those of whom He is the federal head.

Since all mankind fell in Adam and came under condemnation because of his sin and since there is no recuperative power in our fallen nature *(see **Depravity**),* it was necessary, if sinners were to be saved, that the condemning law should be satisfied by one who had no federal connection with Adam and who was therefore free from the imputation of his guilt—one who, nonetheless, must be truly human and able to stand as the federal head of a new race.

Federal theology holds that the Scriptures (see especially Rom. 5 and 1 Cor. 15) teach that the Lord Jesus Christ came in this capacity and sustains this federal relationship to His people. By His life He satisfied the precept of the law and by His death He satisfied its penalty. As the covenant of works was made with Adam and his posterity in him and led to the condemnation of his race, so the covenant of grace was made with Christ and in Him with all His people, by virtue of which God imputes to them the merits of the full obedience of their Head, Jesus Christ.

See *Covenant Theology; Creationism; Traducianism.*

FEMINIST THEOLOGY

A rejection or reinterpretation of Biblical theology on the basis of "the absolute right of women to develop theological understanding rooted in their own realities and experiences" (the words are from a declaration issued by Church Women United, a feminist ecumenical group). Feminist theology operates on the assumption that the Bible and historic Christianity are patriarchal and sexist. That is, that their God is a male God, most of whose prophets and all of whose apostles were males, and whose ministry and leadership were open only to males. According to feminists these theological characteristics are not the result of divine revelation but are a product of the unenlightened and abusive cultures of the times and places in which the Bible was compiled.

Not surprisingly, feminist theology is an extremely radical departure from Biblical Christianity. In some cases it descends to the promotion of witchcraft or the worship of mother earth. At a November 1993 conference in Minneapolis, some 2,000 feminists heard Chinese feminist Kwok Pui-Lan claim, "If we cannot imagine Jesus as a tree, as a river, as a wind, and as rain, we are doomed together." A Korean university professor Chung Hyun Kyung used New Age* techniques to lead the gathering in an attempt to harness the divine energy of the universe. Other speakers turned to pantheistic religions and to the heretical gnostic gospels to "reimagine" a new god and a new way of salvation.

The gathered feminists worshipped a new goddess, Sophia, whom they claimed to be the embodiment of wisdom found in Proverbs 8. According to them, Sophia is "the tree of life to those who lay hold

of her." In praying to Sophia the ecumenical feminists in Minneapolis descended to raw sensualism and sexism. They prayed, "Our maker, Sophia, we are women in your image, with the hot blood of our wombs we give form to new life,…with nectar between our thighs we invite a lover,…with our warm body fluids we remind the world of its pleasures and sensations."

With such degeneracy at the heart of their theology, feminist theologians have a violent hatred of essential Christian doctrine. Speakers in Minneapolis "charged that the church and its belief in the incarnation and atonement of Jesus Christ was a patriarchal construct and had caused oppression of women, violence in the streets, child abuse, racism, classism, sexism, and pollution" (*Christianity Today,* April 4, 1994).

Virginia Mollenkott, an ex-Fundamentalist English professor (and an advisor to the translators of the *New International Version of the Bible*) said, "I can no longer worship in a theological context that depicts god as an abusive parent and Jesus as the obedient trusting child. This violent theology encourages the violence of our streets and nation." Another speaker, Delores Williams, said, "I don't think we need folks hanging on crosses and blood dripping and weird stuff."

The influence of feminist theology is apparent from the attempts to produce gender-neutral Bible translations. This is no innocent reevaluation of the role of women. It is a radical attack on the entire Biblical revelation. It shares the premise of all destructive critical movements that the Bible's description of God is part of man's evolving search for Him, not God's personal self-disclosure to man. It rejects the central doctrines of Scripture, from the transcendence of God to the way of salvation.

It lays outrageous charges at the door of Bible Christianity, charges it does not and cannot substantiate. It is vitriolically false to lay the blame for America's street violence on the gospel. In fact, the evidence is that wherever the gospel penetrates the lives of those involved in that violence they cease from it and live to counteract it. The effects of feminist theology are widespread and dangerous. By redefining and recasting the roles of men and women in both home and church it challenges the husband/wife relationship God ordained at creation and thus undermines the Biblical basis for stable and happy family life. It also challenges the NT model for the government and ministry of the church and replaces divinely revealed norms with the current notions of radical feminists.

In rejecting what it claims to be the male orientation of Scripture for a religious programme of women's rights, or a religion based on women's consciousness, Feminist theology leads women to "another gospel which is not another," but a perversion. As with every other departure from the gospel, it fulfils the word of 2 Pet. 2:19: "While they promise them liberty, they themselves are the servants of corruption."

See **Political Theology**.

FENCING THE TABLE

The term used in Scottish Presbyterianism to describe the special address given before the administration of the Lord's Supper* pointing out the character of worthy communicants according to the Scriptures and strongly warning those who do not display such a character against communicating.

FESTSCHRIFT

German, "feast writing"; a collection of scholarly articles written by colleagues of an eminent scholar in honour of some notable milestone in his career, such as a birthday or retirement.

FIFTH MONARCHISM

A fanatical English millenarian sect, an offshoot of the Levellers,* in the times of Oliver Cromwell. The name came from the idea that the time of the fourth and last of the world empires of Daniel 2, the Roman empire, was about to end and that Christ was just about to return to set up His throne—the fifth universal monarch. Fifth Monarchy men saw it as their task to remove human governments from impeding Christ's way and so to facilitate His coming and His kingdom.

FILIATION

The term used in the discussion of the doctrine of the Trinity to denote the internal and eternal activity of the divine essence, by virtue of which the second person of the Trinity is called "the only begotten of the Father." It is, therefore, synonymous with eternal generation, the communication from all eternity of the divine essence by the Father to the Son.

See **Opera Ad Intra**.

FILIOQUE

A Latin word meaning "and from the Son." It is found in the Western versions of the Nicene Creed in the section that deals with the Procession of the Spirit.* The inclusion of *filioque* asserts that the Spirit proceeds from the Father and from the Son. The word was not in the original formulation of the Nicene Creed, and its adoption by the Western Church was a major reason for the schism in 1054 between it and the Eastern Church, which vehemently opposed its insertion. The reasons for this opposition were partly Scriptural (they hold that John 15:26 speaks only of the Spirit proceeding from the Father—an argument which fails to look at all the Scripture teaching on the subject) and partly a matter of church politics, because this addition had been made without the consent of any ecumenical council.

FIVE POINTS OF CONTROVERSY

Often mistakenly called "The Five Points of Calvinism."* In the years before the Synod of Dort (1618-1619) there were grave controversies in which a group known as the Dutch Remonstrants opposed the accepted

Calvinistic system of the churches represented at the Council. These Remonstrants were led by Jacob Arminius, professor of theology at the University of Leyden from 1602-1609. The Remonstrants, also known as Semi-Pelagians* and more generally, as Arminians,* set forth their position (1611) in contrast to that of the Protestant churches in five points. These are known as the five points of controversy between the followers of Arminius and the followers of Calvin. They are as follows:

1. Conditional Election: From all eternity God determined to bestow salvation on those whom He foresaw would persevere to the end in their faith in Christ. Likewise, He determined to inflict everlasting punishment on those whom He foresaw would continue in their unbelief and resist to the end of their life His divine help.

2. Universal Atonement: The Lord Jesus Christ by His sufferings and death made atonement for the sins of mankind generally and of every individual in particular. However, only believers actually partake of the benefits of that atonement.

3. Depravity: Because of his natural corruption man cannot think or do any good thing, and so true faith (by which alone sinners can partake of the benefits of Christ's atonement) cannot proceed from the exercise either of man's natural faculties or of his free will. It is, therefore, necessary to his conversion and salvation that he be regenerated and renewed by the operation of the Holy Ghost, which is the gift of God through Jesus Christ. Evangelical Arminians still hold to the original Remonstrant statement on this subject, placing the work of the Spirit before the exercise of faith and repentance, though the Remonstrants themselves were led to more and more unscriptural positions by the successors of Arminius and Episcopius.

4. Resistible Grace: This divine energy of the grace of the Holy Spirit heals the disorders of corrupt nature and begins and perfects everything that can be called good in man, so that all good works in man are attributed to God and the operation of His grace. Nevertheless, such regenerating grace may be resisted and rendered ineffectual by the perverse will of the impenitent sinner.

5. Fall from Grace: Believers are furnished with abundant strength and help, sufficient to enable them to triumph over the seductions of Satan and the allurements of sin. However, by the neglect of this help, they may fall from grace, and, if they die in such a state, must finally perish.

The Remonstrants were at first doubtful about this last notion of falling from grace, but later adopted it as an established doctrine.

The so-called *Five Points of Calvinism* were a direct answer to these points made by the Remonstrants. Calvinism does not consist of five points. The five points made by Calvinists were specific responses to the points raised by the Remonstrants. Calvinism goes far beyond them.

*See **Depravity**; **Election**; **Irresistible Grace**; **Particular Redemption**; **Perseverance of the Saints**.*

FIVE WAYS

The five proofs devised and formulated by Thomas Aquinas to demonstrate the existence of God. They are as follows:

1. The proof of *the unmoved mover.* Whatever is moved is moved by something. Since an infinite progression backwards is impossible, we are forced to conclude that there is a force that started it all, that moves others, without itself being moved. Aquinas believed this to be God.

2. The proof of *the first cause.* Every effect must have a cause adequate to produce it. An infinite succession of causes and effects is impossible. Therefore, there must be a cause which itself is uncaused. This is God.

3. The proof of *a necessary source of all contingency.* "We find in nature things that are possible to be and not to be....But it is impossible for these always to exist, for that which is possible not to be at some time is not. Therefore, if everything is possible not to be, then at one time there could have been nothing in existence. Now if this were true, even now there would be nothing in existence, because that which does not exist only begins to exist by something already existing....Therefore, not all beings are merely possible, but there must exist something the existence of which is necessary. But every necessary thing either has its necessity caused by another or not. Now it is impossible to go on to infinity in necessary things which have their necessity caused by another, as has already been proved in regard to efficient causes. Therefore we cannot but postulate the existence of some being having of itself its own necessity, and not receiving it from another, but rather causing in others their necessity. This all men speak of as God." (Aquinas, *Summa Theologica,* part 1, question 2, article 3).

4. The proof of *the highest good.* "Among beings there are some more or less good, true, noble, and the like. But more and less are predicated of different things, according as they resemble in their different ways something which is the maximum, as a thing is said to be hotter as it more nearly resembles that which is hottest; so that there is something which is truest, something best, something noblest, and consequently something which is uttermost being,...and this we call God" (ibid.).

5. The proof of *purpose in the physical world.* There is a discernible purpose in how even the merely material parts of the world work. They act generally in the same way to obtain the best result. "Hence it is plain that not fortuitously, but designedly, do they achieve their end. Now whatever lacks intelligence cannot move towards an end, unless it be directed by some being endowed with knowledge and intelligence; as the arrow is shot to its mark by the archer. Therefore some intelligent being exists by whom all natural things are directed to their end;

and this being we call God" (ibid.).

In all this Aquinas adopted and developed the metaphysics of Aristotle *(see **Aristotelianism).** This type of demonstration is in accord with Aquinas's views of natural theology* and the role of reason to lead to faith. The classical arguments for God's existence* largely follow Aquinas's lead.

FOLK CHURCH

A national church in which citizens of the state are reckoned members of the visible church, much as Israelites were members of the OT church. The concept does not in itself lead to the belief that all such people are true Christians, or lessen the need of personal regeneration and justification. "He is not a Jew, which is one outwardly; neither is that circumcision, which is outward in the flesh: but he is a Jew, which is one inwardly; and circumcision is that of the heart" (Rom. 2:28, 29). Similarly, he is not a Christian who is one outwardly, neither is that baptism which is outward in the flesh.

The concept of a national or folk church has its strengths. For example, it should keep the spiritual concerns of the Word of God at the heart of the affairs of the nation. Again, as Thomas Chalmers argued, only a state church has the resources effectively to evangelize the inner cities and other areas of extreme poverty.

However, it must be admitted that no state church has actually realized the claimed benefits of the system. On the contrary, in every case the notion of a folk church has corrupted true evangelism and has pronounced Christian those who clearly have no Scriptural right to the title. It was this reduction of the claims of the gospel to such a lifeless form that stirred both Soren Kierkegaard and Dietrich Bonhoeffer to emphasize faith as an existential experience of crisis. Their solution ultimately failed to remain faithful to the gospel, but we can well understand Bonhoeffer's rejection of folk church Christianity as "cheap grace."

FOREKNOWLEDGE

The eternal, all-inclusive, all-comprehensive knowledge God has of all creatures and events. The knowledge of God is above time. He knows all things throughout all time simultaneously. But we are limited by time. Our knowledge is gained by a succession of experiences. Thus what is eternally known to God, in all its connections, is from a human standpoint said to be *foreknown.*

In Scripture, the word *foreknowledge* is used also in a much narrower context. According to Rom. 8:29 God foreknows people, not merely the events surrounding them. When Scripture uses the verb *know* of people, it conveys the idea of God's loving purpose. It refers to His eternal decree. 1 Peter 1:2 places election on the ground of foreknowledge, and verse 20 shows that *foreknown* means *fore-decreed.* Acts 2:23 defines foreknowledge as God's *determinate counsel (see **Granville Sharpe Rule).** Thus election proceeds, not upon foreseen faith, but upon the decree of God.

FOREORDINATION

*See **Predestination**.*

FORM CRITICISM

A method of criticizing ancient literature which, when applied to the Bible, claims to uncover the oral traditions behind the literary sources of the Bible. With regard to the OT, form criticism denies the possibility of establishing any credible history of ancient times from the Scripture text. The form critic must get behind the Scripture by using the evidence of the contemporary situation in Israel's neighbouring pagan countries. From this evidence he must reconstruct by a "synthetic creation" method (quite simply, by the use of his imagination) the oral traditions which were finally reduced to writing at a later date.

With regard to the NT, the theory is that the NT books with their references to the supernatural are really late embellishments on the simple oral traditions of the period A.D.. 30-60. Dialectical theologians such as Rudolph Bultmann used this method. So did liberals such as C. H. Dodd *(see **Realized Eschatology).** Dodd described its procedure:

"*Formgeschichte,* or 'Form-criticism,' has taught us that in order to understand rightly any passage in the Gospels we must enquire into the 'setting in life' (*Sitz im Leben*) in which the tradition underlying that passage took form. The original 'setting in life' of any authentic saying of Jesus was of course provided by the actual conditions of His ministry. But the form critics rightly call our attention to the fact that the formed traditions of His teaching, as it reaches us, has often been affected by the changed conditions under which His followers lived during the period between His death and the completion of our Gospels. Its 'setting in life' is provided by the situation in the early Church. It is important to bear this distinction in mind in studying the parables [the subject of Dodd's book]. We shall sometimes have to remove a parable from its setting in the life and thought of the Church, as represented by the Gospels, and make an attempt to reconstruct its original setting in the life of Jesus" (*The Parables of the Kingdom,* p. 111).

Form criticism demands a long period of oral tradition during which the experience of the church led it to interpolate its interpretations into the original sayings of Jesus and the earliest record of them. It therefore constructs a scheme of early history out of the necessities created by its own theological and literary presuppositions. If objective evidence shows that its fundamental idea of a substantial period of oral tradition before the writing of our Gospels is wrong, the entire scheme stands condemned. That is precisely the situation. Renowned papyrologist José O'Callaghan has identified as NT portions papyrus fragments discovered at Qumran that date from

A.D.. 50-70. It is form criticism, not the NT, that is proved unhistorical and unreliable.

See **Criticism**; **Myth**; **Q**; **Redaction Criticism**.

FORM OF GOD

The expression in Phil. 2:6 is of great importance in discussion of the subjects of the Trinity and the deity of Christ. The words *a form of God* cannot be adequately explained except on the basis that the passage teaches the essential deity of Christ and His distinctive trinitarian person. The Greek word *morphe* has no reference to shape, or any other external mark, "but refers to the distinctive nature and character of the being to whom it pertains, and is thus permanently identified with the nature and character. Thus it is distinguished from *schema* ('fashion'), comprising that which appeals to the senses and is changeable. *Morphe,* form, is identified with the essence of a person or thing: *schema,* fashion, is an accident which may change without affecting the form" (M. R. Vincent, *Word Studies in the New Testament: accident* here means a quality not inherent in the essence of a thing). The undoubted force of *morphe* validates the statement of E. H. Gifford: "Morphe is…the Divine Nature actually and inseparably subsisting in the Person of Christ." It is an expression of the essential deity of Christ.

It also has an important witness to give in relation to the doctrine of the Trinity. In Phil. 2:6, as Shedd points out, *morphe* is anarthrous (not having the definite article). Literally, the text reads, "Who being in *a* form of God." That is to say, there is more than one *form,* or personal subsistence, of the divine essence.

FORMAL EQUIVALENCE

The method of Bible translation adopted by the Authorized Version translators and others who seek to represent not merely the general thought of the Scripture text but the very expressions in which it is conveyed. Where possible, formal equivalence translations use a word or phrase in the receptor language for every one in the original. The AV even uses a system of italics to indicate where the translators had to supply words not in the original to give full expression of its meaning in English.

A formal equivalence translation is not always necessarily literal. At times it must translate idiom for idiom. In Gen. 16:12 we learn that Ishmael would dwell "in the presence of all his brethren," but the Hebrew text literally says "in the face of all his brethren." In Gen. 23:11 Ephron offered to give the cave of Machpelah to Abraham, saying, "In the presence of the sons of my people give I it thee." Here the Hebrew word for *presence* means *eye.* No one doubts that in each case *presence* is the proper translation.

Similarly, when the Lord commanded Moses to consecrate the priests the words He used literally mean "fill the hand." This is a Hebraism that in our English idiom signifies "consecrate." In cases such as these, formal equivalence does not call for wooden word-for-word literalness. This would obscure the meaning, not clarify it.

For that reason some conservative translators prefer the term *complete equivalence.* Where a word-for-word representation of the Biblical text in the receptor language yields the meaning of the original precisely they seek to supply it. Where exact literalness is impossible, they supply the free translation that best represents the meaning of the original.

The very words of Scripture are inspired. They are not the disposable garb of God's truth which may be changed without affecting the truth they convey. That is the fundamental truth which formal equivalence and complete equivalence translators seek to maintain as they present people with the word of God in their own tongues.

See **Dynamic Equivalence**.

FORMULA CONCORDIAE

"Formula of Concord," prepared in 1577 for the purpose of settling differences in the Lutheran church, especially on the subject of the Lord's presence in the Eucharist.* It gave the "high" Lutheran view on this subject *(see Consubstantiation).*

FREE WILL

Free will has been variously defined. **1.** It has been called the *freedom of indeterminacy,* which holds that man's will is independent of all previous conditions. This is the claim that free will in man is a total freedom, unaffected by anything that occurred in the past, such as the fall.* This is the theory of most Bible deniers, particularly those of the existential school *(see Existentialism).* **2.** Free will in man has also been called the *freedom of self-determination,* or spontaneity. That is, man's free will consists in his ability to choose according to the disposition, inclination, or bias of his own will. This is the scriptural doctrine.

Because of the fall, man's will is inclined away from God and disposed toward self and sin. Man cannot choose against the bias of his will. And the bias he has toward self and sin is a voluntary bias; it is not imposed upon him by God. Therefore, his choice is truly a free choice, one which carries with it the responsibility for making it.

When free will is understood in this way, it is easy to see how Reformed theologians can on the one hand teach the Biblical doctrine of predestination* while on the other hand maintaining that man is a free and responsible moral agent. Similarly, we can see how we can speak of free will, while holding with Luther the doctrine of the bondage of the will: man acts according to the inclination of his will, but that inclination is ensnared by Satan and sin. In truth, unregenerate man's vaunted freedom of will is freedom to sin, freedom to become an ever greater slave to sin. **3.** A third definition of free will, held by Arminian theologians, goes beyond self-determination to include what is called the power of contrary choice. It is argued that to say that a sinner freely chooses to reject Christ and remain in sin implies that he has the native capability of choosing to receive Christ.

This theory is based upon a fallacy. The power of contrary choice is not the essence of free will, as may be easily shown. God is supremely free. He can choose to do good, but He cannot choose to do anything sinful. His freedom consists in choosing and acting according to the disposition of His will, without the power of contrary choice.

Self-determination alone then is the essence of free will. It is the sinner's free choice. *Free choice* is a choice in full accord with and proceeding from the voluntary disposition of his will. The moral responsibility for such a choice is derived, not from some fancied ability to make the opposite choice, but from the fact that it springs from the voluntary disposition of his will.

See *Self Determination*; *Will.*

FULNESS OF THE HOLY SPIRIT

The NT uses the terms *full* and *filled* to describe the experience of the Holy Spirit every Christian should have. The similarity of the words has led many to see no material distinction in their meanings. However, a study of the NT's usage will show how necessary and beneficial it is to give careful attention to the precise meaning and use of each term.

Fulness as Expressed by the Noun *Pleroma*

All fulness *(pleroma)* dwells in Christ (Col. 1:19; 2:9). All Christians "are complete *(pepleromenoi)* in Him (Col. 2:10). That is, they are *filled full* in Him. That is the position of every Christian by virtue of his being in Christ. In Eph. 1:22, 23 Paul says that God "gave him [Christ] to be head over all things to the church, which is his body, the fulness of him that filleth all in all." Lenski gives the literal sense of this difficult text: "Him he gave as head over everything to the church since she is his body, the fulness of him who fills all things in all ways for himself."

From these texts we gather that there is a fulness that is natural to every Christian. It inheres in the very idea of being in Christ. It is a major part of the Holy Spirit's ministry in believers to lead them to see and appropriate that fulness (1 Cor. 2:9-10). For example, He leads them into *full assurance.* This phrase is commonly taken simply as a reference to assurance of salvation. The NT certainly warrants that, but it speaks of full assurance in three distinct ways: the full assurance of *understanding* (Col. 2:2), of *faith* (Heb. 10:22), and of *hope* (Heb. 6:11). The *full assurance* in each of these texts is the word *plerophoria,* lit. "full-carrying."

Christians who live with a full knowledge of the gospel, in a full faith that Christ is theirs and a full confidence of their security in Him, will live in the fulness of the Spirit as their consistent experience.

Fulness as Expressed by the Verb *Pleroo*

Ephesians 5:18 commands Christians, "Be not drunk with wine, wherein is excess; but be filled with the Spirit." The verb is *pleroo* and the obvious meaning of the verse is that in contrast to a drunkard, who is controlled by alcohol, a Christian should live his life under the control of the Holy Spirit. In other words, the idea of *fulness* here is that of an habitual state. This is confirmed by Acts 7:55, which speaks of Stephen's "being full of the Holy Ghost." The Greek text indicates that he *existed full* of the Holy Ghost (*huparchon pleres*). John 12:3 provides a good illustration. As the fragrance of Mary's ointment filled (*pleroo*) the house, the influence of the Holy Spirit should fill every part of the believer's life.

God commands His people to live full of the Holy Spirit. The significance of this command is clear from Eph. 5:18-6:18. Christians should submit to the Spirit's control in every department of their lives. Paul mentions every major sphere of life: church, home, marriage, parent/child relationships, business, employer/employee relationships, and the whole area of spiritual warfare.

Fulness as Expressed by the Verb *Pletho*

The NT speaks of a sudden infilling of Christians with divine power for the service of God. In these cases it employs the verb *pletho,* as in Acts 2:4: "They were all filled with the Holy Ghost."

The difference between *pleroo* and *pletho* is clear from Acts 19:28, 29, which records the result of the incendiary speech of Demetrius the silversmith to the Ephesian idol makers: "When they heard these sayings, they were full of wrath, and cried out, saying, Great is Diana of the Ephesians. And the whole city was filled with confusion." The idol makers were *full* (*pleroo*) of wrath against the apostles. That was their ongoing attitude to them. The city was brought to a crisis and was suddenly *filled* (*pletho*) with confusion by the accusation laid against the apostles.

We must observe this difference if we are to do justice to all the NT data on the subject of the fulness of the Spirit. The evidence is that the Lord *fills* (*pletho*) with the power of the Spirit those who *are full* (*pleros*) of the Spirit. The similarity of the words causes confusion for many, but the idea is truly scriptural. It is one every Christian immediately recognizes: God imparts power for His service to Christians who are living in submission to the influence and leading of the Holy Spirit.

Fulness of Power

The result of the infilling of the Spirit is always power for service. This power is the authority and ability to be an effective witness for Christ (Acts 1:8; 4:31, 33; 1 Thess. 1:5).

This infilling of power to serve must be renewed for each new challenge. Again and again the apostles "were filled" with power to do the work of God, each filling being a distinct *crisis* experience to empower them for some new service (Acts 2:4; 4:8, 31; 9:17; 13:9).

God is sovereign in the manner, time, and extent of the manifestations of His power. He may choose to send a mighty revival. He may choose to use His people in a much more limited manner. While it is natural that we should desire a great demonstration of the Spirit's power, we must remember that God is sovereign and all-wise in deciding the extent of His Spirit's gracious working. Whatever His purpose as to the extent and precise manner of the Spirit's working at any given time, it is our duty to *exist full* of the Holy Spirit and therefore to be available and fit for use in His service as He directs.

How to Obtain the Fulness of Power

The question of how we may obtain God's power for service is an urgent one. He has given His people encouraging promises, and they have a warrant for their faith in seeking His power for service. Scripture gives us clear guidelines in our quest for the Spirit's power.
1. Live *full* of the Holy Ghost (Eph. 5:18).
2. Desire much of the revelation of Christ in the word. An apprehension of His love will beget in us a love for Him and His service. The more we know of Him, the more we will be moved to bring others to know Him. The assurance of our perfect standing in Him will deliver us from the fear of man and give us boldness to witness.
3. Pray specifically for the gift of the Spirit (Luke 11:13; 24:49; Acts 1:4, 5). The aim in such praying must be the glory of God, not our enjoyment of some esoteric experience. God imparted the power of the Holy Spirit to a praying people at Pentecost. He has not changed. He gives the Spirit's power to those who seek Him (Acts 4:31) and obey Him (Acts 5:32).

FUNDAMENTALISM

The term used to denote a movement which received its name from a set of twelve booklets published between 1910 and 1912, *The Fundamentals: A Testimony to the Truth*. These booklets and the movement that took its name from them sought to establish a testimony to the great basic doctrines of evangelical Protestantism. In May 1919 in Philadelphia, the World's Christian Fundamentals Association was formed with W. B. Riley as its president. It required its members to adhere to nine points of doctrine held to be fundamental:
1. The inspiration and inerrancy of Scripture.
2. The Trinity.
3. The deity and virgin birth of Christ.
4. The creation and fall of man.
5. Christ's substitutionary atonement.
6. The bodily resurrection and ascension of Christ.
7. The regeneration of believers.
8. The imminent and personal return of Christ.
9. The resurrection; eternal blessedness for the redeemed and eternal woe for the unregenerate.

The term *Fundamentalism* came into use in 1920 as a description of the position of the anti-modernist party in the Northern Baptist Convention. It then became the popular name for the evangelical theology of those in various Protestant denominations who were militantly opposed to the modernism* that was then taking over the major denominations of America. Thus from the beginning a Fundamentalist was an evangelical on a crusade against modernistic attacks on the faith. In time, as modernist control of the major denominations and seminaries strengthened, many Fundamentalists felt the need to separate and form new denominations, associations, or independent congregations.

Some evangelicals rebelled against the militant stand of Fundamentalism and developed New-Evangelicalism,* which Fundamentalists see as the old compromise with infidelity in a new garb.

The use of the term *Fundamentalism* has been extended and confused in recent years by its application to the ultraconservative wing of any religion, for example "Islamic Fundamentalism," or "Jewish Fundamentalism." This has given the word the connotation of religious extremism and intolerance. This vicious innuendo allows Bible believers to be dismissed as mindless obscurantists, or treated as a danger to society (for many "fundamentalists," especially of the Islamic type, are terrorists). A 1994 Vatican document, *The Interpretation of the Bible in the Church,* accuses Biblical Fundamentalists of a kind of spiritual terrorism: "Without saying as much in so many words, fundamentalism actually invites people to a kind of spiritual suicide." The Vatican document continues in the same vein: "Its [i.e., Fundamentalism's] relying upon a non-critical reading of certain texts of the Bible serves to reinforce political ideas and social attitudes that are marked by prejudices—racism, for example quite contrary to the Christian gospel."

Fundamentalists may be excused for treating such criticism from the Vatican as an example of boldfaced hypocrisy, for the popes of Rome have done more than any other religious organization to bathe the world in blood. Perhaps the real danger the Vatican perceives in Fundamentalism is the fact that it is seeing great numbers of Roman Catholics, especially in Latin America, converted. Rome's document actually pinpoints a major attraction of Fundamentalism, though it labels it dangerous: "The fundamentalist approach is dangerous, for it is attractive to people who look to the Bible for ready answers to the problems of life." If that is deemed dangerous, Fundamentalists would plead guilty to the charge. They do look to the Bible for divine answers, readily available and clearly comprehensible, to the spiritual, social, and personal

problems they face. They believe the Bible is God's Word and that it has the answers they need.

The Vatican document fosters the widely repeated fallacy that Fundamentalists do not interpret the Bible. The secular press regularly distinguishes between Fundamentalists and rationalistic critics of the Bible by saying that while the latter interpret the Bible, Fundamentalists believe it literally. The fact is that Fundamentalists do interpret the Bible, but they interpret it according to the principles laid down in and demanded by the Bible itself. They refuse to make the Bible the prisoner of whatever rationalistic or philosophic fantasy happens to be in vogue. They refuse to accept that the verbal revelation of Scripture is the historically and culturally conditioned—and therefore unfactual, inadequate, and misleading—garb under which God's abiding truth somehow lies hidden. They look upon such a critical procedure as deceitful or, at best, mere wishful thinking—for if the Bible proves false in its statements of history and dangerous in its statements of political, social, and personal morality, how and why should we take its inner message, conveyed by its flawed and outdated words, as divine?

Fundamentalism is an honest and serious attempt to take the Bible for what it claims to be, and what the Christian church throughout history has acknowledged it to be—the verbally inspired word of God, the only infallible rule of faith and practice. No less a liberal than Adolph Von Harnack admitted that it was Liberalism, not Fundamentalism, that had departed from the views of primitive Christianity on Scripture.

Nowadays, most Fundamentalists are in dispensational churches, and the notion that to be a Fundamentalist requires one to be a dispensationalist is widely held. However, that is not the case. In its early days, Fundamentalism embraced Bible believers from a variety of churches and many were not dispensational in theology.

The definition of a Fundamentalist, adopted in 1980 by the Word Congress of Fundamentalists, makes no connection between dispensationalism* and Fundamentalism. It reads as follows:

"A Fundamentalist is a born-again believer in the Lord Jesus Christ who:

1. Maintains an immovable allegiance to the inerrant, infallible, and verbally inspired Bible.

2. Believes that whatever the Bible says, is so.

3. Judges all things by the Bible and is judged only by the Bible.

4. Affirms the foundational truths of the historic Christian Faith:

a. The doctrine of the Trinity

b. The incarnation, virgin birth, substitutionary atonement, bodily resurrection and glorious ascension, and Second Coming of the Lord Jesus Christ

c. The new birth through regeneration of the Holy Spirit

d. The resurrection of the ungodly to final judgment and eternal death

e. The resurrection of saints to life eternal

f. The fellowship of the saints, who are the body of Christ

5. Practises fidelity to that Faith and endeavours to preach it to every creature.

6. Exposes and separates from all ecclesiastical denial of that Faith, compromise with error, and apostasy from the Truth.

7. Earnestly contends for the Faith once delivered."

This is Fundamentalism's view of itself. It is, to use the title of David O. Beale's history of it, a movement *In Pursuit of Purity* — purity of doctrine, practice, and association, all in submission to the infallible word of God, the Bible.

See **New Evangelicalism**; **Separation**.

FUTURISM

A school of prophetic interpretation, especially of the book of the Revelation. A futurist sees the bulk of the Revelation (from 4:1) as awaiting fulfilment in the period immediately preceding and following the second coming* of Christ. While many futurists admit the use of symbolic language in John's apocalyptic visions, the more literally one interprets those visions, the more certainly he will be a futurist.

See **Historicism**; **Millennium**; **Preterism**.

G

GAP THEORY

The belief of many Bible students that there is a great period of time between the first and second verses of Genesis. Some use this alleged gap to make room for the vast ages claimed for the earth and the fossils in it by modern geologists.

The arguments most popularly employed to support the gap theory are as follows:

1. The verb "was" in the statement, "The earth was without form," properly means "became"; that is, the earth was not created "without form and void."

2. Isaiah 45:18 says that the Lord did not create the earth "in vain," which in the Hebrew is the same as "without form" in Gen. 1:2.

3. The only other places where the Hebrew words translated "without form and void"—*tohu wabbohu bohu*—occur together are Isa. 33:11 and Jer. 4:23. Gap theorists hold both texts to be descriptions of a worldwide judgment, from which they conclude that Gen. 1:1, 2 describes a great judgment that caused the earth to be "without form and void."

4. It is surmised that that judgment followed Lucifer's rebellion. The language of Isa. 14:9-17, Jer. 4:23-27, and Ezek. 28:12-18—taken as references to Satan's sin and judgment—is believed to belong to the gap period.

While the gap theory is popular in dispensational* circles, and even among some Reformed believers, it has never commanded general acceptance. The argument adduced against it are as follows:

1. The verb "was" in Gen. 1:2 is properly translated; it cannot mean "became." If *became* were the meaning, the Hebrew verb *hayah* would have a prefixed *lamed,* which is not the case here.

2. The clause in v. 2a is a noun clause and therefore represents a state of *being,* not of *becoming.* It is also a *circumstantial* clause which in Hebrew syntax must describe what precedes it. Thus "the earth was without form" is a descriptive expansion of the prior statement, "God created the heaven and the earth."

3. The *and* at the beginning of v. 2 is the Hebrew *waw* and is connected with the noun "earth." According to some of the best grammarians, it must therefore introduce an explanation of the preceding statement. This force of the *waw* makes it linguistically impossible to hold that Gen. 1:2 teaches a temporal gap between it and the previous verse. It makes it certain that v. 2 must be understood as describing a state of being that is contemporaneous with the main verb "created" (v. 1).

4. The theories of evolutionary scientists must not be permitted to dictate our interpretation* of Scripture.* The "facts" such scientists present are all based on the presupposition of the truth of the theory of evolution. The book of Genesis presents the framework of events that amply refutes the evolutionary use of geological data without having recourse to an imagined gap of billions of years. The parts of that framework for the interpretation of the phenomena and history of the earth are creation,* the fall,* the consequent curse, and the worldwide flood.

5. Exodus 20:11 refers the creation of the entire universe to the six-day period of Genesis 1. Gap theorists object that the verb "make" in Exod. 20:11 is not synonymous with the verb "create" in Gen. 1:1. But Neh.

9:6 uses the same word as Exod. 20:11 in a context in which it is certainly describing the original creation.

6. The appeal to Isa. 45:18 is fruitless because the context shows that Isaiah's meaning is simply that God's purpose in creating the world was not that it should be "without form," but that it should be inhabited. In other words, Isaiah does not tell us the *state* of the earth when God created it, but the *purpose* for which He created it.

7. The fact that then phrase *tohu wabbohu* is used by the prophets as a poetic description of a great judgment furnishes no logical proof that the phrase in Gen. 1 must describe God's judgment on Satan's sin. That the prophet's use of *tohu wabbohu* is poetic is clear from the fact that even gap theorists must admit that in Isa. 33:11 and Jer. 4:23 the phrase does not describe an absolutely total desolation such as we have in Gen. 1:1, 2.

In the light of the Biblical evidence we conclude that the first two verses of the Bible are not separated by a period of millions of years.

GATHERED CHURCH

The theory of independency* that all the functions and authority for the ministry and government of the church* reside in the membership of each local congregation; indeed, that according to Scripture the word *church* may properly be used only of a local congregation meeting in one place. Thus the concept is equally opposed to episcopacy,* presbyterianism,* the folk church* as understood in state church systems, and the magisterium* claimed by the Roman Catholic church.

GEHENNA

A transliteration of the Greek word *geenna.*

The Hebrew form of the word is *gehinnom,* "the valley of Hinnom." That explains the name and use of the place to describe hell, the place of perpetual punishment.

The Valley of Hinnom was the refuse dump for Jerusalem, a place of perpetual fire, where the bodies of executed criminals were burned. It is thus a fit word to be taken and used in a spiritual sense to describe hell. It appears twelve times in the NT, in eleven of which the Lord Jesus Himself chose the word. Matthew 5:22 speaks of "the hell of fire"; Mark 9:43-47 says that its fire is unquenchable and in it "the worm dieth not and the fire is not quenched"; Luke 12:4, 5 and Matt. 10:28 teach that it is the place into which God casts sinners both body and soul after death.

Thus, *Gehenna* is hell, everlasting hell with unquenchable fire, where with body and soul united, the ungodly endure conscious suffering, without any lessening of its torment. It is, then, synonymous with the lake of fire (Rev. 19:20; 20:10, 14, 15; 21:8), the final abode of the ungodly.

*See **Wrath of God**.*

GEMATRIA

The use of the total numerical value of the letters of a Hebrew word to arrive at a hidden meaning of the word.

GENERAL REVELATION

The revelation of the existence and being of God contained in His works of creation and providence (Ps. 19:1-3; Rom. 1:19, 20). It is not a saving revelation, but shows God's eternal power and Godhead (or sovereignty).

*See **Innate Idea of God**; **Revelation**.*

GENUINENESS

Authenticity. When applied to the books of the Bible, it indicates the canonicity of the book *(see **Canon).*** When applied to a part of the text of a canonical book it indicates that the section under examination has not been corrupted and is therefore actually what the inspired penman wrote. *See **Burgon**; **Textual Criticism of the New Testament**.*

GIFTS OF THE HOLY SPIRIT

A gift of the Spirit is a revelation given by Him in and through a member of the church for the common good of all the members (1 Cor. 12:7).

In Rom. 12:6-8, 1 Cor. 12:2-11, and Eph. 4:11 Paul gives us lists of spiritual gifts. While all originate with the Holy Spirit some are of an entirely supernatural character while others are not. Those that are miraculous involve direct, divine revelation, illumination, and inspiration. It has been the general opinion of the church that the miraculous gifts of the Spirit were intended to be temporary *(see* **Cessationism)**.

Writers ancient and modern have likened the miraculous gifts of the Spirit to the attire of a young bride, important for its purpose, but not her permanent garb. In 1 Cor. 13:11 Paul shows that they belong to the church's infancy and that God's people will be more mature and more certain when they learn to stand on the finished canon of revealed Scripture. Despite this clear teaching, some claim the continuance of the *charismata*—the miraculous gifts of the Spirit—and blame their nonappearance on unbelief.

Indisputably, in the NT the supernatural gifts of the Spirit were intended as special confirmations of God's revelation then in the process of being given (Heb. 2:3-4). It is also noteworthy that in the book of Acts every occurrence of a miracle is in connection with the ministry of an apostle, and no one but an apostle had the right or power to communicate the gifts of the Spirit to another. Clearly, NT miracles were not only accompaniments of divine revelation but were part of it. Indeed Paul actually calls the *charismata* "the manifestation [revelation] of the Spirit" (1 Cor. 12:7), that is, a revelation given by the Holy Spirit.

Redemptive revelation always has three elements: theophany*—God's intervention in His own person; prophecy*—God's intervention with His own word; and miracle*—God's intervention with His own power. These three go together, each validating the other. Thus, true supernatural manifestations of the Spirit do not occur in a period when the Holy Spirit is not giving a new redemptive revelation. A miracle is never a raw demonstration of God's power. It never occurs apart from the revelation of redemption.

This teaches us an important lesson: the supernatural gifts of the Spirit are not in operation today for God has completed His revelation in the NT. The Bible prophesied that they would pass away (1 Cor. 13:8). In the light of all this, those who now claim to exercise the supernatural sign gifts of the apostolic period are in direct contradiction to Scripture. The *giving* of divine revelation includes miracle. The *use* of a *finished* revelation does not.

Nevertheless, the Holy Spirit still gives to His people gifts that are vital to the ministry of the church. The fact that God has removed the supernatural gifts of apostolic times does not mean that there are no gifts of the Spirit in the church today. Some of the Spirit's gifts in apostolic times were not sign miracles. They are still with us, for example, the gifts of pastoring (Eph. 4:11), helps, governments (or, organizers, managers, 1 Cor. 12:28), exhortation (or, encouragement), giving, showing mercy, ministering, and teaching (Rom. 12:6, 7). There is always a need in every church for these gifts to be exercised in the power of the Holy Spirit.

Even the supernatural gifts of the NT period have their reflections in the ordinary ministry of the Holy Spirit in the church to this day. 1 Corinthians 12 mentions nine supernatural gifts. As miraculous manifestations they have passed away to be replaced by the Holy Spirit's use and application of the completed Bible. However, there is a counterpart to each of them. In other words, the church has not lost the ministry of the Spirit. He still does great things for and through His people, using His inspired Word. The Lord has not left His church to flounder. He has provided every energy we need to serve the Saviour and to do His will and work. He has promised every Christian the power of the Holy Spirit. He will keep that promise. Christians need to be sure to seek the true Biblical experience of the power of the Holy Spirit for His service and not be hoodwinked into pursuing an unbiblical counterfeit of the genuine power of God.

See *Holy Spirit, Fulness Of.*

GILGAMESH EPIC

An ancient Babylonian composition recovered from the ruins of the palace library of Assyrian king Ashurbanipal at Nineveh.

The *Epic* describes the exploits of a legendary Sumerian king in the early third millennium B.C. The eleventh tablet records the Babylonian story of the flood. In it Utnapishtim recounted to Gilgamesh that the gods planned to send a terrible flood. Utnaphishtim was commanded to build an ark in preparation for the coming tempest which lasted for six days and six nights.

The Babylonian flood account indicates that the historical reality of the flood was stamped on the consciousness of every nation. There are some similarities between the Biblical account and the *Epic.* Radical critics use this fact to argue that since we know the *Epic* is mythological so is the Bible's flood account. The truth is that the *Epic* represents the original universal consciousness of the flood, though in a debased fashion.

GLASITES

The followers of John Glas, a Scottish Independent minister, whose theories had a wide acceptance far beyond Scotland. In Scotland his followers were called *Glasites,* while abroad they were called *Sandemanians,** after Glas's son-in-law Robert Sandeman, whose writings were a powerful instrument in the spread of the movement.

GLORIFICATION

The perfect conformity of the believer to the image of Jesus Christ, both in body and soul. It is the perfection of sanctification, when our body of humiliation will be conformed to the body of Christ's glory (Phil. 3:21) and we shall be entirely "like Christ" (1 John 3:2). These texts place this event at the second coming* of the Lord Jesus Christ (see 1 Cor. 15:51-53).

See *Resurrection; Heaven.*

GLOSSALALIA

Greek, *glossa,* "tongue, language," and *laleo,* "to speak," translated "speak with tongues" (Acts 2:4; 10:46; 19:6); the practice of speaking in other tongues, usually as part of a religious experience.

In the NT the Holy Spirit gave the gift of tongues to many. These tongues were foreign languages, as on the day of Pentecost (Acts 2:8). In modern Pentecostalism* and in the Charismatic movement* this apostolic gift has allegedly been restored. However, there is little or no similarity between Pentecost and Pentecostalism. In the latter case, the tongues used are rarely foreign languages and even more rarely used to spread the gospel to people of a foreign tongue.

Unscriptural Claims of Tongues Speakers

Many Pentecostalists parade their glossalalia as the proof *par excellence* that their "gifts" are genuinely of God. However, the mere phenomenon of speaking in an unknown tongue, especially in the ecstatic utterances Pentecostalists often claim to be angel tongues, is no proof of the presence and power of the Holy Spirit.

Heathen Tongues Speaking

Merrill F. Unger's *New Testament Teaching on Tongues* gives the following information:

Among Spiritists and Muslims. "That tongues can be and are counterfeited by demon spirits is evidenced by the fact that spiritistic mediums, Muslim dervishes, and Indian fakirs speak in tongues. It must be remembered by those who try to make tongues a badge of spirituality or a status symbol of saints who have attained the height of spiritual experience, that speaking in tongues and their interpretation are not peculiar to the Christian church but are common in ancient pagan religions and in spiritism both ancient and modern."

In Ancient Paganism. "The very phrase 'to speak in tongues…was not invented by New Testament writers, but borrowed from the ordinary speech of pagans. Plato's attitude toward the enthusiastic ecstasies of the ancient soothsayer (*mantis,* diviner) recalls the Apostle Paul's attitude toward glossolalia among the Corinthian believers.

"Virgil graphically describes the ancient pagan prophetess 'speaking with tongues.' He depicts her disheveled hair, her panting breast, her change of color, and her apparent increase in stature as the god (demon) came upon her and filled her with his supernatural afflatus. Then her voice loses its mortal ring as the god (demon) speaks through her, as in ancient and modern necromancy (spiritism)."

In Modern Paganism. "Phenomena of this type are common among savages and pagan peoples of lower culture. Ecstatic utterances interpreted by a person in a sane state of mind have been verified. In the Sandwich Islands for example, the god Oro gave his oracles through a priest who ceased to act or speak as a voluntary agent, but with his limbs convulsed, his features distorted and terrific, his eyes wild and strained, would roll on the ground foaming at the mouth, and reveal the will of the god in shrill cries and sounds violent and indistinct, which the attending priests duly interpreted to the people" (pp. 163f.).

Charles R. Smith, *Tongues in Biblical Perspective,* documents the occurrence of *tongues* in various settings.

In Non-Christian Religions. Having shown the widespread use of tongues in ancient times, he goes on, "Today shamans (witch doctors, priests, or medicine men) in Haiti, Greenland, Micronesia, and countries of Af-rica, Australia, Asia, and North and South America speak in tongues. Several groups use drugs to aid in inducing the ecstatic state and utterances. Voodoo practitioners speak in tongues. Buddhist and Shinto priests have been heard speaking in tongues. Moslems have spoken in tongues, and an ancient tradition even reports that Mohammed himself spoke in tongues. According to his own account, after his ecstatic experiences he found it difficult to return to logical and intelligible speech.

In Mental Illness. "The fact that nonreligious tongues speaking often occurs in association with certain mental illnesses is well documented. Psychiatrists have reported it in association with schizophrenia, neurosis, and psychosis. Probably all psychiatrists and psychologists are aware of the possibility of psychic damage resulting from tongues speaking. It was reported that following the extended tongues meeting held by Aimee Semple McPherson, founder of the Church of the Foursquare Gospel, mental institutions in the area of her meetings were overburdened. The Episcopalian church financed a study commission which concluded that tongues are 'not *per se* a religious phenomenon' and may appear among those 'who are suffering from mental disorders as schizophrenia and hysteria.'

In Spiritism. "Tongues speaking occurs among anti-Christian spiritistic mediums. Contrary to popular belief among tongues speakers, a few years ago the European Pentecostal Conference admitted that 'tongues might occur apart from the Spirit's action.'

In the Demon Possessed. "Even Pentecostal authors grant that there are cases where demonic influence is apparently responsible for tongues utterances. Some feel that this is why 'the gift of discernment of spirits' is necessary" (Smith, pp. 20f).

It is doubtful whether the cases described by Smith may properly be termed "mental illness." But whether the tongues-speaking in those cases arises from a psychological or a demonic source, the argument is equally persuasive. Glossalalia is no proof of the inspiration or power of the Holy Spirit.

Modern Tongues Not the NT Gift

The true gift of tongues in NT times was part of a much greater manifestation of the miraculous power of the Holy Spirit whose signs and wonders were intended to be a divine attestation of the gospel. This supernatural witness was intentionally temporary. Tongues would cease, according to the apostle Paul (1 Cor. 13:8). The time of their withdrawal was the completion of the NT Scriptures (*see* **Cessationism**). Thus in the very nature of the case the tongues-speaking of modern Pentecostal and Charismatic groups is essentially different from the apostolic gift. Perhaps that is why modern glossalalia is almost entirely made up of ecstatic utterances, not foreign languages, and is used for personal devotion, not for preaching the gospel. These were not marks of the genuine apostolic gift.

See **Gifts of the Spirit**.

GNOSTICISM

Greek *gnosis,* "knowledge"; a second-century heresy that challenged and sought to subvert the early church.

Gnostic Doctrines

Gnostics claimed a secret knowledge to which only a small segment of humanity could attain. Those who did were looked on as *pneumatic,* or "spiritual" people. These people alone were led back to the light of the Supreme God.

While the *pneumatic* enjoyed knowledge, a second, inferior class, including the OT prophets, were called *psychic,* people who could not proceed beyond faith. The remaining majority of humanity were called *hylic,* those subject to matter. While the *psychic* were consigned eternally to an inferior destiny than that of the *pneumatic,* the *hylic* were considered hopeless and due to be utterly destroyed.

From this it is clear that Gnosticism was far removed from Christianity. Just how far will be even more evident when we consider its views on the great fundamentals of the faith.

God and Creation. The Gnostics, steeped as they were in the heathen philosophies and theosophies of the East, rejected the monotheism of the Bible. They thought of an absolute, Supreme Being from whom a series of *aeons,* or emanations (i.e., middle beings or inferior gods) proceeded, each *aeon* originating the one following. One of the *aeons,* remote from the Supreme Being, created the world, and did so badly. This *aeon* was identified by the Gnostics as the *demiurge* * or the God of the OT. Sometimes indeed, the Gnostics spoke of him as being hostile to the Supreme Being.

Good and Evil. Gnosticism rejected the Biblical doctrine of sin. Looking on matter as intrinsically evil, and creation as the poor product of an inferior god, the Gnostics held that there were germs of a higher life, rays from the *pleroma,* or fulness of the Supreme God, which were ever struggling to be free—hence the constant struggle between good and evil. Those who had most of this germinal divine life were, of course, the Gnostics.

Christ. Holding that matter was intrinsically evil, the Gnostics repudiated the doctrine of the incarnation of Christ. Some held that His body was a phantom. Others held that Jesus was a mere man upon whom the heavenly Christ came at his baptism, leaving him before his crucifixion.

Scripture. We have noted the Gnostics' view of the OT prophets. They also controverted and corrupted the NT Scriptures. Rejecting the twin doctrines of guilt and atonement, as well as the incarnation of the eternal Son, they had to reject the great preponderance of the Bible's witness.

Gnosticism was a highly speculative heresy attended by mystical rites. For a time it exerted a fascination for many inquiring minds and posed a serious challenge to the church of Christ during the first 150 years of its history.

Gnostic Divisions

Basilides and Valentinus. Within the general framework of Gnosticism, there were many variations. There were Judaizing and anti-Judaizing factions. Some, like Basilides (*circa* A.D. 130) held that every development of God and the world was a development upwards from beneath. Others, like Valentinus (*circa.* A.D. 150) held that the development was (as described above) downward from the Supreme through middle beings.

Cerinthus and Marcion. Cerinthus and Marcion figure largely in any study of Gnosticism. Cerinthus, a contemporary of John in Ephesus, taught that Jesus and Christ must be distinguished, Jesus being merely a man, and Christ being one of the *aeons,* who came upon Jesus at baptism. John addresses this Cerinthian heresy in 1 John 2:22; 4:2, 3.

Marcion (*circa* A.D. 139) is often looked upon as the most Christian of the Gnostics, but he held to the notion that the God of the OT was an inferior God. He held that the Christ of the NT was not the Messiah of the OT and that Christ's body was not a real body. Therefore Christ was not really crucified. Professing to establish his system of belief on *Galatians,* Marcion rejected all the NT except *Luke* and ten of Paul's epistles.

In the end Gnosticism died out as an active religious movement, but many of its esoteric ideas refused to die and came to the surface from time to time. Indeed, much of the philosophy of the New Age movement* has a decidedly Gnostic flavour.

GOEL

The active participle of the Hebrew verb *ga'al,* "to redeem." It is used to describe the redemption of property (Lev. 25:25). It is also used of the kinsman whose duty was to raise up seed to a brother who had died childless (Deut. 25:5). Another duty of a kinsman was that of the avenger of blood (Num. 35:12-34; Deut. 19:1-3).

The prevalent thought in all this is that of the kinsman-redeemer, an apt type and description of the Lord Jesus Christ. The name is used of the Lord, for example, by Job in his famous statement: "I know that my redeemer liveth" (Job 19:25). The outstanding OT example of the *goel* was Boaz (cf. Ruth 3:12; 4:6-10). To fulfil the office of the kinsman-redeemer he had to meet three requirements:

1 He had to be near of kin.
2. He had to be able to redeem.
3. He had to be willing to redeem.

The Lord Jesus Christ perfectly fulfilled the type. In His perfect humanity He is near of kin to us (Heb. 2:16, 17); in His boundless ability He was able to redeem us (Heb. 7:25); and in His infinite mercy He was willing to redeem us (2 Cor. 8:9). *See **Redemption**.*

GOOD WORKS

Works that are pure as to their motive, lawful as to their execution, and God-glorifying as to their aim.

No fallen man can originate such works (Rom. 8:7). Good works are tantamount to merit, for while God is not bound *a priori* to bestow favour on good works, He has promised to do so according to the terms of the Covenant of Works *(see **Covenant Theology**).* Thus, when the Scripture (e.g., Rom. 3:12) declares that no fallen man can originate good works, it is teaching in the most emphatic terms that no sinner can gain salvation by his own merit. In line with this, Protestantism emphasizes the Biblical doctrine of a free justification through faith alone: that is, justification by the merits of Christ, without any contributory merit from the sinner, received by faith, which is itself the gift of God (Eph. 2:8, 9).

While the carnal mind is incapable of originating good works (Rom. 8:7), the "new creature in Christ" (2 Cor. 5:17), the man redeemed and purified by the blood of Christ, is to be zealous of good works (Titus 2:14; Eph. 2:10). These works are the fruit of salvation, not the ground of it. They are produced by the working of the Lord indwelling His people (Phil. 2:13).

GOODNESS OF GOD

A divine attribute that comprehends God's benevolence, complacency, mercy, and grace. A. A. Hodge distinguished these aspects of God's goodness as follows:

"The infinite goodness of God is a glorious perfection which preeminently characterizes His nature, and which He, in an infinitely wise, righteous and sovereign manner, exercises toward His creatures in various modes, according to their relations and conditions."

"Benevolence is the goodness of God viewed generically. It embraces all His creatures, except the judicially condemned on account of sin, and provides for their welfare."

"The love of complacency is that approving affection with which God regards His own infinite perfections, and every image and reflection of them in His creatures, especially in the sanctified subjects of the new creation."

"God's mercy, of which the more passive forms are pity and compassion, is the divine goodness exercised with respect to the miseries of His creatures feeling for them, and making provision for their relief, and, in the case of impenitent sinners, leading to long-suffering patience."

"The grace of God is His goodness seeking to communicate His favours, and, above all, the fellowship of His own life and blessedness, to his moral creatures, who, as creatures, must be destitute of all merit; and pre-eminently His electing love securing at infinite cost the blessedness of its objects, who, as sinful creatures, were positively ill deserving." (A. A. Hodge). *See Love of God.*

GOVERNMENTAL THEORY OF THE ATONEMENT

A false theory which takes its name from the supposed purpose of Christ's atonement* to honour God's moral government by showing His holy displeasure against sin. The theory was propounded as a middle way between the teaching of the Reformers on the atonement and the Socinian view.

Holding that the law of God is merely the product of His will and not an expression of His essential nature, this theory denies that God's justice necessarily demands obedience to all the requirements of His law. Strict justice demands the sentence of eternal death be passed upon the sinner, but this sentence is not strictly executed, for believers go free. And they go free without any satisfaction offered to God for them. God simply sets the penalty aside. The death of Christ did not make a real atonement. It paid only a nominal equivalent of sin's penalty, which God was pleased to accept as such. The only real reason for the death of Christ was to reveal God's displeasure against sin, that God, the moral Ruler of the universe, might be able to maintain His moral government.

The governmental theory was first advocated by Grotius and later taken up by others, including R. W. Dale of Birmingham. It is false at every point.

1. How moral government can be strengthened by punishing a sinless victim, who is not standing as the substitute for others, is a mystery governmental theorists cannot explain.

2. The basic thesis, that Christ's death was to honour God's moral government, is in Scripture a secondary purpose.

3. The moral law is an expression of God's fundamental nature, and is not subject to change.

4. The penalty on sin is not merely meant to deter sinners, but to satisfy justice.

5. The governmental theory allows no direct connection between Christ's death and the salvation of sinners.

6. It fails to show how OT saints were saved.
7. It contradicts the plain statements of the infallible Word, which makes the death of Christ an atoning sacrifice that merits the salvation of all for whom Christ died.

GRACE

A mode of the goodness of God, often described as undeserved favour. It is more than that. It is undeserved favour bestowed upon those who are positively deserving of the wrath of God. Theologians often speak of grace as the goodness of God dealing with the guilt of the sinner's condition, whereas mercy is the goodness of God dealing with the misery of his condition.

See **Common Grace**; **Special Grace**.

GRAF-WELLHAUSEN THEORY

See **Criticism**; **J.E.D.P.**

GRANVILLE SHARPE RULE

A rule of Greek grammar named after Dr. Granville Sharpe, a noted Church of England scholar (1735-1813). His work was thoroughly investigated by Dr. T. F. Middleton, whose study *The Doctrine of the Greek Article Applied to the Criticism and Illustration of the New Testament* (1808) became the standard work on the use of the Greek definite article. In Middleton's words, the Granville Sharpe rule is as follows: "When two or more attributives (i.e., adjectives, participles, descriptive substantives) joined by a copulative or copulatives, are assumed of the same person or thing, before the first attributive the article is inserted, before the remaining ones omitted." Simply put, when two or more nouns (or adjectives or participles) are joined by "and," the first having the definite article and the others not having it, they all refer to the same subject.

Dr. Middleton quotes Plutarch's description of Roscius as *ho huios kai kleronomos*, "the son and heir," where clearly both nouns apply to the same person. Classical Greek furnishes multitudes of examples of the use of this rule. The only exemptions from this uniform use of the article according to Middleton are proper nouns (i.e., names), abstract nouns, and simple names of substances.

The rule has particular importance in the study of the deity of Christ.* For example, Middleton comments on Eph. 5:5, "Instead of rendering 'the kingdom of Christ and God,' we should read, 'the kingdom of Him Who is Christ and God.'"

Bishop Wordsworth in his commentary on Titus 2:13 gives a comprehensive list of quotations from the early fathers on the use of the article, showing the weight of the evidence in support of the Granville Sharpe rule.

GRATUITOUS

Free, gracious. An adjective often used to describe the sovereign election* by God of His people. It is not to be understood loosely in the sense of *motiveless*. Rather it is to be understood as springing from the free grace of God, and not dependent upon any meritorious thing seen or foreseen in the sinner.

Gratuitous is often used of justification.* In Rom. 3:24 we learn that we are "justified freely by His grace." There is a double emphasis upon the thought of freeness here. *Freely* means "without a cause" (cf. John 15:25) —justification is not granted because of any merit in us, but proceeds upon free grace alone.

GREEK (OR EASTERN) ORTHODOXY

In A.D. 1054, there was a schism between the Church of Rome and the Eastern churches, the latter rejecting, among other things, the dogmas of papal supremacy and purgatory. They also deeply resented Rome's action in unilaterally deciding to put the Western belief concerning the procession of the Spirit into the Nicene Creed without the decision of an ecumenical council *(see Filioque)*.

These Eastern churches profess to hold to the doctrine of the ecumenical creeds of undivided Christendom, in particular the creeds of Nicea and Constantinople *(see Nicene Creed).* Thus they call themselves *orthodox.* Despite this protestation, they hold many soul-destroying errors in common with Rome. They hold to the mass* in which they believe there is a real transubstantiation. Worship is highly liturgical, with little emphasis on preaching. They hold a synergistic* view of salvation. They believe tradition* to be equally authoritative with Scripture and rest in the ultimate authority* of the unchanging common mind of the churches, guided by the Holy Spirit. And they practise prayer to and for the dead.

GUILT

To be guilty is to be under condemnation and worthy of punishment. The words *hupodikos* (e.g., Rom. 3:19) and *enochos* respectively bear these meanings (e.g., 1 Cor. 11:27; James 2:10). Thus, guilt is an aspect of sin, expressing the relation sin bears to the justice of God and to the penalty of His law.

Theologians sometimes speak of *potential guilt* and *actual guilt,* based on the double meaning of the word noted above. R. L. Dabney uses this distinction. *Potential guilt* does not mean that any man can be guilty apart from actual sin. Rather it conveys the thought of the sinner's state of demerit or ill-desert, which renders him worthy of punishment. *Actual guilt* denotes the penal enactment of the lawgiver. In this term the emphasis is not so much upon the inherent ill-deserving state of the sinner as upon the obligation of the judge to visit punishment upon him.

See Reatus Culpae.

H

HADES

The Greek equivalent of the Hebrew *sheol*. *Sheol* is translated in the AV "hell," "grave," and "pit," while *hades* is ten times translated "hell," and once "grave."

There has long been controversy over the exact import of the words. There are two views among Bible believers.

Divided Hades View

W. E. Vine expresses what is now perhaps, the most common view: "Hades [is] the region of departed spirits of the lost (but including the blessed dead in periods preceding the ascension of Christ)....It corresponds to 'Sheol' in the OT....It never denotes the grave, nor is it the permanent region of the lost; in point of time it is, for such, intermediate between decease and the doom of Gehenna. For the condition see Luke 16:23-31.

"The word is used four times in the Gospels, and always by the Lord, Matt. 11:23; 16:18; Luke 10:15; 16:23; it is used with reference to the soul of Christ, Acts 2:27, 31; Christ declares that He has the keys of it, Rev. 1:18; in Rev. 6:8 it is personified, with the signification of the temporary destiny of the doomed; it is to give up those who are therein, Rev. 20:13; and is to be cast into the lake of fire, ver. 14" (*Expository Dictionary of New Testament Words*).

Usual Reformed View

Shedd takes another view, rejecting the theory of the divided sheol or hades, holding that the Scripture nowhere warrants our locating paradise in hades. Berkhof in his *Systematic Theology* takes the same view. Shedd's argument may be summed up as follows:

Sheol Means a Punitive Evil. "That Sheol is a fearful punitive evil, mentioned by the sacred writers to deter men from sin, lies upon the surface of the OT, and any interpretation that essentially modifies this must therefore be erroneous."

Sheol Often Means Hell. "Sheol signifies the place of future retribution.

1. This is proved by the fact that it is denounced against sin and sinners, and not against the righteous. It is a place to which the wicked are sent in distinction from the good." Then follows a long list of texts: Job 21:13; Ps. 9:17; Prov. 5:5; 9:18; 23:14; Deut. 32:22; Ps. 139:8; Prov. 15:24; Job 26:6; Prov. 15:11; 27:20. In these last three references, *destruction* is in the Hebrew *Abaddon*. Shedd argues that since *Abaddon* is the Hebrew word for *Apollyon* who is "the angel and king of the bottomless pit" (Rev. 9:11), the use of *sheol* in these texts proves that it denotes hell. "There can be no rational doubt, that in this class of texts the wicked are warned of a future evil and danger. The danger is that they shall be sent to Sheol."

2. A second proof that Sheol is the proper name for Hell, in the OT, is the fact that there is no other proper name for it in the whole volume—for Tophet is metaphorical, and rarely employed. If Sheol is not the place where the wrath of God falls upon the transgressor there is no place mentioned in the OT where it does."

Shedd finds it "utterly improbable" that there should be such silence, when the final judgment is so clearly announced.

3. A third proof that Sheol in these passages, denoted the dark abode of the wicked and the state of future suffering, is found in those OT texts which speak of the contrary bright

169

abode of the righteous, and of their state of blessedness."

Shedd then argues that paradise cannot be placed as a part of sheol: "There is too great a contrast between the two abodes of the good and evil, to allow them to be brought under one and the same gloomy and terrifying term Sheol." Again he lists proof texts: Ps. 16:11; 17:15; 49:15; 73:24; Isa. 25:8; Prov. 14:32.

4. As a fourth proof that sheol signifies the place of future retribution, Shedd cites its inseparable connection with spiritual and eternal death. This is true of hades, as it is used in the NT (Prov. 5:5; Rev. 20:14).

Sheol Often Means the Grave. But, Shedd argues, sheol has another significance: "Sheol signifies the 'grave' to which all men, good and evil alike, go down. That Sheol should have the two significations of hell and the grave, is explained by the connection between physical death and eternal retribution. The death of the body is one of the consequences of sin, and an integral part of the penalty....As in English, 'death' may mean either physical or spiritual death, so in Hebrew, Sheol may mean either the grave or hell. When Sheol signifies the 'grave,' it is only the body that goes down to Sheol. But as the body is naturally put for the whole person, the man is said to go down to the grave, when his body alone is laid in it... When the aged Jacob says, 'I will go down unto my (dead) son mourning' (Gen. 37:35), no one should understand him to teach the descent of his disembodied spirit into a subterranean world. 'The spirit of man goeth upward and the spirit of the beast goeth downward' (Eccl. 3:21)."

Shedd cites the following texts to prove that sheol signifies the grave: 1 Sam. 2:6; Gen. 44:31; Job 14:13; 17:13; Num. 16:33; Ps. 6:5; Eccl. 9:10; Hos. 13:14; Ps. 88:3; 89:48. He goes on, "Sheol in the sense of the 'grave' is represented as something out of which the righteous are to be delivered by a resurrection of the body to glory, but

the bodies of the wicked are to be left under its power. Ps. 49:14, 15; 16:10; Hosea 13:14. St. Paul quotes this (1 Cor. 15:55), in proof of the blessed resurrection of the bodies of believers—showing that 'Sheol' here is the 'grave,' where the body is laid and from which it is raised."

Objections to Idea that Sheol Means Grave. Shedd seeks to answer some of the objections to his last point. He argues that Ps. 16:10 and Acts 2:31 use soul to mean body and points out that in Lev. 19:28; 21:11; 22:4; Num. 6:6; 19:11, 13; Hag. 2:13, the Hebrew word *nephesh,* "soul" is translated properly by "dead body." He also remarks that Acts 2:31 proves that Psa. 16:10 uses *sheol* as he has argued because, "Acts 2:31 asserts that 'David spake of the resurrection of Christ,'...but there is no resurrection of the soul. Consequently it is the body that David speaks of."

Hades Means Hell and Grave. What has been said of *sheol* holds good for *hades.* Mostly, it signifies the place of torment, and in three places (Acts 2:27, 31; 1 Cor. 15:55) it signifies grave.

In reply to the objection that *sheol* and *hades* cannot mean *grave* because there are other words for *grave*—Hebrew *qeber* and Greek *mnemeion*—Shedd replies, "Grave has an abstract and general sense, denoted by Sheol, and a concrete and particular, denoted by *qeber.* All men go to the grave, but not all men have a grave....These remarks apply also to the use of Hades and *mnemeion.*" (All quotations from Shedd's *The Doctrine of Endless Punishment.*)

Summary of Differences

Basically then, there are two views current among Bible believers. We may summarize their differences:

1. The first places paradise (at least until Christ's resurrection) as a compartment of sheol or hades. The second denies this and says the location of paradise as the third heaven (2 Cor. 12:2, 4) is the only location given in Scripture, with no hint of its ever having been located anywhere else.

2. The first emphasizes that *sheol* refers generally to the region of the departed spirits (as does *hades* until the resurrection of Christ). The second repudiates this and holds that "hell" is the proper translation.

3. The first holds that sheol and hades never mean *grave.* The second is equally adamant that in certain texts it does.

4. The first holds that the souls of the wicked and of the righteous both went to sheol in the OT period (and in the NT until the resurrection of Christ). The second holds that in the OT only the souls of the wicked went to sheol and that the saints went to heaven— as Elijah, upon his translation, did. In this particular aspect of the dispute, the upholders of the divided hades view point out that Samuel "came up from the earth" (1 Sam. 28:7-20). Those of Shedd's persuasion answer that this does not change the plain statement of Prov. 15:24 and that Samuel is represented as coming up from the earth "because the body reanimated rises from the grave" (Shedd, *Dogmatic Theology,* 2:602). Furthermore, in the entire narrative, sheol is not once employed.

Doctrinal Implications

There are many doctrinal issues hanging on the view adopted. According to the first view, Christ's soul descended into sheol/hades. Upholders of this view give differing reasons for His descent and speak of various activities while He was there. Most, however, say it was to proclaim His victory and to lead out the saints from paradise into heaven.

Shedd's position denies such a descent into sheol/hades by Christ to preach or proclaim anything. He says that if such a doctrine were true, it would form a fundamental part of the gospel, on a par with the incarnation, and it is inconceivable that it should be so completely passed over in the great dogmatic statements of faith in the NT. Jesus' cry on the cross, "Father, into thy hands I commend my spirit," Shedd takes to be conclusive evidence that He did not go to any underworld of departed spirits, for "the hands of God" could not be taken as a description of any place but heaven.

One reason for opposing "grave" as a translation of sheol or hades is the use the self-styled Jehovah's Witnesses *(see* **Russellites)** make of such a belief. They say *sheol* always means "the grave" and nothing more. However, Shedd's view, with its strong emphasis on *sheol* as a place of dreadful punishment, poses arguments that the Jehovah's Witness sect can never answer.

After observing so many differences of opinion, it is worth noting that both parties hold sheol/hades to be a place of disembodied spirits. As the eternal blessedness of the believers in heaven is to be enjoyed by the entire man, including the body, so the eternal damnation of the sinner in hell is to be endured by the entire man, including the body. Thus hades will give up the dead which are in it and, reunited with their bodies, they will be cast into the lake of fire (Rev. 20:13, 14).

See **Descent into Hell***; Intermediate State.**

HAGGADAH

Hebrew "anecdote, legend"; the name given to traditional stories used in the Jewish Talmud* to expound and illustrate the messages of the law and the prophets.

HAGIOGRAPHA

The Holy Writings; Heb., *kethubim,* the third part of the OT canon,* including the following books: Ruth, Chronicles, Esther, Job, Psalms, Proverbs, Ecclesiastes, Song of Solomon, Lamentations, Daniel, and Ezra.

HAGIOLATRY

The worship of saints.

HALACHAH

Hebrew "rule"; the oral law of Jewish tradition; short sentences intended to interpret the law and apply it to individual cases. These sentences were known as "sentences of the elders" because they were established by authority of the Sanhedrin.

HALF-COMMUNION

The practice of withholding the cup from the laity in the Lord's Supper.*

HALF-WAY COVENANT

The theory adopted by some New England Congregational churches that the privileges of church membership, notably the right to have their children baptized, were not limited to the communicant members of the church but extended to church adherents who, though making no profession of personal saving faith were not living scandalously or in open rejection of Christianity.

The Half-Way Covenant was strongly supported by Solomon Stoddart in Northampton, Massachussetts. It was vigorously opposed by his successor, Jonathan Edwards, who was eventually forced to resign his pastorate because of his stand on the issue.

HEAVEN

The OT word is *shamayim,* "heights," and the NT word is *ouranos,* "sky, air."

The terms are used in various ways to denote the earth's atmosphere (Gen. 1:20), the firmament (Gen. 1:17), and the abode of God (Ps. 2:4) and of His angels (Matt. 22:30). Deuteronomy 10:14 speaks of the "heaven of heavens," and 2 Cor. 12:2 mentions the "third heaven," which is synonymous with "paradise" (v. 4). Hence, the highest heaven, the abode of God, is "the paradise of God" (Rev. 2:7), which the redeemed of the Lord go to inhabit and enjoy eternally. Thus it is called the "Father's house" (John 14:2), prepared for those pre-

pared by grace for it (Matt. 25:34). It is entered by the saved at death (Luke 16:22; 23:43); in it their souls enjoy the presence of the Lord, free from all sin, while their bodies rest in the grave until the resurrection (2 Cor. 5:8; Heb. 12:23; Rev. 6:9). At the resurrection, the bodies of God's people will be raised, glorified, and fitted to partake of the bliss of immortality and eternal joy (1 Cor. 15:53; Phil. 3:21; 1 John 3:2).

The Scripture gives its description of heaven mostly in negative terms because our finite, earth-oriented minds could not comprehend a positive description of its glories. We know that the throne of God and of the Lamb is central (Rev. 4) and that the praise of the Lamb is sung (Rev. 5). From Rev. 21 we learn that there will be no *division* (v. 1, *sea*), *death* (v. 4), *distress* (v. 4, *sorrow*), *disappointment* (v. 4, *crying*), *drudgery* (v. 4, *pain,* Greek *ponos* means "toil"), *darkness* (v. 25), or *defilement* (v. 27).

This is not an idealistic description of some utopia. It is the description of a real *place* (John 14:2), a *country* (Heb. 11:14, 16), and a *kingdom* (Matt. 8:11), of which God's redeemed people are already citizens (Phil. 3:20; *conversation* means "citizenship").

It is obviously a place of rest in all that the merits of Christ's atonement have provided (Heb. 10:12 with Matt. 8:11), a place of great joy (Rev. 5), of perfect fellowship (1 John 3:2), and of perfect service to God, for heaven is the place where His will is done as it ought to be (Matt. 6:10).

See Glorification.

HEILSGESCHICHTE

The German word meaning the "history of salvation." It is used by theologians who view the Bible as essentially such a history. It makes God's redemptive purpose the controlling factor in all theological investigation. It is a legitimate theological method and was adopted by such men as Thomas Chalmers and Jonathan Edwards. Others (e.g., Shedd) objected to it, holding it to be fractional and incapable of covering the whole ground.

In recent times Oscar Cullman responded to Rudolph Bultmann's view that there is no reliable historical evidence underlying the kerygma*—the gospel of Christianity—which must be received by faith that is independent of any historical events. Cullman, on the other hand, insisted God has acted in history in a series of events designed to save His people. These events stretch all the way from the creation to the consummation of the age, with the incarnation of God's Son at the pivotal point in the process.

Heilsgeschichte is used in a special sense by the neo-orthodox to denote a sort of "super history," distinct from real time-space history, in which the events of the Christian faith took place. This is a use orthodox theologians repudiate as antagonistic to the actual and factual historical revelation of Christ recorded in the Bible.

HELL

See **Gehenna**; **Hades**; **Endless Punishment**; **Wrath of God**.

HELLENISM, HELLENIST

Grecianism, Grecians (See Acts 6:1). The Jews of the Western dispersion unavoidably came under the influence of Greek culture, language, and philosophy, which they assimilated to some degree into their understanding and practice of Judaism. The most positive products of Hellenism were the translation of the OT into Greek (*see* **Septuagint**) and the preparation of the Greek-speaking world for the preaching of the gospel.

HENOTHEISM

Greek *henos,* "one," and *theos,* "god"; the belief in one supreme god without denying the existence of other gods; or the ascription of the place of supreme deity to one of several gods in turn.

See **Monolatry.**

HERESY

A deliberate denial of revealed truth, together with the acceptance of error (2 Pet. 2:1). The basic meaning of the Greek word *hairesis* is "choice," giving the meaning of heresy as a self-willed opinion in opposition to Biblical truth. Such opinions frequently gave rise to sects or parties (Acts 5:17; 15:5; 24:5, 14; 26:5; 28:22; 1 Cor. 11:19; Gal. 5:20). A heretic, therefore, is a sectarian. Thus he is to be cut off from church fellowship (Titus 3:10).

See **Schism.**

HERMENEUTICS

Greek *hermeneuo,* "to explain, interpret"; the science of Bible interpretation. Paul stated the aim of all true hermeneutics in 2 Tim. 2:15 as "rightly dividing the word of truth." That means correctly or accurately teaching the word of truth. The apostle boasted that he did not corrupt, or adulterate, the Scriptures (2 Cor. 2:17). A proper hermeneutical approach will enable us to say the same.

Presuppositions

Bible interpretation proceeds upon certain presuppositions that yield certain clear principles by which we must explain the word of God.

The Inspiration of Scripture. Behind the human writers of the Bible books is the true author of each, God Himself (2 Tim. 3:15, 16; 1 Pet. 1:16-21).

The Uniqueness of Scripture. As the word of God, the Bible stands entirely apart from all other literature, sacred or secular. For this reason we cannot approach it in the same way we would approach any other book. It is its own interpreter. The principles by which we seek to learn its meaning are those the Bible itself demands or proposes.

The Unity of Scripture. Though composed of 66 parts, the Bible is one book with one divine author. It does not contradict itself. Where we imagine it does we simply

173

display our lack of understanding of its meaning. Thus we must never interpret any text of Scripture in such a way as to make it contradict another.

The unity of Scripture has other implications. The most obvious feature of the Bible is its division into two Testaments. Any system of interpretation must come to grips with their differences, similarities, and relationship. These matters raise some far-reaching questions, the answers to which will have a strong bearing on our hermeneutics.

The key to answering those questions must be that all Scripture is God's special redemptive revelation, with the person and work of Christ as its focal point. The progressive nature of this revelation must never be forgotten. Thus, while each Testament throws light on the other, the movement is always irreversibly from the Old to the New. "He taketh away the first, that he may establish the second" (Heb. 10:9). The importance of this one-way movement should be clear. There can be no going back to OT shadows that have found their substance in Christ. Those premillennialists who insist that there will be a return to animal sacrifices in the millennium, a view based largely on their interpretation of Ezek. 40-48, fail to hold on to this fundamental principle. A return to animal sacrifices clearly controverts the central message of the book of Hebrews. Any interpretation of an OT prophecy that produces such a conclusion is wrong and must be abandoned. There can be no return to Jewish sacrifices. The religion of the millennium cannot regress from Christianity to OT Judaism.

Not only must the progressive nature of revelation never be forgotten, it must never be abused. That is, it must not become an excuse to deny the plain meaning of OT prophecy, or to replace what the Bible states in the most literal fashion with idealist or spiritualized interpretations. Those who make over to the church all the blessings predicted for Israel while retaining all the curses for the nation (and sometimes both are in the same verse) are abusing the principle of progressive revelation. Those who refuse to see any reference to literal Israel and her future in places such as Zech. 12-14 do the same. This is all the more unreasonable when the language of the prophet plainly aims at describing literal Israel: "Jerusalem shall be inhabited again in her own place, even in Jerusalem" (Zech. 12:6).

Principles of Interpretation

The Protestant Reformation called the church back to the Bible and demanded that it pay attention to the plain sense of Scripture. For centuries the fourfold sense of Scripture had all but closed up the meaning and message of the Bible (see *Allegory).* The Reformers reinstated the literal, or clearly intended, meaning of Scripture as the only legitimate interpretation. This approach depends heavily on a grammatical study of the text and has the invaluable advantage of heeding what is actually written—a procedure which modern schools of hermeneutics have all but given up.

Context. The context of a passage is both immediate and remote. That is, it is in the surrounding verses and chapters of the text being studied but it is also in related passages in other books, especially by the same writer. The proper understanding of a text is always obtained by seeing it in its context.

Scope. The scope of a passage sets the boundaries of what the writer intends to say or teach in it. This will often be the key to understanding a difficult expression or text. Taking note of the writer's aim in writing the passage, and setting the text under consideration in its proper place in accomplishing that aim, will help the interpreter grasp its meaning.

Language. Morphology (the form of words), lexicology (the meaning of words), and syntax (the relationship of words in a sentence or clause) are vital to the understanding of any text. The rules of grammar and the Scripture's usage of language are indispensable to the interpretation of the word.

Figures of Speech. Figures of speech are too often neglected in Bible study. Failure to identify them and give them their natural force often leads to error. E. W. Bullinger's great work on the subject should be on every Bible interpreter's bookshelf. It should be noted that figurative language often occurs in passages that demand a literal interpretation. If I say, "Jim ran off like a frightened deer," I mean that he literally ran off. The presence of the figure *simile* does not alter the literalness of his running off.

Typology. The Bible identifies certain things, people, and events as typical. That is, beyond their place in OT history they foreshadow the realities of the gospel. The ceremonial rites and laws of Israel portrayed the gospel and have been fulfilled by it. They have therefore a unique place in Bible interpretation, but they must never be used to establish a doctrine that cannot be established by the plain statements of Scripture.

Symbolism. Symbols, especially in prophetic passages, must be interpreted as the Bible itself indicates (e.g., Jer. 1:11-16; 24:1-10; Ezek. 37). And it should be noted that the interpretation of a symbol is literal, not symbolic. For example, when Rev. 17:9 tells us that the seven heads of the beast are seven mountains, the mountains are actual mountains, not a further symbol whose meaning we are left to discover (yet even the acute prophetic scholar B. W. Newton fails to observe this in his treatment of the passage).

Poetry. Poetry has its own peculiarities. Insisting on treating poetry as plain prose will not lead to the Scripture's meaning but will obscure it. Learning the features of Hebrew poetry will open the word of God in a wonderful way to the careful student.

Historical Interpretation. Scripture is historically and culturally mediated. That is, God dipped His pen in actual history to give us the Bible. He did not drop it complete out of heaven. The historical background of the writer and those whom he addresses will be of real help in establishing his meaning. Here the study of introduction* is important.

However, we must not carry this emphasis on historical setting too far. The Bible is historically and culturally *mediated* but it is not historically and culturally *conditioned,* as most modern interpreters insist. By *conditioned* they mean that it is locked in its own time and place in history, that it is a product of its time, that its meaning for us depends on our ability to translate its ancient forms (and myths) into a modern equivalent. This has been the general procedure of modern hermeneutical methods.

Rationalist critics employed a *grammatical-historical* method allied to literary criticism. Their evolutionary view of the history of the religion of the Bible governed their approach.

Liberal critics, following Friedrich Schleiermacher and his consciousness theology,* adopted *romanticist hermeneutics* to discover, not what the written words of the Bible actually mean, but what they mean *for me.* In other words, the reader's response took the place of the writer's intent.

Martin Heidegger's early writings led to a school of interpretation that tried to get inside the mind of the writer to discover what he meant. Heidegger's later writings produced what is called *The New Hermeneutic.* This does not try to get inside the writer's mind but inside his *world.* The idea is that it is only by understanding the world projected by a Bible book that we can understand it. This is the adaptation of Form Criticism* to hermeneutics.

All these methods do two things. First, they fasten on to something that is in itself a legitimate idea—historical background, the writer's purpose, the need to apply the message personally—and blow it out of all proportion so as to pervert it. Second, they fail to come to grips with what is actually written.

Dealing with what is actually written is the great task of all true interpretation. That is how the Lord Jesus Christ and His apostles dealt with the Scriptures. Any hermeneutical approach that fails here cannot do justice to Scripture.

See *Exegesis*; *Scripture (Interpretation of)*.

HEXAEMERON
The six-day creation period of Genesis 1.

HEXAPLA
Meaning "sixfold," this is the name given to Origen's version of the OT in six columns. It was produced about A.D. 240 and contained the Hebrew original, a transliteration of the Hebrew into Greek letters, Aquila's Greek translation (A.D.130), Symmachus' idiomatic Greek translation, the Septuagint, and Theodotion's Greek translation (A.D. 180-190).

HEXTATEUCH
The name given by Julius Wellhausen to the Pentateuch and Joshua, to indicate his claim that they manifest a literary unity.

HIGHER CRITICS
See *Criticism*; *J.E.D.P.*

HIGHER LIFE THEOLOGY
The theory that sanctification is a second work of grace, experienced as a post-conversion crisis in which holiness and victory over sin are received by an act of faith. The theory was popularized in America by William E. Boardman, a Presbyterian minister, and in Britain by Robert Pearsall Smith and Hanna Smith. It formed an important part of the Keswick* Convention message from its inception in 1875.

The Smiths combined elements of Wesleyan and Quaker ideas and produced a hybrid theory of sanctification that was at once a crisis experience and a rest of faith, often expressed by the exhortation "Let go and let God." While the founders of the Higher Life movement rejected Wesley's perfectionism,* their own theories led in that direction, producing such claims as "entire sanctification" and cessation from actual commission of sin.

Boardman's criticism that whereas Wesley claimed too much, the Puritans and the Reformed claimed too little, is unfair to the Puritans, but still carries a valuable lesson. It reminds us that while sanctification involves a battle, there is full provision in Christ for His people to enjoy victory in that battle. However, Higher Life claims tend to reduce sin to mere acts and fail to take sufficient note of the persistence of the old man in the believer.

On a positive note, Higher Life theology emphasizes the great truth that the power to overcome sin is not mere will power, but the power of God experienced by faith. That faith, contrary to the Boardman-Smith scheme, is not a single act in a crisis but a constant laying hold of the fulness of Christ to which we have a right because of our justification in union with Him.

HISTORICAL THEOLOGY
The branch of theology that studies the historical development of the understanding and statement of Christian doctrine in the church.

HISTORICISM
A method of interpreting the Book of the Revelation that sees it as a symbolic prophecy of the entire course of the church's history from the first century until the end of time. It is the method most frequently adopted by postmillennialists. See *Futurism*, *Preterism*.

HOLINESS MOVEMENTS
Protestant groups or churches that broadly follow in the tradition of John Wesley and the Methodists in their views of personal sanctification. While not all holiness move-

ments accept Wesley's doctrine of sinless perfection, they do tend to look on holiness as a "second blessing," a "second work of grace" that transforms the Christian's inner life. They also present the view that holiness is not attained by struggle or effort to subdue the flesh but by an act of self-surrender to Christ. In some cases the resultant blessing is called *sanctification,* in others *the fulness of the Spirit,* which in the case of the Pentecostal Holiness movement is associated with the reception of the gifts of the Spirit,* notably the gift of tongues.

See **Glossalalia; Higher Life Theology.**

HOLINESS OF GOD

"The holiness of God is not to be conceived of as one attribute among others; it is rather a general term representing the conception of His consummate perfection and total glory. It is His infinite moral perfection crowning His infinite intelligence and power....Infinite moral perfection is the crown of the Godhead. Holiness is the total glory thus crowned" (A. A. Hodge).

In Scripture, holiness as applied to God is first, His moral purity (Lev. 11:44; Ps. 145:17), and second, His divine majesty (Isa. 6:3; Ps. 22:3; Rev. 4:8).

See **Attributes of God.**

HOLY OFFICE

At one time this was the tribunal of the church of Rome's Inquisition. It still exists to judge anything that Rome considers to be heresy, and examines and prohibits books thought to be injurious to the faith of the faithful.

HOLY SPIRIT

The Holy Spirit is an eternal, essential trinitarian person, a personal subsistence in the divine essence. He exists eternally in perfect union with the Father and the Son. He is commonly referred to as the "third Person of the Trinity."* This description arises out of man's attempt at a logical understanding of the mystery of the Trinity. It is acceptable as long as we remember that it does not infer any inferiority, subordination, or posteriority.

Our study of the Holy Spirit falls under four heads: first, His personality; second, His deity; third, His work; and finally, His fulness in the life of the believer.

The Personality of the Holy Spirit.

The Holy Spirit is a divine person. He is not a mere influence, as Socianism* teaches. Nor is He an official title, or mode of operation, adopted by God in His dealings with His creatures, as Sabellianism* teaches.

Scriptural Proofs of the Spirit's Personality

1. The Lord Jesus Christ speaks of the Holy Spirit as a person (John 15:26, 27; 16:7).

2. The Bible ascribes personal attributes to Him.

　　a. He *speaks* (Mark 13:11; Acts 13:2; I Tim. 4:1; Rev. 2:7).

　　b. He *instructs* (Neh. 9:20; John 14:26).

　　c. He *bears witness* (Acts 5:32; Rom. 8:16).

　　d. He *searches and knows* (1 Cor. 2:10, 11).

　　e. He *quickens* or gives spiritual life (John 6:63).

　　f. He *intercedes* (Rom. 8:26).

　　g. He *sends forth* (Acts 13:4).

　　h. He *appoints overseers* in the church (Acts 20:28).

　　i. He *can be vexed* (Isa. 63:10); *grieved* (Eph. 4:30).

These are attributes of a person, and are sufficient proof of the personality of the Holy Spirit.

The Deity of the Holy Spirit

1. Scripture calls Him God (2 Cor. 3:17; Acts 5:3, 4).

2. It ascribes divine attributes to Him.

　　a. He is *eternal* (Heb. 9:14)

　　b. He is *omnipresent* (Psa. 139:7, "Whither shall I go from thy Spirit?").

　　c. He is *omniscient and all wise* (1 Cor. 2:10).

d. He is *omnipotent* (Zec. 4:6; Rom. 8:11; 15:19)

e. He is *holy,* and according to Isa. 57:15 that is the definitive attribute of God.

f. He is *just and righteous* (Isa. 59:17-19)

g. He is *good* (Neh. 9:20 with Mark 10:18).

h. He is *true* (John 14:17; 15:26; 16:13).

i. He is *sovereign* (Ps. 51:12; John 3:8).

3. It ascribes divine acts to Him.

    a. *Creation* (Gen. 1:2).

    b. The *resurrection* of Christ (Rom. 8:11; 1 Pet. 3:18).

    c. *Regeneration* (John 6:63).

    d. *Inspiration* of Scripture (2 Tim. 3:16 with 2 Pet. 1:10-11, 21).

4. Scripture uses of the name of the Spirit along with that of the Father and the Son in such a way as to prove His proper deity (Matt. 28:19; 2 Cor. 13:14).

5. Scripture's definition of the sin of blasphemy against the Holy Ghost, and its consequences, proves the Deity of the Spirit (Matt. 12:31, 32).

The Work of the Holy Spirit

1. He *convinces* men of sin (John. 16:8; Acts 2:37).

2. He *regenerates,* or quickens (John 3:5, 8). Regeneration, or the new birth, is the "sole and special work of the Holy Spirit" (Octavius Winslow).

3. He *incorporates* everyone whom He regenerates into the body of Christ (1 Cor. 12:13).

4. He *indwells* all believers (John 14:17; 1 Cor. 6:19; Rom. 8:9; Eph. 2:22).

    a. He thus bears witness with our spirit that we are the sons of God (Rom. 8:16).

    b. He proves our adoption as the sons of God (Gal. 4:6).

    c. The indwelling Spirit is the pledge of our entrance into heaven (Eph. 1:14).

    d. He teaches us and guides us into all truth (John 14:26).

5. He *seals* every believer for glory (2 Cor. 1:22; Eph. 1:13; 4:30). To seal means to put a stamp or impress upon. It denotes ownership, approval, or a shutting up to a particular purpose (cf. Matt. 27:66).

6. He is the *author of sanctification* (2 Thes. 2:13; 1 Pet. 1:2).

7. He is the *author of prayer* in the believer (Rom. 8:26; Eph. 6:18; Jude 20; cf. Zech. 12:10).

8. He is the Comforter, or *paraclete* (John. 14:16; 15:26; 16:7). Paraclete comes from the Greek *para,* "beside," and *kaleo,* "to call." It signifies that the Holy Spirit is called to our side as our advocate and our helper, the vicar of Christ on earth, supplying to us what the Lord was to His disciples in the days of His earthly ministry, as the words "another [i.e., *another of the same sort*] Comforter" show.

9. He leads believers to see what God has freely provided for them in Christ (1 Cor. 2:9-12).

10. His supreme work is to reveal and glorify the Lord Jesus Christ (John 16:14; 15:26).

The Fulness of the Holy Spirit
See separate article with this title.

HOMOLEGOUMENA
A term used by Origen to denote those books universally accepted as Scripture. *See **Antilegomena.***

HOMOOUSIOS
Greek, "of the same substance"; the word that denoted Trinitarian orthodoxy in the controversy waged by Athanasius against Arius in the fourth century.

It states the truth that the Son is of the same substance with the Father. Arius proposed the word *homoiousios,* "of similar substance" *(see **Arians**).* The Nicene Creed's * assertion of the Son's consubstantiality* with the Father has ever since been the standard statement of the orthodox understanding of Scripture on the subject.

HUMANISM

In the 16th century, the party of Erasmus and Reuchlin whose academic pursuit was the cultivation of classical literature, the *literae humaniores,* "polite letters." Nowadays the word refers to an entirely different movement and philosophy. It describes the pursuit of purely human interests and ideals, usually considered apart from and antagonistic to any idea of God or His intervention in human affairs. Indeed the *Humanist Manifesto* makes it a fundamental tenet of humanism that man neither needs nor may have salvation from any superhuman source, and specifically not from God.

HUMANITY OF CHRIST

The doctrine that the Lord Jesus had a true human body and a reasonable human soul.

He is called "the seed of the woman" (Gen. 3:15). He was of the seed of David (Rom. 1:3) and is emphatically called a man (1 Tim. 2:5). One of His titles is "the Son of Man" (Matt. 13:37, etc.).

1. He had a true human body. This was plainly laid down by the inspired apostles in opposition to some Gnostics, the *Docetae,* who held that the body of Christ was merely a phantom and not real flesh and blood. Luke 24:39; John 20:27, and many other Scriptures destroy such a myth.

2. He had a reasonable soul. This contradicts the ancient heresy of Apollinarianism.* See Mt. 26:38; Mk. 6:6; Mt. 8:10; Luke 7:9. "Sorrow and wonder are rational emotions, proper to man, but not to God" (Shedd)— i.e., they are positive proof that the Lord Jesus had a true human soul.

See *Theanthropic Person; Unipersonality.*

HUMILIATION OF CHRIST

"Christ's humiliation consisted in His being born and that in low condition, made under the law, undergoing the miseries of this life, the wrath of God, and the cursed death of the cross, in being buried, and con-

tinuing under the power of death for a time" (*Shorter Catechism,* Q. 27).

See *Sufferings of Christ.*

HUTTERITES

The group of Anabaptists* who moved from the Tyrol into Moravia, where they were consolidated under the ministry of Jacob Hutter.

HYLOZOISM

From two Greek words *hule,* "wood," and *zoe,* "life"; the theory atttributed to Strato of Lampsacus, that matter possesses life and that the universe is a vast animal, self-developing unconsciously from all eternity.

HYPERDULIA

In Roman Catholicism, the worship accorded to the Virgin Mary.

Rome has three types of worship: *latria,* belongs only to God; *dulia* is the worship accorded to the saints; while *hyperdulia* is supposed to be inferior to *latria* but superior to *dulia.* Rome's worship of Mary, however distinguished in Latin words, is idolatry, as any reference to Roman Catholic prayers to her and descriptions of her (*mediatrix, co-redemptrix, Queen of Heaven*) will show.

HYPOCRISY

The OT word *chaneph* signifies chiefly "impious" and gives *hypocrisy* the basic significance of godlessness or wickedness. The Greek *hupokrisis* denotes "an actor's response" and brings the meaning of deliberately acting a part. The Greek word *anupokritos* is the opposite of *hypocritical,* and it signifies "sincere" or "genuine" (Rom. 12:9; I Tim. 1:5; James 3:17, etc.). Thus hypocrisy may be summed up as an insincere acting the part of godliness, as a cloak for the practice of wickedness.

HYPOSTASIS

In Greek, *hupostasis* signifies "essence" or "substance." It comes from a word meaning

179

"to subsist," literally "to stand under," and therefore denotes a real, personal subsistence. Philosophically, *hypostasis* emphasized *essence* as distinct from *attributes*. Theologically, it was used, and continues to be used by orthodox trinitarians, as a term to describe any one of the three real and distinct personal subsistences of the one undivided divine essence. That is its meaning in Heb. 1:3. The formula, "One essence (Greek, *ousia*) three subsistences (*hupostasis*)" is the accepted trinitarian statement of the Biblical doctrine of God's tri-unity. See *Trinity.*

HYPOSTATICAL UNION

A term used to denote the union of a perfect human nature with the eternal Logos without confusion of natures in the person of Christ. *Hypostatical* is used to emphasize that it was one subsistence of the divine essence, or, as we would say, one person of the Trinity, namely the Son of God, who took a human nature into union with Himself. The Trinity did not become incarnate; one *hypostasis** did.

HYPOTHETICAL UNIVERSALISM

The theory of the extent of the atonement adopted by the so-called Calvinistic Universalists of the Saumur School. The leading advocates of the theory were Scottish theologian John Cameron and the Frenchman Moses Amyraut, or Amyrald, after whom the whole scheme is usually named *(see Amyraldism).*

Amyrald taught that the divine motive behind redemption was benevolence toward all men, as the result of which God sent his Son to make the salvation of all men possible. He offers salvation to all men, upon condition that they believe in Christ, something which all men have the natural ability to do. However, "as this natural ability was counteracted by a moral inability, God determined to give His efficacious grace to a certain number of the human race, and thus secure their salvation" (Charles Hodge).

Though Amyrald professed allegiance to the canons of the Synod of Dort, his position is clearly a mediatory one between Augustinianism and Arminianism. John Owen analysed the theory as follows: "Christ died for all, but (only) conditionally for some, if they do believe, or will so do (which He knows they cannot do of themselves); and absolutely for His own, even them on whom He purposeth to bestow faith and grace, so as actually to be made possessors of the good things by Him purchased" (*Death of Death*, p. 110).

From Charles Hodge's *Systematic Theology* we note the objections to hypothetical universalism.

1. It is liable to the objections which press both on Augustinianism and Arminianism.

2. It does not remove the difficulties about the reformed doctrine of the Sovereignty of God to which it set out to find an answer.

3. It leaves the case of the heathen who live and die without hearing the gospel out of view—they have not opportunity to repent and believe, and must be viewed as passed over by the decree to grant the grace to believe on Christ. How can there then be a universal hypothetical decree to offer Christ to all men? We are forced back to the sovereignty of God on strictly Calvinistic terms.

4. It supposes the possibility of change or failure in God's purposes. According to Amyrald, God purposed to save all, and out of that benevolent purpose sent His Son to die for all. Only because He had to acknowledge the failure of such a purpose did He elect a people to receive the gift of efficacious grace. But what an unscriptural view of God is this! "It cannot however be supposed that God intends what is never accomplished; that He purposes what He does not intend to effect; that He adopts means for an end which is never to be attained. This cannot be affirmed of any rational being who had the wisdom and power to secure the execution of his purposes. Much less can it be said of Him whose power and

wisdom are infinite" (Hodge, 2:323).

5. According to Scripture the work of Christ perfectly achieves its intended end (Matt. 1:21; Isa. 53:11). "It was intended to save His people, and not merely to make the salvation of all men possible. It was a real satisfaction to justice and therefore necessarily frees from condemnation. It was a ransom paid and accepted, and therefore, certainly redeems. If, therefore, equally designed for all men, it must secure the salvation of all" *(ibid.)*.

6. The gift of Christ secures and necessarily includes all other blessings (Rom. 8:32). Thus all for whom Christ was given must be saved.

7. "The Bible in numerous passages directly asserts that Christ came to redeem His people; to save them from their sins; and to bring them to God" (Eph. 5:25; John 10:15). "As the end precedes the means...then His people were selected and present to the divine mind in the order of thought, prior to the gift of Christ" *(ibid.)*.

8. God's peculiar love for His people, not His general benevolence, was His motive in the plan of redemption. In giving His Son He gives all conceivable and possible good.

Thus Amyraldism's hypothetical universalism fails. Amyrald's motive was to save Calvinism from a sort of reformed scholasticism and to get back to the Calvinism of Calvin in his *Institutes of the Christian Religion.* This is laudable and is similar to the desire of Scotland's Marrowmen *(see **Marrow Controversy).*** However, it is one thing to preach the free offer of the gospel to all men and tell them that if they repent and believe in Christ they will be saved. It is quite another thing to state that God purposed by the death of Christ to save those who in fact perish eternally. The Marrowmen preached the free offer, the Amyraldists preached the error of an unfulfilled divine purpose in the atonement. The theory was doomed to failure, though for a time it enjoyed great acceptance. It was condemned by the Swiss Reformed Church in its *Formula Consensus*

Helvetica of 1675. In due time most of its advocates either returned to the orthodox reformed view or went all the way into Arminianism. However, Amyrald's views continue to influence the so-called moderate Calvinists of today.

I

ICONOCLASM

Greek *eikon,* "image," and *klao,* "to break"; the destruction of images.

During the period 726-843 the Byzantine* church experienced an ongoing controversy on the subject of the veneration of icons. In 726 Emperor Leo III ordered the destruction of all pictures in churches, but by 787 that policy had been reversed and the Seventh Ecumenical Council which met at Nicea condemned the destruction of icons.

In the period of the Reformation, iconoclasm occurred as the result of the desire of the Reformers, especially the Swiss, to conform Protestant worship to the simplicity of the early church. Luther strongly condemned the destruction of images in Wittenberg in 1522 and permitted the retention of pictures and images as edifying ornaments. In sharp contrast, Reformed churches refused to retain icons or images for any purpose, viewing them as breaches of the second commandment. There were serious iconoclastic disturbances in France, the Netherlands, and Scotland—usually a response by what John Knox called "the rascally mob" to violent outrages by the Church of Rome or her political supporters.

ICONOLATRY

The use of icons, images, and physical or pictorial representations in the worship of God.

In Roman Catholicism and Eastern Orthodoxy there is a species of worship given to the icon, professedly not in and for itself (which both systems would agree would be idolatry) but as a representation of Christ. The theory is that the worship belongs to Christ but inasmuch as He is represented by the icon, veneration of the representation is proper. Such fine distinctions are lost on the common worshipper. They are empty sophisms. The decalogue* sets the inviolable standard that there are no representations of deity permissible under any circumstances or as any assistance in worship. *See* **Henotheism**.

IDEALISM

The philosophy, opposite to materialism,* that only that which is mental is real and that the phenomena of the material world are only modifications of mind.

According to this theory, all a man really knows is the thought or feeling of which he is conscious: "He can never be rationally certain whether there is any outward reality corresponding to that inward state or not" (A. A. Hodge). Thus we have the strange situation of the idealist writing great tomes upon his philosophy and never being sure that the books he has written have any objective reality.

I.H.S.

The first three letters of the name *Jesus* in Greek script. Misreading these as Latin letters has produced a mystical symbol widely revered in the Roman Catholic church, which uses them on her altars and consecrated host. Had they been Latin letters they would have read *IES* from *Iesus.* Three meanings have commonly been attributed to *IHS.* These are the "Christian" uses of the acrostic.

1. *Iesus Hominum Salvator,* "Jesus Saviour of men."

2. *In Hoc Signo (vinces),* "In this sign (thou shalt conquer)." This is the message Constantine is alleged to have seen written in the sky as he led his army into battle. It is the slogan of the Jesuits as they conduct their unrelenting campaign against Protestantism.

3. *In Hac (cruce) Salus* "In this (cross is) salvation."

Alexander Hislop in his *Two Babylons* traces the original meaning as *Isis, Horus, Seb,* the Mother, the Child, and the Father of the gods, or the Egyptian trinity.

ILLUMINATION

Enlightenment. Theologically, illumination is used in two ways. First, it describes the work of the Holy Spirit in regeneration whereby He enlightens "our minds in the knowledge of Christ" (*Shorter Catechism,* Q. 31).

Second, it is used of a false theory of inspiration as a mere intensification of the spiritual perceptions which every believer has by the internal enlightenment of the Spirit.

IMAGO DEI, OR IMAGE OF GOD

"God created man . . . after his own image, in knowledge, righteousness and holiness, with dominion over the creatures" (*Shorter Catechism,* Q. 10). NT references such as Col. 3:10 and Eph. 4:24 indicate that knowledge, righteousness, and holiness characterized the state in which man was originally created. Gen. 1:27 teaches that he was created in the image of God, and so we can conclude that his creation in knowledge, righteousness, and holiness constitutes, at least in part, the image of God in man.

We say "at least in part" because there has been a great deal of discussion as to how comprehensively we are to understand the *imago dei.*

Pelagius *(see Pelagianism)* taught that it referred only to man's reason, free will, and power to rule the lower creation.

The Reformers included the idea of original righteousness. Indeed, Luther limited the whole idea of the image of God to man's creation in righteousness, deny-

ing that his rational or moral powers were any part of it. Thus, in Luther's view, man lost the image of God entirely by his fall.* Calvin saw the *imago* as including rational and moral powers.

The references already cited prove that original righteousness (including knowledge and true holiness) is included in the term.

Clearly, this original righteousness was lost by the fall, and man is now "desperately wicked" (Jer. 17:9). But the Scripture continues to speak of the image of God in man after the fall (Gen. 9:6; 1 Cor. 11:7; James 3:9). According to Gen. 9:6 the foulness of murder consists in an attack upon the image of God.

These facts indicate that the "image of God" comprises more than original righteousness. Thus it is taken to include such things as spirituality, immortality, and moral and rational powers. Summarizing, we may say that Reformed theology views the image of God in man as consisting in spirituality, immortality,* intellect and will,* original righteousness, and lordship over the lower creation.

See **Creation**.

IMMACULATE CONCEPTION

A teaching of the Church of Rome that Mary the mother of Jesus was born without original sin.

According to this dogma Christ paid for sinners a debt that had already been incurred. In the case of Mary, He paid for her the debt of sin in order that it might never be incurred. Though Pope Pius IX stated that the Immaculate Conception of Mary was "a doctrine revealed by God" the word of God makes no mention of it whatsoever. Indeed, the evidence is much the other way, for Mary spoke of "God my Saviour." Only sinners need a Saviour.

IMMANENCE

A word used to convey the idea of God indwelling His creation and its processes. It is the counterpart of transcendence,* which emphasizes His distinctness from, and total sovereign superiority over, His creation. Pantheism is immanentistic: it, in fact, identifies God with the universe. Another form of immanence is the notion of theistic evolution: God is viewed as always acting "naturally" (i.e., within the course of nature and by means of natural development) and not supernaturally.

These are unscriptural and clearly erroneous views of the immanence of God. Still, the idea of God's immanence is scriptural. It is not antagonistic to His transcendence. He is immanent in that He is omnipresent throughout His creation (Ps. 139), and yet He is transcendent in that He is personally and essentially distinct from, and infinitely superior to, His creation. This was graphically portrayed to the Israelites by the camp around the tabernacle. The tabernacle, with the pillar of cloud, signified God's presence or immanence. His separation, or transcendence, was signified by the fact that the camp was separated from the tabernacle on all four sides by the Levites and Moses, Aaron and the priests (Num. 1:53; 3:31-38).

IMMEDIATE IMPUTATION

The orthodox doctrine, sometimes referred to as a*ntecedent imputation,* that teaches that the guilt of Adam's first sin was immediately imputed to all his posterity issuing from him by natural generation, in consequence of which they are in time born corrupted and depraved.

See Imputation; Mediate Imputation.

IMMEDIATE WORKS OF GOD

Those works which God does not carry out mediately, or by means of a delegate.

This use of the word becomes very important as we compare Christ's mediatorial functions as our prophet and as our priest. He discharged His prophetic function both mediately and immediately—i.e., through human instruments (1 Pet. 1:10, 11) and in person. However, his priestly function He discharges only in person—i.e., it is His immediate work. Similarly, in regeneration* the Holy Spirit works immediately upon the soul, and for that reason we say that the act of regeneration is accomplished without the use of means.

See Mediator; Priestly Office of Christ; Prophetic Office of Christ.

IMMENSITY OF GOD

The description of the relation of the infinite essence of God to space. He transcends all spatial limitations. "The entire indivisible essence of God is at every moment of time contemporaneously present to every point of infinite space" (A. A. Hodge).

See and compare Omnipresence; Infinity of God.

IMMERSE, IMMERSION

The meaning attributed by Baptists* to the Greek words *baptizo* and *baptisma.* Of the verb *baptizo* they claim, "It always signifies to dip, never expressing anything but mode" (Carson). Thus immersion is held to be the only valid mode of baptism.

On the contrary side, there is ample evidence from Scripture that baptism refers to washing or purification, without specific reference to the mode. In Heb. 9:10 Paul speaks of "divers baptisms" under the OT and in vv. 13, 19, and 21 he details them. There is no reference to immersion, but there is to sprinkling.

Thus while Baptists insist that immersion is the only mode of baptism, most other believers hold that while it is a legitimate mode, it is not set down in the word of God as the exclusive mode.

See Baptism.

IMMORTALITY

The word is used in a restricted sense and unrestricted sense. In the unrestricted sense, it is used only of God (1 Tim. 6:16). Only God has immortality as an original, eternal, and necessary characteristic. In the restricted sense some of His creatures (men and angels) are immortal, in the sense that they have an existence which will never be terminated. The Scripture pictures both saints and sinners as consciously existing after death in a disembodied state. It also speaks of a resurrection of the body and a reuniting of body and soul, so that the whole man enters into eternal bliss or blackness, as the case may be.

From this we conclude the following:

1. God's immortality is true eternity. He is without beginning or end. His is a necessary immortality.

2. The immortality ascribed to creatures is everlasting continuance in existence. They had a beginning and by the mere good pleasure of His will God has constituted them immortal. This is a contingent immortality (not to be confused with the false theory of conditional immortality*). It does not belong to their constitution by necessity, but by divine appointment.

3. For God's redeemed people, immortality means the full enjoyment of the inexpressibly abundant and eternal life purchased by Christ for His people (Rom. 2:7 and 2 Tim. 1:10).

IMMUTABILITY OF GOD

The attribute of God whereby He cannot change or be changed in His essence or perfections.

In Himself He is *absolutely* immutable. In relation to His creatures, He is *relatively* immutable: He will never deviate or show a "shadow of turning" from His revealed purpose and truth (James 1:17; Mal. 3:6; Isa. 46:10; Ps. 33:11).

IMPECCABILITY OF CHRIST

The doctrine that the Lord Jesus Christ not only was *able not to sin,* but that He was *not able to sin.* Thus, not only did He not sin, He could not sin. "He was not only able to overcome temptation, but He

was unable to be overcome by it" (Shedd, *Dogmatic Theology,* 2:330).

Christ had a human nature, and human nature is, considered in itself, capable of falling. But the human nature of Christ was personally united to the eternal Word, or Son of God, who was incapable of falling. It never had any existence apart from this union with the Word. Thus, when speaking of the theanthropic person,* it is both inconceivable and unscriptural to say that the God-man could have sinned. It is vain to say what the human nature of Christ could have done if left to itself. The fact is, it was not and could not be left to itself. The complex person of Christ could do nothing that was detrimental to the glory of the infinitely holy Son of God. The divine nature could never be a party to sin.

It is frequently urged that if Christ could not sin, His temptations were meaningless. But this does not follow. As Shedd points out, "Temptability and peccability may be in inverse proportion to each other, and this proves that the two things are entirely distinct and diverse." It takes a stronger temptation to assail a virtuous person than a debauched person. The principle is clear: the less peccability the greater the temptation's force. Thus in the case of the most virtuous person of all, the God-man, temptation would have reached its highest degree.

The Scripture teaches the impeccability of Christ. Hebrews 13:8 says He is immutable. That could not be, if He had been capable of falling. Hebrews 4:15 says, "Christ was tempted in all points like as we are *choris hamartias." Choris hamartias* means "apart from sin," or "sinlessly" (compare the use of *choris* in Heb. 7:21; 9:18; 9:22). Christ's temptations were unlike ours in that while He was assailed from the outside, there was nothing in Him to desire to embrace that outward temptation. He said, "The prince of this world cometh, and hath nothing in me" (John 14:30).

Shedd and Berkhof defend the truth of Christ's impeccability, though, sadly, no less a theologian than Charles Hodge repudiated it (*Systematic Theology,* 2:457).

See **Temptability**.

IMPETRATION

The accomplishment of redemption by Christ. It is a fundamental truth of Reformed soteriology* that in Christ's atoning work impetration and application are coextensive—i.e., all He accomplished is certainly applied to all for whom He accomplished it.

See **Atonement**; **Priestly Office**.

IMPLICIT FAITH

The term used in Roman Catholic theology when the church or an individual believer does not grasp all the particulars or consequences of an article of revealed truth to which each gives assent. Such particulars or consequences are said to be implicit in the article believed. Roman Catholic apologists have employed this idea to justify their church's definition of Mary's immaculate conception* and assumption* as Christian doctrine. They argue that although these dogmas are nowhere mentioned in Scripture, they are implied by Mary's selection to be the mother of Jesus—i.e., the early church had implicit faith in them. From a Protestant perspective, implicit faith as used by Rome is a sophistical invention to justify her unscriptural additions to the gospel revelation.

IMPUTATION

A forensic term that denotes the reckoning or placing to a person's account the merit or guilt that belongs to him on account of his personal performance or of that of his federal head. While *impute* is used in Scripture to express the idea of receiving the just reward of our deeds (Lev. 7:18; 17:4; 2 Sam. 19:19), *imputation* as a theological term normally carries one of two meanings:

Meaning of Imputation

1. It describes the transmission of the guilt of Adam's first sin to his descendants. It is imputed, or reckoned, to them; i.e., it is laid to their account. (*See* **Traducianism** for a discussion of the ground of such a reckoning; also **Immediate Imputation.**)

2. It describes the act of God in visiting the guilt of believers on Christ and of conferring the righteousness of Christ upon believers. In this sense "imputation is an act of God as sovereign judge, at once judicial and sovereign, whereby He—(1). Makes the guilt, legal responsibility of our sins, really Christ's, and punishes them in Him, Isa. 53:6; John 1:29; 2 Cor. 5:21; and (2). Makes the merit, legal rights of Christ's righteousness, ours, and then treats us as persons legally invested with all those rights, Rom. 4:6; 10:4; 1 Cor. 1:30; 2 Cor. 5:21; Phil. 3:9. As Christ is not made a sinner by the imputation to Him of our sins, so we are not made holy by the imputation to us of His righteousness. The transfer is only of guilt from us to Him, and of merit from Him to us. He justly suffered the punishment due to our sins, and we justly receive the rewards due to His righteousness, 1 John 1:8, 9" (A. A. Hodge, *Outlines of Theology,* chap. 30, Q. 15).

The ground of this imputation is the real, vital, personal, spiritual and federal union of Christ with His people, a union established as the result of the gracious purpose of God.

Imputation, then, is clearly indispensable to the Biblical doctrine of justification.* It has been attacked by modernists and so misrepresented as to be absurd.

Denials of Imputation

A Modernist Denial.

According to J. E. Davey, late Principal of Assembly's College, Belfast, the doctrine of imputation is just "another Form of Transubstantiation." In his book, *The Changing Vesture of the Faith,* Davey wrote, "Protestantism has unwittingly done exactly the same thing (as Romanism). The centre of the orthodox system is a doctrine of atonement resting upon a theory of imputation which is only another form of transubstantiation. Guilt and righteousness are relative terms, which refer to the personal will, and cannot be disassociated from it by any mental jugglery....These words simply represent states of the consciousness, and are in no sense transferable."

Davey's views, propounding a way of salvation almost divorced from what Christ did and possessed by a "simple process of change," are based upon unscriptural notions of guilt and righteousness. He denies any objective reality to them. They are to him mere forms of consciousness. They are to be forgotten, not atoned for. Thus, according to Davey, salvation is accomplished without any imputation of the righteousness of Christ to the believer, without any satisfaction made to divine justice, and without any legal ground for its being established. This is a typical "liberal" gospel, which is not a gospel at all, and can be arrived at only by a wholesale wresting, or ignoring, of Scripture. No more telling commentary on just how vital the doctrine of imputation is to the scriptural scheme of salvation could be given.

Arminian, Lutheran, and Dispensationalist Denials. Objections against the orthodox statement of the imputation of Christ's righteousness to believers come also from various evangelicals, including Arminians, some Lutherans, and dispensationalists.

The argument is usually that "faith is counted for righteousness" (Rom. 4:3, 5). That is, faith is regarded as righteousness. However, that is something the text quoted does not say. Faith is counted *for* or *unto* righteousness, not *as* righteousness. Paul is not teaching that God regarded faith as something it was not. Rather he shows that faith is the instrument by which this righteousness is received.

Proof of the Imputation of Christ's Righteousness

Faith is counted unto believers for righteousness. The question is, "Whose righ-

teousness?" It certainly is not our own. The Bible makes it clear that it is Christ's (1 Cor. 1:30; 2 Cor. 5:21).

Two Kinds of Words in Romans 5:18, 19. The Bible also makes it clear what it means by Christ's righteousness. The terms Paul employs in Rom. 5:18, 19 are exact. Note the *-ma* and the *-is* endings in this text: "Therefore as by the offence *(paraptoma)* of one judgment came upon all men to condemnation; even so by the righteousness *(dikaioma)* of one the free gift came upon all men unto justification *(dikaiosis)* of life. For as by one man's disobedience *(parakoe)* many were made [constituted] sinners, so by the obedience *(hupakoe)* of one shall many be made [constituted] righteous."

The significance of the *-ma* and the *-is* endings should not be overlooked. Paul has been piling up nouns with the *-ma* ending, six of them in verse 16 (*dorema,* "gift," *krima,* "judgment," *katakrima,* "condemnation," *charisma,* "free gift," *paraptomata,* "offences," *dikaioma,* "justification"). In every case the *-ma* ending indicates not only the action but its effect: *dorema* is the gift with its effect; *krima* is the judgment result or verdict; *katakrima* is the adverse judgment result or verdict; *charisma* is the gift of grace and its effect; *paraptomata* means many falls with their results; *dikaioma* is righteousness with its result, namely a verdict of acquittal or justification on the ground of righteousness.

In contrast, the *-is* ending emphasizes the thought of action. Additionally, *parakoe* and *hupakoe* denote respectively the action of disobeying and obeying. With all this in mind we are in a position to grasp the full significance of Paul's statement. Adam's *paraptoma* (v. 18) means his offence and its effects leading to *katakrima,* a verdict of judgment on all men. Even so by the *dikaioma* of Christ, or His justification because of His righteous actions, the *charisma,* or gracious gift, brought for all men a *dikaiosis,* an action declaring them righteous. The ground of these verdicts is stated in verse 19. By Adam's act of disobedience many were constituted sinners. By Christ's action of obedience many are constituted righteous.

Christ's Personal Righteousness Imputed. The point Paul makes about our justification is vitally important: God declared Jesus Christ righteous on the basis of His personal righteousness. He declares believers righteous, not on the ground of any personal righteousness, but on the ground of the righteous action of Christ in His obedience. The entire action of Christ in obeying God, including what theologians term His active obedience as well as His passive obedience (i.e. His obedience both in His life and in His death), is the ground of God's verdict of justification on the believer. The claim that the Bible does not teach that Christ's active obedience was vicarious, or that His personal obedience is imputed to us to constitute us legally righteous before God, is patently groundless. In the one place where the NT formally and extensively deals with the ground of our justification (Rom. 5:12-19) these truths are carefully expounded.

Further Textual Proof. Other texts carry the same message. As God "made him [Christ] to be sin for us," so He made us "the righteousness of God in him" (2 Cor. 5:21). This signifies a legal imputation, not a moral infusion, of righteousness. The "righteousness of God in him" is the righteousness God has provided. And where may we find it? "In him," not in our works, or even in our faith. By faith we receive Christ as our righteousness, but we must never locate the merit of our justification in our act of faith. No action of ours, even our believing, is perfect. Thus no action of ours, even our believing, can be the ground of our justification, which demands a perfect righteousness. It is Christ who "is made unto us righteousness" (1 Cor. 1:30). Thus with Jeremiah we properly call Him *Jehovah Tsidkenu,* "the Lord our Righteousness" (Jer. 23:6).

Consequences of the Imputation of Christ's Righteousness

The truth of the imputation of Christ's righteousness has important consequences for the believer's assurance and serenity. The latter is discussed in contrast with a psychological counterfeit of it under Self-esteem.*

Understanding Imputation Yields Assurance. As long as Christians keep dissecting their own faith to see if they "really" believed, felt enough penitent emotion, prayed the right prayer, or have performed to a sufficiently high standard, they will destroy assurance. There is no perfection in the best we have done or can do. And yet assurance demands a perfect foundation on which to rest. We have that foundation in the perfect righteousness of Christ, which God has made over to the account of every believer. He who believes in Christ stands before God's judgment bar as if he personally had rendered the perfect obedience of the Lord Jesus. We are in Him; He is the head and we are the body. The head suffered for the body's sin; the body receives all the reward of the head's righteousness.

This doctrine will have far-reaching effects in the life of the believer. It will set him free to serve the Lord in love. This is the essence of Christian liberty. As J. Gresham Machen long ago pointed out, this is the liberty from having to establish our own righteousness before God, or having to do something to gain His acceptance. Christ has done all that. Now we serve, not to be justified, but because we are "justified freely by his grace through the redemption that is in Christ Jesus" (Rom. 3:24).

Understanding Imputation Leads to Holiness. Some imagine that the doctrine of free justification and imputed righteousness takes away the motive for holiness and leaves a believer free to sin. Paul answers that objection with a simple question: "How shall we, that are dead to sin, live any longer therein?" (Rom. 6:2)—rather, "How shall we who died to sin live any longer therein?" That is, we

189

died in Christ and rose again in Him (v. 4) and that is the strongest motive for holiness we can have.

INABILITY

The corollary of total depravity *(see **Depravity**);* this term denotes the absence of any ability in fallen man to will that which is good, in the sense of being meritorious in the sight of God. The *Westminster Confession of Faith* sums up the case as follows:

"Man by his fall into a state of sin, hath wholly lost all ability of will to any spiritual good accompanying salvation; so as a natural man, being altogether averse from that good, and dead in sin, is not able, by his own strength, to convert himself, or to prepare himself thereunto" (chap. 9, sec. 3).

This makes man's inability flow from the voluntary disposition of his depraved will. By the fall, man is "utterly indisposed, disabled, and made opposite to all good, and wholly inclined to all evil" (*Confession,* chap. 6, sec. 4).

This inability does not contradict the principle of the freedom of the will *(see **Free Will**).* It does not arise from any constitutional deficiency in the faculties of the soul as created by God. It flows from the voluntary aversion of the human will to God and His law, and therefore is said to be *moral* (stressing the fact that such inability is the result of the exercise of a self-determining responsible, moral agent), and *natural,* in that it is innate in all fallen souls. This inability is said to be *total* or absolute: man's case is, by his own strength and efforts, beyond remedy or hope of change. Thus in Scripture, fallen man is said to be "without strength," "dead," "blind," and "darkened." As Jer. 13:23 puts it, "Can the Ethiopian change his skin, or the leopard his spots? Then may ye also do good that are accustomed to do evil."

INCARNATION

The coming of the *Logos,* or "Word," in the flesh. John 1:14 is the key text: "The

Word was made [became] flesh and dwelt among us." In writing to Timothy, Paul lays this down as the first fundamental doctrine of Christianity: "Great is the mystery of godliness, God was manifest in the flesh" (1 Tim. 3:16).

The NT constantly stresses this point. Christ is said to have "come in the flesh" (1 John 4:2); to have been "sent in the flesh" (Rom. 8:3); to have "suffered in the flesh" (1 Pet. 4:1); to have "died in the flesh" (1 Pet. 3:18); and to have "made reconciliation in the body of His flesh" (Col. 1:21-22). Every spirit that refuses to confess this cardinal truth is expressly declared to be not of God, but to be that spirit of Antichrist (1 John 4:2, 3).

This coming in the flesh was effected by a miraculous conception and virgin birth (Matt. 1:18-20; Luke 1:34, 35; Heb. 10:5). In John 1 there is a striking contrast between the *was (en)* that appears four times in verses 1 and 2, and the *became (egeneto)* of verse 14. *Was* is descriptive of the essential and eternal being of the Word, and His intratrinitarian relations. *Became* expresses His willing assumption of a true human nature into personal union with Himself.

This act of incarnation did not cause any change in the Trinity. The uncreated essence of the *Logos* was not changed. God was not humanized; the human nature of Christ was not deified. The second person of the Trinity entered into a new relation but wrought no change in the essence of the Godhead. *See **Kenosis***.

INCOMPREHENSIBILITY OF GOD

The infinite measure of what God is over what any of His creatures ever perceive Him to be. No finite intelligence can comprehend the infinite. Thus Scripture makes it clear that God infinitely surpasses our understanding of His being and nature (Job 11:7), of the depths of His counsels (Rom. 11:33), and of the purposes of His grace (Eph. 3:8).

Nevertheless, Scripture also teaches the knowability of God. What He has revealed of Himself to us is true and sufficient. Indeed, the Lord Jesus Christ defines eternal life as knowing God and Jesus Christ whom He sent into the world to declare Him (John 17:3; 1:18).

INDEFECTIBILITY

1. One of the notes or marks of the church,* namely her perpetuity and infallibility—i.e., the true church always exists and does so in continued faithfulness to Christ and His gospel;
2. The perseverance of the saints.*

INDEPENDENCY

See **Congregationalism**; **Brownists**; **Gathered Church**.

INDULGENCE

Latin indulgentia, "kindness, tenderness"; in Roman Catholic theology the remission of the punishment of certain sins either in this life, in purgatory, or in both.*

Rome's Definition of Indulgence

Rome defines indulgence as "a remission of the temporal punishment due to sin, the guilt of which has been forgiven." In practice, especially in the days preceding the Protestant Reformation, indulgences became equated with a licence to sin. The theory was, and is, that by some "good work," or some payment to obtain someone else's merit, satisfaction for certain sins may be made.

Indulgences in Modern Romanism

It is commonly thought among Protestants that Rome's doctrine of indulgences died out a long time ago. They imagine that all such ideas belong only to the Reformation* era and before. The facts are far otherwise. Rome still holds to her theory of indulgences. Her latest authoritative productions emphasize this. The *Catechism of the Catholic Church* (1994) quotes extensively

from Pope Paul VI in his *Indulgentiarum Doctrina* ("The Doctrine of Indulgences").

The following quotations show that Roman Catholic dogma on this issue is as unscriptural and superstitious as it was in the medieval times.

Allegedly Founded on Divine Revelation. Paul VI claimed that the doctrine of indulgences was "solely founded on divine revelation, handed down 'from the apostles.'" The reference given to prove this incredible assertion is the Council of Trent session 25 and Matt. 28:18 ("all power is given unto me in heaven and in earth") (*Indulgentiarum Doctrina*, par. 1).

Expiating Each Other's Sins. The pope continued: "Sins must be expiated. This may be done on this earth through sorrows, miseries and trials of this life, and, above all, through death. Otherwise the expiation must be made in the next life through fire and torments of purifying punishments" (par. 2).

According to Rome the temporal punishment due to sin may be alleviated or removed by the merits of Christ and the saints dispensed by the church. Paul VI put it like this: "Following in Christ's steps those who believe in him have always tried to help one another along the path which leads to the heavenly Father, through prayer, the exchange of spiritual goods and penitential expiation. The more they have been immersed in the fervor of love, the more they have imitated Christ in his sufferings. They have carried their crosses to make expiation for their own sins and the sins of others. They were convinced that they could help their brothers to obtain salvation from God who is the Father of mercies" (par. 5).

Rome the Treasure House of Merit. The treasury of all this merit is committed to the church to be conferred on the faithful: "The treasury of the Church is the infinite value, which can never be exhausted, which Christ's merits have before God. They were offered so that the whole of mankind could be set free from sin and attain communion with the Father. In Christ, the Redeemer himself, the satisfactions and merits of his Redemption exist and find their efficacy. This treasury includes as well the prayers and good works of the Blessed Virgin Mary. They are truly immense, unfathomable and even pristine in their value before God. In the treasury, too, are the prayers and good works of all the saints, all those who have followed in the footsteps of Christ the Lord and by his grace have made their lives holy and carried out the mission the Father entrusted to them. In this way they attained their own salvation and at the same time cooperated in saving their brothers in the unity of the Mystical Body" (par. 5).

Help of the Glorified for Sinners Expiating Guilt. This cooperation involves the transfer of merits from saints in heaven to those still expiating their sins on earth or in purgatory: "A perennial link of charity exists between the faithful who have already reached their heavenly home, those who are expiating their sins in purgatory and those who are still pilgrims on earth. Between them there is, too, an abundant exchange of all the goods by which divine justice is placated as expiation is made for all the sins of the whole of the Mystical Body. This is how God's mercy is led to forgiveness and it becomes possible for sinners who have repented sincerely, to share, as soon as they are capable of it, in the full enjoyment of the benefits of God's family" (par. 5).

This merit may be enjoyed only through the ministry of the church and the observance of her sacrament of penance. On that ground, Paul VI confirms the ancient definition and dogma of indulgences for the living and the dead.

The unambiguous testimony of Scripture condemns the entire scheme of indulgences as a baseless fraud.

See Merit.

INFALLIBILITY

That quality of the Bible, the inspired word of God, by which it is free from error, is authentic in its writings, reliable in its revelation, and authoritative in all its communications. In other words, infallibility means that the Scripture, whether considered in its totality, or in any of its parts, cannot fall short of being true, whatever the subject under consideration may be.

See Inspiration.

INFALLIBILITY OF THE POPE

A dogma promulgated in 1870, which ascribes to the pope the power of speaking infallibly, as Christ's vicar on earth, or *ex cathedra,* so that he expresses with divine authority what the church of Christ should believe on questions of faith and morals. It is devoid of scriptural proof and caused the secession from Rome of those known as the Old Catholic church.

See Ultramontanism.

INFINITY OF GOD

"The infinity of God is that perfection of God by which He is free from all limitations" (Berkhof, *Systematic Theology,* p. 59). Obviously, the finite mind cannot define the infinite, for to define is to circumscribe, or set the limits of that which is defined. We can only receive the self-revelation of the infinite God, which describes His perfection. This self-revelation indicates that God's infinity is not a boundless extension of God throughout the universe, as if part of Him were in one place and part in another. God is pure spirit (John 4:24) and therefore has no body and no extension. He is the uncontained and boundless One, who transcends His creation, and is not confused with it (as Pantheism* teaches), or limited by it (as all forms of rationalism* imply).

See Immensity.

INFRALAPSARIANISM

Also known as sublapsarianism; a theory that posits a logical (not a temporal) order in the decrees of God, according to which the decrees to create man and to permit him to fall precede the decree of election—hence *infra-* or *sub-lapsarianism,* "under the fall" (Latin, *lapsus*).

The question of where the decrees of election and reprobation stand in relation to the decrees to create mankind and to permit his fall has engaged the minds of theologians for centuries. Does the decree of election come *after* the decree to permit the fall or before it?

Infralapsarianism, holding that in the decree of election man is viewed as already created and fallen, sees the order of the decrees as follows:

1. The decree to create man.
2. The decree to permit man to fall.
3. The decree to elect certain men, out of the mass of the fallen and justly condemned race, to eternal life, and to pass others by, leaving them to the just consequences of their sins.
4. The decree to provide salvation for the elect (see A. A. Hodge, *Outlines of Theology*).

In contrast, supralapsarianism places the decree of election *before* or *above* (Latin, *supra*) the decree to create man and to permit his fall. It sees the decree of election, therefore, settling not upon created man, but man certain to be created and to fall. Supralapsarians argue that a rational mind first sets down the end it has in view and then proceeds to adopt the means calculated to achieve this end. Thus, they teach that:

1. God first decreed His end, His own glory in the salvation of some and the damnation of others.
2. Then He decreed the means to this end, namely, the election of a people for Himself out of the mass of all those to be created.
3. Next He decreed the creation of those elected and those passed over in the decree of election.
4. Finally, He decreed to provide salvation for His elect.

From this it is clear that supralapsarianism makes the reprobate what they are by divine appointment and settles their eternal destiny without regard to their personal choice. The reprobation of the wicked proceeds on exactly parallel lines to the election of the righteous. Both take place by a sovereign, gratuitous, divine choice without regard to personal merit. This is the theory of double predestination.*

Infralapsarianism denies this and holds that while election is entirely gratuitous and sovereign, reprobation is partly gratuitous and partly judicial. Non-election is sovereign; condemnation is always on account of personal guilt.

Serious consequences follow in the train of each position. Supralapsarianism leads inevitably to hyper-Calvinism and an anti-evangelistic stance. Infralapsarianism allows strict Calvinism to maintain the glory of God's sovereignty while giving due place to His benevolence. It is therefore much more conducive to evangelistic endeavour.

Most Reformed theologians are infralapsarian. Most Reformed confessions have adopted the infralapsarian view, but have not condemned the supralapsarian view. In many ways it seems presumptuous to seek to place any kind of order or succession upon the one indivisible and instantaneous decree of God. The whole manner of argument tends to make man's conceptions of how the mind of God ought to work the rule and measure of God. Perhaps nowhere does the principle of Isa. 55:8, 9 apply more than here. We ought not to seek to be wise above what is written. Passages of Scripture (such as Rom. 9:15-23; 1 Pet. 2:8) that seem to demand a *supra-* or *infra-lapsarian* interpretation should be interpreted by and in the light of the entire body of Scriptural statements on the subject, not by some man-made rational system.

However, given these serious issues, without descending into self-contradictory logical systems, we should strenuously guard against anything that leads to the deadening influence of hyper-Calvinism.

INNATE IDEA OF GOD

The immediate and universal consciousness of the human soul of the knowledge of the existence of God, and, to some extent, of His being. *Existence* here says that God is; *being* says what He is.

The Scriptures speak most fully of this idea of God which is natural to the human mind or which springs from its constitution (Rom. 1:19, 20; 2:14, 15; Ps. 19:1-3; Acts 17:24-28). The *Westminster Confession of Faith* sums up the Scripture teaching:

"The light of nature, and the works of creation and providence, do so far manifest the goodness, wisdom and power of God, as to leave men inexcusable" (chap. 1, sec. 1).

Calvin says, "That there exists in the human mind, and indeed by natural instinct, some sense of Deity, we hold to be beyond dispute, since God Himself, to prevent any man from pretending ignorance, has endued all men with some idea of His Godhead, the memory of which He constantly renews and occasionally enlarges, that all to a man, being aware that there is a God, and that He is their Maker, may be condemned by their own conscience when they neither worship Him nor consecrate their lives to His service" (*Institutes*, 1, chap. 3.1). Again he says, "A sense of Deity is indelibly engraven on the human heart" (3.3). This innate idea, or *sensus divinitatis* ("sense of deity") is not sufficient to give a saving revelation of the will of God, but is a condemning force. Idolatry (Rom. 1:20-25), sensuality (v. 32), unthankfulness (v. 21), and failure to worship God (v. 21) are charged upon the pagan as guilt. Thus far general revelation goes and no further. Only a special revelation can lead to salvation.

INNER LIGHT

The doctrine of the Quakers* that there is in every man, as a supernatural, divine gift, an inward gospel illumination.

According to Robert Barclay's *Apology for the True Christian Divinity,* this light is real spiritual substance. It is not the light of conscience or of reason. It is the gift of God and it is universal. It is God's inward gospel that reaches every creature under heaven, whereas the outward gospel fails to reach many. Sinners may be saved apart from the outward gospel but not apart from the inward: "The gospel is this inward power and life which preacheth glad tidings in the hearts of all men, offering salvation unto them, and seeking to redeem them from their iniquities." While this inner light is sufficient for salvation, it is resistible. It commands us to be saved, but it does not actually save any. Those who reject the inner light will not be saved.

This Quaker doctrine is nothing more than a doctrine of salvation by works and runs contrary to what the Bible teaches on the subject of the standing of the natural man before God (Rom. 1:18-32).

INQUISITION

"Roman Catholic institution for investigation and punishment of those who hold erroneous doctrines. Although John Chrystostom had stated that 'to put a heretic to death would be to introduce upon earth an inexpiable crime,' Catholic bishops began in the Middle Ages to use the power of civil authorities to suppress heresies. In 1229 Pope Gregory IX instituted the Inquisition in southern France with the aid of Dominican monks who investigated Albigenses. Some heretics were being hunted in many countries of Europe, and Franciscans were also used to ferret out misbelievers. The accused were not told who had accused them, were given no counsel, and could be tortured even though some popes opposed torture. The result might be repentance, penance, imprisonment, or burning at the stake. In 1542 the Inquisition was assigned to the Congregation of the Holy Office, which now seeks to guard

the faithful from injurious books and ideas" *(Baker's Pocket Dictionary of Religious Terms)*. The total number of victims of the Inquisition has been calculated to have been between 50 and 68 million.
See **Spanish Inquisition.**

INSCRIPTURATION

The committal to writing of the revealed word of God, according to His command, and accomplished by His inspiration of the human penmen. Inscripturation of the word guaranteed the purity, the preservation, and the worldwide propagation of the deposit.

INSPIRATION

Definition

Inspiration is the work of God, by His Holy Spirit, communicating His word to the writers of the Bible and enabling them to write that word without error, addition, or deletion. Thus, though fallible human penmen were employed, the Holy Spirit ensured the production of infallible writings, true in all respects, both as to their ideas and their words. Thus these writings are, in the strictest sense, God's word, and are therefore authoritative, the final rule of faith and practice.

Bible Claims to Inspiration

The Bible itself claims such inspiration. "Thus saith the Lord," is stamped upon all its parts. The very first chapter of the Bible has "And God said" ten times, and this emphasis is carried throughout Genesis. Speaking of the Pentateuch, Hugh D. Brown considers such references as "The Lord said unto Moses" and comments: "These words seem to stand out as the root and essence, the heart and manifestation, the centre and circumference of the whole Pentateuch, as indeed they are, for while the five books are divided by men into one hundred and eighty-seven chapters, which might, with greater wisdom and continuity of thought, be easily reduced to say, one hundred and

sixty-seven, we have in all, it is computed, five hundred and one distinct assertions in them of supernatural authority, being an average of three such claims in every chapter" *(Critics or Christ,* p. 13).

The same claim to inspiration is found throughout the Bible. There are four unique titles of Scripture that emphasize its inspiration: *the Scriptures of truth* (Dan. 10:21); *the holy Scriptures* (Rom. 1:2); *the oracles of God* (Rom. 3:2); *the sacred letters* (2 Tim. 3:15, Greek). Two NT references sum up all the Bible's claims. 2 Tim. 3:16 says, "All Scripture is inspired of God [or, God-breathed]." 2 Pet. 1:20, 21 says, "No prophecy of the scripture is of any private interpretation [of the prophet's]. For the prophecy came not in old time by the will of man: but holy men of God spake as they were moved by the Holy Ghost."

Christ's Endorsement of Inspiration

The Lord Jesus Christ evidently accepted the Scriptures as the inspired and authoritative word of God. While critics present their revisions of the text and of the canon, He unhesitatingly received and appealed to the entire canon of the OT (Luke 24:44), identical to our OT in the books included. He pre-authenticated the NT Scriptures and gave the promise of the Holy Ghost to guide His apostles "into all truth" (John 16:13).

The Manner of Inspiration

The manner of inspiration is not detailed in Scripture. The Bible propounds no *theory* of inspiration: it merely sets forth the *fact* with its results. Men have adopted theories. Some speak of the inspiration of *illumination* (i.e., that the sacred writers merely enjoyed the illumination granted to every Christian in a preeminent degree). Others speak of the inspiration of *superintendence.* Many orthodox writers have used this term to denote God's oversight of the writers, ensuring the production of an infallible book. Others hold the notion of the inspiration of *elevation*—i.e., the elevation of the natural faculties of the writers by God to a degree not otherwise attainable—making the Bible a merely human and natural book, however elevated. Still others promote the notion of the inspiration of *suggestion,* the theory that God suggested new truths to the minds of the writers.

Among defenders of inspiration, some have advocated the *mechanical* theory, that the writers were like typewriters upon which God punched out the message. Others, the majority, have been content to leave all theorizing about *how* God inspired the Scriptures to the one side, and simply state that He exerted such an influence as to give to the Scriptures divine authority and infallibility. There is strong evidence that God dictated His Word, and yet that He used the writing style of each penman. The whole process was supernatural, and like every other miracle, is not to be rationally explained away.

Characteristics of Inspiration

1. The inspiration of Scripture is *immediate.* That is, it is the direct operation of God upon the human agent, not merely the exercise or elevation of the gifts of literary or religious genius.

2. It is, therefore, *unique.* It can be predicated only of the Bible. Some speak of the inspiration of great poets, playwrights, or musicians, but this is not a theological use of the term.

3. It is *plenary.* The influence of God was sufficient to produce the desired effect—a book inspired and infallible in all its parts. The Bible is the word of God; it does not merely contain it.

4. It is *verbal.* It extends to all the expressions of Scripture, even the words (Matt. 5:18).

5. It is *objective.* It belongs to the Biblical writings in themselves, whether men perceive it or not. This is in direct opposition to the neo-orthodox notion that the Bible may *become* the word of God to different people in particular circumstances.

The Importance of Inspiration

The whole Biblical doctrine of inspiration is rejected by rationalists, modernists, liberals, existentialists, and every school of theology that exalts the consciousness of man to the role of final or supreme arbiter in every issue presented to the human mind. But it is the bedrock of all Christian faith and doctrine. Christianity without an inspired Bible would be a body without a soul, just another speculative philosophy among the many man has produced.

See **Scripture**; **Marks of Scripture**.

INTENTION

The Church of Rome holds that in the administration of a sacrament, the officiating minister must have the intention of doing what the church does; otherwise, though all the external actions are regularly performed, the entire administration is void. In other words, the validity of the sacrament depends upon the secret intention of the officiating minister. Protestants do not leave the recipient at the mercy of the secret will of the minister in this way, but hold that the administration of a sacrament is valid if it is performed with the professed design of complying with the command of the Lord.

INTERCESSION OF CHRIST

The work of Christ in appearing as the advocate of His people at the Father's right hand (Heb. 7:25; 9:11, 12, 24; 1 John 2:1).

There is a perfect agreement among all the aspects of the work of the mediator,* and this is nowhere more clearly seen than in His intercession. His sacrifice and His intercession have the same persons as their subjects. His propitiation is the ground of His intercession, and thus His intercession claims an entrance into heaven for all for whom He suffered: "Father, I will that they also whom thou hast given me, be with me where I am" (John 17:24). "For whomsoever He suffered, He appears for them in heaven with His satisfaction and merit" (John Owen).

INTERDICT

A papal prohibition debarring individuals, parishes, communities, or even nations, from some or all ecclesiastical privileges and functions. At various points in history the pope employed it as a powerful tool to force rebellious princes or citizens into submission to his will. He would deprive them of all priestly ministry. All spiritual services would be suspended. Under Rome's sacerdotal* system priests are indispensable. Access to saving grace is dependent on their ministry. Thus to place a people under interdict was to shut them off from the grace of God. The prevailing ignorance of the gospel meant that there was little chance of withstanding the papal ban. One of the most famous instances of the power of papal interdiction was in England in 1213. To force King John to submit to him, the pope placed the entire nation under interdict. The ploy worked and in a brief time the monarch had to capitulate.

INTERMEDIATE STATE

The term used to describe the state of the soul between physical death and the resurrection.
1. It is a disembodied state (2 Cor. 5:1-8).
2. It is a temporary state (1 Cor. 15:52).
3. For the unsaved, it is a state of suffering (Luke 16:23).
4. For the saved, it is a state of blessedness in the conscious enjoyment of being "with Christ" (Phil. 1:23; cf. 2 Cor. 5:8).
5. It is not a probationary state (Heb. 9:27. See **Second Probation**).
6. It is terminated by the resurrection of the body, when the entire man, body and soul, enters into his final and everlasting state.
See **Gehenna**; **Hades**; **Resurrection**.

INTERNAL CALL

The effectual call of the Spirit, which is spiritual, irresistible, and directed only to the elect. It is distinct from the external call, which is general and which indiscriminately reaches all who hear the gospel (see **Calling**; **Effectual Calling**).

The internal call has the following characteristics:
1. It has God as its author (1 Cor. 1:9; 2 Tim. 1:8, 9; Gal. 1:15; 1 Thess. 5:23, 24; 2 Thess. 2:13, 14; 1 Pet. 5:10). Specifically, it is God the Father who initiates salvation by the call of his sovereign grace (Rom. 8:30; 1 Cor. 1:9; Gal. 1:15; Eph. 1:17, 18).
2. It is an act, not a process (1 Pet. 2:9; 1 Thess. 2:12), as is illustrated in the calling of Lazarus from the dead (John 11:43; Eph. 2:1).
3. It is an effective summons, which cannot be frustrated but is inevitably and invariably followed by justification (Rom. 8:29, 30).
4. It is immutable both in its inherent character (Rom. 11:29) and in its effects (Rom. 8:29-30).
5. It is a high, holy, and heavenly call (Phil. 3:14; 2 Tim. 1:9; Heb. 3:1) both as to its origin and intrinsic character, and as to the destiny to which it conducts.
6. It leads to great spiritual blessings: fellowship with Christ (1 Cor. 1:9) and with the saints (Col. 3:15); the peace of God (1 Cor. 7:15); holiness (1 Thess. 4:7; 5:23-24); light (1 Pet. 2:9); liberty (Gal. 5:13); hope (Eph. 1:18; 4:4); patient endurance (1 Pet. 2:20, 21); and, finally, entrance into God's kingdom and glory (1 Thess. 2:12) or eternal life and glory (2 Thess. 2:14; 1 Tim. 6:12; 1 Pet. 5:10; Heb. 9:15; Rev. 19:9).
7. It imposes practical obligations on God's people (Eph. 4:1, 2; 5:1, 2) because Christians ought to walk in accordance with it (2 Pet. 1:10).

INTRODUCTION

The systematic study of the background against which each book of the Bible is to be understood.

"It deals with matters of language, custom, historical situations, persons, places, and events alluded to in the various books of the Bible" (Gleason L. Archer,

A Survey of Old Testament Introduction, p. 15). It pays particular attention to the subjects of authorship, date and place of writing, purpose, structure, theme or central message, and textual criticism in studying each Bible book.

IRRATIONALISM

Called by some *non-rationalism,* it is the philosophy that reality is contacted by non-rational means, either by intuition, will, emotion, or mysticism. Applied to theology, irrationalism is the belief that God can be contacted in these ways. Thus consciousness theology,* existentialism,* paradox theology,* and mysticism,* are forms of irrationalism.

IRRESISTIBLE GRACE

The sovereign grace of God by which He favours His elect with effectual calling.* It is irresistible in that it is no mere expression of desire that the elect soul should come to Christ and be saved, but an act of divine power that brings him to Christ. It is an indispensable link in the chain of God's eternal purpose (Rom. 8:29-30; cf. Ps. 110:3; Phil. 2:13).

The term *irresistible grace* has reference solely to the grace of God in regeneration.* Many objections to the doctrine are based upon a misconception on this point, since the Bible very clearly speaks of people resisting divine grace.

*See **Internal Call**.*

J

JEDP

The designation of the documents which Higher Critics allege have been combined to form the Pentateuch (see *Criticism*). This *documentary hypothesis* is based on the belief that the Pentateuch is not an historical record but the late compilation of four main sources: *J* is the *Jehovist, who* is identified by his use of the name *Jehovah* for God; *E* is the *Elohist,* who used *Elohim* as his name for God; *D* is the Deuteronomy document; and *P* is the priestly document, identified by the Levitical material in the Pentateuch.

The hypothesis that these alleged sources were combined over a period of time to produce the Pentateuch as we have it was gradually developed in the 18th and 19th centuries. It commenced with the speculations of Jean Astruc in 1753 and culminated in Julius Wellhausen's definitive statement of it in 1876.

According to Wellhausen *J* was a well written narrative, composed in Judah about 850 B.C. *E* originated in the northern kingdom around 750. About one hundred years later, after the fall of Israel, a redactor (editor) combined them into a single work. *D* came from Judah in 621 during Josiah's reform. Another redactor added this to the already combined *JE* document to produce *JED*. Finally, after Judah's exile in Babylon, *P*, the priestly document, was woven into the existing *JED* document.

The *JEDP* hypothesis gained wide acceptance, though some notable scholars contended against it. In addition to the literary, linguistic, and theological arguments that were used against it, there are some obvious reasons for rejecting it.

The *JEDP* hypothesis is based on the fal-lacy that the use of the divine names in the Pentateuch is arbitrary, and that those names are interchangeable without affecting the sense. If those names have a specific meaning that makes them them appropriate to the context of the passages in which they appear, their use cannot be taken as an indication of different authors. They do have distinctive meanings, as Exod. 6:3 makes clear *(see Names of God).*

Another fault of the documentary hypothesis is that it took an evolutionary view of history as its starting point: Israel's worship and laws could not have been so developed at the early stage of human history claimed by the Pentateuch. The discovery of the code of Hammurabi* in 1901 proved how false the evolutionary theory of history was. In fact, archaeological discoveries have shown that the world presented in the Pentateuch was a real world, not a late literary composition.

Modern defenders of the documentary hypothesis have largely abandoned Wellhausen's wholesale denial of the historicity of the Pentateuch. Their revised version is that though the documents *JEDP* are late, the traditions they contain are much older. This modified version has recently been demonstrated false by the discovery in the 1980's of a fragment of the Pentateuch dating from before the destruction of the temple by Nebuchadnezzar. This fragment contains the text of Num. 6:24, 25, the Aaronic blessing (see Amihai Mazar, *Archaeology of the Land of the Bible*). According to the critics, Num. 6:24, 25 belongs to the *P* document, which they claim is post-exilic. The hard evidence provided by the discovery of the Numbers fragment shows how empty that claim is.

199

JANSENISM

The movement in the Roman Catholic church that sought reform on the lines of Augustinian theology, while maintaining all the ecclesiasticism of the papal church. Its founder was Cornelius Otto Jansen (1585-1638), Bishop of Ypres. On the one hand, Jansen opposed the Jesuits and stressed the necessity and irresistibility of divine grace, but on the other hand, opposed the Protestant Reformers, teaching that there is no salvation apart from the Roman church. Jansenism was condemned in 1713 by Pope Clement XI in his famous Bull Unigenitus and was suppressed. In Holland, however, it began a movement that led to the formation of the Old Catholic Church.*

JEHOVAH'S WITNESSES

See **Russellites**.

JEHOVIST

The imaginary writer whose documents higher critics claim lie back of the Pentateuch. His literary contributions are allegedly discernible by his characteristic use of *Jehovah* as the Divine name.

See **Criticism**; **Elohist**; **J.E.D.P.**

JESUITS

A Roman Catholic society formed in 1534 by Ignatius Loyola and officially instituted as an Order of the Roman church by a papal bull* in 1540. According to the bull, the Jesuits were constituted "to wield the arms of God" in obedience to the pope. Their chief aim was to stamp out the Reformation *(see **Counter Reformation**).* This purpose is vividly portrayed by a plaster cast in the Church of the Jesuits in Rome, depicting Loyola with his foot on the neck of Protestantism.

By their oath, Jesuits swear unswerving loyalty to the pope, ascribing to him the power to depose "heretical" kings and states. They renounce any allegiance due to Protestant states.

Ever since their institution their energy and activities have been boundless. They came to have such enormous power that they posed a very real threat to lawful authority in many countries. They were expelled from one nation after another, until finally in 1773 Pope Clement XIV abolished their order entirely. But Pope Pius VII reestablished it in 1814, declaring that "if any should again attempt to abolish it he would incur the indignation of Almighty God and of the Holy Apostles Peter and Paul."

Jesuit philosophy has always been synonymous with deceit, dissimulation, and immorality. It teaches that it is morally acceptable "to do evil that good may come," holding that "the end justifies the means." That moral flexibility has rendered the Jesuits very valuable to the Vatican in many areas. For example, they have taken the leading role in Rome's church-unity dealings with ecumenical Protestants, where their skill in diplomatic duplicity has paid great dividends.

In recent times, however, the order has again become embroiled in controversy within the Roman church. It has championed the cause of liberation theology* in Latin America and, according to some of its members, has departed from its primary task of upholding and advancing the decrees of the pope.

JUDICIAL HARDENING

"A judicial act, wherein God withdraws from sinful men, whom He has not elected to life, for the just punishment of their sins, all gracious influences, and leaves them to the unrestrained tendencies of their own hearts, and to the uncounteracted influences of the world and the devil" (A. A. Hodge).

See **Romans 1:24-28; 9:18.**

JUSTICE

1. The absolute rectitude in the divine nature in virtue of which God is infinitely righteous in Himself.

2. "That phase of God's holiness which is

seen in His treatment of the obedient and disobedient subjects of His government. It is that attribute whereby He gives to everyone what is due him" (Shedd).

Theologians note several distinctions in God's justice in His dealings with His creatures.

1. *Rectoral justice* is God's rectitude as the ruler over the good and the evil. By virtue of this, He lays down a just law, with promises of reward for obedience and threats of punishment for disobedience. God is the lawgiver (Isa. 33:22; James 4:12) whose laws are righteous (Deut. 4:8).

2. *Distributive justice* is God's rectitude in the execution of His law. It relates to His distribution of rewards and punishments (Isa. 3:10, 11; Rom. 2:6; 1 Pet. 1:17). Distributive justice falls into two categories:

a. *Remunerative justice,* or the giving of rewards to men and angels (Deut. 7:9, 12, 13; 2 Chron. 6:15; Ps. 58:11; Mic. 7:20; Matt. 25:21, 34; Rom. 2:7; Heb. 11:26). "Remunerative justice is the expression of the divine love, as retributive justice is of the divine wrath. It proceeds upon the ground of relative merit only. The creature cannot establish an absolute merit before the creator. This is taught by our Lord in Luke 17:10…and by St. Paul in 1 Cor. 4:7…and by God to Job, 41:11" (Shedd). "God's rewards are gracious and spring from a covenant relation which He has established" (Berkhof).

b. *Retributive justice* (sometimes called *punitive* or *vindicative justice*) relates to the infliction of penalties. As noted above, it expresses God's wrath (Rom. 1:32; 2:8, 9; 12:19; 2 Thess. 1:8).

Whereas the merit upon which remunerative justice rewards is relative, the merit upon which retributive justice condemns is absolute. "Divine justice is originally and necessarily obliged to requite disobedience, but not to reward obedience. God does not covenant to punish sin, as He does to reward

holiness" (Shedd). Holiness runs back to God as its author; sin does not. Therefore, the self-determined act of the creature is the ultimate and sole efficient cause for a just God to punish sin.

3. *Corrective justice* is postulated by those who deny the existence of punitive justice in God. They claim that God's punishment of the sinner is always with a view to reform him and to deter others. According to this false theory, the punishment of sin does not have as its primary purpose the maintenance of right and justice. Correction or reformation may result from punishment and punishment may be a deterrent to others, but the primary purpose of God's judgment on sin has respect to His own law and justice.

JUSTIFICATION
Definition of Justification

The establishment of a sinner in a righteous standing before God. The verb *dikaioo* means "to declare or demonstrate to be righteous" (Matt. 11:19; 12:37; Luke 7:29; 10:29). The cognate nouns are *dikaiosune* (Rom. 1:17), *dikaiosis* (Rom. 4:25), and *dikaioma* (Rom. 1:32; 5:16, 18). *Dikaiosune* is always translated "righteousness" and denotes a perfect rectitude according to the standard of God's character revealed in His law. The phrase "the righteousness of God" may denote the divine attribute of righteousness, or in the great soteriological teaching of Romans the righteousness God has provided to give His people a title to eternal life (Rom. 3:22; 5:17, "the gift of righteousness").

Dikaiosis is the action of declaring righteous and *dikaioma* signifies the verdict, the judgment handed down by God. Lenski states the relationship between these two terms: *dikaiosis* is "a declaring righteous (action)"; *dikaioma* is "a declaring righteous and thereby placing in a permanent relationship or state even as the declaration stands permanently (result)." The language of Scripture, therefore, points to justification as God's action in declaring His people righteous and placing them in a state of legal perfection before His law on the basis of the righteousness He provided freely for them in Christ.

There is no more Scriptural or succinct theological definition of justification than that given by the *Shorter Catechism:* "Justification is an act of God's free grace, wherein He pardoneth all our sins, and accepteth us as righteous in His sight, only for the righteousness of Christ imputed to us, and received by faith alone." (Q. 33; *see Westminster Confession of Faith,* chap. 11).

The Two Elements in Justification

The two elements in justification are pardon and imputed righteousness. That is, the total obedience of Christ, both passive and active, avails for the believer. The vicarious atonement* of Christ pays the debt of the believer's sin, satisfies divine justice on his behalf, and renders it possible for God to be just and yet to justify him (Rom. 3:26). The imputed righteousness of Christ gives the believer "the adoption of children" (Gal. 4:5) and the title to eternal life.

Characteristics of Justification

1. Justification is *an act,* not a process (Rom. 5:1). It is something that has taken place in the justified, not something that is constantly taking place.
2. It is an *act of the free grace of God* toward sinners who are personally guilty and deserving of His wrath (Rom. 3:25).
3. It is a *forensic act.* It describes a change in the legal standing of the justified person. It does not describe the inner moral change God effects in all those whom He saves (2 Cor. 5:21). This is a vital truth. "God made him [Christ] to be sin for us" does not mean that Christ became morally corrupted. It solely describes a forensic transaction. Similarly, when as a result of that transaction we are "made the righteousness of God in him" there is no reference to an inner moral change. It does not mean we are made morally sinless or pure. It means that God has radically changed our legal standing before

His law. Thus *justify* means "to declare righteous," not "to make righteous" (see Psa. 51:4). The statement in Rom. 5:19 that through Christ's obedience "shall many be made righteous" uses the verb *kathistemi* which means "appoint, constitute." It describes the place we occupy, not a purification of our nature.

4. It is a *just act* for it proceeds on the ground of the imputed righteousness of Christ (Rom. 5:19). This text makes it clear that the righteousness of Christ's obedience in life and death is imputed as the ground of justification. Christ is the righteousness of the justified (1 Cor. 1:30; Jer. 23:6). This answers the objection that unless justification is an actual infusion of grace and moral purity, God would be lying to declare any man righteous. Paul states bluntly that God "justifieth the ungodly" (Rom. 5:5), not the godly, the sanctified. How can the God of truth declare the ungodly righteous? By crediting all the perfect righteousness of Christ to their account *(see Imputation).*

5. It is a *once-and-for-all act.* It can neither be reversed nor repeated (Heb. 10:2; Rom. 8:30).

6. It is *equally complete* in all the justified. It cannot be increased or decreased (Rom. 5:19; 1 Cor. 1:30). All Christians are not equally mature, or holy. But all believers are equally "justified from all things" (Acts 13:39). They all have the same basis for their acceptance by God, the righteousness of Christ.

7. It invariably *leads to glorification.* No justified person can perish: "whom he justified, them he also glorified" (Rom. 8:30).

8. It is *received by faith* without works (Rom. 3:20-22; 4:1-8, 24; 5:1; Gal. 3:5-12). Some imagine that James contradicts this in James 2:18-26, notably in verse 24, "Ye see then how that by works a man is justified, and not by faith only."

There is no discrepancy between Paul and James. There is a difference of emphasis in response to the particular form of opposition each apostle was combatting. Paul was opposing the legalist who taught justification by works. James was opposing the antinomian *(see Antinomianism)* whose profession of justifying faith was united to a life of blatant ungodliness. Paul teaches that we are justified by faith as the sole instrument of reception, excluding works or any mixture of faith and works. James teaches that the faith that justifies is never alone. It is a living faith and therefore will express itself in good works. Good works are the evidence of the reality of justifying faith, not a substitute for it, a preparation for it, or an addition to it. Buchanan in his *Justification,* terms justification according to Paul *actual justification,* and justification according to James *declarative justification.*

Confusion about Justification

The doctrine of justification lies at the very heart of all Biblical soteriology. Yet prior to the Reformation* confusion reigned on the meaning of the term. Even in very early times, the legal aspect of justification so clearly set forth in the NT was overlooked with the result that it was common for justification to be confused with regeneration or sanctification.

Justification Confused with Regeneration. Thomas Aquinas set the standard for medieval views on the subject. He taught that the first element in justification was the infusion of grace, on the ground of which the second element, pardon for sins, was given. Thus the Roman Catholic doctrine of justification in baptism was laid down. As Aquinas' doctrine was developed, Rome came to assert more and more blatantly that the justification received in baptism could be increased or lost by human activity. This laid the ground for the Tridentine decree that justification depends at least in part upon personal merit.

Justification Confused with Sanctification. Confounding justification and sanctification led to the error of viewing justification as a process (e.g., *Canons and Decrees of the Council of Trent,* chap. 16, canon 24). This characteristic error of Romanism has found acceptance in many other quarters. Many early Anabaptists* espoused it. To this day it is the mark of all false gospels to equate justification with sanctification as the basis of a doctrine of salvation by works.

Distinctions Between Justification and Sanctification. Scripture carefully marks the difference between justification and sanctification. Berkhof notes:

"**1.** Justification removes the guilt of sin and restores the sinner to all the filial rights involved in his state as a child of God, including eternal inheritance. Sanctification removes the pollution of sin and renews the sinner ever increasingly in conformity with the image of God.

2. Justification takes place outside of the sinner in the tribunal of God, and does not change his inner life, though the sentence is brought home to him subjectively. Sanctification on the other hand, takes place in the inner life of man and gradually affects his whole being.

3. Justification takes place once for all. It is not repeated, neither is it a process; it is complete at once and for all time. There is no more or less in justification, man is either fully justified, or he is not justified at all. In distinction from it, sanctification is a continuous process, which is never completed in this life.

4. While the meritorious cause of both lies in the merits of Christ, there is a difference in the efficient cause. Speaking economically, God the Father declares the sinner righteous, and God the Holy Spirit sanctifies him" (*Systematic Theology,* pp. 513, 514).

Justification the Same for OT and NT Believers

This justification is in all respects the same for believers under both the Old and New Testaments (Gal. 3:9, 13, 14; Rom. 4:1-6, 16). Abraham was justified on the very same ground and in the very same way as believers in the NT. We are "blessed *with* faithful Abraham." He is the "father of all them that believe" (Rom. 4:11). David rejoiced in the very same justification we enjoy (Ps. 32: 1, 2; Rom. 4:6). The only righteousness that ever gave any man a title to heaven is the righteousness of Christ freely imputed to him and received by faith alone.

Conclusion

Luther's insight was accurate when he declared the Biblical doctrine of justification to be *articulus ecclesiae stantis aut cadentis,* the article of faith that marks whether a church is standing or falling. Paul realized its immense importance to the entire gospel scheme and pronounced God's curse on anyone, even an angel from heaven, who preached any other gospel (Gal. 1:8, 9). This is the gospel of which the apostle was "not ashamed...for it is the power of God unto salvation to every one that believeth" (Rom. 1:16).

K

KENOSIS, KENOTICISTS

The term *kenosis* comes from the Greek verb *kenoo*, used in Phil. 2:7 and translated "made Himself of no reputation" by the AV. The ARV translated it "emptied Himself," which B. B. Warfield condemned as a mistranslation in this context.

The use of *emptied* reflects the views of a school of thought that developed in the mid-19th century. Their view of *kenosis* was that in the incarnation the divine Logos emptied Himself of His divine attributes. Kenoticists did not agree on the extent of the emptying. Some made it absolute and spoke of the incarnation as divine suicide. Others referred it solely to the Logos's "relative" attributes, those not essential to His Godhead (such as omnipresence, omniscience, and omnipotence), leaving His "absolute" attributes out of the scope of the emptying. Another particularly objectionable notion of some leading kenoticists was the idea that the Logos actually laid aside His Godhood and became a human soul. In their opinion He did not *take* a true human soul into union with Himself, but actually *became* a true human soul. The supposed Scripture basis for this doctrine is principally Phil. 2:6-8, though 2 Cor. 8:9 and John 17:5 are also pressed into service.

These scriptures do not teach what the kenoticists claim. Philippians 2:6-8 shows how Christ "emptied himself." It was not by losing or getting rid of anything but by *taking* something. As an act of love He did not *hold on to* the expression of His divine and sovereign equality with the Father, but made Himself of no reputation, taking the form of a servant and becoming obedient, even unto the death of the cross. As Hebrews 5:8 puts it: "Though He were a Son, yet learned he obedience." What He laid aside was the assertion of His equality, submitting Himself to the obedience of a servant as our Mediator. Thus, He could say "My Father is greater than I" (John 14:28). The "emptying" of Phil. 2:7, then, does not refer to the essential divine nature of the Logos, but to the assertion of divine prerogatives belonging properly to Him. The evidence of Scripture that the Lord Jesus Christ retained His divine nature and attributes after the incarnation is too strong to be shaken by kenotic views (see Matt. 1:23; 11:27; Mark 1:1; John 1:1, 14; 3:13; 14:9; Rom. 1:4; 9:5). Hebrews 13:8 emphasizes the immutability of Christ; the kenotic theory, in effect, denies the whole doctrine of divine immutability (see Mal. 3:6; James 1:17).

After a brief spell of popularity, even among some Reformed theologians, kenoticism lost most of its support.

KERYGMA

A Greek word that appears eight times in the NT and that is translated "preaching" on every occasion (*see* Matt. 12:41; Luke 11:32; Rom. 16:25; 1 Cor. 1:21; 2:4; 15:14; 2 Tim. 4:17; Tit. 1:3). It refers to the message, the emphasis being upon "the substance of what is preached as distinct from the act of preaching" (W. E. Vine). In other words, the *kerygma* is the gospel.

However, the word is used by theologians of the Neo-orthodox school (*see* **Neo-orthodoxy**) in such a way as to distinguish between the essential substance of God's proclamation and the thought and language forms in which the early church conceived the message and wrote it down in the NT.

Thus they use the term *kerygmatic* to describe the church's interpretation of the original message of the historical Jesus.

Rudolf Bultmann adopted this line as he set about "demythologizing" the gospel. By repudiating the doctrines of the virgin birth, miraculous life, atoning substitution, bodily resurrection, and physical ascension of the Lord Jesus Christ, he claimed to be rescuing the *kerygma,* the essential gospel message, so as to be able to present it to "modern man" in a way acceptable to his intellect. Every so-called *quest for the historical Jesus** indulges the same fantasy.

However, the Scriptures and the NT church know no proclamation of God's grace apart from those very doctrines. They are the essence of the message (1 Cor. 15:3-5; 1 Tim. 3:16). The *kerygma* is not something that lies behind their obscuring form; it has no existence apart from them.

See **Myth**.

KETHIB

The Aramaic word *kethib* means "it is written" and describes the consonantal text of the Hebrew Scriptures. "The Massoretic scholars regarded the consonantal text as inviolable. When, therefore, for any reason, of tradition, grammar or propriety, they preferred another reading to that of the consonantal text, the vowels of this reading were attached to the Kethib, while the consonants of it, which could not be inserted into the text, were placed in the margin. This recommended reading in such a case is named Qere." (A. B. Davidson).

See **Masoretes**; **Qere**.

KEYS, POWER OF

The power Christ has invested in His church for its government and discipline. It is a ministerial, not magisterial, power. It is the application of the authoritative commands and teachings of Christ and His apostles to the life and fellowship of the church and its members. Speaking of church officers, the *Westminster Confession of Faith* states, "To these officers the keys of the kingdom of heaven are committed, by virtue whereof they have power respectively to retain and remit sins, to shut the kingdom against the impenitent, both by the Word and censures; and to open it unto penitent sinners, by the ministry of the gospel and by absolution from censures, as occasion shall require" (chap. 30, sec. 2).

According to the Roman Catholic church, the power of the keys is the primacy Christ conferred on Peter with the power to bind and to loose, a power that was transmitted to his successors as bishop of Rome. The Biblical authority for this power is said to be Matt. 16:18, 19. The power of binding and loosing was also conferred on all the disciples (Matt. 18:18), but the primacy was given to Peter alone. From this Rome argues that the pope and the bishops and priests in fellowship with him have the power to grant or deny absolution and that the only way in which a Christian may gain absolution is by confession to a Roman priest.

Even if the Lord Jesus Christ did confer on Peter primacy among the apostles and did give them the power of life and death over souls, there is not the slightest hint in Scripture that these prerogatives were transferable to anyone else, or that they were ever in any way associated with the bishop of Rome. There is no historical evidence that Peter was ever bishop of Rome. Indeed, there is every scriptural reason to dismiss the idea because the NT knows absolutely nothing of diocesan bishops or popes.

The power of the keys in the NT has no relationship whatever to the pretensions of papal or priestly power. The keys of which Christ spoke clearly signify the opening of the doors of the knowledge of the gospel (*see* Matt. 23:13; Luke 11:52), and/or the administration of the house of God. Peter had the privilege of opening the doors of the kingdom to the Jews (Acts 2), to the Samaritans (Acts 8), and to the Gentiles

(Acts 10). This is the only primacy we find for Peter in the NT.

Peter's power to open the kingdom to men was a declarative power. In other words, he opened the kingdom, not by the exercise of any inherent power in him or in his alleged primacy, but by the declaration of the terms of the gospel. On that ground he and the apostles could declare men forgiven or not forgiven, i.e., could declare that they were admitted to or excluded from the kingdom. According to the NT this is the only manner in which Peter and the apostles ever used their power.

The administrative power of binding and loosing of which Christ spoke referred to things, not people. Among the Rabbis *binding* and *loosing* were terms for forbidding and permitting. The apostles exercised this kind of power in the council of Jerusalem when they determined the relationship of believers to the Mosaic ceremonies (Acts 15). Paul's epistle to the Galatians (see also Col. 2:16-23; Rom. 14) gives us another example of this power, while his statements in 1 Cor. 10:18-33 show him setting the limits of what is permissible to Christians interacting with a heathen culture.

The enactments of the apostles of Christ are final and authoritative for the universal church. No pope, church, or council can now bind the consciences of believers by their decrees, unless it is by their promulgation of the enactments of Scripture, or unless, in matters of doubt or dispute among Christians, it is by their exercise of agreed principles among people who freely enter their fellowship in professed acceptance of those principles.

See *Authority*.

KINGDOM OF GOD, OR OF CHRIST

There are few more complex themes in Scripture than that of the kingdom.

The theme of the kingdom defines the mission and message of Christ in the synoptic gospels. Matthew uses the expression *king-dom of heaven* some fifty times and *kingdom of God* only five times. The rest of the NT uses *kingdom of God* or equivalent expressions and the nearest approach to a mention of *kingdom of heaven* is in 2 Tim. 4:18, "his heavenly kingdom."

In common parlance *kingdom* carries the idea of a territory or a realm over which a king exerts his rule. It has that significance at times in Scripture. God's kingdom is the extent of His sovereign rule. In this sense it is universal, for His "kingdom ruleth over all" (Ps. 103:19).

What the Kingdom Is

However, the terms *kingdom of God* and *kingdom of heaven* have a much more specific significance in Scripture. They denote the rule of God through His Son. God's kingdom is *the kingdom of heaven* because it is heavenly in its origin and authority. But the sphere and realization of its rule have to do largely with the earth. Thus it confronts men here on earth with the message that the King Himself has come into the world, preaching repentance and submission to His kingly authority. Those who accept this gracious gospel of the kingdom (Acts 20:24, 25) will at once enter into eternal life and will forever enjoy the security and ecstacy of eternal glory (Matt. 8:11-12; 25:34).

The terms *kingdom of God* and *kingdom of heaven* are synonymous. W. E. Vine sees a dispensational distinction, but the data do not support this. The expressions are used interchangeably (*see* Matt 19:23,24 with Mark 10:23, 24; Matt. 4:17 with Mark 1:15; Matt. 13:11 with Mark 4:11; Matt. 13:31 with Mark 4:30, 31; Matt. 13:33 with Luke 13:20, 21; Matt. 18:3 with Mark 10:15; Matt. 19:14 with Mark 10:14; Matt. 8:11, 12 with Luke 13:28, 29).

The Kingdom Is Present

It Came with Christ. The NT speaks of the kingdom as coming with Christ. It is the kingdom of God's dear Son (Col. 1:13). It is now present (Matt. 12:28; Luke 17:21, where *within you* means "in the midst of you"). For a liberal misuse of this truth, *(see **Realized Eschatology**).*

The Kingdom and Eternal Life. Kingdom of heaven is also a synonym for eternal life (Matt. 19:16, 23). It demands a response of repentance as the only way of entrance (Matt. 4:17). The preaching of the kingdom is the preaching of the gospel of grace (Acts 20:24, 25) promising all who repent and receive Christ an immediate place in God's kingdom.

The Kingdom and the Church. It is clear that the kingdom and the church are closely related. In Matt. 16:16, 18-19 Jesus speaks to Peter about building His *church* and proceeds at once to promise him the *keys of the kingdom.* While *kingdom* and *church* are not altogether synonymous they stand in a special closeness. The kingdom is the mediatorial rule of Christ and the sphere in which He exercises that rule. The church is the fellowship of the people who have received the offer of the kingdom. So, *kingdom* emphasizes Christ's gracious sovereignty, and *church* emphasizes His redeemed people.

The Kingdom Is Future

It Will Come with Christ. The dying thief asked the Lord, "Remember me when thou comest into thy kingdom" (Luke 23:42) and the Saviour immediately assured him of a place in paradise (v. 43). But the thief's words indicate that he was anticipating a future kingly reign for Christ. He was not mistaken, for while the kingdom is in one sense present, in another it is still future. We pray, "Thy kingdom come" (Matt. 6:10). Paul looked forward to Christ's "appearing and his kingdom" and rejoiced that the Lord "will preserve me unto his heavenly kingdom" (2 Tim. 4:1, 18).

Living in the Light of the Kingdom to Come. The Sermon on the Mount (Matt. 5-7) and the various parables of the kingdom Jesus told (Matt. 13, 25) speak of the personal and corporate development of the people of God on earth in submission to the kingship of Christ. These passages deal with the deep ethical, evangelical, and eschatological issues that arise as the gospel confronts men and calls them to Christ. They show that the kingdom is both a present and future kingdom of messianic, or mediatorial, grace.

Millennial Kingdom Is Messianic and Mediatorial. Dispensationalists draw a sharp distinction between *messianic* and *mediatorial* in regard to the kingdom. This is unwarranted. The Scriptures identify the Messiah and the Mediator as the Lord Jesus Christ. There is therefore a deep unity of purpose and operation in every aspect of His kingdom. Dispensationalists see no essential continuity between the present mediatorial kingdom of Christ and His messianic, millennial kingdom. But these cannot be divorced. The whole idea of the kingdom as eternal life for all who respond to Christ in repentance precludes the notion of the Jews of the millennial kingdom being forever an earthly people in contrast with the church of the mediatorial kingdom who are a heavenly people.

Postmillennialists and amillennialists deny any reign of Christ on earth as part of His future kingdom and use the vagaries of dispensationalism* to show the eminent reasonableness of their position. This is as unwarranted as the dispensational theories they despise. The Scripture speaks of "the *ages* to come" (Eph. 2:7). It is a very inadequate treatment of OT and NT prophecy that sees only the eternal state to follow this age. The evidence is that the kingdom to come is both millennial and eternal (Rev. 11:15). The millennial kingdom will be Christ's. It will be a reign of grace. It will mark the fulness of God's purpose for Israel united to the church. The religion of the kingdom will be Christianity with Christ present on earth, not the revived Judaism dispensationalists anticipate.

The Eternal Kingdom. The kingdom is "the everlasting kingdom of our Lord and Saviour Jesus Christ" (2 Peter 1:11). Its full and eternal expression will come when all things are finally summed up in Christ the head (Eph. 1:10) and all other authority and power have been put down never to rise again (1 Cor. 15:24, 25).

The Kingdom Not of This World

From all this it is clear that the kingdom of God must not be thought of in the terms of liberalism and ecumenism, which reduce it to a man-made social order. Paul equates "the gospel of the kingdom" with "the gospel of the grace of God" (Acts 20:24, 25), showing that the kingdom is not the product of any social or political activity. It is not the result of any so-called "liberation" movement. Jesus said, "My kingdom is not of this world" (John 18:36). Social gospellers strive to reverse this divine decree, but their effort is doomed to failure. Christ's kingdom proceeds by other means. It is the product of saving grace, and its subjects are those saved by grace through faith in Christ.

Summary

In summary, then, we note that the kingdom is *historical* for it "comes" in time, and is even now at work in the world (see the parables of Matt. 13). It is *ethical* as the Sermon on the Mount makes clear. It is *spiritual* for it signifies eternal life. And it is *eschatological,* for it is associated with the prophesied consummation of the ages (Matt. 8:11, 12; 13:24-30, 36-43; 25:31-46).

KINGLY OFFICE OF CHRIST

As mediator, the Lord Jesus Christ performs three functions: those of prophet, priest, and king *(see Priestly Office of Christ; Prophetic Office of Christ).* The Shorter Catechism (Q. 26) defines the kingly office of Christ as follows: "Christ executeth the office of a King, in subduing us to Himself, in ruling and defending us, and restraining and conquering all His and our enemies."

Thus the kingship of the Lord Jesus Christ is an integral and essential part of the gospel. Indeed, one title of the gospel is "The gospel of the kingdom." We may sum up the matter as follows:

1. Christ is a king. He has the *title* (Ps. 2:6; Rev. 1:5; 17:14). He has a *crown* (Heb. 2:9; Rev. 6:2; 19:12), a *sword* (Rev. 19:15), and a *sceptre* (Heb. 1:8). He has a *people* who are His loyal subjects and He has all *power* in heaven and in earth (Matt. 28:18; Ps. 135:6).
2. Christ exercises His kingship over both His redeemed people and His enemies. He *draws* His people (John 12:32), *governing* them by His law and love (1 John 2:7, 8), and *subduing* their iniquities (Mic. 7:19). He *restrains* the malice of His enemies, brings to nought every demonic and human plan against God, destroys their pride, and finally *commands* their allegiance (see Gen. 20:6; Job 1:6-12; Phil. 2:9, 10).

As a glorious king, Christ has a kingdom. Samuel Rutherford spoke of His having three kingdoms, but we may regard them better as three ways in which He exercises His Kingly power.

Christ's Kingdom of Government (1 Cor. 15:25; Heb. 1:3; Ps. 103:19; Col. 1:17).

Christ's Kingdom of Grace—His headship in the church as the sole ruler (Eph. 1:20-22).

Christ's Kingdom of Glory, which is really the perfection of His grace. Matthew 19:28 and 25:31 speak of the "throne of his glory" and show Him exercising His kingly power eternally (cf. 2 Peter 1:11). Thomas Watson said, "The Kingdom of grace is glory in the seed; the Kingdom of glory is grace in the flower."

KNOWLEDGE OF GOD

God's knowledge is omniscience. It is infinite knowledge: He knows Himself in His own infinite being; He knows all things possible, whether they ever become actual or not; and He comprehends all these things in one simultaneous act of knowing. This knowledge is known in theology as "the knowledge of simple intelligence" (*scientia simplicis intelligentiae*) or, "necessary knowledge" (*scientia necessaria*), because God's knowledge is simply an act of the divine intellect, not a product of the divine will. God is omniscient by the necessity of His nature. This divine knowledge

1. *Is intuitive, not discursive.* That is, it discerns all things directly in its own light; it does not proceed logically from the known to the unknown.

2. *Is independent.* That is, it is not in any way dependent upon His creatures or their actions. By the light of His own infinite intelligence God knows all things possible; by the light of His own sovereign purpose He knows all things actual and future. The knowledge of things actual, whether past, present, or future, is called *scientia visionis,* "the knowledge of vision"; or it is called "free knowledge," to indicate that with the exercise of the divine intellect is the concurrent action of the divine will, for what comes to pass is the result of the purpose of God.

3. *Is simultaneous, not successive.* Creature knowledge grows; divine knowledge does not. God knows all things in one single act of intuition.

4. *Is essential, not relative.* Man knows things only by their properties; God knows them perfectly and directly in their very essences.

5. *Includes future contingent events.* Events may be uncertain to us for various reasons—for example, because their immediate cause is indeterminate (as in the rolling of dice); or because their immediate cause may be the act of will of a free agent. But these are not uncertain to God. He fully knows the outcome of the rolling of the dice (Prov. 16:33), just as he foreknows the volition of His creatures (1 Sam. 23:11, 12; Acts 2:23; 15:18; Isa. 46:9, 10).

See *Scientia Media.*

KNOWLEDGE OF GOD, MAN'S

1. The innate witness in every man that God is. It is a law written in his heart (Rom. 2:15), something God has shown him and has confirmed by the witness of all creation (Rom. 1:19, 20). Fallen men *suppress* this truth in unrighteousness (Rom. 1:18) but the witness to the Creator from within and around every man is sufficient to leave him "without excuse." Thus the Scripture condemns all professed atheists as *fools* (Ps. 14:1).

2. The intellectual and spiritual apprehension of God as He has revealed Himself in His Word, received by means of the illuminating activity of the Holy Spirit in regeneration and sanctification. This knowledge of God is the very essence of eternal life (John 17:3).

Neo-orthodoxy and existentialism deny the possibility of a real and objective knowledge of God. Bultmann, Barth, and Brunner made faith and knowledge mutually exclusive, so that if we know, we cannot say we exercise faith. But the Scriptures do not oppose the two. In fact, they so join them as to make faith dependent upon a knowledge of God and His truth (1 John 5:13, 20).

Repudiating the knowledge of God, neo-orthodox theologians hold that God is to be encountered, not known. "Persons are met, not thought." This attitude pervades much modern-day evangelism, which invites people to have an encounter with God, with no definite declaration of the gospel. But apart from the doctrinal content of the gospel such "encounters" are delusions. Without a God-given knowledge of God that we can rationally understand, no meaningful encounter can take place.

See *Epistemology.*

KOINE

The common Greek language as distinct from classical Greek. The LXX* and the NT were both written in Koine Greek.

L

LABADISTS

Followers of Jean de Labadie (1610-74), a French Jesuit* who became a Protestant. They existed into the 18th century and cherished such views as holding their property and children in common. They were mystical in outlook and sought to exclude all blemish from the visible church. Despite the Labadist emphasis on purity, Labadie was charged with various inconsistencies, whether fairly or unfairly it is difficult to determine. The group eventually moved to the United States where it petered out.

LAITY

Greek *laos*, "people," a term to designate the members of the church as distinct from its ordained ministers.

LATITUDINARIANISM

The position of those in the Church of England in the 17th and 18th centuries who professed to occupy the middle ground between Puritanism* and high churchism. Latitudinarianism was a movement that gloried in non-dogmatic toleration in matters of theology and invoked "sweet reason" rather than divine revelation as the basis of settling religious questions. Latitudinarians were especially opposed to all emotional expression in religion and thus were antagonistic to what they termed enthusiasm, their equivalent for what we today would term *fanaticism*. Thus they looked with disfavour on the Methodists and rejected the work of revival carried on through them.

LATRIA

In Roman Catholicism, the worship accorded to God alone, distinct from *dulia*,* the worship of the saints, and *hyperdulia*,* the worship of the Virgin Mary. In practice, the distinctions are of little or no use and it is at once apparent from Roman Catholic prayers to Mary that *latria* and *hyperdulia* differ only in name.

LECTIONARIES

The church lesson-books of the ancient Greek church, containing the passages of Scripture assigned to be read on a given day. The lectionaries are often valuable witnesses in defending the purity of the majority text of the NT.

See **Textual Criticism of the New Testament.**

LEGALISM

A term that is used with various meanings.

1. The dogma of salvation by works, the heresy* that man must earn a place in heaven by his personal righteousness.

2. Neonomianism*—the theory that works of obedience are a constituent part of saving faith, rather than its natural fruit. In earlier times neonomianism produced the sterile moralism of moderatism.* Nowadays it has found a place in much evangelical preaching where faith is looked upon as "man's part" in the plan of salvation. As it is often popularly expressed, "God has done His part, now it is up to you to do your part." In the neonomian scheme, this *doing* is the condition of salvation; it is not the fruit of the free gift of saving faith, sovereignly imparted by God to His elect.

3. The Galatian error of preaching faith plus something else to make one acceptable to God. At its worst this form of legalism de-

LEVELLERS

generates into salvation by works. At best it removes the solid basis of Christian assurance for it drives a sincere believer more and more into himself to examine the quality of his work or his faith rather than to the all-sufficient merits of Christ.

4. Sometimes it is used erroneously to describe those who advocate that Christians should be careful to observe the moral law on the ground that whereas the law as a covenant of life is abrogated by the gospel, it still stands as a standard of Christian obedience.

LEVELLERS

A party of radical political reform in England in the days of the Parliamentary-Royalist struggle and during the rule of Oliver Cromwell as Lord Protector. Levellers sought to destroy all social rank, distinction, and privilege, and establish equality in rights and property for men in all stations of life. Hume wrote in his *History of England,* "The Levellers insisted on an equal distribution of power and property, and disclaimed all dependence and subordination" (5:386). The Levellers supported Parliament in the struggle against Charles I but were critical of the regime that replaced him. They alleged that "the army grandees were busy betraying the aims of the revolution by not implementing those social reforms they had believed implicit in all their agreements" (Antonia Fraser, *Cromwell Our Chief of Men,* p. 309). They were particularly scathing in their attacks on Cromwell, of whom they had entertained high hopes. They enjoyed strong popular support among Dissenters and continued to be a thorn in Cromwell's side. Their continuing opposition did much to destabilize the country and undermine the revolution they had helped to launch. In the end they opted for all or nothing. They finally got nothing when, two years after Cromwell's death in 1658, the monarchy was restored under Charles II.

LEVIRATE MARRIAGE

From Latin *levir,* "husband's brother"; the requirement of the Mosaic law that a man should marry the childless wife of his deceased brother. The issue of such a marriage would then be heir to the dead brother's property and would carry on his line (Deut. 25:5-10). From Ruth 4 we learn that in practice the duty of the living "brother" extended beyond the actual fraternal relationship to the closest living relative.

LIBERALISM

The theological movement also known as modernism. *Liberalism* denotes the movement's free criticism of all theological claims. In effect, it is freedom from all restraint imposed by any theological *a priori,* meaning that any Biblical doctrine is open to be denied. *Modernism* denotes its preference for the new over the old.

It is a movement which from its inception—usually attributed to Schleiermacher, though its roots go back much further—fully embraced the so-called "findings" of higher criticism *(see Criticism),* repudiating the doctrines of divine revelation and inspiration, since, according to their theories, the Bible had been disproved at many points by modern scientific investigation. The abandonment of Scripture led to a belief in God that arose out of human consciousness *(see Consciousness Theology),* with the consequent denial of the fundamental doctrines of divine revelation—e.g., the Trinity,* the deity of Christ,* His virgin birth,* His atoning death, and His bodily resurrection.* Jettisoned also were the Biblical teachings of sin* and grace, and the division between saved and lost, with everlasting heaven for the one and everlasting hell for the other. In the place of the gospel of grace, liberalism preached the social gospel, the theological premise of which was "the Fatherhood of God and the Brotherhood of Man."

Liberalism/modernism infected theological institutions and churches across the world. After World War I, it lost much of its appeal and left its most earnest devotees frustrated and in search of a new star to follow. Through the years it reappeared in a variety of guises. Some ex-liberals espoused the dialectical theology of neo-orthodoxy, which Cornelius Van Til aptly termed "The New Modernism." Others turned to even more radical existential systems. Many became religious socialists, adopting the theories of men such as Paul Tillich who reduced God to "the ground of being"—a meaningless abstraction that led some into the so-called Christian atheism of God-is-dead theology.*

See **Rationalism**.

LIBERATION THEOLOGY

A largely Roman Catholic radical and activist philosophy born in Latin America in the 1960's. It sees the great mission of the church, indeed the content of the gospel, to be the freedom of the poor, oppressed, and disadvantaged of the world from cultural, economic, political, and religious tyranny. It is an attempt to redefine Christianity in secular, usually Marxist, terms. It has substituted a message of social justice for the gospel of justification by faith in Christ.

Liberation theology espouses the fundamental error that man's problem is preeminently environmental, that if we solve his social problems we have introduced him to true liberty. All the evidence is to the contrary. Socially liberated sinners are still under the wrath of God and need the message of true liberation: justification by faith in Christ and acceptance with God in Him.

Christian theology does have much to say about the oppression of the poor and needy. It must not be subverted to serve the interests of any supremacist elite. But neither must it be denuded of its glorious mission by making its gospel a mere manual for social amelioration in the here and now.

See **African Theology**; **Black Theology**; **Contextualization**; **Political Theology**.

LIMBO

The Latin word *limbus* means "fringe," and it is used by the Church of Rome in two ways:

1. *Limbus Patrum* is said to have been on the fringe of hell, a place where the OT saints awaited Christ's descent into hades to lead them into heaven.

2. *Limbus Infantum* is said to be the place where all unbaptized infants go after death. Though it is said to be on the fringe of hell, most Roman Catholic writers teach that the tormenting fires do not reach them. In contrast, most Roman Catholics talk about the "natural happiness" of these unbaptized infants in *limbus infantum*—their suffering consists solely in the lack of the "beatific vision" (i.e., entrance into the presence of God in heaven). The *Catechism of the Council of Trent* spoke in much sterner terms as it stated the official position of Rome: "Infants, unless regenerated unto God through the grace of baptism, whether their parents be Christian or infidel, are born to eternal misery and perdition." Revulsion to this Tridentine doctrine led to the adoption of the current "softer" *Limbus Infantum* notions. Needless to say, one is as devoid of scriptural proof as the other.

LIMITED ATONEMENT

Particular redemption.*

LITURGICAL CALENDAR

The Roman Catholic church and others (particularly the Anglican and Lutheran churches, but increasingly to some extent even Dissenting churches) divide the year into various seasons for the celebration of the different aspects of the mystery of Christ's redemptive mission. According to Rome, the liturgical seasons are (1) Advent; preparing for (2) Christmas; (3) Lent; preparing for (4) Easter; (5) Ordinary Time—i.e., the two periods between Christmas and Lent, and between Pentecost, the end of the Easter season, and Advent. In addition, "Sundays, holydays, feasts of Mary, celebrations of saints' days and other feast days light the Church year with warmth to stir the devotion of God's people" (Daughters of St. Paul, *Basic Catechism*).

On the validity of introducing these and other innovations into the practice and worship of the church see *Normative Principle; Regulative Principle.*

LITURGY

The Greek word *leitourgia* is used in the NT with the meaning of "service," or "ministry." "In Biblical Greek [it means] a. the service or ministry of the priests relative to the prayers and sacrifices offered to God: Lk. 1:23; Heb. 8:6; 9:21;...b. A gift or benefaction, for the relief of the needy: 2 Cor. 9:12; Phil. 2:30." (Thayer)

The ecclesiastical usage of the word is different, though clearly derived from the Biblical meaning. Liturgy in this sense is used of prescribed services and formularies to be used in worship, especially with reference to the celebration of Holy Communion *(see Lord's Supper).* The NT nowhere sets down a liturgy in the sense of prescribing forms of service for church worship. The introduction of liturgy helped to mould the thinking of the church in viewing the celebration of the Lord's Supper as a priestly function of sacrifice, so setting the stage for the Romish teaching of the mass* as a true sacrifice, not merely a memorial of Christ's once-for-all sacrifice.

LOCUS CLASSICUS

Latin for "a classical place," a term used in exegesis* to describe a portion that is a celebrated example of the Bible's teaching on a subject. For example, 1 Cor. 13 would be a *locus classicus* on the subject of love.

LOGICAL POSITIVISM

The conjunction of the empiricism* of David Hume with the positivism* of Auguste Comte. Its aim was to develop and systematize empiricism by means of the principles of logic and mathematics. It taught that all reality could be stated with logical or mathematical precision, either in terms of physical objects or of sense experience. In either case, it promoted naturalism with no place for supernaturalism. It therefore denigrated theology as meaningless and was strongly anti-theistic and atheistic.

LOGOS

The title given to the Lord Jesus Christ in John 1:1, 14; 1 John 1:1; Rev. 19:13 and translated "Word." Much has been written to try to connect the NT use of *Logos* as a title for Christ with Greek philosophical uses of it. Much learned discussion has taken place on the "sources of the Johannine concept." Such studies are nonproductive because God alone is the source of John's teaching of the *Logos.* Greek philosophy spoke of a *logos* as the principle of divine reason in the world. The Greeks thought God could not make direct contact with matter and therefore looked on the *logos* as a sort of buffer between God and the material world.

How different is the *Logos* in John's inspired writings. No mere principle, He is truly God as to His essence and yet "with God" (*pros,* "with," in John 1:1 signifies the closest communion), indicating His hypostatic distinction *(see Hypotasis).* Calvin remarks that the title "Word" refers to the fulness of divine wisdom residing in Him, by which all the inspired prophets and apostles communicated God's revelation to men. As the Word, Christ is the perfect self-expression of God, God's message to the world (cf. Heb. 1:1).

LOLLARDS

The followers of John Wyclif (1328-84), who gave Englishmen the first translation of the Bible in their own tongue and who opposed the doctrinal and moral corruption of the papal church in his day.

LONGSUFFERING

An aspect of the infinite goodness of God, "in virtue of which He bears with the froward and evil in spite of their long continued disobedience" (Berkhof).

LORD'S SUPPER

The memorial feast instituted by the Lord Jesus Christ "the same night He was betrayed."

Institution of the Lord's Supper

Berkhof says, "There are four different accounts of the institution of the Lord's Supper, one in each of the Synoptics, and one in 1 Cor. 11. John speaks of eating the passover, but does not mention the institution of a new sacrament. These accounts are independent of, and serve to compliment, one another. Evidently, the Lord did not finish the passover meal before He instituted the Lord's Supper. The new sacrament was linked with the central element in the paschal meal. The bread that was eaten with the Lamb was consecrated to a new use. This is evident from the fact that the third cup, generally called 'the cup of blessing' was used for the second element in the new sacrament. Thus the sacrament of the Old Testament passed into that of the New in a most natural way" (*Systematic Theology*, p. 647).

NT Terms for the Lord's Supper

1 Corinthians 11:20 uses the words *kuriakon deipnon*, "the Lord's Supper," and these supply the designation most favoured by Protestants. 1 Corinthians 10:21 speaks of *poterion kuriou*, "the cup of the Lord," and *trapeza kuriou*, "the table of the Lord." Acts 2:42 (cf. 20:7) speaks of *klasis tou artou*, "the breaking of bread." The references to Christ giving thanks led to the use of the term *eucharist* (Greek *eucharistia*, "thanksgiving"), which in its scriptural setting is plainly unobjectionable; however, later developments tended to link this term with highly ritualistic views of the Lord's

Supper, which in turn led all the way to the Roman Catholic dogma of the Mass.*

Reformed View of the Lord's Supper

Reformed theology's view of the Lord's Supper is ably set forth in chap. 29 of the *Westminster Confession of Faith*. It refers to it as "the sacrament of His body and blood," to be observed "for the perpetual remembrance of the sacrifice of Himself in His death." According to the *Confession* God intends the Lord's Supper to seal to believers the benefits of that sacrifice, aiding their spiritual nourishment and growth in grace, and expressing the "bond and pledge of their communion with Him and with each other, as members of His mystical body."

The Lord's Supper is not a sacrifice offered to God, "but only a commemoration of that one offering up of Himself, by Himself, on the cross, once for all." The *Confession* voices its opposition to the whole Romish doctrine of the mass in the strongest terms: "The Popish sacrifice of the Mass, as they call it, is most abominably injurious to Christ's one only sacrifice, the alone propitiation for all the sins of the elect." The *Confession* goes on to oppose private masses or celebrations of the Lord's Supper, the denial of the cup to the laity, all adoration of the elements, and the entire notion of transubstantiation.

The Presence of Christ and the Lord's Supper

At the Reformation, Protestants agreed that the Romish notion of transubstantiation* was unscriptural, but they disagreed on the subject of Christ's presence in relation to the Supper. Luther taught consubstantiation.* Zwingli denied absolutely any bodily presence of Christ, holding that the Lord's Supper is purely commemorative, though Christ is spiritually present to the faith of believers. Calvin, whose views have become the most widely accepted statement of the Reformed position, agreed with Zwingli that there is no bodily presence of Christ in the sacrament, but he maintained that His spiritual presence is a real presence. Furthermore, he considered it dangerous to reduce the Lord's Supper merely to an act of man in commemorating Christ's death. He looked on it, first and foremost, as a gracious gift of God, and only secondarily as a human act of commemoration. In this way, he sought to emphasize that the Lord's Supper is primarily a divinely appointed means of strengthening the faith of believers. This is the view expounded in the *Confession of Faith.*

LORDSHIP SALVATION

The belief that the acceptance of Christ as Saviour necessarily includes acceptance of Him as Lord. In other words, saving faith inevitably produces the fruit of godly obedience to Christ, and repentance is more than a mere change of mind; it is also a change of heart and life.

This view has become a divisive issue within American dispensationalism.* Professors from Dallas Theological Seminary have strongly attacked it, claiming that it adds works to faith for salvation. Their opponents in turn charge the Dallas position with "easy believism."

The chief promoter of the Lordship Salvation position has been John MacArthur whose book, *The Gospel According to Jesus,* first brought the controversy to the attention of the Christian public. That book established that according to the gospel Jesus taught, to be His disciple was to acknowledge Him as Lord. None can deny that. But this plain fact goes to the very heart of the controversy.

Lordship salvation is *the gospel according to Jesus.* However, dispensationalism has long distinguished between the *gospel of the kingdom* (which Christ preached) and the gospel of the grace of God. MacArthur's opponents insist that faith is a bare belief, and repentance a change of mind, both of which may exist in the soul without any accompanying works of holiness or obedience.

Obviously, the question is, "Did Jesus preach the gospel?" According to Heb. 2:1-4 He preached the very gospel of "so great salvation" that the apostles later preached. To Paul, there was no other gospel and he anathematized any who preached any other message (Gal. 1:8, 9). So Jesus certainly preached the gospel of God's grace, the same gospel His apostles preached, and therefore on the very same terms.

That settles the Lordship Salvation controversy. However the disputants dress their arguments in theological language, the simple matter is that according to the Lord Jesus Christ no man can be His disciple without acknowledging His Lordship. No man can receive Him by faith as Saviour while deliberately rejecting Him as Lord.

Really the Lordship Salvation controversy is the old dispute on the relation of grace to law and of faith to works. We are not saved by works. We are saved by grace through faith. But living faith always produces good works—that is, it acknowledges Christ as Lord (Rom. 10:9). The works prove the reality of the faith that produced them.

LOVE OF GOD

A particular aspect of the goodness of God. Berkhof defines it as "that perfection of God by which He is eternally moved to self-communication." The love of the absolutely holy God cannot find any grounds for its exercise in any fallen creature, and so it is exercised "freely"—i.e., without any meritorious cause in the sinner.

It is exercised in Christ, for God can regard only His own absolute perfection with complacency. Thus God's love is specifically united in Scripture with His gift of His Son (John 3:16) by and in whom His elect are exalted to the highest station (1 John 3:1, 2). This sovereign, saving bestowal of the love of God is described in Scripture as being special, or particular, in that the proper objects of it are God's chosen people (Eph. 1:4, 5; 5:25-27; Rom. 9:13).

LUTHERANISM

The church and theology produced by the 16th century German Reformation under the leadership of Martin Luther. Their major tenets of historical importance were:

1. The Scriptures are the very inspired and authoritative word of God (*sola Scriptura*);
2. Salvation is by grace alone (*sola gratia*);
3. Through faith alone (*sola fide*).
4. Justification* is based squarely on the merits of Christ and His perfect obedience and atoning death, by which the believer has the very righteousness Christ imputed to him.

Nevertheless, some peculiarities about Lutheranism distinguish it from Reformed theology.

1. Original sin:* See the discussion under this head.
2. Person of Christ. Lutherans hold a peculiar view of ubiquity,* believing that the human nature of the ascended Christ received and exercises the perfections of His divine nature (*see* **Communicatio Idiomatum).** The *Formula of Concord**states, "The Son of Man is really, that is, truly and in very deed, according to his human nature, exalted to the right hand of the omnipotent majesty and power of God, since that man was assumed into God when he was conceived by the Holy Ghost in the womb of his mother, and his humanity was then personally united with the Son of God Most High.

"And that majesty, in virtue of the personal union, Christ has always had, but in the state of his humiliation he divested himself of it, for which cause he truly grew in age, wisdom, and favor with God and men. Wherefore he did not always make use of that majesty, but as often as seemed good to him, until after the resurrection, he fully and forever laid aside the form of a servant, but not the human nature, and was established in the plenary use, manifestation, and revelation of the divine majesty, and in this manner entered into his glory (Phil. 2:6f). Therefore now not only as God, but also as man, he knows all things, can do all things, is present to all creatures, has under his feet and in his hand all things which are in heaven, in the earth, and under the earth." (Art. 8, Affirmation 10).

3. Baptism:* see **Baptismal Regeneration.**
4. Lord's Supper:* Lutheranism espoused Luther's notion of consubstantiation,* a theory supported vigorously by the *Formula of Concord* on the basis of the peculiar Lutheran view of the *Communicatio Idiomatum* and of Christ's ubiquity.*
5. Church rites and ceremonies: Whereas Reformed churches adopted the regulative principle* of public worship, Lutheranism took the view that what was not forbidden by God's word was permissible. The *Formula of Concord* states that such ceremonies as are neither commanded nor forbidden in Scripture are not part of worship, and may be changed if the church desires; however, to avoid giving offence or hurting the faith of the weak, the church should show forbearance, i.e., not make unnecessary changes to the ritual received from Rome.
6. Predestination: In response to the crypto-Calvinists within Lutheranism, the *Saxon Visitation Articles* (which though not an official standard of Lutheranism are nevertheless a plain, but very biased, statement of Lutheranism's differences with Calvinism on the subject) condemn the following propositions:
   a. That Christ died only for the elect.
   b. "That the elected and regenerated cannot lose faith and the Holy Spirit, or be damned."
   c. "That those who are not elect are necessarily damned, and cannot arrive at salvation, though baptized a thousand times and receive the Eucharist every day and lead [a] blameless life."
   d. "That not all who are baptized in water, but the elect only, obtain by it the grace of Christ and the gifts of faith."

Thus despite Luther's strong emphasis on the authority of the Word, the centrality of

Christ, and the place of grace and faith in
salvation, Lutheranism has developed into a
sacramentalist church with close affinity to
Rome on baptism and the Lord's Supper,
and with Arminianism on the matter of the
security of the saints.

LXX

The usual abbreviation used to denote
the Septuagint translation of the Old Testament into Greek.

See **Textual Criticism of the Old Testament**.

M

MAGISTERIUM

Latin *magister,* "master"; the authoritative teaching office claimed by the Church of Rome for her pope and bishops. This teaching may be promulgated by an ecumenical council with the pope at its head, by the pope speaking as the alleged head of the universal church, apart from a council, by a papal encyclical, by a decree of a synod of bishops, or by a declaration of a Vatican congregation with the approval of the pope. While Rome says that in the widest sense this teaching authority belongs to the whole church and that all the faithful participate through baptism in Christ's mission as prophet, priest, and king, the reality is very different. The authority to teach in Rome belongs to some by virtue of their office (i.e., the pope and his bishops) and to a much lesser degree to others by their scholarly competence (e.g., theologians). None but the pope or a council headed by him may define dogma.*

MANICHEISM

An ancient heresy which stemmed largely from the aberrations of Manes, who flourished in the middle of the third century, but about whose early life we have little concrete information. He assimilated much of the philosophy of Gnosticism* and taught a form of heathen dualism,* positing two opposing forces, good and evil, in the world. Redemption was the liberation of the good from the dominion of the evil, which in keeping with his Gnosticism was closely associated with matter. Manes viewed Christ in a Gnostic light and denied His resurrection. He taught that Christ helped in the redeeming work of liberating the good from evil domination, and that he (Manes) was his successor in that work. Manicheism had a wide following, absorbing many of the followers of Marcion* into its fold.

MARCION

*See **Gnosticism**.*

MARKS OF SCRIPTURE

The attributes of Scripture.* They may be summarized as follows:

Necessity

Reformed theology holds that the inscripturation of God's special, saving revelation to men was necessary, that it might (a) remain throughout all ages; (b) reach all mankind; (c) be offered to men objectively; and (d) have the testimony to its own truthfulness within itself. Thus, not only is a special revelation from God necessary, but because of Satanic opposition and human blindness and inability, an inspired record and interpretation of that revelation is also necessary. This is what the Scripture is.

Authority

Man ever seeks to constitute himself the final arbiter over all that presents itself to him as revelation, but the Scripture, rejecting such conceited claims to autonomy, asserts its absolute authority over man. Necessity of revelation leads automatically to the authority of that revelation. God has spoken. Obedience to His word is the only appropriate response from man.

Perspicuity

Clearness. All things are not "alike plain in themselves or alike clear unto all" (*Westminster Confession of Faith,* chap. 1, sec. 7), but the great fundamentals of the faith, necessary to salvation, may be understood by those to whom God directs His word, without the appointment of mediate human authorities. This is not to deny the role of preachers and teachers, for the Scriptures testify to the divine appointment of these offices. It is to say, however, that teachers and those whom they teach are alike under the authority of Scripture and that the people have the right to subject any man's teaching to the judgment of the written word. Perspicuity, then, is the assertion that God's people may understand His word without the creation of a clerical caste.

Sufficiency

This flows from the preceding marks and is the assertion that Scripture alone is necessary to convey God's saving revelation, without any mixture of human traditions, inventions, or interpretations.

MARONITES

A sect or community in Lebanon that originally followed the monothelite* heresy on the person of Christ, and that entered the fold of Rome at the time of the Crusades. The Maronite church is one of the Uniate churches, which are found in Eastern Europe and the Middle East. Uniate churches are in full communion with Rome and acknowledge the pope's supremacy, but retain their own liturgy and organization. In the case of the Maronites that organization is headed by a patriarch (of Antioch, as he claims) and eight bishops.

MARROW CONTROVERSY

A controversy which raged in the Church of Scotland, following a decision of the General Assembly in 1720 to condemn a widely circulated book, *The Marrow of Modern Divinity,* written in 1646 in the form of a dialogue by a Gloucestershire scholar, Edward Fisher. The book took its name from the fact that it was composed of extracts from the leading Reformed theologians of the period:

Calvin, Beza, Luther, Reynolds, Hooker, Goodwin, and others.

It dealt with the relation of law and grace. Repudiating both licence and legal bondage, Fisher aimed to show the freeness of the offer of the gospel. *The Marrow* was Calvinistic, not universalist as its opponents charged, but it emphasized the free offer of the gospel to all men.

The views of the book found a ready response in such Scottish ministers as Thomas Boston, James Hog, and Ebenezer Erskine, who with nine other ministers petitioned the Assembly to remove its condemnation. An Assembly Commission reduced the controversy to twelve questions which it put before the "Marrowmen," as they were called. Their answers, chiefly framed by Ebenezer Erskine and Gabriel Wilson, are counted a classic statement of evangelical Calvinism.

The Commission denied the petition, and in this was supported by the Assembly of 1722. This decision did not lead to a disruption at that time, though all candidates for the ministry who were thought to be of a mind with the Marrowmen were greatly hindered from obtaining churches. Both Thomas Boston and Ebenezer Erskine suffered discrimination, finding their way blocked when a change of church was desired. Erskine later led a large and popular secession from the Church of Scotland.

See *Auchterarder Creed.*

MARYOLATRY

Latin *Maria,* "Mary," and *latria,* "worship, adoration"; the worship rendered by Roman Catholics to the Virgin Mary, termed by Rome *hyperdulia.* *

Though Rome makes a semantic distinction between *hyperdulia* paid to Mary and the *latria* paid to God, she essentially deifies Mary. According to Alphonsus Lignori, a Romish saint, Mary is the Queen of Mercy as Jesus Christ is the King of Justice. Vatican II decreed, "The blessed Virgin is invoked in the Church under the titles of Advocate, Helper, Benefactress, and Mediatrix" (*Lumen Gentium,* VIII, par. 62). John Paul II has plainly stated that in Mary "is effected the reconciliation of God with humanity,...[in Mary] is accomplished the work of reconciliation" (*On Reconciliation and Penance,* p. 139).

Rome's Maryolatry is idolatry for in her system, to use E. B. Pusey's words, "Mary is the complement of the Trinity" (*Eirenicon,* II.167).

MASORA, MASORETES

Masora, "tradition" in Hebrew; the Masoretes, a school of Jewish scholars, active between the sixth and eleventh centuries A.D., who have been described as the successors of the scribes *(see Sopherim).* The tradition the Masoretes preserved pertained to the pronunciation of the words of the Hebrew Scriptures. Originally the text was unpointed, that is, without any written directions as to pronunciation. Correct pronunciation, therefore, became a matter of tradition. It was this proper pronunciation the Masoretes were at pains to maintain.

They were also concerned to preserve the accuracy of the text. "These textual scholars counted words, indicated where and in what connection unusual words occurred, marked all peculiarities which they discovered in the text, down to the minutest irregularity in shape or position of the letters. To this work they undertook to confine themselves, professing never to have made or suggested any alteration in the consonantal text as they found it written" (John MacPherson, *New Biblical Guide*).

Correct pronunciation was preserved by the use of vowel points placed above or below the consonantal text. The Masoretic text is the Hebrew text behind our English Bible. *See Textual Criticism of the Old Testament.*

MASS

The centre of the entire Roman Catholic system of worship, the mass purports to be a representation of the sacrifice of Christ. In Roman Catholic worship it is distinct from the laity's participation in Holy Communion. Before the worshippers can participate by receiving a consecrated wafer ("the host"), the officiating priest performs the mass, professedly changing the bread and wine into the body and blood of Christ and offering up a "true, proper, propitiatory sacrifice" to God (*Creed of Pius IV,* * Art. 5; see *Canons and Decrees of the Council of Trent,* sess. 22, chap. 2 and canons 1, 3; Vatican II, *Eucharisticum Mysterium,* Intro. C).

Rome's Definition of the Mass

The Second Vatican Council (in December 1963) produced its document on the *Sacred Liturgy.* In dealing with "the most Sacred Mystery of the Eucharist," it speaks of "the Eucharistic Sacrifice of His Body and Blood," which, it claims, Christ instituted "to perpetuate the sacrifice of His cross throughout the centuries until He should come again." It goes on to speak of the Eucharist as "a paschal banquet in which Christ is consumed."

Obviously, despite the claims of some ecumenists, Rome still clings to her ancient heresy of the mass as a sacrifice. The creed of Pius IV,* an official creed of the Roman Catholic church, laid down that position clearly: "I profess that in the Mass is offered to God a true, proper, and propitiatory sacrifice for the living and the dead."

Transubstantiation

Pius's creed goes on to define Rome's notion of Transubstantiation: "In the most holy sacrament of the Eucharist there is truly, really, and substantially, the body and blood, together with the soul and divinity, of our Lord Jesus Christ; and...there is a conversion of the whole substance of the wine into the blood, which the Catholic Church calls Transubstantiation."

In keeping with this, Vatican II spoke of Christ being consumed or eaten, which is exactly a restatement of the gross views of Humber in 1059: "The very body of Christ is truly held in the priest's hand, broken and chewed by the teeth of the faithful" (Quoted by Berkhof, *History of Christian Doctrines,* p. 253).

Worshipping the Host

Since the bread is changed into the very deity and humanity of Christ, it is not surprising that it is "adored" or worshipped. Before the act of priestly consecration, the wafer is said to be just a wafer. But when consecrated, it becomes the host, to be worshipped as truly God.

Consecration

According to Rome, the efficacy of the sacrament depends on the officiating priest's administration of the sacrament according to the Romish liturgy, and upon his secret intention. The Creed of Pius IV says: "If there is any defect in any of these: namely, the due matter, the form with intention, or the sacerdotal order of the celebrant, it nullifies the sacrament." In the light of this dependence upon a priest's secret intention, Cardinal Bellarmine, one of the greatest ever Roman Catholic authorities, said, "No one can be certain... that he has received a true sacrament, since no sacrament is performed without the intention of the ministers, and no one can see the intentions of another."

Cup Withheld from the Laity

At the order of the Council of Constance (1415), the laity were to be given only the host, not the cup, during Holy Communion, in case a drop of Christ's blood should be spilled. Rome argues that since Christ is entirely present, body and blood included, under each element, the laity need receive only the wafer.

Obligatory Mass Attendance

The Baltimore Catechism, answer 390, states: "It is a mortal sin not to hear Mass on a Sunday, or a holy-day of obligation." As Loraine Boettner aptly remarks, this means "that considerably more than half the claimed Roman Catholic membership throughout the world is constantly in mortal sin." (*Roman Catholicism,* p. 259).

Protestant Repudiation of the Mass

The Reformers totally repudiated the Romish notions of the mass. The *Articles of the Church of England* refer to masses as "blasphemous fables and dangerous deceits," while the *Westminster Confession of Faith* says, "the Popish Sacrifice of the Mass, as they call it, is most abominably injurious to Christ's one, only sacrifice, the alone propitiation for all the sins of the elect."

Ecumenical Compromise on the Mass

It is one of the major aims of the ecumenical movement to find an agreement with Rome on the subject of the mass. The documents produced as a result of the discussions of Protestant and Roman Catholic theologians indicate that a form of words has been devised to satisfy compromising Protestants, while the substance of the Roman Catholic dogma remains unchanged. On such a basis is reunion with Rome seriously proposed and actively pursued.

MATERIALISM

The doctrine that everything that exists is material. To a materialist there is really only one substance in the universe, and such things as intelligence, feeling, conscience,* volitions, and dispositions are but modified properties of matter. Instead of intelligence creating matter, matter evolved into intelligence. Thus materialism is the antithesis of idealism* and antagonistic to all theism.*

As a system of philosophy, materialism is not the creed of the masses, but it finds practical expression in their enchantment with material gain at the expense of their spiritual welfare.

MEANS OF GRACE

"Those institutions which God has ordained to be the ordinary channels of grace, i.e., of the supernatural influences of the Holy

Spirit, to the souls of men" (Charles Hodge, *Systematic Theology*, 3:466).

The *Larger Catechism* defines the means of grace as "the outward and ordinary means whereby Christ communicates to His Church the benefits of His mediation," and identifies them as "all His ordinances; especially the Word, sacraments and prayer; all of which are made effectual to the elect for their salvation" (Q. 154).

The primary means of grace is the word of God, the Bible. Hodge remarks, "The word of God, as far as adults are concerned, is an indispensable means of salvation. True religion never existed, and never can exist, where the truths revealed in the Bible are unknown....The word of God is not only necessary to salvation, but it is also divinely efficacious to the accomplishment of that end" (*ibid.*).

This power is in Scripture by virtue of its divine inspiration.* However, for it to become effective in the souls of men it must be attended by the supernatural power of the Holy Spirit (1 Cor. 2:14; John 8:43, 47; James 1:18). It is by His word that God brings souls to the new birth (1 Pet. 1:23) and calls them to the exercise of faith in Christ (Rom. 10:17). (*See **Regeneration*** for discussion of the apparently—but not really—contradictory point that the Holy Spirit quickens dead souls *immediately,* i.e, without the use of means.)

As a means of grace, the word of God continues to be effective in the souls of believers as the primary means of sanctification (John 17:17). Growth in grace and progress to full spiritual maturity depend on the word of God (1 Pet. 2:2; Heb. 5:12-14).

Prayer is a means of grace. It is by calling on the name of the Lord that men are saved (Rom. 10:13) and it is by continuing steadfastly in apostolic doctrine and fellowship and in prayers that Christians grow in Christ (Acts 2:42).

The sacraments* of baptism* and the Lord's Supper* are also means of grace. They do not communicate grace *opus operatum,** but they are used by the Holy Spirit to quicken the believer's faith in the reality of the things they signify. In this way they are gracious means to sanctification.

It should be noted that the *grace* intended in the phrase "the means of grace" is supernatural, saving grace in the proper sense of that term. It is not *regenerating* grace *(see **Baptismal Regeneration).*** Reformed theology is careful to maintain the distinction between regeneration as the sovereign act of the Holy Spirit creating new life in dead souls and all consequent exercise of that life, both in the initial act of faith in trusting Christ and in all the activities of conversion.* The *grace* in the means of grace is converting and sanctifying grace—and, of course, conversion and sanctification are vital components of our salvation.

MEDIATE IMPUTATION

A theory first advocated by Joshua Placaeus, professor of Theology at Saumur, France, in 1645, opposing the Reformed and Scriptural doctrine of the imputation of the guilt of Adam's first transgression. Berkhof summarizes the theory as follows:

"Adam's descendants derive their innate corruption from him by a process of natural generation, and only on the basis of that inherent depravity which they share with him are they also considered guilty of his apostasy. They are not born corrupt because they are considered guilty in Adam, but they are considered guilty because they are corrupt. Their condition is not based upon their legal status, but their legal status on their condition."

Mediate Imputation is based on certain fallacies:

1. That moral corruption does not in itself include guilt;

2. That human depravity, which is the result of Adam's sin, can be counted as the legal basis for imputing the guilt of that sin (a logical absurdity). In fact, the theory is an

attempt to remove all real imputation of Adam's first sin to his posterity.

MEDIATE REGENERATION

1. The theory of the Saumur school that in regeneration the Holy Spirit supernaturally illuminates the intellect, but does not directly act on the will. Because of His work on the intellect it delivers such sound and practical judgment that the will cannot fail to follow it. This is in contrast to the orthodox teaching of the direct, or immediate, operation of the Holy Spirit on the will.

2. The theory that the Holy Spirit uses the preaching of the Word as a means or instrument to regenerate the soul. Though this sounds scriptural, in fact it is not. The word of God distinguishes between the influence of the Spirit and that of the truth. "Regeneration is a creative act" (Berkhof). The truth of the gospel has a moral impact, but only the Holy Spirit acting directly on the human soul can create life. According to Scripture, the regenerating grace of the Spirit is necessary before a soul is capable of receiving the truth of the Word unto salvation (Acts 16:14; John 6:64, 65).

To sum up: God employs a *creative* word in the act of regeneration. In bringing a soul to conscious decision and faith He uses the *preached* word (Rom. 10:17; 1 Peter 1:23), but the initial creation of life is due only to the direct operation of the Spirit without the use of means (2 Cor. 4:6).

MEDIATOR

Greek *mesites,* from *mesos,* "middle," and *eime,* "to go"; one who goes between differing or contending parties to reconcile them and who represents each part to the other.

Need for a Mediator

The need for a mediator between God and men arises from the fallen state of man: he is now a rebel whose sin against His Creator has brought him under divine condemnation, he has no recuperative power within him, and he cannot expiate his guilt or reverse his depravity. Without a mediator who has the power to address these deep needs, every man must perish. This is the bitter realization Job expressed when he lamented, "Neither is there any daysman betwixt us, that might lay his hand upon us both" (Job 9:33).

In human affairs the work of a mediator usually involves working out a compromise by inducing each party to modify its original position. In the case of the mediator between God and men there can be no place for negotiation or compromise, for the claims of God over sinful men are absolute. In this case the mediator must completely vindicate and satisfy God and yet justify sinners.

Such a work demands a unique person. Thus in Scripture the title of mediator is given only to Christ (1 Tim. 2:5). Some think Gal. 3:19, 20 names Moses as the mediator under the law, but that is a mistake. It is better to see it as a statement that Christ is the one and only mediator between God and men both under the law and the promise. The use of the definite article in the Greek text of v. 20 supports this view. Moses and Aaron in some ways pictured the work of Christ the mediator, but He alone has the title and the position.

A mediator intervenes between two parties and must be acceptable to both and capable of fully representing both.

The mediator between God and men, therefore, must be a theanthropic person,* "God and man in two distinct natures and one person forever" (*Shorter Catechism,* Q. 21). As such He is capable of being God's representative to man and man's representative to God. He is the "daysman" (Job 9:33), or umpire, the efficient peacemaker who brings men nigh to God. He does this by rendering satisfaction to God as the substitute of His people.

All contact between God and men is through this mediator. God deals with men only through Him (Heb. 1:1-3; John 1:18;

Matt. 11:27). Men can come to God only through Him (John 14:6; Acts 4:12).

Offices of Christ the Mediator

In His office of mediator, Christ discharges three functions: prophet, priest, and king (see *Shorter Catechism,* Q. 24-26).

As prophet, by His word and Spirit, He reveals to us the will of God for our salvation *(see **Prophetic Office of Christ**).*

As priest, Christ once offered Himself as a sacrifice to satisfy divine justice and reconcile us to God, and now makes continual intercession for us *(see **Priestly Office of Christ**).*

As king, Christ subdues us to Himself, rules and defends us, and restrains and conquers all His and our enemies *(see **Kingly Office of Christ**).*

The Lord Jesus discharged the functions of a mediator both in His humiliation and His exaltation (see *Westminster Confession of Faith,* chap. 8, sec. 3, 4).

The Work of Christ the Mediator

When we say that Christ discharged the office of a mediator we mean that "Christ, in the work of mediation, acteth according to both natures; by each nature doing that which is proper to itself; yet by reason of the unity of the person, that which is proper to one nature is sometimes in Scripture attributed to the person denominated by the other nature" (*Confession* chap. 8, sec. 7). We may summarize Christ's mediatorial functions:

His Work for Saints:

1. As the daysman (Job 9:33). The word properly signifies one to argue or reprove. By His Spirit accompanying the law, He makes us see that God is righteous and we are the offending party (Job 33:23).

2. As the messenger, or angel, of the covenant* (Mal. 3:1), He comes with God's good news, offering peace to men (Isa. 61:1, 2), and reports our obedience and acceptance to the Father (John 17:14, 25).

3. As our surety, He pays a ransom for us, His own life (Matt. 20:28).

4. As an advocate and friend, He pleads and intercedes for us (1 John 2:1).

5. As our king, He rules us in grace, preserving us as loyal subjects and saints (Col. 3:3; John 10:28).

6. As the bridegroom, He will present us as a holy, chaste virgin in the marriage day, without spot or sin (Eph. 5:27).

Thus, Christ our mediator, as our representative, entered eternally into a covenant of peace with God; then came to earth to be born under the law, and to ratify and seal the everlasting covenant with His own blood, so as to purchase for us all the blessings contained in that covenant. Having shed His blood for us, He now lives to intercede for us and to bring us safely home to glory.

His Work Toward Sinners. As mediator, Christ not only administers the saving provisions of the covenant of grace *(see **Covenant Theology)** to God's elect, but He administers divine judgment to the wicked. At His return he will judge both men and angels (Acts 10:42; 2 Pet. 2:4), a fact solemnly emphasized in the phrase "the wrath of the Lamb" (Rev. 6:16).

MENNONITES

A part of the Anabaptist* movement, named after Dutch Anabaptist* Menno Simons (*circa* 1496-1561). There are still sizeable Mennonite communities in the Netherlands, United States, and Canada. They seem to have little or no common theology, except their opposition to infant baptism and their adherence to pacifism.

MERCY OF GOD

*See under **Goodness of God**.*

MERIT

Properly, the intrinsic value or dignity of a work or service, on account of which it justly deserves a reward from God. Unfortunately, some early fathers used the term very loosely to indicate that which received a reward, without any reference to the ground, or virtue, upon which the reward was conferred. In time this led to the whole monstrous system of Rome's doctrine of merit, which really amounts to salvation by works.

Roman Catholic theologians distinguish between (1) the merit of congruity and (2) the merit of condignity.*

By the first of these they mean that it is "congruous," or fitting, that God should reward those good dispositions which they suppose an unregenerate man can produce without the aid of divine grace. The reward which it is fitting for God to confer is the infusion of grace into the heart.

The merit of condignity is that merit belonging only to the works of the regenerate and produced by the aid of divine grace, which in and of itself (as distinct from mere covenant or promise) deserves God's reward. While there has always been a great deal of disagreement among Romish writers on this point, it is clear that there is a broad agreement on salvation by works. In its mildest form, the Romish position is that through the sacraments, grace is infused into the sinner's heart for Christ's sake and that his subsequent good works merit, or lay a foundation for a just claim to salvation (see **Opus Operatum).**

Indeed, Rome's teaching is that not only can a man so work as to merit salvation, but he can do much more. He can lay up a store of merit which then becomes available to needy souls. Such works in excess of what is needful for personal salvation are called *works of supererogation.** Only a few—the "saints"—are said to have attained to this perfection, and their excess merit is mediated by the pope.

This was the notion that lay behind the promotion of papal indulgences,* which so aroused Luther, and led to the Protestant Reformation. Luther saw this connection, which others missed: he opposed not merely the immoral exercise of the sale of indulgences, giving licence to sin, but the entire pernicious doctrine of merit upon which indulgences were founded.

In Protestant theology, merit is always and only attributed to the obedience of Christ since it alone has the power to procure divine favour.

METAPHYSICS

Greek *meta,* "after," *phusis,* "nature"; the branch of philosophy that seeks to discover or establish, by means of reason, a general theory of the universe and man's place in it. It tries to describe and understand the structure of human thought in its most basic concepts and bring it into a rational system. It explores the meaning of the deepest ideas of the mind, such as existence, essence, truth, reality, time, causation, and ultimately God. It takes its name from the book Aristotle wrote on the subject: he wrote it after his book on physics, hence *meta physics.*

Metaphysics relies either on an *a priori,** or a transcendental,* approach and has been largely dismissed by empiricists. In so far as it proceeds on *a priori* principles, it is an exercise in rationalism.* When it depends on transcendental communications of truth, it is open to even worse abuse. Both approaches are speculative but the latter is closely associated with such pursuits as theosophy,* spiritism,* and the New Age* movement.

The endless theorizing of metaphysicians shows that the fundamental thoughts that engage the human mind are incomprehensible apart from an objective divine revelation. Apart from Scripture man cannot know God, or the truth about the universe and his own place in it. Metaphysical speculation leaves him as much in the dark as when he began.

Empiricism* does not supply the answers either. The physical data gathered in empirical studies may help define the questions but they cannot supply the ultimate answers. Only God can do that and He has done so in the objective revelation of His word, both inscripturated and incarnate.

METEMPSYCHOSIS

Reincarnation, a theory which is totally alien to the word of God. See Hebrews 9:27. See *Pre-existence of Souls*.

MILLENNIAL DAWNISM

See *Russellites*.

MILLENNIUM

The one-thousand-year reign of Christ on earth (Rev. 20:2-7).

Differing Views of the Millennium

Premillennialists place the coming of Christ before the millennium, which they see as the personal reign of Christ on the earth. In the very early church premillennialism, then known as *chiliasm,* was widely accepted. In the Middle Ages, chiliasm was rejected as heretical and this may have been why Luther dismissed it as "the dream" of Christ reigning on earth.

Postmillennialism places the coming of Christ after the millennium, which it conceives as a spiritual presence of Christ working in and through His church to give a golden age, a period of unexampled prosperity in its ministry.

Amillennialism denies the reality of a thousand-year reign, either in the sense in which the premillennialist or the postmillennialist conceives it. The theory rests upon a totally symbolic interpretation of Rev. 20:2-7 and the same type of treatment of the "millennial" passages of the OT. Most present-day amillennialists view these as descriptions of the blessedness the church now experiences. Millennialism, whether pre- or post-, recognizes the 1,000 years of Rev. 20:2-7 as a real indication of time. W. W. Milligan, an amillennialist, writes: "The thousand years mentioned in the passage express no period of time."

Criticism of Each Millennial Position

Amillennialist Position. If a sixfold reference to one thousand years expresses no period of time, what language could be employed to express a period of a thousand years? The presumption must be that the thousand years means just that, at least until it is shown that the passage cannot bear that meaning and must bear a symbolical meaning. It is just on this point that millennialists allege that amillennialists signally fail, for their suggested symbolical interpretations of Rev. 20 are far-fetched and unconvincing.

Postmillennialist Position. Postmillennialism posits a great spiritual improvement right across the world before Christ comes, followed by a brief period of fierce satanic activity. This hardly coincides with the Scripture representations concerning the days preceding Christ's return. Especially, it seems incompatible with the order of events as set forth in Daniel 2—the destruction of the final form of Gentile government followed by the worldwide dominance of the kingdom of God (Dan. 2:34, 35, 43, 44). This same passage also seems to militate against amillennialism, since it speaks of a future kingdom upon the earth, after the final destruction of Gentile power.

Premillennial Position. It is unfortunate that in modern times, premillennialism has become almost synonymous with dispensationalism.* While it is true that dispensationalists are premillennial, premillennialism does not necessarily lead to dispensationalism, with such ideas as the pre-tribulation secret rapture,* and the exclusion of OT believers and future Jewish believers from the covenant blessings and relationship enjoyed by the church. There are valid arguments against such theories, but they do not directly impinge on the doctrine of the millennium.

This is not to say that there are no difficulties involved in the doctrine of an actual millennial reign. The allocation of some portions of the OT to the millennium for their ultimate fulfillment, which premillennialists hold to be their only valid interpretation, raises the thorny problem of alleged references to animal sacrifices in the millennium.

Animal Sacrifices in the Millennium? Premillennialists usually say that such sacrifices will be commemorative of Christ's atonement, as the Lord's Supper* now is. This is a weak response to what every premillennialist recognizes as the strongest challenge to his entire position. Premillennialism would be better served by an unconditional acceptance of the plain teaching of the book of Hebrews that there can be no return to animal sacrifices. It should see that Ezek. 40-48 is not millennial. The temple described is clearly more than something merely ideal, as the amillennialist and postmillennialist hold. Spiritualizing these chapters may produce some sweet devotional applications but it is a very inadequate method of interpretation. If Ezekiel, with his wealth of minute details about the temple he describes, does not describe a real building, words mean nothing.

However, this building may be real without being millennial. Internal evidence leads to the conclusion that God was holding out to the Jews of the exile the promise of a glorious temple in Jerusalem, on condition of their repentance and devotion to Him. They did not fulfil the condition and so did not receive the fulfilment of the promise.

The evidence for this view is as follows:
1. Ezekiel records that the temple he described was promised to the Jews of the Restoration on condition of repentance (43:9-11. Note the *if* in v. 11). Zechariah 6:15 makes the same stipulation and adds, "This shall come to pass, if ye will diligently obey the voice of the Lord your God."
2. The temple was to be erected in Ezekiel's lifetime (43:19-25).
3. The sacrifices associated with this temple were purely OT sacrifices and plainly refer to the period before Calvary (43:17-19).
4. Circumcision is given as a condition for entrance to this temple. The NT makes it clear that circumcision has no sacramental place in the administration of the covenant of grace after Calvary (44:7; cf. Acts 15; Rom. 2:28, 29; Gal. 5:6; 6:15). A return to circumcision would violate the principle Paul set forth in Gal. 2:18: "If I build again the things which I destroyed, I make myself a transgressor."
5. Ezekiel speaks of "the prince" who offers animal sacrifices for himself and for his people (45:17-46:4). If the passage is millennial this prince would have to be Christ. But will *He* offer animal sacrifices? Will He offer animal sacrifices *for Himself?*
6. Ezekiel's prince has sons to whom he gives gifts (46:16). This could not refer to Christ.
7. God warned the prince of whom Ezekiel spoke not to steal from the people by oppression (46:18). This can have no application to Christ or any other millennial ruler in Jerusalem.

These are plain considerations that lead us to see Ezekiel's description as that of a real temple conditionally promised for the time of the return of the exiles from Babylon. Just as God gave Moses the details of the tabernacle and its sacrifices to encourage the Israelites before their entrance into Canaan, He gave Ezekiel the details of the temple and its sacrifices to encourage them before their restoration to the land.

If Ezekiel's temple was part of God's conditional promise to the returning exiles, the glorious changes in the land described in chapter 47 must be additional aspects of the same promise. The parallels between parts of the *Revelation* and Ezekiel's language do not invalidate this position. Revelation 22 adapts the language of Ezekiel 47, but that does not make the Ezekiel passage millennial.

Old Testament millennial references to animal sacrifices in such passages as Zech. 14:16-21 may be taken as prophetic descriptions of actual events in the only language the prophet's contemporaries could understand. Thus the reference to animal sacrifices must be interpreted to mean the spiritual truth signified by those sacrifices, not to the reintroduction of the OT sacrificial system in the millennium.

Toleration in Holding Millennial Views

All three approaches to the subject of the millennium have their problems. The difficulties of fully understanding the Scripture within the system laid down by pre-, post, or a- millennialism should lead us to hold our views in humility and with due love and regard for the equally sincerely held views of differing brethren.

MINIMALISM

1. The approach to historical or theological study that attributes the least meaning or significance to a belief, position, or pronouncement.
2. The views of a school of radical historical critics who refuse to receive the historicity of the people and events mentioned in Scripture without corroborative evidence from contemporary sources, brought to light by historical and archaeological research. Without such evidence, these minimalists hold that the Bible is all but useless as an historical source. In common with many modern historians and archaeologists, they entirely reject the history of the patriarchs and of Israel's exodus from Egypt and conquest of Canaan. They go even further than other critics, however, in rejecting David and Solomon as historical characters. According to this school, the OT histories were produced between the 5th and 2nd centuries B.C. The tiny historical fragments that may be in the OT lie buried under unhistorical traditions that the late writers— i.e., 400-200 B.C.— of Scripture placed in fictitious historical settings. Thus, to minimalists, the Bible is a window into the intellectual and literary period in which it was produced, but not into the world of the periods its histories describe.

MINISTER, MINISTRY

The original meaning of *minister* carries the thought of service. To be a minister is to be in a place of responsibility, but not to be a "lord over God's heritage" (1 Pet. 5:3).

Eph. 4:11, 12 says: "He gave some, apostles; and some, prophets; and some, evangelists; and some, pastors and teachers; for (*pros*, 'with a view to') the perfecting of the saints, for (*eis*, 'in order to') the work of the ministry, for (*eis*) the edifying of the body of Christ." From this passage it is clear that in its widest sense, ministry is the service of the whole church: the saints are perfected in order to do the work of the ministry.

Yet there is a more restricted sense in which *minister* is used. In 1 Tim. 4:6 a good minister is evidently one, like Timothy, set apart to a particular work and place of leadership in the church. To perform this ministry, the apostles ordained elders in every church (Acts 14:23). Paul spoke to Timothy (1 Tim. 5:17) of elders who rule, and elders who labour in the Word and doctrine. In Acts 20:28 he told the Ephesian elders that they were God-appointed bishops. Peter (1 Pet. 5:1-3) speaks to the elders as those who have the bishopric (oversight) over the flock of God, and who have the task of feeding the flock.

Such are the two significations of minister and ministry. Together they form a defence against two extreme views: first, they oppose the Romish notion which makes the church synonymous with, or at least subservient to, the hierarchy; second, they oppose the view which does away with a God-ordained ministry in the church.

The Protestant, and Scriptural, view of the ministry is set out in the *Westminster Confession of Faith:* "Unto this catholic visible Church Christ hath given the ministry, oracles, and ordinances of God for the gathering and perfecting of the saints in this life to the end of the world" (chap. 25, sec. 3).

This makes the ministry a means to the end of edifying the church. Romanism, on the other hand, makes the ministry the end and the church the means. This is a vital point. Much controversy has raged around what constitutes a valid ministry. Rome holds that where there is no valid ministry there can be no church, even where there is a company of professing Christians. A valid ministry, in Rome's sense, means one conferred by bishops, supposedly standing in direct succession to the apostles; thus, without the hierarchy, there can be no church.

The Protestant position is that before any discussion takes place on the validity of a ministry, the first inquiry should be whether or not a company of professing Christians is a true church, in the scriptural sense. What determines the answer here is the presence or absence of the scriptural notes of a true church.* If a company of professing Christians bears the marks of a true church, it may have a valid ministry. In the regular way, this is by "the laying on of hands of the presbytery," i.e., by ordination by those who have themselves been previously ordained to the ministry. However, if in the providence of God, a true church of Christ is placed in such a position that a regular ministry is impossible, that church is entitled to appoint a minister possessed of the Scriptural qualifications, and his appointment to the ministry, though not regular, is nonetheless valid.

MIRACLE

Miracle is a mode of God's special revelation. It has been defined as "an observable phenomenon effected by the direct operation of God's power, an arresting deviation from the ordinary sequence of nature, a deviation calculated to beget faith-begetting awe, a divine inbreaking which authenticates a revelational agent" (*Baker's Dictionary of Theology*).

Cornelius Van Til says, "By miracle God actually reveals His redeeming work in process of fulfillment. Sin brought every sphere of human life in subjection to misery and death; by miracle God brings all these spheres

of life back to health. Through the central miracle of the person and work of Christ the human soul is brought into favour with the living God. Hence in performing His miracles Christ constantly points out that they are symbolical of what He came to do for the souls of men" (*An Introduction to Systematic Theology,* Class Syllabus, p. 135).

This view of miracle does two important things. First, it makes clear the great essential difference between the miracles of Scripture and the fables of Rome. Scripture miracles are no mere arbitrary demonstrations of power; they are the outworking of God's gracious revelation. Second, it answers the common objection against the possibility of miracle, that it constitutes a "violation of the laws of nature," as the celebrated sceptic David Hume put it. The "laws of nature" are merely the way things normally occur in a world ruined by the entrance of sin. Miracle is God in grace fulfilling His purpose to undo the curse of sin. It is sin which is truly abnormal, not the operations of divine grace.

It should be kept in mind that true miracle reveals the redemptive purpose of God. Not all exercise of supernatural power is an evidence of divine operation or proof that the human agent is divinely appointed (Deut. 13:1-4; Rev. 13:15, etc.).

A true miracle will tally with all that the Scripture says of all the modes of special revelation, namely, theophany,* prophecy,* and miracle.

MISHNAH

A collection of ancient oral Hebrew traditions compiled by Rabbi Judah Ha-Nasi (A.D. 135-220). These traditions deal with detailed interpretations and applications of matters dealt with only in principle in the law.

*See **Talmud**.*

MISSAL

In Roman Catholicism, a book that contains all the mass* prayers and readings for a three-year Sunday cycle and a two-year weekday cycle.

MODALISM

Sabellianism,* the view of the Trinity* that denies personal distinctions in the Godhead and makes Father, Son, and Holy Spirit to be three modes of operation of the same divine person, as creation, redemption, and sanctification.

MODERATISM

Moderate was a title claimed by a section of churchmen following the Revolution Settlement of 1689, a settlement that brought the hope of peace and religious liberty to Britain, but especially to the much persecuted Covenanters of Scotland. *Moderate* churchmen welcomed the change in official policy and accepted the legitimacy of the government and the state church of Scotland, in contrast to the Cameronians* who continued to advocate a strict adherence to the terms of the National Covenant of 1638.

However, *moderate* came to be a name of ill repute and reproach among Bible believing Christians. Moderates were "broad churchmen"; that is, they found it easy to conform with the encroachments of the state upon the affairs of the church; they were indifferent to matters of church government (e.g., in Scotland, those who had conformed to the tyranny of prelacy* while the Covenanters suffered, found that they could settle into the reinstated Presbyterian mould with equal ease); they deprecated all interest in "high" doctrine, such as the covenant of grace *(see Covenant Theology),* the Trinity,* the incarnation,* etc.; they reduced the gospel to a cold, lifeless ethical system. They were the compromisers of their day, with love for atheists and deists (not a love that sought to win them, but which settled comfortably with them) but with only a bitter hatred for earnest preachers of the gospel of grace. Archbishop

Tillotson, upon whom George Whitefield passed severe strictures, was the acknowledged star of Moderatism.

Of course, this full-blown Moderatism, (which propounded such heresies as salvation by works, Pelagianism,* universalism,* naturalism, and human reason as the final arbiter in all matters of faith—*see Rationalism)* did not come about all at once. It commenced as a mediating tendency, an indifference to important issues. It proceeded to laxity on matters of doctrine. It embraced the Neonomian* error on justification, which it further worked into a thoroughgoing doctrine of works. It came finally to stand, not for Bible Christianity or anything remotely like it, but for what was "practical." It detested anything which could be looked upon as "enthusiasm," and for this reason, bitterly opposed the evangelical awakening under the ministry of Whitefield and Wesley.

In Scotland, it ranged itself against the Marrowmen *(see Marrow)* and having gained a stranglehold on the courts of the church, so pandered to state control as to force one secession by those who formed the Associate Presbytery; and another by those who became known as the Relief Synod; and finally the disruption of 1843 when Moderate weakness in the face of state tyranny led to the formation of the Free Church of Scotland. Dr. Macleod, in *Scottish Theology,* (p. 204), says: "In more modern speech it [Moderatism] would be described as realist or as ethical or as a species of social regeneration teaching, whose supreme concern was in a pragmatic fashion with tangible results in the region of the conventions of neighbourly life."

The name "Moderate" has again been claimed in recent times by the modern successors of these opponents of God's truth. They bear the same features, they share the same follies, and they produce the same blighting results.

MODERNISM
See Liberalism.

MONARCHIANISM

The name coined by Tertullian to describe a heresy which, though supposedly protecting the unity of the Godhead, actually departed from the revealed truth of Scripture. Monarchianism was of two kinds:

1. *Dynamic Monarchianism* denied the divine personality of the *Logos,* making it a mere power residing in God, as reason resides in man. This impersonal power, though present in all men, specially operated in the man Jesus and finally deified Him. In denying the personality of the Logos, and in making Him and the Holy Spirit mere impersonal attributes of God, Dynamic Monarchianism laid the ground for the later heresies of Socianism* and unitarianism.*

2. *Modalistic Monarchianism.* The view that Father, Son, and Holy Spirit are merely different names for the same divine person, three modes in which God manifested Himself. This heresy, while maintaining the true divinity of Christ, denied the existence of the ontological Trinity.* It was widely known by two other names. In the West it was known as patripassianism,* since it taught that the Father had become incarnate in Christ and had suffered. In the East it was known as Sabellianism,* after Sabellius, one of its leading exponents.

The important thing to note is that it made the Father, Son, and Holy Ghost merely three different modes of revelation and operation of the one divine person.

While dynamic monarchianism survives, at least in part, in modern unitarianism, modalistic monarchianism also survives in some "oneness" sects.

MONERGISM

The doctrine that regeneration* is the work of God unaided by human effort or cooperation.

MONISM

The philosophical belief that the nature of all things is one. In religion it is equivalent to pantheism.* It may be distinguished from pantheism in that whereas it sees all reality as a unified whole, pantheism sees that whole reality as God.

MONOLATRY

The worship of a single deity. It differs from monotheism* in that while it is the worship of a single god it recognizes the existence of other gods.

MONOPHYSITISM

A fifth-century heresy concerning the person of Christ. Monophysites denied that Christ had two distinct natures. They held Him to have but one composite nature.
See Monothelitism; Eutychianism.

MONOTHEISM

The belief that there is but one God. Christian-biblical monotheism teaches that the one true God subsists eternally as Father, Son, and Holy Ghost; the doctrine of Trinity in unity.

MONOTHELITISM

Monothelites were Monophysites who particularly opposed the idea, not only of two natures in Christ, but of two wills in Christ. They held that He had but one nature and one will—some holding that a fusion of the divine and human will occurred to form a third kind of will which then existed alone in Christ, and others holding that the human will was merely absorbed into the divine, so that the latter acted alone.

The Council of Constantinople in 680 laid down the accepted Biblical position: Christ has two natures, and therefore two wills, divine and human. The human is always subordinate to, and in total harmony with, the divine. By its union with the divine will, the human did not cease to be human, but was so exalted as to be always in harmony with the divine.

MONTANISM

About the year A.D. 150 Montanus (of Phrygia in the Roman province of Asia Minor, modern Turkey) with two women, Prisca and Maximilla, set themselves forth as prophets. They were generally orthodox, but believed they had received divine revelations, intimating that the age of the Paraclete had come and that the end of the world was at hand. They also practised a very legalistic asceticism. Their chief failures were their dependence on charismatic gifts, even elevating these over the inspired Scriptures of the NT, and their false prophecies of the imminent end of the world. In some particulars they bear a striking resemblance to elements in the modern Charismatic movement*—not least in the preponderance of women as the possessors of supernatural endowments.

MORAL ARGUMENT FOR GOD'S EXISTENCE

See *Arguments for God's Existence*.

MORAL INFLUENCE THEORY OF THE ATONEMENT

A false theory, first advocated by Abelard (1079-1142), the father of theological rationalism,* in opposition to Anselm (1033-1109), which in reality is not a theory of the atonement* at all, denying, as it does, the very existence of atonement. It is based on the belief that there is nothing in God which necessitates satisfaction for sin. Thus the death of Christ did not satisfy divine justice and was not an expiation for sin. Rather it merely manifested God's love, as He suffered in and with His sinful creatures. According to this theory God is eager to pardon every sinner, without any satisfaction, the only condition being that sinners come to Him with penitent hearts. Clearly such a theory finds no support in Scripture. The death of Christ, truly the supreme manifestation of God's love, is always connected with the thought of a propitiatory sacrifice. This theory allows no real connection between the death of Christ and the salvation of sinners, and therefore fails to do justice to the great Scripture statements of Christ giving "His life a ransom"; of Christ "making peace through the blood of his cross"; and of sinners being "justified by His blood," or "justified freely by God's grace through the redemption that is in Christ Jesus."

MORAL REARMAMENT

A group founded by American Lutheran minister, Frank Buchman, for the purpose of world reform. Buchman was an American Lutheran evangelical who specialized in student evangelism. He worked at Cambridge but transferred to Oxford, where in 1929 he formed the Oxford Group* which in 1938 became Moral Rearmament. It was not an exclusively Christian group but welcomed all of whatever religious background who wished to change society on the basis of Moral Rearmament's four absolutes: absolute purity, absolute unselfishness, absolute honesty, and absolute love. A major means of getting the movement's message to the common people was the use of films and plays. Buchman claimed that the ideals of Moral Rearmament were those of Christianity; however, his theory that he could reform the world to Christian standards apart from Christian doctrine, especially the doctrine of salvation from sin by the merit of Christ's atonement, was doomed to failure.

MORAVIANS

A movement, famed for its pietism* and missionary zeal, which grew out of a branch of the Hussites, upholders of the principles for which John Huss was martyred. This branch was known as the Bohemian Brethren from pre-Reformation times. They were continually persecuted, but in 1722, they created a settlement on land donated by Count Zinzendorf to become the Moravians.

Moravian practices had a large impact on the Methodist revivals under Whitefield and Wesley, and indeed, it was through hearing the Moravian Peter Bohler read Luther's *Preface to the Epistle to the Romans* that John Wesley came to know Christ as Saviour.

MORMONISM

The cult organized by Joseph Smith under the title "Church of Jesus Christ of Latter-Day Saints," at Fayette, New York, in 1830. Smith claimed that the angel Moroni visited him, and that with the aid of Urim and Thummim he translated the golden plates which contained the history of early America "in reformed Egyptian characters." The plates were supposedly hidden from the year A.D. 420 until Smith found them on September 22, 1823. The translation was called *The Book of Mormon*. Hidden since the year 420, it has extensive quotations from the King James Version of the Bible, which dates from 1611! It contains expressions and ideas which are exclusively modern, and "its story of the ancient inhabitants of America, the supposed ancestors of the 'Latter-Day Saints,' contains twelve historical errors" (Van Baalen, *The Chaos of Cults,* p. 152). This garbled production is regarded by Mormons as equal in authority to the Bible. The real origin of the Book of Mormon is far less glamorous than the Mormon tale:

"There is an abundance of incontestable evidence that the origin of the Book of Mormon must be sought in Solomon Spaulding's unpublished and stolen novel, *The Manuscript Found.* The Mormons try to obliterate this evidence by referring to another manuscript, *The Manuscript Story,* by the same Spaulding; they prove that the Book of Mormon is not a copy of the latter manuscript. The unknowing are thus convinced that Joseph Smith did not copy from 'the Spaulding manuscript'; but the real argument, that the 'Golden Bible' is the work of copying and embellishing by Rigdon and Smith, remains unanswered" (Van Baalen, p. 152).

Joseph Smith, the prophet of Mormonism, died when an angry crowd stormed the gaol where he was being kept on charges of gross immorality, counterfeiting, and sheltering criminals.

Brigham Young succeeded him, to lead the majority faction, while a minority followed Smith's son. Young had enjoyed a total of eleven days of formal schooling, and with the tenacity of an uneducated mind he held to the story of Joseph Smith, remaining true to the "prophet" to the end. Young led his Mormons to Utah, where they could then practice polygamy freely, while Smith, Jr., and his followers went to Missouri. These factions disputed bitterly, mostly about polygamy, which the Missouri Mormons wanted to blame on Young. The truth is, however, that Mormonism from the first taught polygamy, and Joseph Smith himself had forty-eight wives. The best evidence against Mormonism is itself. Here are some of its teachings, which stand self-condemned as anti-Christian.

1. *The Fatherhood of God.* "When our father Adam came into the garden of Eden, he came into it with a celestial body, and brought Eve, one of his wives, with him.... He is our father and our God, and the only God with whom we have to do" (Brigham Young, *Journal of Discourses,* 1:50).

2. *God's Unity.* "The passages are numerous in the inspired writings which indicate a plurality of God" (F. D. Richards, *Compendium,* p. 170). "And they (the Gods) said: Let there be light and there was light. And they (the Gods) comprehended the light...and they divided the light." (Joseph Smith, *The Pearl of Great Price,* p. 67)

"Each of these Gods, including Jesus Christ and His Father, being in possession of not merely an organized spirit, but a glorious body of flesh and bones, is subject to the laws which govern, of necessity, even the most refined order of physical existence." (Parley Pratt, *Key to the Science of Theology,* p. 42).

3. *God's Trinity.* "The Father has a body of flesh and bones as tangible as man's; the Son also; but the Holy Ghost has not a body of flesh and bones but is a personage of spirit....Were it not so, the Holy Ghost could not dwell in us. A man may receive the Holy Ghost, and it may descend upon him, and not tarry with him" (Joseph Smith, *Doctrine and Covenants,* p. 462).

4. *Polygamy.* "Jesus Christ was a polygamist; Mary and Martha, the sisters of Lazarus, were his plural wives, and Mary Magdalene was another. Also, the bridal feast of Cana of Galilee, where Jesus turned the water into wine, was on the occasion of one of his own marriages" (Brigham Young, quoted in *Wife No. 19,* chap. 34, by Ann Eliza Young).

"We say it was Jesus Christ who was married (at Cana, to Martha and Mary), whereby he could see his own seed before he was crucified. The reference is to Isaiah 53:10" (Orson Hyde, cf. *The True Origin of Mormon Polygamy,* by C. A. Shook, p. 207).

5. *Virgin Birth.* "When the Virgin Mary conceived the child Jesus, the Father had begotten him in his own likeness. He was NOT begotten by the Holy Ghost. And who was the Father? He was the first of the human family....Jesus, our elder brother, was begotten in the flesh by the same character that was in the garden of Eden, and who is our Father in Heaven" (Brigham Young, *Journal of Discourses,* 1:50).

6. *Justification.* "The sectarian dogma of justification by faith alone has exercised an influence for evil since the early days of Christianity" (James E. Talmadge, *The Articles of Faith,* p. 120).

"Abraham received concubines and they bare him children, and it was accounted unto him for righteousness. Go ye therefore and do the works of Abraham, enter ye into my law, and ye shall be saved. But if ye enter not into my law (of polygamy), ye cannot receive the promise of my Father, which he made unto Abraham" (Joseph Smith, *Celestial Marriage,* par. 12, 14).

"Now, that the blessing of redemption from individual sins, while free for all to attain, is nevertheless conditioned on individual effort, is as plainly declared as is the truth of unconditional redemption from the effects of the Fall" (James E. Talmadge, p. 42).

Much more could be added to illustrate Mormon heresy on such subjects as sin, inspiration, etc., but these excerpts are sufficient to demonstrate the innate anti-Christianity of the system.

MORTAL SIN

The Church of Rome distinguishes between mortal sin and venial sin.* Mortal sin is said to be any great offence against the law of God or of the church, and is so named because it is considered to be deadly to the soul, leading to eternal hell. According to Rome, it may be pardoned upon confession, though an indefinite amount of punishment in purgatory* is needed to expiate it. Thus, to die in mortal sin is to go straight to hell, where no alleviation of suffering can be obtained through prayers and masses. The soul dying in mortal sin is deprived of all sanctifying grace and is irremediably lost. But those guilty of mortal sin can have pardon if in life they confess it and obtain absolution from a priest. In this way, and by the grace inherent in the sacraments of baptism and penance *(see **Opus Operatum**),* the eternal punishment due to mortal sin is cancelled. The temporal punishment of purgatory remains, though this may be reduced in duration by penance,* paying for masses, almsgiving, indulgence, etc.

Venial sin is said to be a small and pardonable offence against God or our neighbour. Being comparatively light sins, they do not need to be confessed, but can be expiated by good works, prayers, extreme unction,* and the sufferings of purgatory.

Needless to say, the whole elaborate distinction, with its attendant fallacies of auricular confessions, human merit, priestly pardons, and purgatorial expiation, is without any base at all in Scripture.

MSS

Manuscripts. The extant Greek MSS of the NT, of which there is an abundant supply—more than 5,000 in all—represent different kinds of material, different styles of writing, and different periods of copying.

Some were written on papyrus, a material used from very ancient times and made from a kind of sedge. John refers to papyrus in 2 John 12. Some very ancient papyrus fragments of NT portions have been discovered, but papyrus was highly perishable, and the majority of very ancient papyrus copies of the NT have perished.

Parchment—strictly, the skin of very young calves—and vellum—strictly, the skin of sheep or goats—were also used as writing material. The two words are usually employed interchangeably, but generally vellum belongs to the oldest MSS while parchment was used for later ones. Codices Aleph, Vaticanus, *Alexandrinus,* and *Claromontanus* are on vellum of the finest quality. *Aleph* is of antelope skin and the leaves are so large that a single animal's skin would provide only two leaves. Some of these skins were reused, but the strokes of the original writing are usually still discernible. Such MSS are called *palimpsests* or *codices rescripti.*

Style varied in different centuries, a fact which enables scholars to ascribe an accurate age to a MS. Some MSS were written in uncials, i.e., capital letters formed separately and, in the earlier specimens, without any space between words. Uncial MSS date from the fourth to the tenth centuries. Other MSS were written in cursive letters, or the "running hand" of small letters joined together to form separate words, with a complete system of punctuation. The cursive MSS stretched from the ninth or tenth century until the invention of printing.

There are few MSS of the entire NT. The practice was to copy the Gospels in one volume and the Acts and the Epistles in another volume. Since little use was made of Revelation in the public readings of the church, fewer copies were made of it. With all the MS material, there is an abundant supply of witnesses to the original NT text. The vast majority of these agree, clearly witnessing to a Greek text which, as Burgon* ably shows, was the prevalent text in the church from the very earliest times. Variations from this common text are mainly based on a few ancient codices: Codex *Sinaiticus* (*Aleph*—4th century), *Vaticanus* (B—4th century), and to a lesser degree, *Alexandrinus* (A—5th century), *Ephraemi* (C—5th century) and *Bezæ* (D—"the singular codes," a particularly corrupt codex* dated to the 6th century).

The majority text, or traditional text, as it is sometimes called, is the text behind our Authorized Version.

See **Textual Criticism***.*

MURATORIAN CANON

The oldest extant list of NT books, probably from the second century. A fragment of some eighty-five lines, written in Latin, it omits 2 and 3 John, 1 and 2 Peter, and Hebrews, and includes some uncanonical material.

MYSTICAL THEORY OF THE ATONEMENT

An unscriptural theory of the atonement,* which resembles the moral influence theory* in that it denies any work of satisfaction* in the death of Christ. However, it conceives the change effected in man, "not as an ethical change in the conscious life of man, but as a deeper change in the subconscious life which is brought about in a mystical way" (Berkhof).

Proponents of this theory view the incarnation as the divine life entering into the life of humanity with the view of exalting it to the plane of the divine. They view the human nature of Christ as corrupt and disposed to evil, but hold that it was kept from actual sin through the influence of the Holy Spirit. The Holy Spirit gradually purified this corrupt nature, until finally in the death of the cross it was completely purged of its original depravity and reunited with the divine nature. This is looked upon as redemption for human nature generally, since in the incarnation of Christ, the divine life entered the streams of humanity and acted as a transforming leaven.

A theory riddled with falsehood, it impugns the doctrine of the sinlessness of Christ *(see Impeccability of Christ),* pays no attention to man's guilt as distinct from his pollution, and makes no provision for the redemption of those who lived before the time of Christ.

MYSTICAL UNION

"That intimate, vital and spiritual union between Christ and His people, in virtue of which He is the source of their life and strength, of their blessedness and salvation" (Berkhof).

In the terms of the covenant of redemption *(see Covenant Theology),* Christ was appointed the federal head of God's elect, the last Adam (1 Cor. 15:22, 45), the one who, on behalf of His people, assumes all the obligations under the covenant of works, which the first Adam failed to discharge.

In virtue of this federal union, there is a ground for the legal imputation of our guilt to Him and of His righteousness to us, with the resultant forensic benefits to us of justification* and adoption.* Subjectively, or in the experience of the believer, this eternally established union is effected by the Holy Spirit in a supernatural way. Though we often speak of the believer being "united to Christ by faith," this is not to deny the mystical work of the Spirit in effecting the union; it is, rather, merely an acknowledgment of the fact that by the exercise of saving faith, the believer personally receives Christ and enters into the enjoyment of all the benefits of our union with Him.

When we speak of union, or being "in Christ," to use the Scriptural phrase, we should remember that we do not use the term to indicate any confusion of personality between Christ and His people. On the other hand, we mean more than a mere association. The Spirit of Christ dwells in the believer and the believer dwells in Christ, in a union which is, therefore—

1. *Spiritual* (1 Cor. 12:13; 1 John 4:13).

2. *Vital*—i.e., our spiritual life is sustained by the life of Christ through the indwelling Spirit (Gal. 2:20).

3. *Total*—i.e., it includes our entire person, spirit, soul, and body (1 Cor. 6:15, 19).

4. *Federal and legal,* so that all our legal and covenant liabilities rest upon Christ, and all His legal and covenant merit is accrued to us (Rom. 5:12, 18, 19). In other words, by virtue of this union, God treats the believer as He treats Christ (Rom. 8:17).

5. *Eternal*—i.e., it was laid down in the eternal decree of God and it is, in fact, everlasting, being indissoluble (John 10:28; Rom. 8:35-39). A. A. Hodge sums up: "This union is between the believer and the person of the God-man in His office as Mediator. Its immediate organ is the Holy Spirit, who dwells in us, and through Him we are vitally united to and commune with the whole Godhead, since He is the Spirit of the Father as well as of the Son—John 14:23; 17:21, 23."

MYSTICISM

The search for a higher initiation into spiritual mysteries, or a higher consecration to spiritual realities, or a union with deity, by a withdrawal from the external world and by means of contemplation. In this way, mystics profess to apprehend truths which are beyond the understanding. While some have sought to conjoin mysticism and Christianity, the two are mutually exclusive. Christianity is, first and foremost, an *objective* divine revelation through which the Holy Spirit communicates a *subjective* revelation in the souls of God's elect. "Higher consecration" can be experienced only through a progressive sanctification or conformity to Christ, which is a work of God's Spirit, not the product of a course of contemplation.

However, Christian meditation, as distinct from a humanistic or pantheistic type of contemplation, is a sanctifying virtue, too little practised by God's people. "Think on these things" (Phil. 4:8) and "Meditate on these things" (1 Tim. 4:15) are scriptural precepts. To meditate deeply and continuously upon a scriptural theme, in a prayerful spirit, will mortify the flesh, and be a means of sweet communion with the Lord.

MYTH

The proper definition of *myth* is a fiction or a fable, as distinct from what is genuine and true. In this sense the Greek *muthos* is used five times in the NT—1 Tim. 1:4; 4:7; 2 Tim. 4:4; Tit. 1:14; and 2 Peter 1:16.

The term *myth* was used by existential theologian Rudolf Bultmann (1884-1976) in a totally different way. Though he would no doubt have maintained the basic definition, Bultmann claimed that much of what the Bible set forth as historical fact was merely myth. To him, myth in Scripture was anything which could be accepted by modern scientific man. In other words, the entire supernatural element of Scripture had to be rejected as myth. Thus, according to Bultmann, there was no evidence in the Gospels of the historical Jesus.

He set out to *demythologize* the Bible, and by removing those elements which modern man found unacceptable, to render the Kerygma,* or essence of the gospel, credible to him.

This is really the old higher criticism,* only going about the task in a slightly different fashion. Higher criticism, liberalism,* existentialism,* and neo-orthodoxy* all concur in making man the measure of God, man's reason the measure of truth, and man's credence the measure of the content of the

gospel. Such notions put these theories outside the pale of Christianity. Whether men will hear or whether they will forbear, the great appeal of Christianity is "to the law and to the testimony" (Isa. 8:20) with its full and historical revelation. If men find this incredible, it is not because of the untruthfulness of the revelation, it is "because there is no light in them." Bultmann's demythologizing of Scripture is a blind man's denial of the existence of sunlight and his subsequent attempt to pull the sun out of the heavens.

See **Theology of Crisis**; **Quest for the Historical Jesus**.

N

NAMES OF GOD

The names of God in Scripture are divine self-revelations. They are not human attempts to describe Him or evidence of developing Jewish consciousness of Him, as documentary theories* of the OT suggest (see *J.E.D.P.*). Theologians distinguish God's names as follows: proper names, essential names (His attributes), personal names (*Father, Son, Holy Spirit*). Our concern here is with God's proper names, or *nomina propria.*

Proper Names in the Old Testament

El, Elohim. Since these names are not used exclusively of the true God they are not strictly *nomina propria,* and are included among them only to show that they are distinct from the essential names. This double usage exactly parallels our English use of *God* or *god.* As a divine title, *El* signifies the strong one. *Elohim* (a plural word, the singular form of which is *Eloah,* Deut. 32:15, 17) speaks of God as the strong and mighty one, the object of fear. The singular rarely occurs, except in poetry. The plural does not denote a plurality of gods. Some regard it as an indication of the doctrine of the Trinity, while most treat it as a plural of majesty, used to intensify and magnify the ideas of strength and might.

Elyon. This signifies the high and exalted one. The AV translates it as "the Most High" (Gen. 14:18-20), who is "over all the earth" (Ps. 83:18).

Adonai. This plural form with a singular suffix is uniquely a title of the true God. It signifies the supreme master or sovereign, the almighty ruler to whom all are subject. The AV translates it "Lord."

The singular *ha'adon* occurs only infrequently, always as a divine title (an important OT witness to the essential deity of the Messiah, Mal. 3:1).

El-shaddai. This speaks of God as the all-powerful Lord of all creation, the source of comfort and assurance to His people (Gen. 17:1). The AV typically translates it "Almighty God."

Jehovah. This is the incommunicable name, the name of God as the covenant God, the great *I AM* (Exod. 3:14), the absolute and immutable one, who will ever remain faithful in all His covenant engagements. The AV translates it as "LORD."

Jehovah (*Jah* is a contraction used in poetic portions) has no plural form and never takes a suffix. For example, in Ps. 8:1 we have *Jehovah adonenu,* "LORD our Lord," but nowhere do we read of "our" or "my" Jehovah. *Jehovah tsebaoth* means "Lord of Hosts," referring primarily to the angelic hosts. *(See **Tetragram.**)*

Ab, Father. While *Father* is a personal name, it is also a proper name with reference to God as the Creator of all men and, especially, as sustaining a saving covenant relation to all His elect. These He regards as His children. It is popularly thought that *Father* is exclusively a NT description of God, but that is not so (e.g., Deut. 32:6; Ps. 103:13; Isa. 63:16, 64:8). It signifies that God is the Creator and sustainer, caring for and protecting His children.

Proper Names of God in the New Testament

Theos. "God," the NT equivalent to *El* in the OT.

Hupeistos theos. "The most high God" (Mark 5:7), equivalent to *Elyon* in the OT.

Pantokrator, Theos Ho Pantokrator. "The Almighty," or "omnipotent God" (2 Cor. 6:18; Rev. 19:6). It is equivalent to *El-shaddai* in the OT.

Kurios. "Lord." It is used of Christ and of God, and is equivalent to *Adonai* or *Jehovah* in the OT.

Pater, Abba, Father. See *Ab, Father* under OT entries above.

NANTES, EDICT OF

The decree issued by Henry IV of France, April 13, 1598, guaranteeing to his Protestant subjects freedom to worship God according to their conscience and the enjoyment of their civil rights and privileges. It was confirmed in 1610 by Louis XIII and again in 1662 by Louis XIV. Despite these confirmations many of the provisions of the Edict were repealed by ordinances that forbade the profession of the Reformed faith and imposed severe penalties on such profession. Finally, on October 18, 1685, Louis XIV revoked the Edict of Nantes altogether.

The revocation permitted the destruction of Protestant churches, called for the closure of Protestant schools, banned all Protestant worship, public or private, forbade Protestant parents to instruct their children in the Protestant faith but commanded them to rear them in Roman Catholicism, and banished all Protestant pastors from France. Any Protestant attempting to escape from France faced severe penalties: women faced a sentence of life imprisonment and men of servitude in the galleys. Despite the danger, many left France for Britain, Holland, Germany, Switzerland, and America. The loss to France was incalculable both in economic and spiritual terms. Wherever the French Protestants settled they enriched the land of their adoption, particularly Britain where they made a vital contribution to the development of the nation's manufacturing industries.

NATURAL LAW

Moral principles that allegedly exist in the very nature of things, discernible by human reason and self-evidently commended to human conscience, apart from the revelation of Scripture.

Protestant View of Natural Law

Richard Baxter defined natural law as "objectively, that signification of God's will concerning man's duty, which was discernible in the universal nature of things in all God's works; but principally in man's own nature, as related to God and all persons, and things about him" (*End of Doctrinal Controversies,* p. 113). Baxter draws a distinction between this objective law and man's subjective knowledge or interpretations of it. In other words, these subjective interpretations of natural law, even when collected and systematized by a society of people, cannot be termed natural law. They are not law but subjective reflections upon law, and they may be more or less right or wrong.

To put this another way, God has written His law on men's hearts. He has implanted within their very constitution an acknowledgment of right and wrong, i.e., He has given them a moral nature. He holds them responsible to Him for what they do with the revelation around them and within them. But sinful man naturally perverts that revelation. All men recognize a distinction between right and wrong, but determining what is right and what is wrong is an entirely different matter. There is no natural standard common to all men for making that judgment. In some societies monogamy is "natural," in others polygamy. In some cultures theft and even murder are accepted as natural. Some societies are patriarchal and some matriarchal. Some, like ancient Sparta, naturally glorify courage but encourage lying and deceit, and make the discovery of a crime a greater evil than the crime itself.

Depraved men have perverted the law in their hearts almost endlessly. That is why man's reflections on the law of nature are not themselves a law but must be brought to an objective standard by which they must be judged. That standard cannot in the very nature of the case be the nonverbal natural law of which those reflections are divergent interpretations. In the final analysis, all we can authoritatively say about God's natural law is what He has told us about it in His Biblical revelation.

This distinction between the objective law of nature and man's subjective view of it is important.

First, the Scriptures are clear that God has written His law upon the hearts of men (Rom. 2:14, 15). He has also surrounded man with eloquent witnesses to Himself. His entire creation speaks to men of His glory, wisdom, power, and Godhead (Ps. 19:1-2; Rom. 1:19, 20). There is in God's creation a natural revelation of the Creator that addresses man's reason and commands his conscience. That objective reality is the law of nature.

Second, we must remember that man is fallen and his understanding is darkened. The light that is in him is darkness. He is wilfully blind to the light of natural revelation and deaf to the commands of natural law, except as he reworks them according to his own will. Additionally, all creation has felt the impact of man's sin and is no longer in its "natural" state. So, while the witness of nature leaves man without excuse, and every attempt at a moral system attests that the law of God is written on man's heart, fallen man will never find in natural law a sufficient basis for his rule of life.

Since nature is no longer truly "natural" and therefore no longer entirely normative, and because "sin put man's eyes out" (to use Cornelius Van Til's telling phrase), fallen man will always twist the testimony of nature to establish moral standards that are in utter defiance of God's written law in Scripture. He may at times approximate the moral standards the Lord reveals in His word, and this may be traced either to some influence felt from the witness of Scripture or to the action of the Holy Spirit in His operation of common grace.*

Roman Catholic View of Natural Law

Roman Catholic theology has usually given a much greater prominence to natural law. The Protestant position reflects Protestantism's full acceptance of the necessity and sufficiency of Biblical revelation, especially in its statements regarding the fall of man and its consequences. Rome has always been weak on these two fundamentally important doctrines: the doctrine of Scripture and the full impact of Adam's apostasy. She therefore accords the term *law* to non-scriptural material and attributes to unregenerate man's reason the ability rightly to interpret the data placed before it. To a Roman Catholic theologian "Natural law means the whole order of things, which, by the will of God, defines us as human persons and contributes to human development." It is "the obligation, built into nature, to use reason in moral judgment" (R. P. McBrien, *Catholicism,* pp. 994, 995).

Rome uses this view of natural law to commend her position, for example, on abortion and contraception to an increasingly secular age. Where people will not listen to Scripture, they will listen to natural law!

Natural Law As the Ground for Making Common Cause with Secularists

Increasingly, Protestants, in academia and in politics, have been appealing to the concept of natural law as a means whereby Christians and non-Christians can reach a consensus on moral issues. It is eagerly grasped as a point of contact with secularists. In reality, it provides little or no ground for agreed moral standards. This is clearly evidenced by the skepticism with which Rome's natural law pronouncements on the subjects of contraception and abortion are greeted by the secular world and even by many of her own people.

Reason divorced from faithful submission to divine revelation acknowledges a variety of responses to such moral issues to be "natural." Commenting on Rome's dogma on contraception, the *New Dictionary of Theology* has this telling criticism: "To attribute this dogma to 'natural' law, when the overwhelming majority of men and women cannot, in good conscience, regard a responsible use of all such means of contraception as 'intrinsically immoral' seems to undermine the very basis of the doctrine"—i.e., the theory of natural law.

The Relativism of Natural Law

Nowadays, natural law is generally looked at in very relativistic terms. It is no longer the absolute statement of moral duty it was once proclaimed to be. The fact is, it was always a relativist concept; but in earlier times it stood related to cultures that were based, at least in a general way, on the concept of the absolute truth of the Christian faith. Natural law was interpreted from that standpoint and received by the people because they were culturally preconditioned to do so. That is no longer the case, with the result that natural law theorists appear to be reading back into nature the conclusions they have already reached in the culture they accept.

Fallen man needs special revelation. Law must be grounded in God, our Creator and Redeemer in Christ. The solemn fact—at first disheartening, even devastating to those engaged in the attempt—is that there is no neutral ground, no commonly accepted body of authoritative truth between Christians and the ungodly. In fact, rather than being disheartening, this is a call to evangelism, an evangelism conducted in absolute confidence in the power of the word of God (Heb. 4:12) and the gospel of Christ (Rom. 1:16) to transform individuals and nations. When "God who commanded the light to shine out of darkness" shines in men's hearts "to give the light of the knowl-

edge of the glory of God in the face of Jesus Christ" (2 Cor. 4:6) He will conform them to His law. Men are never brought to obedience to the law by law, whether revealed or natural, but by the gospel.

NATURAL REVELATION
*See **Revelation**.*

NATURAL THEOLOGY

The science which on the principles of human reason and conscience, considering the evidences of God's works in creation and providence, seeks to construct a scientific knowledge of God—i.e., it seeks to ascertain (1) Is there a God? (2) What is His nature? (3) In what relation does He stand to man? But human reason, darkened by the entrance of sin, is unable to achieve this goal. God has truly revealed Himself in nature, but sinful man is unable to interpret this revelation aright, being spiritually blind.

While fallen man cannot construct a scientific knowledge of God by the study of nature alone, he has the inescapable knowledge of God's "eternal power and Godhead" clearly written on his heart (Rom. 1:20; 2:15). Using the clear light of special revelation *(see **Revelation**)* the regenerate mind can find a glorious revelation of God in His works of creation and providence (Ps. 19:1).

NEO-ORTHODOXY

Also known as Barthianism, after Karl Barth (1886-1968), a Swiss theologian and the acknowledged leader of the neo-orthodox school. Neo-orthodoxy, as its name suggests, was supposed to represent a return to Biblical orthodoxy and a repudiation of liberalism,* with its optimistic views of man as innately good. Barth rejected the subjectivism of liberalism and claimed to be going back to the great principles of the Protestant Reformation, placing his emphasis on the transcendence of God, the sinfulness of man, and the centrality of Christ. His theology was to be a theology of the Word.

On the face of it, neo-orthodoxy therefore appears to be a laudable movement. On closer examination, however, the semblance of orthodoxy disappears and we are left with all the follies of modernism.

Barth, and the host of neo-orthodox writers who followed him, either deny or dismiss as irrelevant the concrete historicity of the facts of the gospel narrative. The resurrection of Christ is a case in point. The neo-orthodox profess belief in the resurrection, but they effectively remove it from the realm of concrete history into a sort of super-history, which is not to be confused with historical facts. Historical events have no religious or theological significance. Neo-orthodoxy can deny the historicity of the recorded circumstances surrounding Biblical events and still maintain that those events truly occurred in heilsgeschichte,* or the history of salvation. Barth adopts this approach to every great historical fact of the Biblical revelation of God's saving grace.

For example, the fall is not something which occurred at a definite point of time in history. It is something which happens in every man. In other words, neo-orthodoxy professes that the truths of the gospel can only be understood existentially (see *Existentialism),* which is really just another way of saying, "They are real to me, and their concrete history is beside the point."

This acceptance of existentialism is basic to neo-orthodoxy and has reduced the movement to the very subjectivism it avowedly set out to repudiate. Being an existential movement, it also has always opposed propositional statements of Christian doctrine such as creeds, confessions, etc. It views theology as a series of paradoxes to which there are no solutions (see *Dialectic Theology).*

Though claiming to present a theology of the Word, Barth and all the neo-orthodox school deny that the Bible is the very word of God. They speak of the inspiration of Scripture and of its unique witness to Christ, but they do not intend to convey the notion that the Bible is the word of God. Parts of the Bible may *become* the word of God to the individual believer. Exactly which parts may become the word of God is a cause for dispute.

They all accept that the Bible is a human production and therefore subject to error, but where to draw the line is the problem. Denying that the supernatural content of the NT had any historical reality, Rudolf Bultmann proposed a thorough programme of demythologizing the Bible *(see Myth).* Barth was critical of the extent of Bultmann's aims, but in the final analysis, the dispute came down to the personal preferences of the contending parties, with their own subjective notions as to what is essential to the *Kerygma,** the essential message of the gospel.

Thus neo-orthodoxy fails to escape the follies of the liberalism to which it was supposed to be the answer. It ultimately falls into the mire of subjectivism and makes man and his reason the measure of God and His word. It is merely modernism dressed up, or, as Cornelius Van Til styled it, "The New Modernism."

See *Theology of Crisis.*

NEO-PAGANISM

A term used in two ways:

First, it is used by some Christian writers to describe the earth worship of the New Age Movement.* It manifests a strong hatred for all things Christian. Its philosophy is well expressed in Ernest Callenbach's *Earth's Ten Commandments:*

1. Thou shalt love and honor the earth for it blesses thy life and governs thy survival.
2. Thou shalt keep each day sacred to the earth and celebrate the turning of its seasons.
3. Thou shalt not hold thyself above other living things nor drive them to extinction.
4. Thou shalt give thanks for thy food to the creatures and plants that nourish thee.
5. Thou shalt limit thy offspring as multi-

tudes of people are a burden unto the earth.

6. Thou shalt not kill nor waste earth's riches upon weapons of war.

7. Thou shalt not pursue profit at the earth's expense but strive to restore its damaged majesty.

8. Thou shalt not hide from thyself or others the consequences of thy actions upon the earth.

9. Thou shalt not steal from future generations by impoverishing or poisoning the earth.

10. Thou shalt consume material goods in moderation so all may share earth's bounty.

Second, *neo-paganism* is used by others to describe modern occult religions, particularly witchcraft. In this sense it is "the revival of the old gods and goddesses of pre-Christian polytheistic mythologies, mystery cults, and nature religions, such as Celtic, Greek, Egyptian, Roman, and Sumerian" (C. S. Hawkins, *Goddess Worship, Witchcraft and Neo-Paganism,* p. 7). It includes the tribal religions of North American Indians, and Shamanism* as well as Druidic cults that evoke the religion of prehistoric Ireland.

On the other hand neo-paganism includes new religions that have sprung out of the fantasies of science fiction. Neo-pagans reject organized religion as a patriarchal ("Our Father, which art in heaven") prop of Western, male-dominated society. They adopt feminism's* goddess worship, often identifying the goddess as man's inner divinity.

These two aspects of neo-paganism merge in their pantheistic nature worship and in their utter rejection of the Christian revelation.

NEONOMIANISM

From two Greek words *neos,* "new," and *nomos,* "law." *Neonomian* was the name given to the followers of Richard Baxter, who adopted a basically Arminian view of the doctrine of justification by faith. Reformed theology was careful to teach that "the sinner who believes in Christ is fully accepted before God on the ground of His Son's obedience which He yielded to that law which man's sin had broken" (John MacLeod, *Scottish Theology,* p. 134) and that faith is a gift, an inwrought grace, and is the instrument whereby justification is received—not the condition upon whose fulfilment by man justification is granted. In contrast to this, the Baxterian school, fearing that the Reformed doctrine favoured Antinomianism,* espoused a new, erroneous view of justification. MacLeod sums up their position:

"The followers of Baxter went by the name of Neonomians. This name they got from their type of teaching which at this point was of a generally Arminian character. They spoke of a new law of works, compliance with whose demand was held graciously to be a righteousness that won life for the Christian. The Gospel that calls for faith was to them such a new law as called for faith and sincere obedience; and they made the endeavour to pack into the faith that it calls for as much as possible by way of resolution and effort and achievement of a moral character. There was to be seen in this teaching so much of a return to Roman doctrine which ascribes justification to more than the faith which receives the atonement" (p. 139).

The Neonomians' desire to escape antinomianism was laudable, but their solution was foolish and unscriptural. They failed to distinguish between the law as a covenant of life and death, and the law as a rule or standard of life—the "index to the will of God for the obedience of His creatures" (MacLeod). Paradoxically, in this failure they were in virtual agreement with the very antinomians they opposed, though each side, of course, repudiated this distinction for its own peculiar reasons.

The neonomianism of Richard Baxter was the result of his acceptance of the views current among the later French Huguenots. He embraced their Amyraldism,* the halfway house to Arminianism* on the doctrine of the atonement, and ended up as the champion of Arminian views of justification. This had unfortunate results. It halted any chance of Nonconformist unity in England and it spread into Scotland where it ultimately led to the legal preaching of the self-styled Moderates *(see Moderatism).*

Though the name neonomian is no longer in use, its salient features are very much to the fore in many areas of modern evangelicalism. Today we would call it legalism.*

NESTORIANISM

Nestorius, appointed Bishop of Constantinople in A.D. 428, rightly opposed giving Mary the title "Mother of God," but wrongly held that she gave birth to a man who was accompanied by the Logos. Nestorianism, therefore, seeking to do justice to the true humanity of Christ, failed to do justice to the unity of His person and to the union of the Logos with a human nature in Christ. In effect, it made Christ two distinct persons. "Instead of blending the two natures into a single self-consciousness, Nestorianism places them alongside of each other with nothing more than a moral and sympathetic union between them" (Berkhof). Nestorius was deposed in 431 at the Council of Ephesus and banished in 436. *(See Eutychianism,* the contemporary and opposite heresy on the person of Christ.)

NEW AGE MOVEMENT

A loose association of individuals and organizations seeking to penetrate and capture Western culture with Eastern mysticism and Hindu philosophy. New Agers differ from each other in many of their ideas and interests, and no one can speak for the entire movement; however, they share a belief, taken from astrology, that the Age of Aquarius is soon to dawn and that it will be a time of harmony and enlightenment.

Though the New Age movement is very diverse and loosely structured, it is nevertheless coordinated. It is an eclectic patch-

work of many religious, philosophical, and occult ideas. In addition to its Hinduism, it has major elements of Transcendental Meditation,* spiritism,* astrology, theosophy,* mysticism,* neopaganism,* and the 1960s hippie movement.

The central ideas of the New Age movement are monism,* pantheism,* and mysticism. Its pantheism leads it to see all as God and God as all. New Agers loudly proclaim man's deity. Indeed they make his enlightenment on this point their equivalent of the new birth and term it "God-realization," "self-realization," or "self-actualization." This enlightenment is "personal transformation." When "a critical mass" of personally transformed people take responsibility for the world's social and political affairs we will have a "planetary transformation" ushering in the Age of Aquarius, the New Age. This is the New Age vision of Utopia, a new world order with one world government run on the principles of socialism and practising New Age religion.

Being pantheistic, the New Age movement denies that man is a sinner or that he needs salvation. He simply needs to realize his divinity. Being God, every man creates his own reality. Thus, everything anyone does is the action of God.

There is no such distinction as right and wrong, good and evil. According to New Age celebrity Shirley MacLaine, "There is no evil—only lack of knowledge." Again: "Until mankind realizes that there is, in truth, no evil, there will be no peace" (*Dancing in the Light,* pp. 259, 357, quoted by Ron Rhodes, *The New Age Movement,* p. 91).

Inconsistently, New Agers look on peace as good, and war as bad. Conservation is good and ecological destruction is bad. On the basis of their beliefs, however, we are justified in asking why one should be considered better than the other, since all are part of the total reality which is God.

The New Age denial of the existence of evil and of the distinction between right and

245

wrong has far-reaching consequences. It undermines any foundation for ethical conduct. It removes all shame from the worst atrocities evil men have ever committed. It excuses and even encourages base and vicious behaviour. Denying any absolute moral code, it promotes relativism in morals. While it would be wrong to lay all the blame for the emergence of relativism in morals at the door of the New Agers, it would be true to say that they have encouraged and popularized it. They have provided an excuse for those seeking an escape from moral absolutes. People creating their own reality, thereby exercising their inner divinity, are apt to recognize no law outside of themselves and no good beyond their own desires.

New Agers try to escape this criticism by invoking the twin theories of reincarnation and karma. Karma is the "debt," or accumulated merit, a person accrues by his actions in this or previous lives, on the basis of which he will be reincarnated in a more or less desirable state. This is what New Agers mean by *good karma* and *bad karma*. None of this makes the slightest sense given the basic New Age idea that there is no evil. There is nothing in New Age philosophy to establish any ground for regarding one thing as better than another.

As mentioned already, New Agers are eclectic in their beliefs. They claim enlightenment from many sources. They even cite the Old and New Testaments, perverting their plain meaning and attributing a hidden, occult message to their words. They also appeal to other religions, holding that there is a "seed of God" in each of them (here they seem to forget that if all is God and God is all, the world's religions are not only seminally divine but entirely divine). New Agers also claim to be receiving new revelations of truth from a variety of sources, including spirit guides, disembodied human spirits, UFOs or "space brothers." These sources make their revelations through "channellers," or mediums.

Techniques used by New Agers to draw people into their movement may be psychological, mystical, occult, or spiritistic. It could be argued that there is of necessity a spiritist element in every technique they employ. Meditation, especially combined with relaxation exercises such as yoga (the aim of which is to unite the individual with the universal soul), and guided imagery (or, visualization, the idea of mind over matter, the claimed ability to make changes in the physical universe by exercising the power of the mind), leading to altered states of consciousness (mystical experiences in which a person's normal consciousness gives place to states of higher awareness of spiritual truth communicated directly to his mind) are favourite New Age methods.

New Agers are hard at work to spread their religion and to bring their vision to pass. They have made their presence, or their philosophy, felt in many fields. In psychology they have popularized the human potential movement, telling people, "You are your own god," or "You can create your own reality." This approach has many applications. It is very much a part of the secular self-esteem* psychologies that are currently so popular. (There are "Christian" uses of this concept but they sound more New Age than Christian). It is also a much used technique in business seminars and has been adopted by many leading companies to train their managers. The *Wall Street Journal* reported, "Business after business is putting its managers into 'New Age seminars.'...All promise 'consciousness raising' and non-religious conversion resulting in a 'changed person'" (Feb. 9, 1989, quoted by Rhodes, p. 23). These business seminars have been fertile recruiting grounds for the New Age movement—not surprisingly since the conversion the *Wall Street Journal* wrote about is not "nonreligious" but overtly religious.

In the field of education these same psychological approaches with their emphasis on self-esteem and human potential are popular and widespread. So are other New Age ideas, such as visualization, confluent education (in which children are led to recognize their inner divinity), and the theory of beneficial rebellion against parental beliefs and standards (beneficial because it leads children to enjoy their "freedom").

In the entertainment industry actress Shirley MacLaine has been a popular and prolific advocate of the New Age movement. Even her most extreme statements, such as those quoted above, have not aroused the sense of public outrage one would have expected, and MacLaine is treated by the media as a celebrity who deserves to be heard.

New Agers have played a large part in the environmental movement. The rationale behind their conservation appeals is the notion that the earth is a living organism that must be protected. The New Age way to achieve this is through nuclear disarmament, decreasing world population, cutting back on man's use of the earth's resources, and the adoption of socialism on a worldwide scale (though the New Agers who conduct the business seminars mentioned above practise capitalism very successfully, receiving millions of dollars for their efforts).

Not everyone who supports one or all of the points on this agenda is a New Ager, but New Age presuppositions underlie much of the political pressure exerted in furtherance of these aims. New Age success in this area has been considerable as seen in the growth in "Mother Earth" phraseology and the annual observance of Earth Day in increasingly New Age terms. The "Green Party" that has entered the political arena in various countries proceeds on a largely New Age basis.

It is clear that the New Age movement is an all-out attack on Christianity and its formative role in the development of Western culture. It has gathered an impressive list of public advocates, including even some from the scientific community who claim to find support for it in Einstein's theory of relativity and in quantum physics. The science New

Agers claim is as bogus as the support they claim from the words of Christ. The New Age movement is a dangerous delusion, the existence of which may be seen as an evidence that one of its postulates is correct, namely, that this present age is coming to a close—for it is part of that "strong delusion" that will deceive the nations prior to the second coming* of the Lord Jesus Christ.

NEW BIRTH
*See **Regeneration**.*

NEW ENGLAND THEOLOGY
The schools of theological thought that commenced with Jonathan Edwards (1703-58) and concluded with E. A. Park (1808-1900). The feature of New England theology was not a theological conformity or consistency with Edwards or with historic Calvinism.* It was rather the conjunction of very precise forms of reasoning on abstruse matters of philosophy and theology with a strong interest in practical and ethical concerns.

Edwards combined his speculative theology with an intense personal devotion and a powerful experience and defence of revival. In later years other New England theologians continued to display the same philosophical and ethical combination without maintaining the purity of Edward's Calvinism. After Edwards, the New England schools betrayed a gradual movement toward the position of mediate imputation,* the natural ability of the human will (in contrast to its moral inability), man's active participation in regeneration,* and acceptance of general atonement.*

NEW EVANGELICALISM
A title coined in 1947 by a Boston minister, Harold J. Ockenga, to denote the views of evangelicals who repudiated ecclesiastical separation and practised infiltration and inclusivism. New evangelicals claimed to remain true to Protestant orthodoxy, but

professed to see the need for a dramatically new approach to the world of science and scholarship, as well as to society in general. They gave four reasons for their emergence.

First, they wished to place an emphasis on scholarship that they charged was lacking in the old evangelicalism, or fundamentalism.* The Associated Press quoted Ockenga: "The evangelical believes that Christianity is intellectually defensible, that the Christian cannot be obscurantist in scientific questions pertaining to creation, the age of man, the universality of the flood, and other debatable Biblical questions....The new Evangelical is willing to face the intellectual problems and meet them in the framework of modern learning" (AP, Dec. 8, 1957).

Ockenga's new evangelicalism sounds very much like old-line modernism.* Old evangelicals did not shirk the intellectual rigours of defending their Biblical faith. Men such as J. Gresham Machen could not by any stretch of the imagination be termed "obscurantist," but they stood firmly by the reliability and historicity of the Biblical record. New evangelicalism commenced by doubting both those positions and has continually retreated from them.

Second, new evangelicals wished to abandon the old confrontational spirit of earlier days. They had no stomach for the fight in which fundamentalism had long been engaged with modernism. With the passage of half a century, new evangelicals have travelled so far from anything remotely like a confrontation with the enemies of the gospel that they now cooperate in literary productions and even in evangelistic crusades with avowed liberals and Roman Catholics. E. J. Carnell, a leading thinker in the formative years of the new evangelical movement, accused fundamentalists of having shifted doctrine into the place that love should occupy. He charged that this "places believers at the disposal of demonic pretence, for not only is Satan an accomplished student of

Scripture, but the demons often address Jesus with language used by angels" (Carnell, *The Case for Orthodox Theology*, p. 137).

Carnell's statement is amazing—and typical of the topsy-turvy reasoning of new evangelicals. It is possibly demonic to love Biblical truth and confront apostasy, but it is fine to compromise God's word in order to embrace serious error and those who spread it. Using that kind of logic, new evangelicals can participate in the World Council of Churches* and pretend that in essential matters evangelicalism and Roman Catholicism embrace a common faith.

Third, new evangelicals wished to be more open to modern scientific theory, especially the theory of evolution. They had the view that a person could be both an evangelical and an evolutionist. Carnell accepted "threshold evolution," while others taught "progressive creationism"—a euphemism for theistic evolution. Softness toward, or even open acceptance of evolution, is common in the learned treatises of new evangelicals on such issues as the Biblical account of creation, the age of the earth, and the flood. Carnell wrote, "Since Orthodoxy has given up the literal-day theory out of respect for geology, it would forfeit no principle if it gave up the immediate creation theory out of respect for paleontology" (Carnell, p. 95).

Fourth, new evangelicals wished to become more involved than old evangelicals had been in addressing the problems of society. They decided to participate fully in societal efforts to deal with such issues as social justice, racism, capitalism, the profit motive, and similar social concerns. Old evangelicals had been involved, in varying degrees, in a number of social concerns. They had pursued their goals as part of their evangelistic ministry, without compromising their theological principles. The new evangelicals took a different course. Their attitude was, and is, that they should unite with any society or reform movement, regardless of the company they must keep in doing so, unless the group specifically rules out redemption as a means of fulfilling its aims. Since liberals, Roman Catholics, and people of any other religious persuasion would not deny redemption (however they may define it) some role in the solution of society's problems, new evangelicals could fit in anywhere.

These four reasons for the emergence of the movement would be better described as *excuses*. Building on such a base, new evangelicalism has become a movement of compromise. This is nowhere more evident than in its attitude to the Bible. New evangelicals have espoused such views as *modified inerrancy* —the Bible is inerrant on the subjects it addresses, but not necessarily in the terms in which it speaks of them; and *limited infallibility*— the Bible is infallible only in matters of faith and practice.

Those who accept modified inerrancy profess orthodoxy but feel free to deny the factuality of countless historical statements of Scripture, e.g., the serpent's conversation with Eve (Gen. 3). Following James Orr, the theologian they look on as the forerunner of their position, modified inerrantists accept the presence of *pseudonymity*— in plain language, *forgery*— in Scripture, as well as legends masquerading as history (as in Jude's reference to Enoch and his prophecy, Jude 14, 15). They accept that there are degrees of inspiration and therefore "minor errors in the *matter* of the [Biblical] record" (James Orr, *Revelation and Inspiration,* p. 215).

Those who adopt the view of limited infallibility go even further. Apart from the subject of salvation, they feel free to give up any part of Scripture (see Daniel P. Fuller, "Benjamin B. Warfield's View of Faith and History," in *Bulletin of the Evangelical Theological Society,* vol. 11, no. 2, pp. 82, 83). They may abandon the Bible's chronology and history, and even admit errors in its doctrine (Dewey M. Beegle, *Scripture, Tradition and Infallibility*).

Such views are neither *new* nor *evangelical.* They belong to modernism and open infidelity. Yet they are the views of many who profess to be evangelicals, people who have appropriated an honoured name and prostituted it in advancing the very theology that evangelicalism historically opposed with all its power.

New evangelicalism is widely accepted. It has affected churches and seminaries in varying degrees. Its spirit of compromise is now accepted by many as Christian love. It has created the theological basis and the psychological mood for the inclusivism practised by many evangelistic and para-church organizations—e.g., Billy Graham's fellowship with the church of Rome, and the joint worship and action of evangelicals and non-evangelicals in *Promise Keepers* and in anti-abortion groups.

Compromise with theological error and fellowship with those from whom the Scripture commands separation betoken a movement that is on a swift downward career to open apostasy.

NICENE CREED

The name is taken from Nicea in Bithynia where the first ecumenical* council was held in A.D. 325. At that council the scriptural doctrine of the consubstantiality* of the Son was declared. In 381 the second ecumenical council was held in Constantinople and this added to the Nicene Creed the scriptural teaching on the deity and personality of the Holy Spirit. In 569, at Toledo, the Western Church added the famous "filioque"* clause. Thus, in its final form, the Nicene Creed is a full statement of Biblical trinitarianism.

The full text of the Nicene, or more properly the Nicene-Constantinopolitan, Creed is as follows:

"We believe in one God, the Father, the Almighty, maker of heaven and earth, and of all that is unseen. We believe in one Lord, Jesus Christ, the only Son of God, eternally begotten of the Father, God from God, Light from Light, true God from true God, begotten, not made, one in Being with the Father. Through him all things were made. For us men and for our salvation he came down from heaven: by the power of the Holy Spirit he was born of the Virgin Mary, and became man. For our sake he was crucified under Pontius Pilate; he suffered, died, and was buried. On the third day he rose again in fulfillment of the Scriptures; he ascended into heaven and is seated at the right hand of the Father. He will come again in glory to judge the living and the dead, and his kingdom will have no end. We believe in the Holy Spirit, the Lord, the giver of life, who proceeds from the Father and the Son. With the Father and the Son he is worshiped and glorified. He has spoken through the Prophets. We believe in one holy catholic and apostolic Church. We acknowledge one baptism for the forgiveness of sins. We look for the resurrection of the dead, and the life of the world to come. Amen."

NIHILISM

From Latin *nihil,* "nothing"; it is used in various senses. Philosophically, nihilism is the belief that there is no basis for knowledge or truth, and no meaning or purpose to existence. Consequently it rejects and opposes all customary, especially Christian, beliefs about religion and morality. It is a sort of moral anarchism in which we can know nothing to be true or right, or indeed anything but a speck of meaninglessness in the midst of cosmic confusion and darkness. As is usually the case, philosophy has consequences in real life and this one is no exception.

Politically, it is used as a loose description of any revolutionary, terrorist movement that seeks to overthrow an orderly society. In precise terms, it is the doctrine that all current social, political, and economic institutions must be destroyed to make way for new institutions.

Often philosophical and political nihilism combine, as in the case of the Russian Nihilists (1860-1917) and of the modern Marxist or Trotskyite terrorist groups that attacked various European countries, notably Germany, Italy, and France, in the last third of the 20th century.

NOMINALISM

A school of late medieval scholastic thought that held that "universals," or abstract terms describing universal principles, were nothing more than necessities of thought, or conventions of language, and had no real existence. Its emphasis was always on the individual term, person, or situation.

In this nominalists opposed the realists.* Nominalists were Franciscans, who purported to reflect Augustine's theological emphasis *(see **Augustinianism),** and the realists were Dominicans, who reflected the position of Thomas Aquinas. They disagreed about the relation of reason to faith and the efficacy of sacramental grace. In the latter the nominalist position stressed the necessity of prevenient grace* to enable the recipient to benefit from the grace conveyed by a sacrament.* According to the nominalists this prevenient grace was received either mystically or by doing the best one could. It created a merit* of congruity whereby the grace of the sacrament could be bestowed as a fitting reward. As the controversy progressed each side proceeded to extremes in stating their positions. As a result nominalism came to be regarded as propounding utterly speculative ideas on the arbitrary nature of grace. Realism, on the other hand came to be viewed as being rationalistic.

NORMATIVE PRINCIPLE

The theory held by Lutherans and Anglicans that what is not forbidden in Scripture is admissible in the practice, worship, and government of the church. It is the opposite of the regulative principle* generally adopted by Calvinists. Adherents of the regulative principle ask, "Where does Scripture command or sanction a particular practice or form?" Those who hold the normative principle ask, "Where does Scripture forbid it?"

Martin Luther, while holding tenaciously to the principle of *sola Scriptura,* "by Scripture alone," in matters of doctrine, nonetheless condemned no ceremony unless it was opposed to the gospel. If a form or practice was not forbidden by the Word, he allowed it to remain. In this way he conformed the worship of the new Lutheran churches to what the people were used to in the old papal church.

The Church of England agreed with the Lutherans, not with the Calvinists. Article 20 of the *Thirty-Nine Articles* (1571) states, "The Church hath power to decree Rites or Ceremonies, and authority in controversies of faith. And yet it is not lawful for the Church to ordain anything that is contrary to God's word written....As it ought not to decree anything against the same, so besides the same ought it not to enforce anything to be believed for necessity of salvation." In other words, the church may introduce or allow ecclesiastical practices as long as they are not forbidden in Scripture, but it may not make anything part of the faith necessary to salvation except what the Scripture expressly lays down as such.

NOVATIANISTS

Followers of Novatian, a Roman presbyter who disputed the title to the bishopric of the church of Rome in the third century. Novatian was inflexible in his opposition to the readmission to the church of any who had lapsed under persecution, and when he learned that Cornelius, who took a much softer line, had been elected bishop in place of the martyred Fabian, he refused to acknowledge him. He himself was then ordained bishop by a number of like-minded clerics, thus starting the first of history's many controversies as to who was rightfully bishop of Rome. A church council condemned Novatian and he was forced to give way.

He still refused to fellowship in the Catholic church and formed his followers into a separate sect. This sect, which persisted beyond the fifth century, continued Novatian's exclusion of all who had lapsed under persecution. Their view was based on Heb. 6:4-6, and their thinking was as follows: the church could not receive unpardoned sinners into its fellowship; it could grant pardon only by baptism, which could not be repeated; therefore baptized persons who had lapsed could not be forgiven or readmitted to fellowship. From this Novatianists developed a theory of the church as the assembly of the *katharoi*—"pure ones"—and this has invested them with a peculiar interest to those who imagine a *trail-of-blood* succession of independent Baptist churches *(see **Baptist).** The fact is, however, that Novatianist dogma was far removed from the beliefs of Baptists.

The Catholic church sought the re-entry of Novatianists into the church upon reconciliation (Council of Nicea, A.D. 325). The councils of Laodicea (367) and Constantinople (381) added the condition of full and written proof that Novatianists had anathematized their former heresies. Later councils added to these conditions until at last Novatianists were not regarded as Christians at all and had to accept another baptism if they were to gain admission to the Catholic church.

O

OBEDIENCE OF CHRIST

Christ's filial submission to His Father's will in coming into the world, becoming subject to the law to fulfil and satisfy both its precept and its penalty. As a true man He fully entered into all that it meant to be "made under the law" (Gal. 4:4). In perfectly meeting its standard, he endured temptation and suffered in body and in soul.

He obeyed *graciously* and as a matter of choice. His eternal Sonship* neither implied nor involved subordination nor obedience. He did not obey *because* He was a Son but *despite* that fact (Heb. 5:8).

He obeyed *sinlessly* (Phil. 2:5-8; Heb. 7:26; 2 Cor. 5:21; 1 Pet. 2: 22; 1 John 3:5).

He obeyed *vicariously* and *representatively* (Rom. 5:16-19) and is therefore the ground of His people's justification.*

See **Imputation**.

OCCULT

Latin o*ccultus,* "concealed"; it is a term that is sometimes loosely employed to describe anything that is mysterious. It is, however, more commonly used to denote the study, pursuit, or practice of the mystic arts such as black magic, witchcraft, necromancy, spiritism, astrology, and the diverse methods of "spiritual enlightenment" found in the New Age* movement, including channelling and visualization.

OFFICES OF CHRIST

See **Mediator**, **Kingly Office**; **Priestly Office**; **Prophetic Office**.

OLD CATHOLIC CHURCH

First formed by a Dutch separation from Rome in 1723, following the pope's condemnation of Jansenism* in the bull* Unigenitus (1713) and Rome's refusal to allow a Dutch archbishop to be chosen locally. These Old Catholic seceders were joined by others who repudiated the Vatican Council of 1870, with its decree of papal infallibility. The Old Catholic church holds to the doctrines of the first seven ecumenical councils and has set out its position fully in the *Declaration of Utrecht* (1889). It maintains a married clergy and since 1932 has been in full communion with the Church of England.

OMNIPOTENCE

The all-powerfulness of God, His unlimited ability to act according to His own perfect will. Theologians sometimes speak of God's power being limited by His own will and by the nature of things—i.e., He cannot work an essential contradiction. These are foolish quibbles. To be able to do whatsoever He wills is no limitation. Contradictions are nonentities. To say God cannot create a nonentity is to say, "God cannot create nothing." By the act of creation, it would not be *nothing* any longer.

See Jer. 32:17; Mt. 19:26; Luke. 1:37; Rev. 19:6.

OMNIPRESENCE

God's presence in every point of space with His whole being. Immensity stresses the transcendence of God, that He is not subject to the limitations of space; omnipresence stresses His immanence in His creation, that He fills all space. He is not extended through space, for God is pure spirit and has no extension.

Some theologians, such as Samuel Clarke, speak of infinite space as an attribute of God.

Others prefer to speak of all things being simultaneously present to God rather than God being present in all places.

OMNISCIENCE
*See **Knowledge of God**.*

ONLY BEGOTTEN
Greek *monogenes;* it declares the unique relationship of the Son of God to His Father. B. B. Warfield says, "The adjective 'only begotten' conveys the idea, not of derivation and subordination, but of uniqueness and consubstantiality: Jesus is all that God is, and He alone is this."
*See **Eternal Generation**.*

ONTOLOGICAL ARGUMENT FOR GOD'S EXISTENCE
*See **Arguments for God's Existence**.*

ONTOLOGICAL TRINITY
Ontology is the science of real existence, or absolute reality, as distinct from things as they appear to us to be. Thus when theologians speak of the ontological Trinity—Cornelius Van Til makes frequent use of the term—they mean that God exists from all eternity as the triune God, Father, Son, and Holy Spirit, as revealed in the word of God; that this is not merely a human conception of Him, but that it is absolutely, eternally, and necessarily what God is and how God exists.

The fact that the persons of the Trinity operate according to a certain order or pattern in the economy of creation and redemption has given rise to the term "economical trinity." But it should always be remembered that God is not described as triune because He deals with His creatures in this fashion. Rather the economical Trinity is based on the ontological Trinity: God demonstrates His trinal distinctions in His dealings with His creatures, because He is essentially and necessarily triune.

OPERA AD EXTRA
Called, by some theologians, *notae externae,* they are "the activities and effects by which the Trinity is manifested outwardly. They are the following: (1) Creation, preservation, and government of the universe. (2) Redemption. (3) Inspiration, regeneration, and sanctification. The first belongs officially and eminently to the Father; the second to the Son; the third to the Holy Spirit" (Shedd).

OPERA AD INTRA
Also called *notae internae,* these are the activities of the Trinity that are within the divine essence and confined to it—unlike the *opera ad extra* which go outside of the divine essence and produce external results. Thus they are referred to as immanent and intransitive activities, or as constitutional and necessary activities. "The internal works or actions of God are those which the Persons perform and exercise one toward another" (Ursinus). The eternal generation of the Son and the procession of the Spirit are the *opera ad intra.*

OPUS DEI
Latin, meaning "the work of God"; the name of a controversial organization in the Roman Catholic church. Founded in Spain in 1928 by a Spanish priest Josémaria Escriva, Opus Dei now boasts some 80,000 members worldwide. Its full title is *The Personal Prelature of the Holy Cross and Opus Dei.* (A personal prelature is like a bishopric with people but without a defined territory.)

Escriva saw his organization as a means of protecting and promoting traditional Roman Catholic theology and spirituality. It is something of a papal army of priests, university professors, teachers, and workers throughout the world, dedicated to carrying out the programmes of the Vatican. Escriva insisted that Opus Dei be a lay, rather than a religious, society. At first it aimed particularly at intellectuals but now boasts that it includes thousands of working men and women in its ranks.

Opus Dei has aroused suspicion both within and outside the Roman Catholic church. Roman Catholic religious groups such as the Jesuits* have been suspicious of its lay structures while some bishops have been suspicious of its members being outside local diocesan control and accountable to Opus Dei's leadership. Politicians, especially in Italy, have accused Opus Dei of being a sort of Vatican Mafia, though hard evidence is difficult to obtain. Escriva died in 1975 and was beatified* in 1992.

OPUS OPERATUM

Equivalent to *ex opere operato;* a Latin phrase employed by Roman Catholic theologians to signify that the benefit of a sacrament is conferred "by virtue of the work wrought." In other words, the grace is in the sacrament which conveys it to the passive recipient without the necessity of faith and repentance. Cardinal Bellarmine said that the administration of a sacrament is called *opus operatum,* so that "it confers grace by virtue of the sacramental act itself."

ORDINATION

The act of initial induction into a ministry by the presbytery (1 Tim. 4:14), expressing its judgment that one who has received a call from a local church to the office of teaching or ruling elder is indeed called and qualified by God. By the laying on of hands the candidate is set aside for the office to which he has been called, and that calling is thereby publicly acknowledged and confirmed. In the case of ministerial candidates called to missionary work, the call of a local congregation is not deemed necessary, and the presbytery will ordain a candidate of whose gifts and calling by the Lord they are sure.

*See **Church (Government of)**.*

ORDO SALUTIS

The order of salvation, the process by which the work of salvation, wrought in Christ, is realized in the hearts of God's elect. "It aims at describing in their logical order, and also in their interrelations the various movements of the Holy Spirit in the application of the work of redemption" (Berkhof).

The Bible nowhere explicitly sets out such an order, though Rom. 8:29-30 may be considered as an approach to such a definitive statement. On the basis of this, most Reformed theologians (see *Westminster Confession of Faith,* chap. 3, sec. 6) describe the *ordo salutis* as regeneration, calling, conversion, repentance, faith, justification, adoption, sanctification, perseverance of the saints, and their final glorification—all this depending on our union with Christ, a union first established by divine election in the covenant of redemption.

*See **Covenant Theology**.*

ORIGINAL RIGHTEOUSNESS

The perfect conformity of man as first created to the law of God. Sometimes the term *natural righteousness* is employed with the same meaning. It must be kept in mind, however, that "natural" implies only that such righteousness belonged to man's nature as it came from the hand of its Creator. It does not imply that it is necessary to human nature, so that man would not be a real man, or a responsible moral agent, without it. Fallen man is every bit as responsible as unfallen man.

ORIGINAL SIN

Fallen man's natural sinfulness, the hereditary depravity* and corruption of human nature because of Adam's fall.* Though it inheres in human nature and is propagated by natural generation, it does not arise from anything in man's original natural constitution.

Reformed Position

Calvin said, "Man is corrupted by a natural depravity, but which did not originate from nature. We deny that it proceeded from nature, to signify that it is rather an adventitious quality or accident, than a substantial property originally innate. Yet we call it natural, that none may suppose it to be contracted by every individual from corrupt habit, whereas it prevails over all by hereditary right" (*Institutes*, 2:1.11). "On account of the corruption of human nature, man may be justly said to be naturally abominable to God" (ibid., 2:1.11).

"Sin has possessed all the powers of the soul, since Adam departed from the fountain of righteousness. For man has not only been ensnared by the inferior appetites, but abominable impiety has seized the very citadel of his mind, and pride has penetrated into the inmost recesses of his heart" (2:1.9).

In tracing Paul's doctrine of original sin, Calvin concludes "that man is so totally overwhelmed, as with a deluge, that no part is free from sin: and therefore whatever proceeds from him is accounted sin; as Paul says that all the affections or thoughts of the flesh are enmity against God, and therefore death (Rom. 8:6-7)."

Hence, though sin in man is not a material principle in human nature (as Manicheism* holds) or an original, or necessary part of it, the soul of fallen man "is not only wounded, but so corrupted, that it requires not merely to be healed, but to receive a new nature" (2:1.9). Calvin thus safeguards the doctrine against Pelagianism* of every degree. Furthermore, he does not make corruption something in our nature but yet in some way distinct from our nature. He acknowledges that in its first state human nature was holy, but he proves from Scripture that it has degenerated from that state. Now it is not merely overcome by corruption, it is in itself corrupt—"man is of himself nothing else but concupiscence [lust]," and "abominable impiety" is the ruling principle of his unrenewed mind.

Lutheran Position

Lutherans debated and rejected the idea that original sin "is properly and without any distinction the very nature, substance, and essence of corrupt man, or at least the principal and pre-eminent part of his substance, namely rational soul" *Formula of Concord,* Art. 1). They hold that even after the fall* there is a distinction between man's corrupt nature and original sin "which adheres in the corrupt nature and also corrupts the nature" (*ibid.,* Art. 1). The nature of man is God's work, original sin is the devil's work (*ibid.,* Affirmative 1) and "the distinction between our corrupt nature and the corruption which is implanted within the nature, and through which the nature is corrupt, can be easily discerned" (Affirmative 2). None but God can separate the nature from the corruption within it, but He will certainly sever one from the other by means of death and resurrection (Affirmative 3). Despite this insistence that man's nature is distinct from the corruption that now resides within it and thereby corrupts it, Lutheranism seeks to avoid the notions that man's nature is fundamentally good (as God's creature) and that corruption is something alien to it, or "merely the liability and debt of another's transgression, transmitted to us apart from any corruption of our nature" (Negative 8.1). The formulators of this Lutheran standard desired to ensure that no attack could be made upon God's goodness and wisdom on account of the corruption of man's nature. God did not create it corrupted.

As believers in creationism* these Lutheran fathers believed that God has continued to create souls and that His creation could not be corrupt as it comes from His hand; that is, man is not corrupted because of some concreated necessity or because of his finiteness. Their desire to show that man's corruption does not come from his original constitution and is not the natural consequence of his humanness is Scriptural and praiseworthy, but their statements are open to two major objections:

First, they tend to a materialistic view of nature and corruption, though Lutherans would protest such a conclusion and point to the *Formula of Concord's* strong denunciation of Manicheism.* But the notion that an uncorrupt, pure soul is created by God and united with a physical body by the act of conception, and that by that union the soul becomes corrupt seems to fall into the very dualism and materialism of Manicheism that the *Formula* so roundly condemns.

Second, the way Lutherans describe the distinction between the nature of man and the corruption in it, has led to a modification of the original stand of Luther on the subject of the total inability of fallen man's will to originate anything good or pleasing to God. McClintock and Strong quote Charles O. Krauth's summary of Lutheran doctrine, which includes the statement, "The depravity of man is total in its extent, and his will has no *positive* ability in the work of salvation, but has the *negative* ability (under the ordinary means of grace) of ceasing resistance" (emphasis is added). This ignores the fact that such cessation of resistance is in itself a good work; it is, indeed, a good work that flies in the face of the evil inclination of the unrenewed will. This is certainly a serious modification of Luther's view.

The somewhat dialectical pronouncements of the *Formula of Concord* may be contrasted to the Reformed statement of the doctrine of original sin in the *Westminster Confession of Faith* (chap. 6, sec. 2-4): "By this sin [our first parents] fell from their original righteousness, and communion with God, and so became dead in sin, and wholly defiled in all the faculties and parts of soul and body. They being the root of all mankind, the guilt of this sin was imputed, and the same death in sin and corrupted nature conveyed to all their posterity, descending from them by ordinary generation. From this original corruption, whereby we are utterly indisposed, disabled, and made opposite to all

good, and wholly inclined to all evil, do proceed all actual transgressions."

Roman Catholic Position

Rome holds that "all men are implicated in Adam's sin" (*Catechism of the Catholic Church,* ¶ 402); however, in Roman Catholic theology this implication is limited and falls far short of the Protestant doctrine. "Although it is proper to each individual, original sin does not have the character of a personal fault in any of Adam's descendants. It is a deprivation of original holiness and justice [righteousness], but human nature has not been totally corrupted" (*ibid.,* ¶ 404).

Rome admits that original sin causes every person to be "inclined to sin—an inclination to evil that is called *concupiscence*" (¶ 405), but insists that this concupiscence* is not in itself sin.

The heart of Rome's position lies in her failure to understand the truth of concreated holiness.* She sees man's original holiness as a gift *superadded* to his nature. He lost this by the fall, but the loss did not involve the radical ruin of his moral constitution.

Rome teaches that "baptism, by imparting the life of Christ's grace, erases original sin and turns a man back toward God" (¶ 405, *see **Baptismal Regeneration**)*. Despite this, concupiscence and a nature "weakened and inclined to evil" ensure that he will continue to have "a hard battle" with sin (¶ 407-409).

Pelagian and Arminian Positions

*Pelagianism** entirely rejects the doctrine of original sin and confines sin to separate acts of the will,* which retains the power to choose sinlessly as much as sinfully.

*Arminianism** is semi-Pelagian* in its position on original sin. It agrees with Pelagians that sin consists in separate acts of the will, and that the guilt of Adam's first sin is not transmitted to his descendents. It disagrees with Pelagians in that it holds that fallen man is depraved, though not totally, and that the pollution of Adam's first sin is transmitted to his descendants.

Summary

Original sin is the natural sinfulness of Adam's descendants, by natural generation. The designation *original sin* signifies the following:

1. This sinfulness is derived from Adam the original root of the entire race.

2. It is inherent in Adam's posterity from the womb; it is not the result of environment or imitation.

3. It is the root of all the actual transgressions each sinner commits. Rome's idea that though the root has been removed by baptism, the fruit remains is both illogical and unscriptural.

4. It consists of original guilt and original pollution. Guilt signifies a liability to punishment. Pollution signifies the absence of original righteousness and the presence of evil. Pollution involves guilt; there is no such thing as guiltless pollution. The Arminian view that pollution alone, not guilt, is transmitted from Adam to his posterity is based on an unscriptural view of man's sinfulness, and obviously views pollution as a moral disease which is guiltless *per se.*

See **Depravity**; **Inability**; **Transmission of Sin**.

ORTHODOXY

Consistency in doctrine with the revelation of Scripture. To this definition Rome would add the traditions of the church and the teaching of the fathers, but Protestantism* limits the authority to establish a doctrinal norm to the inspired word of God. That is not to say that it has no place for creeds or confessions but holds that they must be judged by the Bible. They cannot become an additional source of revelation or authority.

OXFORD GROUP

A group founded at Oxford University in 1929 by American Lutheran minister, Frank Buchman, with a program for world reform. In 1938 it became Moral Rearmament.*

OXFORD MOVEMENT

See **Anglo Catholicism**; **Tractarianism**; **Puseyites**.

P

PAEDOBAPTISM

From the Greek *paidion,* "a young child, or infant"; infant baptism. At the time of the Reformation, Anabaptists* rejected paedobaptism, while the Reformed churches, believing it to be a sign and seal of the covenant of grace, argued that Scripture warranted the baptism of the children of believing parents because such children were included by God in His covenant promises.
*See **Baptism; Baptismal Regeneration; Means of Grace.***

PANENTHEISM

A term invented to provide a philosophical basis for process theology.* It should be distinguished from pantheism.* Pantheism identifies God with the universe. Panentheism is the notion that the universe is God but that God is more than the universe. In other words, though the universe is part of the reality of God it is not all of that reality. God is something which the universe is not. God may be looked on as the soul of the universe and the universe as the body of God. Viewed in this way, the universe is God while God is greater than the universe just as the body of a man is the man but his soul is not limited to the body.

PANTHEISM

From two Greek words, *pan,* "all," and *theos,* "God"; a theory that denies the transcendence of God, refusing to recognize Him as a being distinct from creation. Thus it identifies God and the universe; all is God and God is all. Theologically, it is the denial of the personality of God.

Far from the absolute and sovereign Being presented in Scripture, the god of the pantheist is an "eternal becoming" (Berkhof), who developed into personal consciousness in the consciousness of man. Through the influence of Schleiermacher's Consciousness Theology,* this notion became the dominant heresy of nineteenth-century theology. Barth, who was schooled in Schleiermacher's system, repudiated its pantheistic base and emphasized the transcendence of God, speaking of Him as "wholly other"; although by embracing existentialism he remained a captive of subjectivism, the very thing he professed to eschew.

PAPYRUS

*See **MSS**.*

PARADIGM

Greek *para,* "by," *deigma,* "example"; a pattern or model. It has two main uses:
1. In theology a paradigm is a model that sets the norm for understanding and interpreting the gospel. Nowadays we hear a lot about a *paradigm shift.* This describes the adoption of a new motif for interpreting the entire Biblical message. It is usually a tool to validate a new theology or practice, even at the expense of invalidating the plain meaning of the Biblical text. For example, by moving away from Christ's atoning death and bodily resurrection as the paradigm that defines the gospel in terms of personal redemption from sin unto God, to a totally unscriptural interpretation of His emphasis on freedom, or love and justice, liberation theologians have invented a paradigm that proclaims the gospel in terms of "social justice," or freedom from political, economic, or social oppression or repression. In this way they can validate anything from ter-

rorist revolutions to the acceptance of homosexual lifestyles.

2. Form criticism* uses *paradigm* for the narratives of the gospel, usually ending with a saying of Jesus, that the original gospel preachers used as examples of "that which Jesus was and brought into being," (Martin Dibelius). Thus to a form critic, a paradigm is an oral tradition, possibly historical, or partly historical, about what Jesus really was and did, that provided an example for the evangelists to use in their ministry.

Like every other attempt to get behind the text of the NT to discover an oral tradition, which over a period of time became embellished with mythological material before it was written in the NT, this view of paradigm is fundamentally wrong. If the gospels are an inspired and honest record of the Son of God the form critical approach is wrong. If they are not, we are left in a darkness that no amount of form criticism can ever penetrate. The Biblical paradigm to adopt with regard to the gospel narratives is found in texts such as 2 Pet. 1:16-19. This sets the norm for our understanding of the gospels. They are accurate, historical, inspired, and trustworthy, and should be treated as such.

PARADOX THEOLOGY
See **Dialectic Theology**.

PAROUSIA

A Greek word usually translated "coming" in the NT. Its basic significance is "presence" (Phil. 2:12), or "arrival" (1 Cor. 15:23; 2 Cor. 7:6). It is used for the coming of both Christ and the antichrist (2 Thess. 2:1, 8).

The NT describes the *parousia* of Christ in a variety of ways:

1. The *parousia* of the Son of Man (Matt. 24:3, 27, 37, 39).

2. The *parousia* of the Lord (1 Thess. 3:13; 4:15; 5:23; 2 Thess. 2:1; James 5:7; 2 Pet. 3:4).

3. The *parousia* of Christ (2 Pet. 1:16).

4. His *parousia* (1 Cor. 15:23; 1 Thess. 2:19; 2 Thess. 2:8; 2 Pet. 3:4; 1 John 2:28).

5. The *parousia* of the day of God (2 Pet. 3:12).

In ancient times, *parousia* was popularly used of the arrival of a king. That makes it a fitting word to denote the second coming* of the King of Kings.

Dispensationalists have claimed that *parousia* is particularly a Pauline word and is used to denote the pre-tribulation coming of Christ to rapture His church, as distinct from His post-tribulation revelation or appearing. However, a glance at the above-listed texts will show how groundless is such a claim. More thoughtful writers of that school do not now make the claim in quite such terms. W. E. Vine claims:

"When used of the return of Christ, at the Rapture of the Church, it signifies not merely His momentary coming for His Saints, but His presence with them from that moment until His revelation and manifestation to the world. In some passages the word gives prominence to the beginning of that period, the course of the period being implied, 1 Cor. 15:23; 1 Thess. 4:15; 5:23; 2 Thess. 2:1; James 5:7, 8; 2 Pet. 3:4. In some, the course is prominent, Matt. 24:3, 37; 1 Thess. 3:13; 1 John 2:28; in others the conclusion of the period, Matt. 24:27; 2 Thess. 2:8."

This is all purely imaginary, not warranted by the texts and invented to bolster the preconceived theory of a pre-tribulation coming of Christ. According to this scheme the Lord Jesus used *parousia* with very different significances in Matt. 24, almost in the same breath, without any intimation of His change of meaning. Furthermore, it is not consistent with itself. Vine holds that 1 Cor. 15:23 and 1 Thess. 4:15 both speak of Christ's "momentary coming for His saints." Obviously they do both speak of the same event, but 1 Cor. 15:52 indicates that this "momentary coming" is at the last trump—which cannot be before the tribulation period, because that period is characterized by seven trumps (Rev. 8:6) in keeping with what the Lord Jesus said in Matt. 24:29-31. The fact that the NT sets forth the "glorious appearing" as our "blessed hope" (Titus 2:13, see **Granville Sharpe Rule**) and that the church is referred to Christ's revelation for her comfort (2 Thess. 1:7; see 1 Cor. 1:7; 1 Pet. 1:7, 13; 4:13) shows how baseless is any theory that would either distinguish, as to time, the *parousia* from the *appearing*, or make the *parousia* cover two second comings and an extended period of time, as Vine's scheme does. The simple truth of the matter is that *parousia* is a designation of the one second coming of Christ and is contemporaneous with His appearing or revelation. They are but different descriptions of the same event.

PARTHENOGENESIS

Greek, *parthenos*, "virgin," *genesis*, "birth"; virgin birth.*

PARTICULAR REDEMPTION

The doctrine that the purpose of God in the work of Christ was actually to save His elect, not to make the salvation of all men possible. Christ died to purchase a people, not a possibility.

*See **Atonement; Five Points of Controversy; Calvinism.***

PASCHAL CONTROVERSY

The difference of opinion and practice that agitated the early church regarding the proper observance of the Lord's death and resurrection at Easter. Some believed that the church should strictly observe the very date of the crucifixion, the fourteenth of Nisan, and the resurrection three days later. Others believed that the Lord Jesus died on a Friday and rose again on the following Sunday, making it the Lord's Day. Thus they observed Good Friday and Easter Sunday on those days irrespective of whether they fell on the original dates.

*See **Quartodecimanism**.*

PASTORAL THEOLOGY

That branch of theological study which deals with a pastor's personal and official duties as an undershepherd to whom Christ has committed the solemn task of feeding and leading the flock of God according to the word of God.

*See **Practical Theology**.*

PATRIPASSIANISM

Latin *pater*, "father," and *patior*, "to suffer"; a name for Modalistic Monarchianism* which expresses the mistaken view that since God is one indivisible *person* it is correct to say that the Father suffered for our redemption. *See also **Sabellianism**.*

PATRONAGE

The right of a patron to appoint the pastor of a local church (*see **Advowson*** for the operation of this system in the English church). In the Scottish church a patron was generally a landowner whose means enabled him to assume responsibility for the payment and housing of a minister.

The Scottish practice of patronage arose in the Middle Ages as pious landowners built and endowed churches to which they appointed priests. After the Reformation the patronage was continued despite that the *First Book of Discipline* and the *Second Book of Discipline* called for its discontinuance. It often led to bitter controversy as patrons installed ministers who were not wanted by the parishioners. Consequently there were frequent resentment and agitation to establish the right of a congregation to call their minister. Division was inevitable. The issue of patronage was a major cause of the Disruption of 1843 which gave birth to the Free Church of Scotland.

PAULICIANS

An ancient witness against the errors that had taken hold in the Eastern Church, much as the Waldenses* were in the West. They flourished in the East from the mid-seventh century until the tenth. During the eighth to the tenth centuries they were transported to Thrace and from there they spread across Europe.

The charges levelled against them by their enemies give us a good idea of their adherence to scriptural truth. "Among the prominent charges urged against the Paulicians before the Patriarch of Constantinople in the eighth century, and by Photius and Petrus Siculus in the ninth, we find the following— that they dishonoured the Virgin Mary, and rejected her worship; denied the life-giving efficacy of the cross, and refused its worship; and gainsaid the awful mystery of the conversion of the blood of Christ in the Eucharist; while by others they are branded as the originators of the Iconoclastic heresy and the war against the sacred images. In the first notice of the secretaries in Western Europe, I mean at Orleans, they were similarly accused of treating with contempt the worship of martyrs and saints, the sign of the holy cross, and mystery of transubstantiation; and much the same too at Arras" (Elliott, *Horae Apocalyticae,* 2:277).

PELAGIANISM

Named after Pelagius, a fifth-century British monk who denied the doctrines of original sin* and the transmission of Adam's guilt to his posterity, Pelagianism became one of the most persistent heresies to corrupt the gospel of salvation by grace.

Pelagius and his immediate followers held that human nature was not ruined and inclined toward sin by the fall.* Thus they taught the natural ability of every soul to do good, since God creates each one with as much natural ability as He bestowed on Adam. Pelagius taught that sin* consisted only in separate acts of the will. To him, there was no such thing as a sinful disposition. In keeping with this, he held that Adam was not created positively holy, but with his will* equally balanced between good and evil. He explained the fact of the universality of sin

as the result of the imitation of the habits of other sinners.

Thus, Pelagianism has no place for the doctrines of grace* and the sovereignty of God.* Indeed, it has no place for redemption,* holding that man's free will* is sufficient for the practice of virtue, helped by the law of God and the example of Christ, which make holiness easier to practise.

The term *Pelagian* has also been used more loosely. William Cunningham says, "In ordinary usage, Pelagianism is commonly employed as a general designation of defective and erroneous views in regard to the extent and consequences of human depravity and of the necessity of special divine agency in conversion and sanctification."

Semi-Pelagianism started as a halfway house between Augustine's defence of the doctrine of grace and Pelagius's denial of it. Semi-Pelagianism held on to the notion that the fallen human will had some power to incline to good, but accepted the necessity of grace for salvation. However, this grace is given after the first step is taken by the will of man. Thus, man does not receive Christ because of grace, but receives grace after he decides to receive Christ.

Arminianism tends toward Semi-Pelagianism, though Arminius himself and others like John Wesley, have held (inconsistently, in the light of their other views) to total depravity* and the necessity of grace to precede and cause any decision of the human will to turn to Christ *(see Prevenient Grace).*

PENALTY OF THE BROKEN LAW

All the just consequences of sin. The Scripture denominates these under one word, "death" (Gen. 2:17). This includes natural, physical death (Ecc. 12:7), moral and spiritual death (Matt. 8:22; Eph. 2:1; 1 Tim. 5:6), and eternal death, the second death (Rev. 20:6-14).

A. A. Hodge remarks, "The instant the law was violated its penalty began to operate, although, on account of the intervention of the dispensation of grace, the full effect of the sentence is suspended during the present life. The Spirit of God was withdrawn the instant man fell, and he at once became spiritually dead, physically mortal, and under sentence of death eternal."

PENANCE

A sacrament of the Roman Catholic church "by which sins committed after baptism are forgiven through the absolution of the priest" (*Baltimore Catechism*). Roman Catholics are taught that penance helps them to make up for the temporal punishment they must suffer for sin, but since penance given by the priest does not always make full satisfaction for the sins in question, they should do other acts of penance in an effort to gain indulgences, or remissions from the punishments of purgatory.

The whole unscriptural notion is based on Rome's perverted system of merit.* Bishop Fulton J. Sheen wrote, "Through them [i.e., penances], the Church gives her penitents a fresh start. And the Church has tremendous spiritual capital, gained through centuries of penance, persecution, and martyrdom; many of her children prayed, suffered and merited more than they needed for their own individual salvation. The Church took these superabundant merits and put them into the spiritual treasury, out of which repentant sinners can draw in times of spiritual depression." *(See Supererogation).*

As well as highlighting the anti-Biblical and anti-Christian character of the Romish doctrine of penance, this statement serves to show, on the authority of one of Rome's most eminent 20th-century American bishops, that modern Rome has not shifted from the counterfeit gospel which the Reformers exposed and repudiated in the 16th century.

PENTECOSTALISM

The name chosen by churches that stress a post-conversion experience they describe as "the baptism in the Spirit," evidenced by the reception of the *charismata,* or supernatural gifts of the Holy Spirit,* especially *glossalalia,* speaking in tongues.

Pentecostal Roots

Pentecostalism claims the Holiness and Higher Life movements that began to flourish in the 19th century as its true roots. These movements emphasized a post-conversion "second blessing" and a baptism of the Spirit to impart power for service. Their views, Pentecostalists claim, paved the way for their movement. This claim appears to have an element of truth in it, in that Pentecostalism did flourish among members of Holiness groups, especially in the United States. However, many who strongly believed in the baptism of the Spirit to impart power for service, for example R. A. Torrey, and most of the supporters of the Keswick movement, rejected the Pentecostalist view of a restoration of the supernatural gifts of the apostolic period to the modern church. They particularly rejected the Pentecostalist insistence on speaking in tongues as the initial evidence of the baptism of the Spirit.

The Beginning of Pentecostalism

In the United States. Pentecostalism began January 1, 1901 when Agnes Ozman spoke in tongues at Bethel Bible School, Topeka, Kansas. The school was operated by Charles F. Parham who launched the view, now widely accepted among Pentecostalists, that speaking in tongues is the initial evidence of the baptism in the Spirit. The further evidence, he claimed, was the restoration of the NT charismata to the church, particularly the gift of supernatural healing. Indeed, this claim was developed to teach another widely held Pentecostalist position, namely that "healing is in the atonement." By this Parham and those who have followed him hold not merely that Christ's atonement has purchased eternal glorification for the believer's body—what Paul calls "the redemption of our body" (Rom. 8:23), which awaits the second coming* of Christ—but that it purchased for every Christian deliverance from every bodily sickness.

From 1906-09 "the Azusa Street Revival" gave Pentecostalism a worldwide prominence. The Azusa Street Mission in Los Angeles was an unpromising place for such a forward thrust. According to the *Los Angeles Times* it was a "tumble down shack." However, under the ministry of a black preacher from Texas, William J. Seymour, it became the scene of a prolonged Pentecostal event that attracted people from around the nation and the world, and sent them back with a burning zeal to see the new movement established in their own localities.

In Europe. In Europe, Pentecostalism started with the ministry of Thomas Ball Barratt, an English-born naturalized Norwegian. Barratt visited America and received the Pentecostalist experience in New York. He returned to Norway where he organized Pentecostalist meetings. Among his visitors was an Anglican clergyman from Sunderland, England, J. A. Boddy, who brought Barratt to England for special meetings that introduced Pentecostalism to Britain. Barratt had a similar influence in Germany, Switzerland, Denmark, and Finland, where his visits led to the establishment of Pentecostalist churches.

Growth of Pentecostalism

Prior to 1945. Though the growth of Pentecostalism was comparatively slow before World War II, the major Pentecostalist denominations were formed during that period. In America, the Pentecostal Holiness Church, the Church of God (Cleveland, Tennessee), the Church of God in Christ, the Assemblies of God, and the Pentecostal Church of God all came into existence before 1920. In Britain, the Apostolic Faith Church was formed by William Oliver Hutchinson. The Welsh assemblies in this group withdrew in 1916 to form the Apostolic Church. In 1915 George Jeffreys vis-

ited Northern Ireland where he formed the Elim Evangelistic Band, which later became the Elim Pentecostal Church. In 1924 some seventy independent Pentecostalist churches amalgamated to form the Assemblies of God of Great Britain and Ireland. Later (1940) Jeffreys left the Elim movement to form the Bible-Pattern Church Fellowship.

After World War II. After World War II, Pentecostalism experienced a worldwide growth, particularly through the efforts of American evangelists and faith healers, such as Oral Roberts and T. L. Osborne. Another leading cause of the spread of the movement was the emergence of the Full Gospel Business Men's Fellowship International which introduced Pentecostalism to many from mainstream churches and gave it much needed respectability. In America, Pentecostalists gained acceptance in mainstream Evangelicalism,* becoming charter members of the National Association of Evangelicals, though they were (and are) strongly opposed by Fundamentalist churches.

In Latin America and Africa, Pentecostalism met with great success. Indeed, by 1990, according to the *Dictionary of Pentecostal and Charismatic Movements*, there were 193,678,230 Pentecostalists worldwide, making Pentecostalism the largest Protestant grouping in the world. If Charismatic church members are included, this number soars to 372,651,280. However, this number is greatly inflated by the inclusion of over 45 million Roman Catholics and over 187 million members of denominational churches, whom the Pentecostal *Dictionary* claims as Pentecostal believers.

Pentecostal Theology

Historically, Pentecostalism was mainly a holiness movement that accepted the fundamental truths of the Protestant faith, though it was mostly Arminian* in its soteriology.* It suffered a major division on the doctrine of the Trinity* when very early in its existence (1916) the Assemblies of God had to face the withdrawal of a number who had espoused Sabellianism.* These became a "oneness" denomination, a "Jesus only" people who ascribed to Jesus the deity of the Father, the Son, and the Holy Spirit.

Pentecostalism and Neo-Pentecostalism

Since about 1970 Pentecostalism has become known as *Classical Pentecostalism* to distinguish it from *neo-Pentecostalism* (the experience and practice of Pentecostalist distinctives by people who remain members of mainline Protestant denominations) and from *Roman Catholic Charismatic Pentecostalism.*

The emergence of these groups has posed a major problem for many classical Pentecostalist churches that traditionally have seen themselves as Protestant and have been antipathetic to the ecumenical desire for union with Rome. In most cases, the anti-ecumenical stance of Pentecostalist churches has weakened in the light of the Charismatic Movement's* emphasis on the very experiences Pentecostalists claim to be proof of the baptism in the Spirit. Charismatic inclusivism has swept aside generations of Pentecostalist separatism.

PERFECTIONISM

The theory that sinless perfection is attainable in this life. The proponents of perfectionism include Pelagians, Romanists, Arminians, Wesleyans, and the Oberlin school of theologians (e.g., Charles Finney). These groups present conflicting ideas of sin, law, our relation to law, the role of grace, and exactly what is to be understood by *perfection.* Their point of agreement is that men may perfectly fulfil all that God at present requires them to be or do. We may compare and contrast their views.

Sin

Pelagians deny the pollution of human nature while the others accept it; but, as Berkhof rightly points out, "They all agree, however, in externalizing sin." For example, Rome's position is that the concupiscence* which continues to indwell renewed men is not in itself sin.* It is the fuel for actual sin, but "sin consists only in the consent of the will to the impulse of concupiscence" (A. A. Hodge). This is "externalizing sin."

Grace

Pelagians, holding to the idea of the natural ability of the human will to keep the laws of God, deny the need for, or exercise of, supernatural grace* in the attainment of perfection. The others hold that grace is necessary, though Rome's idea of grace is that it is received "through those sacramental and priestly channels which Christ has instituted in His Church, especially in the observance of works of prayer, fasting, and alms-deeds, and the acquisition of supererogatory merit by the fulfilment of the counsels of Christ to chastity, obedience, and voluntary poverty" (A. A. Hodge, summarizing the Council of Trent's position). Thus, even grace, in Rome's system, is by works!

Law

Pelagians, Rome, and the Oberlin school hold that the law which renewed men may fully keep in this life is the moral law of God. Arminians and Wesleyans deny this, believing that the law they perfectly keep is the new law of faith and evangelical obedience. Pelagians hold that man can perfectly keep the original moral law in all its parts. Rome holds that God in grace and for the sake of Christ adjusts the law's standards to our present capacities. The Oberlin school of Finney holds that it is justice, not grace, which adjusts the demands of the law!

What Perfection Really Entails

Pelagians mean complete sinless perfection, as complete as Adam's at his creation. Rome means fully keeping the divine law (adjusted to our deteriorated capacities!), and even doing more than is commanded, though (unless enabled as a special privilege) renewed men will fall into venial* sins every day. Finney held that a Christian may be "according to his knowledge, as upright as God is," and as "perfectly conformed to the will of God as is the will of the inhabitants of heaven."

Arminians and Wesleyans mean by perfection "entire sanctification," which every believer must attain before death, though most do so not long before death. This entire sanctification does not remove the "infirmities of the flesh" and of the natural temperament, nor does it exclude liability to mistakes—i.e., it is not perfect conformity to the moral law—but it does exclude all inward disposition to sin and all outward acts of sin and brings the soul to a state where it is governed by perfect faith in Christ and perfect love to God. In this way Christians fulfil the law of Christ, under which they are now held in a state of probation—i.e., failure means damnation, the popularly known dogma of "saved today, lost tomorrow." John Wesley acknowledged that "involuntary transgressions of a divine law, known or unknown," are "naturally consequent on the ignorance and mistakes inseparable from mortality." He also stated that entire sanctification and obedience "cannot bear the rigour of God's justice, but needs atoning blood," so that even the most perfect "must continually say, 'Forgive us our trespasses.'"

Most modern holiness movements generally follow the Wesleyan pattern. Some of them speak of "getting the root out"; but on closer examination they are found, like these systems we have examined, to detract from the sinfulness of sin and the strict application of the law of God. The only perfectionists, in the strictest use of the term, are the Pelagians. They, in this heresy, are consistent with their fundamental error. They are wrong, but consistently wrong. As for the rest, by tampering with the Biblical doctrine of sin and by dragging down the standards of the law of God to coincide with our ca-

pacities, they arrive at a doctrine of perfection. But it is perfection without substance.
*See **Sanctification.***

PERICOPE DE ADULTERA

The twelve verses from John 7:53-8:11, which contain the history of the woman taken in adultery. This is one of only two extensive sections of the NT upon whose authenticity modern textual critics have been able to cast doubt. The other portion is the last twelve verses of Mark's gospel. In both cases, as Dean Burgon* demonstrated, the weight of evidence for the genuineness of the verses assures them of their place in the NT.
*See **Textual Criticism of the New Testament***.

PERMISSIVE DECREE

In Reformed theology it is usual to speak of God's decree regarding sin as a permissive decree. By this is meant that God's decree rendered the sinful acts of His creatures absolutely certain, but God did not effectuate them by operating immediately upon the will of the creature. Rather, he determined not to hinder the sinful self-determination* of the creature's will and to regulate and control the results of this sinful self-determination. See Ps. 78:29; 106:15; Acts 14:16; 17:30. The permissive decree is not a conditional decree, it is absolute.
*See **Decrees of God***.

PERSEVERANCE OF THE SAINTS

"They whom God hath accepted in His Beloved, effectually called and sanctified by His Spirit, can neither totally nor finally fall away from the state of grace; but shall certainly persevere therein to the end, and be eternally saved. This perseverance of the saints depends not upon their own free will, but upon the immutability of the decree of election, flowing from the free and unchangeable love of God the Father; upon the efficacy of the merit and intercession of

Jesus Christ; the abiding of the Spirit, and of the seed of God within them; and the nature of the covenant of grace: from all which ariseth also the certainty and infallibility thereof" (*Westminster Confession of Faith*, chap. 17, sec. 1, 2). This statement contains certain key elements:

1. God's elect will certainly be eternally saved.

2. Those who have once been regenerated by the Holy Spirit can never completely fall from that state and be lost.

3. This perseverance is the perseverance of God in His love and grace toward His people; it is not something which depends upon human power or activity. Berkhof defines it as "that continuous operation of the Holy Spirit in the believer, by which the work of divine grace that is begun in the heart, is continued and brought to completion."

4. Thus it is an aspect of the Spirit's sanctifying grace: it is perseverance in holiness. It is what is popularly known as the eternal security of the believer. But to avoid the idea that a person who once made a profession of faith but has since lived in sin with no marks of holiness about his life, can comfort himself in being eternally secure, the Reformed statement of the doctrine emphasizes the certainty of perseverance in holiness if we have truly believed—not the certainty of salvation if we once professed to believe. Possessors of eternal life are secure; mere professors have neither life nor security.

5. Nevertheless, true believers may fall into sin (*Westminster Confession of Faith*, chap. 17, sec. 3), causing great hurt, grieving the Spirit and even incurring temporal judgments; but they can never be abandoned by the Lord who chose and regenerated them.

The Scripture clearly teaches this perseverance of the saints: Rom. 11:29; John 10:28; Phil. 1:6; 2 Thes. 3:3; 2 Tim. 1:12; 1 Pet. 1:5.

The church of Rome with its semi-Pelagianism* and its doctrine of free will,* rejects the doctrine of security for the justi-fied. "If anyone maintain that a man once justified cannot lose grace, and, therefore that he who falls and sins never was truly justified, let him be accursed" (Council of Trent, sess. 6, canon 23).

Arminians, including Wesleyans, also reject it. Their views of election, the purpose of the death of Christ, grace, and free will all lead to this conclusion. In this they seem more consistent than many modern evangelicals who wish to espouse these views but still hold on to "eternal security." A common objection to the doctrine is that it leads to laxity and even antinomianism,* but such an objection can have no force against the doctrine of perseverance in holiness, which is the very opposite to justifying unholiness. Objections based on the warnings of Scripture or the exhortations to believers to strive are also based on a misconception of the doctrine or of the scope and meaning of the Scripture texts.

PERSONAL PROPERTIES OF THE TRINITARIAN PERSONS

That "Father," "Son," and "Holy Spirit" are not merely nominal distinctions in the Godhead, but personal, is evidenced by the fact that Scripture reveals their incommunicable personal properties. The Father begets, the Son is begotten, and the Spirit proceeds from the Father and the Son. The Father neither is begotten nor does He proceed. Agreeably with the personal distinctions indicated by these incommunicable properties, the persons of the Trinity speak of each other as "I," "Thou," and "He."

*See **Opera Ad Intra**.*

PERSONALITY

"Personality is marked by two characteristics: (a) self-consciousness; (b) self-determination. Self-consciousness is, first, the power which a rational spirit has of making itself its own object, and, secondly, of knowing that it has done so.... If the first step is taken, and not the second, there is consciousness but not self-consciousness, because the subject would not in this case, know that the object is the self. And the second step cannot be taken if the first has not been. These two acts of a rational spirit, or mind, involve three distinctions in it, or modes of it. The whole mind as a subject contemplates the very same whole mind as an object....And the very same whole mind also perceives that the contemplating subject and the contemplated object are one and the same essence or being" (Shedd).

Self-determination* is freedom to act according to the inclination, bias, or disposition of the will.* Together, self-consciousness and self-determination constitute personality. Thus we speak of God as a personal God. Shedd sees in the trinal distinction noted in self-consciousness, a proof of the doctrine of the Trinity. Man's self-consciousness is patterned after God's, not vice versa, and thus it is no objection to say that since these distinctions in human self-consciousness do not yield a trinity in man, they cannot do so in God. Our knowledge of personality leads us to expect the Scriptures to speak of a trinal distinction in the personal God. The nature of that distinction is a matter of pure revelation. It is something upon which fallen man cannot begin to speculate—and Scripture reveals that in the divine essence the trinal distinctions are personalized, as Father, Son, and Holy Spirit, each with personal properties which cannot be attributed to the others.

See Ego; Trinity.

PESHITTA

The ancient Syriac, or Aramaic, translation of the OT was given this name, which means "simple." However, it was also given to the Syriac translation of the NT, the oldest translation known, dated around A.D. 100. It witnesses to the traditional text* of the NT.

Its value as a witness is lessened by scholars who wish to follow the minority text, represented chiefly by Codex Vaticanus and Codex Sinaiticus *(see Textual Criticism of the New Testament).* They hold it to be not the Old Syriac version, but a much later revision of it. It would destroy their textual theories to have a translation, evidently based on the traditional text, dated almost from the days of the apostles, for their whole thesis is that the traditional text represents a later revision of the text. F. C. Burkitt produced what has become the accepted theory: the Peshitta was the work of Rabbula, Bishop of Edessa from A.D. 411-435. Arthur Vööbus trenchantly dismissed Burkitt's theory: "This kind of reconstruction of textual history is pure fiction without a shred of evidence to support it" (*Early Versions of the New Testament,* p. 100). Indeed, the evidence is very clearly against Burkitt's theory. Rabbula was a Monophysite,* an opponent of the Nestorians.* It is certain that both Nestorians and Monophysites accepted the Peshitta as their authoritative Scriptures. This is perfectly understandable on the assumption of its early date, but it is utterly incredible that the Nestorians would unanimously and almost immediately have adopted a late work produced by their strongest opponent. Both Scrivener and Burgon* show that the evidence for the great antiquity of the Peshitta is strong (Scrivener, *Introduction to the Criticism of the New Testament;* Burgon, *Traditional Text of the Holy Gospels*), and its value as a witness to the traditional text is, therefore, of unimpaired importance.

PETROBRUSIANS

Followers of Peter de Bruys who around A.D. 100 began to speak out against the corruptions of the church of Rome and her clergy. He denied infant baptism, the sanctity of consecrated buildings, the use of crosses, the doctrine of the real presence* of Christ in the Lord's Supper,* and prayers for the dead.

PIETISM

A movement in the Lutheran church in the 17th century, reacting against dead orthodoxy and aiming at a revival of piety and vital godliness. P. J. Spener, its chief mover, emphasized informal prayer meetings and Bible study. Pietism did not itself become an organized movement, but it had a profound influence on the early Moravians, and through them, on the awakening of missionary vision. It also greatly affected John Wesley, and through him, the English-speaking countries of the world. Indeed, it still influences much of modern-day evangelicalism. Its emphasis is a healthy one, so long as it is within the framework of the great objective truths of the gospel. If that proviso is neglected, it leads to a very basic denial of the faith—witness the fact that Halle University, founded on the principles of pietism, became a centre of such emphasis on individual experience that it produced the pure subjectiveness of Schleiermacher's consciousness theology.*

PLATONISM

A form of philosophic idealism taught by Plato of Athens (circa 427-347 B.C.), the pupil of Socrates. Plato was convinced that absolute standards of virtue and truth existed, that goodness came from true wisdom, and that evil came from ignorance and folly. As he pondered the problem of how to know the absolute standards he believed existed, he concluded that human reason had to transcend the study of things as we see and experience them. He was influenced by the thinking of Pythagoras and his mathematical studies. The mathematicians had developed theorems in which geometric bodies were perfect. In real life, however, a triangle drawn in the dust is not perfect. Plato saw in this an answer to his problem of knowledge. Like the triangle in the dust, all things here on earth, including man and his virtues, are imperfect; but behind and beyond these imperfect forms there are the true forms of things, the patterns and archetypes of all we find in our world of experience. These ideal patterns are knowable by the application of human reason and Plato saw it as the job of the philosopher to pursue this goal. In Plato's most important work, *The Republic,* Socrates (all Plato's works are in dialogue form and he makes Socrates the expounder of his ideas) likens men to prisoners in an underground cave. They are chained and have their back to the light. They see the shadows cast by the light on the wall of their cave but mistake them for realities. True knowledge comes, not by treating the shadows as if they were substantial but by turning around to face the light. When a man does that, he leaves his cave of shadows and sees the real things—the archetypal forms—face to face.

Plato believed in one God, the supreme form of good which is the cause of all being and knowing. He also believed in the immortality of the soul, though he held the idea of reincarnation. His philosophy had a profound effect on the development of how Christians presented their beliefs to the world. Starting with Justin Martyr, the early apologists incorporated Plato's ideas into their statement of Biblical revelation.* His philosophy came to be the accepted dress in which the theology of revelation was presented. This synthesis of theology* with Platonic philosophy is known as Neoplatonism. It was developed in the school of Alexandria in the third century A.D. but was rooted in the ideas of Plotinus (A.D. 205-270), a non-Christian philosopher in that city.

This synthesis continued to have a dominating impact on theological thought until Thomas Aquinas promoted the dialectical logic of Aristotle. The great division between realism* and nominalism* in scholastic theology was largely the division between Platonism (adopted by the Realists) and Aristotelianism* (adopted by the nominalists). The baneful impact of Greek philosophy upon theology was noted by Cornelius Van Til. In his judgment, "The God of Greek philosophy is either exclusively deistic or exclusively pantheistic" (*A Survey of Christian Epistemology,* p. 16).

POLISH BRETHREN

An Anabaptist* group of Socinian* views.

POLITICAL THEOLOGY

A theological method of contextualization* that relates religion to the political situation of the society in which it exists. While it may recognize the importance of a personal reception of grace and a personal relationship with God, it refuses to see the great themes of the gospel solely or chiefly in terms of individual salvation. It holds that those themes—peace, justice, reconciliation, freedom, etc.—must be seen in a social setting. The leading exponent of political theology, Roman Catholic theologian J. B. Metz, asserts that such kingdom themes "cannot be made radically private affairs … cannot be entirely interiorized and spiritualized as corresponding to the individual's longing for freedom and peace. They make the individual free with regard to the society around him, in the sense of committing him to it in a free critique of it" (*Sacramentum Mundi,* vol. 5, p. 36, quoted in *New Dictionary of Theology,* p. 521).

C. Wigglesworth of the Church of Scotland's Board of World Mission and Unity argued that "Scripture requires this concern, with its witness to Jesus in moral conflict with the religious and political leaders of his society, his cross set up in public, and his church called, as bearer of his eschatological message, to similar encounters with the political world. The church is an institution within society with a series of crucial, liberating tasks: first, concern for the individual, especially the person who is a victim of impersonal technology devoted to bettering the future of the rich; secondly, a message that the future depends on God;

thirdly, love expressed in social terms by bringing justice and peace to all, even in extreme situations to the extent of calling for revolutionary change for the sake of the victims of present systems; and fourthly, a changed view of itself which accepts internal criticism of its leadership (a problem for the Roman Catholic church especially), welcomes truth from outside and is prepared to oppose the political powers that be" (*New Dictionary of Theology,* p. 521).

By such means political theology validates such things as liberation theology,* African theology,* Black theology, revolutionary theology,* and feminist theology.* Some new evangelical* theologians have responded positively to its approach. Conservatives have seen it for what it really is, a rejection of the gospel in the terms in which the Biblical text states it. The paradigm* Wigglesworth adopts is patently one he imposes on the Scriptures, not something they impose on us. To make the fact that the Romans crucified Christ publicly a reason for making the church a political pressure group or revolutionary movement is absurd. To define the Biblical doctrine of Christian liberty in terms of political and economic "freedom" is heretical. To turn the church's ministry into one of political conflict is to fly in the face of the response of the NT church to the gross inequities they faced from the Roman authorities. If Rom. 13 and 1 Pet. 4:12-16 are true, Wigglesworth's paradigm is false.

Of course it is impossible for the Christian church to live and witness in this world without affecting political theory and practice. Indeed it ought never to fear to speak boldly to call national leaders and society at large to the moral absolutes of the law of God and to repentance toward God and faith in the Lord Jesus Christ. Its message of gospel truth will transform lives spiritually, and when that power is felt in a sufficiently large number of people, the effect on the nation will be dramatic. But the church of Christ must never forget the words of its Master: "My kingdom is not of this world: if my kingdom were of this world, then would my servants fight" (John 18:36). As Andrew Melville told Scotland's King James VI when the monarch tried to change the constitution of the church: "There are two kings and two kingdoms in Scotland: there is King James, the head of the commonwealth; and there is Christ Jesus, the king of the church, whose subject James the sixth is, and in whose kingdom he is not a king, nor a lord, nor a head, but a member." The church's role in the political life of a nation, as distinct from the involvement of individual Christians, will of necessity be indirect, in that its task is not to develop into a political pressure group but to be faithful to the truth of the gospel of Christ. When the church is used of God to build up His kingdom by leading sinners to evangelical repentance* and saving faith,* it is most effective in changing the society in which it is called to labour.

The difficulty facing the church in relating its theology to the political system under which it lives and serves is obvious. The Reformers, the Puritans, the Covenanters and many others are standing proof of that. The dangers involved in making the church's task a political one should be equally obvious. The marriage of religion and political philosophy and ambition has produced many horrors, from the Crusades to the Inquisition to Nazism to some modern Marxist revolutionary movements. When the church defines her task in terms of political and social action rather than in terms of spiritual activity (that will have not only spiritual but social and political implications)—and this is precisely what political theology proposes—she will fail both God and man.

When the church is faithful and successful in its stand for the gospel of Christ it will often face great suffering. It may be drawn into deep conflicts; but it must never allow itself to become the political pawn of any man or movement, the theological cover they need for the furtherance of their agenda. The church must follow its own agenda, or rather that of its Master: "Go ye therefore, and teach all nations, baptizing them in the name of the Father, and of the Son, and of the Holy Ghost: teaching them to observe all things whatsoever I have commanded you: and, lo, I am with you alway, even unto the end of the world" (Matt. 28:19-20). That is not a commission "to do political theology" but one to engage in evangelistic outreach to lead people of every nation to the knowledge of eternal salvation.

POLYTHEISM

Belief in many gods. *See Theism*.

POSITIVISM

The philosophy which was presented as a coherent system by French philosopher Auguste Comte (1798-1857), though it was foreshadowed in the philosophies of Locke and Hume. It teaches that knowledge consists of or is derived from actual facts, meaning mathematics and the scientific method of observation and experiment. The German theologian Albrecht Ritschl (1822-1889) adopted a positivist approach to theology, limiting it to what our religious feelings value as factual and practical *(see Pragmatism)*. To Ritschl, religious doctrines are merely value judgments. He considered love to be the fundamental determination in the Christian view of God and aimed through this attribute to solve the problems of the world and to show the world that it owed its existence to God.

Thus Ritschl carried the idea of Schleiermacher *(see Consciousness Theology)* a step further: the latter elevated human religious consciousness to the role of final arbiter, Ritschl set up human values as to what is practicable. As with every other false philosophy, positivism arrogates to the human mind the throne of supreme judgment.

See Ritschlianism.

POSTMILLENNIALISM

The belief that Christ's second coming* will be preceded by the Millennium,* a golden age of gospel blessing upon the ministry of the church. At Christ's coming there will be the general resurrection, the general judgment, followed by the creation of the new heavens and the new earth, and the eternal state.

PRACTICAL THEOLOGY

That branch of theological study that covers all the "practical" parts of a pastor's work. It is almost another name for pastoral theology,* concentrating on the "official duties" mentioned under that head. It includes such subjects as homiletics, worship, liturgy, catechetics, pastoral care and counselling, church administration, church growth and church planting, and ethical responses to the problems that arise from the advance of technology (such as the moral decisions that have to be made because of advances in medical procedures).

PRAGMATISM

The philosophy that defines truth as that which produces good works. Therefore, pragmatists count as "true" whatever "works," or produces effects they judge beneficial. Thus they recognize no absolute moral standard and adopt the moral theory of relativism.* The Bible is directly contrary to pragmatism, teaching that works are judged by truth. According to Scripture, divine revelation determines what is true and provides the basis and standard for judging action. When the Lord Jesus said, "By their fruits ye shall know them," He was not saying that truth is determined by behaviour, but that the reality or otherwise of a person's belief in the truth is shown by his behaviour. The folly of pragmatism is that without a prior standard of good and evil, we cannot speak of some works being good and others evil.

See **Ritschlianism**.

PRAXIX

A term popular in political theology* and liberation theology* to denote religious faith in action to make the world a better place. That is the idea behind the popular phrase "doing theology." Studying theology emphasizes orthodoxy in doctrine; doing theology emphasizes social and political involvement, usually with a corresponding decrease in interest in doctrinal purity.

PRECEPTIVE WILL OF GOD

God's command to His moral creatures to do what He says to be right and wise for them to do. Some see a difficulty in reconciling the preceptive will of God and His decretive will, that is, the purpose of His eternal decree. A. A. Hodge says, "They are not inconsistent. What He wills as our duty may very consistently be different from what He wills as His purpose. What is right for him to permit may be wrong for Him to approve, or for us to do." For example, it is right for God to command repentance and faith from all men (His preceptive will, Acts 17:30), even those He has not elected to eternal life (His decretive will, Acts 13:48).

PREDESTINATION

In the widest sense, predestination "is the theological doctrine…that from eternity God has foreordained all things which come to pass" (Boettner). In this sense it is synonymous with God's decree. However, it is most frequently used in a narrower sense, "as designating only the counsel of God concerning fallen men, including the sovereign election of some and the most righteous reprobation of the rest" (A. A. Hodge).

In this sense, predestination is in two parts, election and reprobation (see *Westminster Confession,* chap. 3, sec. 3, 7).

Election has no other basis than the good pleasure of God. It is not conditional, it does not rest upon any foreseen act of faith. Rather, faith is part of the blessing the elect are chosen to receive (1 Pet. 1:1, 2; Eph.

2:8-10; Phil. 1:29). Reprobation also has its basis in the good pleasure of God (Rom. 9:11-18). However, while election is purely sovereign, taking no account of the personal deserts of the objects of it, reprobation, while certainly sovereign, is also judicial and does take account of the guilt of the sinner. The *Westminster Confession of Faith* (chap. 3, sec. 7) states the Reformed position clearly: "The rest of mankind, God was pleased, according to the unsearchable counsel of His own will, whereby He extendeth or withholdeth mercy as He pleaseth, for the glory of His sovereign power over His creatures, to pass by, and to ordain them to dishonour and wrath for their sin, to the praise of His glorious justice" (Rom. 9:18-22; 2 Tim. 2:19-20; Jude 4; 1 Pet. 2:8).

Thus reprobation has two parts to it: (a) Preterition, or the passing over of some in the decree of election. This is the sovereign prerogative of God. As Calvin long ago pointed out, God owes no man anything, and no man can justly argue against the righteousness of God in passing him by in election, so leaving him to his own sinful self-determination. (b) Condemnation is the act of the sovereign judge. It is passed upon sinners. No man will be damned except for sin.

Viewing predestination as composed of election and reprobation is often referred to as double predestination.* While some represent double predestination as the twin discretionary acts of a sovereign God, both without reference to anything but God's good pleasure, it is better and more scriptural to mark the distinction between election and reprobation set out above, and evidently sanctioned by the language of our Confession.

PRE-EXISTENCE OF SOULS

The theory that the souls of men existed in a previous state. The theory can take various forms: (a) It can be presented as the belief that all souls exist in a treasury from which they are called forth to inhabit men. (b) It can be presented as a blatant belief in reincarnation, holding that occurrences in a former life have some power to determine the present condition of a soul. (c) Origen taught that man's present material existence is a punishment for sins committed in a previous existence. (d) Mormonism teaches that the soul, which is synonymous with spirit, is with God in heaven until sent to indwell the newly conceived baby. None of these theories can claim any support for their ideas from the word of God. All shades of reincarnation and its attendant notions are foreign to Scripture. The Bible teaches that souls, upon quitting this life, enter into everlasting blessing in the presence of God or everlasting punishment in separation from God (Phil. 1:23; 2 Cor. 5:6-8; Luke 12:4, 5).

See **Soul**; **Traducianism**.

PRELACY

Episcopacy.*

PREMILLENNIALISM

The belief that Christ's second coming* will occur before the millennium,* and that he will then reign for 1,000 years on the earth. It is often mistakenly equated with dispensationalism,* which is premillennial in its eschatology;* however it long predates dispensationalism. The distinction is frequently made by speaking of *historic premillennialism,* from which dispensationalism is a departure.

PREPARATIONISM

The view that sinners must be spiritually prepared in order to receive the promises and invitations of the gospel, usually by a sufficient amount of conviction of sin wrought in them by an application of the law of God. It effectively changes Christ's commission to His people to "go into all the world and preach the gospel" (Mark 16:15). Certainly we must set the gospel in its Biblical relation to the law and must labour to bring sinners to a sense of their need of Christ, but we must also recognize that the grace they need is saving grace—and that is what God promises to all who receive Christ as He is freely offered in the gospel. The tendency of preparationism is toward hypercalvinism* and is anti-evangelistic. It is also virtually a doctrine of works. Essentially it is a doctrine of how to make sinners acceptable enough to God to receive saving grace, though its proponents would strongly deny this conclusion and proclaim their belief in sovereign grace. No doubt they do believe in sovereign grace but their preparationist ideas are inconsistent with that belief. It is more in line with the Roman Catholic notion of the merit* of congruity, the idea that an unregenerate man may display such dispositions as will make it fitting for God to confer regenerating grace.

PRESBYTERIANISM

The form of church government based on the spiritual oversight of elders or presbyters. Presbyterianism proceeds upon a collation of the Scripture rules regarding church government and the consistent application of those rules to our own situation. In this way, it is shown that the inspired apostles committed the ordinary administration of the divine ordinances, and the ordinary regulation of church affairs, to rulers or office bearers, not to the general body of church members; that these office bearers were of two kinds, presbyters (also called bishops) and deacons; that the presbyters were of two kinds, those who taught and ruled and those who only ruled; that the spiritual affairs of the church were administered by the elders, and that its temporal and secular affairs were managed by them in conjunction with the deacons. Furthermore, there is clear Scripture evidence that, at least in some cases, several congregations were placed under one presbyterial government, and that there was a subordination of

the local church court (i.e., its elders) to this general presbytery.

John Calvin set forth the fullest scriptural exposition of this theme. William Cunningham remarks: "[Calvin's] leading principles were these: That a separate ministry is a standing ordinance appointed by God, provision being made in His Word for preserving and perpetuating it in the church in a regular manner; and that ministers who have been duly and regularly set apart to the work are alone warranted, in all ordinary circumstances, to administer God's ordinances of public preaching and the sacraments; that presbyters, or ordinary pastors of congregations, are fully authorized to discharge all the ordinary duties necessary in the administration of the affairs of the church—including, of course, the ordination of other pastors" (*Historical Theology*, 2:518). After mentioning Calvin's repudiation of episcopacy,* Cunningham goes on to emphasize his principle "that a distinction between the office bearers and the ordinary members of the church is established by Scripture, and ought to be permanently observed" (*ibid.*).

Thus the hierarchical system of prelacy* is denied. But, from all that has been said, so is the principle of independency.* Presbyterianism, laying great stress on portions like Acts chapters 1, 6, 15, lays down these general positions:
1. The unity of the church. The Scripture picture is not one of a great number of totally independent churches. Acts 15 makes that clear.
2. Ultimate ecclesiastical authority is not vested in the local church, but in a presbytery made up of elders from the constituent congregations. In Acts 15 the principles of the lesser church court being subordinate to the greater is also established.
3. The equality of the elders is also set forth. At the general council in Jerusalem (Acts 15) there is no hint of a hierarchy, and the language of Galatians 2 confirms this. Indeed, the Greek of Acts 15:2 makes it clear that

the apostles sat on that council as elders, while the Greek of verse 6 indicates that there were elders who were not apostles. The distinction between elders who rule and elders who rule and teach is made in 1 Tim. 5:17, but both have equal standing and power in the courts of the church.

4. The right of the people to a real part in the government of the church, by means of electing the office bearers of the church. Acts 1 and 6 give instances of this in the early church; yet, as Acts 15 shows, this part in government does not warrant the practice of independency. Some claim that Acts 15:12 indicates that the decision of the council in Jerusalem was the decision of the entire congregation, which was present for the meeting. However, this view is unwarranted, for the following reasons:

a. Verse 2 specifically states that the question was for "the apostles and elders."

b. This interpretation of v. 12 proves too much for the independents, because it then presents the case of one congregation deciding issues for other congregations. Is that independency? Furthermore, there surely was more than one congregation in Jerusalem after all those years (cf. Gal. 2:1) of fruitful gospel preaching. Thus, we have many congregations meeting to discuss and decide issues for other (absent) congregations. Is this independency?

c. *Multitude* in v. 12 means merely the whole assemblage or gathering, and is quite consonant with the view that it means the gathering of the elders.

d. When the whole church is referred to, as in v. 22, that very phrase is employed. Evidently, the entire church associated itself with the decision reached by their elders.

These general points give us the essence of Presbyterianism, and show it to be a form of church government "founded on and agreeable to the Word of God,"

to use the temperate language of the Scottish ordination* formula.

PRESUPPOSITIONALISM

The system of Christian apologetics* pioneered by Cornelius Van Til of Westminster Theological Seminary, based on the theological writings of Abraham Kuyper. Van Til believed that the Bible never sets out to "prove" the truth of God's existence or of the gospel by human reason. Rather, it presupposes God (Gen. 1:1; Heb. 11:6).

The God of the Bible is the absolute, eternal, ontological Trinity,* who has revealed Himself in His word, the Bible, the focus of which is His final personal self-expression in the self-attesting Christ (Heb. 1:1-3). Thus God is not a fact of the universe, or the mere force behind the universe. He is not something whose existence may be questioned or denied while we yet come to true conclusions about the facts of the universe. The God of the Bible is necessary to the existence of all the facts of the universe. He created them and only in Him can they have their true meaning. It is by Christ that all things cohere (Col. 1:17).

This is what a Christian presupposes in all his reasoning about God, truth, causality, factuality, and man. Conversely, this is what every non-Christian denies in his reasoning. In other words, it is impossible to approach any of these subjects apart from a presuppositional bias.

Van Til criticized the usual apologetic approach of Christians who try to use the "brute facts" of the universe, as he called them, to convince antitheists, as if both parties held these facts in common as a point of contact between them. His criticism was that this approach failed to expose and challenge the antitheistic bias in all non-Christian thought, but rather accepted it. Furthermore, the God "proved" by such methods is always less than the true God, the God of Scripture.

Van Til believed that we must never accept that the mind of fallen man is capable of thinking about anything without a sinful bias or that it can ever arrive at the truth apart from God. Christians may, for the sake of argument, reason with sinners on their own presuppositional ground with a view to showing the absurdity of their system—for no matter how hard unbelievers try, they can never make the facts of God's creation "fit" an antitheistic system. They are God-created facts.

Having shown the absurdity of antitheistic systems, the Christian's task is to proclaim, not to "prove," the Biblical revelation. Sinners are wilfully blind to the truth of God. They suppress the witness that is all around them and within them (Rom. 1: 18-20; 2:15). Their problem is not factual but spiritual. Presuppositionalism aims at freeing Christians to attack the entrenched positions of antitheistic intellectuals with confidence, knowing that the power of the gospel is not in rational proofs but in the self-attestation of the One who is the truth.

Van Til gives this description of his presuppositional system in his *Survey of Christian Epistemology:* "Every system of thought necessarily has a certain method of its own. Usually this fact is overlooked. It is taken for granted that everybody begins in the same way with an examination of the facts, and that the differences between systems come only as a result of such investigations. Yet this is not actually the case. It could not actually be the case. In the first place, this could not be the case with a Christian. His fundamental and determining fact is the fact of God's existence. That is his final conclusion. But that must also be his starting point. If the Christian is right in his final conclusion about God, then he would not even get into touch with any fact unless it were through the medium of God. And since man has, through the fall in Adam, become a sinner, man cannot know and therefore love God except through Christ the Mediator. Scripture is the Word of Christ, the Son of God and Son of man. No sinner knows any-

thing truly except he knows Christ, and no one knows Christ truly unless the Holy Ghost, the Spirit sent by the Father and the Son, regenerates him. If all things must be seen 'in God' to be seen truly, one could look ever so long elsewhere without ever seeing a fact as it really is. If I must look through a telescope to see a distant star, I cannot first look at the star to see whether there is a telescope through which alone I could see it. If I must look through a microscope to see a germ, I cannot first look at the germ with the naked eye to see if there is a microscope through which alone I can see it. If it were a question of seeing something with the naked eye and seeing the same object more clearly through a telescope or a microscope, the matter would be different. We may see a landscape dimly with the naked eye and then turn to look at it through a telescope and see it more clearly. But such is not the case with the Christian position. According to it, nothing at all can be known truly of any fact unless it be known through and by way of man's knowledge of God.

"But if it be readily granted that a Christian begins with a bias, it will not be so readily granted that his opponents also begin with a bias. Yet this is no less the case. And the reason for this is really the same as that given above in the case of the Christian. We may again illustrate with our telescope analogy. The antitheist is one who has made up his mind in advance that he will never look through a telescope. He maintains steadfast in his conviction that there are some facts that can be known truly without looking through a telescope. This much is implied in the very idea of starting to see whether there is a God. It will be observed that even to say that there are some facts that can be known without reference to God, is already the very opposite of the Christian position. It is not necessary to say that all facts can be known without reference to God in order to have a flat denial of the Christian position. The contention of Christianity is exactly that there is not one fact that can be known without God. Hence if anyone avers that there is even one fact that can be known without God, he reasons like a non-Christian. It follows then that such a person in effect rejects the whole of the Christian position, the final conclusions as well as the starting point. All that means that such a person has at the outset taken for granted that there is no God in whom alone 'facts' can be known. In other words such a person has taken for granted that God at least is not such a 'fact' that he is related to every other 'fact' so that no other fact can be understood without reference to the 'fact' of God" (pp. 5, 6).

The last sentence of this quotation sums up the whole position. This is what presuppositionalism is all about. If we recognize this we will be able to see Van Til's wisdom in insisting that Christians cannot hope to establish the truth about God and the gospel by adopting the presuppositional position of unbelievers.

PRETERISM

A method of interpreting the book of the Revelation as a description of conditions in the first century A.D. Preterists see the book as a protest in apocalyptic terms against the tyranny of imperial Rome, not as a prophecy of end-time conditions and events.

One may accept that the Revelation exposes conditions in the first century without going to the extreme of Preterism. The letters to the seven churches, as Sir William Ramsay has shown in his *Letters to the Seven Churches,* are more fully comprehensible if we understand the story of the cities in which they were located. However, it is a very different thing to hold that all the data of the book refer to events in the first century, even before A.D. 70, as some preterists insist. Chapter 4:1 refers to the great body of the book to what happens "hereafter," or in the future from John's point in time. To see the first and the clearly implied second resurrection, the judgment of the living and the

dead, the creation of a new heavens and a new earth, and the new Jerusalem as symbols of first century events is fanciful.

The conviction that this is a book that is ultimately eschatological is not something we impose on the book but something that arises out of its own language and descriptions. *See Futurism, Historicism.*

PRETERITION

Preterition is the sovereign decision of God in His eternal decree* to pass over some and leave them to their self-determined sinfulness, while He graciously elects others, equally sinful in themselves, unto eternal salvation. Preterition does not make any man a sinner. The guilt of sin is chargeable to none but sinful man himself. Nor is preterition the ground on which sinners are condemned to hell. Condemnation is a judicial act and proceeds solely on the ground of personal guilt.*
See Predestination.

PREVENIENT GRACE

Latin *pre,* "before," and *venire,* "to come"; grace that must precede certain actions of man to enable him to perform them.

Evangelical Arminians, following John Wesley, hold that prevenient grace is the grace God gives a sinner to enable him to exercise the faith on the basis of which he is regenerated.

Some evangelicals, who do not think of themselves as Arminians mainly because they do not believe in Arminianism's* "saved and lost" theory, have a similar view. They speak of prevenient grace as the ability to exercise saving faith that God has given to all men through the merits of Christ's death. They view regeneration* as the result, not the cause, of faith.

In Roman Catholic theology, prevenient grace is grace necessary to receive the benefit of the grace conveyed by a sacrament.*

All these theories of prevenient grace are deficient. The Arminian and the evangelical views appear to be weak attempts to evade the force of the Reformed doctrine of irresistible grace* and effectual calling.* They both make saving faith the action of unregenerate man. According to Scripture, it is the action of the new man. Faith* is the result, not the cause, of regeneration (Rom. 8:7; 1 Pet. 1:2).

The Roman Catholic use of prevenient grace is an obvious invention to provide support for Rome's unscriptural system of sacramentalism.*

PRIESTHOOD OF ALL BELIEVERS

The right of all believers in Jesus Christ to approach God without any intermediary other than the Lord Jesus Christ. Christ is the only mediator* (1 Tim. 2:5) and through Him all Christians have direct access to the Father (Eph. 2:18). Peter calls Christians "a holy priesthood" and "a royal priesthood" (1 Pet. 2:5, 9). They have sacrifices to offer, but not of an expiatory nature. Christ has "offered one sacrifice for sins forever" (Heb. 10:12). The sacrifices we offer are spiritual (Rom. 12:1; Heb. 13:15, 16).

The NT knows no other priesthood in the church.* It has no official rank of priest that renders a class of men the necessary dispensers of the grace of God, without whom Christian life cannot proceed. That is the invention of the church of Rome and is a mark of her apostasy* from the truth of the gospel. In her system grace is conveyed sacramentally, *opus operatum,** and the sacraments demand the service of a priest. It is strictly a system of priestcraft that brings its followers under bondage and denies them the essential rights and privileges all the members of the NT church enjoyed.

The power of priestcraft in the Roman system has been evidenced many times in history. Every time the pope placed a people under interdict,* he was saying in effect that he was shutting heaven to them—and he used that power to impose his political will on superstitious men untaught in the truths of the gospel. It was one of the great accomplishments of the Reformation* to sweep away this monstrous system and to proclaim that sinners have direct access to God through the merits of Christ to obtain from Him directly the saving grace they need, and that saints have unrestricted access to the throne of grace, without any sacerdotal* intrusion by any man.

PRIESTLY OFFICE OF CHRIST

One of the three functions of Christ as mediator, the others being His prophetic office and His kingly office. The *Shorter Catechism* (Q. 25) defines the priestly office of Christ as "His once offering up of Himself a sacrifice to satisfy divine justice, and reconcile us to God; and [His] making continual intercession for us." It is important to emphasize that these two aspects of the priestly work of Christ have the same scope. That is, they have respect to the same persons. He intercedes for all for whom He died.

In the past, some Arminians have made much of the distinction between impetration,* or the obtaining by Christ of the benefits of redemption, and the application of those benefits to particular souls. Impetration, they hold, has respect to all men, but application only to believers. Amyraldians *(see **Amyraldism)** also made this distinction. But both impetration and application have the same persons in view. This can be seen in the two parts of Christ's priestly ministry. Dare any man say that Christ obtained eternal redemption for those for whom, according to His own words, He explicitly excluded from His intercession (John 17:9)? The *Westminster Confession of Faith* (chap. 8, sec. 8), draws attention to the fact that Christ intercedes for, and thereby applies His redeeming grace to, all for whom He died.

Finally, it should be noted that Christ executes His priestly office directly or immediately, not mediately. He does not act as our priest through agents or delegates. OT priests were types of Christ our priest, not delegates. We read in Hebrews 7:24 that He exercises an unchangeable, or untransferable, priesthood. It is particularly important to remember this in the light of the claims of the Roman Catholic church and others that their ministers are really priests acting for Christ in the dispensing of grace to men. Shedd has well said, "The Romish theory of an ecclesiastical priesthood acting, since Christ's ascension, as the delegates and agents of the great high priest, has no support in Scripture."

PRIMITIVE STATE

The state of Adam, as God created him, prior to his fall into sin *(see Fall)*. The *Westminster Confession of Faith* (chap. 4, sec. 2) states, "God...created man, male and female, with reasonable and immortal souls, endued with knowledge, righteousness, and true holiness, after His own image, having the law of God written in their hearts, and power to fulfill it; and yet under a possibility of transgressing, being left to the liberty of their own will, which was subject unto change. Beside this law written in their hearts, they received a command not to eat of the tree of the knowledge of good and evil; which while they kept, they were happy in their communion with God, and had dominion over the creatures."

Man's primitive state,* then, was one of mutable perfection. He was created in the image of God,* a rational and moral free agent, in righteousness and true holiness, with dominion over the other creatures of earth. "Righteousness" declares that man was created sinless; "holiness" declares that God created the dispositions of his will* in a state of conformity to, and inclination toward, His law. Thus man was not created in a state of mere equilibrium, finely balanced between good and evil. He was created positively holy and righteous (Ecc. 7:29; *see Regeneration*). This scriptural view of man's primitive state enables us to understand the gravity of the fall. Obviously, it was no mere upset of the balance in man. It was much more radical than that. It was the wrecking of a holy disposition in man and its replacement with a sinful and godless disposition. It depraved and corrupted his entire nature. Man's primitive perfection was mutable, for his original state was one of probation,* under the terms of the covenant of works.

*See **Covenant Theology***.

PRINCETON THEOLOGY

The exposition and defence of the Reformed faith in the 19th and early 20th centuries by the theologians of Princeton Seminary. The leading figures were A. A. Alexander, Charles Hodge, A. A. Hodge, J. W. Alexander, J. A. Alexander, B. B. Warfield, and J. Gresham Machen. Princeton theology employed the Scottish Common Sense* philosophy and promoted strict adherence to a Calvinistic federal theology and, in times of denominational drifting, to the Westminster Standards* as the authentic confessional position of Presbyterianism.* It laid great emphasis on the inspiration* and authority* of Scripture, holding that the Bible is God's verbally infallible word—a fact they maintained on the twin bases of its own internal testimony to itself and external proofs that this testimony is true.

PROBABILISM

The Roman Catholic teaching that where a line of action is merited by a solid probable opinion, it is permissible, even though a more probable opinion militates against it. It is a theory adopted and perfected by the Jesuits,* as a method of justifying almost any action taken by Rome and her minions. Probabilism is still the teaching of Rome.

PROBATION

Probation is a trial. The word is used to convey the situation in which Adam was placed under the covenant of works. *(See **Covenant Theology**.)*

1. Adam was placed in a covenant relationship. Hosea 6:7 says, "They like men [Hebrew, "like Adam"] have transgressed the covenant." So Adam transgressed a covenant.
2. The covenant under which Adam was placed was the covenant of works. Genesis 2:17 clearly shows this.
3. The condition of the covenant was perfect obedience (Gen. 2:17).
4. The promised reward for perfect obedience was life. This is implied in Gen. 2:17, and the principle is stated again and again in Scripture (Lev. 18:5; Ezek. 20:11, 13, 21; Luke 10:28; Rom. 10:5; Gal. 3:12). In Rom. 7:10 Paul notes that the commandment was unto life.
5. The penalty of the covenant: the punishment for failure was death (Gen. 2:17). The whole race was on trial in Adam, fell with him, and sinned in him (Rom. 5:12). This is the only occasion of probation in this sense of the word. The notion of dispensationalists that God has placed man in a series of probationary situations, each holding the possibility of gaining eternal life, has no basis in Scripture.

Also unbiblical is the notion that the period between death and the resurrection (see **Intermediate State**; **Purgatory**) is a period of probation and gospel opportunity. The Scripture holds out no hope of repentance and salvation after death. Berkhof lists the following among his arguments against the theory:
1. The state of unbelievers after death is represented in Scripture as a fixed state (Luke 16:19-31; John 8:21, 24; 2 Pet. 2:4, 9; Jude 7-13; cf. I Pet. 3:19).
2. The final judgment in Scripture always has reference to deeds done in the flesh, not in the intermediate state (Matt. 7:22, 23; 10:32, 33; 25:34-46; Luke 12:47, 48; 2 Cor. 5:9, 10; Gal. 6:7, 8; 2 Thes. 1:8; Heb. 9:27).
3. The notion, which undergirds the theory that only the conscious rejection of Christ and His gospel causes men to perish, is

unscriptural. Man is lost by nature—by nature he is a child of wrath (Eph. 2:3).
*See **Second Probation**.*

PROCESS THEOLOGY

The theological system that grew out of the philosophical speculations of Alfred North Whitehead and Charles Hartshorne. Its premise is that reality is a process of becoming. This is true of God: He is the eternal and absolute mind of which the universe is the body. Thus God and the universe are viewed in pantheistic terms, though process theologians argue that as a person may say, "I am my body, but I am more than my body," so God is more than the universe. In this view, the evolution of the universe is really the process of God's becoming. This leads naturally to the notion that every event in history is incarnational, for it shows God acting and becoming. Hence the Biblical doctrine of the incarnation* and deity of Christ* must be abandoned. Process theologians speak of Christ's life and death inaugurating a new way of living for man. They produced a major step forward in human evolution by giving us the church, which was a new kind of human community. This, according to process theology, is the real meaning of the resurrection.

Process theology posits the notion that every event is not only incarnational, and therefore God-determined, but self-determined. Thus even God cannot predict the future, which must remain unknown until it decides its own shape. In this way process theology repudiates the Biblical doctrines of general and special revelation,* prophetic utterance and its fulfilment, and of course a verbal, inspired, and inerrant Word.

In the light of all this, process theology has to redefine the idea of redemption and salvation, which become descriptions of a person's willingness to join in the community of the church, the body of Christ. Why this should be superior to any other way of life is difficult to see since every event is incarnational. Though process theologians would deny it, their theory destroys the essential difference between sin and virtue, since every event is God's activity in the historical process.

Some process theologians, notably the Roman Catholic Teilhard de Chardin, have sought to impart a more orthodox gloss to their theories by insisting that the entire cosmic order is evolving toward a goal, the "Omega Point," which is Christ. Indeed this optimistic note runs through much of process theology. Though God cannot predict the future, he never forgets an event of the past, and He uses the past not only to give meaning to it but to present new possibilities to the future. However, since the future is completely open and unpredictable, there would appear to be little reason for the process theologians' hope of a time when evil will be overcome and there will be a universal community of love and peace.

Process theology, in the final analysis, is the full expression of the error of old line rationalistic liberalism,* namely, the acceptance of the theory of universal evolution* and its application to religion and theology. It depersonalizes God, denies the doctrine of creation, repudiates the truth of an objective general and special revelation, compromises the doctrine of sin, jettisons the doctrines of the incarnation, atonement, and resurrection of Christ, reduces salvation to a mere acceptance of communality, and gives up the Biblical message of a heaven to gain and a hell to shun.

PROCESSION OF THE SPIRIT

"Theologians intend by this phrase to designate the relation which the third Person [of the Trinity] sustains to the first and second; wherein, by an eternal and necessary—i.e., not voluntary—act of the Father and the Son, their whole identical divine essence, without alienation, division, or change, is communicated to the Holy Ghost" (A. A. Hodge).

Another word for the procession of the Spirit is spiration, bearing the same theological meaning, viz., the necessary communication from all eternity of the fulness of the divine essence by the Father and the Son to the Spirit.

See **Opera Ad Intra**; **Eternal Generation**; **Filioque**; **Holy Spirit**.

PROPHECY

Prophecy is a mode of special revelation* that has been defined as God's interpretation of redemptive truth to fallen man. The fall involved man in repudiating God as the ultimate interpreter of truth and in substituting his own interpretation. Thus, by the special revelation of His redemptive purpose, God reasserted Himself as the ultimate interpreter of truth. Hence, prophecy emphasizes that truth is not to be arrived at as long as man assumes himself to be the final arbiter. All true theology* is, therefore, theocentric and not anthropocentric.*

Again, this view of prophecy indicates that it was no mere foretelling of future events. False prophets did that, and fulfilment was in itself no guarantee that the prophet was of God—though obviously non-fulfilment proved that he had not spoken from God. True prophecy was a redemptive revelation—i.e., it revealed some part of God's purpose of redeeming grace. Each part of true prophecy had "its meaning in relation to Christ and as a part of the revelation of Christ" (Van Til).

Furthermore, true prophecy stands in conjunction with the other modes of special revelation, theophany* and miracle.* This is the full test of every professed prophet of the Lord. False prophets claimed visions from the Lord and made their predictions, claiming the attention of the people. How could the false and the true be distinguished? Deuteronomy 18:21, 22 and Jer. 28:9 show that the most basic test was to see if their predictions came true. In the case of true prophets, they always did; in the case of false prophets, they usually did not. But Moses reminded the Israelites of the possibility of a false prophet's prediction being fulfilled (Deut. 13:1-4), emphasizing the need for a fuller, final, test to distinguish between the false and the true. That test, as already indicated, was that any particular prophecy must relate to all other true prophecy, theophany, and miracle. In other words, true prophets ministered in complete harmony with prior divine revelations—note in Deut. 13:1-4 the emphasis on the "commandments" given by the Lord and compare 1 Cor. 14:32. Isaiah 8:20 is the normative standard in this respect. Again, true prophets ministered in relation to the appearance of God among His people: in the tabernacle, in the temple, and finally in Christ. In addition, their ministry was proved by signs and wonders, the seals of the Lord.

No one of these alone would be a sufficient proof of the divine origin of a prophecy, but taken together they provide a foolproof method of judgment.

PROPHETIC OFFICE OF CHRIST

One of the three functions of Christ as mediator,* the others being priest and king *(see **Kingly Office of Christ**; **Priestly Office of Christ**).*

"Christ executeth the office of a prophet, in His revealing to the church, in all ages, by His Spirit and word, in divers ways of administration, the whole will of God, in all things concerning their edification and salvation" (*Larger Catechism,* Q. 43). Passages such as John 1:18; Heb. 1:1, 2; Matt. 11:27 present Christ as the great declarer and revealer of God, while Acts 3:22, 23 quotes Moses' prophecy in Deut. 18:15, 19 as a direct reference to Him: He is the prophet of whom it was said, "Him shall ye hear in all things whatsoever he shall say unto you." Unlike His priestly office, which Christ executes immediately, or without the use of delegates or agents, His prophetic office is executed both immediately and mediately.

Christ executes the prophetic office immediately—i.e., personally and directly—in His theophanies in the OT; in His incarnation, by His own words and works (Luke 24:19; John 10:37, 38). He executes His prophetic office mediately or through delegates: through the Holy Spirit (1 Peter 1:10-12; 3:19, 20); and through the Christian ministry, first by inspired apostles and later by teachers and preachers (Ephesians 4:11, 12).

PROPITIATION

The appeasement or turning away of God's wrath against sinners by means of an atoning sacrifice. In Romans 3:25 Christ is said to be a propitiation. The Greek term is *hilasterion,* which is translated "mercy-seat" in Hebrews 9:5. The LXX used the same word for *mercy seat.* There are some who hold that such should be the rendering in Romans 3:25, but the AV translation of a propitiation, or a *propitiatory sacrifice,* is preferable. The mercy seat was sprinkled with the blood of atonement* and is therefore called the *hilasterion,* the "propitiatory," or place of propitiation, because when the blood was sprinkled, God's wrath was turned away. That is what Romans 3:25 teaches. Christ, by the shedding of His blood, turned away God's wrath. Cognate words are used in Heb. 2:17, 1 John 2:22, and 4:10 showing that the Lord Jesus, by the shedding of His own blood, has propitiated God and delivered His people from divine wrath.

The whole idea of the wrath* of God is discountenanced by modern sceptical theologians. C. H. Dodd is a case in point: "He denies that 'the wrath of God' denotes anything more than a process of cause and effect whereby disaster inevitably follows sin" (Leon Morris). But all the arguments of men of Dodd's persuasion cannot shake the fact of the "wrath of God revealed" (Rom. 1:18) in the inspired Word. John Owen, "the prince of Puritan divines," lists four essential elements in any propitiation:

1. An offence to be taken away.
2. A person offended who needs to be pacified.
3. An offending person; one guilty of the offence.
4. A sacrifice or some other means of making atonement for the offence.

Propitiation proves that the atonement is objective, that it makes its primary impression on God, not man *(see* **Atonement).** Martyn Lloyd-Jones's sermon on Romans 3:25, in his first volume of studies in Romans, gives a very good exposition of propitiation and disposes of current critical views. *See* **Expiation, Satisfaction.**

PROTESTANTISM

The Biblical system of faith and practice rediscovered by the Reformation* in the 16th century. The name was originally used in 1529 in the Diet of Spires when Luther's supporters protested against the repeal of a more tolerant edict of 1526, but it soon came to have a wider significance. It pointed up two things: (1) the Reformers' protest against the unscriptural dogma and practice of Rome; (2) their witnessing to the scriptural truth abandoned by Rome. The basic significance of the Latin word *protestatio* is witness, and witnessing to the truth was the major work of the Reformation. "The Bible, the Bible only, the religion of Protestants," succinctly expresses this emphasis. The following article from McClintock and Strong aptly sums up the heart of Protestantism:

"Protestantism is the advocacy of the authority of the Sacred Scriptures above and without any other. The Romanist and Jew hold to tradition as having the warrant of authority, but the Protestants refuse to yield to any arguments not clearly and directly drawn from the sacred Word of God. There arise, of course, various questions as to what this Word is, and how it is to be interpreted. In regard to the former, the Protestant holds that the Holy Bible is composed only of the canonical writings of the Old and New Testaments, while the Roman Catholics also ascribe canonical authority to the so-called Apocrypha of the Old Testament. The right of interpretation the Roman Catholic Church claims to be hers alone, while the Protestant Church concedes this right in a stricter sense to every one who possesses the requisite gifts and attainments, but in a more comprehensive sense to every Christian who seeks after salvation proceeding upon the principle that Scripture is its own interpreter according to the *analogia fidei.* With this is connected the assumption of the Roman Catholic Church that the Vulgate version, which it sanctions, is to be preferred to all other versions as the authentic one, and is to a certain extent of equal importance with the original, while Protestants regard the original only as authentic.

"The object of Protestant Christianity is freedom from that ecclesiasticism which the primitive Church was unacquainted with, and which owes its origin and development to the medieval Church. 'The Reformation, viewed in its most general character,' says Ullymann (*Reformers Before the Reformation,* 1:13), 'was the reaction of Christianity as Gospel against Christianity as law.' It is therefore inconsistent for Anglican High-Churchmen and their followers on this side of the Atlantic to assert that Protestantism is simply negative. It is positive as well, for it not only discards one interpretation of Christianity, but espouses another. It denies the right of the Church to stand in authority of the individual, but it gives a circumscribed and well-defined liberty to the individual—not absolute license. 'The liberty which the Reformers prized first and chiefly,' says Prof. Fisher (*Hist. of the Ref.,* p. 9), 'was not the abstract right to choose one's creed without constraint, but a liberty that flows from the enforced appropriation by the soul of truth in harmony with its inmost nature and its conscious necessities.' The nature of Protestantism, the essence of Protestantism, the principle of Protestantism, is freedom, but freedom only from the restraints of man, from a tyranny of conscience, from all systems which had previous to the great Reformation been imposed upon man without any divine warrant. It is freedom on the basis of obedience to God and to his holy Word. It is that freedom which consists in the cheerful and ready obedience to the divine Word and to the divine Will. It is the freedom of the republic, and not the license of the commune; it is the liberty of common-sense, and not the enthusiasm of the idealist. 'The principle of Protestantism,' says Dr. Schaff, 'is evangelical freedom in Christ, its aim to bring every soul into direct relation to Christ. Romanism puts the Church first and Christ next; Protestantism reverses the order. Romanism says, Where the Church is (meaning thereby the papal organization), there is Christ; Protestantism says, Where Christ is, there is the Church; Romanism says, Where the Catholic tradition is, there is the Bible and the infallible rule of faith; Protestantism says, Where the Bible is, there is the true tradition and the infallible rule of faith; Romanism says, Where good works are, there are faith and justification; Protestantism says, Where faith is, there are justification and good works. Romanism throws Mary and the saints between Christ and the believer; Protestantism goes directly to the Saviour. Romanism proceeds from the visible Church (the papacy) to the invisible Church; Protestantism from the invisible Church (the true body of Christ) to the visible. Romanism works from without, and from the general to the particular; Protestantism from within, and from the individual to the general. Protestantism is a protest against the tyranny of man on the basis of the authority of God. It proclaims the Bible to be the only infallible rule of Christian faith and practice, and teaches justification by grace alone as apprehended by a living faith. It holds up Christ as all in all, whose word is all-sufficient to teach, whose grace is all-sufficient to save. Its mission is to realize the universal priesthood and kingship of all believers by bringing them all into direct union and fellowship with Christ' (*Christian Intelligencer,* Jan. 14, 1869). Dr. Hagenback objects to this reduction of Protestantism to one fundamental principle and offers three as its basis—viz., (1) the real principle, living faith in Christ; (2) the formal principle, the authority of the Scriptures as a rule of faith; (3) the social principle, forming a community, of which Christ is the individual head, and of which all the members are priests unto God. In this division every essential characteristic of Protestantism seems to have been considered."

PROTEVANGELIUM

Greek *protos,* "first," *euangelion,* "gospel"; used as a title for the first Messianic promise in Gen. 3:15. This promise contains a prophecy of the coming of a great deliverer of fallen man, who would be born of a virgin *(see Virgin Birth)* and would utterly defeat the old serpent, Satan,* who had just procured the fall* of the human race.

PROVIDENCE

The efficacious administration by the all-wise God of His eternal decree.* Berkhof defines it as "that continued exercise of the divine energy, whereby the Creator preserves all His creatures, is operative in all that comes to pass in the world, and directs all things to their appointed end."

Reformed theologians have usually stressed the two elements in providence—preservation and government—while some give particular prominence also to the idea of concurrence or cooperation, as the manner in which God preserves and governs the world: i.e., divine power cooperates with created power, in keeping with the laws of their operation, to cause them to act as they do *(see Concursus).* The doctrine of providence guards Christian theology from the opposite evils of deism* and pantheism.* It presents a God who is in control over every part of

His creation. Berkhof lists eleven areas of providential control, as follows:

"**1.**The universe at large, Ps. 103:19; Dan. 4:35; Eph. 1:11.
2. The physical world, Job 37:5, 10; Ps. 104:14; 135:6.
3. The brute creation, Ps. 104:21, 28; Mt. 6:26; 10:29.
4. The affairs of nations, Job 12:23; Ps. 22:28; 66:7; Acts 17:26.
5. Man's birth and lot in life, 1 Sam. 16:1; Ps. 139:16; Is. 45:5; Gal. 1:15-16.
6. Outward successes and failures of men's lives, Ps. 75:6, 7; Luke 1:52.
7. Things seemingly accidental or insignificant, Prov. 16:33; Mt. 10:30.
8. The protection of the righteous, Ps. 4:8; 5:12; 63:8; 121:3; Rom. 8:28.
9. Supplying the wants of God's people, Gen. 22:8, 14; Deut. 8:3; Phil. 4:19.
10. Giving answers to prayer, 1 Sam. 1:19; 2 Chr. 33:13; Ps. 65:2; Mt. 7:7; Luke 18:7, 8.
11. The exposure and punishment of the wicked, Ps. 7:12, 13; 11:6."

From such a list, it is easy to see why theologians usually speak of general providence (God's control over the universe generally) and special providence (God's care for individual parts of His creation). Some indeed speak of a third division, very special providence, for while the term *special providence* is often used to designate God's special care for His rational creatures, they wish to draw attention to His particular care for His elect, those who stand related to Him as sons in the covenant of grace.*

See **Sovereignty of God**; *Theodicy.*

PSYCHOLOGY

Greek *psyche,* "soul," *logos,* "word"; the study of the mind and mental processes, feelings, and desires; or of the behavior and experience of man and animals. As a professedly scientific discipline it is bound to an empirical* approach. In fact it often proceeds upon fundamentally flawed presuppositions, as in the case of Sigmund Freud

with his hatred of God and his bizarre and degenerate theory of the Oedipus complex. The study of human behaviour and experience may yield a great deal of factual data but those data must always be explained within some interpretive framework. Secular psychologists find that framework in their secular worldview* and make man the explanation of his own condition. What is observed within the spectrum of human behaviors and experience is human and must be accepted as such. Blame and guilt are misplaced. Undesirable behaviors and experience are symptoms of a breakdown of mental health and must be understood and resolved psychologically. Since the time of Freud that has meant psychoanalytically.

This secular view has all but captured public opinion with the result that psychological therapies and therapists abound. Psychological counselling appears to many to be the answer to almost any mental or emotional need. This idea has invaded even the evangelical church. Historically, there has been a branch of theology* known as "psychology." As a subdivision of anthropology,* the study of the human soul as God's creation, psychology was pursued on the basis of the Bible's teaching regarding man's creation,* fall,* depravity,* and renewal in mind and will* in Christ the Redeemer. Pastoral counselling proceeded along these lines and sought to lead the counselled person to see his problem in Biblical terms. It gave him the clear commands of Scripture on the behaviors that troubled him and encouraged him to hope because of the sufficiency of God's gracious provision in Christ.

Nowadays, however, there is a widespread perception that psychology, not theology, is the answer for the mental and emotional problems of men. If "mental problems" refer to some kind of brain damage or malfunction then the need is a medical one; however terms like "mental health" and "mental illness" are freely used to describe conditions in people who do not suffer from any neurological impairment. The terms "mental problems" and "emotional problems" are usually employed of moods, feelings, or perceptions that are directly connected with wrong behaviour or wrong reactions to the challenges presented by our environment. In other words they are connected with sinful, unbelieving actions or reactions. Much of what secular psychology terms "sickness" the Bible calls "sin." To secular psychologists such a diagnosis is judgmental. However, to a Christian it opens the door of hope. Once we can identify a problem as sinful according to some specific statement of Scripture we know what to do with it. The Bible has a clear answer for all sin* problems. Christ has made provision for His people to have victory over sin. Once we accept the philosophy of secular psychology, however, we compound the problem: we misdiagnose it and we shut off the Biblical answer to it.

The consistently Biblical approach has fallen into disuse even among many evangelicals. More often than not ministers defer to psychologists and psychiatrists as physicians of the mind, forgetting that the care of souls is a spiritual task which God has committed to His church. Frequently "Christian psychologists" will seek to marry the theories of secular psychologists to the Bible. The result is usually a radical reinterpretation of Scripture. Often a Scripture text will be forced to provide support for some psychological "insight" which then will be paraded as a Biblical principle.

The effects of all this are unhealthy. First, there is an underlying naturalizing tendency. The supernatural work of the Holy Spirit is downplayed, and even His sovereign act in regeneration* is demoted to the level of a mere human decision to change. Second, the Biblical diagnosis of man's sin and guilt* is diluted. Instead of confronting sinners with their guilt, a psychological approach seeks to understand how they have been victimized. It does not blame, it excuses. Third, the Biblical answer is obscured. The psy-

chological approach appears sympathetic but it is actually destructive. Until a man faces the fact of his guilt and sin he is cut off from the experience of God's mercy in Christ who came "to call…sinners to repentance" (Matt. 9:13). Fourth, humanistic substitutes for Biblical truths are welcomed. A striking example of this is the wide acceptance and preaching of the concept of self-esteem.* What we should be expounding is the truth of justification* by grace* through faith* in the merits of Christ, and the free imputation* of Christ's righteousness to believers. The self-esteem concept is a counterfeit of this fundamental gospel truth—yet nowadays many pulpits resound to the cries of self-esteem but are silent on justification and imputation.

As noted, psychological research may uncover patterns of human behaviour and emotions and provide valuable data to be studied and interpreted. Only God our creator can provide the truth which can enable us to make sense of these data. The truth about man, the needs of his soul and the answers to them, must come from God. They are not discoverable from within man. Fallen man, with every part of his being corrupted by sin, is incapable of interpreting himself aright. He starts off with the idea of his own independence from God, thus basing all his subsequent interpretations on a fallacy. Wrong premises lead to wrong conclusions.

So it is to theology, not psychology, we need to turn for the most basic insights into the mental and moral constitution of man, and for answers to his mental, emotional, and behavioural needs. Given a Biblical theological base, there is room for inductive psychological case studies, but without such a starting point, psychological studies are bound to lead to more or less false conclusions.

Older Protestant theology adopted a view of the mental and moral constitution of man which divided the powers of the soul* into two categories, understanding* and will.* Later theologians divided them into three categories, intellect, sensibility, and will—the view most commonly held today. The older psychology includes moral desires and affections under the will, the later does not. In this the older psychology is more correct theologically, and has the support of Scripture.*

PUNISHMENT
See under **Endless Punishment**; **Hell**; **Justice of God**.

PURGATORY
A place of suffering, where, according to Roman Catholic and Eastern Orthodox dogma, those who die at peace with the church, and not in a state of mortal sin,* are purified and made fit for heaven. The theory is that all unbaptized adults and all baptized adults dying in mortal sin go straight to hell. Saints and martyrs go straight to heaven, but the vast majority of the faithful must endure purgatorial fire.

"According to the Holy Fathers of the Church, the fire of purgatory does not differ from the fire of hell, except in point of duration" *(Manual of the Purgatorial Society).* As to duration, Cardinal Bellarmine said: "There is absolutely no doubt that the pains of purgatory in some cases endure for entire centuries" (quoted by Roman Catholic writer J. M. Haffert). Release from purgatory is supposed to be expedited by masses for the departed suffering soul, leading to the justifiable charge that purgatory is Rome's gold mine—especially when it is conceded by Rome that the massing priest has no way of knowing when a soul is released from purgatory. All that is paid to deliver souls from purgatory is paid for nothing, for the existence of such a place is nowhere intimated in Scripture. Rather, all the scriptural evidence, indeed the very essence of the gospel of grace, argues strongly against the whole notion of purgatorial fire. As Loraine Boettner said, "It is safe to say that

no other doctrine of the Church of Rome, unless it be that of auricular confession, has done so much to pervert the Gospel or to enslave the people to the priesthood as has the doctrine of purgatory."

PURITAN THEOLOGY
The term given to the theological mood and method of the 17th century Puritans. There were major theological differences among the Puritans, notably on the subject of relationship to the national church, but also on matters such as church government, the extent of the atonement* and its relation to God's decree of election,* and the law and the believer. For example, Amyraldian* views of the atonement were quite prevalent; and Richard Baxter adopted Neonomianism.* Nevertheless it is permissible to speak of Puritan theology for all the Puritans shared some important fundamental views that shaped their theological approach.

They all had a deep respect for Scripture,* which they accepted as the inspired and authoritative word of God. The use they made of Scripture—whether in Bunyan's allegories, *Pilgrim's Progress* and *The Holy War,* in expository sermons, or in formal theological treatises—was extensive and profound.

They shared a reverential awe of the transcendent majesty of God. Stephen Charnock's *Discourse on the Existence and Attributes of God* was and remains a penetrating work to glorify God and to humble the heart of man. The Puritans majored on the great central themes of the gospel with powerful intellectual rigour. They investigated the relation of law to gospel with great precision and insight—so much so that their conclusions are sorely needed in the modern church. They set forth the Biblical doctrines of justification and sanctification with scholarly acumen and pastoral passion. Puritan theologians were physicians of the soul. They thoroughly understood man's nature and temptations because they had grasped the Bible's doctrine of the fall* and sin.* They had experienced the things they spoke about. They were not ivory-tower theorists but men who had to prove their own teaching in the battles of real life. They were particularly deeply instructed, and therefore were able to instruct others, in the glories of the person and work of Christ. John Owen's works such as *The Doctrine of Justification by Faith, through the Imputation of the Righteousness of Christ,* and *The Mortification of Sin in Believers* are outstanding examples of Puritan power in applying the Bible to the needs of the soul. Puritans showed a depth of understanding that is almost incredible. Thomas Brook's *Sweet Remedies Against Satan's Devices* lays bare the workings of Satan and shows how they may be dealt with scripturally, with an almost overwhelming wealth of detail.

Despite the intellectual rigour of the Puritans, their theology was not a mere academic exercise. It was almost uniformly Calvinistic. Owen's *Display of Arminianism* and his *Death of Death in the Death of Christ* are still unanswerable Biblical demonstrations of the gospel as Calvinists understand it. Even such weighty tomes as these were intended to be intensely practical. Puritan theology aimed to inform the mind and to challenge the conscience. It called for every part of life, every element in our belief and behaviour, to be made subject to the Lordship of Christ and to the authority of the word of God.

It was also evangelistic. Puritan evangelism was a far cry from the easy believism of modern times. It sought to do a deep law work—i.e., to apply the law of God to the conscience* to bring conviction of sin—and then present Jesus Christ as God's remedy, to be received by faith. At times Puritan theology lapsed into preparationism* but anyone who reads Alleine's *Alarm to the Unconverted,* or Baxter's *Call to the Unconverted* cannot help but feel the power of the Puritan passion to bring the lost to Christ.

We should never forget that Puritan theology was preeminently a preaching theology. The Puritans were powerful expositors of the word of God. Their expositions are of lasting value. Thomas Watson, Thomas Manton, Richard Sibbes, and a host of others represent the British pulpit at its best. They had a mighty impact on their own age and have continued to exert a blessed influence on succeeding ages. Their age is gone forever but the truths they taught, and the devotion and passion with which they taught them, are timeless.

Thankfully there has been something of a revival of interest in the Puritans and their writings. If the Puritans could speak to all who are showing an interest in them, they would undoubtedly tell them not to try to be a reincarnation of a 17th-century preacher but to fill the heart and mind with God and His Word, both incarnate and inscripturated, until these are the great joy of the soul and the chief end of our existence. For that is the genius of Puritan theology.

PUSEYITES

The name given to the Anglo-Catholic party in the Church of England in the 19th century. The name was for Edmund Pusey, who adopted Roman Catholic views of sacramentalism,* especially baptismal regeneration.* They were also called *Tractarians* * and the *Oxford Movement.* *

Q

An abbreviation of the German *quelle,* "source"; the designation given by NT critics to the supposed Aramaic original of the sayings of Jesus. The argument for its existence is that the Lord and His apostles all spoke Aramaic while the Gospels are written in Greek. How and when did the transfer take place? Source critics hold that the Gospels would likely have been written first in Aramaic and only later produced in Greek. They appeal to the witness of Papias and Jerome. According to Papias, Matthew wrote the *logia* in Hebrew (taken by many to mean Aramaic), and Jerome spoke of a Hebrew Gospel. While critics are not fully agreed on the matter, many identify the documents mentioned by Papias and Jerome with their claimed "Q document." Some critics have gone so far as to produce their version of this mythical document.

There is no evidence that the Gospel narratives ever appeared in any literary form before they were written in their present Greek form. There is good reason to believe that the Greek text of Mark has been traced as far back as the middle of the first century (*see **Quest for the Historical Jesus*** for evidence of this). This argues strongly against anything but a Greek original of the Gospel narratives—for if Mark needed no Aramaic stage to transfer the gospel into Greek there is no good reason to suppose it for Matthew or Luke.

QERE

Meaning "to be read," this word denotes a marginal correction or substitution in the Hebrew scriptures. Any departure from what is written *(kethib),* even in cases when a copyist's error is evident, was marked by the Masoretes* in a special way. So that there could be no tampering with the text, the consonants of the uncorrected word were allowed to stand, but the vowel signs of the corrected form were placed under it. This produced an impossible reading, forcing the reader to refer to the corrected reading (*qere*) in the margin or footnote.

QUAKERS

Popular name for the Society of Friends, founded in England by George Fox in 1668. They took the name *Quakers* because they were said to "tremble at the word of the Lord." Quakers have no ministers and observe no sacraments. Their chief feature is a belief in Inner Light, or direct illumination from God, which they elevate to a place of spiritual authority, superior even to the Bible.

The breakaway *United Society of Believers in Christ's Second Appearing* was popularly known as the *Shakers* on account of their convulsive movements during their meetings. Ann Lee, a Manchester textile worker generally referred to as *Mother Lee,* led this group into the United States. Shakers were sure that Christ's second coming* was about to take place. In view of this, though they were renowned for their industry, they disallowed marriage, and have faded almost out of existence.

QUARTODECIMANISM

The belief of a number of early Christians in Asia Minor that Easter should be observed on the fourteenth Nisan, irrespective of the day of the week that may happen to be. In contrast, the Western church determined at the Council of Nicea (A.D. 325) that the crucifixion should be commemorated on the Friday of the week, whether or not it fell on the fourteenth, and the resurrection on the following Lord's day.

See **Paschal Controversy**.

QUEST FOR THE HISTORICAL JESUS

The attempt by various schools of liberal, rationalist, and neo-orthodox theology to get behind the narratives of the gospels and the teachings of the NT epistles about the Lord Jesus Christ to discover who He really was and what He really did and said. Inherent in the entire procedure is the theory that the NT is largely unhistorical in its records and untrustworthy in its doctrine of Christ—certainly not divinely inspired and authoritative.

The foundation of this procedure is the rejection of the supernatural. Any narrative that records the supernatural is *ipso facto* unhistorical. Another premise is that the NT narratives are a late compilation of early oral data which has been mythologized—i.e., embellished with the addition of the growing belief in Jesus' divinity—to create the official "ecclesiastical" Christ. Thus to reach the historical Jesus the critics must remove the later embellishments. To use Bultmann's language, they must "demythologize" it.

The quest for the historical Jesus is an entirely unwarranted exercise in infidelity. The more we learn about the writing of the NT books the more it is confirmed that they are not late productions but exactly what they claim to be, records from the apostolic age, written by the people whose names they bear.

Radical critics reject that conclusion on *a priori** grounds. When in 1972 Jose O'Callaghan, a Jesuit priest and one of the world's leading papyrologists, identified a fragment from Qumran cave 7 as Mark 6:52, 53 he was derided and denounced. The fact that no other possible identification could be proposed did not seem to matter. The trouble for radical criticism was

that O'Callaghan's find dated the Gospel of Mark at least as far back as A.D. 50-55. He went on to make eight other NT identifications among the fragments from Qumran 7, dating them between A.D. 50 and 70. (The passages are Mark 4:28; 6:48; 12:17; Acts 27:38; Rom. 5:11-12; 1 Tim. 3:16; 4:1-3; 2 Pet.. 1:15; James 1:23, 24—See *The First New Testament,* by David Estrada and William White, Jr.)

Obviously such discoveries demolish the various theories critics have adopted about a long oral tradition that became corrupted and then was written down in the books of the NT to make later myths look like original history.

For the historical Jesus we need look no further than the NT. It is historical, reliable, inspired, and authoritative. Any Jesus other than the one presented in the NT is a character of fiction.

See **Form Criticism**; **Myth**.

QUIETISM

A small Roman Catholic movement in 17th-century France, which sought to achieve a condition of mind in which the believer is filled with God Himself, while his own will is completely destroyed. This meant that all desire, and therefore all work, had to be renounced, as in a mystical sense the believer experienced death to self. B. B. Warfield said, "Quietism, which is on the passive side resignation, on the active renunciation, and in its lowest reaches becomes a placid acceptance of the lot that has come to us, in its highest reaches rises into disinterested love" (*Counterfeit Miracles,* p. 223).

R

RABBINISM

The development in Judaism after the Babylonian exile* and especially after the destruction of the temple, of a special class of expert interpreters of the Mosaic legal code. Since all of Jewish life was governed by that code the rabbis became something of a spiritual aristocracy.

See **Talmud**.

RANSOM-TO-SATAN THEORY OF THE ATONEMENT

The notion that by His death Christ paid a ransom to Satan to remove his right of power over man.

This was the theory of Origen (*ca.* A.D. 85-251), who based it upon such texts as 2 Tim. 2:26, 1 Tim. 1:20, and 1 Cor. 5:5. However, these texts speak of the tyrannical power exercised by Satan and should be interpreted in the light of the principles laid down in John 8:34 and Rom. 6:16. They contain no reference to any legal right over man to which Satan can lay claim. The uniform testimony of Scripture is that Christ paid the ransom price Godward to free His people from divine condemnation.

RAPTURE

The Latin verb *rapio* means "to snatch, or seize." The English word *rapture,* derived from it, has a double usage. Generally it means "ecstatic delight," but in popular theology it means "the catching up" of the church* to meet the Lord at His second coming.* Dispensationalists usually term this "the rapture," or "the secret rapture," and they place it before the great tribulation.* They profess to find Scripture warrant for their theory in such texts as 1 Thess. 4:16,

17; 1 Cor. 15:51, 52; and Matt. 24:40, 41. Actually, these texts strongly oppose their view of a two-stage coming of Christ and the secret removal of the church from the earth before the tribulation.

1. 1 Thessalonians 4:16 can hardly be pressed into service as proof of anything secret—a noisier or more public passage would be difficult to imagine. Furthermore, the Greek usage of the NT precludes the notion that our rising "to meet" the Lord is followed by His turning back the way He came. The Greek words here employed (*eis apantesin*) appear three other times in the NT (Matt. 25:1, 6 and Acts 28:15). In each case it is the party going out to the meeting that turns back, after the meeting, in the direction from which it just came. The same is true in 1 Thessalonians 4; the Lord comes on His way and those who rise to meet Him return to earth with Him. It is significant that the Scripture nowhere has any reference to "the coming of the Lord to the air."

2. 1 Corinthians 15:51, 52 is obviously a description of the same event as in 1 Thess. 4:16, 17, and so it is understood by dispensationalists. However, 1 Cor. 15:52 places the rapture "at the last trump," which cannot be before the tribulation, because there are seven trumpets sounded during that period. It is futile for dispensational writers to claim, as they have, that "this last trumpet has nothing to do with the trumpets of the Apocalypse" (*The Advent Witness*). Such a statement is mere wishful thinking without the slightest warrant from the word of God. Revelation 8-11 presents the only series of trumpets in Scripture. Thus I Cor. 15 clearly places the rapture of 1 Thess. 4 after the tribulation, in keeping with the words of our Lord in Matt. 24:29-31.

3. Matthew 24:40, 41 speaks of one being taken and the other left, and this is generally understood to describe the secret rapture. But does it? Let the verses be read in context and their import is apparent. "For as in the days that were before the flood they were eating and drinking, marrying and giving in marriage, until the day that Noah entered into the ark, and knew not until the flood came and took them all away; so shall also the coming of the Son of man be. Then shall two be in the field; the one shall be taken, and the other left" (vv. 38-40). Who shall be taken? Who was taken in Noah's day? The flood took the ungodly away. And "so shall also the coming of the Son of man be." The ungodly are the ones taken, and this agrees perfectly with the Lord's teaching in the parable of the tares and the wheat in Matt. 13:24-30; 36-43. There He says, "let both grow together until the harvest," which He interprets as "the end of the world." First to be taken will be the tares, the "children of the wicked one" (vv. 30, 38-41).

Such is the primary textual evidence usually adduced for the dispensationalist view of the rapture. In fact, as indeed some dispensationalists have admitted, there is no direct statement of a secret pre-tribulation rapture in the Bible.

RATIONALISM

From the Latin *ratio,* "reason," the philosophy that elevates human reason as the sufficient, supreme, and final arbiter in every realm of human experience.

Pure rationalism was the idea that reason alone, with no help from the experience of the senses, was the source of all knowledge. *Empirical rationalism* made use of the senses to produce its data and set up the scientific method as the source of knowledge—i.e., knowledge is gained only by investigation and verification. In both cases, human reason is still the only source of knowledge.

Theological rationalism is of various kinds. Deists and pantheists *(see **Deism; Pantheism**)* deny the need for, or the possibility of, a special, supernatural revelation.* The main body of rationalists attribute to human reason the exclusive power of formulating religious truth. They profess to admit some sort of a divine revelation, but they reserve to human reason the authority and ability to sit in judgment on such revelation.

Thus they repudiate the supernatural element in Scripture as unreasonable. Rationalists at one time argued that the Bible did not teach the reality of miracle,* but in the ensuing controversy they were forced to abandon their position. However, they did not abandon their rationalism. They simply shifted their ground and repudiated the divine record as unhistorical.

Rationalism still poisons modern religious thought at many points. The Bultmann segment of the neo-orthodox school is blatantly rationalistic *(see **Myth**; **Neo-Orthodoxy**; **Theology of Crisis**).* The rest of the movement does not escape either, but covers its rationalism behind a welter of confusing expressions.

*See **Criticism**; **Liberalism**.*

REAL PRESENCE

The presence of the real substance of Christ's body in or with the bread and wine at the Lord's Supper.* Rome maintains the doctrine of a real presence by teaching transubstantiation;* Luther maintained it by teaching consubstantiation.*

Reformed theology rejects both these notions. The *Westminster Confession of Faith* expresses the Reformed view: "The body and blood of Christ [are] not corporally or carnally in, with or under the bread and wine; yet [are] as really, but spiritually, present to the faith of believers in that ordinance, as the elements themselves are to their outward senses" (chap. 29, sec. 7).

REALISM

A late medieval scholastic doctrine, associated with the Dominican order and based on the theology of Thomas Aquinas. It stressed the objective reality of things apart from the person thinking about them. It looked on universal principles as real and reasonable forerunners and helpers of faith. It took a strong view of the reality of sacramental grace acting *opus operatum.** On both these issues it was fiercely opposed by the nominalists.*

Christian realism is how some Roman Catholic theologians describe their church's "distinctively Catholic way of integrating the pluralism of philosophies underlying its various theological and doctrinal orientations" (R. P. McBrien, *Catholicism,* p. 1178). Stripped of obscurity this means that the Roman Catholic church has a unique way of reconciling the contradictory elements that comprise its life and theology. That way is by means of *critical realism.* It rejects *naive realism,* the idea that knowledge comes from simply taking a good look at objective facts. McBrien claims that *biblicism* is a form of *naive realism* that Rome especially repudiates. *Biblicism* in Rome's estimation is the belief that the Bible is a book with a clear meaning. McBrien gives an example of the error of depending on the clarity of the Bible: "The requirements of Christian existence are clear. The answers are readily available in the pages of Sacred Scripture." Ultimately, Rome's so-called Christian realism degenerates into raw subjectivism: "Critical realism insists that all reality is 'mediated by meaning'—i.e., the real is what we *judge* to be true, on the basis of our experience" (McBrien, p. 1254).

REALIZED ESCHATOLOGY

A description of two very different theological positions.

1. It describes the eschatology* of those amillennialists who adopt preterism.*

2. It describes the theory of C. H. Dodd

(1884-1973) that the Lord Jesus Christ did not understand the kingdom of God* in any future, apocalyptic sense. This is the usual sense of the term. Given Dodd's reputation as perhaps the leading British NT scholar of the 20th century, and his widespread influence on theological studies and on Bible translation (he was chairman of the *New English Bible* translators), an examination of his views is worthwhile.

Dodd stressed Christ's teaching that the kingdom was already present, interpreting this to mean that the only end-time He envisaged was the time already present. Thus, his theory was called "realized eschatology," in contrast to the futurist eschatology envisaged by men like Albert Schweitzer (1875-1965).

Basing much of his theory on Christ's parables, Dodd explained his position as follows:

"The predictions of Jesus have no long historical perspective. They seem to be concerned with the immediate developments of the crisis which was already in being when He spoke, and which He interpreted as the coming of the Kingdom of God. But this does not mean...that He believed that history would come to an end shortly after His death. The eternal significance of history had revealed itself in this crisis. Whether its subsequent plan would be long or short, men would henceforth be living in a new age, in which the Kingdom of God, His grace and His judgment, stood revealed. Hence there is a place for ethical teaching, not as 'interim ethics,' but as a moral ideal for men who have 'accepted the Kingdom of God,' and live their lives in the presence of His judgment and His grace, now decisively revealed.

"The experience of many generations has no doubt brought a growing understanding of the meaning of that revelation, and the attempt to live by the ethical standards of Jesus has had results in history. We may yet hope to understand Him better, and to see His ethical principles more fully embodied in our social life. But of all this we hear nothing in His sayings. He points His hearers directly from the historical crisis in which they were involved to the eternal order of which that crisis was a mirror" (*The Parables of the Kingdom,* pp. 108, 109).

Here Dodd spells out his liberal creed and vision. The kingdom of God is a present-day social order, increasingly conformed to the ethical standards of the teachings of Christ. The judgment of God is not some future event; it is here and now. The only eschatology of which Christ spoke was the application of His ethical principles to our earthly society in the present age.

As a profound NT scholar, Dodd was aware that his theory directly contradicted the NT's own record and interpretation of the sayings of Jesus. When faced with Christ's sayings likening His kingdom to something that grows over a period of time and reaches its consummation at a future point in history, Dodd invoked form criticism,* on the basis of which he denied the authenticity of the statements in question (Dodd, chaps. 4-6). In his comments on the parables in Matt. 13:33-37 and Luke 12:35-38, Dodd denied that "Jesus Himself taught His disciples to expect His second advent after a long and incalculable interval" (p. 165). He attributed the expectation of a second coming to the church's misapplication of Christ's original message. Referring to eschatological parables, he said, "They were intended to enforce His appeal to men to recognize that the Kingdom of God was present in all its momentous consequences, and that by their conduct in the presence of this tremendous crisis they would judge themselves as faithful or unfaithful, wise or foolish. When the crisis had passed, they were adapted by the Church to enforce its appeal to men to prepare for the second and final world-crisis which it believed to be approaching" (p. 174).

In Dodd's "realized eschatology," the sayings attributed to Jesus that point to His future coming and reign were later church interpretations, not the authentic words of Christ Himself. Dodd admitted that "Jesus employed the traditional symbolism of apocalypse to indicate the 'otherworldly' or absolute character of the Kingdom of God" (p. 197). The church later misunderstood these as predictions of Christ's second coming and the establishment of a future kingdom.

In Dodd's scheme the resurrection of Christ, His 40-day sojourn with the disciples before His ascension, and His second coming, are all reduced to non-literal events. Indeed, Christ's death, resurrection, glory, and coming are one single event (pp. 97-101). The only sense in which Christ rose in triumph or will come again is in the spread of His ethical teachings through human society. Even this Christ did not predict. For Him, and for us, the eternal order has already come. The new heaven and new earth are now present.

People lose sight of the fact that the eternal and absolute "entered decisively into history" (p. 203). Thus the church needs to proclaim the gospel of the kingdom to each generation. It prays, "Thy kingdom come," and "Even so, come, Lord Jesus." God's answer to these prayers is in the "Sacrament of the Eucharist," which "recapitulates the historic crisis in which Christ came, lived, died and rose again," and which "in its origin and in its governing ideas...may be described as a sacrament of realized eschatology" (p. 203). Beyond that, there is no expectation of any personal return or reign of Christ: "We have, it appears, no warrant in the teaching of Jesus for affirming that the long cycles of history will lead eventually to a millennial 'Kingdom Come' on earth" (p. 209).

Dodd's emphasis on the kingdom as already present is in itself perfectly scriptural. His emphasis on the decisive entrance of God into history in the person of Christ is a welcome counterbalance to neo-orthodoxy's* rejection of the historical revelation of the gospel. But his denial of the actual resurrection and second coming of Christ is plainly unscriptural. Indeed, it is explicitly antichristian.

Dodd's entire scheme depends on the reliability of form criticism. If its conclusions are deeply flawed—and they are—he has no warrant for his rejection of the recorded sayings of Christ that clearly contradict his view.

See **Kingdom of God**.

REATUS CULPAE, REATUS POENAE

Two phrases used in discussion of the guilt* of sin.* *Reatus* in Latin means, "the state or condition of an accused person." *Reatus culpae* signifies the state of being guilty in the sense of being worthy of blame. *Reatus poenae* signifies the state of being guilty in the sense of being worthy of punishment. This distinction is of importance in federal theology* especially in considering the imputation* of our guilt to Christ as our substitute. Only the guilt of *punishment* was imputed to Him, not the guilt of *blame.* He did not become personally sinful by bearing our sins.

Some theologians teach that the distinction should also be applied in considering the imputation of Adam's first transgression. They hold that whereas Adam alone is *blamed* for that sin, all humanity has been accounted guilty in the sense of liability to punishment for it. Thus Berkhof says, "The guilt of Adam's sin, committed by him as the federal head of the human race, is imputed to all his descendants" (*Systematic Theology,* p. 246). Here *guilt* means *reatus poenae:* the penalty is imputed. But this seems to miss the point of Romans 5:12, especially the force of the Greek aorist tense of the verb in the last clause: "As by one man sin entered into the world, and death by sin; and so death passed upon all men, in that all sinned." This last clause means "on the ground of the fact that all sinned." So the penalty of that first sin is laid upon Adam's posterity, because—in the sense of blame—

they are held to have been personally guilty of it in him.

Both *reatus culpae* and *reatus poenae* are imputed to Adam's posterity. Only *reatus poenae* is in view in the imputation of our sin to Christ. This distinction is supported by the language of Rom. 5:15, 16 where Paul uses the language of contrast as well as comparison in describing our union with Adam and with Christ.

RECAPITULATION THEORY OF THE ATONEMENT

The idea, which was held by Irenaeus of Lyons, that "Christ recapitulates in Himself all the stages of human life, including those which belong to our state as sinners" (James Orr). Berkhof further explains the theory: "By His incarnation and human life He reverses the course on which Adam by his sin started humanity and thus becomes a new leaven in the life of mankind. He communicates immortality to those who are united to Him by faith and effects an ethical transformation in their lives, and by His obedience compensates for the disobedience of Adam."

The theory is deficient, hardly meriting the description "theory of the atonement," since it has no place for Christ's atoning work. It is devoid of scriptural proof.

RECEIVED TEXT

See **Textual Criticism of the Old Testament**, and **Textual Criticism of the New Testament**.

RECENSION

A term used in textual criticism* meaning a revision of the text of Scripture based on a critical examination of available sources or variant readings.

RECONCILIATION

"To make reconciliation (which Christ is said in many places to do), it is required, first, that the wrath of God be turned away, His anger removed, and all the effects of enmity on His part towards us; secondly, that we be turned away from our opposition to Him, and brought into voluntary obedience" (John Owen, *Death of Death,* p. 151).

The basic NT words *katallage,* "reconciliation," and *katallasso,* "to reconcile," denote a change or exchange of money, and paint a picture of two parties, formerly at enmity, settling their differences, by one paying the balance or exchange. In terms of Biblical doctrine, reconciliation is the removal of the enmity between God and the sinner, and the establishment of a new relationship of peace and friendship between them, on the ground of Christ's payment of everything due to God and His holy law because of sin. Accordingly, in Scripture, reconciliation is ascribed to the merit of the blood shedding of Christ (Rom. 5:10; 2 Cor. 5:18; Eph. 2:13, 14; Col. 1:20).

RECONSTRUCTIONISM

A version of Reformed, postmillennial theology that emphasizes the concepts of theonomy and dominion. It was founded by Orthodox Presbyterian theologian Rousas J. Rushdoony.

A Reconstructionist's Definition

Rushdoony's *Chalcedon Report* frequently carries an outline of reconstructionist positions by Andrew Sandlin. It reads:

"A Christian Reconstructionist is a *Calvinist.* He holds to historic, orthodox, catholic Christianity and the great Reformed confessions. He believes God, not man, is the center of the universe—and beyond; God, not man, controls whatever comes to pass; God, not man, must be pleased and obeyed. He believes God saves sinners—He does not help them save themselves. A Christian Reconstructionist believes the Faith should apply to all of life, not just the 'spiritual' side. It applies to art, education, technology, and politics no less than to church, prayer, evangelism, and Bible study.

"A Christian Reconstructionist is a *Theonomist.* Theonomy means 'God's law.'

A Christian Reconstructionist believes God's law is found in the Bible. It has not been abolished as a standard of righteousness. It no longer accuses the Christian, since Christ bore its penalty on the cross for him. But the law is a description of God's righteous character. It cannot change any more than God can change. God's law is used for three main purposes: First, to drive the sinner to trust in Christ alone, the only perfect law-keeper. Second, to provide a standard of obedience for the Christian, by which he may judge his progress in sanctification. And third, to maintain order in society, restraining and arresting civil evil.

"A Christian Reconstructionist is a *Presuppositionalist.* He does not try to 'prove' that God exists or that the Bible is true. He holds the faith because the Bible says so, not because he can 'prove' it. He does not try to convince the unconverted that the gospel is true. They already know it is true. They need repentance, not evidence. Of course, the Christian Reconstructionist believes there is evidence for the faith—in fact, there is nothing but evidence for the faith. The problem for the unconverted, though, is not a lack of evidence, but a lack of submission. The Christian Reconstructionist begins and ends with the Bible. He does not defend 'natural theology,' and other inventions designed to find some agreement with covenant-breaking, apostate mankind.

"A Christian Reconstructionist is a *Postmillennialist.* He believes Christ will return to earth only after the Holy Spirit has empowered the church to advance Christ's kingdom in time and history. He has faith that God's purposes to bring all nations—though not every individual—into subjection to Christ cannot fail. The Christian Reconstructionist is not utopian. He does not believe the kingdom will advance quickly or painlessly. He knows that we enter the kingdom through much tribulation. He knows Christians are in the fight for the 'long haul.' He believes the church may yet be in her infancy. But he believes the Faith will triumph. Under the power of the Spirit of God, it cannot but triumph.

"A Christian Reconstructionist is a *Dominionist.* He takes seriously the Bible's commands to the godly to take dominion in the earth. This is the goal of the gospel and the Great Commission. The Christian Reconstructionist believes the earth and all its fulness is the Lord's—that every area dominated by sin must be 'reconstructed' in terms of the Bible. This includes, first, the individual; second, the family; third, the church; and fourth, the wider society, including the state. The Christian Reconstructionist therefore believes fervently in Christian civilization. He firmly believes in the separation of church and state, but not the separation of the state—or anything else—from God. He is not a revolutionary; he does not believe in the militant, forced overthrow of human government. He has infinitely more powerful weapons than guns and bombs—he has the invincible Spirit of God, the infallible word of God, and the incomparable gospel of God, none of which can fail.

"He presses the crown rights of the Lord Jesus Christ in every sphere, expecting eventual triumph."

Reconstructionists emphasize their Calvinism* and presuppositionalism.* Certainly there is much in Sandlin's statement that every Calvinist and presuppositionalist would heartily endorse. Despite that, many convinced Calvinists and presuppositionalists are not reconstructionists. The heart of their dispute with reconstructionism lies in the movement's idea of theonomy.

Theonomy
Justified By Grace, Sanctified By Law. Theonomy reaches to the Christian's personal life and then to the nations of the world through the church's work and witness. On the personal level, reconstructionism strikes a welcome note against the antinomianism* inherent in much of modern evangelicalism,

particularly in dispensationalism.* But it goes too far. According to Rushdoony, "Man's justification, is by the grace of God in Jesus Christ; man's sanctification is by means of the law of God" (*Institutes of Biblical Law,* p. 4). Again, "The law is the way of sanctification" (p. 3). These statements set law as the antithesis of grace. They present a theory of sanctification* that is not by grace but by works of law.

The NT paints a very different picture. Christ "is made unto us…sanctification" (1 Cor. 1:30); "The life that I now live in the flesh, I live by the faith of the Son of God, who loved me, and gave himself for me" (Gal. 2:20). These apostolic declarations show that grace received through faith is the way of sanctification. Romans 6, with its emphasis on *knowing* and *reckoning* on our union with Christ as the basis of yielding our bodies as instruments of His service, makes the same point. Sanctification will produce obedience to God and His moral law, which is the abiding standard of holy obedience, but it is grace received through faith that produces and empowers obedience.

Though reconstructionists vehemently deny it, their view of sanctification is a species of legalism.* Taken seriously—especially in the light of their insistence of the permanence of the civil laws of Israel for the believer—it is difficult to see that a Christian could ever escape a sense of bondage and defeat.

Calvin's View of Law "Heretical Nonsense." Reconstructionists also apply their concept of theonomy to states and nations. They deny the classic Reformed view of the law of God that distributes it under three categories, moral, civil, and ceremonial, and holds that the last two have been abolished under the gospel. The *Westminster Confession of Faith* clearly states this position (chap. 19, sec. 3-5). Of particular importance is its statement, "To them [Israel] also, as a body politic, he gave sundry judicial laws, which expired together with the state of that people, not obliging any other now, further than the general equity thereof may require" (sec. 4).

Against this Rushdoony says, " it is a serious error to say that the civil law was also (i.e., with the ceremonial law) abolished, but the moral law retained" (*Institutes of Biblical Law,* p. 304). He boldly labels Calvin's view, with which the *Confession* is in complete accord, "heretical nonsense" (p. 9). Calvin described the position now advocated by reconstructionists as "dangerous and seditious," and "false and foolish" (*Institutes,* 4: chap. 20, ¶ 14).

Problem of Reconstructionist Use of OT Civil Laws. The matter at issue is whether the laws God gave to govern the theocratic state of Israel are binding on every state in every place. Calvin thought they were not; Rushdoony says they are. The reconstructionists' insistence on this point, where they openly depart from the very *Confession* they claim to adhere to, runs into a serious problem: the complete silence of the NT on the application of Israel's civil code to the nations to which the apostles took the gospel. Arguments from silence are always questionable but in this case the silence is very significant. If the reconstructionist is right in defining the church's commission in theonomic terms (see below) it is inconceivable that the NT would fail to give us plain testimony to the apostles' obedience to the Saviour's mandate. Rushdoony's case sounds good but lacks clear NT evidence.

Logical Inconsistency. It also lacks logical consistency. In his *Institutes* Rushdoony argues that the civil law* is moral and therefore permanent. Then he uses it as case law which evidences the principles of the moral law under the circumstances mentioned. He interprets these case law examples to apply them to modern situations. Today only antinomians deny that the moral law has implications for modern society, that its demands are permanent. Only antinomians refuse to acknowledge that OT case laws give us examples of the moral principles of the decalogue* in concrete situations, and that the demands of the moral law must be established by applying the principles laid down by the word of God. All orthodox believers accept these truths.

Rushdoony, however, goes a lot further. He claims that the case laws themselves are moral and permanent. But that is to ignore the intrinsic nature of case law: its form and continuance depend on the nature and continuance of the cases it was designed to cover.

Deuteronomy 22, for example, states a number of case laws. If these are still binding then reconstructionists must seek to introduce the following to the moral code of the church and the state: every new house must have a battlement for its roof (v. 8); no vineyard may be sown with divers seeds (v. 9); a garment may not be made from mixed materials, as wool and linen (v. 11); everyone should have fringes on his clothing (v. 12); a betrothed girl who has had sexual relations with a man in the city must die, while if it happened in the open field she may live (vv. 23-27); if a man lays hold of an unbetrothed girl and lies with her he must pay her father fifty shekels and marry her (v. 29). Deuteronomy 25:5 adds another part to the civil code: the duty of a man to marry the childless wife of his dead brother.

It is not enough for reconstructionists to spiritualize these commands, or to modernize them by eliciting what they take to be the abiding principles in them. They set them on the same level as the decalogue and demand that we regard them as equally permanent. Yet their own treatment of those laws shows that they do not take the laws themselves as permanent but merely as passing examples of how the permanent principles set forth in the ten commandments should be applied to situations not mentioned in the moral law.

This is how Rushdoony uses the command, "Thou shalt not muzzle the ox that treadeth out the corn" (Deut. 25:4). He treats it as an elaboration of the eighth commandment, "Thou shalt not steal," (Exod. 20:15) and goes on to notice Paul's use of it in 1 Cor. 9:9, 10, 14 and 1 Tim. 5:18. Paul argues, "Does God take care for oxen? or saith he it altogether for our sakes? For our sakes, no doubt, this was written."

Paul's Treatment of an OT Civil Law. Two things stand out in Paul's treatment of the OT law:

First, he seems to indicate quite clearly that the actual Mosaic statute was not binding and that his only purpose in citing it had nothing to do with oxen. The morally binding principle required a just remuneration for those who labour in the work of God. Now in the Rushdoony scheme, what would a state have to place on its statute books? Cases change with time and place, and of necessity the expression of how the moral law applies to them must change too. Only the ten commandments were inscribed in stone.

Second, Paul limits his application of the OT case law to the church. The texts quoted above would have been a golden opportunity for him to have stated the position so beloved of reconstructionists, that the entire Mosaic corpus is binding on states and nations—and if God expects them to pay just wages surely the church should do the same. But he does not do so, with the result that reconstructionists are forced to look elsewhere for support for their thesis.

Dominion

Stating that Abraham and Israel were commanded to subdue the earth and bring it to obedience to God's law, Rushdoony claims this is still the purpose and mission of the church. The premise is faulty. God spoke to Abraham and Israel about a particular area of the earth. He did not give them a mission of world dominion.

Reinstating Man in the Covenant of Works?

Rushdoony argues that the purpose of Christ was to reinstate man in the original covenant relationship in which he stood before the fall* (pp. 3, 14). That is, it is the purpose of the covenant of grace to put man back under the covenant of works. It is difficult to understand Rushdoony's statements in any other sense. He goes on to say, "The fulfilment of that covenant is their [the elect's] great commission: to subdue all things and all nations to Christ and His law-word" (p.14). This redefines the church's mission. It is a reckless innovation to make such a definition when Christ and His apostles have by word and deed shown us that the great commission was never expressed or carried out in anything like the terms Rushdoony employs. His new mission tends toward state reform, with state churches, rather than a programme of soul-winning evangelization. It appears to offer a vision of renewal from the top down (from government to people) rather than from the bottom up. That would be a reform without much corresponding spiritual change in the populace.

We should note something significant in this entire scenario. Reconstructionists place great stress on the law as covenant. They insist that the mission of the church is to call the nations back to the covenant of the law-word; however, as far as unsaved people are concerned this must be a bare covenant of works. Now it is true that every unconverted sinner stands under the law as a covenant of works and is condemned by it. But is it the mission of the church—is it the gospel message—that the nations of the world should arrange their affairs by obedience to the covenant of works? And if they sought to do so, would that be an evidence of the great spiritual regeneration postmillennialists envisage before Christ returns?

Postmillennial Basis

Postmillennialism Essential. All reconstructionist visions of theonomic dominion over the nations depend on the validity of postmillennial eschatology.* If it can be shown that Christ's return is imminent, or that He will return and then rule on the earth (or, indeed, if Amillennialism* can be proved scriptural) the entire scheme of Christian reconstructionism falls to the ground.

Postmillennialism Questionable. There is good ground to dispute the postmillennial vision of the future. It appears clear from Zech. 12-14 that there is a day yet future when "Jerusalem shall be inhabited in her own place, even in Jerusalem" (12:6—a text that is difficult to spiritualize); when the Lord "will pour upon...the inhabitants of Jerusalem the spirit of grace and of supplications: and they shall look upon me whom they have pierced" (12:10). The timing of that day appears from 14:4 to be at the second coming of the Lord Jesus Christ. Significantly, it is after this that "the Lord shall be king over all the earth" (14:9). That this is speaking of the millennial earth and not the eternal state is clear from verse 16 where the prophet refers to "every one that is left of all the nations which came against Jerusalem." This passage (and it is just one of many possible examples) undermines the entire postmillennial programme. Without it, on their own confession, reconstructionism's carefully constructed scheme fails.

Christ's Eschatological Purpose Our Immediate Purpose? We may remark that Rushdoony's proposal to make Christ's *eschatological* purpose the *immediate* purpose of the church (*Institutes,* p. 3) is without warrant. The worldwide reign of Christ awaits His return. In the meantime we evangelize; we do not dominate by the imposition of the law of Moses.

Positive Features

Notwithstanding these criticisms, reconstructionism has some positive features. It restates the old truths of Calvinism without apology in the hostile environment of modern humanism.* It reminds men and nations that they are accountable to God. It holds out the gospel of justifying grace as the only hope for sinners. It calls on Christians to

become positive instruments for moral and spiritual renewal in every area of life, including matters of state. Many reconstructionists are active in evangelism and in sound social and political endeavours. These are not small matters. Neither are they the exclusive property of reconstructionism. Its most attractive features are those which are not the core essentials of its theory.

See Law of God.

RECUSANT

A term from English law dating back to the time of Elizabeth I, describing a person who refused or neglected to attend the worship of the established church on Sundays or other appointed days. Recusants may have been Roman Catholics or Protestants but there were additional penalties levied against the former who were termed *popish recusants.* Protestant recusants received relief under the Toleration Act when William and Mary ascended the throne. Popish recusants received partial relief in 1791 and complete relief in the Catholic Emancipation Acts of 1829.

REDACTION CRITICISM

A widespread modern approach to Biblical criticism, devised by some pupils of Rudolph Bultmann (1884-1976). They reject his thesis that the Gospels supply no evidence of the historical Jesus, and set out upon "a new quest" for Him. Their redaction criticism proceeds upon the belief that each Gospel's writer or editor (*redactor*) freely "restated" the material that came to him, in order to further his own particular theological interests.

The criteria by which redaction critics argue their case are highly sceptical. One popular standard of judgment is to consider false anything attributed to Jesus in the Gospels that could plausibly have been spoken by His contemporaries. Another standard of judgment rejects the genuineness of any saying attributed to Him that expresses later church teaching—far from being the authentic words of Jesus, such sayings were creations of church tradition which redactors later attributed to Him.

D. A. Carson commented on these criteria: "From these two criteria alone (and there are others of similar ilk), the only sayings of Jesus that scholars may judge to be authentic are those that are idiosyncratic. Such criteria have been criticized repeatedly. Jesus was, after all, a first-century Jewish man. To begin by arguing that he must not sound like one is akin to arguing that Churchill must never sound like an Englishman. To turn around and say that Jesus must not sound like the church, either, is to assume that perhaps the most influential man in history never said anything that the church believed, cherished, and passed on" (*Christianity Today,* April 25, 1994, p. 32).

REDEMPTION

In a general sense, the saving purpose and revelation of God in Christ Jesus. In a more particular sense, the deliverance of God's elect from a state of sin into a state of salvation by the means and merit of the ransom paid by Christ on their behalf. "Redemption, which in the [Greek] Scripture is *lutrosis* sometimes, but most frequently *apolutrosis,* is the delivery of any one from captivity and misery by the intervention *lutrou,* of a price or ransom. That this ransom, or price of our deliverance was the blood of Christ is evident. He calls it *lutron,* Matt. 20:28; and [it is called] *antilutron,* 1 Tim. 2:6—that is, the price of such a redemption, that which was received as a valuable consideration for our dismission" (John Owen, *Death of Death,* p. 147).

In many modern translations the word *deliverance* appears in place of *redemption.* This reflects the opinion that whatever the inherent meaning of the Greek terms, the NT uses them in a non-technical sense to mean nothing more precise than deliverance. This is an assumption far removed from the facts of the case.

The etymology and usage of the Greek words involved argue very strongly for the precise meaning given by Owen. The Greek words *lutron, lutrosis,* and *apolutrosis* are derived from the verb *luo,* "to loose." B. B. Warfield notes:

"When applied to men, its common meaning is 'to loose, release, set free,' especially from bonds or prison, and so, generally, from difficulty, or danger. It developed a particular usage with reference to prisoners, which is of interest to us. In this usage, it means, in the active voice, 'to release on receipt of ransom,' 'to hold to ransom,' 'to ransom' in the common use of that word, passing on to a broader usage of simply 'to redeem.'…It also acquired the sense of paying debts, and, with reference to wrong-doings, a sense of 'undoing' or 'making up for,' which is not far removed from that of making atonement for, them" (*Biblical Foundations,* pp. 200, 201).

This is the root from which the word *lutron* is derived. The *lutron* was the instrument by which the action in the verb *luo* was accomplished—i.e., it was the ransom because of which the release took place. This was the sense of the word as it appears in first-century papyri documenting the emancipation of slaves. "The essential meaning of the term [is] just the price paid as a ransom in order to secure release" (Warfield, p. 204). Thus the idea of ransom that was present in *luo* came by association to be the central meaning of the verb *lutroo.*

This is the chief term the NT uses to express the idea of redemption. It has one meaning only: to release by the payment of a ransom. That ransom price was the sacrificial death, the atoning blood, of the Lord Jesus Christ (Tit. 2:14).

The NT also employs the Greek verb *exagorazo* to denote Christ's ransom of His people from the curse of the law (Gal. 3:13; 4:5). John used *agorazo* without the prefix in Rev. 5:9 where the glorified saints praise the Lamb, "Thou hast redeemed us to God by thy blood." In Rev. 14:3, 4 the 144,000 are

301

said to have been redeemed (*agorazo*) from among men. This word means "to buy out," and was used in NT times for purchasing a slave in order to give him his freedom. The idea is similar to that in *lutroo.* The NT language leaves us in no doubt that God's elect were sinners and slaves who could be released from the curse of the broken law of God only by means of the ransom Christ paid on their behalf at Calvary (1 Pet. 1:18, 19).

In the NT, *redemption* not only denotes the present deliverance from sin believers enjoy (Eph. 1:7), but the future deliverance of their bodies from all the effects of sin (Rom. 8:23). Thus in Eph. 1:14 and 4:30 redemption is viewed as future. The deliverance has been purchased and is now the possession of all believers, but the full effects of that purchase await the coming again of our Lord Jesus Christ when our vile bodies will be changed to be like His glorious body (Phil. 3:21; 1 John 3:2).

See *Goel.*

REFORMATION

The 16th-century movement which exposed and opposed the apostasy of Romanism and rediscovered and republished the pure gospel of the NT. The Reformation was essentially a movement of the Word and deserves the description given it by Philip Schaff in the *History of the Christian Church:* "The Reformation was a republication of primitive Christianity, and the inauguration of modern Christianity. This makes it, next to the Apostolic age, the most important and interesting portion of church history" (7:1, AP&A edition).

Schaff succinctly states the need for the Reformation: "The hopelessness of expecting any permanent reform from the papacy and the hierarchy was demonstrated in the last years of the period, 1460-1517, when ecclesiastical Rome offered a spectacle of moral corruption and spiritual fall which has been compared to the corrupt age of the Roman Empire" (6:2).

The Reformers attacked Rome at the very heart of her corruption, namely her debasement of the gospel of free grace to a system of human merit. Luther told Erasmus, in his *Bondage of the Will,* that the real issue was the Reformed emphasis on the total inability of man's will to produce spiritual good, with the necessary consequence that salvation, far from being dependent in any degree on human merit, is of free and sovereign grace. The doctrine of justification* obtained only on the merits of Christ's obedience and received by faith without works, became in Luther's words, *Articulus stantis et cadentis ecclesiae,* "the article of a standing or falling church" (i.e., the doctrine by which we may judge whether a church is standing true to Christ or has fallen into apostasy).

The Reformation produced theologians of the highest class. Calvin ranks first in theological genius, his *Institutes of the Christian Religion* being the leading statement of the Reformed faith. Luther, in his *Bondage of the Will,* produced one of the greatest theological classics of all time. Zwingli, Bucer, Oecolampadius, Bullinger, Melancthon, Beza—the list goes on—all championed the cause of the gospel of grace.

On the great fundamentals of the gospel the Reformers were one, but they differed on a number of secondary matters. As a result, the Reformation developed into two main strands, the Lutheran and the Calvinistic, while outside the main movement, the Anglicans* and the Anabaptists* represented yet other variations.

Some historians refer to the mainstream and Anglican Reformation movements as the *magisterial Reformation* and the movement of the Anabaptist and Spiritualist groups as the *radical Reformation.* This distinction is more or less arbitrary. It begs the question raised by the term *radical Reformation* for, as any Protestant of the Lutheran or Calvinistic persuasions would justifiably argue, even the best of the Anabaptists did not show themselves more radical in the sense of really going back to the NT roots of Christianity than did the mainstream Reformers. Indeed on many vital issues they stopped far short of the roots and made little, if any, progress on the Romish position—e.g., in areas such as the doctrine of original sin* and justification* by faith. The term *magisterial Reformation* is objectionable because it is an Anabaptist mischaracterization of the work of the mainstream Reformers and because it has in it the suggestion of Erastianism.*

REFORMED FAITH, REFORMED THEOLOGY

Popularly known as Calvinism,* it is the system of doctrine regarded as consistently Biblical by the Reformed churches, i.e., those Protestant churches historically associated with Calvin and Geneva. It is most cogently set forth in such symbols* as the *Heidelberg Catechism,* the *Canons of the Synod of Dort,* and the *Westminster Standards.* *

As a systematic and Biblical theology, the Reformed faith gives proper prominence to the sovereignty of God* in His eternal decree and its execution because it is consistently a theology of the word of God, whose revelation is sufficient and whose authority is final.

The Reformed faith is also a system of covenant theology,* at least for its Presbyterian proponents. Others, notably some Baptists* of Calvinistic persuasion, reject covenant theology as an integral part of the Reformed faith; but even these will agree with the central conviction of their covenant brethren that there is a grand unity in God's purpose and method of saving sinners, in both the OT and the NT.

See Doctrines of Grace.

REGENERATION
Definition

"Regeneration is that act of God by which the principle of the new life is implanted in man, and the governing disposition of the soul is made holy... and the first holy exer-

cise of this new disposition is secured" (Berkhof). This is the usual sense of the word, though in Scripture the same Greek word *palingenesia* is also employed in a totally different way (Matt. 19:28) as the equivalent of "the restitution [or restoration] of all things" (Acts 3:21).

In its theological sense, regeneration deals with the beginning of the new life in the believer. The terms *birth, born,* or *begotten* (John 1:13; 3:3-8; 1 Pet. 1:23; 1 John 2:29; 3:9; 4:7; 5:1, 4, 18; James 1:18) signify this beginning of new life. Ephesians 2:5 uses the verb *quicken* (or *make alive*) to denote the same thing (cf. Col. 2:13), while verse 10 uses the verb *create,* which also emphasizes the beginning of new life (cf. 2 Cor. 5:17; Gal. 6:15, which speak of a "new creature," and Eph. 4:24, "the new man"). By noting these terms we may set forth the leading characteristics of regeneration.

Characteristics

1. It is the work, or more properly the *act,* of God (Eph. 2:1-10). The creature has no power in originating this new life. The creation of new life is called a "new birth" or a "birth from above" (John 3:3; *anothen* signifies "from above"), or a "birth of the Spirit" (John 3:5). **2.** Man is passive in regeneration. He receives this gracious act of God, but being naturally "dead" (Eph. 2:1) he cannot contribute to it. Pelagians look upon regeneration as the free will* of man choosing in a new way. Arminians adopt the theory of synergism,* literally, "a working together," in which they see the human and divine wills actively cooperating in regeneration. The Biblical and Reformed position is that regeneration is monergistic; i.e., it is the result of God working alone. A dead man can do nothing to contribute to his own resurrection, just as Lazarus in his grave could do nothing to cooperate with the Lord in his resurrection. **3.** The result of regeneration is a "new man," "a new creature." This renewal affects both the understanding and the will.

a. The understanding is enlightened (2 Cor. 4:6; 1 Cor. 2:12, 13; Eph. 1:18; Phil. 1:9; Col. 3:10; 1 John 4:7; 5:20).

Shedd remarks, "The distinguishing peculiarity of the knowledge produced by regeneration is, that it is experimental. By this is meant, that the cognition is that of immediate consciousness. This is the highest and clearest form of cognition. When, for example, the truth that God is merciful is stated in language, the natural man understands the language grammatically and logically, but nothing more. He has no accompanying consciousness of God's mercy. In common phrase, he does not feel that God is merciful. But a knowledge that is destitute of inward consciousness is an inferior species. It is a blind man's knowledge of colour. ...It is quasi-knowledge; such as Christ refers to, when He says of the natural man: 'Seeing he sees not; hearing he hears not.'"

The state of natural man's mind is said to be one of "ignorance" (John 8:19; Heb. 5:2; Rom. 10:3; 2 Pet. 3:5; 1 Pet. 1:14) and "darkness" (Eph. 4:18). In contrast, the quickened or regenerated soul is brought into "God's marvelous light" (1 Pet. 2:9).

b. The will is renewed. The *Larger Catechism* (Q. 67), in defining effectual calling, says, "He doth, in His accepted time, invite and draw them to Jesus Christ, by His Word and Spirit; savingly enlightening their minds, renewing and powerfully determining their wills, so as they (although in themselves dead in sin) are hereby made willing and able freely to answer His call..." (Rom. 9:16; Phil. 2:13; Ps. 110:3).

4. Regeneration is accomplished without the use of means, in the strict sense of the term, for it is an act of direct, divine creation. God speaks and it is done (1 Pet. 1:23). Paul's statement, "Faith cometh by hearing, and hearing by the word of God" (Rom. 10:17) does not run counter to this. God acts directly in the act of creating spiritual life in a dead soul, but He calls forth the first exercise of faith by that new creation through His word.

5. Regeneration precedes, and is the immediate cause of, conversion. "The Holy Spirit acts in regeneration, and as a consequence the human spirit acts in conversion" (Shedd). The instantaneous act of regeneration gives rise to the continual activity of conversion, namely the growing exercise of faith and repentance. J. I. Packer says: "In John's Gospel and First Epistle the figure of new birth...is integral to the presentation of personal salvation....In the Gospel, Christ assures Nicodemus that there are no special activities—no seeing or entering God's kingdom, because (he had) no faith in himself—without regeneration (John 3:1 ff.); and John declares in the prologue that only the regenerate receive Christ and enter into the privilege of God's children (John 1:12-13). Conversely, in the Epistle, John insists that there is no regeneration that does not issue in spiritual activities. The regenerate do righteousness (1 John 2:29) and do not live a life of sin (3:9; 5:18; the present tense indicates habitual law-keeping, not absolute sinlessness, cf. 1:8-10); they love Christians (4:7); believe rightly in Christ and experience faith's victory over the world (5:4). Any who do otherwise, whatever they claim, are still unregenerate children of the devil (3:6-10)" (*Baker's Dictionary of Theology,* pp. 440, 441).

A Wider Use of the Term By Reformed Writers

This fact—i.e., that the implanting of the principle of new life (the new birth) leads to the exercise of spiritual activities—and the added fact that the Scriptures speak in a few places of saved people needing or experiencing renewal (Eph. 4:22-25; Rom. 12:2; 2 Cor. 4:16), gave rise to a rather confused and indiscriminate use of the term *regeneration* in theological literature. We have been discussing it in its narrow sense, marking its distinction from conversion. In earlier days, however, theologians used it in a much wider sense to indicate not only the new birth, but all that issues from it.

Calvin's Use of It. Thus Calvin (*Institutes,* 3: 3, ¶9) says, "I apprehend repentance to be regeneration, the end of which is the restoration of the divine image within us. In this regeneration, we are restored by the grace of Christ to the righteousness of God from which we fell in Adam. And this restoration is not accomplished in a single moment, or day, or year; but by continual even tardy advances the Lord destroys the carnal corruptions of His elect."

Resulting Confusion. Such a statement is not wrong. In fact, it stresses some vital truths, as for instance, that regeneration is not a complete and perfect change in the nature of the whole man, rendering him incapable of sin. Calvin needed to emphasize this against the views of some Anabaptists.* So his representation, one which is generally followed by Protestant writers of the Reformation and Puritan periods, is understandable. It fails, however, to mark the distinction between regeneration, in which God alone acts, and conversion, in which the human will works. This confusion is still evident in many quarters today.

Distinction Between Regeneration and Conversion. The distinction between regeneration and conversion is vital. Shedd sums it up: "Regeneration, accordingly, is an act; conversion is an activity, or a process. Regeneration is the origination of life; conversion is the evolution (development) or manifestation of life. Regeneration is wholly an act of God; conversion is wholly an activity of man. Regeneration is a cause; conversion is an effect. Regeneration is instantaneous; conversion is continuous."

See *Effectual Calling*.

REGULATIVE PRINCIPLE

The theory of church government and worship that stipulates that not only church doctrine but church practice, must be based on clear scriptural warrant. That is, we must have a clear Biblical command or precedent, expressed or implied, for all we introduce into the work and worship of the church. It is the position laid down in the *Westminster Confession of Faith* and is the opposite of the normative principle* espoused by Lutherans and Anglicans.

In its statement on the Holy Scriptures the *Confession* says, "The whole counsel of God, concerning all things necessary for his own glory, man's salvation, faith, and life, is either expressly set down in Scripture, or, by good and necessary consequence may be deduced from Scripture: unto which nothing at any time is to be added, whether by new revelations of the Spirit, or traditions of men. Nevertheless, we acknowledge …that there are some circumstances concerning the worship of God, and government of the Church, common to human actions and societies, which are to be ordered by the light of nature and Christian prudence, according to the general rules of the Word, which are always to be observed" (chap. 1, sec. 6). In its chapter on "Religious Worship and the Sabbath" the *Confession* applies these general principles to the particulars of worship and practice: "The acceptable way of worshipping the true God is instituted by himself, and so limited by his own revealed will, that he may not be worshipped according to the imaginations and devices of men, or the suggestions of Satan, under any visible representation, or any other way not prescribed in the Holy Scripture" (chap. 21, sec. 1).

These balanced statements avoid the extreme of allowing into the church's worship and government whatever is not expressly forbidden in the Word and the opposite extreme of demanding that every detail of our practice should have an explicit command of Scripture before it is allowable. Many things—e.g., the time and frequency of church services, the particular order of service in public worship, the length of services and sermons, the taking of minutes in session meetings, etc.—are not given us in Scripture.

"The light of nature and Christian prudence"—sanctified common sense—will show us the proper course to adopt. But that course must always be in strict accord with all that God has declared in His word. A. A. Hodge commented on the *Confession's* statement (chap. 1, sec. 6):

"They [the Scriptures] do not descend in practical matters into details, but, laying down general principles, leave men to apply them on the exercise of their natural judgment, in the light of experience, and in adaptation to changing circumstances, as they are guided by the sanctifying influences of the Holy Spirit. This liberty, of course, is allowed only within the limits of the strict interpretation of the principles taught in the Word, and in the legitimate application of those principles, and applies to the regulations of the practical life of the individual and of the Church, in detailed adjustments to changing circumstances."

REINCARNATION

Also called metempsychosis;* essentially the Buddhist and Hindu notion of transmigration.* It is the theory that after death the soul may return to this life in a new body or form. It is foreign to the Biblical teaching of death and judgment (Heb. 9:27), and to the entire revelation of salvation in Christ.

RELATIVISM

The denial of any absolute standard of truth and morality.

In epistemology* relativism is the theory that truth is relative to the position of the recipient. Thus there is no universal truth. Truth varies according to the people and conditions involved. This ancient fallacy has become popular in recent years. The notion of "what is true for you may not be true for me" has become a guiding principle in many people's lives. This philoso-

phy defines truth in John Dewey's terms that what works is true, or that a statistical average of human behaviour under given conditions must be true.

This idea carries over into the field of ethics.* If what works is true, then what works is right. According to the relativist, the idea of what is right can never be settled by divine law, but by the cultural norms. Furthermore, the validity of any decision or behaviour must be judged in the context of the situation in which the subject finds himself. This is known as situation ethics, the idea that the moral quality of an action is not determined by any absolute standard of right and wrong but by the situation in which a person makes his ethical choices.

This ethical relativism has opened the door for the acceptance by society of all sorts of deviant behaviour, from abortion-on-demand, to homosexuality, to euthanasia.

Many people see the moral morass into which moral relativism has brought the nation as a threat to the very fabric of society. However, among them are those who, though decrying relativism in morals, uphold the same theory with regard to truth. Without absolute truth there are not absolute standards for life. But given that Jesus is "the Way, the Truth, and the Life" (John 14:6), and that God's "word is truth" (John 17:17), the Bible is a sufficient statement of moral standards for all men, in all places, at all times.

RELIGIOUS EXPERIENCE

Subjective feelings that result from the real or alleged actions of God upon the human soul or spirit. The work of the Holy Spirit* in convicting men of sin, leading them to the assurance of faith,* enlightening them as to the fulness of God's provision in Christ (Eph. 1:17-23), and enabling them to "be filled with all the fulness of God" (Eph. 3:19), is the true essence of religious experience.

Fellowship with God and the sense of His withdrawal, as with Job and even with our

Lord Jesus Christ, are real. The quickening and reviving grace of God's Spirit is real. The "righteousness, peace, and joy in the Holy Ghost" which characterize the kingdom of God (Rom. 14:17) are real. The deliverance God gives His people from fear, granting them the spirit "of power, and of love, and of a sound mind" (2 Tim. 1:7), is not a mere psychological phenomenon. It is a real experience of God.

The measure of all claimed religious experience is Scripture (1 John 4:1-6). Some things that are claimed to be religious experiences are mere productions of the flesh. Some are the delusions of demons. No religious experience may be admitted as authentic merely because the subject of it invokes the name of Christ, or even because he offers supernatural power to validate his claim. A false prophet may support his lies with miracles (Deut. 13:1-5). That does not alter the fact that his experiences are not of God. The pythoness of Acts 16 obviously had experience combined with supernatural power, but Paul cast out of her the evil spirit that was the source of both (Acts 16:18).

Observing Scripture as the objective standard to judge all claimed religious experience is vitally important. This has never been more true than today when there are so many Charismatics claiming to have heard God, seen Christ, visited heaven, or received some other special visitation from on high. Usually the light of Scripture will expose these claims for the counterfeits they are.

Care must be taken to avoid psychologically induced copies of genuine religious experiences. For example, at times people who witnessed certain effects of a powerful move of the Holy Spirit in revival set out to duplicate those effects in the mistaken belief that they were reproducing the authentic work of the Spirit.

Anything that must be worked up or produced by mood-controlling techniques is obviously not the work of the Holy Spirit. He is sovereign and free. Like the wind, He blows where He wills (John 3:8). He is God's gift to His people and through their faithful exercise of the means of grace*—the Word, the sacraments,* and prayer—will give them a genuine experience of the fulness of their Saviour.

See **Fulness of the Spirit**.

REMONSTRANTS

See **Dutch Remonstrants**; **Five Points of Controversy**.

REPENTANCE

"Repentance unto life is a saving grace, wrought in the heart of a sinner by the Spirit and word of God, whereby, out of the sense and sight, not only of the danger, but also of the filthiness and odiousness of his sins, and upon the apprehension of God's mercy in Christ to such as are penitent, he so grieves for and hates his sins, as that he turns from them all to God, purposing and endeavoring constantly to walk with Him in all the ways of new obedience" (*Larger Catechism,* Q. 76).

In this definition we may note the following:

1. Repentance is necessary for sinners to be saved. It does not merit pardon, but pardon is not to be had without it (Luke 13:3. See *Westminster Confession of Faith,* chap. 15, sec. 3).

2. Repentance is a grace. God imparts it as a gracious gift (2 Tim. 2:25).

3. It is wrought by the Spirit (Zech. 12:10) by the normal means of the word of God (Acts 11:18-21).

4. It involves seeing and feeling sin to be not only deadly to the soul, but a filthy and hateful thing in God's sight (Ezek. 18:28-32; 36:31; Ps. 51:4).

5. It also involves a basic change of attitude to sin. It produces sorrow for and hatred of sin, with a purpose to forsake it and serve God, instead of the former love for it (2 Cor. 7:11; Jer. 31:18, 19; Acts 26:18).

To summarize the Biblical teaching, we may say that repentance has three elements.

First, repentance is a *change of mind.* It includes a *realization* of sin, or as the Scripture puts it, "the knowledge of sin" (Rom. 3:20).

Second, repentance is a *change of emotion.* It includes *regret* for sin, not merely for its consequences. This regret is emphasized by the Greek verb *metamelomai* (2 Cor. 7:8-10) which signifies literally a change in what one cares for, and hence regret or sorrow.

Third, repentance is a *change of will.* It includes a *repudiation* of sin, a basic change of purpose toward sin. This change of disposition from sin to God is emphasized by the Greek words most frequently employed for the verb "repent," and the noun "repentance," viz., *metanoeo* and *metanoia. Meta* means "after" and *noeo* means "to perceive," from *nous,* "mind." Thus, repentance is basically "a perception after," or "a change of perception, or mind." But this change is more than intellectual. *Metanoia* indicates a definite purpose to forsake sin and obey God. Shedd remarks, "Repentance is turning to God as the chief end of existence, and away from the creature as the chief end" (*Dogmatic Theology,* 2:529).

See **Conversion***.*

REPROBATION

See **Predestination***.*

RESTORATIONISM

1. Universalism; the belief that all God's rational creatures will ultimately be brought into a state of happiness and holiness. Some of this persuasion hold that this restoration will occur after some period of suffering to atone for personal guilt. Others teach that all men at death enter into heaven, with no need of any punishment or expiatory sufferings. This notion is a favourite one in Unitarianism. Its supporters appeal to such passages as Acts 3:21; Rom. 5:18, 19; 1 Cor.

15:22; Eph. 1:10; Col. 1:19, 20. They impose upon these an interpretation which is at variance with the plain statements of Scripture, and which a careful examination of the context renders impossible. The Bible doctrine is totally opposed to either view of universal salvation.

2. The belief of many in Pentecostalism* and the Charismatic movement* that God has begun to restore the supernatural signs of the apostles to the church to produce the greatest revival in history prior to the second coming* of Christ.

At the beginning of the 20th century Charles Parham and others promoted the restoration of the gift of tongues* as the token of this restoration. In the middle of the century William Branham and others promoted supernatural healing as the sign of a new Pentecost. Toward the end of the century restorationist claims have become more and more outlandish. God, we are assured, is not only restoring apostolic gifts, He is restoring apostles and even "super apostles" to the church.

The "Kansas City Prophets," Bob Jones and Paul Cain, claimed: "No apostle who ever lived equalled the power of these individuals in this great army of the Lord in these last days. No one ever had it, not even Elijah or Peter or Paul, or anyone else enjoyed the power that is going to rest on this great army" (Quoted by Frank Hanegraaff, *Counterfeit Revival,* p. 15).

RESURRECTION

The raising of the dead to life. Scripture speaks of a spiritual resurrection of souls dead in sins to newness of life in Christ (Eph. 2:1-4). This should not obscure its fundamental use of the term: the actual raising of the dead, both body and soul, to life.

The Scripture speaks of the resurrection of a number of people as special miracles of divine power (e.g., Lazarus in John 11). It also speaks of the final resurrection of the righteous dead and of the wicked dead. Of course it pays special attention to the resurrection of the Lord Jesus Christ.

Necessity of Christ's Resurrection

The historical, factual reality that the Lord Jesus Christ rose again from the dead in the body in which He had been crucified is the cornerstone of Christian doctrine. The whole corpus of Christian doctrine stands or falls with it. From beginning to end, divine revelation presents to us the reality of the supernatural, and it need not surprise us that the miraculous occurrence of Christ's resurrection should hold a place of such importance.

OT Expectation. In OT times, faith in the reality of resurrection was very evident. According to Heb. 11:19, Abraham was willing to sacrifice Isaac, in the assurance that God would raise him from the dead. Job 19:26, 27 and Dan. 12:2 are explicit affirmations of faith in the resurrection, while Isa. 26:16-19 is looked on by many as the single most important passage on the subject in the OT. This hope of personal resurrection is vitally connected with the prophesied resurrection of the Messiah (Ps. 16:10; Acts 2:27, 31).

NT Fulfilment. In the NT, we read of Christ bringing life and immortality to light through the gospel (2 Tim. 1:10), and He did this first by preaching, "I am the resurrection and the life" (John 11:25); then by rising from the dead in fulfilment of His own promise so to do; and finally by guaranteeing His people "because I live, ye shall live also" (John 14:19). "The resurrection of Christ is held forth as a pledge and promise of His people's resurrection, and as the sure foundation of their hope (1 Cor. 15:12-19; 2 Cor. 4:14; Rom. 8:11)" (W. W. Clarke).

Evidence of Christ's Resurrection. The resurrection of Christ is attested by incontrovertible evidence. By every law of literature and evidence, the testimony of the witnesses to Christ's resurrection, recorded in the NT, must be received as true. The apostles were eye-witnesses of the risen Christ, and the dramatic change in their lives after meeting Him precludes the possibility that they invented the story. Thomas Sherlock's *Trial of the Witnesses of the Resurrection of Jesus,* which is old but not obsolete, subjects their recorded testimony to all the rigours of courtroom cross-examination and vindicates it at every point. Add to that testimony, the evidence of the empty tomb, and it becomes clear why the resurrection has been termed "the best attested fact in history."

Denials of Christ's Resurrection

Opposition to Christ's resurrection is never based on factual evidence. Rather, it is an expression of a preconceived notion of its inherent impossibility. To such a prejudice we may well answer, as Paul did to Festus, "Why should it be thought a thing impossible with you that God should raise the dead?" To make human notions of possibility the measure of God's power is as bankrupt logically as it is theologically. Opposition to our Lord's resurrection is usually presented under one of the following arguments:

The Swoon Theory. According to this, He did not really die; He merely swooned. Thus, His resurrection was merely a return to consciousness. William Milligan in his classic treatment of the subject, *The Resurrection of our Lord,* ably disposes of this theory. He quotes the admission of the infidel critic, David Strauss, whose work *Leben Jesu* violently attacks orthodox Christianity, to show its weakness: "It is impossible that one who had just come forth from the grave half dead, who crept about weak and ill, who stood in need of medical treatment, of bandaging, strengthening and tender care, and who at last succumbed to suffering, could ever have given to the disciples the impression that he was a conqueror over death and the grave—that he was the Prince of Life—which lay at the bottom of their future ministry. Such a resuscitation could only have weakened the impression which He had made upon them in life and in death—or at most could have given it an elegaic voice—but could, by no possibility, have changed their sorrow into enthusiasm, or elevated their reverence into worship" (Milligan, pp. 254, 255).

Thus, the swoon theory is inherently impossible. But suppose, for a moment, that it were possible. What kind of a person does it make Christ to be, who, knowing that His disciples mistakenly believed Him to have risen from the dead, imposed upon their credulity and left them to their delusion? Where is the evidence that such monstrous wrongdoing may justly be attributed to the Lord Jesus Christ? The very suggestion is enough to destroy the theory which gave birth to it. It is a baseless piece of wicked imagination, untrue to the evidence, and incapable of giving even a viable suggestion of what happened to Jesus afterwards: He could not have ascended, if He did not rise from the dead, so when and where did He ultimately die? What became of His body? The theory has no answers. It is a fallacy.

The Fraud Theory. Some have charged that the disciples practised a fraud, having stolen the body of Christ from the tomb. The Jews anticipated this line of argument (Matt. 28:13), but it remains as baseless now as it was then. Let any candid person examine the lives of these same disciples and show evidence that their entire ministry was built upon a gigantic fraud. It is impossible and has been recognized to be so, even by those who do not believe in the resurrection of Christ.

The Vision Theory. This is the idea that the disciples thought so much of Christ that they *thought* they saw Him! They were in such an excited state of mind that when Mary Magdalene, "a sensitive and nervous woman," came to report that she had seen the Lord, it was like a spark igniting tinder, and soon they were all aflame with similar visionary experiences.

Modern deniers of the resurrection have long loved this theory—but it is as baseless as the rest, for it, too, fails to answer to the facts of the case.

1. The disciples were not excited; they were depressed, following Christ's death.
2. They did not expect a resurrection.
3. Mary Magdalene's report did not act like a spark which set their fervour alight; it was treated with scepticism (Luke 24:11).

Recognizing these difficulties, some supporters of the vision theory advanced the view that God sent these visions, making them seem very real! But where is the need to surmise this supernatural intervention of God, to escape that other supernatural intervention, the resurrection? Furthermore, can men be serious, can they even pretend to the name Christian, when they advance a notion that God practised a deliberate deception on His people and made this deception the basic thrust of their evangelistic ministry?

The Myth Theory. This is the theory, advanced in one form by David Strauss and in another form by the neo-orthodox school of Rudolph Bultmann. Strauss held the resurrection story to be a myth constructed from some first-century legends. The neo-orthodox view is no real advance on this. Bultmann *(see **Myth**)* abandoned the historicity of the resurrection. It did not happen—but it stood for something! It was a symbol which embodied "the real Easter faith." The only reason for asserting this was that Bultmann had the idea that the supernatural could not take place in history. He had decreed it impossible, so the resurrection did not take place—though it (nonexistent as it is!) does stand for our "Easter faith." Neoorthodoxy, with its love of paradox theology, therefore, presents faith in a risen Lord, who did not rise from the dead.

Consequences of Christ's Resurrection

The resurrection of Christ has far-reaching consequences. It is the completion of His earthly ministry, the commencement of His exaltation, the attestation of all His claims (Rom. 1:4), the answer to all His foes, and the assurance and anticipation of the bodily resurrection of all who have died in Christ.

Resurrection of Saints and Sinners. Believers will rise from the dead (1 Cor. 15; 1 Thess. 4) and they will receive glorified bodies, like unto Christ's body (Phil. 3:20, 21; 1 Cor. 15; 2 Cor. 5). Unbelievers will rise also (John 5:28, 29). The resurrection of believers is "blessed" (Rev. 20:6), but that of unbelievers is "unto damnation" (John 5:29).

There has been controversy as to whether both believers and unbelievers will be raised at one and the same time. Reformed theologians, usually holding to a postmillennial view, have for the most part answered in the affirmative. Premillenialists hold that the "first resurrection" (i.e., of believers) precedes the resurrection of "the rest of the dead" (Rev. 20:5). Both take place in "the last day," or the day of the Lord, one at the beginning of that day, and one at the end. Critics of this view repeatedly claim that the Bible nowhere describes a divided resurrection. But the claim is false. Daniel 12:2 very clearly does so. Anyone who denies this text's reference to a divided resurrection must conclude that it teaches a *partial resurrection.* One thing it does not teach is a *simultaneous* resurrection of all men. The Hebrew of the verse yields only one meaning: "Many (not *all*) of them that sleep in the dust of the earth shall awake, *these* (the *many* who awake) to everlasting life, and *those* (who do not awake with those already mentioned) to shame and everlasting contempt."

See Millennium.

REVELATION

This term has a double usage:

1. The *apokalupsis,* Christ's second coming* (e.g., 2 Thess. 1:7).

2. The knowledge God gives to His creatures, especially His self-disclosure by whatever means He chooses, but definitively in the Bible as His inspired word.

From this it is clear that Scripture is not the sole means of divine revelation, but it is the controlling one. It testifies that God speaks through His creation. Fallen man, however, cannot interpret creation aright. He needs the controlling word of Scripture to keep him right.

Thus the study of revelation must include *general,* or *natural, revelation* and *special revelation,* noting their separate characteristics and relationship.

General or Natural Revelation.

God has revealed Himself in His works of creation,* hence the term "natural" revelation. This revelation of God in nature is accessible to all mankind without distinction, hence the term "general" revelation. The Scriptures speak of this revelation (Acts 14:17; Rom. 1:20; Ps. 19:1). This revelation was first made to Adam before the fall.* It was not merely external and objective, but was accompanied by an internal and subjective revelation—i.e., unfallen man had by creation the power to see and interpret the external revelation aright. The fall robbed man of that inner light and left him blind and darkened.

Natural revelation is still operative, as Ps. 19:1 shows, but the blinded mind of fallen man cannot by its own power perceive and interpret it properly. Furthermore, natural revelation, addressed as it was originally, to unfallen man, has nothing to say to fallen man about salvation. It is inadequate to lead a sinner to a saving knowledge of God. This inadequacy does not stem from any defect in the revelation itself because it is perfect for its God-ordained purpose, but from the fact that man, because of sin, now occupies a very different position, and has very different needs, from unfallen Adam. While natural revelation is incapable of revealing salvation to sinners, it still leaves them "without excuse" and accuses and condemns them because of their sin (Rom. 1:19-21; 2:15). Thus, it takes the form of a "moral" or "religious" consciousness, a "God-consciousness," derived from God the Creator, which stamps God's law, and man's breach of it, upon the conscience.

Special Revelation

Since general revelation has no reference to redemption, a special revelation is necessary, if God is to convey any message of grace to fallen men. Special revelation is the revelation by God of His redemptive purpose, using various infallible means.

Modes of Special Revelation. God has revealed His redemptive purpose in three ways or modes: *theophany,** in which He intervened in human history in His own person; *prophecy,** in which He intervened with His own word; and *miracle,** in which He intervened with His own power.

Marks of Special Revelation. The marks of this special revelation are the following:

1. It is *supernatural.*
2. It is *addressed to men as sinners.*
3. It can be *properly understood and received only by faith.* As we have noted, the internal subjective revelation in unfallen man enabled him to perceive and interpret the external, objective revelation. In the case of special revelation the same truth applies. If it is to become a saving revelation, it must be accompanied by an internal revelation, the work of the Holy Spirit* enlightening the mind and imparting the gift of faith.*
4. It is *written* (Isa. 8:19, 20; Hosea 8:12), "those former ways of God's revealing His will to His people being now ceased," (*Westminster Confession of Faith,* chap. 1, sec. 1).
5. It is *inspired and infallible,* comprising all the Scriptures of the Old and New Testaments (2 Tim. 3:16; 2 Pet. 1:20, 21). God's special revelation is identified with the Bible as His written word. From Heb. 1:1 we know that God used many means of communicating His will, and the Bible is one of these. However, the Bible is the only record of all the rest, and thus special revelation is limited to the Scriptures. Daniel (9:2) "understood by books," though he was himself a prophet, and this emphasizes the perpetual validity and authority* of scriptural revelation.

6. It is *redemptive.* This is true of both its doctrines and historical events. The Biblical history of God's dealings with His people is factual and revelational and is the basis upon which the doctrinal principles of Scripture stand. "The static truth depends upon the active deed" (J. Barton Payne, *The Theology of the Older Covenant*). For example, the truth of our justification is based solidly on the historical event of Christ's resurrection (Rom. 4:25). Apart from the historical reality of the event, the doctrine based upon it is invalidated.

The importance of this Biblical position is seen in a twofold opposition to neo-orthodoxy.

a. Barth's so-called "theology of the Word" denies the true historicity of much of the Biblical narrative. Other neo-orthodox leaders, following the lead of Bultmann, blatantly ridicule as myth much of what the Bible teaches as history *(see Myth).* In spite of this, they profess to maintain the doctrinal principles drawn from these events. But both must stand or fall together.

b. Neo-orthodoxy denies the reality of "propositional revelation," that is, the communication by God in inspired writings of factual knowledge, especially the propositions of truths about Himself. J. Barton Payne summed up this attitude as limiting God's contacts with men "to 'existential' encounters of personalities." (*Existential* stresses the view that God and man consciously meet as free agents and in the free exercise of their own wills; *see Existentialism).* Such existential encounters are viewed as the substance of special revelation, valid in themselves apart from any external, authoritative standard. Thus, the Bible is not a divine revelation *per se* but may become so to one existentially encountering God.

Against all this, the Biblical teaching of special revelation emphasizes the objective and immutable reality of God's redemptive revelation, both in the Bible's historical record of events and in propositional truths.

7. It is *Christocentric.* Its focus is the person and work of the Mediator (Heb. 1:1-4). All creation finds its ultimate explanation in the eternal Word (John 1:3) and thus all divine revelation centres on Him (Heb. 1:1). The written word points to the incarnate Word as its central theme. Thus, Christ in Scripture is the essence of divine revelation.

8. It is *objectively complete.* The Bible is the full objective record of the unfolding of redemption. In connection with this unfolding drama, God gave many particular revelations. But redemption is complete in Christ (John 19:30; Col. 2:10) and therefore special revelation cannot now be found beyond the NT Scriptures.

Revelations of the Spirit to God's people always have reference to this completed word, as in Eph. 1:17, where it is said to be "in the knowledge" of Christ, and as in 1 John 5:1, 2, where the testimony of truth rests upon the historical revelation of the incarnate Christ.

Unity of Divine Revelation

In speaking of general and special revelation, we ought not to view them as two entirely separate revelations. Scholasticism* in effect did this and ended up with a dualism in which human reason, employing the data of natural revelation, attained to a scientific knowledge of God; and faith, accepting the data of special revelation, attained a knowledge of such mysteries as the Trinity,* the incarnation,* and redemption,* which are not rationally demonstrable. Having accepted these by faith because they are revealed, the schoolmen then sought to demonstrate their reasonableness. Thus they adopted a dual structure: a knowledge of God revealed supernaturally and received by faith, and another system of scientific theology produced by the application of human reason to the natural revelation.

The Protestant Reformers rejected this dualism* and asserted the unitary nature of divine revelation. Berkhof sums up their views: "In His supernatural revelation He republished the truths of natural revelation, cleared them of misconception, interpreted them with a view to the present needs of man, and thus incorporated them in His supernatural revelation of redemption" *Systematic Theology,* p. 38).

Saving Revelation

Special revelation has redemption for its subject. It is a message of the light of eternal life. Fallen man is spiritually blind and dead. All the light in the world cannot in itself enable him to see. He needs something more than light, or information. He needs sight to see the light. To put it another way, he needs God to do a subjective work within him to enable him to respond to the objective revelation presented to him.

Thus the Bible speaks of regeneration* as a divine revelation within us: "The god of this world hath blinded the minds of them which believe not, lest the light of the glorious gospel of Christ, who is the image of God, should shine unto them....For God, who commanded the light to shine out of darkness, hath shined in our hearts, to give the light of the knowledge of the glory of God in the face of Jesus Christ" (2 Cor. 4:4, 6).

Berkhof notes that God "provided a cure for the spiritual blindness of man in the work of regeneration and sanctification, including spiritual illumination, and thus enabled man once more to obtain true knowledge of God, the knowledge that carries with it the assurance of eternal life" (ibid., p. 38).

REVIVAL

Literally, a coming to life from the dead (1 Kings 17:22; Rom. 14:9). As distinct from resurrection,* the term is used, however, to denote a quickening and kindling of *spiritual* life in an individual Christian, church, community, or country. In this view it is a work of God's Spirit, dispelling the darkness and deadness of spiritual declension.

True revival always brings a fresh and vivid scriptural emphasis on the holiness and justice of God; on His judgment on sin; on true repentance and the reception of Christ by faith. The presence of God in awful and overwhelming power is the hallmark of revival, as He moves in glorious gospel triumph, bringing new life to His church and salvation to many souls. Such a revival leaves a lasting mark.

Frequently, *revival* is used to describe a special evangelistic effort. In this sense it is said to be "conducted" or "scheduled." However, this confuses *evangelism,* which is man working for God, with *revival,* which is the sovereign work of God on behalf of men.

REVIVISCENCE

A Roman Catholic term denoting "the revival of grace from a character sacrament received in mortal sin. If a person receives a character sacrament in the state of mortal sin, the grace of that sacrament is not given. But that grace 'revives' and is applied to the individual as soon as contrition blots out the sin." (Richard P. McBrien, *Catholicism,* p. 1255).

See **Character Sacrament**.

RIGHTEOUSNESS OF GOD

The term is used to describe the following:

1. The inherent rectitude of the divine nature (John 17:25; *see* **Holiness of God**).

2. God's attitude toward every violation of His holy law (Rev. 16:5).

3. The imputed righteousness of Christ to believers (Rom. 3:21, 22; *see* **Imputation**).

The first two portray aspects of God's *justice* in Himself and in relation to sinners. The third describes the exercise of His *grace,* on the ground of Christ's redemption, to satisfy the standards of His justice, in providing a free and perfect righteousness for His believing people (Rom. 3:24-26).

See **Justification.**

RITSCHLIANISM

The liberal theology of Albrecht Ritschl (1822-1889), which sought to apply positivism* and pragmatism* to theology.* Ritschl rejected speculative rationalism* on the one hand and subjective mysticism* *(see* **Consciousness Theology)** on the other hand. He therefore sought to exclude both the intellectual and the emotional from his theological premises. Though he called for a return to the historical records about Christ in the Bible, Ritschl repudiated orthodox Christianity. He made religious knowledge the result of value judgments— i.e., to him, truth was what the individual thought to be of worth. This is just as subjective as the system of Schleiermacher, which Ritschl opposed.

Building upon this pragmatic approach, in contrast with the dogmatic approach of an orthodox Bible believer, Ritschl looked on the kingdom of God* as "the organization of humanity through action inspired by love." Justification* and redemption* were the individual's identification with the community, and reconciliation was the result of believing from the example of Jesus that God is love and that we are forgiven.

Although the dominance of Ritschl's school stretched only from about 1875 to 1914, its influence can be seen in the social gospel* *(see* **World Council of Churches**, **Life and Work Movement),** and the view that the kingdom of God is a state of human society produced by human endeavours. It can also be traced in the neo-orthodoxy* of Karl Barth, who has been called "Ritschl's great successor." Though the hermeneutical approach is different, the message and mission of the various types of political theology* essentially share Ritschl's definition of salvation in social terms, as well.

RITUALISM

The use of prescribed liturgies, rites, ceremonies, and vestments in religious worship. The 19th-century ritualists in the Church of England *(see **Puseyites)** introduced the use of Romish vestments into Anglican worship.

ROMAN CATHOLIC THEOLOGY

The theological system of the Roman Catholic church, as set forth in her official creedal documents. Of these the *Decrees of the Council of Trent* and the *Documents of the Second Vatican Council* are the most influential.

Rome's theology revolves around her view of the magisterial power of the pope and the bishops. She makes the church the vehicle and judge of divine revelation.* She has adopted a system of sacramental grace that necessitates the recognition of a special priestly hierarchy—i.e., grace can reach sinners through the sacraments which only consecrated priests have the power to administer. Rome's priesthood is a sacrificing priesthood and the central act of her worship is the mass* in which she claims to offer a true propitiatory sacrifice for the sins of the living and the dead. Along with this sacramentalism,* Rome propounds a theory of synergism* in which she has a highly developed theory of human merit.* The effect of this is to produce a gospel of works, though Rome maintains that she teaches salvation by grace.

Central to the entire system of Roman Catholic theology is her view of authority.* She claims to accept the entirety of Scripture but to it she adds two things that effectively negate that claim:

First, she adds church tradition,* which she claims to be apostolic but for which there is no support in the known words or actions of the apostles.

Second, she adds the church's authority to interpret Scripture so that it means what she determines it means. The result of all this is to establish Roman Catholic dogma on papal tradition* and authority.

On such a basis almost anything except gospel purity is possible. Rome's departures from Bible Christianity are legion: her elevation of Mary to be co-Redemptrix and co-Mediatrix; her invocation of a multitude of saints (some of whom she now admits never existed); her blasphemous dogma of the mass; her teaching of transubstantiation;* her rejection of justification* by faith alone; her sacerdotalism;* her theory of sacramental grace conferred *opus operatum;** her dogmas of human merit, works of supererogation;* indulgences;* and purgatory;* as well as the entire system of the papacy—these are just some of the marks of her apostasy.*

Some evangelicals have held dialogue with some Roman Catholics and have produced joint declarations that maximize points of apparent agreement. Roman Catholic theology may be stated in terms that may sound evangelical, but only by careful editing. When consistent Roman Catholics and evangelicals agree on definitions of the gospel it is because they are using the same words with entirely different meanings in mind. To parade this as some significant step forward in Christian understanding and unity, as the signatories to *Evangelicals and Catholics Together* did, is more than a little disingenuous.

Roman Catholic theology is the antithesis of evangelical Protestantism.* Rome rejects or seriously modifies every aspect of Biblical revelation evangelicals hold to be essential to the gospel. When we see Rome's departure from the faith on such fundamental matters as authority, the atonement* of Christ, and man's acceptance with God, we can only conclude that her theology is not Christian, or even sub-Christian, but anti-Christian.

ROSARY

A string of prayer beads used by Roman Catholics. When blessed, these beads are supposed to be "enriched with many indulgences for reciting the prescribed prayers" (Daughters of St. Paul, *Basic Catechism,* p. 148). This catechism says: "The complete rosary consists of fifteen decades, but it is divided into three distinct parts, each containing five decades. The first part is called the Five Joyful Mysteries, the second part, the Five Sorrowful Mysteries, and the third part, the Five Glorious Mysteries" (p. 18).

ROSETTA STONE

A basalt slab found in 1799 by French soldiers digging the foundations for a new fort in Rosetta, Egypt. It contained an inscription in Egyptian hieroglyphic script, in a later common Egyptian or Demotic script, and in Greek. It provided the key to deciphering the hieroglyphic script which had so puzzled scholars. Jean-François Champollion used the Rosetta Stone to unravel the mystery first of the Demotic and then of the earlier Hieratic script.

The Rosetta Stone is now in the British museum.

RULING ELDER

In a Presbyterian church, a member of the session* who is not a teaching elder (meaning an ordained minister* of the gospel). *See* **Presbyterianism.**

RUSSELLITES

The proper name for the self-styled "Jehovah's Witnesses." In 1879 Charles Taze Russell founded Zion's Watchtower and in 1881, the Watchtower Bible and Tract Society.

As a man, Russell was unprincipled. He lied under oath in court, when asked if he knew Greek. He was summoned for fraud

against his wife and divorced by her. He was charged with selling "miracle wheat" at an exorbitant price and of inducing sick people to sign over their fortunes to his organization. All the while, he berated the churches for being in business for money!

As the founder of a cult, Russell was equally unprincipled and dangerous. "Pastor" Russell (though he was never ordained to the ministry) claimed to be such a Bible teacher that it would be better for readers to read his notes on Scripture and leave the Bible unread, than to read the Bible and neglect his notes! He died in 1916 and was succeeded by "Judge" J. F. Rutherford, a lawyer who vied with his mentor in boldness.

In 1931 the name "Jehovah's Witnesses" was coined to distinguish the main body of the cult from a breakaway group.

Russellite Dogma

1. Russellism looks on reason as a foundation upon which "we have endeavoured to build…the teachings of scripture in such a manner that, so far as possible, purely human judgment may try its squares and angles" (Rutherford). "Let us examine the character of the writings claimed as inspired, to see whether their teachings correspond with the character we have reasonably imputed to God" (Rutherford). Thus Russellites will change Scripture translations in an arbitrary way to bring the teaching into line with their preconceived "reasonable" ideas.

2. Russellism denies the deity of Christ.* It is Arian in character *(see **Arianism).**

3. Thus it denies the doctrine of the Trinity,* to which it has referred as "that notorious, pagan doctrine, the Trinity."

4. Russellism reduces atonement* to a mere "at-one-ment," i.e., reconciliation to God without any sacrifice of propitiation.* Russell taught that reconciliation* was in two parts:

    a. The work of reconciliation by the man Jesus; and

    b. Man's return to God of his own free will, the condition for such a return having been met by what Jesus did. This work of atonement is not complete and "the little flock" (the Russellites) are said to be "joint sacrifices, joint-mediators, joint-reconcilers, joint-at-one-ers," who shall thus be "privileged to be joint heirs in the Millennial Kingdom and partakers of his divine nature." Thus in the Russellite view of salvation, man always acts first, and God accepts the act.

5. Russellism denies all divine retribution, holding that man is so constituted as to be incapable of suffering God's wrath.* It is vehement in its denunciation of any who preach the reality of a place of torment *(see Endless Punishment).*

6. It also denies the bodily resurrection* of Christ, holding that He was raised "a spirit being of the highest order of the divine nature." "The man Jesus is dead, forever dead" (Russell).

7. It holds a peculiar view of eschatology.* According to it—

a. The time of the end began in 1799.

b. Christ's second coming took place in 1874.

c. The Day of Jehovah began in 1914.

d. The Messenger of the Covenant (the Lord Jesus) came to His temple (the Russellites) in 1918 and so began "the day of our Lord Jesus Christ," and the judgment of the house of God. Thus Christ has already come, the battle of Armageddon is just about to happen, and immediately the Millennium will follow.

e. All this gives rise to the notion of two sections to the kingdom, the heavenly part and the New World Order on earth.

The Heavenly Kingdom

Since 1914 Christ has been ruling in His heavenly kingdom. By *Christ,* Russellites understand something different from the rest of us. "Christ is composed of Jesus, the great and mighty head, and 144,000 members" (Rutherford). These 144,000 are a special class, all resurrected since 1918, called variously "the mystery class," "the bride class," or "the anointed class." These are "Christ the body," while Jesus is "Christ the head." This special class enjoy the heavenly kingdom, ruling as Christ.

The New World Order

Following the battle of Armageddon, the millennium will begin. In it "millions now living," who desire righteousness but do not know the way, will be given a chance for a place in the New World Order. There will be great miracles of healing, so that "the most sceptical, it is to be hoped, will believe that the Lord Jesus reigns" (Rutherford). There will be a resurrection of those who have died without the knowledge of Christ, and they will be given a minimum trial period of 100 years (for which Isa. 65:20 is cited!). Only a small number will remain disobedient, and they will be annihilated. All the rest, i.e., those "other sheep," who are not of the 144,000 who reign in the heavenly kingdom, will constitute the New World Order in God's everlasting kingdom.

Russellism is a thoroughgoing rationalistic system of anti-Christianity, built by unscrupulous men, using the most arbitrary forms of Scripture exegesis.

Russellites have proved themselves a formidable proselytizing force, printing hundreds of millions of pieces of literature, including their own *New World Translation of the Bible* (which rides roughshod over the conclusions of the most eminent Hebrew and Greek scholars, to establish the Russellite position), and sending forth thousands of "ministers" across the world on a crusade (in their words) of "liberty for the prisoners held in ignorance and superstition in the Devil's organization and its religious prison-houses."

A more complete example of "strong delusion" would be difficult to find.

S

SABBATH

Hebrew, meaning "rest, cessation"; the name of the weekly day of rest ordained by God at creation* (Gen. 2:2-3). The next reference to the sabbath is found in Exod. 16 at the time of the giving of the manna (vv. 16-30). Observance of the sabbath was included in the decalogue* (Exod. 20:8-11) and violation of it was a capital offence in Israel (Exod. 31:14). It was chiefly a day of rest, but the religious significance of the day was marked by extra offerings in the tabernacle.

Other feast days were called sabbaths (Lev. 16:31, etc.), and each seventh year was a sabbatic year.

An Enduring Obligation

Much controversy has raged around the question as to whether the fourth commandment is still binding on God's people, and, if it is, whether the first day of the week is to be regarded as the Christian sabbath.

There are good reasons for believing that the observance of the sabbath remains as a moral duty.

It Is Part of the Moral Law. It is commonly stated that Christians are not under law, but under grace, and that, therefore, the fourth commandment is not binding upon Christians. The reasoning here is grossly defective, for could not the same be said in regard to each of the other commandments in the decalogue? Antinomians argue that the same *should* be said of all the commandments, holding that these are not to be regarded as a rule of life for Christians. Paul's assertion that we are "under the law to Christ" (1 Cor. 9:21) clearly removes the argument, as does the fact that the NT quotes or refers to each of the commandments—plain evidence of their morally-binding character for the people of God.

The Sabbath Was Made for Man. The Lord Jesus said plainly, "The sabbath was made for man" (Mark 2:27)—not just for Jews, but for man generally. Despite this, some argue that the fourth commandment is the only one of the ten that is not repeated in the NT. Therefore, we are told, it is not binding on Christians.

A Keeping of Sabbath Remains. We may question if the NT really remains silent on the matter. Heb. 4:9, 10 says, "There remaineth therefore a rest to the people of God. For he that is entered into his rest, he also hath ceased from his own works, as God did from his." Throughout Heb. 4, the Greek word *katapausis* is used to signify "rest." In verse 9 the word is *sabbatismos,* which means "a sabbatism" or "a keeping of sabbath." Any exegesis* of Heb. 4 must take note of and do full justice to the introduction by the Holy Spirit of this word. Every exegesis that removes all reference to the keeping of the sabbath from the apostle's argument fails to do justice to the special character of the word and furnishes no real reason why *katapausis* should not have been used.

The most popular interpretation of the verse is to make it refer to the future rest of the redeemed in heaven,* and, it is said, the word *sabbatismos* is introduced to lend emphasis to the idea. But why then is it dropped in v. 10? If the text (Heb. 4:9) had appeared in our version as, "Therefore, there is left to the people of God a keeping of sabbath," it is doubtful if any Bible reader would have imagined a reference to heaven.

The word *remaineth* is important. The original verb is *apoleipomai,* and it signifies "to be left from something going before." What is it that is left to the people of God? A keeping of the sabbath, for that is the only meaning that the word *sabbatismos* can have. John Owen held that it was "undeniably manifest that the apostle here proves and asserts the granting of an evangelical sabbath, or day of rest, for the worship of God to be constantly observed."

The Seventh Day or the First? But if the keeping of the sabbath is binding on God's people, two questions remain to be answered:

1. Why do we not hold the Jewish sabbath, the seventh day of the week, instead of the first day of the week?

2. How should we interpret Paul's words in Col. 2:16, 17, "Let no man judge you in eating and drinking, or in respect of a feast day, or a new moon, or of sabbaths, which are a shadow of things to come."

These questions are closely related, and the answer to the second contains the answer to the first. Paul's argument in Col. 2:16, 17 refers to Jewish sabbaths. According to the inspired apostle, seventh-day sabbath keeping is not binding on the people of God. As we have seen from Heb. 4:9, a keeping of sabbath is binding on Christians. Clearly another day is laid before Christians for their observance. This is in harmony with the fourth commandment.

Seventh Day Not Fixed by the Fourth Commandment. Robert Nevin, in *Misunderstood Scriptures,* argues, "It is not true that the Fourth Commandment specifies or fixes any one day of the week to be observed as the sabbath. Let us examine its terms. 'Remember the sabbath day to keep it holy'—literally, the day of the sabbath, or the day of rest—not the seventh day of the week. 'Six days shalt thou labour and do all thy work'—not the first six days of the week. 'But the seventh day is the sabbath of the Lord thy God'—not, the seventh day of the week, but

plainly the day coming after the six days of labour, whatever days of the week these might be....And, in conclusion, 'the Lord blessed the sabbath day (or the day of rest) and hallowed it.'" God's institution, therefore, is for one day out of seven.

First Day Demanded by Hebrews 4:10. Hebrews 4:10 emphasizes the change of day from the seventh to the first day of the week. The creation sabbath recalled God's rest at the end of His creative activity. The Christian sabbath should recall the rest of Christ. That is what Paul is teaching: "He [Christ] that is entered into his rest, he also hath ceased from his own works as God did from his." The first day of the week, the resurrection day, called "the Lord's day" (Rev. 1:10), meets all the requirements and has the sanction of apostolic example (e.g., Acts 20:7; 1 Cor. 16:2). Thus Heb. 4:10 establishes "the change of the day from the seventh to the first day of the week, to commemorate Christ's resurrection on that day, His resting from His works as God did from His own. This is commemorated by its being the first day of the week, while at the same time the commemoration of creation is not lost sight of since it is still the seventh portion of time" (Nevin).

Historical Development of First Day Sabbath

It Started with the Apostles. We frequently hear the Seventh Day Adventist charge that Constantine changed the day for sabbath observance from Saturday to Sunday. This is untrue. The early church very clearly observed the first day of the week as its day for public worship (Acts 20:7; 1 Cor. 16:2). Just why Christians should have met on the first day of the week has never been satisfactorily answered by upholders of the seventh-day sabbath. Their practice is a mystery to us unless we recognize that it had apostolic sanction.

It Became the Law of the Roman Empire. In 321 Constantine issued regulations against working on Sunday. He *enforced* the observance of the first day of the week, a very different thing from *commencing* it. In 789 Charlemagne used the fourth commandment to validate his enforcement of sabbath observance.

It Was Widely Received in Protestantism. In Reformation times, Luther rejected sabbath-keeping, though Calvin maintained it, stoutly defending the observance against the criticism of "those restless souls" who decried it as Judaism. The Puritans strongly adhered to sabbath observance, as did Scottish Presbyterians.

The *Westminster Confession of Faith* (chap. 21, sec. 7, 8) sums up the Protestant view:

"As it is of the law of nature, that, in general, a due proportion of time be set apart for the worship of God; so, in his Word, by a positive, moral, and perpetual commandment, binding all men in all ages, he hath particularly appointed one day in seven for a sabbath, to be kept holy unto him; which, from the beginning of the world to the resurrection of Christ, was the last day of the week; and, from the resurrection of Christ, was changed into the first day of the week, which in Scripture is called the Lord's day, and is to be continued to the end of the world, as the Christian sabbath. This sabbath is then kept holy unto the Lord, when men, after a due preparing of their hearts, and ordering of their common affairs beforehand, do not only observe an holy rest all the day from their own works, words, and thoughts about their worldly employments and recreations; but also are taken up the whole time in the public and private exercises of his worship, and in the duties of necessity and mercy."

This position has generally prevailed among Protestants, though the Seventh Day Baptists (1671) reverted to the observance of the Jewish sabbath (as did the Seventh Day Adventists in 1845). Under the influence of dispensationalism* observance of the Christian sabbath has largely been abandoned by great numbers of Christians, though God's promise is still "If thou turn away thy foot from the sabbath, from doing thy pleasure on my holy day; and call the sabbath a delight, the holy of the Lord, honourable…then shalt thou delight thyself in the Lord; and I will cause thee to ride upon the high places of the earth, and feed thee with the heritage of Jacob thy father: for the mouth of the Lord hath spoken it" (Isa. 58:13, 14).

SABELLIANISM

A form of Unitarianism named after Sabellius, a third-century African bishop; the heresy of modalistic monarchianism. It is the view that God is not only one single essence but one single person. Thus, the names *Father, Son,* and *Holy Spirit* are not personal names but modes or relations of the one divine person in His dealings with man. According to Sabellians, the term *Father* referred to this one divine person when His incomprehensible greatness and sovereignty were in view. *Son* referred to His revelation to men and His becoming incarnate. *Holy Spirit* referred to His operating immediately upon the creature in the works of creation, providence, or grace.

In modern times, Swedenborgianism* and some so-called "oneness" sects have adopted Sabellian views.

See **Eternal Sonship**; **Trinity**.

SACERDOTALISM

The assumption of the powers of a sacrificing priesthood, by professed ministers of Christ; the use of such supposed supernatural, sacrificing powers to exercise authority and control over the laity.

See **Priesthood of Believers**.

SACRAMENT

"A sacrament is an holy ordinance instituted by Christ, wherein, by sensible signs, Christ, and the benefits of the new covenant, are represented, sealed, and applied to believers" (*Shorter Catechism,* Q. 92). Thus a sacrament includes and indicates the following:

1. *An outward, visible sign.* Augustine called it "a visible sign of invisible grace instituted for our justification." While the latter part of his definition smacks of sacramentalism,* the emphasis on a visible sign is essential to the existence of a sacrament.

2. *An inward, spiritual grace.* A sacrament signifies an inward work of grace, without which the outward symbol is an empty form, devoid of spiritual reality. The inward work of grace consists in the riches of Christ, not, as Rome holds, an addition to human nature that enables man to do good works.

Some have described a sacrament as a visible enactment of the gospel proclamation. A sacrament does proclaim the gospel. But there is more to it than proclamation. It signifies the general truth of the gospel along with a definite gracious promise given by God and accepted by us. Thus, it serves "to strengthen our faith with respect to the realization of that promise, Gen. 17:1-14; Exod. 12:13; Rom. 4:11-13" (Berkhof).

3. *A union between the sign and the grace it signifies.* Berkhof terms this union "the essence of the sacrament."

Rome holds that it is a physical union, so that the sign necessarily includes the grace* it signifies *(see **Opus Operatum**).*

Lutherans hold that it is a local union, as if the sign and the thing signified occupied the same portion of space, so that whoever receives the sign, even an unbeliever, necessarily receives the grace signified by it.

Reformed theology holds that the union is spiritual, or relative and moral. That is, where a sacrament is received by faith, the grace signified by it is communicated.

Protestants hold that Christ instituted two sacraments, baptism* and the Lord's Supper,* corresponding to the two OT sacraments, circumcision and the passover. In keeping with the truth of Christ's finished atonement,* baptism and the Lord's Supper are bloodless, even the latter holding no element of sacrifice within it.

Rome has added five other sacraments—confirmation,* penance,* holy orders, marriage, and extreme unction.* The Council of Trent said that Christ instituted all seven sacraments, but this is a delusion, the NT recording only two.

Protestants believe that the observance of baptism and the Lord's Supper is necessary in the sense that it is obligatory because it is commanded in Scripture. Rome views the sacraments as absolutely necessary to salvation* *(see **Sacramentalism**),* a view that denies the spiritual character of the gospel dispensation and that equally denies the statements of Scripture regarding true faith being the only instrument for the reception of salvation (John 3:36; Acts 16:31).

Since ancient times the use of the term *sacrament* to describe the ordinances of baptism and the Lord's Supper has evoked controversy. In the Reformation period many preferred the terms "sign" or "mystery." Today many Protestants use only the word *ordinance.* Part of the antipathy toward *sacrament* arises from its misuse to denote its alleged power to confer the grace it signifies. However, the ancient use of the Latin *sacramentum* has led Protestants to see it as a useful term to retain. Charles Hodge gives the development of its usage: "In classical usage the word *sacramentum* means, in general, something sacred. In legal proceedings the money deposited by contending parties was called *sacramentum,* because when it was forfeited it was applied to sacred purposes....Then in a secondary sense it meant a judicial process. In military usage it expressed the obligation of the soldier to his leader or country; then the oath by which he was bound; and generally an oath; so that in ordinary language *sacramentum dicere,* meant to swear" (*Systematic Theology,* 3:485, 486).

SACRAMENTALISM

The view that ascribes such importance to the sacraments as to make them absolutely necessary to salvation and conveyors of divine grace, *opus operatum.**

SACRAMENTARIAN

The name given in the 16th century to Zwinglians and Calvinists who repudiated the Lutheran notion of consubstantiation* and the Roman Catholic dogma of transubstantiation *(see* **Mass***)* and denied the so-called "real presence"* in the Lord's Supper,* holding that the bread and wine were no more than symbols of the body and blood of Christ.

SACRIFICE

An offering rendered to God and designed to satisfy Him. In the OT most sacrifices were bloody. Of the five kinds of sacrifice in the Levitical system, only the meal offering was unbloody. The other four, the burnt offering, the peace offering, the sin offering, and the trespass offering were all bloody sacrifices, and were designed to propitiate God.

Scriptural Significance of Sacrifice

"The common doctrine of these sin offerings is, (1) That the design of such offerings was to propitiate God; to satisfy His justice, and to render it consistent and proper that the offence for which they were offered should be forgiven; (2) That this propitiation of God was secured by the expiation of guilt; by such an offering as covered sin, so that it did not appear before Him as demanding punishment; (3) That this expiation was accomplished by vicarious punishment; the victim being substituted for the offender, bearing his guilt, and suffering the penalty which he had incurred; (4) That the effect of such sin offerings was the pardon of the offender, and his restoration to favour and to the enjoyment of the privileges which he had forfeited. If this be the true Scriptural idea of a sacrifice for sin, then do the Scrip-

tures in declaring that Christ was a sacrifice, intend to teach that He was the substitute for sinners; that He bore their guilt and suffered the penalty of the law in their stead; and thereby reconciled them unto God; i.e., rendered it consistent with His perfections that they should be pardoned and restored to the divine fellowship and favour" (Charles Hodge, *Systematic Theology,* 2:499).

Origin of Sacrifice

While Gen. 3:21 does not explicitly mention the slaughter of an animal, it infers a sacrifice, for God made coverings of skins to clothe Adam and Eve after the fall.* It is significant then that God Himself made the first sacrifice. At Calvary He also made the last sacrifice.

There has been much debate as to the origin of the practice of sacrifice among men. If this interpretation of Gen. 3:21 is accepted, the subject is settled, for obviously it came as a revelation from God. Conservatives normally trace sacrifice to a divine revelation* and command whereas liberals find its roots in the primitive religious consciousness of early man. Even some conservatives do not trace it to God's command. H. C. Leupold says, "Since no commandment is recorded authorizing or requesting sacrifice from man as a thing divinely sought, we are, no doubt, nearer the truth when we let sacrifices originate spontaneously on man's part as a natural expression of a devout spirit and of gratitude toward the omnipotent Giver of all good things.... If sacrifice had originated in a commandment of God, it might well be thought of as a thing of sufficient importance to be permanently recorded in divine Scriptures" (Leupold on Gen. 4:3-5). This view fails to do justice to the Scripture data and leads to dangerous conclusions in expounding the cases of Cain and Abel in connection with which Leupold made this statement. In Heb. 11:4 we are told that Abel offered "by faith." In Rom. 10:17 we are told explicitly, "Faith cometh by hearing and hearing by the word of God." Abel could not have offered a sacrifice by faith without a definite revelation from God on the subject. And since Genesis 4 gives us the first record of man offering a sacrifice, we can conclude only that it was by a direct revelation from God that sacrifice was instituted among men.

No Expiatory Sacrifices After Calvary

The Scriptures teach that the sacrifice of Christ was perfect and complete, putting an end to all other propitiatory offerings (Heb. 10:12, 14). The prayers, praise, gifts, faith, and bodies of God's people are called sacrifices, but this is a metaphorical use of the term. These offerings are not expiatory, and indeed can be acceptable to God only on the grounds of Christ's sacrifice. Particularly we should note that the Lord's Supper is nowhere set forth in Scripture as an expiatory sacrifice or a continuation of Christ's sacrifice. The popish notion of it as an unbloody sacrifice *(see Mass)* is foreign to God's word. "Finished," was Christ's triumphant cry from the cross, and to that all Scripture agrees.

SADDUCEES

A small but wealthy party of aristocratic and rationalistic priests in the days of Christ. They rejected the doctrine of immortality,* according to Josephus (*Antiquities,* 18:1.4), the resurrection* of the body, and eternal rewards and punishments. The etymology of the name is uncertain. Some believe it denotes the sons of Zadok (2 Sam. 8:17); others refer it to members of the *sundikos,* or supreme council, and still others derive it from the Hebrew *tsaddiq,* "righteous."

As to their origin, the Sadducees probably sprang from a Hellenizing party of Jews who supported the infamous Antiochus Epiphanes in the second century B.C. They professed subjection to the law, and therefore Christ used the law to confound their heresy (Matt. 22:23-33).

SAINT

The leading idea in the word is *separation* unto the Lord, *holiness.* A saint is literally a "holy one." In the NT the word is always used in a corporate sense, referring to the body of believers. Saints are such by the call of God (Rom. 1:7), and they bear the marks of conformity to His will (Eph. 5:1-3). The term is used of the faithful in Christ Jesus, the brethren (Eph. 1:1; Col. 1:2). All God's people are saints (Eph. 1:15; 3:8; 3:18; 6:18). The Scripture nowhere countenances the Roman Catholic restriction of sainthood to a few particularly holy people, worthy to be venerated, approved by special supernatural signs, and able to be intermediaries between the petitioning believer and the Lord.

See Canonization.

SALVATION

The comprehensive term to describe the complete deliverance that God, through the person and work of Christ, and by the operation of the Holy Spirit, gives to His people. It includes all the other soteriological terms *(see Soteriology):* regeneration,* conversion,* justification,* adoption,* sanctification,* and glorification.*

The Scriptures show fallen man in a dead and desperate state (Eph. 2:1-3). He needs to be saved (Acts 4:12), or he must perish (John 3:3). But, being depraved and dead in sins, he cannot do a thing to effect his own salvation (Eph. 2:9; Titus 3:5). Only Jesus Christ can save (Matt. 1:21; Acts 4:12; 15:11; Eph. 2:8-10). His whole purpose in coming into the world was salvation (1 Tim. 1:15), and this He purchased by the sacrifice of Himself on the cross (Heb. 5:8, 9; 9:12). The only merit upon which a sinner may be saved is Christ's merit (Rom. 5:18, 19). Even the act of faith (Acts 16:31; Rom. 5:1), by which a man reaches out and receives Christ, is a divine gift, given on the ground of His righteousness (Eph. 2:8; Phil 1:29; 2 Pet. 1:1).

The salvation which Christ imparts to His people is all-embracing. As to time: it deals with the past, the present, and the future (1 Cor. 1:18; Rom. 5:9). As to the entire man: it deals with spirit, soul, and body (1 Thess. 5:23). It gives us a new legal standing (Rom. 5:1; Gal. 4:5), makes us partakers of the divine nature (2 Pet. 1:4), renewing us after the image of God (Eph. 4:24; Col. 3:10), and assures us of eternity with Christ in the heaven He has gone to prepare (John 14:1-3). It is an irreversible work—the Scripture speaks of the lost being saved, but never of the saved being lost.

SALVATION HISTORY
See Heilsgeschichte.

SANCTIFICATION
The verb "to sanctify" may mean two things:
1. To consecrate, or set apart for a sacred use or purpose (John 10:36).
2. To purify, or make holy (John 17:17; 1 Cor. 6:11; Heb. 13:12).
When the doctrine of sanctification is in view, the latter meaning of the verb is more prominent. It is true that the NT uses the term to express the fact that believers have been sanctified once and for all in Christ (Heb. 10:14). They have been set apart once and for all by virtue of their union with Him. Nevertheless in the discussion of the doctrine of sanctification the sense of the verb is preeminently to purify or make holy.

Shaw on the *Westminster Confession of Faith* says: "The sanctification of believers consists in the purification of the pollution of sin and the renovation of their nature after the image of God." The *Shorter Catechism* (Q. 35) gives a lucid definition: "Sanctification is the work of God's free grace, whereby we are renewed in the whole man after the image of God, and are enabled more and more to die unto sin, and live unto righteousness" (see *Westminster Confession of Faith,* chap. 13).

The Fact of Sanctification
The *Westminster Confession of Faith* speaks of persons being really and personally sanctified. This is in opposition to the antinomians *(see Antinomianism).* As their name suggests, antinomians deny that God demands or expects any obedience to the law from believers. They maintain that sanctification is accomplished only by the holiness of Christ being imputed.

When Paul presented the truth of a comprehensive, free justification his critics charged him with antinomianism. His argument in Rom. 3 and 6 is to repudiate that charge. He establishes that only justification through an imputed righteousness, received by faith without works, can place a sinner in the state in which he can bring forth holy works as the fruit of filial love. Thus the *Westminster Confession of Faith* emphasizes that every justified believer is really and personally sanctified from the pollution of sin by the means of the indwelling Spirit of God and through the virtue of the death of Christ.

Contrast Between Sanctification and Justification
Sanctification is a work of grace* that is gradual and progressive. It relates to the conflict with and the victory over indwelling sin. There is a dying more and more unto sin and a living more and more unto righteousness. The word *work* to describe sanctification is used in contrast to the word *act* to describe justification.* Shaw remarks that sanctification and justification differ in the following:
1. *Their nature.* Justification is a relative change in state; sanctification is a real change of the whole man.
2. *Their order.* Justification precedes sanctification; for imputed righteousness precedes implanted and inherent holiness.
3. *Their matter.* The matter of justification is the righteousness of Christ imputed. The matter of sanctification is an inherent righteousness communicated.

4. *Their form.* Justification is a judicial act by which the sinner is pronounced righteous. Sanctification is a moral act, or rather a series of acts, by which a change is effected in the qualities of the soul.

5. *Their properties.* Justification is perfect at first and is equal in all believers. Sanctification is imperfect at first and exists in different degrees of advancement in different individuals.

6. In justification we receive a *title* to heaven. Sanctification gives us a *meetness* for heaven and a capacity of enjoying it.

Cause of Sanctification

According to the statement of the *Westminster Confession of Faith,* the *moving* cause of sanctification is the grace of God (Titus 3:5), the *meritorious* cause is the blood and righteousness of Christ (Titus 2:14), and the *efficient* cause is the Spirit of God (1 Pet. 1:2; 2 Thess. 2:13). Thus, the source of sanctification is the Lord Himself.

This needs to be noted because Pelagians, Romanists, and Arminians all agree on one point—that man has in himself the ability to attain a state of fulfilling all his obligations *(see **Perfectionism**; **Pelagianism**; **Arminianism**).* It is true that Arminians hold that sanctification is not effected through the strength or merit of man, but rather that it is of grace for Christ's sake, by the Holy Spirit through the instrumentality of faith in the Lord Jesus Christ. But this statement is nullified by their failure to see faith as being entirely the gift of God and in no way the product of man. Thus Arminians must be included with those who oppose the orthodox position.

To the Pelagian, sin* consists not in any disposition of the will, but merely in acts. God's law is not an inflexible rule laid down in His word—the only requirements that God lays down are those that men have the ability and opportunity of recognizing. Since the Pelagians do not believe in the depravity of human nature and the immutability of God's

law, they can talk about men reforming their actions. That is their idea of sanctification.

Rome also holds that sin consists of deeds, teaching that in baptism original sin has been taken away. In essence the popish view of sanctification is that God does not ask men to perform impossibilities, and so He graciously lowers the standards of His requirements to accommodate His people, thus enabling them to attain to observance and obedience.

Arminians in their endeavours to establish their doctrine of perfect sanctification also hold that God does not command men to do that which it is impossible for them to do. But Arminians hold that the standards of God's law cannot be lowered and that men cannot attain to these standards. Thus they teach that all God now requires of His people are faith and evangelical obedience—a standard to which they can perfectly attain.

Characteristics of Sanctification

It Is Imperfect in This Life. The *Westminster Confession of Faith* states the teaching of the word of God very clearly on this point. All the above theories hold that perfection is possible in this life. However, it can be seen that their perfection is not really perfection at all. The Romanist still has his venial sins and the Arminian still has "infirmities." The perfection of Wesley is what he termed perfect love, i.e., the love of God filling the heart and dominating every act of the soul. It is attained by a single act of faith, although it is preceded and followed by a gradual work (although how a gradual work can follow perfection is something of a mystery). This perfection is something that every heir of glory must experience. Despite this, Wesley admits that man does not have the ability to fulfil the original law of holiness under which Adam was created, nor does it exclude liability to mistake or to the infirmities of the flesh or natural temperament. These are to be confessed and cleansed, even though according to Wesley the believer is so sanctified as to have all inward disposition to sin and all outward commission of sin eradicated. The position of Arminianism on the subject of sanctification is self-contradictory. Their perfection is achieved by refusing to see "infirmities" as sin, or by substituting an easier standard than the moral law of God. This is an error to be avoided. Sanctification is progressive and gradual, but the nearer a Christian gets to God in this life the more conscious he will be of sin. He may have Christian victory, but that is vastly different from sinless perfection (Rom. 7:18, 23; Gal. 5:16, 17; Phil. 3:12-14; Heb. 12:23; 1 John 1:9).

Hebrews 12:23 speaks of the spirits of just men made perfect. As just men they went to heaven. There they were made perfect. Thus sanctification is completed at death. (See A. A. Hodge's *Outlines of Theology,* chap. 35, question 23ff.).

It Is the Fruit, Not the Cause of Salvation. Sanctification is the exercise of the Holy Spirit in the renewed soul. In regeneration* the soul is renewed, and the Spirit comes to indwell it. Sanctification is the exercise or the outworking of the Spirit's graces in the life. This is emphasized to show that sanctification with its works of holiness is, in Scripture, represented as flowing from, not conducting to, salvation.

It Affects the Entire Person. The whole man is sanctified (1 Thess. 5:23). Shaw: "As original corruption pervades the whole man so sanctifying grace extends to every part. Thence our nature is renewed after the image of God, is called the new man because the holiness commenced by sanctification possesses and enables the whole man." That sanctification affects not only the spiritual life but the physical part of man is clear from 1 Cor. 6:19.

It Is Effected by Internal and External Means.
1. The internal means of sanctification are faith (Gal. 5:6), hope (Rom. 5:5), joy (1 Pet. 1:8, 9), and peace (Phil. 4:7). The exercise of any of these graces increases holiness in the believer.
2. The external means of sanctification are the Scriptures (John 17:17; 1 Pet. 1:22, 23; 2:2), prayer and communion at the Lord's table (Acts 2:42), and discipline (John 15:2; 1 Cor. 11:32; Heb. 13).

It Is Both a Duty and a Grace. Regeneration is the work of God solely and therefore it is a grace. In sanctification the believer cooperates with the Spirit of God in the use of the means provided and thus it is not only a grace of the Spirit but is also the duty of the Christian (e.g., Phil. 2:12, 13).

SANDEMANIANISM

The theology and church practices of the Glasites.* Robert Sandeman (1718-1771) was the son-in-law of John Glas, a Scottish Independent minister of mainly Calvinistic persuasions. Sandemanianism was an attempt to get back to primitive, apostolic Christianity. It was based on a fiercely independent theory of the church.* Its chief interest for the study of theology today is its insistence that saving faith is nothing more than an intellectual belief in the resurrection of Christ, a matter still hotly disputed among dispensationalists* in the lordship salvation* controversy, and even among the Reformed.

SANHEDRIN

From the Greek *sunedrion,* "council"; a Jewish council of ecclesiastical leaders, presided over by the high priest. While the Rabbis held that it was a continuation of the Mosaic advisory board of elders (Exod. 24:1), there is no provable connection. In the time of Christ, the Sanhedrin acted largely as an advisory body to the Roman governor, but had power to make final decisions on matters of the interpretation of Jewish law and even to act in criminal cases, subject to the governor's approval. This is the council before which the Lord Jesus (Matt. 26:59) and the apostles (Acts 4:15-18; 22:30; 23:1) were brought.

SATAN

Hebrew word meaning "adversary"; a finite created spirit with unspeakable malignity toward God and men. He is first referred to in Genesis 3 as a deceiver. In Gen. 3:15 he is cursed and condemned to be broken by the seed of the woman, a reference to the virgin-born Redeemer. The Lord Jesus Christ referred to this in John 12:31, 32, for Calvary doomed Satan and loosed God's elect from his baneful grip.

Satan's history, titles, activity, and end are clearly set forth in Scripture.

Satan's Titles

The Bible names and describes Satan in many ways: *Abaddon* (Rev. 9:11); *accuser* (Rev. 12:10); *adversary* (1 Pet. 5:8); *angel of the bottomless pit* (Rev. 9:11); *the anointed Cherub that covereth* (Ezek. 28:14); *Apollyon* (Rev. 9:11); *Belial* (2 Cor. 6:15); *Beelzebub* (Matt. 12:24); *the devil* (Matt. 4:1); *God of this world* (2 Cor. 4:4); *Lucifer* (Isa. 14:12); *murderer* (John 8:44); *prince of devils* (Matt. 12:24); *prince of the power of the air* (Eph. 2:2); *tempter* (Matt. 4:3); *unclean spirit* (Matt. 12:43); *strong man* (Matt. 12:29); *wicked one* (Matt. 13:19).

Satan's History

Satan is a finite creature, the recognized head (Matt. 12:24) of the fallen angels of whom we read in 2 Pet. 2:4 and Jude 6.

It is generally believed that the language of Isa. 14:14 and Ezek. 28:13-17 has its deepest and truest meaning in reference to Satan and that pride and desire for worship led to his fall (see Matt. 4:9). Thus, in his first assault on mankind, he attacked Eve at the exact point of his own rebellion. In his *Principles of Prophetic Interpretation* (pp. 43, 44), John Wilmot suggests an alternative view. He holds that Satan desired to usurp the place God had decreed for man as the image of God and the lord of all the earthly creation and that this is what led to his rebellion.

Exodus 20:11 makes it clear that Satan's creation came within the six days of Genesis 1, so his fall must have been soon after his creation and his attack on man would probably have been very soon after his creation. *Lucifer* (Isa. 14:12) means "light-bearer," indicating that he was of a high rank among the angels (Ezek. 28:14). This may explain how he can so easily transform himself into an angel* of light (2 Cor. 11:14).

Satan's use of a serpent in Gen. 3 fits this deceptive appearance. The serpent is secret and silent in motion. Its nature is poisonous, its embrace is destructive, and it has fatal powers of fascination—a very apt form for the arch-deceiver to assume. The fall of Satan is recorded by the Lord Jesus in Luke 10:18 (cf. Ezek. 28:15), and he is under the control of the Lord (Job 1:7-12, etc.). His end is described in Rev. 20:10.

Satan's Activity

Satan heads a host of activities in this world. The unclean spirit is represented as restless and relentless (Job 1:7; Matt. 12:43-45).

1. He afflicts God's people, as God permits (Job 1:12).

2. He claims authority over this world (Luke 4:6)—though his claim is false, for he is subject to God.

3. He dominates and captivates sinners (Acts 26:18).

4. He blinds unbelievers' minds (2 Cor. 4:4).

5. He wrestles against the saints (Eph. 6:12).

6. He inspires lying wonders (2 Thess. 2:9).

7. He tempts to sin (Gen. 3:4).

8. He slanders the saints (Job 1:9-11).

9. He accuses them (Rev. 12:10).

10. He inflicts disease (Job 2:7).

11. He opposes prayer (Zech. 3:1).

12. He removes the good seed of the gospel (Matt. 13:19).

13. He sows tares (Matt. 13:38, 39).

14. He ruins human bodies and souls (Luke 9:42).

15. He lies (John 8:44).

16. He instigates sin (John 13:2).

17. He seeks to devour souls (1 Pet. 5:8; Rev. 2:10).

18. He deceives (2 Cor. 2:11; 11:3).

19. He possesses some human beings (John 13:27).

20. He speaks through men, even believers, at times (Matt. 16:22, 23).

Satan's End

Satan's end is utter defeat and destruction. Revelation 20:2-3 says he will be cast into the bottomless pit, where he will be bound for the duration of Christ's millennial reign. Verse 10 of the same chapter records his final doom in the lake of fire and brimstone where he will be tormented day and night forever.

SATISFACTION

"A full, valuable compensation, made to the justice of God, for all the sins of all those for whom [Christ] made satisfaction, by undergoing the same punishment which, by reason of the obligation that was upon them, they themselves were bound to undergo" (John Owen, *Death of Death,* p. 157).

The etymology of the word signifies "doing enough," and it is used to convey the truth that Christ by His active and passive obedience—i.e., His life and death—has satisfied the demands of the justice and law of God in the place of, and for the benefit of, His elect.*

The word *satisfaction* does not occur in Scripture, but was borrowed from Roman law by Anselm (circa 1033-1109). *(See Satisfaction Theory of the Atonement.)*

Charles Hodge worked out the doctrine in his *Systematic Theology:*

"There are…two kinds of satisfaction, which as they differ essentially in their nature and effects, should not be confounded. The one is pecuniary or commercial, the other penal or forensic. When a debtor pays the demand of his creditor in full, he satisfies his claims, and is entirely free from any further demands. In this case the thing paid is the precise sum due, neither more nor less. It is a simple matter of commutative justice; a *quid pro quo;* so much for so much. There can be no condescension, mercy, or grace on the part of a creditor receiving the payment of a debt. It matters not to him by whom the debt is paid, whether by the debtor himself, or by some one in his stead, because the claim of the creditor is simply upon the amount due and not upon the person of the debtor. In the case of crimes the matter is different. The demand is then upon the offender. He himself is amenable to justice.… In case a substitute is provided to bear the penalty in the place of the criminal, it would be to the offender a matter of pure grace, enhanced in proportion to the dignity of the substitute, and the greatness of the evil from which the criminal is delivered. Another important difference between pecuniary and penal satisfaction, is that the one *ipso facto* liberates. The moment the debt is paid the debtor is free, and that completely. No delay can be admitted, and no conditions can be attached to his deliverance. But in the case of a criminal, as he has no claim to have a substitute take his place, if one be provided, the terms on which the benefits of his substitution shall accrue to the principal, are matters of agreement, or covenant between the substitute and the magistrate who represents justice. The deliverance of the offender may be immediate, unconditional, and complete, or, it may be deferred, suspended on certain conditions, and its benefits gradually bestowed.

"As the satisfaction of Christ was not pecuniary, but penal or forensic; a satisfaction for sinners, and not for those who owed a certain amount of money, it follows—

1. That it does not consist in an exact *quid pro quo,* so much for so much. This…is not the case even among men.…The punishment for the offence is something different from the evil which the offender himself inflicted. All that justice demands in penal satisfaction is that it should be a real satisfaction, and not merely something graciously accepted as such. It must bear an adequate proportion to the crime committed. It may be different in kind, but it must have inherent value....All, therefore, that the Church teaches when it says that Christ satisfied divine justice for the sins of men, is that what He did and suffered was a real adequate compensation for the penalty remitted and the benefits conferred. His sufferings and death were adequate to accomplish all the ends designed by the punishment of the sins of men. He satisfied justice. He rendered it consistent with the justice of God that the sinner should be justified. But He did not suffer either in kind or degree what sinners would have suffered. In value, His sufferings infinitely transcended theirs....

2. The satisfaction of Christ was a matter of grace. The Father was not bound to provide a substitute for fallen men, nor was the Son bound to assume that office. It was an act of pure grace....All the benefits, therefore, which accrue to sinners in consequence of the satisfaction of Christ are to them pure gratuities; blessings to which in themselves they have no claim. They call for gratitude, and exclude boasting.

3. Nevertheless, it is a matter of justice that the blessings which Christ intended to secure for His people should be actually bestowed upon them. This follows, for two reasons: first, they were promised to Him as the reward of his obedience and sufferings....It follows, secondly, from the nature of a satisfaction. If the claims of justice are satisfied they cannot be again enforced. This is the analogy between the work of Christ and the payment of a debt. The point of agreement between the two cases is not the nature of the satisfaction rendered, but one aspect of the effect produced. In both cases the persons for whom the satisfaction is made are certainly freed. Their exemption or deliverance is in both cases, and equally in both, a matter of justice. This is what the Scriptures teach when

they say that Christ gave Himself for a ransom. When a ransom is paid and accepted, the deliverance of the captive is a matter of justice. It does not, however, thereby cease to be to the captives a matter of grace....

4. The satisfaction of Christ being a matter of covenant between the Father and the Son, the distribution of its benefits is determined by the terms of that covenant. It does not *ipso facto* liberate. The people of God are not justified from eternity. They do not come into the world in a justified state. They remain (if adults) in a state of condemnation until they believe" (2:470-472).

Hodge does not appear to do justice to the doctrine that Christ's death is a payment. Despite his explanation in note 3, he also seems inconsistent in holding that Christ's satisfaction was not a *quid pro quo* (an agreed payment for an agreed result). He argues that if it were, salvation* would be a matter of justice, not grace. But at the same time he holds that God's justice demands the salvation of those for whom Christ died.

Furthermore, the idea of pecuniary satisfaction does not diminish the element of grace, for the payment was made by God in the person of His Son. It seems to miss the mark to make pecuniary satisfaction "the precise sum, neither more nor less," as if it quantified the value of Christ's sacrifice. Sin against the infinitely holy God needed a satisfaction of infinite value. God could ask no more and Christ paid no less.

Hodge is undoubtedly right in attributing an infinitely greater value to Christ's sufferings than anything sinners could endure. However, his view that the sufferings of Christ and of sinners differ not only in degree but in kind hardly reflects the statements of Scripture (e.g., Gal. 3:10, 13; Rom. 5:6 and 6:23; 2 Cor. 5:21).

Finally, the idea that the satisfaction of Christ does not *ipso facto* (i.e., by the very deed) liberate is a very incomplete statement. True, God's people do not come into the world in a justified state, but as far as God's purpose in relation to His elect is concerned, they are viewed as already justified and glorified (Rom. 8:29, 30) on Christ's merits.

Since sin is a debt as well as a crime (Matt. 6:12), Christ's satisfaction is pecuniary as well as penal.

See **Propitiation**.

SATISFACTION THEORY OF THE ATONEMENT

The name given to the theory advanced by Anselm (1033-1109). Berkhof summarizes and criticizes it as follows:

"The theory of Anselm is sometimes identified with that of the Reformers, which is also known as the satisfaction theory, but the two are not identical. Some seek to prejudice others against it by calling it 'the commercial theory.' Anselm stressed the absolute necessity of the atonement by grounding it in the very nature of God. According to him sin consists in the creature's withholding from God the honour which is His due. By the sin of man God was robbed of his honour, and it was necessary that this should be vindicated. This could be done in either of two ways: by punishment or by satisfaction. The mercy of God prompted Him to seek it in the way of satisfaction, and more particularly through the gift of His Son, which was the only way, since an infinite satisfaction was required. Christ rendered obedience to the law, but since this was nothing more than His duty as man, it did not constitute any merit on His part. In addition to that, however, He also suffered and died in the performance of His duty; and since He as a sinless being was under no obligation to suffer and to die, He thus brought infinite glory to God. This was a work of supererogation on the part of Christ, which merited, and also brought a reward; but since Christ as the Son of God needed nothing for Himself, the reward was passed on to sinners in the form of the forgiveness of sins and of future blessedness for all those who live according to the commandments of the gospel. Anselm was the first to work out a rather complete doctrine of the atonement, and in many respects his theory points in the right direction. However, it is open to several points of criticism.

1. It is not consistent in its representation of the necessity of the atonement. It ostensibly does not ground this necessity in the justice of God which cannot brook sin, but in the honour of God which calls for amends or reparation. He really starts out with the principle of 'private law' or custom, according to which an injured party may demand whatever satisfaction he sees fit; and yet argues for the necessity of the atonement in a way which only holds on the standpoint of public law.

2. This theory really has no place for the idea that Christ by suffering endured the penalty of sin, and that His suffering was strictly vicarious. The death of Christ is merely a tribute offered voluntarily to the honour of the Father. It constitutes a supererogatory merit, compensating for the demerits of others; and this is really the Roman Catholic doctrine of penance applied to the work of Christ.

3. The scheme is also one-sided and therefore insufficient in that it bases redemption exclusively on the death of Christ, conceived as a material contribution to the honour of God, and excludes the active obedience of Christ as a contributing factor to His atoning work. The whole emphasis is on the death of Christ, and no justice is done to the redemptive significance of His life.

4. In Anselm's representation there is merely an external transfer of the merits of Christ to man. It contains no indication of the way in which the work of Christ for man is communicated to man. There is no hint of the mystical union of Christ and believers, nor of faith as accepting the righteousness of Christ. Since the whole transaction appears to be rather commercial, the theory is often called the commercial theory."

SAUMUR SCHOOL

Because of the views of some of its professors, the French Protestant school at Saumur is associated with three main departures from the orthodox Reformed faith: mediate imputation,* mediate regeneration,* and hypothetical universalism.* The name of Joshua Placæus is most closely identified with the first of these, while that of Amyrald is identified with the other two *(see Amyraldism).*

SAVING FAITH

See Faith.

SCHISM

The Greek word *schisma* literally denotes a rent, or cleft (cf. Matt. 9:16; Mark 2:21); hence metaphorically, discord or division (John 7:43; 9:16; 10:19). This is its meaning in 1 Cor. 1:10; 11:18; 12:25.

1 Corinthians 12:25 is vital to a proper understanding of a schism: "That there should be no schism in the body; but that the members should have the same care one for another." Thus, schism is a rending of the body of Christ. It is a sin that exhibits a carelessness about the welfare of the body in general and its other members in particular. It is a sin against charity, a selfish introduction of dissention and division where there ought to be mutual tolerance and love.

This distinguishes schism from scriptural separation.* Scripturally, heretics *(see Heresy)* must be rejected (Titus 3:10) for they are schismatics from the body of true believers, having followed a self-willed opinion in preference to God's revealed truth. Thus, separation from a communion on the grounds of the purity of fundamental Christian doctrine is not schism. For example, Calvin argued that the scriptural marks of a true church are the preaching of the pure gospel and the valid administration of the sacraments. Rome did not maintain these basic marks of a true church. Therefore, in separating from her the Reformers were not guilty of schism. Rome was the party, or

sect, guilty of schism, for she had departed from the faith of the gospel.

The same argument holds good today. In an age when ecumenism is rampant, those who stand for Biblical separation are denounced as schismatics, and are frequently likened to such sects as the Donatists.* But no Christian can deny that the ecumenical movement progresses by compromising the essentials of the gospel. Christians should therefore separate from ecumenical churches. The same goes for churches where modernism* and liberalism* dominate.

It is not right to remain in such fellowships merely because they nominally retain their ancient confessional standards. The argument is frequently put, for example, that while a Presbyterian church retains the *Westminster Standards*, it would be schism to separate from it. However, when the Reformers separated from Rome, she avowed her acceptance of the ancient creeds of the church. But that did not make her a pure church. It merely denoted the fact that lying and falsehood were added to her other impurities. Calvin said, "If the Church is 'the pillar and ground of truth' (1 Tim. 3:15), it is certain that there is no church where lying and falsehood have usurped the ascendancy." If that was true of Rome with her professed acceptance of the ancient creeds of the church, it is no less true of those once Protestant churches that are seeking reunion with an unrepentant Rome, or are open to all great doctrinal impurity.

To sum up: schism is an expression of self-will or of heresy that leads to the setting up of sects—any group that is built on heresy is a schism from the body of Christ. Separation is on Biblical grounds, is commanded by the Lord (Eph. 5:11; 2 Cor. 6:14-18; 1 Tim. 6:3-5), and aims at maintaining essential Christian doctrine and practice.

SCHOLASTICISM

From the Latin *schola*, "school"; the general name of the theological systems of the

Middle Ages—hence the term "schoolmen" for its practitioners. It mingled theology with Greek philosophy, using the latter to reconcile faith and reason. Anselm's dictum, "I believe that I may understand," expressed the idea of the earlier schoolmen that having accepted the truths of special revelation* by faith, they had to proceed to demonstrate the rationality of these truths. In their attempt to erect a natural theology* they set down three ways in which man may determine the attributes of God:

1. *The way of causality,* arguing from the world as an effect to the idea of God as the First Cause and Almighty Ruler;

2. *The way of negation,* by which they removed all the imperfections seen in creation and posited the opposite perfection as belonging to God;

3. *The way of eminence,* by which they ascribed to God in a most eminent degree the relative perfection found in His creatures.

Thomas Aquinas rejected the idea of a rational demonstration of the mysteries of the faith, except in those areas where special revelation dealt with truths that were also part of natural revelation. He proposed a system of theology to be accepted by faith on the basis of supernatural revelation, and another system of scientific theology raised on the ground of natural revelation interpreted by the light of human reason. It was this dualism that the Protestant Reformers rejected as they strove to do justice to the Scriptural teaching on the natural blindness of fallen man.

Scholastic theology prepared the way for Rome's system of salvation by human merit. Whereas Anselm and others held orthodox views on original sin, the usual scholastic view limited the results of the fall* in a semi-Pelagian way.

Under Aquinas's influence Roman Catholicism officially adopted sacramentalism* *(see **Opus Operatum**).* "The emphasis was not on grace as the favour of God shown to sinners, but on grace as a quality of the soul, which might be regarded as both uncreated (i.e., as the Holy Spirit), or as increated, or wrought in the hearts of men by the Holy Spirit. This infused grace is basic to the development of the Christian virtues, and enables man to acquire merit with God, to merit further grace, though he cannot merit the grace of perseverance. This can only be obtained as a free gift of God" (Berkhof, *Systematic Theology,* p. 429).

Scholasticism—and this is still true of Roman Catholic theology—confused regeneration* and justification,* making the latter include the former, regarding it as an activity in which man cooperates with God. In justification man was viewed as forgiven and then actually made righteous. Aquinas changed the order, and his view became the prevalent one. He taught that because grace is infused at baptism, the soul is made righteous, and then is forgiven. This view led to the general acceptance of the idea that man can by his works merit forgiveness.

Scholasticism boasted many acute thinkers, among whom Soctus Erigena, Anselm, Peter Abelard, Thomas Aquinas, William of Occam, and Duns Scotus have achieved prominence. However, the scholastic emphasis on rationality in many cases led to absurdity, so that by Reformation times scholasticism was synonymous with triviality and irrelevance.

SCIENTIA MEDIA

Literally, "the middle knowledge"; a theory of God's knowledge of the free actions of men. It was introduced by the Jesuits* and adopted by Lutherans and Arminians. It is called "middle knowledge" because it is supposed to occupy the middle ground between the *knowledge of simple intelligence* (by which God knows all things, whether actual or possible) and the *knowledge of vision* (by which is meant His knowledge of all things that actually come to pass). This middle knowledge is supposedly grounded, not in the eternal purpose of God, but in His foresight of the creature's free choice. This free choice is seen in Pelagian terms *(see **Pelagianism**).*

The entire idea, by which it is intended to reconcile God's foreknowledge* and man's freedom of will, is built upon the imagined possibility that much of what comes to pass is not because of the divine will or purpose, but is the product of the unfettered choice of the creature. God can foresee these things because He is omniscient; this foresight is called *scientia media.* The entire theory is based upon a fallacy, for the Scripture teaches that God works all things according to His own will (Eph. 1:11; Phil. 2:13; Acts 2:23; Rom. 9:16).

*See **Sovereignty of God.***

SCRIPTURES

The inspired word of God, the Old and New Testaments, the only rule of faith and practice.

Inspiration of Scripture

God is the author of every word of Scripture (2 Tim. 3:16; 2 Pet. 1:19-21; *see **Inspiration**; **Canon of Scripture**).*

Authority of Scripture

The authority of the Scriptures is based, not on the testimony of men, but wholly upon God. It is full and final. All matters are to be judged in the light of Scripture and every opinion to be settled by it (Isa. 8:20).

The Authentication of Scripture

Scripture does not depend on human reasoning to "prove" it. It carries its own evidences internally, though due to the innate blindness of fallen man these can be savingly perceived and received only as a result of the inward work of the Holy Spirit in the heart. The *Westminster Confession of Faith* (chap. 1, sec. 5) says:

"We may be moved and induced by the testimony of the Church to an high and reverend esteem of the Holy Scripture, and the heavenliness of the matter, the efficacy of the doctrine, the majesty of the style, the consent of all the parts, the scope of the whole, (which is to give all glory to God,) the full discovery it makes of the only way of man's salvation, the many other incomparable excellencies, and the entire perfection thereof, are arguments whereby it doth abundantly evidence itself to be the Word of God; yet, notwithstanding, our full persuasion and assurance of the infallible truth, and divine authority thereof, is from the inward work of the Holy Spirit, bearing witness by and with the Word in our hearts."

The Sufficiency of the Scriptures

The *Westminster Confession* defines the sufficiency of Scripture (chap. 1, sec. 6): "The whole counsel of God, concerning all things necessary for his own glory, man's salvation, faith, and life, is either expressly set down in Scripture, or by good and necessary consequence may be deduced from Scripture: unto which nothing at any time is to be added whether by new revelations of the Spirit, or traditions of men. Nevertheless, we acknowledge the inward illumination of the Spirit of God to be necessary for the saving understanding of such things as are revealed in the Word; and that there are some circumstances concerning the worship of God, and government of the Church, common to human actions and societies, which are to be ordered by the light of nature and Christian prudence, according to the general rules of the Word, which are always to be observed."

There are two important considerations here:

1. The Bible is complete in itself, to which there is to be no addition, but the illumination of the Spirit of God is necessary if it is to be savingly understood (Luke 24:45).

2. The sufficiency of the Scriptures is not to be understood as a setting forth of every detail of church worship and government. Rather, there are general rules which must be followed and applied in "Christian prudence" *(see **Regulative Principle**).*

The Perspicuity of the Scriptures

God has given His people a word they can understand. Thus Protestantism has maintained the perspicuity of the Bible against Rome's dependence on church tradition and her denial of the right of every Christian to interpret Scripture for himself. While all things are not equally plain in God's word, everything necessary to salvation is perfectly clear (Ps. 119:105, 130; 2 Tim. 3:15-17). The fact that God addresses His word either to all men or to the body of believers generally, proves the Protestant position, while the solemn warning of Rev. 22:18 removes the validity of Rome's appeal to any authority outside of the Bible itself.

Interpretation of Scripture

"The infallible rule of interpretation of Scripture is the Scripture itself" (*Westminster Confession of Faith,* chap. 1, sec. 9). "The Holy Spirit who inspired the Scriptures is the only adequate expounder of His own words, and He is promised to all the children of God as a Spirit of light and truth" (A. A. Hodge). Thus ecclesiastical or traditional authority cannot settle the true meaning of any Scripture.

The basic rule of interpretation is laid down by the Holy Spirit in Rom. 12:6, "according to the proportion [or analogy] of the faith." That is, the general teaching of Scripture on any subject governs the interpretation of any particular passage. No Scripture may be interpreted in a way that conflicts with the general teaching of the Bible. Passages that are particularly difficult must be interpreted in the light of other clearer passages.

Paul exhorted Timothy (2 Tim. 2:15): "Study to show thyself approved…rightly dividing the word of truth" or "cutting the word of truth straight." That is the constant task of Bible interpretation. *(See **Hermeneutics**.)*

Key to Scripture

The key to Scripture is Christ (Luke 24:27, 44; Acts 10:43). He is the great subject of the Biblical revelation, from Genesis to Revelation. The written word witnesses to the incarnate Word and vice versa.

Integrity of the Scripture Text

Concerning the OT text, B. E. Nicholls wrote: "Such was the impression on the mind of the Jews of the Divine origin of their Scriptures, that, according to the statements of Philo and Josephus, they would suffer any torments, or even death itself, rather than change a single point or iota of them: and a law was enacted by the Jews, which denounced him to be guilty of inexpiable sin who should presume to make the slightest alteration in their Sacred Books. They have never dared to annex to them any historical narrative since the death of their last prophet Malachi. They closed the Sacred Volume with the succession of their prophets. Our Lord declared the Old Testament, as the Jews possessed it in His time, to be the Word of God; He adopted the three-fold division of it into 'the Law, the Prophets, and the Psalms,' which the Jews adopt, to comprehend all the Old Testament as we now have it: and though He frequently charged the Jews with making the Word of God of none effect by their traditions, He never accused them of corrupting the text. The books of the Old Testament which we receive as canonical, are acknowledged by both Jews and Christians to be those which existed in our Saviour's time: and by the confession of both parties, they have been handed down to us uncorrupted and unchanged."

As to the NT text, we have abundant evidence from ancient MSS copies, versions, lectionaries, and quotations in the works of early Christian writers, of the state of the original text. That text was widely distributed and independently copied throughout the early churches, so that corruptions, intentional or innocent, are capable of being identified and the pure text maintained. Conservative scholars refer to this text as the majority text or the traditional text,* and it essentially corresponds with the text underlying our Authorized Version of the Scriptures *(see Textual Criticism of the New Testament).*

Amid the wreckage of all that is merely human, the Bible stands, textually pure despite all the malice of wicked men against it. As Bishop Jewel long ago remarked, no tyrant has been able to consume the Bible, no tradition to choke it, no heretic successfully to corrupt it. "The Word of the Lord endureth forever. And this is the Word which by the gospel is preached unto you" (1 Pet. 1:25).

SEAL

The Bible uses the term both literally (Gen. 38:18, 25; 1 Kings 21:8, etc.), and figuratively.

There are two outstanding examples of its literal use:

1. The tomb of Christ was sealed (Matt. 27:66). Probably wax was poured on a rope stretched across the stone at the mouth of the tomb and then stamped with a seal while it was still soft.

2. The book that John saw (Rev. 5:1) was sealed with seven seals, a reminder of the perfect authenticity and authority of the message it contained.

When used figuratively *seal* "sometimes denotes ownership or responsibility (Eph. 1:13; 2 Tim. 2:19). It might also denote such things as security (Eph. 4:30); authenticity (John 3:33); privacy or secrecy (Dan. 12:4; Rev. 10:4); proof of genuineness (1 Cor.9:2)" (*Baker's Dictionary of Theology*).

SECOND COMING

The "blessed hope" (Titus 2:13) of the people of God is based on the promise of the Lord Jesus Christ, "I will come again" (John 14:3). The angelic word to the disciples on the Mount of Olives after the ascension of Christ was, "This same Jesus, which is taken up from you into heaven, shall so come in like manner as ye have seen him go into heaven" (Acts 1:11).

It is clear that the return of Christ will be personal, visible, literal, and physical. His feet shall stand on the Mount of Olives (Zech. 14:4), and every eye shall see Him (Rev. 1:7). It is called His "glorious appearing" (Titus 2:13), for He will come in all the glory of His Father and will be attended by angelic hosts (Mark 8:38; 2 Thess. 1:7, 8) as well as by His glorified saints (1 Thess. 3:13; 4:15-17; 1 Cor. 15:51-53).

A Single Event

Historically, Christians have looked upon the second coming of Christ as a single event, the various aspects of which are denoted in the NT by the use of the words *parousia, apokalupsis,* and *epiphaneia.* "*Parousia,* the most frequently used, is an ordinary word indicating arrival or consequent presence (Phil. 1:26), but as applied to Christ it is doubtless intended to have a somewhat technical force such as it had in the Hellenistic age for denoting the arrival of a king or a person of prominence. The other terms are picturesque. Of these, *apokalupsis* (2 Thess. 1:7) means an unveiling, and thus takes account of Christ's withdrawal to heaven before His final denouement (cf. Col. 3:3-4, where the verb *phaneroo* has much the same force). Similarly, the verb *ophthesetai* (He shall appear), used in Heb. 9:28, is chosen with the background of the tabernacle and the Day of Atonement ritual in view, when the high priest emerged before the people after being in the most holy place. The word *apokalupsis* connotes more than visibility in contrast to invisibility. It suggests the consummation of God's purpose and the sharing of the saints in it. Then shall we know even as we have been known. Finally, *epiphaneia* (2 Tim. 4:1) suggests the public, open character of Christ's appearing. It readily associates with itself the idea of glory (Titus 2:13), and it is suitable for suggesting an appearing which is sudden, conspicuous, and overwhelming in its effects on hostile powers (2 Thess. 2:8)" (*Baker's Dictionary of Theology*).

Theory of a Two-Stage Coming

Thus, *parousia, apokalupsis,* and *epiphaneia* are three descriptions of one event. Since the mid-19th century, however, the idea of a two-stage second coming has gained ground among many Christians. This view is closely associated with dispensationalism* and teaches that Christ will come secretly to remove His church before the great tribulation* and will then return with all His saints at the end of the tribulation period. It is alleged that the blessed hope of the church is the pre-tribulation rapture* and that this is different in time from the glorious appearing. 1 Thessalonians 4:15-17 is frequently cited in proof of this secret pre-tribulation coming of Christ for His people.

The theory raises many theological questions of the deepest significance, associated with its dispensational bias. Furthermore, the Scriptures cited in favour of it do not bear the weight placed on them by the advocates of the rapture idea. The construction of the Greek in Titus 2:13 *(see Granville Sharpe Rule)* makes it clear that the blessed hope and the glorious appearing are one event. 1 Thessalonians 4:15-17 describes the resurrection* of the saints. How can this take place before the great tribulation when according to Rev. 20:4, 5 some of those raised in the first resurrection die during the tribulation? A comparison between 1 Thess. 4:15-17 and 1 Cor. 15:51, 52 will indicate that the same event is in view in both places. 1 Cor. 15:52 clearly says that it takes place "at the last trump." How could this precede the tribulation period with its seven trumpets (Rev. 8:2)? And how could it precede the post-tribulation coming of Christ, when (Matt. 24:31) there will be "a great sound of a trumpet?"

Clearly, there is one second coming and He whom the Father told to "sit Thou at my right hand, until I make thine enemies thy footstool" (Ps. 110:1; Acts 2:34, 35) will not leave that position just as antichrist is about to assume his greatest dominion on earth.

"When He Shall Appear"

The second coming of Christ will have a special significance for Israel (Zech. 12:10). It will consummate the hope of the saints, when the dead shall be raised incorruptible and the living shall be instantly glorified (1 Cor. 15:51-52; 1 Thess. 4:13-18; Phil 3:21). Christ will be admired by all His saints (2 Thess. 1:10) and will proceed to reward His servants (Rev. 22:12; 1 Cor. 3:12-15; 4:5). He will also, at the instant of His coming, destroy the forces of antichrist (2 Thess. 2:8-10) and the world of the ungodly (2 Thess. 1:7-10).

See Millennium.

SECOND PROBATION

The idea that in the intermediate state* salvation will again be offered to those who died without Christ. Advocates of the theory hold that the offer is on the same terms as the present gospel invitation, namely by faith in Christ as Saviour. No one will be damned without being given this test, and those who are finally condemned will be condemned only because they have rejected this grace. In contrast to this, the Scripture represents the state of believers and unbelievers after death to be fixed (Luke 16:19-31; John 8:21, 24; 2 Pet. 2:4, 9; Jude 7-13). Now is the accepted time, now is the day of salvation (2 Cor. 6:2), not later. After death, there is judgment (Heb. 9:27), not a period of probation and gospel grace.

SECT

A faction, guilty of schism* from the church.

SECULARISM

A philosophy which attempts to achieve human betterment without reference to God or religion. It is based on the assumption that materialism* is true. It is thus man-centered, materialistic, and temporally oriented. It is expressed in modern man's trust in science over God and in his preoccupation with this world over the world to come. It is the full harvest of Enlightenment* philosophy, a harvest of desperation and a sense of meaninglessness that has spawned the widespread breakdown of modern society.

Secularism is most obvious in the separation of the state—its laws, government, courts, and political and social policy—from all religious (i.e., Christian) moorings. It is more than the separation of church and state as envisaged, for example, in the United States' constitution. It is the separation of the state from God to establish its dependence upon the faith of secular humanism.*

Secularism takes on a particularly reprehensible aspect when it invades the church. There it asserts, "Religion is a private, not a public matter" and shows its concern to be "this worldly" rather than "other worldly." It redefines the gospel, the mission of the church, and the manner and sphere of Christian life in terms of social action and human relationships. It is worldliness, fulfilling the old saying, "I looked for the church and I found it in the world; I looked for the world and I found it in the church."

Secularism is disastrous alike for the church, for the state, and for the individual. It is the epitome of man's depraved and corrupted state and is the very essence of man's age-old rebellion against God. Far from being the answer to the needs of men it is a problem that needs the solution provided by the gospel and received through repentance and faith.

SEE

Literally, "a seat," Latin, *sedes* of a bishop, which is officially called a throne, Latin *cathedra*. Thus, when the pope makes an official pronouncement, he is said to speak *ex cathedra*.

In ecclesiastical usage *see* is synonymous with *diocese*, the area over which a bishop exercises jurisdiction.

SEED OF RELIGION, SEMEN RELIGIONIS

That principle implanted in man by his creation in the image of God, by which he has an innate knowledge of God.
See **Innate Idea of God**.

SELF-DETERMINATION

Responsible moral agency. "When we say that an agent is self-determined, we say two things: (1) That he is the author or efficient cause of his own act, (2) That the grounds or reasons of his determination are within himself" (Charles Hodge, *Systematic Theology*, 2:295).

The self-determination that renders man a responsible moral agent must be distinguished from the notion of the *self-determination of the will*. Self-determination of the will signifies that the will is always self-moved, with absolute freedom of choice, a freedom it may use completely arbitrarily. The idea of a self-determined will is open to criticism on two grounds:

1. It separates the choices, or volitions, of the will from all the other constituents of a man's character, making the will operate, not on account of anything in the agent, but by its own inherent self-moving power. "In this case, the volition ceases to be a decision of the agent, for it may be contrary to that agent's whole character, principles, inclinations, feelings, convictions, or whatever makes him what he is" (Hodge, 2:295).

2. It makes the power of contrary choice an essential element in self-determination. That is, a person cannot be held a responsible moral agent unless he has the ability to decide against the prevailing inclination of his will, thus originating a new inclination *(see Free Will)*. But this power of contrary choice is not of the essence of moral responsibility and liberty. God is supremely free, yet He "cannot lie" (Titus 1:2). He has no power to sin. Fallen man's inclination is selfish, sinful, and depraved. All his volitions proceed from that inclination. He is

personally the author of these volitions, for they are in accordance with the prevailing inclination of his will. He has no power to originate a new inclination, as Arminians imagine. Only God can do that for him (John 6:44; Eph. 4:24; Col. 3:10). Thus godly volitions are the acts of a renewed will, for the "carnal mind" or unrenewed will is incapable of them (Rom. 8:7).

SELF-ESTEEM

Self-acceptance; recognition of one's value as a person; the ability to feel at home with one's self as he is. It is based on the recognition of personal identity, independent of the opinions of others or of one's own merits and characteristics. It is the esteem a person has for himself for what he is.

Secular psychology,* not having any understanding of sin and depravity, freely employs this concept. Carl Jung called the self "God." New Age psychology with its inherent pantheism* emphasizes the deity of every man. On such premises it is easy to see why everyone should esteem himself.

However, it is a very different matter for Christians. We recognize that secular psychology and the New Age movement* are wrong in their denial of man's status as a fallen creature of God. Given this Biblical doctrine, we may ask what reason a man has for self-esteem in the terms set forth above. Some Christian psychologists who promote the concept of self-esteem face very real difficulties in such NT statements as Gal. 2:20: "I am crucified with Christ: nevertheless I live; yet not I, but Christ liveth in me: and the life which I now live in the flesh I live by the faith of the Son of God, who loved me, and gave himself for me." They argue that all Paul is doing is condemning self-centred living. As we shall see, he is doing much more than that; but even if the argument could be sustained in this case it would hardly meet the objection to self-esteem therapy as a Christian discipline from Rom. 7:18: "I know that in me (that is, in my flesh,) dwelleth no good thing: for to will is present with me; but how to perform that which is good I find not." Clearly this goes deeper than egocentricity and describes a fundamental reality of the natural man. His nature is corrupted and his will* depraved.

These same Christian psychologists have a problem with the idea of "dying to self," limiting its meaning also to the idea of ceasing to live selfishly. The trouble with this professedly Christian use of self-esteem is that it fails to understand the nature of sin.* Thus its therapeutic value is a mere surface treatment.

Yet we must never forget that God has placed the value of a human soul above the combined wealth of all the world (Mark 8:36). However, this realization does not lead to some feeling of self-esteem. It leads rather to a deep conviction of sin and need, for this soul stands in danger of being eternally lost. Any self-acceptance in a soul standing on the brink of hell is surely misplaced.

The Bible gives a man no reason to look complacently on himself while he remains an enemy of God. Once that man has received Christ and has been justified by faith, God gives him the perfect ground on which to be at home with himself while avoiding the snare of self-promotion or self-centredness. That ground is in the imputed righteousness of Christ. God looks on a believer as perfectly righteous and acceptable because he is in Christ and is robed in His righteousness (Rom. 5:18-19; 1 Cor. 1:30; 2 Cor. 5:21; Eph. 1:6; Isa. 61:10; Jer. 23:6).

With this assurance a believer can be honest with himself and face his sins and shortcomings. He feels guilty about these, but he knows what to do about that guilt: he knows to bring it to the cross and receive the cleansing of the blood of Christ from its pollution (1 John 1:7-9). However, he does not live under guilt. As a justified man, in Christ he has a perfect legal standing before God, a perfect acceptance, because he has a perfect righteousness. That righteousness is outside of himself. It is in Christ. God accepts him, not on the basis of what he is or has done, but on the basis of Christ's perfect obedience unto death for him. God will never deal with him apart from Christ and will never deal with Christ apart from him, for he is "in Christ."

Thus his acceptance with God does not depend on how well he performs or on what characteristics or acquirements he has. On this basis, he is free to live his life by faith in the light of God's declaration of his acceptance. He is free to accept himself in Christ because God does so. This is the meaning of Paul's statement in Gal. 2:20. "I have been crucified with Christ" refers to our identification with Christ in His death. Believers died in Christ's death, rose again in His resurrection,* and ascended to glory in His ascension (Eph. 2:6). The way for a Christian to live his life "in the flesh" is "by the faith of the Son of God, who loved me, and gave himself for me." In this way a believer is free from tying his acceptability to his performance, talents, or accomplishments. Since he does not have to work to become acceptable, but is so because of Christ's righteousness imputed to him, he is free to seek to be and do his best because he is already and unchangeably acceptable to God.

In the NT the great key to free, joyful Christian living is not in any psychological concept of self-esteem but in the central doctrine of the gospel, the doctrine of justification* by grace* alone, on the merits of Christ alone, received by faith* alone. Self-esteem is the world's way of seeking the peace of soul that justifying grace brings, while rejecting that grace. It has no place in Christian pastoral theology.* To a Christian, it is a poor, secular substitute for the spiritual provision our heavenly Father has made for us in imputing the righteousness of Christ to us.

SELF-EXISTENCE

Aseity;* the eternal, necessary, and uncaused being of God.

SEMI-ARIANISM

The compromise view between the position of the orthodox party and the Arians *(see **Arianism)** at the Council of Nicea in Bithynia, in A.D. 325. The orthodox party held to the scriptural doctrine that the "Lord Jesus is, as to His divine nature, of the same identical substance with the Father." The Arians held the Son to be merely a creature, though the greatest of all creatures. The Semi-Arians denied on the one hand that the Son was a creature, and on the other hand that He was God in the same sense as the Father is God. They taught that while the Father is eternally and essentially God, the Son was derived from Him by an act of the Father's will. Thus the Son's is not a necessary, but a contingent, existence. The orthodox party used the Greek word *homoousion,* "of the same substance," to teach the great mystery of the scriptural doctrine of the Trinity,* that the persons of the Trinity are the same numerical essence. The Semi-Arians used the term *homoiousion,* "of like or similar substance," to denote their view of the derived being of the Son.

Regarding their doctrine of the Holy Spirit,* most Semi-Arians denied His personality* and regarded the term as descriptive of a divine energy or as synonymous with the word of God. Some adopted the Arian position that He was the first and most glorious creature of the Son.

SEMI-PELAGIANISM

A middle ground between Augustianism* and Pelagianism.* Augustine denied the saving merit of human works and strongly propounded the doctrines of predestination* and sovereign grace. Under the leadership of Cassian (d. *circa* 440), Vincent of Lerius (d. *circa* 450), and Faustus of Reghuim (d. *circa* 485), the Semi-Pelagians admitted that Adam's sin injured all his posterity, and continued to affect them both in body and soul, but they denied that fallen men were spiritually dead. They held them to be merely enfeebled and in need of the assistance of divine grace which they understood to be the influence of the Holy Spirit in the Scriptures. They taught that because of man's free will* and ability to do good, the human will cooperates with the Holy Spirit in regeneration* *(see Synergism).* Indeed, the beginning of salvation* lies with the sinner, whose efforts are assisted by God. In keeping with such views, the Semi-Pelagians denied God's sovereign election of His people.

While the name *Semi-Pelagian* has now largely passed out of use, its leading features live on, even in many evangelical circles.

SEPARATION

The word has an extensive Biblical usage with the common theme that God's people are a distinctive, peculiar people. The Lord made a clear separation between Israel and the heathen nations (Lev. 20:24; 1 Kings 8:53). Mixed marriages were forbidden (Deut. 7:3) and severely judged in the days of Ezra and Nehemiah (Ezra 10:11; Neh. 13:3).

Separation is essential to holiness and is the basic idea in sanctification.* This was clearly taught in the Levitical distinction between clean and unclean (cf. Lev. 11:20-25) and by the law of the Nazarite (Num. 6:1-8). Separation is essential to service (Num. 18:14; 16:9), a fact that the NT also stresses (Acts 13:2; Gal. 1:15). In these texts separation is seen not merely to be *from* certain evil things but *to* God and His service.

The Scripture uses separation in an evil sense to describe apostates who divide themselves from the body of Christ by false teaching (Jude 19).

It also uses the term to denote the Christian's duty to "have no fellowship with the unfruitful works of darkness" (Eph. 5:11).

In this connection 2 Cor. 6:14-18; Rom. 16:17; 1 Tim. 6:3-5; and 2 John 10, 11 are explicit and form the basis for the doctrine of ecclesiastical separation. This is the repudiation, as to Christian fellowship and cooperation, of those guilty of heresy,* schism,* or open sin and disobedience. (For a discussion of the grounds of scriptural separation from a professedly Christian communion and the difference between such separation and sinful division, *see Schism*).

SEPTUAGINT

The Greek version of the OT, commonly abbreviated as *LXX.* The name signifies the "seventy" and derives from the story that it was the work of seventy (rather, seventy-two) scholars who translated it from the original Hebrew. It was executed in Alexandria about two and a half centuries before Christ. For six centuries it was the Bible of the Hellenistic Jews in Egypt, Palestine, Western Asia, and Europe. "It created a language of religion which lent itself readily to the service of Christianity, and became one of the most important allies of the gospel. It provided the Greek-speaking church with an authorized translation of the Old Testament, and, when Christian missions advanced beyond the limits of Hellenism, it served as a basis for fresh translation into the vernacular" (H. B. Swete, *An Introduction to the O.T. in Greek,* p. 433).

SESSION

1. Christ's appearance at the right hand of God as our sovereign high priest, pleading the virtue of His once-for-all atoning sacrifice on behalf of His people (see Ps. 110:1; Acts 2:34, 35; Heb. 1:3; 9:24; 10:12; 1 Pet. 3:22).

2. In Presbyterianism,* the board of elders governing the local church.

SEVENTH-DAY ADVENTISM

A movement, organized in 1860, that grew out of the prophetic teachings of William Miller, who on the basis of the Year-Day Theory* calculated from Dan. 8:14 that Christ would return to earth in 1843. This was later amended to October 22, 1844, and when that date passed without the appearance of Christ, one of Miller's followers provided an escape from embarrassment. He received a "vision" of Christ standing at the altar in heaven, from which he concluded that Miller's date had been right, though he had got the place wrong. Christ had returned, not to earth but to cleanse the heavenly sanctuary!

Seventh-Day Adventism (SDA) took up this idea about Christ's return and made it a principal part of their belief. So much for the *adventism* in the name.

The "seventh-day" part arose from the fanciful theories of James White and his wife Ellen, on the message of the three angels in Rev. 14:6-11. These three angels were supposed to symbolize by their messages "the three parts of the genuine movement" begun by Miller. Mrs. White, who became the "prophetess" of SDA, held that the third angel's message called men to honour the seventh-day sabbath. She based her interpretation on another "vision," so that the entire system ultimately rests on two claimed visions.

Van Baalen in *The Chaos of Cults* lists four areas in which SDA deviates from Bible Christianity:

1. *The doctrine of soul-sleep between death and the resurrection.** Against this see Luke 16:22-30; Phil. 1:23, 24; 2 Cor. 5:1-8; Ps. 73:24; Rev. 6:9, 10.

2. *The doctrine of the annihilation of the wicked.* Against this see Rom. 2:6-9; Rev. 20:13; John 3:36; Rev. 20:10.

3. *The doctrine of the atonement.** Mrs. White taught that for 1,800 years Christ pleaded in the Holy Place in the heavenly sanctuary for penitent sinners, but their sins remained on the record because Christ's atonement remained unfinished. He needed to go in, as the High Priest did on the day of atonement, and purge the inner sanctuary. This He commenced in 1844. How? By His investigative judgment of His people, upon examination of whom He showed the Father those "who through repentance of

sin and faith in Christ, are entitled to the benefits of the atonement." Carrying the parallel with the day of atonement still further, Mrs. White taught that the scapegoat upon which the sins of God's people were laid was Satan,* "upon whom the sins of the truly penitent will be finally placed." Thus, Satan is the bearer of the sins of the saved! Nowhere in all Scripture is there a hint of such a monstrous dogma—see John 1:29; 1 Pet. 2:24. The sacrificial victims in the OT symbolism all typify Christ *(See **Azazel**).*

This apostasy from the orthodox scriptural doctrine of the atonement lies at the heart of SDA. Mrs. White in *The Great Controversy* (p. 489) wrote, "We dissent from the view that the atonement was made upon the cross, as is generally held." Again: "We are now living in the great day of atonement. In the typical service, while the high priest was making the atonement for Israel, all were required to afflict their souls by repentance of sin and humiliation before the Lord, lest they be cut off from among the people. In like manner, all who would have their names retained in the book of life, should now, in the few remaining days of their probation, afflict their souls before God by sorrow for sin and true repentance. Now, while our great High Priest is making the atonement for us, we should seek to become perfect in Christ....It is in this life that we are to separate sin from us, through faith in the atoning blood of Christ. Our precious Saviour invites us to join ourselves to Him, to unite our weakness to His strength, our ignorance to His wisdom, our unworthiness to His merits" (ibid., p. 623).

All this is dangerous heresy. It makes salvation a cooperative work between Christ and the sinner *(see **Synergism**).* It ignores the scriptural representations of the death of Christ as the ransom, the price of redemption (Matt. 20:28). It contradicts the plain record of Scripture, which describes God's people as already redeemed (Eph. 1:7; Col. 1:14; 1 Pet. 1:18, 19) by saying that their sins still stood on record for 1,800 years (cf. Ps. 103:12; Isa. 43:25; 44:22, 23) and that the present state of believers is one of probation* (cf. 1 John 3:1, 2).

4. *The seventh-day sabbath.* SDA regards the use of the first day of the week as the mark of the beast. Mrs. White identified the first beast in Rev. 13 as the papacy, and the second as the United States government because of its enactment of various "Sunday laws." SDA concentrates its attack on Sunday worship, not usually volunteering information about its peculiar adventist ideas with their shocking corollaries in the area of the atonement.

Undoubtedly many sincere Christians have been ensnared by SDA. Indeed, the evidence is that William Miller, from whom the germ of the movement came, was a humble Bible-believing Christian, mistaken but saved. Many of SDA members have come out of churches in which they observed the first day of the week. They ought to be very careful about adopting the SDA exegesis of Rev. 14 identifying the mark of the beast as the observance of the sabbath on the first day of the week, for vv. 9-11 show that any who ever wear this mark can never be saved. It is in keeping with the rest of the cult's confused thinking to overlook the simple fact that by their own exegesis most of them are doomed never to be saved!

SHEKINAH

The glory of God. J. Barton Payne (*Baker's Dictionary of Theology,* p. 484) summed up the Scripture evidence as follows:

"While Scripture denies any permanent localization of God it does describe, simultaneously with his transcendence, his 'glory,' or apprehensible presence. Glory may be expressed in God's 'face,' 'name' (Exod. 33:18-20), 'Angel'—pre-incarnate appearances of Christ—or 'cloud' (Exod. 14:19). Shekinah concerns the cloud, which surrounded the glory (40:34), like thunderheads through which lightning flashes

(19:9, 16). The shekinah first appeared when God led Israel from Egypt and protected them by 'a pillar of cloud and fire' (13:21; 14:19). The cloud vindicated Moses against 'murmurers' (16:10; Num. 16:42) and covered Sinai (Exod. 24:16) as he communed there with God (vs. 18; cf. 33:9). God 'dwelt' (25:8) among Israel in the tabernacle, 'place of dwelling' (vs. 9; cf. 1 Kings 8:13), a type of his dwelling in heaven (1 Kings 8:30; Heb. 9:24). The cloud filled the tabernacle (Exod. 40:34-35; cf. Rom. 9:4); and post-biblical usage accordingly designated this permanent, visible manifestation shekina, 'dwelling (of God's presence).' Shortly thereafter consuming fire twice 'came forth from before the Lord' (Lev. 9:23, 24; 10:2). Specifically, God appeared 'in the cloud upon the mercy-seat, which is upon the ark' (Lev. 16:2; Exod. 25:22; cf. Heb. 9:5).

"The shekinah guided Israel through the wilderness (Exod. 40:36-38); and, though the ark's loss meant 'Ichabod (no glory)' (1 Sam. 4:21), the cloud again filled Solomon's temple (1 Kings 8:11; cf. 2 Chron. 7:1). Ezekiel visualized its departure because of sin (Ezek. 10:18) before the temple's destruction, and Judaism confessed its absence from the second temple. The shekinah reappeared with Christ (Matt. 17:5; Luke 2:9), true God localized (John 1:14; *skene,* 'tabernacle'; cf. Rev. 21:3 = *shekina?*), the glory of the latter temple (Hag. 2:9; Zech. 2:5). Christ ascended in the glory cloud (Acts 1:9) and will some day return (Mark 14:62; Rev. 14:14; cf. Isa. 24:3; 60:1)."

SHEOL

The OT equivalent of the NT *hades.**

SHEPHERDING MOVEMENT

A movement within the Charismatic Movement* that grew out of the home churches of the 1960's and 1970's. It places a strong emphasis on leadership, oversight, and accountability. In the Shepherding Movement every member is accountable to a group leader who in turn is accountable to the church elders both for his own life and the lives of those in his group. The elders are responsible to pastors, and the pastors to apostles. The apostles are subject to each other.

Leadership and oversight in this movement may extend to direction in decision making from choosing a marriage partner to buying or selling a house. In 1975 Pat Robertson and other Charismatic leaders strongly condemned the movement. Robertson called it "witchcraft" and likened it to the Jim Jones cult. It was clear that the pyramids of sheep and shepherds were being abused. One allegation was, "Down through the pyramid went the orders,... while up the same pyramid went the tithes" (*Dictionary of Pentecostal and Charismatic Movements,* p. 784).

Leaders of the Shepherding Movement sought to rectify the situation and build safeguards into their system. Still their movement suffered various divisions and by 1986 what was left of the original movement (Christian Growth Ministries) announced the end of their organizational ties. However, various churches remain committed to the principles of the Shepherding Movement and maintain an affiliation with each other on that basis.

SIMONY

From the name of Simon Magus (Acts 8:18-20), who thought that the power of the Holy Spirit could be bought; the sale or purchase of ecclesiastical position or office. This evil, though condemned by the plain teaching of Scripture (cf. Acts 8:20) and by the Council of Chalcedon in 451, became widespread in medieval times and was one of the corruptions the Reformers battled against. The practice was dealt with only very slowly in England, where the monarch assumed the pope's power, including trafficking in ecclesiastical preferment. It was a source of much contention in Scotland as

the Presbyterians opposed the impositions of the Episcopal party.

SIMPLICITY OF GOD

More fully stated as the *Unity of Simplicity,* this is the divine attribute of indivisibility. Particularly, *simplicity* emphasizes that the three persons of the Trinity* are not three parts of which the divine essence is composed. It also teaches that there can be no distinction between the divine essence and the divine attributes. God is not an eternal essence to which attributes have been added. He is not essence *plus* attributes. He is essence *in* attributes.

SIN

Essence of Sin

The Hebrew and Greek words used for *sin* in Scripture mean "to miss, or to fail to hit the mark," and thus "to err from a rule or law." In the light of this the *Shorter Catechism* defines sin as "any want of conformity unto or transgression of the law of God." Berkhof elaborates on this, defining sin as "lack of conformity to the moral law of God, either in act, disposition or state." In Berkhof's definition the triple reference to "act, disposition or state" is important.

Sin in Scripture is used to describe any act of transgression of God's law (e.g., James 1:15). *Disposition* refers to the determination of the will.* In Romans 7:8 sin is used to describe the evil disposition of man's fallen will. This disposition is the voluntary product of a rebellious and lawless self-determination.* *State* emphasizes the fact that fallen man's condition is also sin. In Luke 6:43-45 the Lord Jesus clearly lays down the position that the state of man's soul produces his sinful disposition, which in turn produces sinful acts. Thus the underlying state of the sinner is sinful.

The standard against which sin is to be judged is the law of God. This fact stresses that a sinner is a moral agent, or one possessed of intelligence, conscience,* and free will.* It should be remembered that free will is the power of a moral agent to choose according to the disposition of his will. This definition of free will is one that will become very important at a later state in our discussion, in dealing with the twin truths of total depravity* and total inability.* With all this in mind we may make some observations on the nature of sin.

Sin is a real evil. It is unrighteousness, or crookedness, a failure to be right, straight, upright or true (1 John 5:17). It is a real perversion of human nature that results in a definite force of rebellion against God.

Sin is a moral evil. It is wrong. The Bible refers to it as "iniquity," that which is wrong in its very nature. It is a violation of God's law (1 John 3:4). God's law is the absolute unchangeable and irreversible standard of true morality, and all transgression of that law is essentially immoral.

Sin is a judicial evil. The literal force of 1 John 3:4 is that "sin is lawlessness." Therefore, the sinner will be arraigned before the judgment bar of God (Acts 17:31; Eccles. 12:14).

Sin is a personal evil. The Scripture refers to it as "trespass," a word that emphasizes the truth of the second clause of Isaiah 53:6, "We have turned everyone to his own way." Sin is the voluntary act, disposition, or state of the individual, and of the sum of all the individuals that comprise the race, apart from grace.

Sin is a universal evil. All the world is guilty (Rom. 3:19). All have sinned (Rom. 3:23; 1 John 1:8, 10). "There is no man that sinneth not" (1 Kings 8:46). The universality of sin is an important fact, which no serious thinker can deny. It strongly presupposes the reality of the fall* and the union of all mankind in Adam in his fall.

Sin is a comprehensive evil. Pelagianism teaches that sin consists only in personal acts of transgression of a known law. Such acts do not render a man's natural state corrupt, so that, while he is liable to punishment (i.e.,

guilt) because of his sinful acts, he retains the power to cease from sin. Thus sin incurs guilt,* but not corruption—and since it does not produce a sinful state, Adam's guilt cannot be imputed to his posterity. But from what we have noted above, sin is more than mere acts. It covers disposition and state as well. Thus, sin is both guilt and corruption. Guilt is the liability of a sinner to punishment for the violation of God's law. It is the sinner's demerit or ill-desert which, on the ground of divine justice, must be punished. Note this carefully, for the obligation to satisfy divine justice not only spells the doom of the sinner, but sounds the note of gospel hope, because clearly guilt may be removed by the satisfaction* (or full payment of the penalty) of the law, either personally or by a substitute. Sinners could never personally pay the penalty of the broken law without perishing, but Christ has made a full payment for all His people. His satisfaction of God's justice (Rom. 3:25) perfectly vindicates God's law and justifies or frees from condemnation all His believing people. *(See Reatus Culpae, Poenae.)*

Guilty sinners are naturally and necessarily polluted (see Job 14:4; Jer. 17:9; Matt. 7:15-20; Rom. 8:5-8; Eph. 4:17-19).

Entrance of Sin

The origin of sin is an "inexplicable mystery" (A. A. Hodge). We can say that it originated in the angelic world and, after the satanic temptation of Eve, entered the human race. Genesis 3 records the history of the event and such passages as 2 Cor. 11:3 and 1 Tim. 2:14 show that the story is historical, not allegorical. Sin entered the world by the voluntary act of man, though how a will created positively holy could respond to wicked temptations is not clear. What we do know is that God is not the author of it (James 1:13).

Effects of Sin

The entrance of sin into the world had immediate and enduring effects. Generally, the result was death—physical, spiritual, and eternal (Rom. 6:23; 5:12), both for Adam and for his posterity.

Effect of Sin on Adam

The immediate effects of sin are apparent in Gen. 3: the shame of guilt (v. 7); separation from God (v. 8; Isa. 59:2; Eph. 4:18); and suffering and grief because of God's curse (vv.16-19).

The effect of sin on Adam's will was particularly ruinous. He replaced a godly disposition with a selfish, sinful one and so wrecked the original constitution of the will. From the moment of sin's entrance all his choices sprang from a depraved disposition.

Effects on Adam's Posterity

Adam's sin depraved and corrupted all his offspring, born of natural generation. This is true not only in the general sense that children often suffer as the result of their parents' sins, but in the specific sense that Adam is the natural root and legal representative of the race, and because of all men's union with him in his first transgression, God imputes or attributes the guilt of that sin to all. Rom. 5:12 says categorically (and the reference is to Adam's first transgression) "death passed upon all men for that all have sinned." We were "in Adam" when he sinned, and we sinned in him and fell with him in his first transgression. Both the guilt and the pollution were charged upon the entire race.

Pelagians deny the imputation of Adam's sin to his posterity, and Roman Catholic theology is severely tainted with Pelagianism* at this point. Arminianism* is semi-Pelagian, holding that the pollution or corruption of Adam's sin was inherited from him, but denying the judicial imputation of the guilt of his fall. But Romans 5:12 is explicit—punishment is laid upon all because of that first sin, proving that the guilt of the fall is indeed imputed.

The moral and spiritual effects on Adam's posterity of his fall into sin, then, are:

1. Original sin* or the absence of original righteousness and the corruption of the whole nature. This corruption is total depravity. "Total depravity means the entire absence of holiness, not the highest intensity of sin" (Shedd, *Dogmatic Theology,* 2:257. See Gen. 6:5; Jer. 17:9; Rom. 3:10-19; 8:7).

2. Actual transgressions as the result of Adam's fall (see James 1:14, 15; Eph. 2:2, 3; Matt. 15:19).

3. Everlasting punishment, the just sentence of God's law (Rom. 6:23; Ezek. 18:4). The full and final expression of this sentence is "the second death," or the lake of fire for evermore (Rev. 20:15). "Sin when it is finished bringeth forth death" (James 1:15).

Sin took man from Eden to destruction. It is the story of paradise lost. In the light of the terrible picture Scripture paints of sin we are driven from every hope of salvation by human merit to Him who is called "the last Adam," in whom we have the glorious gospel of paradise regained.

SINLESSNESS

See **Impeccability**; **Perfectionism**.

SMALCALD ARTICLES

The declaration of Protestant faith, in 28 folio pages, drawn up by Martin Luther in 1536 to highlight the irreconcilable differences with Romanism.

SOCIAL GOSPEL

The redefinition of the gospel by early 20th-century liberalism* in terms of social justice and the amelioration of societal conditions. It was rooted in the legitimate Christian concern for the poor but became much more. It became the message of those who thought they could create the kingdom of God* on earth by social action. It went hand in hand with a denial of the Bible as the word of God and of the central doctrines of the historic gospel. It especially believed in the perfectibility of man's nature and therefore was optimistic about the future of society. World War I and the Great Depression destroyed much of its optimism about man and society; however, its central ideas live on in the various liberation theologies* that abound today.

SOCINIANISM

The heretical system named after an Italian theologian, Faustus Socinus (1539-1604). Socinus denied the doctrine of the Trinity,* going further even than the ancient Arians by making Christ to be a mere man with no existence prior to His birth in Bethlehem. Socinus held to the doctrines of the virgin birth,* the sinlessness and the resurrection* of Christ, and taught that following His ascension all power was given to Him as God's viceroy over all creation. On account of this, Christ is called God and is a proper object of worship.

Socinus held that men owe their salvation to Christ as their prophet teaching them the truth; as their priest, interceding for them; and as their king, exercising His power for their protection and help. But he denied that Christ offered any atonement* or satisfaction* to God for sinners, advocating the example theory of the atonement.* He held that sinners are pardoned and accepted by God, through divine mercy, on the ground of their own repentance and reformation.

Socinus also denied the Scripture doctrines of the deity and personality of the Holy Spirit,* predestination,* original sin,* total inability, and endless punishment. Socinus made Cracow in Poland the centre of his labours and found great acceptance there. The Polish Brethren,* an Anabaptist group, were largely Socinian.

Socinianism became dominant in many circles in the English-speaking churches in the 18th century, and in 1774 the first Socinian church was formed in London (see **Unitarianism**).

Socinus was the forerunner of present-day liberals and modernists (see **Liberalism**), who, while repudiating his nobler views of Christ as virgin-born, sinless, and risen from the dead, have based their theology on his denial of the Biblical doctrine of Christ's person and work.

SON OF PERDITION

A title used twice in the NT, first of Judas Iscariot (John 17:12) and second of the coming antichrist (2 Thess. 2:3). The Greek *apoleia,* "perdition," means destruction, ruin, or loss. It does not indicate extinction of being but destruction of well-being and hence has the idea of perishing. *Son of perdition,* then, signifies the proper destiny of the one described.

SOPHERIM

A Hebrew word meaning "scribes"; it is used to describe those who arose under Ezra, the "ready scribe," and whose activities extended to A.D. 200. Their aim was to reproduce the pure standard text of the Hebrew Scripture. W. H. Green wrote: "It was their function, as they understood and expressed it, 'to put a hedge about the law,' i.e., to ascertain, defend, and perpetuate the true interpretation of Scripture, and to preserve it from any possible error in transmission" (*General Introduction to the Old Testament: The Text,* p. 146).

See **Textual Criticism of the Old Testament**.

SOTERIOLOGY

The doctrine of salvation;* the branch of systematic theology* that deals with the work of Christ the redeemer, and its application to the elect by the Holy Spirit. Soteriology, then, comprises the following subjects: the mediatorial offices of Christ (see **Mediator**; **Kingly Office**; **Priestly Office**; **Prophetic Office**); the atonement,* regeneration,* conversion,* justification,* adoption,* sanctification,* and the means of grace.*

SOUL

The NT usage of *psuche,* soul, is analysed by W. E. Vine (*Expository Dictionary of New Testament Words*) as follows:

Usage of the Term

"*Psuche* denotes the breath, the breath of life, then the soul, in its various meanings. The N.T. uses may be analysed approximately as follows:

1. The natural life of the body, Mt. 2:20; Luke 12:22; Acts 20:10; Rev. 8:9; 12:11; cp. Lev. 17:11; 2 Sam. 14:7; Esth. 8:11;
2. The immaterial, invisible part of man, Mt. 10:28; Acts 2:27; cp. 1 Kings 17:21;
3. The disembodied (or 'unclothed' or 'naked,' 2 Cor. 5:3, 4) man, Rev. 6:9;
4. The seat of personality, Luke 9:24, explained as = 'own self,' ver. 25; Heb. 6:19; 10:39; cp. Isa. 53:10 with 1 Tim. 2:6;
5. The seat of the sentient element in man, that by which he perceives, reflects, feels, desires, Mt. 11:29; Luke 1:46; 2:35; Acts 14:2, 22; cp. Ps. 84:2; 139:14; Isa. 26:9;
6. The seat of will and purpose, Mt. 22:37; Acts 4:32; Eph. 6:6; Phil. 1:27; Heb. 12:3; cp. Numb. 21:4; Deut. 11:13;
7. The seat of appetite, Rev. 18:14; cp. Ps. 107:9; Prov. 6:30; Isa. 5:14 ('desire'); 29:8;
8. Persons, individuals, Acts 2:41, 43; Rom. 2:9; Jas. 5:20; 1 Pet. 3:20; 2 Pet. 2:14; cp. Gen. 12:5; 14:21 ('persons'); Lev. 4:2 ('any one'); Ezek. 27:13; of dead bodies, Numb. 6:6, lit., 'dead soul'; and of animals. Lev. 24:18, lit., 'soul for soul';
9. The equivalent of the personal pronoun, used for emphasis and effect—first person, John 10:24 ('us'); Heb. 10:38; cp. Gen. 12:13; Numb. 23:10; Jude 16:30; Ps. 120:2 ('me'); second person, 2 Cor. 12:15; Heb. 13:17; Jas. 1:21; 1 Pet. 1:9; 2:25; cp. Lev. 17:11; 26:15; 1 Sam. 1:26; third person, 1 Pet. 4:19; 2 Pet. 2:8; cp. Ex. 30:12; Job 32:2, Heb. 'soul,' Septuagint 'self';
10. An animate creature, human, or other, 1 Cor. 15:45; Rev. 16:3; cp. Gen. 1:24; 2:7, 19;
11. 'The inward man,' the seat of the new life, Luke 21:19 (cp. Mt. 10:39); 1 Pet. 2:11; 3 John 2.

"With (10) compare *a-psuchos,* soulless, inanimate, 1 Cor. 14:7.

"With (6) compare *di-psuchos,* two-souled, Jas. 1:8; 4:8; *oligo-psuchos,* feeble-souled, 1 Thess. 5:14; *iso-psuchos,* like-souled, Phil. 2:20; *sum-psuchos,* joint-souled ('with one accord'), Phil. 2:2."

Origin of the Soul

There are three views of the origin of the soul: creationism;* pre-existence of souls;* and Traducianism.*

Faculties of the Soul

The faculties of the soul are comprehended under the understanding and the will.* In speaking of these faculties it is important not to consider the soul as composed of so many parts. It is one immaterial, indivisible agent, and its faculties are the capacity of this one agent to discharge various functions separately or concurrently. "Thus, it is not true, in fact, that the understanding reasons, and the heart feels and the conscience approves or condemns, and the will decides, as different members of the body work together, or as the different persons constituting a council deliberate and decide in mutual parts; but it is true that the one indivisible, rational, feeling, moral, self-determining soul reasons, feels, approves or condemns and decides" (A. A. Hodge).

Dichotomy or Trichotomy

The distinction between soul and spirit has long been disputed. Dichotomists hold that man is constituted of body and soul. Trichotomists hold to the tripartite nature of man—spirit, soul, and body. Dichotomists hold that the general tenor of Scripture supports their view. Trichotomists point particularly to 1 Thess. 5:23 and Heb. 4:12 to show support for their view. It appears that the argument is reduced to the meaning of the word *parts.* Trichotomists feel grave difficulties in making soul and spirit two separate substances, while dichotomists cannot avoid admitting the "distinction" between soul and spirit, and therefore speak of the spirit as "the animating principle," and the soul as "the animated result." This appears to be trichotomic in all but name.

A Dichotomist Argument. John Laidlow, a dichotomist, sets out the historical, Biblical development of the Hebrew words *ruach* (spirit) and *nephesh* (soul) and the meaning of their NT equivalents, *pneuma* (spirit) and *psuche* (soul) in his work *The Bible Doctrine of Man* (pp. 88, 89): "*Nephesh* is the subject or bearer of life. *Ruach* is the principle of life; so that in all the Old Testament references to the origin of living beings, we distinguish *Nephesh* as life constituted in the creature, from *Ruach,* as life bestowed by the Creator. The life indicated by both these terms is that of man and the lower animals alike. A 'living soul' is a living creature in general, or an animated being. It is used in Gen. 1:30 of every creature that has life, and in Gen. 2:7 to express the result, even in man, of the divine creative breath. So also *Ruach* and its kindred term *Neshamah* are used for the principle of life, in man and brute alike. It is the '*nishmath* of life' that makes man a living soul (Gen. 2:7). It is the '*Ruach* of life' that animates all the creatures who were threatened by the flood (6:17), and all those who entered into the ark (7:15). It is the '*Nishmath-ruach* of life' which denotes those who perished in the waters (7:22). These passages prove that no distinction is made in Genesis between the life principle in animals generally and in man. But, what is of more importance, they call attention to a usage which is practically uniform, of putting 'spirit' (*Ruach* or *Neshamah*) for the animating principle, and 'soul' or 'living soul' (*Nephesh hayyah*) for the animated result. This primary distinction of the two terms, when applied to physical life, has passed over from the Hebrew of the Old Testament to their Greek equivalents in the New Testament, and suggests a reason for their respective employment, even where the meaning goes beyond the merely physical. If *psuche* thus means the entire being as a constituted life, we see why it is used in such an expression as that of John 10:11, 'He giveth his life (*psuche,* not *zoe* nor *pneuma*) for the sheep.' If *pneuma* is the life principle bestowed by and belonging to God, we see its propriety in John 19:30, 'He gave up the ghost (*pneuma*).'"

A Trichotomist Response. Laidlow goes on to distinguish the use of these words when applied to the life of the mind as distinct from mere "physical life," and holds that when referred to the life of the mind, spirit and soul are synonymous. However, David W. Kerr (*Baker's Dictionary of Theology*) argues, "In the O.T. the functions of the soul and spirit sometimes coincide, especially where mental or emotional activities are considered. This is because the soul is the visible life through which the spirit expresses itself....Since the N.T. has a word for mind, which the Hebrew did not have, there are cognitive functions ascribed to the spirit in the O.T. which are not in the New."

In the unity of the human being there is obviously a diversity, and spirit and soul can be distinguished almost as cause and effect. There is no easy way in which to compartmentalize them, as Heb. 4:12 should remind us. Only God using His word can divide one from the other. One popular way of summarizing man is to view the body as world-consciousness, the soul as self-consciousness, and the spirit as God-consciousness. However, it is a shallow analysis, for can the body have any consciousness apart from the soul? Or the soul apart from the spirit?

The Immortality of the Soul

The immortality of the soul is clearly taught in Scripture. The following are plain OT evidences of the doctrine:

1. Its doctrine of *Sheol;**

2. Its warnings against consulting the dead or "familiar spirits" (people who purported to call up the spirits of the dead to give messages to inquirers on earth, Lev. 19:31; 20:27; Deut. 18:11; Isa. 8:19; 29:4);

3. Its teaching on the subject of the resurrection* (Job 19:23-27; Ps. 16:9-11; Isa. 26:19; Dan. 12:2);
4. Its testimony to the conscious bliss of believers after death (Ps. 16:9-11; 17:15; 73:23, 24, 26).

The NT is even clearer:
1. The souls of believers survive death (Matt. 10:28; Luke 23:43; John 11:25f; 14:3; 2 Cor. 5:1-8).
2. The souls of the wicked also survive death (Matt. 11:21-24; Luke 12:4-5; Rom. 2:5-11; 2 Cor. 5:10).
3. Believers enjoy blessedness after death (Matt. 13:43; 25:34; Rom. 2:7, 10; 1 Cor. 15:49; Phil. 3:21; 2 Tim. 4:8, etc.). "The immortality of believers is not a bare endless existence, but a rapturous life of bliss in communion with God and with Jesus Christ, the full fruition of the life that is implanted in the soul while still on earth" (Berkhof).
4. The wicked endure endless punishment and torment after death (Luke 12:4, 5; 16:19-31; Rev. 20:12-15). Christ's words "where the worm dieth not and the fire is not quenched" (Mark 9:43, 46, 48) can be understood to teach only continued, conscious suffering in the fires of hell. This endless punishment is called "losing the soul" (Mark 8:36), "perishing" (John 3:16), and the "second death" (Rev. 20:14), because though it is a conscious existence, it is not worthy of the name life, cut off eternally, as it is, from God and any exercise of His mercy.

SOUL SLEEP

The notion that the soul sleeps between death and the resurrection.* This theory was held by some Anabaptists* and is the teaching of modern-day Seventh Day Adventism.* It rests upon the assumption that the use of the term *sleep* in Scripture to describe death, means cessation of consciousness and is not used metaphorically of the dead body. The evidence that the metaphorical use (e.g., 1 Thess. 4:13) is what the Scripture intends is summarized by W. E. Vine in his *Expository*

Dictionary of New Testament Words:

"This metaphorical use of the word sleep is appropriate, because of the similarity in appearance between a sleeping body and a dead body; restfulness and peace normally characterize both. The object of the metaphor is to suggest that, as the sleeper does not cease to exist while his body sleeps, so the dead person continues to exist despite his absence from the region in which those who remain can communicate with him, and that, as sleep is known to be temporary, so the death of the body will be found to be....

"That the body alone is in view in this metaphor is evident, (a) from the derivation of the word *koimaomai,* from *keimai,* to lie down (cp. *anastasis,* resurrection, from *ana,* 'up,' and *histemi,* to cause to stand); cp. Is. 14:8, where for 'laid down,' the Septuagint has 'fallen asleep': (b) from the fact that in the N.T. the word resurrection is used of the body alone; (c) from Dan. 12:2, where the physically dead are described as 'them that sleep (Sept. *katheudo,* as at 1 Thes. 5:6) in the dust of the earth,' language inapplicable to the spiritual part of man; moreover, when the body returns whence it came, Gen. 3:19, the spirit returns to God who gave it, Eccles. 12:7.

"When the physical frame of the Christian (the earthly house of our tabernacle, 2 Cor. 5:1) is dissolved and returns to the dust, the spiritual part of his highly complex being, the seat of personality, departs to be with Christ, Phil. 1:23. And since that state in which the believer, absent from the body, is at home with the Lord, 2 Cor. 5:6-9, is described as 'very far better' than the present state of joy in communion with God and of happy activity in His service, everywhere reflected in Paul's writings, it is evident the word 'sleep,' where applied to the departed Christians, is not intended to convey the idea that the spirit is unconscious."

SOVEREIGNTY OF GOD
Definition of Sovereignty

The Bible presents to us the God who reigns, who is in control, and who is not bounded or limited by the dictates of His creatures, or by the circumstances of time. "Whatsoever the Lord pleased, that did He in heaven, and in earth, in the seas, and in all deep places" (Ps. 135:6). This perfect freedom is the essential element in God's sovereignty. His will is supreme and unfettered. "I am God, and there is none else; I am God, and there is none like me, declaring the end from the beginning, and from ancient times the things that are not yet done, saying, my counsel shall stand, and I will do all my pleasure.... I have purposed it, I will also do it" (Isa. 46:9-11).

This is the testimony of all Scripture. From Genesis to Revelation, God is presented as the supreme, almighty, and sovereign One. He is called, "the most high God, possessor of heaven and earth" (Gen. 14:19). His supreme will cannot be frustrated by any of His creatures, for we read, "He doeth according to his will in the army of heaven, and among the inhabitants of the earth: and none can stay his hand, or say unto him, What doest thou?" (Dan. 4:35).

The NT sums up these glorious statements with such descriptions of God as, "the only Potentate, the King of kings, and Lord of lords" (1 Tim. 6:15); "Alpha and Omega, the beginning and the ending...which is, and which was, and which is to come, the Almighty" (Rev. 1:8).

In these statements of God's sovereignty, we note the deliberate emphasis placed on God's will. God is a rational being, and His actions are the result of His free and voluntary decision. Thus, behind all the powerful acts of God in time lies His sovereign eternal purpose. In writing to the Ephesians, Paul speaks of God's "good pleasure which he hath purposed in himself" (Eph. 1:9), and of "the purpose of him who worketh all things after the counsel of his will" (1:11). This purpose is called His "eternal purpose which He purposed in Christ Jesus our Lord" (3:11), and it assures us that all things that come to pass fall within the plan of God.

The *Shorter Catechism* defines this purpose of God, using the term *decrees:* "The decrees of God are His eternal purpose according to the counsel of His will, whereby for His own glory, He hath foreordained whatsoever comes to pass" (Q. 7).

Characteristics of Sovereignty

The characteristics of this eternal and sovereign purpose are as follows:
1. It is *founded upon infinite wisdom.*
God works all things according to His all-wise counsel (Job 12:13; Eph. 1:11).
2. It is *eternal.*
It is expressly said to be eternal (Eph. 3:11; cf. Acts 15:18; Eph. 1:4; 2 Thess. 2:13; 2 Tim. 1:9).
3. It is *universal.*
It includes "whatsoever comes to pass" (see Ps. 135:6; Isa. 46:9-11; Dan. 4:35; Eph. 1: 9-11); *whatsoever* extends to the following:
    a. The good actions of men (Eph. 2:10).
    b. The wicked actions of men (Acts 2:23; 4:27, 28; Ps. 76:10; Prov. 16:4).
    c. So-called accidental events (Prov. 16:33).
    d. The means as well as the end (2 Thess. 2:13; Eph. 1:4; 1 Pet. 1:2).
    e. The time of every man's death (Job 14:5; Heb. 9:27; Rev. 1:18).
The case of Hezekiah (Isa. 38:1-5) is often cited as proof against this. But the statement of the prophet merely told Hezekiah the natural result of his illness. It was not a statement of God's purpose—that was given in verse 5, and it was perfectly fulfilled.
4. It is *unchangeable.*
There is no defect in God's planning, so it needs no alteration. No creature's action takes place outside of His control and purpose, so it cannot be upset by unforeseen circumstances. God Himself does not change, but remains faithful. Thus there is no possi-

bility of any alteration in His eternal purpose, a fact that is set forth in the Word for our comfort (Mal. 3:6; Num. 23:19; Job 23:13; Isa. 46:10).

Some object to this, pointing to those places in Scripture where God is said to have "repented." They insist that this indicates a change of mind or purpose. However, in Hosea 11:8, 9 we have God's own interpretation of His "repentings." He uses this very word to show that He is not a man (who is changeable), but God. The "repentings" of God are included in His eternal purpose. The change they describe is not in the mind of God but in the attitude or circumstances of His creatures, and consequently in His treatment of them. For example, when a sinner repents, God does not continue to deal with him as if he were still in sin. Thus, when God says that He repents, He uses the word figuratively to denote His attitude to a changed situation, a change which itself is included in the scope of His decree.

5. It is *absolute.*

That is, it is unconditional. It does not depend for its fulfilment upon anything which itself is not decreed. For example, God decreed to save sinners on the ground of the death of Christ. Now, Christ was killed by ungodly men who are justly held accountable for their crime, but nonetheless their sinful action was part of the "determinate counsel and foreknowledge of God" (Acts 2:23). Again, God decreed that through faith in Christ sinners would be saved. But faith is not a condition left for man to fulfil apart from God. Rather it is God's gift, decreed from all eternity (1 Pet. 1:1, 2).

Efficacious and Permissive Decrees

God's purpose is one and indivisible, but it comprehends two ways of effecting the thing decreed. The term *efficacious decree* is used to describe the divine purpose as it determines an event either by physical or natural causes (Job 28:26), or by the immediate operation of God upon the will* of His

creatures (Eph. 2:1; 2 Tim. 1:9; Eph. 2:10; 4:24). The term *permissive decree** is used of God's purpose in relation to sin. It renders the event certain, but not by the immediate action of the divine will upon the human (Acts 14:16; Ps. 106:15). The permissive decree, then, is a decree not to hinder the sinful self-determination* of the creature's will but to make it certain and to regulate and control its result.

Sovereignty and Creation

Why did God create? Was He obliged to? Had He no choice in the matter? Was there some lack in His own nature that could be fulfilled only by what He created? The answer to these questions will help us to a clear view of the sovereignty of God in creation.* To the last three questions above the answer is a resounding "No!" God did not have to create anything. It was His own free choice to create. His nature is absolutely perfect, lacking nothing, and cannot be made more perfect or happy by His creatures. Romans 9:5 describes God as "blessed forever," that is, eternally and perfectly blessed in Himself.

So, why did God create? The Bible gives the answer. In Rev. 4:11 we read, "Thou hast created all things, and for thy pleasure they are and were created." God's sovereign good pleasure is the sole reason for creation. We would do well to ponder again the words of Ps. 135:6: "Whatsoever the Lord pleased, that did he in heaven, and in earth, in the seas, and all deep places."

Not only is the good pleasure of God the cause for creation, it is also the purpose of it. In Rom. 11:36 we read: "For of him, and through him, and to him, are all things: to whom be glory for ever." Solomon put it succinctly: "The Lord hath made all things for Himself" (Prov. 16:4).

God has made differences in the glory of the heavenly bodies (1 Cor. 15:41); differences among the angels (1 Tim. 5:21); differences on the earth—differences in geography, climate, resources, animal life, and plants; and differences among men (1 Cor. 4:7). The reason and the purpose of such variety as God has created are to be found only in His sovereign good pleasure. He is sovereign and so it seemed good in His sight (Matt. 11:26).

Sovereignty and Providence

God is not only the creator, but the governor of all His creation (Ps. 103:19). He controls the elements, the winds and the waves obeying His voice (Luke 8:25). He brought the flood upon the earth in Noah's day (Gen. 6:17) and the plagues on Egypt in Moses' day (Exod. 9:23-26). He gives rain or drought (Amos 4:7), snow or ice (Ps. 147:15-18), heat or cold (Matt. 5:45; Ps. 147:17).

He Controls the Animal Creation. He brought the animals before Adam to be named (Gen. 2:19); He led those appointed to safety in the ark to enter it and thus escape the flood (Gen. 6:19, 20). It was at His command that the flies, the locusts, the lice, and the frogs plagued Egypt. At His word Balaam's ass spoke, Darius' lions were impotent against Daniel but devoured his enemies, ravens fed Elijah, two she-bears vindicated Elisha's honour, a great fish swallowed Jonah and later deposited him alive on dry land, and another fish of divine appointment carried a coin in its mouth to Peter to pay tribute for him and for his Master.

He Controls All Men, the Reprobate As Well As the Elect (Prov. 21:1; Jer. 10:23).

God Controls Both Angels and Demons. The angels of heaven do His pleasure (Ps. 103:20, 21). The demons of hell obey His voice (Mark 1:27), and Satan himself is subject to His control (Job 1:6-12; Matt. 4:11). Isaac Watts sang of this sovereignty:

There's not a sparrow or a worm,
But's found in His decrees,
He raises monarchs to their throne
And sinks them as He please.

Every Christian celebrates the same truth each time he prays as the Lord Jesus taught His people to pray, "Thine is the kingdom, and the power, and the glory" (Matt. 6:13), and each time he draws sweet consolation from the assurance of Rom. 8:28: "We know that all things work together for good to them that love God, to them who are the called according to his purpose." How can we know any such thing but by knowing that our God is sovereign and is in control?

Sovereignty and Salvation

God's Election* Is Sovereign. In Rom. 8:28 the words "the called according to his purpose" clearly indicate that God's sovereignty operates as really in salvation* as in providence.* "Salvation is of the Lord" (Jonah 2:9). God from all eternity chose a people for Himself (Rom. 8:28, 30; Eph. 1:4; Deut. 7:7, 8).

Christ's Atonement* Is Sovereign. Christ died, in fulfilment of the terms of the covenant of redemption,* as the surety* and substitute for those people whom He calls His "sheep," His "own," His "church," and "the men which thou gavest me" (John 10:15; 13:1; Eph. 5:25; John 17:6).

Christ's Intercession* Is Sovereign. Christ, as mediator and great High Priest, intercedes for all for whom He died (Isa. 53:12). He Himself stated expressly that He did not pray for the world, but only for those whom the Father had given Him out of the world (John 17:9).

Regeneration* Is Sovereign. The Holy Spirit regenerates these same people, applying to them the merits of Christ's mediation, and of His work we read, "The wind bloweth where it listeth [pleaseth]....so is every one that is born of the Spirit" (John 3:8).

Repentance and Faith* Are Sovereign Gifts. Repentance and faith are gifts of God (Acts 5:31; Eph. 2:8, 9; Phil. 1:29). Willingness to receive Christ is the inclination of a renewed will—i.e., a will upon which the regenerating Spirit has already wrought (Rom. 8:7; John 14:17; 1 Cor. 2:14).

Salvation is all of God, and all of grace.* He planned it; He purchased it; He applies it. He says, "Therefore hath he mercy on whom he will have mercy, and whom he will he hardeneth" (Rom. 9:18). God owes mercy to none, and He gives it to whom He will, for the glory of His own Name and in accordance with His own good pleasure.

Sovereignty and Human Responsibility

Many object to this Biblical truth on the ground that it destroys human responsibility. But does it? No! Man, as God's rational creature, is responsible for all his inclinations and actions. The Bible makes this clear, and sees no contradiction between this truth and that of divine sovereignty. However, we should remember that while man is responsible, he is not free. By the fall, he became a slave of sin and is unable to will spiritual good. He cannot alter the disposition of his will from its enmity against God, nor is there anything in him by nature that would even influence him in that direction. This is the plain Biblical doctrine of human inability.* But man's inability in no way lessens his responsibility, for that very inability is the direct result of his wilful and sinful condition.

How God controls and directs the self-determining acts of man's will, doing no violence to his constitution and maintaining him as a fully responsible moral agent, is not revealed in Scripture. The word of God tells us that He does it, and we rejoice to believe that it is so.

God rules. His eternal plan is being perfectly fulfilled. His counsel stands. The heathen may rage and the people imagine vain things; the rulers of earth may set themselves against our sovereign God, but He "sitteth in the heavens" (Ps. 2), doing His will in heaven, earth, and hell.

SPANISH INQUISITION

Baker's Pocket Dictionary of Religious Terms describes it thus: "Special investiga-tion (1478-1820) of heresy in Spain and Spanish America. Never completely approved by the papal office, and sometimes acting in defiance of the pope, it suppressed with unusual cruelty and severity heretics, Catholics who were believed insincere, and Protestants. Beginning with investigation of converted Jews and Moslems, it included even Ignatius of Loyola, Theresa of Avila, and several bishops in its suspicions. Among the objects of its wrath were freemasons, blasphemers, bigamists, homosexuals, married priests, mystics, Jansenists, humanists, philosophers, and writers of books which had not been approved. Under the notorious inquisitor Tomas de Torquemada probably two thousand victims were burned. Thirty thousand may have been killed during the whole Inquisition."

This estimate of the number of victims is too low. John B. Wilder (*The Shadow of Rome,* p. 87) reckoned that between 50,000,000 and 68,000,000 suffered under Rome's inquisition, with 300,000 being burned in Spain.

The statement that the Spanish Inquisition was "never completely approved by the papal office" is questionable. The inquisitors could not have carried on their campaign of cruel repression apart from the pope's authority, and he certainly sought to strengthen papal power by their efforts. The wider use of the Inquisition by the pope and by the congregation of the Holy Office indicates very clearly the official Romish attitude to the methods and aims of the Spanish Inquisitors.

SPECIAL GRACE

The sovereign operation of God's goodness within His elect, whereby He savingly applies to them the work of redemption accomplished for them by Christ (*see Internal Call*).

SPECIAL REVELATION

See Revelation.

SPIRATION

See **Procession of the Spirit.**

SPIRIT

Hebrew *ruach,* Greek *pneuma.* The origin of the human spirit is ascribed to God (Num. 16:22; Heb. 12:9). Man cannot retain his spirit (Eccles. 8:8; Ps. 104:29) which, at his death, returns to God who gave it (Eccles. 12:7). W. E. Vine, *Expository Dictionary of New Testament Words,* summarizes the NT use of *pneuma:*

"**1.** The wind, John 3:8 (where marg. is perhaps to be preferred); Heb. 1:7; cp. Amos 4:13, Sept.;

2. The breath, 2 Thess. 2:8; Rev. 11:11; 13:15; cp. Job 12:10, Sept.;

3. The immaterial, invisible part of man, Luke 8:55; Acts 7:59; 1 Cor. 5:5; James 2:26; cp. Eccles.. 12:7, Sept.;

4. The disembodied (or 'unclothed,' or 'naked,' 2 Cor. 5:3, 4) man, Luke 24:37, 39; Heb. 12:23; 1 Pet. 4:6;

5. The resurrection body, 1 Cor. 15:45 [It is better to see this as a reference to the aseity* of our Lord and His power to impart life]; 1 Tim. 3:16; 1 Pet. 3:18 [It is better to see this as a reference to the Holy Spirit];

6. The sentient element in man, that by which he perceives, reflects, feels, desires, Matt. 5:3; 26:41; Mark 2:8; Luke 1:47, 80; Acts 17:16; 20:22; 1 Cor. 2:11; 5:3, 4; 14:4, 15; 2 Cor. 7:1; cp. Gen. 26:35; Isa. 26:9; Ezek. 13:3; Dan. 7:15;

7. Purpose, aim, 2 Cor. 12:18; Phil. 1:27; Eph. 4:23; Rev. 19:10; cp. Ezra 1:5; Ps. 78:8; Dan. 5:12;

8. The equivalent of the personal pronoun, used for emphasis and effect; 1st person, 1 Cor. 16:18; cp. Gen 6:3; 2nd person, 2 Tim. 4:22; Philem. 25; cp. Ps. 139:7; 3rd person, 2 Cor. 7:13; cp. Isa. 40:13;

9. Character, Luke 1:17; Rom. 1:4 [In contrast to this, most commentators take *spirit* here to refer to Christ's divine nature]; cp. Num. 14:24;

10. Moral qualities and activities: bad, as of bondage, as of a slave, Rom. 8:15; cp. Isa. 61:3; stupor, Rom. 11:8; cp. Isa. 29:10; timidity, 2 Tim. 1:7; cp. Josh. 5:1; good, as of adoption, i.e., liberty as of a son, Rom. 8:15; cp. Ps. 51:12; [Calvin, Hodge, Haldane, etc., take the "spirit of adoption" to mean the Holy Spirit]; meekness, 1 Cor. 4:21; cp. Prov. 16:19; faith, 2 Cor. 4:13; quietness, 1 Pet. 3:4; cp. Prov. 14:29;

11. The Holy Spirit, e.g., Matt. 4:1; Luke 4:18;

12. 'The inward man' (an expression used only of the believer, Rom. 7:22; 2 Cor. 4:16; Eph. 3:16); the new life, Rom. 8:4-6, 10, 16; Heb. 12:9; cp. Ps. 51:10;

13. Unclean spirits, demons, Matt. 8:16; Luke 4:33; 1 Pet. 3:19; cp. 1 Sam. 18:10;

14. Angels, Heb. 1:14; cp. Acts 12:15;

15. Divine gift for service, 1 Cor. 14:12, 32;

16. By metonymy, those who claim to be depositories of these gifts, 2 Thess. 2:2; 1 John 1-3;

17. The significance, as contrasted with the form, of words, or of a rite, John 6:63; Rom. 2:29; 7:6; 2 Cor. 3:6;

18. A vision, Rev. 1:10; 4:2; 17:3; 21:10."

For the distinction between soul and spirit, *see* **Soul.**

SPIRITISM

The belief, and the system of doctrines based on the belief, that the spirits of the dead can communicate with the living through the office of a medium and that this communication is beneficial to the living, a source of helpful information from the superior spirit world. Spiritistic beliefs are of a pantheistic nature, with their assertion of Infinite Intelligence, of which the phenomena of nature are expressions. Spiritism denies the possibility of forgiveness, and identifies heaven and hell with the here and now. It is thoroughly anti-Biblical and anti-Christian. The Scripture injunctions against spiritism are clear: Exod. 22:18; Lev. 20:6; Deut. 18:11, 14, 15, 20; Isa. 8:19, 20, etc. The wrath of God is denounced on it and its devotees.

SPIRITUALITY OF GOD

Berkhof (*Systematic Theology,* pp. 65, 66) says: "The Bible does not give us a definition of God. The nearest approach to anything like it is found in the word of Christ to the Samaritan woman, 'God is Spirit,' John 4:24. This is at least a statement purporting to tell us in a single word what God is. The Lord does not merely say that God is a spirit but He is Spirit....

"By teaching the spirituality of God theology stresses the fact that God has a substantial Being all His own and distinct from the world, and that this substantial Being is immaterial, invisible, and without composition or extension. It includes the thought that all the essential qualities which belong to the perfect idea of Spirit are found in Him: that He is a self-conscious and self-determining Being. Since He is Spirit in the most absolute, and in the purest sense of the word, there is in Him no composition of parts. The idea of spirituality of necessity excludes the ascription of anything like corporeity to God, and thus condemns the fancies of some of the early Gnostics and medieval Mystics, and of all those sectarians of our own day who ascribe a body to God. It is true that the Bible speaks of the hands and feet, the eyes and ears, the mouth and nose of God, but in doing this it is speaking anthropomorphically or figuratively of Him who far transcends our human knowledge, and of whom we can only speak in a stammering fashion after the manner of men. By ascribing spirituality to God we also affirm that He has none of the properties belonging to matter, and that He cannot be discerned by the bodily senses. Paul speaks of Him as 'the King eternal, immortal, invisible' (1 Tim. 1:17), and again as 'the King of kings, and Lord of lords, who only hath immortality, dwelling in light unapproachable; whom no man hath seen, nor can see; to whom be honour and power eternal,' 1 Tim. 6:15, 16."

SPIRITUALITY OF THE LAW

"The law is spiritual" (Rom. 7:14). It does not command bare, external obedience. God desires truth in the inward parts (Ps. 51:6) and forbids sinful heart attitudes even though they may hide behind an outward compliance with the letter of the law. This is the meaning of Christ's teaching in Mt. 5:21-48. "Ye have heard it said...but I say unto you," is not to be construed as Christ enlarging the scope of the law. Rather He is showing the real force of the commandments, which the Pharisees proudly claimed to keep, but which in truth they broke. Thomas Watson in his work on the *Ten Commandments* lists the following rules of interpretation of the law of God, to emphasize its spirituality:

"*Rule 1*. The commands and prohibitions of the moral law reach the heart. (1) The commands of the moral law reach the heart. The commandments require not only outward actions, but inward affections; they require not only the outward act of obedience, but the inward affection of love. 'Thou shalt love the Lord thy God with all thine heart.' Deut. 6:5. (2) The threats and prohibitions of the moral law reach the heart. The law of God forbids not only the act of sin, but the desire and inclination; not only does it forbid adultery, but lusting (Mt. 5:28): not only stealing, but coveting (Rom. 7:7). 'Man's law binds the hands only, God's law binds the heart.'

"*Rule 2*. In the commandments there is a *synecdoche*, more is intended than is spoken. (1) Where any duty is commanded, the contrary sin is forbidden. When we are commanded to keep the Sabbath-day holy, we are forbidden to break the Sabbath. When we are commanded to live in a calling, 'Six days shalt thou labour,' we are forbidden to live idly, and out of a calling. (2) Where any sin is forbidden, the contrary duty is commanded. When we are forbidden to take God's name in vain, the contrary duty, that we should reverence his name, is commanded. 'That thou mayest fear this glorious and fearful name, the Lord thy God,' Deut. 28:58. Where we are forbidden to wrong our neighbour, there the contrary duty, that we should do him all the good we can, by vindicating his name and supplying his wants, is included.

"*Rule 3.* Where any sin is forbidden in the commandment, the occasion of it is also forbidden. Where murder is forbidden, envy and rash anger are forbidden, which may occasion it. Where adultery is forbidden, all that may lead to it is forbidden, as wanton glances of the eye, or coming into the company of a harlot. 'Come not nigh the door of her house,' Prov. 5:8. He who would be free from the plague, must not come near the infected house. Under the law the Nazarite was forbidden to drink wine; nor might he eat grapes of which the wine was made.

"*Rule 4.* Where one relation is named in the commandment, there another relation is included. Where the child is named, the father is included. Where the duty of children to parents is mentioned, the duty of parents to children is also included. Where the child is commanded to honour the parent, it is implied that the parent is also commanded to instruct, to love, and to provide for the child.

"*Rule 5.* Where greater sins are forbidden, lesser sins are also forbidden. Though no sin in its own nature is little, yet one may be comparatively less than another. Where idolatry is forbidden, superstition is forbidden, or bringing any innovation into God's worship, which he has not appointed. As the sons of Aaron were forbidden to worship an idol, so to sacrifice to God with strange fire, Lev. 10:1. Mixture in sacred things is like a dash in wine, which though it gives a colour, yet does but debase and adulterate it. It is highly provoking to God to bring any superstitious ceremony into his worship which He has not prescribed; it is to tax God's wisdom, as if He were not wise enough to appoint the manner how he will be served.

"*Rule 6.* The law of God is entire. The law is all connected. The first and second tables are knit together; piety to God, and equity to our neighbour. These two tables which God has joined together, must not be put asunder. Try a moral man by the duties of the first table, piety to God, and there you will find him negligent; try a hypocrite by the duties of the second table, equity to his neighbour, and there you will find him tardy. If he who is strict in the second table neglects the first, or he who is zealous in the first, neglects the second, his heart is not right with God. The Pharisees were the highest pretenders to keeping the first table with zeal and holiness; but Christ detects their hypocrisy: 'Ye have omitted judgment, mercy and faith,' Mt. 23:23. They were bad in the second table; they omitted judgment, or being just in their dealings; mercy in relieving the poor; and faith, or faithfulness in their promises and contracts with men. God wrote both the tables, and our obedience must set a seal to both.

"*Rule 7.* God's law forbids not only the acting of sin in our own persons, but being accessory to, or having any hand in, the sins of others."

STATES OF CHRIST

The word *state* refers to a person's position or standing, especially in relation to the law. It is distinct from a *condition,* which refers to a person's mode of existence, and is particularly dependent upon circumstances. For example, a criminal is found guilty and therefore is in a *state* of condemnation, which may lead to a *condition* of imprisonment or punishment of some kind. With reference to Christ, we speak of His state of humiliation* and exaltation.* Berkhof (*Systematic Theology,* p. 331) remarks:

"In theology the states of the Mediator are generally considered as including the resulting conditions. In fact, the different stages of the humiliation and of the exaltation, as usually stated, have a tendency to make the conditions stand out more prominently than the states. Yet the states are the most fundamental of the two and should be so considered. In the state of humiliation Christ was under the law, not only as a rule of life, but as the condition of the covenant of works, and even under the condemnation of the law; but in the state of exaltation He is free from the law, having met the condition of the covenant of works and having paid the penalty for sin."

STOICISM

The philosophy, originated about 300 years before Christ by Zeno, that virtue is the only worthwhile aim and that a virtuous man, by the use of right reason, can discover his proper place in the universe and achieve happiness whatever his circumstances. Stoicism was pantheistic, making all things, including God, to be "fragments of the divine force." It was also fatalistic, holding that all that happens does so from the internal necessity of the universal being. Happiness consisted in realizing the futility of opposing the inevitable and in recognizing one's proper place and submitting to it. Anything that would hinder such resignation, as passions, must be suppressed.

STRUCTURAL ANALYSIS

In theology,* a method of dealing with the text of Scripture that grew out of the theory of structuralism developed by some French linguistic philosophers. These philosophers held that language and narrative, especially of folk literature, reflect the deep structures that govern society.

Applied to the Bible, structuralism examines the language of the text to lay bare the structures that governed the thinking of the society that produced it. For the most part, structuralists will look on the events in the text as myth,* not historical steps in God's special revelation.* Some join the study of the structural patterns of the society that allegedly produced the Biblical text with

those of the society that receives it. They then compare the two to show the development of the myth from its inception to its modern interpretation.

SUBLAPSARIANISM
Infralapsarianism.*

SUBORDINATION

The idea that the three persons in the Godhead differ in rank, or even, as Origen taught, in essence. Orthodox theologians are usually careful not to go beyond the language of Scripture and so deny any superiority or inferiority of dignity, rank, or essence, or any posteriority in time, among the persons in the Trinity,* while holding to the Scripture statements regarding the eternal generation* of the Son and the procession* of the Spirit. They insist that the essence of God is indivisible and belongs equally to the several persons of the Trinity. Charles Hodge comments upon Calvin's argument:

"If the distinction between the Father and the Word be attentively considered, we shall say that the one is from the other. If, however, the essential quality of the Word be considered, in so far as He is one God with the Father, whatever can be said concerning God may also be applied to Him the Second Person in the glorious Trinity. Now, what is the meaning of the name Jehovah? What did that answer imply which was spoken to Moses? I AM THAT I AM. Paul makes Christ the author of this saying. This argument is conclusive. If Christ be Jehovah, and if the name Jehovah implies self-existence, then Christ is self-existent. In other words, self-existence and necessary existence, as well as omnipotence and all other divine attributes, belong to the divine essence common to all the persons of the Trinity, and therefore it is the Triune God who is self-existent, and not one person in distinction from the other persons. That is, self-existence is not to be predicated of the divine essence only, nor of the Father only, but of the Trinity, or of the Godhead as subsisting in three persons. And, therefore, as Calvin says, when the word of God is used indefinitely it means the Triune God, and not the Father in distinction from the Son and Spirit."

SUBSISTENCE

A technical word that indicates a personal mode of existence of the divine substance. Thus in the Godhead, there is but one substance but three subsistences. By a "personal mode of existence" is meant a mode or "form" (Phil. 2:6) of the divine essence characterized by certain personal distinctions.

See **Trinity**.

SUBSTANCE

Essence; in the study of the Biblical doctrine of the Trinity, it is used to denote the single, indivisible divine essence, as distinct from the three personal subsistences of the Father, Son, and Holy Spirit.

SUBSTITUTION

The penal sufferings of Christ in the place of His people, by virtue of which they are saved. The satisfaction* offered by Christ was not for Himself, but for others. In Matt. 20:28 and Mark 10:45 the preposition "for" is *anti* and indisputably means "instead of" (cf. *anti* as used in Matt. 2:22 "in the room of"; Matt. 5:38, "an eye for an eye"; Luke 11:11, "Will he for a fish give him a serpent?").

In most Scripture passages that speak of Christ's death "for" His people, the preposition *huper* is employed (cf. Luke 22:19, 20; John 6:51; 15:13; Rom. 5:6-8; 8:32; 2 Cor. 5:14, 15; Gal. 3:13; Eph. 5:2, 25; 1 Tim. 2:5, 6; Heb. 2:9; 1 Pet. 3:18). Like the English "for," it may mean "for the benefit of," or "instead of." In 2 Cor. 5:20, 21 *huper* certainly means "in place of" (cf. Philem. 13 and 2 Cor. 5:14). A comparison of 1 Tim. 2:5, 6 with Matt. 20:28 will show that Paul uses *huper* to convey the very same thought as Christ who used *anti*. In passages such as 1 Cor. 15:3, "Christ died for [*huper*] our sins," the idea of substitution must be admitted, as it makes no sense at all to say that Christ died for the benefit of our sins.

Christ's substitution for sinners is the highest exhibition of God's mercy. Shedd remarks: "So far as the penalty is concerned, retributive justice would be satisfied if the whole human race were punished forever. (The law as precept, however, would not be satisfied. This proves that endless punishment is not excessive punishment. It still leaves the sinner in debt. According to strict justice, the law could require from the lost an active as well as a passive obedience; perfect obedience in the present and future, as well as suffering the penalty for past disobedience.) And if there had been no attribute but retributive justice, this would have been the course that he would have taken.... He would not have allowed a substituted satisfaction of justice, and still less provided one. It is important to notice this fact, because it shows the senselessness of a common objection to the doctrine of vicarious atonement, namely that it is incompatible with mercy....The ready answer is, it is mercy to the criminal to permit the substitution of penalty, and still more to provide the substitute after the permission.... For, the vicarious atonement of Christ is the Sovereign and the Judge putting Himself in the place of the criminal" (*Dogmatic Theology,* 2:382, 383).

SUFFERINGS OF CHRIST

Berkhof gives a comprehensive statement of the subject (*Systematic Theology,* pp. 336-343).

"Several points should be stressed in connection with the sufferings of Christ.

> **a.** He suffered during His entire life. In view of the fact that Jesus began to speak of His coming sufferings towards the end of His life, we are often inclined to think that the final agonies constituted the whole of His sufferings.

Yet His whole life was a life of suffering. It was the servant-life of the Lord of Hosts, the life of the Sinless One in daily association with sinners, the life of the Holy One in a sin-cursed world. The way of obedience was for Him at the same time a way of suffering. He suffered from the repeated assaults of Satan, from the hatred and unbelief of His own people, and from the persecution of His enemies. Since He trod the wine-press alone, His loneliness must have been oppressive, and His sense of responsibility, crushing. His suffering was consecrated suffering, increasing in severity as He approached the end. The suffering that began in the incarnation finally reached its climax in the passio magna at the end of His life. Then all the wrath of God against sin bore down upon Him.

b. He suffered in body and soul. There has been a time when the attention was fixed too exclusively on the bodily sufferings of the Saviour. It was not the blind physical pain as such that constituted the essence of His suffering, but that pain accompanied with anguish of soul and with a mediatorial consciousness of the sin of humanity with which He was burdened. Later on it became customary to minimize the importance of the bodily sufferings, since it was felt that sin, being of a spiritual nature, could only be atoned for by purely spiritual sufferings. These one-sided views must be avoided. Both body and soul were affected by sin, and in both the punishment had to be borne. Moreover, the Bible clearly teaches that Christ suffered in both. He agonized in the garden, where His soul was 'exceeding sorrowful, even unto death,' and He was buffeted and scourged and crucified.

c. His sufferings resulted from various causes. In the last analysis all the sufferings of Christ resulted from the fact that He took the place of sinners vicariously. But we may distinguish several proximate causes, such as—(1) The fact that He who was the Lord of the universe had to occupy a menial position, even the position of a bond-servant or slave, and that He who had an inherent right to command was in duty bound to obey. (2) The fact that He who was pure and holy had to live in a sinful, polluted atmosphere, in daily association with sinners, and was constantly reminded of the greatness of the guilt with which He was burdened by the sins of His contemporaries. (3) His perfect awareness and clear anticipation, from the very beginning of His life, of the extreme sufferings that would, as it were, overwhelm Him in the end. He knew exactly what was coming, and the outlook was far from cheerful. (4) Finally, also the privations of life, the temptations of the devil, the hatred and rejection of the people, and the maltreatment and persecutions to which He was subjected.

d. His sufferings were unique. We sometimes speak of the 'ordinary' sufferings of Christ, when we think of those sufferings that resulted from the ordinary causes of misery in the world. But we should remember that these causes were far more numerous for the Saviour than they are for us. Moreover, even these common sufferings had an extraordinary character in His case, and were therefore unique. His capacity for suffering was commensurate with the ideal character of His humanity, with His ethical perfection, and with His sense of righteousness and holiness and veracity. No one could feel the poignancy of pain and grief and moral evil as Jesus could. But besides these more common sufferings there were also the sufferings caused by the fact that God caused our iniquities to come upon Him like a flood. The sufferings of the Saviour were not purely natural, but also the result of a positive deed of God, Isa. 53:6, 10. To the more special sufferings of the Saviour may also be reckoned the temptations in the desert, and the agonies of Gethsemane and Golgotha.

e. His sufferings in temptations. The temptations of Christ formed an integral part of His sufferings. They are temptations that are encountered in the pathway of suffering, Mt. 4:1-11 (and parallels); Luke 22:28; John 12:27; Heb. 4:15; 5:7, 8. His public ministry began with a period of temptation, and even after that time temptations were repeated at intervals right on into dark Gethsemane. It was only by entering into the very trials of men, into their temptations, that Jesus could become a truly sympathetic High Priest and attain to the heights of a proved and triumphant perfection, Heb. 4:15; 5:7-9. We may not detract from the reality of the temptations of Jesus as the last Adam, however difficult it may be to conceive of one who could not sin as being tempted."

"THE DEATH OF THE SAVIOUR. The sufferings of the Saviour finally culminated in His death. In connection with this the following points should be emphasized:

a. The extent of His death. It is but natural that, when we speak of the death of Christ in this connection, we have in mind first of all physical death, that is, the separation of body and soul. At the same time we should remember that this does not exhaust the idea of death as it is represented in Scripture. The Bible takes a synthetic view of death, and regards physical death

merely as one of its manifestations. Death is separation from God, but this separation can be viewed in two different ways. Man separates himself from God by sin, and death is the natural result, so that it can even be said that sin is death. But it was not in that way that Jesus became subject to death, since He had no personal sin. In this connection it should be borne in mind that death is not merely the natural consequence of sin, but above all the judicially imposed and inflicted punishment of sin. It is God's withdrawing Himself with the blessings of life and happiness from man and visiting man in wrath. It is from this judicial point of view that the death of Christ must be considered. God imposed the punishment of death upon the Mediator judicially, since the latter undertook voluntarily to pay the penalty for the sin of the human race. Since Christ assumed human nature with all its weaknesses, as it exists after the fall, and thus became like us in all things, sin only excepted, it follows that death worked in Him from the very beginning and manifested itself in many of the sufferings to which He was subject. He was a man of sorrows and acquainted with grief. The Heidelberg Catechism correctly says that 'all the time He lived on earth, but especially at the end of His life, He bore, in body and soul, the wrath of God against the sin of the whole human race.' These sufferings were followed by His death on the cross. But this was not all; He was subject not only to physical, but also to eternal death, though He bore this intensively and not extensively, when He agonized in the garden and when He cried out on the cross, 'My God, my God, why hast thou forsaken me?' In a short period of time He bore the infinite wrath against sin to the very end and came out victoriously. This was possible for Him only because of His exalted nature. At this point we should guard against misunderstanding, however. Eternal death in the case of Christ did not consist in an abrogation of the union of the Logos with the human nature, nor in the divine nature's being forsaken of God, nor in the withdrawal of the Father's divine love, or good pleasure from the person of the Mediator. The Logos remained united with the human nature even when the body was in the grave; the divine nature could not possibly be forsaken of God; and the person of the Mediator was and ever continued to be the object of divine favor. It revealed itself in the human consciousness of the Mediator as a feeling of God-forsakenness. This implies that the human nature for a moment missed the conscious comfort which it might derive from its union with the divine Logos, and the sense of divine love, and was painfully conscious of the fulness of the divine wrath which was bearing down upon it. Yet there was no despair, for even in the darkest hour, while He exclaims that He is forsaken, He directs His prayer to God.

b. The judicial character of His death. It was quite essential that Christ should die neither a natural nor an accidental death; and that He should not die by the hand of an assassin, but under a judicial sentence. He had to be counted with the transgressors, had to be condemned as a criminal. Moreover, it was providentially arranged by God that He should be tried and sentenced by a Roman judge. The Romans had a genius for law and justice, and represented the highest judicial power in the world. It might be ex-pected that a trial before a Roman judge would serve to bring out clearly the innocence of Jesus, which it did, so that it became perfectly clear that He was not condemned for any crime which He had committed. It was a testimony to the fact that, as the Lord says, 'He was cut off out of the land of the living for the transgression of my people, to whom the stroke was due.' And when the Roman judge nevertheless condemned the innocent, he, it is true, also condemned himself and human justice as he applied it, but at the same time imposed sentence on Jesus as the representative of the highest judicial power in the world, functioning by the grace of God and dispensing justice in God's name. The sentence of Pilate was also the sentence of God, though on entirely different grounds. It was significant too that Christ was not beheaded or stoned to death. Crucifixion was not a Jewish but a Roman form of punishment. It was accounted so infamous and ignominious that it might not be applied to Roman citizens, but only to the scum of mankind, to the meanest criminals and slaves. By dying that death, Jesus met the extreme demands of the law. At the same time He died an accursed death, and thus gave evidence of the fact that He became a curse for us, Deut. 21:23; Gal. 3:13.

"THE BURIAL OF THE SAVIOUR. It might seem that the death of Christ was the last stage of His humiliation, especially in view of one of the last words spoken on the cross, 'It is finished.' But that word in all probability refers to His active suffering, that is, the suffering in which He Himself took an active part. This was indeed finished when He died. It is clear that His burial also formed a part of His humiliation. Notice especially the following: (a) Man's returning to the dust from which he is taken, is represented in Scripture as part of the punishment of sin, Gen. 3:19. (b) Several statements of Scripture imply that the Saviour's abode in the grave was a humiliation. Ps. 16:10; Acts 2:27, 31; 13:34, 35. It was a descent into hades, in itself dismal and dreary, a place of corruption, though in it He was kept from corruption. (c) Burial is a going down, and therefore a humiliation. The burial of dead bodies was ordered by God to symbolize the humiliation of the sinner. (d) There is a certain agreement between the stages in the objective work of redemption and the order in the subjective application of the work of Christ. The Bible speaks of the sinner's being buried with Christ. Now this belongs to the putting off of the old man, and not to the putting on of the new, cf. Rom. 6:1-6. Consequently also the burial of Jesus forms a part of His humiliation. His burial, moreover, did not merely serve to prove that Jesus was really dead, but also to remove the terrors of the grave for the redeemed and to sanctify the grave for them."

See **Descent into Hell**.

SUFFRAGAN

In Episcopalianism, the title given to a bishop who assists a diocesan bishop. The word comes from the Latin *suffragor,* "to vote for," or "to support." When diocesan bishops join with archbishops and vote in council, they, too, are called *suffragans,* but this is a minor use of the term.

SUMMUM BONUM

Latin meaning "the highest good"; the supreme value in ethics* or theology.* Many have held the highest good to be the beatific vision, or full knowledge of God with accompanying joy, which awaits the saints in heaven* (1 Cor. 13:12; 1 John 3:2) but which some mystics have held to be possible while still on earth. To Reformed theologians, the *summum bonum* must always be the glory of God.

SUPEREROGATION

In Roman Catholic theology,* works of supererogation are works over and above what God commands. These are conceived as being meritorious in the sight of God, and indeed can avail for others. Thus Rome teaches the fiction of a great treasury of merit available to needy souls, provided by the excess obedience and righteousness of the saints who voluntarily did more than God commanded.

See **Merit**; **Penance**.

SUPERNATURALISM

In theology the acceptance of the special revelation (*see* **Revelation**) of God in the Bible, including all its record of His miraculous interventions in the course of history.

See **Miracle**.

SUPERSESSIONISM

The derogatory term, used especially by Jewish scholars and others involved in Jewish studies, to describe the Biblical belief that NT Christianity is the fulfilment and completed significance of OT teachings. Statements such as Christ's in John 14:6 or Peter's in Acts 4:12 would be labelled *supersessionist.* The term is a handy tool to stir up Jewish opposition to the gospel by teaching that Christianity supersedes Judaism. This carries the connotation of Christian triumphalism and of the removal of the religion of the OT. In fact, the NT speaks of the clearly temporary economy of the OT finding its full and final meaning and expression in Christ and His gospel. This, for example, is the great theme of the book of Hebrews.

SUPERSTITION

An irrational belief or practice, judged according to the standard of the word of God. The word comes from two Latin words, *super,* "above," and *stare,* "to stand." Any belief or practice that "stands above" God's revealed truth, whether it be the poor, foolish notion of a backward heathen or the learned speculation of a modernist or infidel scholar, is *superstition.*

SUPRALAPSARIANISM

See discussion under **Infralapsarianism.**

SURETY

Technically, documents that guarantee a contract. This idea of a guarantee is carried over into scriptural teaching. In Heb. 7:22 Christ is called our surety. It was in that capacity that He died for us, thus guaranteeing the salvation of those for whom He died. As our surety, Christ guaranteed a full legal satisfaction* for our sin, and our deliverance upon His payment of our debt. The *language and undertaking* of a surety (and nothing more, for this is not a *type* of Christ's suretyship) are clearly set out in Genesis 43:9 and 44:32, where Judah becomes surety for the safe return of Benjamin. "Let me bear the blame" (the words of Judah) would apply equally to Christ if one of those for whom He became surety should perish. Thus, the fact that Christ is our surety makes His people sure of heaven.*

SWEDENBORGIANISM

The teaching and movement of Emmanuel Swedenborg (1688-1772), a clairvoyant who adopted Sabellianism,* who rejected most of the Bible and particularly such doctrines as a literal resurrection,* salvation* by grace,* and the imputation* of Christ's righteousness. Swedenborg, undoubtedly a genius and a great scholar, claimed to have direct revelation from God. His system was one of autosoterism.* In 1745 he received a revelation about the New Jerusalem Church, by which title his followers were known. Swedenborg refused to read theology* in case he would be misled, but he claimed that spirits guided his hand while writing his own theological theories. His system is not Christian, but spiritistic. Swedenborgianism is now very

small though the occasional endorsement of some famous people helps the convention of the New Jerusalem gain respectability—e.g., Thomas Carlyle was influenced by Swedenborg's ideas and the famous Helen Keller was a Swedenborgian.

SYLLABUS OF ERRORS

Eighty allegedly heretical doctrines or practices denounced in the encyclical of Pope Pius IX in 1864. The errors are ranged under the headings of Modern Liberalism, Pantheism, Naturalism and Absolute Rationalism, Socialism, Communism, Secret Societies, Bible Societies, and Liberal Clerical Societies. In 1907 Pius X issued a syllabus of 65 heretical propositions. It is interesting to note that the papacy today is openly advocating many of the "errors" of a former allegedly infallible pope.

SYLLOGISM

Deductive, as opposed to inductive, reasoning. Formally, a syllogism is constructed of two premises, a major and a minor, containing a common term, which is absent from the conclusion; e.g., all men are sinners (major premise); I am a man (minor premise); therefore, I am a sinner (conclusion).

SYMBOL

In theology, the name given to a creed.* Thus, the *Westminster Standards** are the *symbols* of Presbyterianism.*

SYNCRETISM

From the Greek verb *sunkretizein,* "to combine"; the movement to unite, not merely the churches of Christendom, but all these with all other religions; the movement for a one-world religion.

See **Ecumenical Movement**; **World Council of Churches**.

SYNERGISM

From the Greek *sun,* "with," and *ergon,* "work." It means cooperation and is used to teach that man works together with God to effect his salvation. One particularly prevalent form of this notion is that in regeneration* the sinner cooperates with the Holy Spirit. Semi-Pelagians, teach that man indeed takes the first step and is then helped by divine grace. Arminians hold that while God makes the first move, He cannot complete the work of regeneration without the consent and cooperation of the sinner.

Reformed theology rejects all this and honours the Biblical doctrine that "salvation is of the Lord." Dead sinners (Eph. 2:1) cannot cooperate to produce regeneration any more than Lazarus could cooperate in his own resurrection. Any activity on his part was the result of the divine impartation of life, a proof of it, but in no way a contributory factor to it.

SYNOD

In Presbyterianism,* the church court midway between a presbytery and a general assembly. It is divided into three or more presbyteries. Where there is no general assembly, the synod becomes the highest court of the church.

In Roman Catholicism, a synod is any official meeting of the church at international, national, regional, or diocesan level.

SYNOD OF DORT

A council of leading European Calvinists that met from November 13, 1618, to May 9, 1619, to consider the points controverted by the followers of Arminius (*see* **Arminianism**). It was made up of pastors, elders, and theological professors from the churches in Holland and deputies from the churches of England, Scotland, Hesse, Bremen, the Palatinate, and Switzerland. All Reformed churches accepted the Cannons of the Synod of Dort "as a true, accurate and eminently authoritative exhibition of the Calvinistic system of Theology" (A. A. Hodge).

See *Five Points of Controversy*; *Calvinism*.

SYSTEMATIC THEOLOGY

Theology is the science of God; the formulation and exposition of the scriptural revelation* concerning God and His relations to His creatures. Today, it is frequently defined as the science of religion, dwelling mainly on man's worship* and relation to God. As a definition this is defective, because God, who should be the chief object and theme in all theological investigation, is included only by inference. The use of the word *science* is important in the definition of theology. "Science is profound and self-consistent knowledge" (Shedd). Systematic theology, or dogmatic theology as it is also called, is the systematic statement of doctrinal propositions formulated from the data afforded by God Himself in His own inspired word. It is thoroughly Biblical, or it ceases to be what it claims.

The true method, therefore, of systematic theology is theocentric (God-centred). It starts with God, making the Trinity its basis. All other methods are fractional and open to great abuse. Schleiermacher's consciousness theology, for example, is anthropocentric* (man-centred), as are most modern treatments of the subject. However, the only truly Christian and comprehensive method is to make the Trinity the starting point and the inspired revelation of Scripture the data.

Shedd rejects a Christological approach as fractional and not truly systematic, but theologians such as Witsius, Edwards, and Chalmers have employed it. There is no good reason why, accepting the basic premise that the Trinity is our starting point and Scripture our data, the Christological method should not be adopted. Our knowledge of God consists in a knowledge of Christ (2 Cor. 4:6). Apart from Him we cannot even read the revelation in nature aright. Thus the Trinity is not to be understood apart from Christ.

That makes the Christological method truly theological. Since all God's revelation and work culminate in, and are in order to,

His redemptive purpose, and since it is in this redemptive purpose that the glory of God is most fully revealed (cf. Eph. 3:10, 11), it is possible to view redemption as the great unifying principle in all theological study, with the eminent advantage that the purpose of God in redemption is kept before us at every step.

This is no mean advantage and may well serve to avoid the tendency of some theologians to abstract (and even idle) speculation. No part of divine revelation is meant to portray truth in the abstract. All special revelation is redemptive, and thus to read each part of it in the light of redemption is logical and, most important of all, scriptural. It could indeed be argued that a systematic approach to theology finds its highest expression in the Christological method, because it starts off with the open acknowledgement of the light of the complete Biblical revelation—and of course that complete revelation is aglow with the centrality of the Redeemer and His work.

T

TALMUD

A body of ancient Jewish literature consisting of two parts, the Mishnah and the Gemara. The *Mishnah,* "teaching," is the text of oral laws and traditions edited by Rabbi Judah Ha-Nasi (A.D. 135-220). The *Gemara,* "learning," is a commentary on the Mishnah by the Amoraim, the interpreters of the law, between the third and the sixth centuries. There are two versions of the Talmud, the Babylonian and the Palestinian, differing mainly in that the discussions in the *Gemara* are by Babylonian or Palestinian Amoraim respectively.

TARGUM

The translation into Aramaic of the Hebrew Scriptures, first orally (some hold that Neh. 8:8 refers to such oral translation) and later in written form. Some targums are literal translations, while others are interpretive expansions of the text, containing much illustrative material.

TELEOLOGY

The doctrine that behind all things there is a final cause, and that all developments occur according to design or purpose.

See **Arguments for God's Existence**; **Dysteleology**; **Theodicy**.

TEMPORAL POWER

The authority claimed by the pope over nations and their rulers. Assuming that he is the supreme moral leader of the world, the pope claims the right to direct all nations and his faithful followers in them. Historically, popes have not limited their exercise of temporal power to mere direction. They have often employed coercion, either in the form of spiritual censures *(see* **Interdict),** of deprivation of office, or of an attempt to subvert the allegiance of subjects to their rulers.

TEMPTABILITY OF CHRIST

The susceptibility of Christ to temptation.

Christ's impeccability* has often been denied (e.g., by Charles Hodge, *Systematic Theology,* 2:457) on the ground that a person who cannot sin cannot be tempted. Christ was tempted, and therefore, it is argued, He was capable of sin (though in fact He did not sin).

The argument is based on a fallacy. Christ was tempted, for as a true man, He was open to all forms of human temptation, both physical and mental, with the all-important reservation noted in Heb. 4:15, "yet without sin." The Greek *choris hamartias* means "without sin," or "apart from sin" (compare the use of *choris* in Heb. 7:20, 21; 9:18, 22). "Our Lord was not tempted by the sinful lusts of pride, ambition, envy, malice, hatred, anger, jealousy, avarice, gluttony, voluptuousness, drunkenness; in short, by evil desire or concupiscence of any kind" (Shedd, *Dogmatic Theology,* 2:343). The assaults upon Christ were real and powerful, through the channel of His human nature, but in Him there was no responsive evil inclination or concupiscence. As He said, "The prince of this world cometh, and hath nothing in me" (John 14:30).

The human nature of Christ was susceptible to temptation, and if left to itself, was peccable. But the human nature of Christ never had even a moment's existence apart from union with the eternal Logos who, as God, is omnipotent, intemptable, and impeccable. The union of the human and divine natures in Christ's theanthropic person* means that while by virtue of His human nature He was temptable, by virtue of His divine nature He was impeccable. The argument that temptability and impeccability are mutually exclusive, or that the temptations of an impeccable person are unreal, not only contradicts the Scripture's plain declarations about the person of Christ, but also runs counter to human experience. The following points are important:

"Temptability, and peccability may be in inverse proportion to each other" (Shedd, 2:338).

"There may be the very greatest degree of temptation, where there is no possibility at all of its succeeding" (2:339).

"As there may be the most violent attack upon a strategic point where there is an invincible power of resistance, so there may be the most extreme and powerful of temptations addressed to a person in whom there is absolute impeccability" (2:340).

"Neither let it be supposed that our Lord's temptations were slight, because they were sinless. An innocent temptation may be greater in its force than a sinful one. Christ was solicited by sinless temptation more strongly than any man ever was by sinful temptation. No drunkard, or sensualist was ever allured by vicious appetite so fiercely as Christ was by innocent appetite, when after the forty days 'he was an hungered.' For the stress of the appetite was supernaturally heightened in this instance. A natural appetite may be stronger, and more difficult to control, than an unnatural and vicious one. The craving of the glutton for artificial sauces, and highly seasoned food, is not so intense as the hunger of the traveller in the desert who is upon the brink of starvation" (2:340, 341).

While some question the reality of Christ's temptations, others misunderstand their nature and describe them in such terms as to make it appear that Christ had to struggle with the same sinful inward lusts that afflict us. Some of the statements in the book promoted by the Promise Keepers movement, *The Masculine Journey,* express this view. It is therefore vitally important to grasp the fulness of the Scripture's teaching on our Lord's temptations. Shedd's treatment of the subject is excellent:

"The reasons why Christ was tempted are the following:

1. The suffering involved in his temptations was a part of his humiliation and satisfaction for sin. A tempted being is, in so far, a sufferer. Hence we have reason to believe that no temptation is experienced in the heavenly world.

2. In submitting to temptation, Christ sets an example to his disciples, of constancy in obedience and resistance to evil. Believers are bidden to 'look unto Jesus, who for the joy that was set before him endured the cross, despising the shame,' and to 'consider him that endured such contradiction of sinners against himself lest they be wearied and faint in their minds,' Heb. 12:2, 3.

"The fact that Christ was almighty and victorious in His resistance, does not unfit Him to be an example for imitation to a weak and sorely tempted believer. Because our Lord overcame His temptations, it does not follow that His conflict and success was an easy one for Him. His victory cost Him tears and blood. 'His visage was so marred more than any man,' Isa. 53:11. There was 'the travail of his soul,' Isa. 52:14. In the struggle he cried, 'O my Father, if it be possible let this cup pass from me!' Matt. 26:39. Because an army is victorious, it by no means follows that the victory was a cheap one....

3. By this almighty and victorious resistance of temptation, Christ evinced His power to succour those that are tempted, and to carry them through all temptation. He showed that He is Lord and conqueror of Satan, and his kingdom. Col. 2:15, 'Having spoiled principalities and powers, he made a show of them openly, triumphing over them.' Ps. 2:2, 4,

'The kings of the earth set themselves against the Lord's anointed. He that sitteth in the heavens shall laugh; the Lord shall have them in derision.' 1 Cor. 15:25, 'He must reign till he hath put all enemies under his feet.' Heb. 2:10, 'It became him for whom are all things, to make the captain of their salvation perfect through sufferings.' The 'perfection' spoken of here is not sanctification from sin; but a suitable preparation and accomplishment for his mediatorial office and work by trial and grief, whereby he is able to sympathize with those that are tempted. Hence *teliosai* and not *hagiazein* is the word employed.

1. In the first place, then, the Redeemer of sinful men must be truly human, not weakly human; unfallen man, not fallen; the ideal man, not the actual [i.e., man as he should be, not as he is by the fall]; temptable not peccable. He must be truly human, in order to be assailable by temptation and thereby able to sympathize with every tempted man. In order to sympathize with a person, it is not necessary to have had exactly the same affliction that he has. It is only necessary to have been afflicted. A different kind of affliction may make a man all the more sympathetic. Because Christ was sinlessly tempted, he feels a deeper and more tender sympathy with sinfully tempted man, than he would had he been lustfully and viciously tempted. And this, for three reasons. (a) Lustful desire deadens the sensibility, and blunts the tenderness and delicacy of the nature. (b) There is much selfishness in the sympathy of vice with vice; of one drunkard with another. Misery loves company. But the sympathy of a benevolent temperate man for a drunkard is disinterested. (c) The strength and reality of sympathy are seen in the amount of self-sacrifice that one is willing to make for the miserable, rather than in the mere fact that one has felt precisely the same misery himself. Tested by this, Christ has infinitely more sympathy for man than any man has had,

or can have. 'Greater love hath no man than this, that a man lay down his life for his friends,' John 15:13. One man may know very vividly from personal experience how another man feels, and yet not be willing to undergo any suffering for him for the purpose of delivering him from suffering. Drunkards have a common feeling of misery, but they do not make sacrifices for one another. On the contrary, they 'bite and devour one another,' Gal. 5:15. Satan well knows from personal experience what remorse is, and how his fellow-angels suffer from remorse, but he has no disposition to help them at his own expense.

2. Secondly, the Redeemer of man must not be weakly and peccably human, because he must be 'mighty to save, travelling in the greatness of his strength,' Isa. 63:1. He must have power to overcome all temptation when it assails himself personally, in order that he may be able 'to succour them that are tempted' Heb. 2:18. Fallen and helpless man cannot trust himself to one who is himself liable to fall from God. The second Adam must be mightier to repel temptation than the first Adam. And certainly if good and evil were so proportioned to each other in Christ that they trembled in the balance, as they sometimes do in his disciples, no fallen man could go to him with confidence of victory over evil. After the cry, 'O wretched man that I am: who shall deliver me from the body of this death?' there would not be the exulting shout, 'I thank God through Jesus Christ our Lord.' If Christ could meet all the temptations that approached him through his innocent and sinless human nature, from the wiles of Satan, and from suffering positively inflicted by eternal justice upon the sinner's voluntary substitute; if Christ could meet this vast amount of temptation with only a feeble finite will not reinforced and strengthened by an infinite will; he would not be 'mighty to save,' nor would he 'travel in the greatness of his strength'" (*Dogmatic Theology,* 2:345-349).

TERRITORIAL CHURCH

The "theory of church government which assumes that the ruler of a country possesses, by virtue of his sovereignty, the right to govern the Church, if Protestant, which has been established within his realm" (McClintock and Strong). This theory asserted the right of a ruler to determine the creed of his subjects according to his personal beliefs, and had the effect of making citizenship practically synonymous with church membership. As a result, Europe boasts many "Christian" countries, whose citizens are nominally church members but are strangers to any real or saving knowledge of the gospel.

TESTAMENT

See Covenant.

TETRAGRAM OR TETRAGRAMMATON

The Hebrew name for *Jehovah,* translated LORD in the AV. (For a defence of *Jehovah* as the correct vocalization, *see* **Yahweh.**)

TEXTUAL CRITIC

A scholar whose expertise in the Biblical and related languages and in history equips him to examine the extant witnesses to the texts of the OT and NT, with a view to identifying and removing any errors that have been introduced into them either innocently by copyists' mistakes, or by design. Popularly the word *critic* is often equated with unbelief and a destructive purpose. However, though many critics display blatant unbelief, without the exercise of the discipline of the textual critic we would not have any current copies of the Hebrew or Greek texts of Scripture. The Jewish scribes—the Sopherim—were textual critics. Erasmus, Stephens, the Elzevirs, Beza, Burgon,* and Scrivener were textual critics just as surely as Tischendorf, Tregelles, Westcott and Hort, and modern scholars such as Metzger and Aland. That is not to say that their presuppositions and methodologies are equally

valid, but that the popular notion that there is something inherently evil in being a textual critic is unfounded.

A sterling example of the good that textual criticism may do is the work of Jose O'Callaghan, a Jesuit priest and one of the world's leading papyrologists, who in 1972, to the consternation of the world of liberal scholarship, identified a fragment from Qumran cave 7 as Mark 6:52, 53. He dated this fragment to at least A.D. 50-55. He went on to make eight other NT identifications among the fragments from Qumran 7, dating them between A.D. 50 and 70. (The passages are Mark 4:28; 6:48; 12:17; Acts 27:38; Rom. 5:11, 12; 1 Tim. 3:16; 4:1-3; 2 Pet. 1:15; James 1:23, 24—see *The First New Testament,* by David Estrada and William White, Jr., p. 138). Eminent supporters of the traditional NT text such as W. N. Pickering (*The Identity of the New Testament Text*) have hailed O'Callaghan's work. This is a case where the text critical studies of a scholar who is far from the theological positions of Bible believing-Protestants nevertheless have destroyed the foundations of the liberal characterization of the NT as the product of second-century editors.

Without the work of dedicated scholars who have given their lives to the study of the text of Scripture, we would have no way of benefitting from the MS copies of the word of God. The difficulties of penetrating the mysteries of the ancient scripts, to say nothing of those of the scribal habits of ancient copyists, demand a scholarly expertise that few possess. Some Hebrew letters are distinguished by only subtle differences. Consider the similarity in appearance of the letters ר and ד, ב and כ, ה and ח, ט and מ, ו and י, ם and ס, and ע and צ. This similarity placed great demands on ancient copyists and led to innocent errors. The presence of such unintentional copyist's errors, as well as abbreviations, and even some deliberate corruption of the text, makes the work of the textual scholar indispensable.

Ronald Cooke, an uncompromising Fundamental scholar, responding to those who see in every textual critic "the trail of the serpent," wrote, "I thank God for those who wrestled in ancient times to pass on the Scriptures in some version which has come down to us, no matter how feeble. I thank God for modern men who wrestled with a mountain of manuscripts to come to a good text, for most of us could not wrestle with even one manuscript to come to an understanding of it" (*Honesty and the KJV,* p. 75).

The presuppositions of each textual critic will govern his presentation of and conclusions from the empirical data. We must be aware of that and make a clear distinction between the data and the critic's use of it. However, modern textual critics have not created the data. Some people speak of, say, "the Westcott and Hort text" as if those two Cambridge scholars produced the text. Every reading they considered was ancient. Their choices in many cases were wrong and the reason for them (their presuppositions) unwarranted. But choices have to be made by all who study the ancient witnesses to the text of Scripture. Even within the traditional text MSS there are textual variations that can be settled only by careful textual criticism. Those who demand an uncritical acceptance of the Received Text* of the NT must face this. They have simply opted to live with the critical decisions of textual critics of the 16th and 17th centuries.

That those decisions were not set in stone is clear from the fact that the AV itself does not stick entirely to the Received Text. What is needed is not a blanket condemnation of textual critics, or a blind adherence to what we have become used to, but an objective method of handling the data of the Bible text that fully acknowledges the unique character of Scripture as the inspired word of God. If that is done, the traditional text of Scripture will stand vindicated as a faithful representation of the original. In those places about which some critics still raise questions a collation of the objective evidence will lead to a certain resolution. That is the limited but important area of labour of the textual critic.

TEXTUAL CRITICISM

The investigation of the text of the Old and New Testaments with the aim of setting forth the authentic readings of the autographs,* as against spurious readings which have found their way into some manuscripts *(see* **MSS),** either from copyists' errors, or by design. It is sometimes referred to as *lower criticism* as distinct from *higher criticism (see* **Criticism).**

There is a marked difference in the criticism of the OT and the NT. Whereas in the NT there is a vast array of MS witnesses to the original text, in the OT there is a relative scarcity of MS material by which to examine the purity of the Masoretic Text *(see* **Masora),** the Hebrew text that conservative scholars accept as a pure descendent of the original OT text.

The OT was written in Hebrew, except for three brief sections (Dan. 2:4-7:28; Ezra 4:8-6:18; and 7:12-26), one verse (Jer. 10:11), and one word (Gen. 31:47) which are in Aramaic. The NT was written in Greek, though its writers, with the possible exception of Luke, were all Jews. The choice of Greek, the international language, reflects not only the widespread dispersal of the Jews—and the gospel is "to the Jew first"—but the great missionary calling of the church to go into all the world with the gospel (Mark 16:15).

None of the original manuscripts, the autographs, of either Testament survives. The same is true of every ancient literary work. However, in the case of the Bible its divine author has providentially guaranteed that we possess the authentic text of the original writings through the preservation of a great many copies.

Hand-copied MSS are particularly liable to suffer from scribal errors, and even intentional alteration. Edward F. Hills (*The King James Version Defended*, p. 1) likens the damage to the text of ancient literary works to that which a ship's cargo is liable to suffer if transferred from vessel to vessel. This is a good picture. The cargo of words of any ancient MS was open to damage in the two ways already mentioned, by accident or by design. It is the task of textual criticism to locate and remove from our modern printed versions of the Hebrew and Greek texts—and hence from our translations made from those texts—the alterations that copyists introduced. In this work the large number of available MSS, or parts of MSS, especially in the NT, is of great help because when the MSS are examined and compared the errors of copyists or editors will become apparent.

Unintentional Errors

Anyone who has ever done much hand copying will readily appreciate that all copyists are prone to certain kinds of innocent mistakes.

Errors of Omission. Haplography: a letter, syllable, or word that is repeated in the text is copied only once. In Isa. 26:3, 4 the First Qumran Isaiah Scroll omits the verb "trust" at the end of verse 3. The Received Text rightly has the consonants *BTWH BTHW* ("he trusts, trust ye") but the scroll omits the first of these.

Homoeoteleuton (from the Greek, meaning "similar ending"): occurs when the copyist's eye skips from a word or words to the same or similar words further down the text, thus omitting what lies between. Codex A (the Alexandrian MS) omits 1 Corinthians 9:2 because the same four words end vv. 1 and 2. Evidently, the copyist, looking away from the MS from which he was copying to finish writing verse 1, turned his eye back and struck the second occurrence of the words *humeis este en kurio*, "you are in the Lord." Continuing from there he proceeded to verse 3.

Errors of Addition. Dittography: a copyist inserts twice what appeared only once in the original. In Ezekiel 48:16 the Masoretic text repeats the word *hamesh*, "five," to read "five five hundred," instead of simply "five hundred." In Acts 27:37 Codex B (the Vatican MS) repeats the letter *o,* giving the reading that there were "about seventy-six," instead of two hundred and seventy-six, people in the ship that carried Paul.

Errors of Transposition. Transposition of letters or words are to be expected in all copying.

Itacism: the interchange of vowels. A celebrated case of this is to be found in Revelation 1:5 where Christ is praised because he "washed us from our sins in His own blood." By copying *u* instead of *ou* some MSS changed the verb to "loosed," a change reflected in many modern translations.

Fission: divides one original word into two words in the copy. C. D. Ginsburg argued that Isa. 9:3 in the Masoretic text furnishes an example of this (*see **Textual Criticism of the Old Testament** for Ginsburg's treatment of this text).

Fusion is the opposite error of joining together two separate words in the original to form only one in the copy. Isaiah 3:15 provides a simple example. In the Masoretic text the letters *MLKM* appear as one word which means "their king." This makes no sense in the context but the Masoretes, followed by our AV, recognized that here there were originally two words *MaH LaKeM,* "What mean ye?" or, "What is the matter with you?" An important example of fusion was noted by Jerome when he translated the OT from Hebrew into Latin. In translating Lev. 16:8 he saw that the word *LaAZAZeL* was in fact two words *LaEZ AZAL,* meaning simply "for the goat of sending away." The AV has rightly followed this analysis of the words, with the translation "for the scapegoat." Some modern versions maintain the fused form of the Hebrew consonants and translate "for Azazel,"* making this a proper name which, according to some commentators, signifies the devil. By recognizing that we have a case of fusion in the text we avoid all the confusion that follows any attempt to understand *azazel* as a proper name.

Contracted and Abbreviated Forms. Some frequently used or very familiar words were copied in abbreviated form and at times later copyists misunderstood the contractions. In Rom. 12:11 the phrase "serving the Lord" reads "serving the time" in the Received Text. The word "Lord" was contracted to *KO* in the MSS and evidently a copyist mistook this for *KRO,* the contraction for *kairos,* "time." In 1 Cor. 12:13 we read of being made to "drink into one Spirit," which some MSS have as "into one drink." The contraction for *pneuma,* "Spirit" was *PMA* which someone copied as *POMA,* "drink."

These and other scribal inaccuracies are to be found in every MS copy of the books of the Bible. This need hardly surprise us. If a few hundred honest and faithful Christians were given the task of copying the Gospel of Luke, it is highly likely that they would all commit some errors. One may omit a line in 3:28 and make the verse read that Melchi was the son of Cosam, instead of the son of Addi. Another may insert a word twice, while someone else may misspell a word. However, it is inconceivable that all or most of our copyists could commit the same unintentional errors. Thus by checking their productions against each other the exact text of the original could be discovered. The same holds good for the MSS of the Bible. Unintentional copyist errors can be isolated by a comparison of the great mass of MSS.

Intentional Errors

Not all changes introduced into the Bible text in the course of copying were innocent or accidental. The Pentateuch was deliberately altered by the Samaritans for sectarian purposes. Some orthodox Jewish scribes also altered the text of Scripture for dogmatic reasons. In the NT also, deliberate falsifica-tion of the inspired text occurred *(see **Textual Criticism of the New Testament***; ***Textual Criticism of the Old Testament).***

Different Factors in Considering the OT and NT Text

A separate treatment of the Old and New Testaments is necessary, not only because they were written in different languages, but because very different factors and circumstances entered into the transmission of copies of their texts. Whereas in the case of the NT there is a vast abundance of MS material dating back to within a century or so of the original writing, in the case of the OT there are comparatively few MSS, most of which are of a late date. Despite such differences, we will find that the same basic approach to the question of establishing the authentic text holds good in both cases.

TEXTUAL CRITICISM OF THE NEW TESTAMENT

Given the length and complexity of this article, we will commence with a thesis—a brief statement of the position adopted—followed by a simple glossary of essential terms and an outlined plan of the study.

Thesis

God, who inspired the NT, has providentially preserved its text in the great number of ancient witnesses (MSS, etc.) still available. Over 90% of the NT text is beyond dispute, down to the smallest details. As for the remainder, some 85% of the MSS agree in presenting a common text. This common text is strongly corroborated by the witness of ancient versions and quotations from church fathers and is the authentic representation of the original text. Despite the variations in the ancient manuscripts, we may ascertain the authentic reading in every case by following the testimony of the overwhelming majority of the ancient witnesses. This objective approach will establish the traditional text of the NT as the authentic text.

Glossary

Codex. An ancient bound folio copy of MSS, somewhat resembling a modern book.

Conflation. The fusion of two or more variant readings to produce a new reading.

Conjectural Emendation. The practice of extreme eclecticists who believe that in cases where they judge that none of the NT MSS preserves the original reading, they may emend the text by supplying a reading they believe, or guess, would better suit the passage. Conjectural emendation, therefore, is a critic's "improvement" of the NT text by inserting what he thinks the inspired writer *should* have written, in preference to what, according to the MSS, he *did* write.

Derived Text. A Greek text or text-type produced by a process of editing older texts; therefore, a secondary text, not a primary witness to the original form of the text.

Eclecticism. The theory that a textual critic is free to choose among variant readings according to his assessment of their probability, based on his opinion of the history of the text and of which reading best suits the author's style. Ecclecticists often differ widely on their judgment on these matters.

Edition. A critical Greek text in printed form. The *Textus Receptus* is such an edition, as are the Westcott and Hort text, the United Bible Societies' text, and Hodges and Farstad's *Majority Text.*

Emendation. The correction of current editions of the Greek text by the adoption of what are claimed to be "better" readings, i.e., readings that more accurately reflect the original text.

Manuscript. A handwritten copy of the Greek text. The word is usually written in an abbreviated form: MS (manuscript, singular), MSS (manuscripts, plural). Manuscripts may be *uncial,* written in capital letters, or *miniscule,* written in smaller *cursive* script, the joined letters of a "running hand."

Received Text. The name translates the Latin *Textus Receptus,* which the Elzevirs used to describe their edition of the traditional text. It is closely identified with the editions of Erasmus, Stephens, and Beza.

Recension. An ancient critical revision of the Greek text. *Critical* here means that ancient scholars examined the available MSS and evaluated the claims of their variant readings to a place in the text.

Text-Type. A group of MSS that exhibit a common text.

Transcriptional Probability. According to eclecticists, the probable explanation of how variant readings came to exist. Eclecticists believe that the reading they deem *most* probable should be inserted in the NT text as the genuine reading.

Variant Reading. A variation in content or wording of a portion of the Greek text as exhibited by different MSS.

Version. A translation from the original language. The LXX* is a version of the OT. Similarly, the Peshitta,* Old Latin, and Coptic are NT versions, as are the AV, RV, RSV, NEB, NASB, and NIV.

Plan of the Article

The Ancient Evidence for the NT Text:
    Papyrus Fragments
    Old Uncials
    Miniscules
    Church Lectionaries
    Ancient Versions
    Patristic Citations

Ancient Text-Types:
    Critics suggest four text-types.
    The Alexandrian Text-Type
    The Western Text-Type
    The Caesarean Text-Type
    The Traditional Text (Byzantine, Majority)

While there are many variant readings among these text-types, the same fundamental text appears in every text-type.

Displacing the Traditional Text:
    Ever since the 17th century there had been some textual scholars who rejected

the TT as the authentic NT text, but in 1881 two Cambridge scholars, B. F. Westcott and F. J. A. Hort, replaced it with a critical text as the basis for the translation of the NT in the RV. Hort used the following lines of argument:

1. *The argument from genealogy:* the TT is an ancient official revision made at Antioch under Lucian. The great number of MSS are copies and copies of copies of this single edition. In this way Hort eliminated the strength of the witness of the majority MSS.

2. *The argument from age:* the TT is a late text not found in the earliest MSS or in the earliest quotations from the church fathers.

3. *The argument from conflation:* the TT joins readings from other texts to make one reading. It is therefore a derived and secondary text.

Hort Refuted

1. There was no Antiochan revision.

The dominance of the TT is the result, not of church authority, but of the ancient acceptance of its position as the pure representation of the original text.

2. The TT is not a late text.
- The charge of lateness.
- Evidence that the TT is not a late text.
- In dealing with MSS, "old" does not necessarily mean "pure"—evidence of early deliberate corruption of the text.
- Reason extant copies of the TT are not as old as those of the Alexandrian text.

3. The TT is not a derived and secondary text.
- The charge of conflation unprovable.
- Conflation chargeable against the Alexandrian and Western MSS.

A Plea for Consistency

Conservative scholars do not reject the Masoretic text of the OT (the TT of the OT), though the very same charges are made against it as are made against the TT of the NT. The OT text has come to us through an official revision, its MSS are of

late date, and some critics charge it with conflation. Despite all this, conservatives do not repudiate the Masoretic text. Why then do some of them reject the TT of the NT in the face of less substantial charges?

Establishing the NT Text

There are two ways of proceeding.

1. The *eclectic* method—the critic "chooses" the "best" reading.

2. The *objective* method—the strength of ancient evidence establishes the *true* reading.

Eclectic Method:

1. Five canons, or rules of criticism.

2. These canons are often unworkable.

3. Eclecticism leaves the pure text of God's word forever beyond our reach.

Objective Method:

Following the great majority of witnesses from throughout the ancient church will establish the TT as the authentic NT text. John Burgon, Dean of Chichester, proposed seven "notes of truth" by which to establish the true reading of a disputed text:

1. Antiquity.

2. Consent of witnesses.

3. Variety of evidence.

4. Respectability of witnesses.

5. Unbroken tradition.

6. Context, or the evidence of a manuscript's accuracy in the context of a disputed reading.

7. Internal evidence, or reasonableness. This refers to a very small number of places involving grammatical or geographical blunders, or other such impossibilities.

Does It Make Much Difference?

1. We must not *overstate* the importance of textual variations. The poorest Greek text that could be produced from the available MSS would not alter one doctrine of the faith.

2. However, we must not *understate* the importance of textual variations. Some weaken the NT's witness to certain doctrines. And eclecticism as a method of establishing the text has a very real effect on the doctrine of the inspiration and trustworthiness of Scripture.

Features of the Traditional Text

1. It differs from the Alexandrian text.

- Mark 16:9-20
- John 7:53-8:11
- 1 Tim. 3:16

2. It differs from the *Textus Receptus.*

- These differences are few and small.
- The most significant involve three full verses and over twenty parts of verses. The most obvious of these are Luke 17:26; Acts 8:37; 1 John 5:7; and Acts 9:5, 6.

Conclusion

The TT is preserved in the majority MSS of the Greek NT. The editions of the text produced during and after the Reformation, including the *Textus Receptus,* are representatives of the TT. Since the AV was translated from an edition of the TT, the charge that it was translated from "a few inferior manuscripts" is false. That charge is applicable only to such modern translations as are not based on the TT, e.g., the RV, RSV, NASB, NEB, GNB, and NIV.

Textual criticism of the NT is the scholarly examination of the MSS witnesses to the NT text, with a view to the identification and removal of errors that have been introduced into them during centuries of hand-copying, either innocently by copyists' errors or intentionally for dogmatic purposes (*see Textual Criticism*).

The Ancient Evidence for the NT Text

The NT books were probably written originally on papyrus scrolls (2 John 12; 3 John 13), none of which has survived. However, each scroll was copied, and each copy was used to produce further copies. This process was continued for some 1,400 years until the invention of printing, after which few hand copies were produced. In all, there are 5,338 Greek MSS or parts of MSS of the NT now known to be in existence. In addition, there are hundreds of copies of ancient translations and thousands

of quotations of the NT in the writings of the church fathers. So there is abundant evidence for the NT text.

Papyrus Fragments. All of these sources are of value in establishing the text of the original, though obviously the Greek MSS are of the greatest importance. Of these MSS the oldest are papyrus fragments of varying size representing every NT book except 2 Timothy. They date from the second to the eighth centuries A.D., with over fifty of them coming from the third and fourth centuries and are designated by numbers, P1-P88. They are written in capital letters, i.e., *uncial* script without separation of words.

Old Uncials. Also written in uncials are the old MSS from the fourth century onwards, which are written on vellum or parchment (i.e., prepared animal skins) instead of papyrus. That parchment was in use in apostolic and pre-apostolic times is clear from Paul's request in 2 Tim. 4:13, "Bring the books, but especially the parchments." However, the earliest MSS of the NT written on skins are from the 4th century, Codex Vaticanus (abbreviated as B) and Codex Sinaiticus (abbreviated as ℵ, Aleph). In all, there are 268 known uncials.

Miniscules. At the beginning of the ninth century, MSS began to be copied in miniscule script, i.e., a script of small letters in cursive style, or as we would say, in a running hand. The advantages of this style fairly quickly displaced the use of uncial script. These miniscules number 2,792.

Church Lectionaries. Many MSS (2,193) are in the form of church lectionaries dating from the sixth century. These are not written in regular sequence but are daily and weekly readings from the Gospels and Epistles. J. W. Burgon* explained their format:

"The Gospels always stand in the following order: St. John: St. Matthew: St. Luke: St. Mark. The lessons are brief—resembling the Epistles and Gospels in our Book of Common Prayer. They seem to me to fall into two classes: (a) Those which contain a lesson for every day in the year: (b) Those which only contain lessons for fixed Festivals and the Saturday-Sunday lessons" (*Causes of Corruption in the Traditional Text,* p. 68).

The practice of publicly reading the Scriptures in church services led to the multiplication of these lesson books. Thus throughout the ancient church the very words of Scripture were preserved. However, as we shall see, the practice of omitting passages that did not suit the purpose of a particular lesson became a source of some confusion about the actual wording of the NT text.

Ancient Versions. Ancient versions of the NT give evidence of the text from which they were translated. They include the Peshitta* (Syriac or Aramaic), Coptic, Armenian, Ethiopic and Latin translations. Their use in NT textual criticism is greater than that of the versions in OT criticism. The reason for this is simple: the much fuller MS support for the NT text falls into clear groups, or text-types, and it is of great value to trace the agreement of a version with a given text-type. In this way the transmission and geographical spread of the text-type can be historically established.

Patristic Citations. A similar role belongs to the quotations of the NT in the writings of the ancient fathers. These quotations are so numerous that a substantial portion of the entire text of the NT could be produced from them alone. The weakness of the witness of these citations is threefold.

First, it is a fragmentary witness, not continuous, and may be inconclusive, or missing altogether, just where we need a clear, unequivocal testimony.

Second, the fathers at times quoted loosely, or from memory, and therefore fail to give a clear witness to some disputed readings.

Third, their own works have been subject to generations of copying, with all the problems that involves.

However, despite these drawbacks, their citations from the NT have great value. J. W. Burgon, who catalogued over 86,000 patristic citations in sixteen folio volumes, showed their importance: "Every attesting Father is perceived to be a dated MS and an independent authority" (*Revision Revised,* p. 297).

Ancient Text-Types of NT MSS

Textual critics divide the MSS into three (or four, according to some) "families" or major text-types.

The Alexandrian Text. This includes the oldest extant MSS—e.g., P75 and P66 in the Gospels, P46 in Paul's epistles, P72 in Peter and Jude, Codex B, Codex ℵ (Aleph) and other MSS.

The Western Text. This is headed by Codex D and is undeniably ancient. Some of its peculiar readings are found in some of the Alexandrian MSS, as for example, in P66 (in John 6-7) and Codex Aleph (in John 1-8). However, the Western text is notoriously corrupt. According to Gordon D. Fee, it reflects at times "an uncontrolled, sometimes 'wild,' tradition of copying and translating" ("The Textual Criticism of the New Testament," in *Biblical Criticism: Historical, Literary and Textual,* p. 136). It adds significantly to the text of Scripture, making the text of Acts about ten percent longer than in all the other MSS. Despite this evident corruption, Codex D is held by some critics to have the original reading in some places where it stands alone among NT MSS.

The Caesarean Text. Some scholars claim that the Caesarean text is a separate text-type, but others hold that it is nothing more than a mixture of the other text-types.

The Traditional (Byzantine or Majority) Text (TT). The TT is the text found in 80-90% of all known MSS. For about 1,500 years it was the dominant and well-nigh universally accepted Greek text of the NT. With the rebirth of classical studies at the end of the medieval period, Desiderius Erasmus produced a printed edition of the

Greek NT based on this text. The TT was the basis for many subsequent editions. In 1550 Robert Stephens produced his third edition, which in due time became the text that the translators of the AV used along with Theodore Beza's edition of the Erasmus text. In 1633 Bonaventure and Abraham Elzevir produced an edition of the TT in the preface of which they wrote, "Therefore thou hast the text now received by all: in which we give nothing altered or corrupted." Consequently, this edition came to be known as the *Textus Receptus,* the "Received Text."

Agreement and Variant Readings. Fundamentally, all these text-types exhibit the same text. The variant readings affect only a small percentage of the text. Stewart Custer of Bob Jones University has noted, "In about 90% of the manuscripts' readings all the manuscripts are agreed. This is unquestionably the wording of the original text" (*The Truth About the King James Version Controversy,* p. 5).

It is also true that every fundamental doctrine can be clearly established from the 90% of the text which is beyond dispute. However, the following deviations from the text which historically has been received as the word of God are important. According to Burgon's notation, using the *Textus Receptus* as a standard of comparison:

Codex B omits at least 2,877 words; adds 536; substitutes 935; transposes 2,098; and modifies 1,132. A total of 7,578 differences.

Codex Aleph omits 3,455 words; adds 839; substitutes 1,114; transposes 2,299; and modifies 1,265. A total of 8,972 differences. The variations are far from being the same in both codices. The fact is that they disagree with each other as markedly as they do from the commonly received text.

Codex D omits 3,704 words; adds 2,213; substitutes 2,121; transposes 3,471; and modifies 1,772; giving a total of 13,281 variations from the standard text.

Thus, the extent and significance of textual variations, though limited, demand attention.

Displacing the Traditional Text

The *Textus Receptus* was received by all, or almost all. In the two centuries following the Elzevirs' work a number of scholars worked to reverse the acceptance of their edition. The names of John Mill, Richard Bentley, J. A. Bengel, J. J. Griesbach, J. M. A. Sholtz, Carl Lachmann, S. P. Tregelles, and Constantin Tischendorf are foremost in this effort. These critics took the position that in places the *Textus Receptus* did not preserve the authentic reading of the original and they proposed that the oldest extant MSS were more reliable.

Tregelles may be taken as a fair representative of the ideas of the opponents of the TT: "We are able to take the few documents…and safely discard…the $^{89}/_{90}$ [of all known MSS, i.e., the TT] or whatever else their numerical proportion may be."

However, all the efforts of such critics had little real effect in displacing the TT. That dubious honour belongs to two Cambridge scholars, B. F. Westcott and F. J. A. Hort. They collaborated to produce a new critical edition of the Greek text, though the theory which formed the rationale for their textual choices was Hort's.

When Hort approached the MSS of the NT he had to do something to remove the tremendous advantage which the TT had in the sheer weight of numbers of witnesses. Anybody knows that in a court of law, if eight out of ten witnesses agree on their version of an event, and there is no inherent impossibility in their story, and if the other two witnesses contradict each other, no sane jury will hesitate to accept the majority testimony. Hort knew that this was exactly the case with the MSS of the NT. What could he do to discredit the majority testimony? His answer had the genius of simplicity. He attacked the TT on three fronts:

The Argument from Genealogy. He claimed that the TT was the result of an official revision executed under Lucian in Antioch in the 4th century. The majority of MSS represent generations of copying this official edition of the text. If we could draw their family tree, they would all go back to that one officially edited MS. Thus, far from being a majority, the TT MSS are really a minority.

The Argument from Age. He claimed that the TT was a late text since it is not found in the oldest MSS and its distinctive readings are not found in the writings of the church fathers before the Council of Nicea (A.D. 325).

The Argument from Conflation. He claimed that the TT was a derived, or secondary, text because it evidenced a tendency to conflict—i.e., it combines different readings from other MSS into one reading—and because it reads more smoothly, a fact Hort took as evidence of the work of an editor.

On the strength of these arguments the TT was overthrown and today the minority text is the basis for almost all new Bible translations.

Hort Refuted

Hort was wrong on each of point of his analysis. Modern critics recognize this, at least to a certain extent, though they still retain his antipathy to the TT.

No Antiochan Revision. The notion of an official revision of the NT text in Antioch in the fourth century is manufactured history. There is not a shred of evidence to support Hort's idea. Indeed, it bears the marks of pure myth on its very surface. For example, one of the fathers whose writings evidence the TT is Athanasius, the great defender of trinitarianism against Arianism. Now Lucian, Hort's nominee as the producer of the supposed parent MS of the TT, was an avowed Arian. Does anyone seriously think that Athanasius would give up an older and better-attested text in favor of one produced by an Arian? The idea is ludicrous.

Modern critics have given up referring to a Lucianic revision. But they still speak of "the framers of the text" (B. M. Metzger, *A*

Textual Commentary on the Greek New Testament, p. xx) to indicate their belief that there was a *policy* of revision, if not a single authoritative revision. However, this shift gains nothing. A series of revisions must surely have left some historical trace. An official policy that led to the sudden and lasting dominance of the so-called Antiochan revision (critics like to call it "the Byzantine text") and the displacement of all other text-types could not fail to be noted in church history. But there is no historical evidence for any Antiochan revision. The reason is not difficult to find: There was no such revision. (Even if there had been, this would rather establish the TT than weaken its authority, for surely the leading scholars of the ancient church were in a better position to know which MSS were deviants than critics of the 19th and 20th centuries who have to work with only a portion of the evidence the earlier scholars had to work with.)

The removal of the Antiochan revision theory is fatal to any case against the TT. If the TT *is* a secondary, derived, and inferior text, how are we to explain its uniformity and its universal dominance from the 4th century onwards? Hort's answer was that it was promulgated by church authority. That answer has been shown to be historically untenable. Fee tries to find an answer by positing the authority of Chrysostom and by theorizing that copying of the Greek MSS almost died out outside the Greek church, so that the TT represents no more than the tradition of medieval Greek Orthodoxy (*Journal of the Evangelical Theological Society [JETS]* 21/1, March 1978, pp. 19-33).

Fee's answers are as empty as Hort's. It has been well established, even by scholars not at all friendly to the TT, that Chrysostom could not have been responsible for the establishment of the TT (see Kirsopp Lake, *The Text of the New Testament,* p. 53; Metzger, "The Lucianic Recension of the Greek Bible," in *Chapters in the History of the New Testament Textual Criticism,* pp. 21, 22). Nor is there historical proof of Fee's assertion about the disuse of MS copying in most of Christendom (see Zane C. Hodges, *JETS,* 21/2, June 1978, p. 150).

There is a simple answer to the question of the dominance of the TT: it represented the ancient text and was the pure descendant of the autographs. There is no answer to the establishment of the TT—no justice to the transmissional history of the text—unless the theory that it represents a late, inferior text is abandoned.

Hort's idea of *genealogy* has had to be dropped as comprehensively as his manufactured history of a *Lucianic revision.* It was on the basis of genealogy that Hort turned the majority into a minority. But now the whole notion of genealogy has had to be given up. Over a hundred years ago Burgon said of the majority MSS:

"Hardly any have been copies from any of the rest. On the contrary, they are discovered to differ among themselves in countless unimportant particulars; and ever here and there single copies exhibit idiosyncrasies which are altogether startling and extraordinary. There has therefore demonstrably been no collusion—no assimilation to an arbitrary standard, no wholesale fraud. It is certain that every one of them represents a MS., or a pedigree of MSS., older than itself" (*Traditional Text of the Holy Gospels,* pp. 46, 47).

Thirty years later, Alexander Souter was still answering this with the old Hort line: "The old unscientific method of textual criticism was to construct the text from the consensus of the majority of witnesses. What nineteen out of twenty witnesses read must be right against that which was read by the twentieth. This erroneous method of criticism is corrected by the application of the principles of genealogy of manuscripts" (*The Text and Canon of the New Testament,* p. 115). Alas for Souter! It was he who was being unscientific and false to history. It was Burgon who was precisely accurate, as Wilbur N. Pickering showed:

"Even Hort acknowledged the presumption inherent in superior number. 'A theoretical presumption indeed remains that a majority of extant documents is more likely to represent a majority of ancestral documents at each stage of transmission than vice versa.' The work of those who have done extensive collating of MSS has tended to confirm this presumption. Thus Lake, Blake, and New found only orphan children among the MSS they collated, and declared further that there were almost no siblings—each MS is an 'orphan child.' This means they are independent witnesses, at least in their own generation" (*The Identity of the New Testament Text,* pp. 130, 131).

We must note the force of these quotations. According to Souter, the only way to overthrow the testimony of the TT is by means of the theory of genealogy. Without that theory, we must construct the NT text on the consensus of the majority of the majority MSS. But the theory of genealogy is dead. In reality, there are no *families* in the MSS. The similarities of Codices B and Aleph have led to their being grouped in the so-called Alexandrian family of MSS. The resemblances cannot be denied, but they are not sufficient to establish genealogy. Of B and Aleph Burgon rightly noted: "It is in fact *easier to find two consecutive verses in which these two MSS differ the one from the other, than two consecutive verses in which they entirely agree*" (*Revision Revised,* p. 12; emphasis his).

The Western family, according to Sir Frederick Kenyon, "is not so much a text as a congeries of various readings, not descending from any one archetype, but possessing an infinitely complicated and intricate parentage" (*Handbook to the Textual Criticism of the New Testament,* p. 356).

As we have seen, the TT is not a family either. The study by Lake, Blake, and New, quoted by Pickering (p. 52), makes this statement about the majority MSS of the TT:

"There are cognate groups—families of distant cousins—but the manuscripts which we have are almost all orphan children without brothers or sisters. Taking this fact into consideration along with the negative result of our collation of MSS at Sinai, Patmos, and Jerusalem, it is hard to resist the conclusion that the scribes usually destroyed their exemplars when they had copied the sacred books" ("The Caesarean Text of the Gospel of Mark," *Harvard Theological Review*, 31 (1928):348, 349).

Now, if there are no families of texts, if in other words genealogy is a baseless fiction, why do textual critics still hold out against the TT? Fee gives a rare insight into the true attitude of minority text advocates: "It is surely dubious procedure to accept or reject a reading solely because it is found in a certain text-type; on the other hand, such groupings, especially of the later (Byzantine) MSS [i.e., the TT], greatly reduce the work of sifting a multiplicity of MSS" (*Biblical Criticism*, p. 138). So a nonexistent system of genealogy is built upon an insubstantial idea and is maintained so that a certain class of critics will not have to spend time and energy examining the vast storehouse of textual material in the TT MSS!

Summarizing, we may say that the attempt to deprive the TT MSS of their overwhelming advantage by making them all the offsprings of one fourth-century MS produced as the result of an official revision of the text at Antioch, is a failure. Each TT MS is an independent witness to the original text. As Jakob Van Bruggen puts it, the uniformity in the TT "rather points in the direction of a simultaneous turning-back in various centres to the same central point of the original text. This text was sought in the oldest and most faithful manuscripts, and people conformed to it after centuries of textual disintegration" (*The Ancient Text of the New Testament,* p. 21).

The TT Is Neither a Late Nor an Inferior Text

Jacob Geerlings has stated that the TT's "origins as well as those of the other so-called text-types probably go back to the autographs" (*Family E and Its Allies,* p. 1). Disregarding the impossible notion that both majority and minority texts go right back to the autographs we note that Geerlings' research led him to recognize that the TT's claim to antiquity was in no way inferior.

Despite the evidence to the contrary, statements like Custer's are common: "The Byzantine text originated in the middle of the fourth century" (Custer, p. 6). "The Byzantine text is later than the others and is a derived text" (p. 9). Custer argues that the earliest MS evidence for the majority text is from Codex W which is from the fourth or fifth century. Since some Alexandrian MS evidence dates from the second century, he concludes that the Alexandrian text has a two-century advantage over the TT. He continues,

"Some will say, 'But could not these Byzantine manuscripts be copied from earlier sources?' Yes, of course. But what is sauce for the goose is sauce for the gander as well. The Alexandrian manuscripts were also copied from earlier sources, which would put the evidence for them back into the first century! The plain truth of the matter is that the Alexandrian text has a two-century advantage over the Byzantine text in age" (Custer, pp. 9, 10).

This "plain truth" obviously escaped Jacob Geerlings whose studies led him to the conclusion that the TT went back to the autographs. Custer assumes that the papyrus fragments are entirely on the minority text side. They certainly have clear affinities with the minority text, but upon statistical analysis they also display a fairly strong support for TT readings (see Pickering, pp. 55, 56).

The argument of "sauce for the goose and sauce for the gander" misses the point. No sane defender of the TT denies the very early date of the Alexandrian MSS and the text behind them. Clearly both they and the TT can be traced right back to early times, but no Bible believer can hold that both go back to the autographs. One is a corruption of the other. The question is, which one? H. C. Hoskier conducted a monumental study of Codex B, the most important of the Alexandrian MSS, and concluded, "The maligned Textus Receptus served in large measure as the base which B tampered with and changed" (quoted by Pickering, p. 60). This conclusion explains why the TT was recognized universally in the church from the fourth century as the purest representation of the autographs and makes the Alexandrian, Western, and Caesarean texts corrupted offshoots which have been preserved in only a handful of MSS.

It is freely admitted that the available MSS of the TT are more recent than those of the minority text. But we must not forget what is evident in the study of the OT text, that old MSS are not necessarily better MSS, and that a young MS may exhibit a text that is both older and purer than that of older extant MSS. What is true of the OT is just as true of the NT. Two things support this contention: (a) the greatest deliberate corruption of the NT MSS occurred in the first two centuries; and (b) there are good reasons why the majority text does not have MSS and patristic citations as early as those of the minority text.

Deliberate corruption of the text. It comes as something of a shock to people who have become accustomed to hearing that we must return to the text of the "most ancient witnesses," to learn just how early men began to corrupt the NT text. Dionysius, Bishop of Corinth, wrote to Soter, Bishop of Rome (168-176 A.D.), complaining that certain "apostles of the devil" had "filled with tares" some of his writings, "cutting out some things and adding others." Then he added the much graver charge that some had also corrupted the Scriptures: "It is,

therefore, not to be wondered at if some have attempted to adulterate the Lord's writings also" (Eusebius, *Ecclesiastical History,* in *Nicene and Post-Nicene Fathers,* second series, 1:199, 200).

F. H. A. Scrivener, after reviewing the evidence of the church fathers, concluded, "The worst corruptions to which the New Testament has ever been subjected, originated within a hundred years after it was composed; that Irenaeus and the African Fathers and the whole Western, with a portion of the Syrian Church, used far inferior manuscripts to those employed by Stunica [the chief editor of the *Complutensian Polyglot,* the first printed edition of the NT, 1514], or Erasmus, or Stephen thirteen centuries later, when moulding the Textus Receptus" (*Introduction to the Criticism of the New Testament,* 2:264).

Burgon correctly discerned the hand of Satan in the early corruption of the NT text: "Vanquished by the Word incarnate, Satan next directed his subtle malice against the Word written....Hence the extraordinary fate which befell certain early transcripts of the Gospel. First, heretical assailants of Christianity,—then, orthodox defenders of the Truth,—lastly, and above all, self-constituted Critics....—such were the corrupting influences which were actively at work throughout the first hundred and fifty years after the death of St. John the Divine. Profane literature has never known anything approaching to it,—can show nothing at all like it" (*Revision Revised,* p. 334. See Burgon's *Causes of Corruption in the Traditional Text* for a full examination of the subject).

The evidence of the deliberate falsification of the text for dogmatic purposes is now generally accepted. Hort denied it, but his denial is rejected even by critics who have followed his lead in overthrowing the TT. The acknowledgment of deliberate corruption seriously compromises the usually accepted canons of criticism upon which eclecticism proceeds. The bare fact that the

Alexandrian MSS are the oldest we possess in no way guarantees that they represent the purest text.

Reason for the lateness of majority witnesses. The oldest MSS we now possess are of papyrus and are all from Egypt. The reason for this is simple. Only in a climate such as Egypt's could papyrus be preserved over a long period of time. The Dead Sea Scrolls found in the Judaean desert furnish another good example of the kind of environment necessary for such preservation. The early church did not have the benefit of such climatic conditions outside Egypt.

This is admitted even by opponents of the TT. Bruce Waltke speaks of "the relatively damp, hostile climate of Palestine in contrast to the dry climate of Egypt, so favourable to the preservation of these materials" (*Biblical Criticism: Historical, Literary, and Textual,* p. 48). Fee agrees: "Because papyrus is naturally perishable, few of the early copies have survived except in the dry sands of Egypt" (*Biblical Criticism,* p. 130). It is not to be wondered at that we do not possess very early MSS from areas where it was well nigh impossible for them to be preserved.

Another important factor must be kept in mind. We are told that the fathers from the ante-Nicene period do not quote the TT, from which it is inferred that before the Council of Nicea they did not know of it. Van Bruggen deals with Hort's use of this argument:

"The value of Hort's argument is limited even more drastically when he has to admit that we only have clear patristic material from the period 175-250 A.D. It surely did not escape Hort that two of the Greek Fathers in this period mentioned by him (Ireneaus and Hippolytus) lived in the West. The other two (Clement of Alexandria and Origen) come from Egypt. This means that we are left with a blank spot on the map: what would the text of the Church Fathers from Antioch have looked like in this period? We do not know. That we encounter text-usage which is not clearly Byzantine [i.e., TT] in the writings that have been preserved for us is not surprising. These Church writers used the texts that were current. The form of their text is not necessarily better. ...The pressing question is whether they lived at a time and in a region in which the textual tradition was at its best, or in a time and region in which this tradition was disturbed by all sorts of influences in the 2nd century" (*Ancient Text,* p. 22, 23. We should note, however, Hoskier's contention that Hippolytus's verbatim quotations from 1 Thess. 4:13-17 and 2 Thess. 2:1-12, which predate both B and Aleph by a hundred years, are "found generally on the side of the 'later' MSS," quoted by Pickering, p. 65).

Van Bruggen's point is significant. We have no very early evidence from the Eastern fathers. As soon as their witness becomes available it supports the TT. That the text was the current text in the East in earlier times must be gathered from the fact that in the earliest available Eastern witnesses (the beginning of the fourth century) it is already the unquestionably accepted text.

Clearly, what we have in the oldest MSS and patristic citations is an Egyptian text. There is no reason to doubt that the text used in Antioch in the very earliest times, were it available, would be that to which the Greek fathers whose writings we possess all bear witness. As Van Bruggen has pointed out, the question is whether Egypt in the second and third centuries was a place in which the textual tradition was maintained at its purest.

Our contention is that it was not. Rather it was a place where the text was corrupted on a significant scale. The papyrus discoveries indicate that there were various text-types current in ancient Egypt. They also show that some of the readings of the TT, rejected by modern criticism because of their absence from Codices B, Aleph, and D, are really genuinely original readings. Eclecticist

Gunther Zuntz admitted, "A number of Byzantine readings, most of them genuine, which previously were discarded as 'late,' are anticipated by P46. Our inquiry has confirmed what was anyhow probably clear enough: the Byzantines did not hit upon their readings by conjecture or independent error. They reproduced an older tradition" (*The Text of the Epistles. A Disquisition upon the Corpus Paulinum*, p. 55).

All this indicates that Egypt was a melting pot for all sorts of textual variants. No original MS of Scripture was addressed to anyone in Egypt. The MSS copied there were made from copies produced in places unknown and under circumstances unknown. There is evidence of their contamination by heretical (and by mistaken orthodox) emenders. All this was exacerbated by the practice of the two greatest Alexandrian scholars of the period, Clement and his pupil and successor, Origen.

Burgon stated, "The mischief done by Origen in this department...is not to be told" (*Revision Revised,* p. 292). Benjamin Wilkinson said: "When we come to Origen, we come to the name of him who did the most to create and give direction to the forces of apostasy down through the centuries.... Origen's corrupted manuscripts of the Scriptures are well arranged and balanced with subtlety" ("Our Authorised Bible Vindicated," *Which Bible,* p. 192).

Summarizing, we note (1) that the TT cannot justly be termed a late text; (2) young MSS can, and in this case demonstrably do, contain an old text; (3) reliance on old Alexandrian MSS is misplaced because they represent only a local Egyptian text, with no witness from the Eastern churches to whom much of the NT was originally directed; (4) such reliance is not only misplaced, but it also ignores the fact of wilful corruption of the text in Egypt; (5) the absence of the TT (as a text-type, as distinct from individual readings) from ancient Egypt provides no reason to deny its

acceptance in the primitive Eastern church. Thus, the second of Hort's three lines of argument is as empty as his first. The same is true of his third line of attack.

The Majority Text Is Not a Derived Text

Custer put the case against the TT succinctly: "It is also clear that the Byzantine text is a derived text. It obviously incorporates into itself the earlier readings found in both the Alexandrian and Western texts.... A clear example of the derived nature of the Byzantine text [the TT] is found in Luke 24:53 in which the disciples are described as being in the temple 'praising and blessing God' (E VIII century, etc.). The Alexandrian text has the reading 'blessing God' (P75 II-III century, etc.). The Western text has the reading 'praising God' (D V-VI century, etc.). The Byzantine text simply put both readings together rather than omit one reading" (Custer, p. 10).

This is a plain and persuasive statement based on Hort's notion of conflation. Two questions arise. Does the TT conflate the other two text-types, as claimed? If it does, is this sufficient ground to brand the entire text late and derived?

After thirty years of investigation, Westcott and Hort produced the grand total of *eight* instances of alleged conflation. In every case there is good reason to believe that the Western and Alexandrian texts were guilty of omissions and that the TT retained the full original reading. It has often been claimed that Hort could have cited more examples had he wished. Why did he not do so? In over a hundred years since Hort, critics have been able to find only a very few other places which they can with any semblance of probability term conflations. The scarcity of the examples calls for another explanation.

When it is recognized that each of the minority text MSS shows a large number of omissions from the TT, is it much wonder that in a handful of places they should remove different phrases from the same verse? In Custer's example the Alexandrian editors deemed "praising" to be superfluous and omitted it, while their Western counterparts chose to excise "blessing." This is a far more probable answer than the Hortian dream of conflations.

Scrivener, a contemporary of Westcott and Hort and possibly the leading textual authority of his day, says of Luke 24:53: "The assumption of course is that the Syrian [TT] reading is a *conflation* of those of the other two classes, so forming a full but not overburdened clause. But if this *praejudicium* [prejudice] be met with the plea that D and the Latins [the Western text] perpetually, B and its allies [the Alexandrian text] very often, seek to abridge the sacred original, it would be hard to demonstrate that the latter explanation is more improbable than the former" (*Introduction,* 2:293).

The appeal to conflate readings can never rise above the level of a prejudice. Let that be carefully noted. "Dr. Hort's other examples of conflation have the same double edge as Luke 24:53....they prove nothing to anyone who has not made up his mind beforehand as to what the reading ought to be" (Scrivener, 2:293). Such is the weight of proof from conflate readings. Opponents of the TT have no legitimate reason for their complacent dismissal of that text as "derived" and, therefore, secondary.

But suppose there *were* instances of conflation in the TT. Would that fact justify stigmatizing the *entire* text as derived and secondary? Certainly not. Here the followers of Hort are not consistent, for the text which they so strongly advocate has its own signs of conflation! Yet they do not on that account stigmatize it as derived and secondary.

Pickering lists some conflations in the Western and Alexandrian MSS. "There is another consideration which is fatal to Hort's purpose. He claimed that inversions

do not exist; but they do. He himself cited one of each kind; D conflates in John 5:37 and B conflates in Col. 1:12 and 2 Thess. 3:4. Further, in Matt. 4:13, John 5:37, and Acts 10:48 the 'Western' text conflates the 'Syrian' [TT] and 'Neutral' [Alexandrian] readings. Codex B has other conflations—Mark 1:28, 1:40; John 7:39. Codex Sinaiticus has conflations—John 13:24; Rev. 6:1, 2, 5, 7, 8 and in Rev. 17:4 a conflation of the two main cursive bodies for that book! The 'Neutral' text conflates in Luke 10:42. P46 and a conflate B and the 'Byzantine' text in 1 Cor. 7:34!" (Pickering, p. 60).

In view of these examples, those who hold that conflation in the TT invalidates the entire text should reject both the Western and Alexandrian texts as well. Most critics are not willing to go that far; they inconsistently reject the TT and hold on to the minority text.

Refutation of Hort's main arguments shows that the majority text was displaced without any good reason. Since these arguments were first advanced there have been no new objective grounds discovered by textual critics for the rejection of the TT. There are, in fact, no good reasons to depart from that text.

A Plea for Consistency

Bible believers are divided over what is the best NT text. We have quoted Stewart Custer, a godly Fundamentalist scholar, in favor of the Alexandrian text. Great defenders of the faith like B. B. Warfield and J. Gresham Machen took the same view. Equally great men of God have taken the opposite position, men like Burgon, Scrivener, Hoskier, and Dabney.

It does no good for God's people to engage in bitter controversy with each other over this issue and to vilify one another in terms that are far from becoming to the gospel of Christ. What is needed is honest discussion of the issue. In that discussion we should aim for consistency. Every charge that is made against the TT of the NT in rejecting its claim to be the standard text, is also made against the Masoretic Text (MT). *(See Textual Criticism of the Old Testament.)*

1. Do some Bible believers reject the TT of the NT because it is said to be an official revision of the earlier text? The MT is an official revision of the Hebrew text—but no Bible believer would on that account reject it. So why reject the majority NT text on that ground?

2. Do some reject the TT of the NT because its extant MSS are all late? Do they hold that only by the use of the oldest available MSS can we arrive at a pure text? Then why do they not apply this equally to the MT? The absence (until very recently) of MSS support for the MT older than the 10th century A.D. led no sober critic of the days before the discovery of the Dead Sea Scrolls to reject the MT in favor of the text of the LXX or the Samaritan Pentateuch. Why then, should the overwhelming majority of available NT MSS stretching right back to the fourth century be so dogmatically dismissed?

3. Are conflate readings the reason for repudiating the NT TT? Then why not for the same reason reject the MT, against which the same charge has been made?

If the MT, the TT of the OT, is accepted as standard, why do conservative scholars not follow parity of reasoning in dealing with the NT text? It appears that in practice Bible believers who reject the TT of the NT follow two very distinct methodologies of criticism in respect of the Old and New Testaments. If their canons of NT criticism prove false and misleading when applied to the OT, is it not obvious that their basic textual approach is wrong?

Amazingly, J. H. Skilton of Westminster Theological Seminary, stating that the same principles of criticism are valid in both Testaments, followed the Masoretic text as the standard text of the OT, and accepted Hort's arguments for the inferiority of the TT of the NT (see "The Transmission of the Scriptures" in *The Infallible Word,* p. 193). A consistent approach is urgently needed in establishing the texts of both Testaments.

Establishing the New Testament Text

Basically there are only two ways to go about establishing the text of the NT:

1. The eclectic method of opponents of the TT in which the critic "chooses" the "best" reading.

2. The objective method in which the weight of ancient evidence establishes the *true* reading.

The Eclectic Method. This method leaves the critic free to apply arbitrary canons of criticism and then choose the reading he judges to be best. Employing the same canons, critics may arrive at very different conclusions, for eclecticism is, at bottom, deeply subjective. The canons that the critics have adopted are arbitrary, frequently untenable, and in practice often cancel each other out—thus making even more room for the full use of the critics' subjective judgments. Eclectic criticism normally proceeds upon these basic principles:

1. The briefer reading is to be preferred.

2. The more difficult reading is also preferable.

3. The reading that best suits the context is preferable.

4. The reading that accords best with the writer's style is preferable.

5. The reading that best explains the origin of competing readings should be adopted.

Eclectic critic E. C. Colwell has admitted that these frequently cancel each other out and demand virtual omniscience on the part of the critic ("Biblical Criticism: Lower and Higher," *Journal of Biblical Literature,* 67 (1948):4-5; "External Evidence and New Testament Criticism" in *Studies in the History and Text of the New Testament,* p. 4). Even with such inbuilt weaknesses eclecticism is the method most in favor with textual critics. Fee has written: "There is among...scholars a methodological consensus, namely that both internal evidence (matters of author's style and scribal habits) and external evidence (value placed upon the MSS that support a variant) must be given full consideration in making textual choices. As B. M. Metzger recently put it: 'Textual criticism is an art as well as a science, and demands that each of the variants be evaluated in the light of the fullest consideration of both external evidence and internal probabilities'" (*JETS,* 21/1, March 1978, p. 19).

Metzger's statement is a fair description of what we could term the majority eclectic position. A minority of eclecticists wish to remove external evidence altogether as a major factor in choosing a reading. No defender of Biblical inspiration would follow this extreme line, but even the moderate eclecticism of Fee poses a real threat to the integrity of the NT text. The danger of eclecticism is that it effectively abandons parts of the inspired text as hopelessly beyond our reach. Van Bruggen has made the significant point that the characteristic mark of twentieth-century textual criticism is uncertainty (*Ancient Text,* p. 9-11). He shows, for example, that the text published by the United Bible Societies is a consensus text, the mean of the opinion of five scholars— Aland, Black, Martini, Metzger, and Wikgren. Metzger's commentary shows that "there are many readings which have been chosen only by the majority of the committee." The result of such a method is to enthrone uncertainty and to remove any ground of ascertaining what the Holy Ghost actually said.

The Objective Method. There is a better way than any form of eclecticism. It is the way of following objectively the great body of the evidence of the ancient data. No one has expounded the objective method of textual criticism better than J. W. Burgon. In brief, what Burgon calls for is the consent of the widest possible spectrum of ancient witnesses. He appeals to a verifiable objective standard. He repudiates conjectural emendation which according to Hort "depends for its success so much on personal endowments, fertility of resource in the first instance, and even more an appreciation of language too delicate to acquiesce in merely plausible corrections" (Westcott and Hort, *The New Testament in the Original Greek,* p. 71). Burgon seeks to remove the critic's subjective notions by denying the validity of Hort's idea of "transcriptional probability," which he vividly describes as "about as useful a substitute for proof as a sweet-pea for a walking stick" (*Revision Revised,* p. 396).

The objective method pleads for the evidence of the case to be allowed a careful hearing, apart from the imagined histories of text-types and families. Recognizing that corruptions found their way into the Greek text at a very early stage, both by copyists' errors and by malice, the objective method holds that by collating the evidence from the MSS, church lectionaries, early versions, and patristic citations, the united testimony of what Burgon called "catholic antiquity" will be heard. That text which has prevailed from the very early church, in a variety of geographical locations, throughout the period of antiquity, has every legitimate claim to be regarded as the true text.

Burgon set out seven "notes of truth" by which to judge competing readings:

1. *Antiquity.*

Antiquity does not mean dependence on any single ancient "authority" to the exclusion of, or in preference to, others. That would lead us back to Hort's theory of probability. Antiquity appeals to the whole body of ancient witnesses, what Burgon called "consent without concert," that is, agreement without collusion or contrivance. No fragment of the ancient witness can take the place of the entire testimony of ancient times. Burgon wrote, "I decline to accept a fragment of Antiquity, arbitrarily broken off, in lieu of the entire mass of ancient witnesses" (*Traditional Text,* p. 31).

Scholars have varying ideas of what time period constitutes antiquity. Westcott and Hort thought it ended before the year 400, Tregelles extended that to about 500, and Burgon extended it through the seventh century. Obviously, it is a relative term.

Wherever the line is drawn, antiquity is only one note of truth. "Age will not confer any exclusive, or indeed paramount, power of decision....It cannot be said to cover the whole ground" (*Traditional Text,* p.43).

Today it is common to equate age alone with superiority. The oldest MSS are held to be the best, simply because they are the oldest witnesses we possess. But this facile assumption is far from satisfactory, for there are clearly demonstrable cases where the oldest witnesses exhibit a corrupt text—e.g., P66, P75, and B in John 5:2, reading "Bethsaida" for "Bethesda." Such agreement in error shows that age alone does not guarantee accuracy.

2. *Number, or Consent of Witnesses.*

Opponents of the TT often say, "Witnesses are to be weighed, not counted." This *weighing* is usually a plea for the eclecticist's right to pass his subjective judgment on the value of each witness. But the consent of independent witnesses, widespread as to location and time, cannot be so easily dismissed. This was the error of Tregelles who, as we have noted, said eighty-nine ninetieths of the MSS could safely be disregarded in favour of the minority.

Burgon's view followed the objective method: "When therefore the great bulk of the witnesses—in the proportion suppose of a hundred or even fifty to one—yield unfaltering testimony to a certain reading; and the remaining little handful of authorities, while advocating a different reading, are yet observed to be unable to agree among themselves as to what that different reading shall precisely be—then that other reading concerning which all that discrepancy of detail is observed to exist, may be regarded as certainly false" (*Traditional Text,* p. 47).

3. *Variety of Evidence, or Catholicity.*

By this Burgon meant witnesses of different kinds, from different countries, in the production of which there could have been no collusion. "Variety may not fairly be claimed for readings which are not advocated by more than two distinct specimens of ancient evidence" (referring to MSS, lectionaries, versions, patristic citations). "Number ensures...genuine testimony. False witness is thus detected and condemned, because it agrees not with the rest. Variety is the consent of independent witnesses" (*Traditional Text,* pp. 58, 50).

4. *Weight, or Respectability of Witnesses.*

This deals with the credibility of witnesses, *judged by their own performance,* not by some critic's preconceived judgment of them. If a MS is seen to be continually corrupted, obviously its value in any disputed reading is impaired. By that standard, the oldest uncials "can be objectively, statistically shown to be habitual liars, witnesses of very low character, therefore. Their respectability quotient hovers near zero...Since the modern critical and eclectic texts are based precisely on B and Aleph and other early MSS, convicted liars all, it is clear that modern scholars have severely ignored the consideration of respectability as an objective criterion" (Pickering, p. 135).

5. *Continuity, or Unbroken Tradition.*

Genuine readings leave traces throughout the entire period of church history. If a reading suddenly appears, say in the Middle Ages, then it may safely be dismissed as spurious. There should be an unbroken tradition of transmission for a reading from antiquity.

This "note of truth" appears at first sight to be a case of special pleading on Burgon's part. He seems to assume the point he should be proving, for his argument comes down to saying, "The true text is the traditional text; therefore, the traditional text is the true text." However, appearances are deceptive and Burgon's argument is not really begging the question. If we remember God's promise to preserve His word for the use of His church, we may conclude that *therefore* He did not leave the church without access to His word in a large number of places for over a thousand years. If that is so, a genuine reading must bear the mark of unbroken tradition—a conclusion that militates against the few MSS undergirding the modern eclectic editions of the text.

6. *Context, or Evidence of the Entire Passage.*

Any reading which openly contradicts its context is clearly not genuine. However, since this note may very easily become an excuse for subjective judgment, *context* is used with a more precise meaning: if in the context of a disputed reading a MS is found to be largely corrupted, then its witness in the point in question is greatly diminished.

7. *Internal Evidence, or Reasonableness.*

Again this is used in a restricted sense to denote some sure marks of corruption, e.g., the appearance in B and other Alexandrian MSS of "Bethsaida" for "Bethesda" in John 5:2. Thus Burgon's appeal to internal evidence is not the eclecticist's notion of intrinsic probability. "This 'note' has nothing to do with the 'internal evidence' [of the eclecticist]. It is only rarely applicable and concerns readings which are grammatically, logically, geographically, or scientifically impossible" (Pickering, p. 137).

These seven notes of truth form the objective method of textual criticism with its emphasis on verifiable criteria. "The true reading of passages must be ascertained, with very slight exception indeed, from the preponderating weight of external evidence, judged according to its antiquity, to number, variety, relative value, continuousness, and with the help of the context" (Burgon, *Traditional Text,* p. 67).

It should be kept in mind that *all seven* of these notes form the objective method. The strength of this method lies in the cooperation of all these principles of procedure. If this approach to the text is consistently followed and applied, the TT, the majority text of the NT, will unquestionably be established as the authentic text and the eclectic editions of the text will suffer the fate the few old uncials now revered by most critics suffered some 1,500 years earlier—abandonment as inferior.

In recent years, Burgon's objective approach has received renewed attention with the production in 1982 of *The Greek New Testament According to the Majority Text,* edited by Zane C. Hodges and Arthur L. Farstad. Though the Hodges and Farstad text reflects the readings in the majority of MSS, the editors did not seek to employ Burgon's broader appeal to the united testimony of catholic antiquity. The Hodges and Farstad *Majority Text* is essentially the same as the *Textus Receptus,* though there are a few significant differences. For example, the *Majority Text* does not include the familiar words of Acts 8:37 and 1 John 5:7. These are instances when the *Textus Receptus* actually reflects a *minority* tradition.

Hodges and Farstad state that their work is not final or definitive. It is a welcome start, but much work remains to be done. Especially in the book of the Revelation, Hodges and Farstad's methodology is defective, depending on a reworking of Westcott and Hort's discredited genealogical idea, and we yet await an edition of the true majority text of that book. Indeed, we still await a serious attempt to carry on the work Burgon and William Miller commenced in their *Traditional Text of the Holy Gospels* (1896), and produce an edition of the NT that is firmly settled on the entire body of ancient objective evidence.

Of the two possible methods of proceeding in textual criticism—the eclectic and the objective—the objective method should be the choice of Bible-believers. Believing scholarship and eclecticism are strange bedfellows. Eclecticism is inherently self-contradictory. We have noted that its two primary canons frequently cancel each other out. They demand virtual omniscience of the critic. "The...rule about choosing what could have caused the other readings requires that the student know everything in Christian history, which could lead to the creation of a variant reading" (E. C. Colwell, *Biblical Criticism,* pp. 4, 5).

The eclectic view of the NT text supposes that the word of God cannot be known in its purity. But the Lord Jesus Christ promised that not one particle of His word would pass away. This is hardly consistent with the view that in many places the actual words of the Holy Ghost are lost to God's people in the midst of a mass of competing readings.

The text of Scripture has been preserved by the gracious and powerful providence of God its author. It is surely time for Bible-believing scholars to repudiate the eclecticist's endless "probabilities," and the inbuilt uncertainty of his method, and to employ their time and God-given talents in the establishment of the TT of the NT. This is the text which the Lord has preserved throughout church history and which, we are confident, He will continue to watch over in fulfillment of His promise to preserve His word.

Does It Make Much Difference?

1. We must not *overstate* the scope or importance of textual variations.

It is easy to overstate the differences between the text as it appears in a critical edition such as Westcott and Hort's or the United Bible Societies' Greek New Testament and as it appears in the *Textus Receptus* or in Hodges and Farstad's *Majority Text.* No edition of the Greek text, whether based on the Alexandrian MSS or the TT, would erase or alter a single doctrine of the Christian faith.

E. F. Hills gives the celebrated words of Richard Bentley (in 1713) in answer to the sceptic Anthony Collins who claimed that textual criticism had rendered the Biblical text uncertain. Bentley rejected this idea:

"The real text of the sacred writers does not now (since the originals have been so long lost) lie in any single manuscript or edition, but is dispersed in them all. It is competently exact indeed even in the worst manuscript now extant, choose as awkwardly as you can, choose the worst by design, out of the whole lump of readings....Make your 30,000 [variant readings] as many more, if numbers of copies can ever reach that sum: all the better to a knowing and serious reader who is thereby more richly furnished to select what he sees genuine. But even put them into the hands of a knave or a fool, and yet with the most sinistrous and absurd choice, he shall not extinguish the light of any one chapter, nor so disguise Christianity but that every feature of it will still be the same" (*King James Version Defended,* p. 108).

This view has been repeated over and over again since Bentley's day, and of course there is truth in it. However poorly or wilfully eclectic critics do their work, they cannot rob us of the truth of the gospel, so well attested is every doctrine in the 90% of the text that is beyond dispute. Undoubtedly, this is the providence of God.

2. We should not *understate* the scope and importance of textual variations.

While it is true that no doctrine is jeopardized or removed from Scripture by following any critical edition of the text, there are variant readings that very clearly call fundamental doctrines into question. For example, one corrupted MS of Matt. 1:16 reads that Joseph begot Jesus. That reading stands in shameful isolation but has yet found its way into the footnotes of some modern translations. Given the prevalence of eclecticism, it may be only a matter of time until some critics include that corrupt reading in the NT text. The doctrine of the virgin birth of Christ would stand on the strength of other clear evidence in the NT, but that raises a second problem: adopting such a corrupt reading would introduce contradiction into the NT text, thereby undermining another very important doctrine, namely, the veracity and trustworthiness of Scripture.

Understating the importance of textual differences also calls certain divine promises into question. The Bible claims that "every word of God is pure" (Prov. 30:5). All God's words are preserved (Psalm 12:7). Every Scripture is inspired and profitable to God's people (2 Timothy 3:16). Christ says that man shall live "by *every* word that proceedeth out of the mouth of God" (Matthew 4:4).

How can we hold these claims, if God's actual words have passed totally beyond our reach in many places? When the Bible says, "Forever, O Lord, thy word is settled in heaven" (Psalm 119:89), surely the meaning must include the idea that God has promised to ensure that neither Satan nor anyone else will be able destroy its text. Is this not a doctrine of Christianity? How can we hold on to the doctrine of an infallible Bible while at the same time teaching that in many instances the church not only does not know, but has no way of ever knowing, what the Bible actually says?

Many take the line set out by Theodor Zahn in 1909: "It has never yet been established from ancient citations, nor made really probable on internal grounds, that a single sentence of the original text has disappeared altogether from the text transmitted in the church, that is, of all the manuscripts of the original and of the ancient translations" (quoted by Hill, *King James Version Defended*, p. 109). In other words, God has preserved His word somewhere, but just where is impossible to tell! How are inspired, infallible Scriptures, which can never be ascertained to belong to the text of Scripture, be "profitable for doctrine" to God's church?

So, without trying to make too much of the textual variations we must yet recognize the importance of a trustworthy, objectively verifiable methodology that allows us to achieve certainty as to the text of Scripture.

The only method that is capable of doing justice to all the facts of the case is that set out above as the objective method.

Features of the Traditional Text

The TT preserved in the majority of ancient witnesses differs quite largely from the critical editions that depend on the Alexandrian MSS. It differs also from the *Textus Receptus,* though these differences are much less numerous and significant than those with the Alexandrian MSS.

Differences Between the TT and the Alexandrian. The Alexandrian-based critical texts either omit or enclose in brackets (to indicate grave doubt) forty-five entire verses of the NT as represented in the TT. They are Matt. 12:47; 17:21; 18:11; 21:44; 23:14; Mark 7:16; 9:44, 46; 11:26; 15:28; 16:9-20; Luke 22:20, 43, 44; 23:17; 24:12, 40; John 5:4; 7:53-8:11; Acts 15:34; 24:7; 28:29; and Rom. 16:24.

In addition there are 134 verses of which significant portions have been omitted or bracketed and in almost 200 other places the name of one of the persons of the Godhead has been dropped or bracketed. Approximately 400 more verses have omissions that yield a discernible difference in translation if not always in the overall meaning of the verses concerned. It is obvious that such an amount of deviation is not to be brushed aside lightly.

We cannot here enter into a detailed discussion of these differences. There are three crucial examples that clearly show the basic difference in methodology between advocates of the Alexandrian-based text and of the TT: Mark 16:9-20, John 7:53-8:11, and 1 Timothy 3:16. Not only do these passages show how critics have gone about their work, but they enjoy a very full body of objective evidence that the reading of the commonly received text is the authentic original reading. Despite this evidence eclectic critics have repudiated the received readings either by outright omission or by some mark of doubt being placed at the disputed text.

1. *Mark 16:9-20.*

Concerning this, A. Plummer wrote: "When we examine the external evidence, the question seems to be at once decided in favour of the disputed twelve verses. With the exception of four MSS...and two other uncial MSS...the longer ending follows v. 8 without a break, in every known Greek MS. It is also found in seven representatives of the old Latin...in Syr. Cur. [Cureton's Syriac], in the Memphitic and the Gothic. Finally, the Christian writings which exhibit clear evidence of the influence of Mark exhibit evidence that these verses were accepted as belonging to the gospel....This external testimony to the genuineness of the twelve verses seems to be not only conclusive, but superabundant" ("The Gospel According to Mark" in *Cambridge Greek Testament for Schools and Colleges,* p. xiv).

Despite this "superabundant" evidence, Plummer rejected the portion entirely and held that it was "one of those sure results of modern criticism which ought no longer to need to be proved," that it be recognized as spurious. His sole argument for this extraordinary verdict was the validity of the Westcott and Hort text-type theory. That is still the only reason for its exclusion from the sacred text or for its being branded as doubtful.

2. *John 7:53-8:11.*

The evidence in favour of John 7:53-8:11 is also strong. Jerome testified to finding the disputed verses in the Greek and Latin MSS (A.D. 415). It is, therefore, attested by both the Western text and the TT. Augustine (A.D. 400) told how the verses came to be missing in some MSS. "Certain persons of little faith, or rather enemies of the true faith, fearing, I suppose, lest their wives should be given impunity in sinning, removed from their manuscripts the Lord's act of forgiveness towards the adulteress" (Hills, *Believing Bible Study,* p. 123).

It is argued against the passage that it is not found in the same place in all the MSS that display it. Therefore it is most likely a piece of floating tradition. Again, it is argued that the early Greek fathers do not quote it. Actually, the silence of the Greek fathers helps to explain the omission of this passage from some MSS. The ancient church used the lectionary system in worship and the lesson for Pentecost overleaped these verses, not because they were not authentic, but because they were not to the point for the lesson on that day. Since the Greek fathers' comments were usually upon the portions set out in the lectionary, they would probably not comment on these verses. The genuineness of the passage is attested by its very full MS support and only by an eclectic disregard for that substantial evidence can the verses be denied or questioned.

3. *1 Timothy 3:16.*

This text provides one of the greatest affirmations of the deity of Christ in Scripture: "God was manifest in the flesh." The Alexandrian-based texts replace "God" with "who." *God* is found in almost every available Greek MS where the text is found, apart from the few Alexandrian MSS. It is widely quoted by the early fathers and it was the reading in the church lectionaries. The origin of the reading "who" is not difficult to imagine. In ancient MSS the word "God" was abbreviated $\overline{\Theta C}$ and "who" was OC. That "who" is an impossible reading is clear from the context. The order of the opening words in the Greek is "great is of godliness the mystery," followed by the contested $\overline{\Theta C}$ or OC. That the reading cannot be OC—"who"— is evident from the fact that *mystery* is a neuter and *who* is a masculine. Grammatically, a "mystery who" is impossible. For that reason, some copyists who had the corrupted reading "who" before them, changed it to "that" to make it agree with "mystery." But there can be no doubt that the text originally was, "God was manifested in the flesh."

It is a great shame that such an outstanding statement of the deity of Christ should have been even called in question. It is true that there is plenty of other proof of the doctrine but that is no reason to be complacent about throwing away one of the greatest and clearest statements on the subject the Holy Spirit ever made.

From this necessarily brief treatment of the differences between the TT and the Alexandrian-based text it is clear that our modern critical texts have never got away from Westcott and Hort's fatal dependence on the few Egyptian and Western witnesses. Burgon, after long and careful study of those MSS, emphatically stated: "Without a particle of doubt...ℵ B D are *three of the most scandalously corrupt copies extant:*—exhibit *the most shamefully mutilated* texts which are anywhere to be met with:—have become by whatever process (for their history is wholly unknown), the depositories of the largest amount of *fabricated readings,* ancient *blunders,* and *intentional perversions of the Truth,*— which are discoverable in any known copies of the Word of God" (*Revision Revised,* p. 16. Emphases in the original).

The purpose of such an observation is not to ignore the 90% agreement of all NT texts but to show that it is utterly unwarrantable to take the flawed MSS of the minority text as the basis for our English translations of the NT. That was what Burgon was opposing at the time of the production of the Revised Version. Since almost every subsequent modern translation has followed the minority MSS, Burgon's strictures on those MSS are still relevant.

Differences Between the TT and the Textus Receptus

Pickering states, "When all the evidence is in I believe the *Textus Receptus* will be found to differ from the Original in something over a thousand places, most of them being very minor differences, whereas the critical texts will be found to differ from the Original in some five thousand places, many of them being very serious differences" (p. 177).

Comparing the *Textus Receptus* with the *Majority Text* of Hodges and Farstad's edition, the number of variants is more in the region of 1,300-1,500, about half of which are in the book of the Revelation. For the most part the differences are small—case endings and word order, for example. Many of the differences are incapable of being translated. Furthermore, the true TT has not yet been definitively established, especially in the book of the Revelation. There Hodges and Farstad attempt to apply the Westcott and Hort notion of genealogy to the MSS. Genealogy cannot be made to work; we still await the application of Burgon's principles to the Greek text. Thus we cannot be absolutely certain just how many deviations the *Textus Receptus* will finally show from the TT. Especially in the book of the Revelation, the *Textus Receptus* may well be vindicated in places where now it shows a deviation from the Hodges and Farstad text. There is still a lot of work to be done to collate the MSS of the TT.

Even now the area of variation is small, as all critics admit. There are only three verses retained by the *Textus Receptus* and omitted by the Hodges and Farstad *Majority Text.* In two dozen other places (eight in Revelation) the *Majority Text* omits parts of a verse of a significant size. Considering that there are some 8,000 verses in the NT, the close agreement of the texts can be seen. The truth is that the *Textus Receptus* and the Hodges and Farstad text are very similar editions of the TT.

Our appeal has been to an *objective, verifiable standard* to decide disputed readings. We have argued against the subjective preferences of any critic, liberal or conservative. We must retain the same principle in dealing with the *Textus Receptus.* Personal preference and long usage cannot justify retaining any reading that does not have MS support. We cannot castigate eclecticism in the advocates of the Alexandrian MSS and then adopt it ourselves to retain one or two ill-attested readings in the *Textus Receptus.* We must maintain a rigorous objectivity.

If we follow this procedure, Luke 17:36 will not be in the text (though the words will not be lost, for they are retained in Matthew 24:40), and Acts 8:37 and 1 John 5:7 will also find no place. It is a telling fact that such a great champion of the traditional text as Burgon never at any time sought to argue that there was any MS basis for the retention of these verses.

R. L. Dabney sought to defend the retention of 1 John 5:7 on the basis of the Old Latin version, and also somewhat tentatively suggested a grammatical argument based on internal evidence (*Discourses Evangelical and Theological,* 1:377, 378). The reference to the Old Latin version is certainly interesting. It follows the line of argument laid down by Cardinal Wiseman (1802-1865) in his scholarly work on the version and shows that the reading dates all the way back to the middle of the second century—probably to an even earlier date. Furthermore, the Old Latin version is generally a witness to the TT, though in places it has incorporated readings from the Alexandrian MSS.

Dabney's argument from internal evidence is cogent. However, after all such argumentation, the conclusive fact remains: there is no MS authority for the retention of 1 John 5:7. We cannot plead for an objective method of textual criticism—a method that demands verifiable MS evidence for every reading admitted to the text—and retain a reading that cannot be found in one single Greek MS before the 16th century.

Saul of Tarsus' encounter with Christ on the Damascus road is related in Acts chapters 9, 22, 26. In the *Majority Text* Acts 9:5, 6 reads: "And he said, Who art thou, Lord? And the Lord said, I am Jesus whom thou persecutest. But arise and go into the city

and it shall be told thee what thou must do." Some familiar expressions are missing: "It is hard for thee to kick against the pricks. And he trembling and astonished said, Lord, what wilt thou have me to do? And the Lord said unto him…." These words are missing from Acts 9:5 because of lack of MS support, but they are not lost to us, for very similar words are retained in 26:14 and 22:10. It would appear that to fill out the narrative details in chapter 9, an early editor or copyist took a couple of details from Paul's own words in these later chapters and interpolated them.

Summarizing, the *Majority Text* and the *Textus Receptus* are not absolutely identical, but are extremely close in their presentation of the TT. We must seek the TT according to the principles set out above. The changes resulting in our *Textus Receptus* will be few and not very significant.

Conclusion

The TT is based on the united witness of the majority of MSS, church fathers, and ancient versions. The TT is the only text that can be established with any semblance of objectivity and verifiability. The vast numerical superiority the MSS of the TT enjoy over the minority text cannot be adequately explained except as a special providence of the Lord to preserve the integrity of His word.

The editions of the Greek text issued around the time of the Reformation—those of Erasmus, Stephens, and the Elzevirs—all reflect the TT. Since the AV was translated from this text the charge that it was translated from "a few inferior MSS" is false. The truth is that it was translated from an excellent text, which needs only slight correction to be brought into exact correspondence with the flawless originals. The versions that are truly open to the charge of being translated from a few inferior MSS are those modern translations that are not based on the TT but on the minority of flawed Alexandrian MSS—translations such as the RV, RSV, NASB, NEB, REB, and NIV.

TEXTUAL CRITICISM OF THE OLD TESTAMENT

Until recently the oldest known witness to the Hebrew text was a fragment of Deuteronomy (5:16-18 and 6:4, 5)—the Nash Papyrus—dating from around the beginning of the Christian era. In 1979, however, an important fragment of the OT text was discovered in a repository of a burial cave at Ketef Hinnom, Jerusalem. The fragment was the text of the Aaronic blessing of Num. 6:24-25 and it was inscribed on a silver sheet (see Amihai Mazar, *Archaelogy of the Land of the Bible*). This fragment dates from before the destruction of the temple by Nebuchadnezzar. (For its importance to Higher Criticism, *see JEDP Theory.*)

Before 1947, the most ancient OT MS was the Leningrad MS of the Pentateuch which experts date at A.D. 916. Thus the MS evidence available was almost 1,500 years after the close of the canon, which in turn was some 1,000 years after Moses was inspired to write the Pentateuch.

Then, in 1947, some very ancient scrolls were discovered at Qumran near the Dead Sea. The Dead Sea Scrolls (DSS) contain at least a fragment of every OT book except Esther. Included among them are two virtually complete scrolls of the prophecy of Isaiah.

D. R. Ap-Thomas summed up the impact of the DSS on our knowledge of the Hebrew text: "A study of these MSS shows, briefly, three things: (a) as already known, the Biblical text was preserved in many slightly different forms, of which the present Masoretic Text was one; (b) the general superiority of the M.T. over any other text-form is confirmed; (c) considerable caution is needed in emending the M.T. on the basis of the Dead Sea Scrolls' texts" (*A Primer of Old Testament Text Criticism,* p. 17).

The outstanding point confirmed by the DSS is the wonderful level of accuracy and purity maintained throughout the centuries of copying which produced the text contained in the late, medieval MSS upon which our current Hebrew Bibles and all our translations rest. This *Textus Receptus* of the OT is called the *Masoretic Text* (MT), after the Jewish scribes who flourished from the sixth century until the tenth century A.D. A brief history of this MT and the men whom God used to preserve it will be helpful.

The History of the OT Text

The Sopherim, or scribes, followed in the train of Ezra in copying the MSS of the OT. They took very great pains to ensure that the text they transmitted was pure and authentic. They were so jealous for the purity of the text that they would produce no separate treatise of their own thoughts or expositions of Scripture, lest these should somehow be mistakenly inserted into the inspired word.

The Sopherim as Text Critics. They did, however, exercise their text-critical skills. According to C. D. Ginsburg there are fifteen words in the printed Hebrew Bibles that present an abnormal appearance, and they represent the results of the critical efforts of the Sopherim (*Introduction to the Hebrew Bible,* pp. 318-334). Ginsburg's edition of the Masora also lists 134 places where the Sopherim, out of a mistaken reverence for the Lord's name, altered *Jehovah* to *Adonai.* Finally, the Masora carries a notation marking the *tiqqune sopherim,** the emendations of the scribes.

The Sopherim were followed in the work of copying and guarding the text by the *Zugoth* (the pairs of textual scholars); the *Tannaim* (the teachers) who, as well as producing accurate copies of the Scripture, wrote down their oral tradition, called Mishna; the *Amoraim* (the expositors) who produced a commentary on the Mishna, called the Talmud;* and in the sixth century A.D. by the *Masoretes.*

The Masoretes. Masora means "tradition" and it was the aim of the Masoretes to reproduce with the utmost fidelity the traditional text which they had received. Their work was based on the textual labours of Rabbi Akiba in the early part of the second century A.D. By Akiba's time the text had been closely scrutinized and standardized by the scribes—that is, variant texts which were recognized as corruptions of the original were rejected and the traditional text was universally accepted among Jewish scholars.

Edward F. Hills remarked of the Masoretes, "These Masoretes took extraordinary pains to transmit without error the Old Testament text which they had received from their predecessors. Many complicated safeguards against scribal slips were devised such as counting the number of times each letter of the alphabet occurs in each book. Also, critical material previously perpetuated by oral instructions was put in writing" (*King James Version Defended*, p. 93).

Bruce K. Waltke describes the Masoretes' minute analysis of the text of Scripture: "In their endeavour to conserve the consonantal text, they hedged it in by placing observations regarding the external form of the text in the margins. In the side margins they used abbreviations (*Masorah parvum*), in the top and bottom margins they gave more detailed and continuous explanations (*Masorah magnum*), and at the end provided alphabetical classification of the whole Masoretic material (*Masorah finalis*). In addition to these annotations made directly in the text, they compiled separate manuals called *Ochlah we-Ochlah*" ("The Textual Criticism of the Old Testament," in *Biblical Criticism, Historical, Literary and Textual*, p. 60).

This vast amount of scholarly labor was expended so that the purity of the text of God's word would be safeguarded amid the production of multiplied copies. That ancient text was a consonantal text; that is, it was written without any indication of vowel pronunciation. As long as Hebrew was a living language the absence of vowels presented no great problem; they were simply supplied in the reading. However, when Hebrew

ceased to be the everyday language of the people, a system of vocalization had to be introduced to indicate the proper pronunciation and meaning of the text.

The first attempt at this was the use of three consonants *(he, waw,* and *yod)* as *matres lectionis,* i.e., to represent vowel sounds. *He* represented *a, waw* either *u* or *o,* and *yod* either *i* or *e.* This partial attempt at vocalization was followed by the Masoretic method of using dots and dashes below and above the consonantal script. In this way, the traditional vocalization of the words was maintained and yet the consonantal text was not altered.

Kethib and Qere. The Masoretes carried to great lengths their determination not to alter the text handed down to them. Even in the case of a plain copyist error they made no change in the consonantal text but drew attention to it in a marginal note. They allowed the uncorrected consonants to stand in the text but placed with them the vowel signs of the corrected word. This, of course, produced an unpronounceable form and the reader was forced to stop and note the copyist's slip. The uncorrected form is called *kethib** ("it is written") and the corrected form in the margin is called *qere** ("to be read"). An example of a Masoretic notation of a scribal error is in Ezekiel 42:16 where by the transposition of the letter *aleph* a copyist made the text read "five cubits reed." The Masoretes pointed out that this ought to read "five hundred reeds," and this is the reading in our printed editions of the Hebrew Bible.

The Accuracy of the OT Text

What some have called the "unbelievable achievement" of the Jewish scribes in faithfully preserving the OT text must be attributed to the providence of the Lord. Without such providential goodness, the level of purity achieved in transmitting the text of the OT over so many centuries would indeed be unbelievable.

According to Robert Dick Wilson (1856-1930), one of America's greatest OT scholars, variant readings in the Hebrew MSS are very few: "An examination of the Hebrew manuscripts now in existence shows that in the whole Old Testament there are scarcely any variants supported by more than one manuscript out of 200 to 400, in which each book is found, except in the full and defective writing of the vowels. This full or defective writing of the vowels has no effect either on the sound or the sense of the words" (*A Scientific Investigation of the Old Testament,* p. 69). Wilson estimated that there was, on average, less than one variant reading per page of the Hebrew Bible (*ibid.,* p. 70). Remembering his point that most have scanty MS authority we can readily appreciate how the word "unbelievable" could be used to describe such an achievement.

The accuracy with which the OT text has been transmitted is evidenced by its exactness in recording the names of foreign kings which also appear in ancient documents discovered in recent times. Wilson notes that in contrast with some notable failures of secular historians in this area, "the evidence shows that for 2,300 to 3,900 years the text of the proper names in the Hebrew Bible has been transmitted with the most minute accuracy" (*ibid.,* p. 82).

Though the number of variant readings in the MT MSS is small, there is substantial disagreement between the MT and other ancient witnesses. For example, in 1 Samuel 14:41 the Septuagint (LXX) has 28 words which are missing from the MT. Conservative scholar Gleason L. Archer, in common with most critics, holds that here the MT is deficient because of a classic case of *homoeoteleuton* (*A Survey of Old Testament Introduction,* p. 57). But is this so? Is it not rather a case of the LXX attempting to fill out and explain the traditional text? Clearly, we need a consistent methodology to guide the discipline of textual criticism, otherwise

it can degenerate into "every man doing that which is right in his own eyes."

Witnesses to the OT Text

The available witnesses to the text include the MT, the DSS, the Samaritan Pentateuch, the targums,* the LXX, and the ancient versions.

The Masoretic Text. The primary witness to the OT text is the consonantal text reproduced by the Masoretes. In his work on the OT text Ernst Wurthwein says, "Since M [the MT] depends on direct transmission in the original language, and was handed down with great care, it deserves special attention in every case. Today, the earlier tendency to underestimate the value of M in favour of the Greek translation, or even in favour of modern conjectures, has been almost entirely given up, since M has revealed itself repeatedly as the best witness to the text" (*Text of the Old Testament,* translated by P. R. Ackroyd, p. 77).

Where the Masoretic pointing is impossible, a better understanding of its text may be obtained by a different vocalization or even by a different division of words. Isaiah 9:3 in the AV reads, "Thou hast multiplied the nation and not increased the joy: they joy before thee according to the joy in harvest, and as men rejoice when they divide the spoil." This translates the MT as it now stands. However, the negative in "not increased the joy" is a problem since the entire verse is about the joy that follows when the Lord multiplies the nation. So how does the "not" appear? Liberals have long trotted out this text as an evidence against the verbal inspiration of the Bible. As usual, they are wrong. The official Masoretic solution is to suppose that a copyist mistook the word "to him" as "not." Both are pronounced *LO,* though written slightly differently. The difficulty of this explanation is that it places the word "to him" before the verb instead of after it as is usual in Hebrew. According to C. D. Ginsburg the real answer lies in the Masoretic division of words. He argues that if the Hebrew *LO* is recognized, not as a separate word, but as the last syllable of the preceding word, the problem is resolved and the clause would then read, "Thou hast increased their rejoicing."

The number of such places is not large. Wurthwein gave his opinion that "it is clear from the history of the text that the vocalization of M has not the same significance as the consonantal basis, and the alterations in the vowel signs do not really rank as emendations" (*ibid.*, p. 78). This is true only in a very limited number of cases. The Masoretic pointing preserves the original vocalization of the text and should be maintained unless it is plainly impossible.

The Dead Sea Scrolls. We have already noted Ap-Thomas' summary of the value of the scrolls. They generally support the MT and, therefore, furnish clear evidence of the antiquity of that text, even though the oldest Masoretic MSS date from as late as the 10th century A.D. Similar support comes from other ancient MSS discovered in the Judaean desert at Wadi Marabbaat and at Nahal Hever. The Minor Prophets Scroll, discovered in 1955, dates from the second century A.D. and has the consonantal text preserved by the Masoretes.

There are some places in the OT where there is no Masoretic correction of what appears to many to be an error. In these places critics generally favor a "pre-Masoretic" reading found in the DSS, on the grounds that it represents an older and purer form of the text. But a "pre-Masoretic" reading is not necessarily older than a Masoretic reading. The proto-Masoretic text existed at Qumran and elsewhere along with the divergent texts. It was the trunk and they were the branches. The most important contribution of the DSS to textual criticism is still their demonstration of this fact.

The Samaritan Pentateuch. The Samaritans have a copy of the books of Moses which differs from the MT in some 6,000

places. Most of these are merely matters of spelling, but there is evidence of deliberate alteration of the text for sectarian purposes. There are other indications that the Samaritan Pentateuch is a derived and secondary text whose variant readings are no ground for emending the received MT. Modern critics tend to value it highly as an aid to textual criticism, but as long ago as 1815 Gesenius, declared it to be almost useless for that purpose.

The Septuagint. The LXX was translated to meet the needs of Alexandrian Jews in the third century B.C. At least the Pentateuch was translated at that time with the rest of the OT following over a long period. The level of translation is very erratic. Waltke (*Biblical Criticism,* p. 69) quotes the following scholarly appraisals of the LXX translations. Concerning the translation of Isaiah, I. L. Seeligman said, "We shall not, however, do the translator any injustice by not rating his knowledge of grammar and syntax very highly." According to H. S. Nyberg, Hosea in the LXX is "overly composed of gross misunderstandings, unfortunate readings and superficial lexical definitions." Of Lamentations, B. Albrektson said, "LXX, then, is not a good translation in this book." G. Gerleman said that the translator of Job "had not mastered the difficulties of the original." Waltke speaks of the vocalizations adopted by the LXX in the Psalms, even when the translator was working from the same consonantal text as the Masoretic, as "erratic and intrinsically improbable" (p. 61).

From all this we can understand G. Bertram's statement, "The Septuagint belongs more to the history of Old Testament exegesis than to that of the Old Testament text" (quoted by Wurthwein, p. 50). There are other factors that militate against the use of the LXX to emend the MT. Its own text has been corrupted through generations of copying, and significantly, in the Pentateuch, where its translation reaches its highest level, it is clearly derived from an ancestor of the

Samaritan Pentateuch. Some critics are willing to abandon the MT when the LXX and the Samaritan Pentateuch agree against it. The fact that they are traceable to one common ancestor destroys the value of their agreement and it is unwarrantable to emend the MT on this basis.

There was a time in the not too distant past when some critics exalted the LXX over the MT simply because the LXX MSS were older. As in NT textual criticism, there is a school of critics to whom *older* means *better.* In the case of the LXX and the MT MSS, the older MSS are certainly not better. Even if we could discover the original of the LXX translation, its age would not make it a better text than the Masoretic. Wurthwein asks: "Even if we did possess this original text, could we then prefer it to M merely on the grounds of its age? This raises the question of the Hebrew text used by [the LXX]. Is it necessarily better because it is older than M?" (*Text of the Old Testament,* p. 47).

Targums. These Aramaic translations were at first oral (Nehemiah 8:8), were committed to writing, and then acquired the status of official translations for Aramaic-speaking Jews. Some of them were literal translations while others were interpretive expansions containing a lot of illustrative material. They at times give interesting insights into the text, but they are only a secondary witness and are not a primary standard by which to emend the received text.

Ancient Versions. Ancient versions such as the Syriac, the Italic, and the Latin Vulgate translated by Jerome from the Hebrew text (the Old Latin version was translated from the LXX) provide evidence of the text from which they were translated. Jerome's work has suffered much textual contamination, but where his original text can be discerned it is a witness to the text preserved by the Masoretes.

The Masoretic Witness to the Text. Another important witness in the text criticism of the OT is that of the Masoretes

themselves. In addition to their *kethib-qere* notations, the Masoretes used the note *sebir,* "supposed," to indicate a reading they judged to be a correction of the text. They also placed dots over words in fifteen places to indicate some peculiar meaning which tradition attached to them. They inverted the letter *nun* in nine places. The inversions distinguish these *nuns* from those in the text and critics believe they indicate a Masoretic question about the proper position in their respective books of the verses concerned. Some of the most important critical notations of the Masoretes are of the 134 places where they report the Sopherim's substitution of *Adonai* for *Jehovah.*

In thirty-two places the Masoretes marked alternate readings which were found in an ancient codex carried to Rome in A.D. 70 after the fall of Jerusalem by the Roman general Titus. They also listed the *tiqqune sopherim,* or emendations of the scribes. These eighteen corrections which the Masoretes attribute to the Sopherim were mostly intended to remove anthropomorphic references that the Sopherim considered derogatory to the dignity of the Lord. The difficulty with these corrections, and others that scholars add to the list, is to know if indeed the Sopherim did actually make all of them. This is a case where an examination of other independent witnesses is necessary. In the majority of the places involved the LXX agrees with the present MT.

A very interesting place where the LXX agrees with the *tiqqune sopherim* is in 1 Samuel 3:13, where the AV translates the MT, "His sons made themselves vile." The verb *QALAL* simply means "to curse." As the text now stands it is followed by the word *LAHEM,* "to them," and literally reads, "His sons cursed to them." Now *QALAL* takes a plain accusative, not a dative and this anomaly in the text is explained by the Masoretes' note that the text originally read "cursed God." He was the object of the cursing or blasphemy of Eli's sons, a statement that the Sopherim wished to soften out of deference to Eli as the priest of God. By removing two letters they created an impossible reading which left the full wickedness of Hophni and Phinehas out of the text, to be remembered through the Masoretic tradition and the witness of the LXX, and through the grammatical difficulty of the reading they created.

Another text where the *tiqqune sopherim* should be recognized is 2 Samuel 16:12. Here translators have had a difficult time. The AV abandons the Hebrew text and follows the LXX, but notes the Masoretic *qere* in the margin. The RSV and the NEB also follow the LXX. The RV follows the Hebrew *kethib* in its translation and notes the LXX reading in the margin. All is clear, however, when we realize that to remove an anthropomorphism the scribes transposed two letters to make the word *B'YNW,* "with His eye," into *B'WNY,* "on my iniquity." The text simply says, "It may be that the Lord will behold with His eye, and that the Lord will requite me good for his cursing this day."

One final example of a correction of the Sopherim will suffice. 2 Samuel 12:14 records Nathan's charge against David: "By this deed thou hast given great occasion to the enemies of the Lord to blaspheme." According to Rashi, one of the greatest of the Masoretic doctors, the original reading was much harsher, for the object of the verb was "the Lord," not "the enemies of the Lord." That the Masoretic tradition here is authentic is shown by the fact that the verb cannot mean "cause to blaspheme," but simply "to blaspheme." Now, David did not blaspheme the Lord's enemies, as a literal translation of the text as it stands would demand. What Nathan said to him was, "Thou hast blasphemed [reproached, reviled, or contemned] the Lord." This agrees with David's own confession in Psalm 51:4, "Against Thee, Thee only, have I sinned."

Principles of OT Textual Criticism

We are now in a position to make some observations about the principles upon which any investigation of the text must proceed.

1. The Masoretic Text, the OT *Textus Receptus,* is the best and purest witness to the original text. This has been the general position of Bible translators ever since this text became available to them. Their confidence was not diminished because the MS evidence for it came from MSS of late date. Age in itself is no guarantee of textual purity. The discoveries in the region of the Dead Sea have demonstrated this.

2. According to the unanimous opinion of textual critics, the MT is the result of an official revision executed by Jewish scholars in the first and second centuries A.D. Its total acceptance to the exclusion of divergent text-types came about as the result of this revision. However, no reputable critic, and certainly no Bible-believing scholar holds that the MT's being an official revision weakens its authority or constitutes it an inferior text. Rather, it is recognized that it was officially adopted because it represented the traditional text in its purest form.

3. According to some critics, the MT exhibits some conflate readings, that is, readings that combine two different accounts of the same or similar incidents. Conflation is difficult to prove for it is just as defensible to hold that briefer variant readings have been produced because some reviser edited out what seemed superfluous. But even if we allow, for argument's sake, that the MT contains instances of conflation, this is not held by any reputable critic to invalidate the entire text or to reduce it to the status of a derived and, therefore, secondary text.

4. The inferiority of the Alexandrian text of the LXX, and of the Hebrew MSS from which it was translated, is established, even though this Hebrew text can be traced back to very ancient times. If the LXX is not a sufficient basis for emending the MT, how much less is the practice of *retroversion* which some critics hold dear. Retroversion is the creation of a hypothetical Hebrew text by translating the Greek of the LXX back into Hebrew. Such a text has no value as a tool to emend the MT.

5. The Samaritan Pentateuch has suffered extensive emendation by Samaritan sectaries. The deliberate depravation of the text renders it unfit to be received either in place of, or as a standard for emending, the MT.

6. The MT was itself emended by orthodox Jewish scribes out of mistaken ideas of protecting the Lord's honour. Such emendations must be corrected, but their presence does not alter the position of the MT as the primary witness to the original.

7. In view of all this, the MT is accepted as the standard text, which should be emended only if its own witness is not consistent, or is contextually or linguistically impossible. Where emendation is necessary it should be carried out only on the basis of the verdict of the majority of available witnesses.

This insistence on the majority-text MSS being the sole ground upon which to correct the *Received Text* is far reaching. No sane critic, and certainly no believer in the inspiration and providential preservation of Scripture, would dream of rejecting the witness of the MT or of the majority of available witnesses on the authority of one MS, or even of an entire tradition such as the Samaritan Pentateuch or the LXX.

That being so, how much more must we insist that the inspired word of God is not to be "corrected" according to the conjectural emendations of uninspired critics. There was a time when critics indulged rather freely in the supposed "art" of saying what the text should have read. In more recent times, even liberal scholars have acknowledged the danger of conjectural emendation, though they insist that when neither the MT nor any other ancient witness offers "a probable text," conjecture is in order. Even some conservative and evangelical scholars endorse this. If by conjectural emendation these critics meant a differing pointing than the Masoretic, or a different division of words, while maintaining the integrity of the consonantal text, they might have a point. But they mean more. They call for the invention of a new reading because they can make nothing of those available in the MSS. This is not acceptable. If there are cases where the critic must admit that he does not know enough to do justice to the reading of the MSS, so be it. Wurthwein says, "As our knowledge in several of these fields is still limited and open to discussion, and subjective judgments are particularly easy to make, it would be a good thing if there were more restraint and self-criticism than is normal" (*Text of the Old Testament,* p. 79). It is better scholarship to admit one's ignorance or inability than to eject from the sacred text what God has providentially preserved.

The result of all this is that we have preserved for us by divine providence the very word of God in the OT Scripture. As Wilson said—and though the discovery of the DSS has changed the situation, his fundamental point is still valid—variants are neither very numerous nor well attested.

Critical Canons. Critics have laid down certain canons by which they proceed. Most prefer the more difficult reading; usually the briefer reading; and the reading that best explains the origin of competing readings. Such a procedure is often impossible as these canons come into conflict with each other. This leaves the door wide open for eclecticism, the critic's subjective exercise of choice among readings which, theoretically, have equal claim to be genuine.

In the case of the OT, while some liberals try to follow the eclectic line, conservative scholars practically ignore the man-made canons and follow the MT in identifying the authentic word of God. They do not try to establish a text founded on the oldest readings. They follow the MT, correcting it only when the preponderating witness of the MS evidence, including that of the MT MSS, demands it.

This is a consistent treatment of the MSS of the OT. It honours the unique character of the inspired word of God. It recognizes that a book which God has breathed and whose very words He has undertaken to preserve (Ps. 12:7; Matt. 5:18) cannot be approached in the same way as a piece of purely human literature. Furthermore, it recognizes that in the light of God's promised preservation the true text is that which has been maintained in use among His people through the centuries.

Even those conservative scholars who would demur at the manner in which we have stated the position, in practice come to the same conclusions about the text. If they were to follow these principles, and come to similar conclusions, in the area of the NT text, Bible-believing churches would have been spared a lot of needless anxiety and dispute (see **Textual Criticism of the New Testament**).

TEXTUS RECEPTUS

1. Latin meaning "The Received Text," a name for the edition of the Greek NT produced by the Elzivir publishers in 1633, in the preface of which they wrote: "Therefore thou hast the text now received by all: in which we give nothing altered or corrupted." Popularly, the name is given to the traditionally accepted NT text, the *Majority Text* as opposed to the critical, eclectic editions based on a tiny minority of MSS. See **Textual Criticism of the New Testament**.

2. Sometimes this designation is given to the Masoretic text of the OT. See **Textual Criticism of the Old Testament**.

THEANTHROPIC PERSON

Theanthropic, from two Greek words, *theos,* "God," and *anthropos,* "man," is the word used to describe the complex person of Christ the redeemer. He is both God and man (see **Deity of Christ**; **Humanity of Christ**) in two distinct natures. In opposition to the conflicting views of Eutychianism* and Nestorianism,* the orthodox doctrine of the person of Christ is, in the words of the *Shorter Catechism,* "The only redeemer of God's elect is the Lord Jesus Christ, Who, being the eternal Son of God, because man, and so was, and continueth to be, God and man in two distinct natures, and one person, for ever" (Q. 21). The following points need to be kept in mind:

1. The divine nature in Christ's person is the eternal *Logos* or "Word" (John 1:1, 14).

2. The incarnation was not a transubstantiation of the divine nature into a human nature. There is no confusion of natures in Christ. In Him, deity did not become humanized or humanity deified. There was a *union* of two natures, not a transmutation. A divine person graciously united a human nature with Himself. *(See* **Communicatio Idiomatum.***)*

3. Thus, there is only one person in Christ *(see* **Unipersonality***).*

4. The divine nature is the base of Christ's theanthropic person—a point of great significance in discussing the impeccability* of Christ.

5. The dominance of the divine nature also helps to explain the words of Mark 13:32, often quoted to show that there were things of which Christ was ignorant. Bengel and, long before him Augustine, held that the meaning is simply that it was not among Christ's instructions to *declare* when the day of the Lord would occur. *Know* means "make known," as in 1 Cor. 2:2 (cf. Gen. 22:12). In Acts 1:7 Christ says that the Father has put the declaration of times and seasons in His own power. The God-man, on account of His eternal deity, has a full knowledge of all things that the Father knows (John 5:20), though as mediator He must await the Father's time to declare them.

6. The union of the two natures in Christ began in time and continues forever (Heb. 13:8).

7. The incarnation made no change in the Trinity.* There are still three persons in the Trinity, for the Logos did not unite with a human *person*, but with a human *nature*.

Well could Paul cry, "Great is the mystery of godliness: God was manifest in the flesh" (1 Tim. 3:16).

THEISM

Broadly, belief in a god. In this sense, animism,* pantheism,* and polytheism* are all forms of theism. Christian theism is the belief in the triune God revealed in the Bible.

The *Shorter Catechism's* description of God is a succinct summary of Christian theism: "God is a Spirit, infinite, eternal and unchangeable in His being, wisdom, power, holiness, justice, goodness and truth....There is but one only, the living and true God.... There are three Persons in the Godhead, the Father, the Son, and the Holy Ghost: these three are one God, the same in substance, equal in power and glory" (Questions 4-6).

*See **Trinity**.*

THEISTIC EVOLUTION

The theory that God, having performed the primary creative act, used the process of evolution to develop the universe over a very long period of time. The theory labours under the problems of seeking to force Scripture into the mould of current sceptical thought, of the intrinsic scientific impossibility of evolution, and of denying, or evacuating of their native force, the plain statements of Scripture on the subject of creation.*

THEOCRACY

From *theos*, "God," and *kratein*, "to rule," it means "rule by God" and describes the control of Israel's national affairs by the Lord as their supreme lawgiver and ruler. Unlike any other form of government, theocracy gives the absolute authority of God to every law He revealed to control and direct all personal and public morality in both religious and social life.

The term is also used loosely to describe any attempt to establish the government or the moral code of a nation on religious belief or Biblical authority.

THEODICY

From *theos*, "God," and *dike*, "justice," the theological or philosophical vindication of the justice of God, in view of His toleration of the existence of evil, both in the sense of wickedness and of calamity, in the world. G. C. Berkouwer defined it as "a justification of God's providential rule" (*The Providence of God*, p. 232).

Berkouwer continued, "It attempts to prove that in spite of all the enigmas and all criticisms God's governing of the world is holy, good, and just. Theodicy is an attempt to defend God against all complaints or accusations by demonstrating the meaningfulness and purposefulness of God's activity in the world and in human life. It presupposes the seriousness of all sorts of doubts and criticisms and assumes that there are empirical facts which cause tensions and pose problems in connection with the Divine rule. We find in every theodicy a consideration of such problems as these: human suffering, tragedy and misery, death, sin, and the numerous shocking events which almost daily bewilder us. Can all these evils—to our joy and comfort—be included in the whole of things, in a system in which all tensions are resolved and which affords us a harmonious perspective of and insight into the world? This question arises with particular acuteness in relation to our confession of God's Providence over all things. How is it possible to rhyme the frightening realities of life with the omnipotence of God over this world? Is there a demonstrable relation between God's omnipotence and His goodness? Questions like these theodicy attempts to answer."

The question is often asked, "If God is all-powerful and all-loving why does He not intervene to stop all the evil and suffering in the world?" Faced with this question, liberals often conclude that God cannot be both omnipotent and good, and usually attribute His toleration of evil and suffering to some limitation of His power.

Some simplistic evangelicals adopt a species of *dualism* in which God is responsible for all the good and Satan for all the evil, as if God and Satan were locked in a struggle in which Satan is not entirely under God's control. While it is undoubtedly true that Satan's malignancy causes much suffering in the world, the question remains, "Why does God allow it?" Dualism has no answer; indeed, it flies in the face of the Biblical testimony to God's sovereignty.

Others invoke God's hidden purpose as the answer to the problems theodicy attempts to answer. God permits evil, but He has an ultimate purpose of good in doing so. This is very true (John 5:3), and it has the advantage of reminding man that he is neither all-knowing nor all-controlling, but must walk by faith. But in itself this *teleological* theodicy does not go far enough.

The Scripture acknowledges that the whole creation groans with suffering and bondage (Rom. 8:22). However, it does not admit us to the mystery of God's eternal decree to permit sin. It simply assures us that God is not the author of sin and is infinitely righteous in His person and working. Sin is the self-determined choice of the creature. Scripture therefore attributes all the sin and suffering in the world to the wilful choice of sin by our first parents and to the curse that sin brought on them and their descendants (Rom. 5:12; Gen. 3:16-19).

This is not to say that each instance of suffering or calamity is the immediate result of some specific sin of the sufferer (John 5:2-3), but that all suffering is ultimately the result of man's rebellion against God. The world is under the curse of sin, and the wrath of God is justly manifested against all ungodliness and unrighteousness of men (Rom.

1:18). Divine wrath is not merely future, but present, and explains some of the suffering in the world.

However, even God's redeemed and justified people are not delivered from participation in the sufferings of the world. Job was the best of men, but God allowed him to suffer more than most. The history of the church of Christ is a long record of how "bad things happen to good people." How can this be?

Paul explains that though Christians are now pardoned and justified, the *redemption of their bodies* awaits the second coming* of Christ (Rom. 8:23). Until then, they are not delivered from the temporal and physical results of the fall*—they suffer, sicken, and die as other men.

This reference to *redemption,* however, provides the key to a believing theodicy. The cross and the resurrection of Christ remove any question about the reality of either God's love for sinners or His power to deliver them. Even as His wrath is revealed against ungodliness and unrighteousness, He is pursuing His redemptive purpose and will not leave it short of complete fulfilment. In that fulfilment, God promises His people a new heaven and a new earth, in which perfect righteousness and perfect happiness dwell side by side (Rev. 21:1-5).

It is in this light that the Christian views suffering and calamity: "Our light affliction, which is but for a moment, worketh for us a far more exceeding and eternal weight of glory; while we look not at the things which are seen, but at the things which are not seen: for the things which are seen are temporal; but the things which are not seen are eternal" (2 Cor 4:17-18). We freely confess that we cannot penetrate the purposes of God (Rom. 11:33), but we know that His purpose in Christ is what controls all His dealings with us and the world. We are assured, therefore, that "all things work together for good to them that love God, to them who are the called according to his purpose" (Rom 8:28). God always deals well with His people, even when He permits them to suffer—sometimes especially when He permits them to suffer (Ps. 119:65, 67, 71).

This is the response of faith. It recognizes that we cannot start with the problem of evil and reason our way up to God, either to justify or criticize Him. We must start with God as we know Him in Christ, and deal with the perplexities of life in the light of that knowledge.

Unbelievers respond to pain and suffering in the very opposite manner. They maintain their rebellion against God and then defiantly demand to know why God allows them to suffer, as if they deserved something better from Him. Those who most loudly criticize God for allowing suffering and calamity are usually the very people who wish to reserve to themselves the right to think and act independently of Him. That was the essence of the sin that introduced suffering into the perfect world in which God first placed man. It is thoroughly hypocritical for sinners to delight in indulging in the very thing that brought suffering into the world and then blame God for their suffering.

Ultimately, then, the need for a theodicy with which to meet the criticisms of unbelievers emphasizes that unrepentant sinners live under a series of delusions: they do not admit the wickedness and guilt of their sin; they do not grasp the awful truth of the justice and wrath of God; they make human reason the judge of divine wisdom; they demand relief from suffering without salvation from sin. The greater tragedy is that unless the very God whom they vilify enters into their lives in redeeming grace, they will forever suffer the torments of hell in which they will have to acknowledge the goodness of God and will yet curse Him as they suffer His wrath (Luke 16:23-25; Matt. 8:12—note the frequent occurrence of Christ's statement that in hell there will be weeping, wailing, and gnashing of teeth: Matt.

13:42, 50; 22:13; 24:51; 25:30; Luke 13:28. "Gnashing of teeth" denotes bitter resentment, Acts 7:54).

THEOLOGY

Greek *theos,* "God," and *logos,* "word"; the systematic study of the being, attributes, purposes, and works of God, and of the world, man, and history in relation to Him. It is usually referred to as a science, because it should be conducted by the investigation of the objective data of divine revelation, which has its full expression in the written and incarnate word—i.e., in the Bible and its Christ-centred message. Indeed, theology used to be called the queen of the sciences.

This basis in an objective, divine revelation is what marks the difference between theology and philosophy or metaphysical speculation. However, with the spread of subjectivism and the decline into more and more man-centred methods, much of what passes for theology grows increasingly like speculative philosophy.

*See **Systematic Theology**; **Biblical Theology**.*

THEOLOGY OF CRISIS

The theology of neo-orthodox theologian Emil Brunner (1889-1966), set forth by him in his book of that name, *The Theology of Crisis*. It is existential* and dialectic.* It views man as living in a contradiction: he lives and yet he does not live—in Brunner's words, "Vitality and mortality always go together." Man is in contradiction to God's will to which he is antagonistic. But God has resolved this contradiction and overcome this antagonism, by giving a self-revelation "through His personal word." This "personal word" is not identical either with Scripture or with the historical Jesus. The historical Jesus is "the incognito" under which the word was revealed. Only faith can penetrate the disguise. This faith intensifies the feeling of contradiction; it is "the

405

crisis of the incurable disease." It is a perpetual crisis or decision. It does not lead to the possession of life: "The life of the Christian is never a possession, but remains as it begins, a decision....Faith is, and remains, a decision; and therefore it remains a principle of crisis for all life....The Christian then is to be recognized as such not by the fact that he has overcome the contradiction, but by the fact that he knows, while standing in the contradiction, that it has been overcome of God."

Thus Brunner's idea of faith is existential, not Biblical. It is a leap into the darkness of a contradiction, but a leap which removes the darkness with which the revelation of God is shrouded. It is a faith which intensifies the contradiction, while imparting the knowledge that the contradiction has been overcome. It is a never-ending decision which cannot enter into the possession of life.

This existential faith decides, without any objective basis for its decision. It obtains its knowledge (?) of God's personal word subsequent to its decision. The decision is not the result of a divine revelation; it is in order to it. It is a leap in the dark.

To such follies men sink when they make faith a human decision, instead of the gift of God (Eph. 2:8, 9). Far from being a leap in the dark, faith's way is lit by the promise of the written word applied to the heart by the Holy Spirit. On Brunner's reckoning, a poor sinner could never be sure that if he came by faith to Christ he would be graciously received.

Brunner's theology of crisis espouses similar views to those of Rudolf Bultmann *(see Myth),* so that when Brunner speaks of the word and revelation, he does not mean the Bible. Similarly, when he speaks of the personal word, he does not mean the historical Christ. God's word is hidden in the Bible, to be discovered by faith. The personal word is disguised under the historical Jesus, also to be discovered by faith.

Brunner lays emphasis on man's sin and separation from God, but fails to understand human depravity.* This is clear from his rationale for his theory of the word and revelation of God appearing *incognito* in the world. He argues that "the natural man receiveth not the things of the Spirit." Therefore, revelation and the personal word are not to be found in all the world or in history, except in disguise. In other words, the basic reason for the world's non-perception of God's revelation is the hiddenness of the revelation. Contrary to this, the Scriptures teach (2 Cor. 4:4-6) that the glory of God shines in the face of Jesus Christ. The trouble is that men, depraved by sin and dominated by Satan, are blinded.

Brunner's position, then, basically is merely a dressed-up version of the old modernism* against which he inveighs so heavily. He criticizes modernism for its "optimistic" view of man, and rightly so, but he fails to escape it himself. God has not disguised His revelation. His glory is revealed in the face of Jesus Christ. Man's depravity blinds him to the light. The trouble is not that God has covered up the light, but that men are wilfully blind to it.

Brunner's defective views of human sinfulness are also apparent from his continual emphasis on man's ability to decide in favour of God and to "let God speak to him." Such thinking belies his claim to be presenting the transcendent and sovereign Lord.

Brunner confesses himself to be "an adherent of a rather radical school of biblical criticism, which, for example, does not accept the gospel of John as an historical source, and which finds legends in many parts of the synoptic gospels." How strange that such a position should take the name of orthodoxy! How strange that it should propose "a theology of the word," when the very Gospel in which the personal word is most fully set forth (John 1:1-14) is rejected as unhistorical! And how strange that this theology should parade the reality of its faith, when its entire system involves a rejection of so much that the Bible and the Lord Jesus claimed to be true.

Brunner rejects the "ancient cosmology and Israelitish chronology" of the OT. He vehemently opposes the doctrine of the verbal inspiration* of Scripture. He criticizes Fundamentalism* and "orthodoxy in general" as a "petrification of Christianity."

This last phrase may well give us a key to Brunner's thinking. He obviously repudiates the idea of fixed truth and absolute authority, outside of man. To be sure, he professes to abjure the rationalist's notion of the supremacy of man's reason. He tells us that by man's criticism of Scripture reason must not "again make itself master of the Bible." But, having rejected the Bible as the very word of God, the only ground for believing anything about the "personal word," and about God's resolution of "the contradiction," is purely subjective. For that reason, Brunner's faith can never lead to the possession of life and to the assurance, "I am a Christian." His apparently Biblical language flatters only to deceive.

Brunner's theology of crisis is merely old-line modernism married to an esoteric knowledge which is paraded as existential faith. The modernist pronounces the Bible to be unhistorical and untrue in many vital areas, full of myth and legend, and goes on to reject the supernatural person and work of the redeemer portrayed in the Bible, reducing the Lord Jesus Christ to an erring, human teacher. Brunner and the neo-orthodox movement agree with modernism's rejection of Scripture but want to retain faith in the "personal word," who is hidden under the errors and myths of the Bible, and even under "the historical appearance of the human personality of Jesus," but who is "revealed" to those who "let God speak to them."

By this revelation, God "requires us to make a decision between his will and ours. This choice is the essence of faith." Since this revelation is not synonymous with the Bible, it may be found as much through the philosophy of a heathen thinker as through the Scriptures. Like Barth, Brunner held that revelational material was not given to one people as distinct from others.

All this is merely a form of modernism that fears to be consistent with itself, but that still hates the old theology of the written and inspired word. Brunner, like neo-orthodoxy generally, is neither *neo* nor orthodox, and clearly falls within the sweep of the condemnation of Isa. 8:20.

THEOLOGY OF DECOLONIZATION

A synthesis between Ethiopianist Theology* and Black Theology.* Dibinga Wa Said described it as follows:

"Black Theology in the United States and the Ethiopianist Theology of African Independent Churches represent a Theology of Decolonization. It is defined as a scientific enterprise of which the main purpose is the liberation of the Wretched of the Third World from spiritual-socio-politico-economic colonialism, imperialism, and neo-colonialism. As a radical call for a new creation, this Theology of Decolonization addresses itself primarily to the situation of the oppressed, and provides some means for their liberation from the white man's exploitation of man by the inhuman. Moreover, Theology of Decolonization seeks for a God and a Jesus who can respond to the cry of the oppressed and liberate them from spiritual imperialism, psychological terrorism, intellectual atrocities, and academic genocide which the white establishment has inflicted upon the oppressed for more than 529 years" (*Harvard Theological Review,* October 1971, p. 518).

As with every kind of liberation theology,* the theology of decolonization is basically a racist, socialist programme, not a theology in any real sense of the term.

THEOLOGY OF RELIGIONS

The study of the relationship of Christianity to other religions. This relationship may be stated by an inclusivist, exclusivist, or pluralist theology of religion.

The *inclusivist* holds that while Christianity is the best and fullest way of knowing and worshipping God, it is not the only way. Each of the world's great religions offers another way of knowing God. The *pluralist* goes even further and holds that Christianity is one way of knowing God, but that it stands on a par with the other religions of the world. The *exclusivist* holds that Christ is the focus of all divine revelation and that He is to be found only in Christianity. All other religions are false representations of God and offer no authentic or saving knowledge of Him.

The Bible itself is clearly exclusive in its claims for Christ and His gospel. Jesus said, "I am the way, the truth, and the life: no man cometh unto the Father but by me" (John 14:6). Again, John 3:36 says, "He that believeth on the Son hath everlasting life: and he that believeth not the Son shall not see life; but the wrath of God abideth on him." Later John wrote, "He that hath the Son hath life; and he that hath not the Son of God hath not life" (1 John 5:12). Peter proclaimed, "Neither is there salvation in any other: for there is none other name under heaven given among men, whereby we must be saved" (Acts 4:12).

The apostles proclaimed to Jews and Gentiles their need of Christ. They did not enter into dialogue with other religions to find the truth. They did not present the gospel as one way among many, or even as the best way. The Christ they preached was the only way, outside of which men were "dead in trespasses and sins," and were "without Christ being aliens from the commonwealth of Israel, and strangers from the covenants of promise, having no hope, and without God in the world" (Eph. 2:1, 12). Without Christ, without hope, without God—that is the human condition apart from gospel grace. But "God…is rich in mercy" (Eph. 2:4) and has a message for the world, a message that is the "power of God unto salvation to every one that believeth, to the Jew first and also to the Greek" (Rom. 1:16). That message is the very heart of the Christian mission to the world. It has never been better expressed than in the words of the Lord Jesus Christ Himself: "God so loved the world, that he gave his only begotten Son, that whosoever believeth in him should not perish, but have everlasting life" (John 3:16).

THEOPHANY

A manifestation of God; frequently employed to denote a pre-incarnation appearance of Christ and therefore often called a *Christophany.* Theophany, along with miracle and prophecy, is a mode of special revelation.* Cornelius Van Til discussed this mode of special revelation as follows:

"After the entrance of sin God could no longer walk and talk with man in the familiar way in which he had walked and talked with him before the fall. But through the 'special principle' of which Christ is the center, this became possible and actual again. Christ is the Immanuel. [By special principle Van Til means the work of redemption.]

"We must be careful here not to understand this work by which he brought God near to us in a metaphysical sense. It is a common mistake of modern theology to mix the categories of the ethical and the metaphysical. Man was a creature in paradise, man remained a creature after he fell into sin, man remains a creature when he is redeemed, and man will remain a creature when he goes to heaven. His metaphysical status cannot, in the nature of the case, be changed. The transformations that take place are ethical.…

"Barthianism, though it seems to be strongly opposed to modern theology, confuses the metaphysical and the ethical. It constantly speaks as though man is to be condemned simply because he is temporal. Instead of providing a deep concept of sin this makes room for a more superficial concept of sin. A man who is under the judgment of God by virtue of creation, will not feel and should not feel that he is responsible for sin. It is only the person who knows that man was made perfect but wilfully fell into disobedience against God, who will feel guilty for his sin.

"John speaks of Christ as the Immanuel when he exultantly declares: 'And the Word became flesh, and dwelt among us (and we beheld his glory, the glory as of the only begotten of the Father), full of grace and truth' (John 1:14). This dwelling of God with man reached its climax, as far as the present age is concerned, in Christ's appearance in the flesh, and will reach its highest climax when 'the tabernacle of God shall dwell with men' (Rev. 21:3). (Van Til, *An Introduction to Systematic Theology,* 1951 class syllabus, p. 127).

THEOSIS

A popular heresy in the Eastern Orthodox church that regards salvation as deification, man becoming divine. According to this theory man is called to be a god and the grace of God in Christ accomplishes this end. One Orthodox theologian, Constantine Cavarnos, held that deification "is the final end for which man was created" (*Orthodox Iconography*, p. 45).

*See **Apotheosis**.*

THEOSOPHY

From *theos,* "God," and *sophia,* "wisdom," it means divine wisdom. However, as a title it has been assumed by a cult that has been described as the "apostate child of Spiritism mixed with Buddhism" (J. K. Van Baalen).

In 1875 the Theosophical Society was founded in New York by "Madame" Blavatsky and Colonel Olcott. After they had visited India they added Hindu and Buddhist elements to their original ideas, which Blavatsky described as "Spiritualism, but under another name."

Madame Blavatsky's most famous follower was Mrs. Annie Besant, who like the founder, left her husband and later converted to Theosophy. Mrs. Besant had an adopted son, Krishnamurti or Krishnaji, whom she claimed was the new Messiah, the re-incarnation of the World Teacher. This World Teacher stands as the Supreme Teacher at the head of the Great Brotherhood of Teachers who are "divine men made perfect," and "the finished products of human evolution." These are the Mahatmas, whose habitat is Tibet and who become incarnate in the body of a Theosophist to supervise human evolution. When the Supreme Teacher becomes incarnate, we have a Christ on earth.

Theosophy's notion of God is pantheistic.* God is the great impersonal *It.* Theosophy postulates the evolution of humanity over a period of 18 million years. It believes in the pre-existence of souls and their reincarnation countless times, until each soul is fit to be absorbed by the great impersonal *It.* This absorption is the Buddhist idea of nirvana. Theosophy, therefore, is autosoteric.*

The source of the Theosophist's alleged knowledge, and the inspiration of his evolution, is spiritistic.* Theosophy holds the notion that the natural body is threefold, consisting of a physical body, an astral body, and a mental body. During sleep or in a trance, man leaves his physical body, and in his astral and mental bodies dwells in the astral world, whence he obtains deeper knowledge and advances in his evolution toward perfection. It uses the practice of yoga to hasten the perfection of the soul's evolution.

Theosophy is at once heathen and truly ecumenical for it views all religions as fundamentally one. Mrs. Besant wrote: "Every religion has a note of its own, a colour of its own, that it gives for the helping of the world...; blended together they give the whiteness of the truth, blended together, they give a mighty chord of perfection." Contrast John 14:6; Acts 4:12.

THEOTOKOS

"The bearer of God"; in Roman Catholic theology, the title accorded to Mary as the "Mother of God." Though no less a theologian than Charles Hodge sanctioned the use of the title "Mother of God," there is no scriptural foundation for it. The divine second person of the Trinity was not conceived in Mary. Only the human nature which He took into personal union with Himself was formed in her womb and of her substance. She is the mother of Jesus as to His humanity; she is not the mother of God.

Yet *theotokos* may have a legitimate use in orthodox theology to emphasize that the one whom Mary bore was truly "God manifest in the flesh" (1 Tim. 3:16). He was the God-man, even when His human substance was yet being formed in Mary's womb. The union of the divine and human natures in Christ took place at the point of conception, so that it was the entire theanthropic person* that Mary carried within her. In this sense, *theotokos* expresses a necessary scriptural idea. It is to be regretted that because of Rome's support of its Maryolatry* with the illegitimate title "Mother of God," and her association of that title with *theotokos,* Protestant theology has largely ignored the benefit of maintaining *theotokos* as a legitimate description of Mary—or rather, as a witness to the uniqueness of the one she bore.

THOMISM

The philosophical and theological system of Thomas Aquinas (1225-74). His scholasticism* propounded the idea that revelation* and reason, both coming from God, cannot be in contradiction and so, applying the philosophy of Aristotle, he erected a rational interpretation of nature, law, ethics, and revelation.

See Natural Law.

TIQQUNE SOPHERIM

"Emendations of the Scribes"; the alterations to the Hebrew text allegedly introduced by the scribes to remove anthropomorphic references to God. The Masora* marks these places. In Gen 18:22 the scribe altered "The Lord stood yet before Abraham" to "Abraham stood yet before the Lord." The other texts usually cited as examples are Num. 11:15; Num. 12:12; 1 Sam. 3:13; 2 Sam. 16:12; 1 Kings 12:16; 2 Chron. 10:16; Job 7:20; Job 32:3; Ps. 106:20; Jer. 2:11; Lam. 3:20; Ezek. 8:17; Hosea 4:7; Hab. 1:12; Zech. 2:12; Mal. 1:13. Traditionally there were said to be eighteen *tiqqune sopherim,* but the number seems somewhat arbitrary.

Textual critics* believe there are many more than eighteen emendations, and various editions of the Masora give differing lists of eighteen corrections. In some of these places it appears clear that the Sopherim did indeed emend the text. However, there is no evidence that they did so in all the cases attributed to them.

TONGUES, GIFT OF

See Glossalalia; Gifts of the Spirit; Holy Spirit; Pentecostalism; Charismatic Movement.

TOTAL DEPRAVITY

See Depravity; Inability.

TRACTARIANISM

The Oxford Movement, made up of a group of Anglican ministers at Oxford—including John Henry Newman, its leader, and E. B. Pusey—which in 1833 launched a series of *Tracts for the Times.* These tracts culminated in *Tract 90* by Newman, advocating the interpretation of the formularies of the Church of England in a Roman Catholic sense. Hence Tractarianism, with its sacramentalism,* became known as Anglo-Catholicism.*

Newman joined the Roman Catholic church and became a cardinal. Many Anglo-Catholics followed his lead back to Rome, but many more stayed within Anglicanism to assume an influence on the bench of bishops far beyond the movement's numerical strength among the laity.

TRADITION

That which has been handed down to us from the apostles as the faith once for all delivered to the saints.

According to the Roman Catholic church, tradition "includes Scripture, the essential doctrines of the church, the major writings and teaching of the Fathers, the liturgical life of the church, and the living and lived faith of the whole church down through the centuries" (R. P. McBrien, *Catholicism,* p. 1258). Thus to Rome, tradition is greater than Scripture,* though, she would claim, always scriptural. In Romanism, tradition is the word of God by which faith and practice are directed. Scripture is part of that word, but not the entirety of it. Against all this, Protestantism contends for the sufficiency of Scripture. R. P. Blakeney enumerated and answered the leading arguments Romanists employ in favour of tradition as a rule of faith and practice:

"**1.** Bellarmine argues that Scripture is not necessary, from the fact that before the Mosaic age, there was no written rule of faith. This, however, when the result is considered, may be adduced as an argument against tradition, for it is written in reference to the days of Noah, 'And God looked upon the earth, and behold, it was corrupt: for *all flesh had corrupted his way upon the earth,*' Gen. 6:12. Besides, there was no such need of a written law, then, as now. The lives of Adam and Methuselah occupied a space of 1650 years, which rendered the transmission of the precepts of religion, which were then but few, comparatively secure; but, notwithstanding, how lamentable was the result!

2. Some passages of Scripture are quoted by Romanists in support of this dogma. The following text is referred to, (in conjunction with John 21:25):—'And many other signs truly did Jesus in the presence of his disciples, which are not written in this book,' John 20:30. We do not deny that much of what Jesus did is not written, but we maintain, that *what is written is sufficient;* for the next verse declares, 'But these are written, that ye might believe that Jesus is the Christ, the Son of God; and that believing ye might have life through his name,' John 20:31.

3. Again, they refer to John 16:12, 'I have yet many things to say unto you, but ye cannot bear them now.' This passage only proves, that, *before* the resurrection, the disciples were not fully instructed in all the truths of the Gospel. On the day of Pentecost, the Holy Spirit was poured out upon the disciples, who were then guided into all truth according to the promise given in John 16:13. This text does not set aside the Protestant doctrine, that the Bible contains all that is necessary to salvation.

4. So also are the following texts quoted:— 'Now I praise you, brethren, that ye remember me in all things, and keep the ordinances,' 1 Cor. 11:2. This passage does not prove that what was so delivered by the Apostle, in so far as it was necessary, was not written.

5. 'And the rest will I set in order when I come,' 1 Cor. 11:34. This refers to discipline. We believe that all that is necessary to the good order of the Church is contained in the Bible.

6. 'Stand fast, and hold the traditions which ye have been taught, whether by word, or our epistle,' 2 Thess. 2:15. We do not deny that what is contained in Scripture was first taught by word; but we believe that all of what was necessary to salvation, in the teaching of Christ and His Apostles, is committed to writing by inspiration of the Spirit. Were the Apostles now alive, we should receive with equal veneration their word, whether delivered orally, or by writing. If the Church of Rome can only prove that her traditions are apostolic, we shall receive them; *but this she cannot do.* The Bible alone contains what the Apostles taught.

7. The exhortations to Timothy to 'keep that which was committed to his trust,' 1 Tim. 6:20; and to 'Hold fast the form of sound words,' 2 Tim. 1:13, are also quoted; but they only prove the necessity of adhering to the teaching of the Apostles, which no Protestant denies. They do not affect our belief, that the Bible is the only certain record of that teaching.

8. 'I had many things to write, but I will not with ink and pen write unto thee: But I trust I shall shortly see thee, and we shall speak face to face,' 3 John 13, 14. Can the Romanist prove that the things not written in this epistle, are not written in other portions of Scripture? Who denies that there were many things said and done, both by Christ and His Apostles, which are not written?—for 'the world itself could not contain the books that should be written,' John 21:25. We have certain warrant of inspiration for believing that sufficient is recorded in the Bible; for St. John says, 'But *these are written,* that ye might believe that Jesus is the Christ, the Son of God; and that believing ye might have life through his name,' John 20:31. Let Rome produce her apostolical traditions, and we shall receive them." (*Manual of the Romish Controversy,* pp. 27-29).

TRADITIONAL TEXT

The name preferred by J. W. Burgon* and many upholders of the *Received Text* of the NT for the Greek text found in the vast majority of MSS.

See **Textual Criticism of the New Testament**.

TRADUCIANISM

The theory of the specific unity of the human race in Adam, and of the propagation of the soul* as well as the body. While creationism* holds that God infuses a newly created soul into each propagated body, traducianism holds that both are descended by ordinary generation from Adam. Thus, we were really, not merely

ideally, in him when he sinned and justly became liable to punishment.

Adam's first sin is imputed to all his posterity, and traducianists believe that "participation is the ground of merited imputation" (Shedd, *Dogmatic Theology,* 2:29).

If we were not personally guilty of Adam's first sin, on what ground could the justice of God charge it upon us? Augustine used this argument in support of traducianism. According to De Marets (Maresius), "He constantly held it [traducianism] in order to save the justice of God; because it is difficult to show the justice of infusing a soul newly created, and destitute of sin, and having no guilt of its own, into a vitiated body, by whose concupiscence and lust it is stained and burdened, is exposed to many and great evils in this life, and condemned to everlasting punishment hereafter." We can see how the mercy of God would grant us a gratuitous imputation of righteousness to save our guilty souls, but can we see any scriptural basis for the theory that God creates sinless souls, places them in sinful bodies, and immediately charges them with guilt by reason of that union?

This is a serious weakness in the creationist theory. There is another: creationism appears to make sin more a matter of the physical constitution than of the will.* However, the whole culpability of sin lies in the voluntariness of the sinner. If the theory of creationism is incapable of embracing this fundamental fact it stands condemned.

The transmission of sin from Adam to his posterity argues for traducianism. Tertullian's maxim was: "The transmission of sin, the transmission of the soul." Shedd said: "Moral corruption, resulting from the first transgression, could not be transmitted and inherited unless there were a vehicle for its transmission; unless there were a common human nature, both as to soul and body, to convey it" (*ibid.,* 2:33).

Some theologians hold that there is no direct Biblical evidence to indicate either traducianism or creationism. Shedd disagrees and cites a number of texts, especially using Gen. 2:1-3, which teaches that God "rested from all His work which he had created and made" (cf. Ex. 20:11; Heb. 4:4). How can the "rest" of a finished creation and the ceaseless work of creating countless millions of souls both be true?

The chief objection used against traducianism is that it endangers the sinlessness of Christ. Creationists contend that if Christ's soul was not a sinless new creation direct from the hand of God, but derived directly from Mary and remotely from Adam, He would be a sinner. If this argument were true, it would be fatal to traducianism. But is it true?

The argument about sinlessness proceeds on the assumption it poses a problem only for traducianism. That is not so, for it affects creationism in just the same degree. Creationism holds that the physical constitution is propagated from Adam and is corrupted by his sin. It is just as logical to say that this endangers the sinlessness of Christ as it is to make that charge against traducianism. The fact is that Christ was supernaturally born. His was a miraculous conception. Reformed theology has always held that the human nature, born of the flesh of Mary, was perfectly sinless in order to be united with the eternal Word. It requires no more of a miracle to extend this to the soul and body than to limit it to the body.

TRANSCENDENCE

The theological term that emphasizes the distinction of God from His creation, and His sovereign exaltation over it. In the popular phrase of Barth, God is "wholly other." He is not part of the universe. He is not the sum of the parts of the universe. He is not the soul of the universe. He is the eternal, uncreated, absolute, self-contained, self-existent, sovereign Creator by whose will and power all things exist. They depend on Him for their being, He depends on none.

Rejection of, or rebellion against, this essential truth lies at the root of many theological heresies. Pantheism,* panentheism,* liberalism,* God-is-dead theology,* process theology,* and various forms of political theology* show how truth perishes once we lose sight of the transcendence of God.

*See **Immanence**.

TRANSCENDENTAL MEDITATION

An ancient Hindu discipline of meditation based on pantheistic mysticism* and popularized, almost trademarked, in the 1960's and 1970's by the Maharishi (meaning "Great Sage") Mahesh Yogi. According to this Indian guru, who attracted a lot of public support from musical, sports, and film stars, peace and serenity can be had only if one proceeds beyond the normal states of consciousness—sleep, dreaming, wakefulness—to a fourth state. He must learn to meditate so that he may transcend to the state of "pure bliss consciousness," a state of "pure awareness," in which he is tuned into "creative intelligence."

Transcendental meditation became popular in the hippie movement. It has since lost its prominence as a movement, but its basic theory is now an integral part of the New Age* movement's philosophy.

TRANSCENDENTALISM

A form of irrationalism,* it is the theory of Immanuel Kant that knowledge and truth are discoverable by an investigation of the mind rather than by sense perception. It was adapted and popularized in America by Ralph Waldo Emerson. Schaff-Hertzog summarizes Emerson's theory as follows:

"[He sought] on a consistently naturalistic basis to inspire the individual and fortify his self-reliance. Nature as a whole, it was said, corresponds to the individual, so the knowledge of the self is the foundation of all knowledge. Thus the intuitive and introspective study of self is placed above natural science, history, and all material values."

Transcendentalism suited Emerson's theology. As a Unitarian, he rejected the Bible as God's authoritative revelation. Loosed from the authority of the divine, he posited an inherently antichristian trust in human intuition, ignoring the fact that man is a fallen creature whose mental processes have been darkened by sin and cannot therefore be either normative or decisive in establishing truth.

TRANSMIGRATION OF SOULS

The removal of a soul from one body to another; reincarnation* as taught in Buddhism and Hinduism.

TRANSUBSTANTIATION

See Mass.

TRENT

The Council of Trent was held at Trent, Italy, from 1545-1563. It was Rome's principal instrument in the Counter Reformation.* It formulated her response to the Protestant doctrine of free, gracious justification, received by the imputation of Christ's righteousness through faith without works. That response was so carefully worked out that Rome has never altered it, and the first and second Vatican Councils did not even attempt an updating or rewording of the Tridentine formula. Though Rome does not hurl her anathemas quite so freely or publicly as Trent did, Trent is still the authentic voice of the Roman Catholic church—as is evident from the frequency with which Vatican II documents and the *Catechism of the Catholic Church* appeal to it as proof of their propositions.

TRIBULATION

The Greek word *thlipsis* means "affliction." The term is used to refer to the period of trial and terror affecting the Jews and the saints of God at the end of this age, immediately before the second coming* of the Lord Jesus Christ. It is usually referred to as "the great tribulation," or, as the Greek of Rev. 7:14 puts it, "the tribulation, the great one." Thus, the phrase "the great tribulation" is a perfectly scriptural one (cf. also Matt. 24:21).

There are many passages of Scripture to be studied to gain a thorough understanding of the subject and its background events, such as Jer. 30; Dan. 2, 7, 8, 9, 11, 12; Zech. 12-14; Matt. 24; Luke 21; 2 Thess. 2; Rev. 4-19.

Description of the Great Tribulation

1. It is *yet future.* Matt. 24, etc., have not yet been fulfilled.

2. It will be a time of *unparalleled persecution* (Jer. 30:7; Dan. 12:1; Matt. 24:21).

Details of the Great Tribulation

1. *It is associated with Antichrist* and the setting up of his image* (Dan. 7:8, 21, 25; 8:8-12, 23-25; 9:27 with Matt. 24:15).

2. *It centres on the Jews in their own land* (Jer. 30:7; Dan. 11:41).

3. *It spreads over the earth against all the saints of God* (Dan. 7:25; Mt. 24:9; Rev. 13:6-8).

4. *Refusal to worship the beast (Antichrist) or bear his mark is the thing that causes Jews and Christians to be persecuted* (Rev. 13:15-18—the instrument of persecution will be the false prophet: this is what apostate religion will lead to).

5. *The power that energizes all this terror is that of the Devil* (2 Thess. 2:9; Rev. 12:12. Cf. Dan. 8:24; Rev. 13:4). Yet God will overrule, for He will use even this as His chastisement upon the Jews to save a remnant and fully restore them (Jer. 30:11). Revelation 9:21 and 18:23 list "sorceries," or "enchantment with drugs" as part of the devil's policy. The increasing emphasis on these in modern society is neither accidental nor unexpected.

The Duration of the Tribulation

The period from Antichrist's making a covenant with the Jews until the end of the age is seven years. The time of persecution starts halfway through that period and lasts for three and a half years (Dan. 9:27, cf. Dan. 7:25; Rev. 11:3; 12:6, 14). This time is set and fixed (Dan. 12:7), for the Lord will curtail the tribulation for His elect's sake (Matt. 24:22).

Deliverance from the Great Tribulation

Some expect a secret return of the Lord to rapture the church before the tribulation. There is no scriptural foundation for this.
1. God's elect will endure the tribulation (Matt. 24:22).
2. The saints who will possess the kingdom for ever and ever will be in it (Dan. 7:18, 22).
3. Some quote Rev. 3:10 to show that Christians will be "kept" from the tribulation. However, even allowing that this text refers to the tribulation, it is clear that keep does not signify removal, but preservation (John 17:11). The Jews have an almost identical promise that they will be "saved out of it" (Jer. 30:7), but they will certainly not be raptured out of the earth.
4. The tribulation will terminate in the coming of the Lord (Matt. 24:29-31). Christ speaks of the sounding of a trumpet at His return at the end of the tribulation. Now Paul tells us that the resurrection of the saints and their rising to meet the Lord in the air takes place "at the last trump" (1 Cor. 15:52; 1 Thess. 4:16). Therefore, since the last trumpet sounds at the rapture* of the saints, this event cannot take place before the end of the tribulation. For further proof see Rev. 20:4, 5, which teaches that some who are raised in the first resurrection die during the tribulation; so they could not be raised before the tribulation.

During the tribulation God's witness and wrath will be against His people's persecutors. Saints will be overcomers (Rev. 11; 12:11). Christ's coming will spell vanquishment (2 Thess. 2:8) for the enemy and victory for His people (Dan. 2:44; 7:13-14, 18; 2 Thess. 1:7-9).

TRICHOTOMY

Belief in the tripartite nature of man as spirit, soul, and body, thus making a distinction between spirit and soul. For a fuller discussion of trichotomy and dichotomy, see Soul.

TRIDENTINE

Of or concerning the Council of Trent.*

TRINITY

The self-revelation of God in Scripture that His indivisible, personal essence exists eternally and necessarily as Father, Son, and Holy Spirit; and that these three are not merely nominal distinctions but personal subsistences in the divine essence.

It has been said that if you try to comprehend the doctrine of the Trinity you may lose your mind, and if you deny it you will lose your soul. The finite mind of man cannot possibly comprehend the infinite God. So a complete understanding of the doctrine of the Trinity is not attainable by us. However, we may obtain a knowledge of the Trinity from God's revelation of Himself in His word, and although the knowledge so gained by our finite minds is incomplete, it is nonetheless true knowledge.

God's revelation of Himself lies at the heart of all He has revealed in His word. In a very real sense, our understanding of any part of the Scripture revelation is dependent upon our acceptance of God's revelation of Himself, a revelation which is denoted by the term Trinity. It has been aptly said, "The Trinity is the point in which all Christian ideas and interests unite; at once the beginning and the end of all insight into Christianity."

Defining Our Terms

Trinity. "The word trinity is derived from Latin and Greek terms meaning three in one, or the one which is three, and the three which are one.…The word is not found in the Scriptures. Technical terms are, however, absolutely necessary in all sciences. In this case they have been made particularly essential because of the subtle perversions of the simple, untechnical Biblical statements by infidels and heretics. The term, as above defined, admirably expresses the central fact of the great doctrine of the one essence eternally subsisting as three Persons, all the elements of which are explicitly taught in the Scriptures" (A. A. Hodge).

Person. The original meaning of the Latin word *persona* is far removed from its present sense and it is an even larger step from the present sense of the word to the scriptural and theological meaning when applied to the Godhead. But despite its imperfection as a term, there is none better in man's vocabulary. In everyday usage, the term *person* denotes an entirely separate and distinct rational individual. It does not have this meaning when referred to the persons in the Trinity. A divine person, to use John Calvin's words, is "a subsistence in the divine essence—a subsistence which, while related to the other two, is distinguished from them by incommunicable properties."

Deniers of the Trinity

These fall into two main classes:
1. Arians and Socinians, who deny the deity of Christ and of the Holy Spirit.
2. Sabellians who hold that the Biblical Trinity is an economical one, not an essential one. That is, the names Father, Son, and Holy Spirit are different names for the one divine person under different relations or fulfilling different offices.

It is commonly, and mostly frivolously, objected that the doctrine of the Trinity makes three Gods, while the Scripture teaches "there is one God." Another objection is that God cannot be both one and three. Such objections either miss the point or set out to misrepresent the orthodox position.

The doctrine of the Trinity emphasizes the unity of the divine essence. What theologians call His "numerical essence" is one and indivisible. Each trinitarian person possesses the undivided essence, not a *fragment* of it. To imagine the three persons of the Godhead each having a third of the divine essence is an absurdity, for infinity cannot be fragmented or fractionalized. As the *Shorter Catechism* put it, "There are three Persons in the Godhead, the Father, the Son, and the Holy Ghost: these three are one God, the same in substance, equal in power and glory" (Q. 6).

Again, the doctrine of the Trinity does not teach that God is one and three in the same sense. Obviously that would be absurd. However, there is no contradiction in saying that God is one as to His eternal spiritual essence and that that divine essence exists necessarily in three modes, each of which is spoken of in Scripture in personal terms.

Furthermore, we do not hold that God is three *and* one, but that He is three *in* one, and one *in* three *(see **Circuminsession**).* We state the doctrine this way, not because we can understand it (if any mind could understand the infinite God, that mind itself would be infinite), but because the word of God warrants such statements. Indeed, the teaching of the Scriptures concerning God cannot be fully and faithfully interpreted apart from such trinitarian statements.

Scripture Proof of the Doctrine of the Trinity

To prove the Trinity we need prove only the following propositions from Scripture:
1. That God is one. Deuteronomy 6:4 establishes that beyond all doubt: "The Lord our God is one Lord."
2. That the Father is truly God, that the Son is truly God, and that the Holy Spirit is truly God. 1 Corinthians 8:6 teaches "there is one God the Father"; John 1:1-3 clearly established the proper deity of the Son; while Acts 5:3-5 does the same concerning the Holy Spirit *(see **Deity of Christ**; **Holy Spirit**).*
3. That yet the Father is not the Son; the

Son is not the Father; and neither of them is the Holy Spirit.

This can be clearly seen from the plain statements of Scripture. Consider the following evidence:

Genesis 1:26: "And God said, Let us make man in our image, after our likeness." Up to this point in the creation story, God has used the language of command, but now He uses the language of consultation. With whom is He taking counsel? We answer, with Himself in the persons of the blessed Trinity.

To avoid this evidence of eternal personal distinctions in the Godhead, some hold that here God consults with angels. Absurd! Where does the Scripture ever teach that angels had a part in the creation of man? The Scriptures do teach, however, that the divine persons in the Godhead were active in creation (Gen. 1:2, referring to the Holy Spirit, and John 1:1-3, referring to the Son). What proves that God consulted with Himself and not with angels, is the statement of Gen. 1:27, "So God created man in his own image," with no mention of angels at all.

If God consulted with Himself, what can the significance of the *us* be, except to emphasize a real plurality of persons in the Godhead?

Isaiah 48:16: "The Lord God, and his Spirit, hath sent me." The context after v. 12 shows that the speaker is Messiah. He is clearly a divine person because in v. 12 He says, "I am he; I am the first, I also am the last" (compare Rev. 1:8, 11-13). In v. 16 He says, "From the time it was, there am I and now the Lord God, and His Spirit, hath sent me." What stronger evidence could be given of three divine persons, distinct one from another as to their personal properties, in the unity of the divine essence?

Many other Scriptures may be cited showing the Father speaking to the Son and vice versa, and all these would be added proof that the Father and the Son are so far distinguished as to be able to hold conversation one with another.

Summary

Since there is one God, and since the Father is God, the Son is God, and the Holy Spirit is God, and since these three are clearly distinguished in Scripture, we are left with the glorious truth of the Trinity—one God eternally existing as Father, Son, and Holy Ghost, each indwelling the other and each possessing, not in part, but entirely, the infinite essence of the one divine Being. Contemplating such a majestic mystery of revealed truth, we are constrained to cry out with heaven's seraphim, "Holy, holy, holy, is the Lord of Hosts" (Isa. 6:3).

TRIPLEX DIVISION

The tripartite arrangement of the OT canon* as the Law, the Prophets, and the Hagiographa (or Holy Writings).

*See **Scriptures.***

TRISAGION

From the "holy, holy, holy" of Isaiah 6:3, and meaning "thrice holy," it refers to an ancient liturgical hymn, now used in the Greek Orthodox and the Roman Catholic churches.

TRITHEISM

The perversion of the doctrine of the Trinity,* propounding the theory that there are three Gods, distinct in essence, not one God in three personal subsistences.

TRUTH OF GOD

A. A. Hodge described it as follows: "The truth of God, in its widest sense, is a perfection which qualifies all his intellectual and moral attributes. His knowledge is infinitely true in relation to its objects, and his wisdom unbiased either by prejudice or passion. His justice and his goodness, in all their exercises, are infinitely true to the perfect standard of his own nature. In all outward manifestations of his perfections to his creatures, God is always true to his nature—always self-consistently divine. This attribute, in its more special sense, qualifies all God's intercourse with his rational creatures. He is true to us as well as to Himself; and thus is laid the foundation of all faith, and therefore, of all knowledge. It is the foundation of all confidence—first, in our senses; second, in our intellect and conscience; third, in any authenticated supernatural revelation.

"The two forms in which this perfection is exercised in relation to us are, first, His entire truthfulness in all His communications; second, His perfect sincerity in undertaking and faithfulness in discharging all His engagements."

TSEBAOTH

Hebrew, meaning "hosts." *Jehovah Tsebaoth,* "Lord of Hosts," is frequently found in the OT. Some interpreters understand the hosts to refer to the armies of Israel, and others to the stars. Most, however, refer it to the angelic hosts (1 Sam. 4:4; 2 Sam. 6:2; Isa. 37:16; Hos. 12:4, 5; Ps. 80:1, 4ff.; 89:6-8). "Jehovah of hosts, then, is God as the King of glory, who is surrounded by angelic hosts, who rules heaven and earth in the interest of His people, and who receives glory from all His creatures" (Berkhof, *Systematic Theology,* p. 50).

TÜBINGEN SCHOOL

The movement initiated by F. C. Baur (1792-1860) at Tübingen University. Baur's basic supposition was that there was a continual conflict in the NT church between the theologies of Peter and Paul and their respective followers. He held that all genuine NT writings must evidence such a Pauline-Petrine tension, and in this way arrived at the conclusion that very little in the NT was genuine. He allowed only Romans, the Corinthian epistles and Galatians to be genuine.

Baur's method was professedly historical, but it proceeded on the first error every historian must avoid: manipulating the data to coincide with a prior supposition

of what history *must* say if we are to accept its witness. From such a flawed basis Baur produced a system of NT criticism that was a delusion, the "findings" of which break down continually before the factual testimony of the NT.

TYPE, TYPOLOGY

"A type is a shadow cast on the pages of OT history by a truth whose full embodiment or antitype is found in the NT revelation" (*Baker's Dictionary of Theology*). The legitimacy of recognizing typology in Biblical exegesis is established by the NT itself.

First, the NT uses a number of terms that confirm the presence of typology in Scripture: (1) *tupos,* "type" (Rom. 5:14; 1 Cor. 10:6, 11); (2) *skia,* "shadow" (Col. 2:17; Heb. 8:5; 10:1), which is really an outline or image of the full revelation of the NT cast by OT ceremonies; (3) *hupodeigma,* "copy" (Heb. 8:5, "example"; 9:23, "patterns"). This word is compounded of *hupo,* "under," and *deiknumi,* "to show," and denotes what is shown under or privately, and thus a "sign suggestive of anything, the delineation or representation of a thing, and so a figure, copy" (Vine); (4) *semeion,* "sign" (Matt. 12:39), in this connection, a token or an indication of a coming event; (5) *parabole,* "figure," or "parable" (Heb. 9:9; 11:19). The word comes from *para,* "beside," and *ballo,* "to throw," and so means to throw things side by side with a view to marking comparison or resemblance; (6) *antitupos,* "antitype" (Heb. 9:24; 1 Pet. 3:21, "figure"), an event, person, or circumstance in place of (*anti,* that is, fulfilling or corresponding to) the type; (7) *allegoreo,* "to allegorize," or speak in such a way that facts are used to illustrate principles (Gal. 4:24). "The allegorical meaning does not do away with the literal meaning of the narrative. There may be more than one allegorical meaning though, of course, only one literal meaning. Scripture histories represent or embody spiritual principles, and these are ascertained, not by the play of the imagination but by the rightful application of the doctrines of Scripture" (Vine).

Obviously such a widespread NT usage denotes the existence of typology and declares its use legitimate.

Second, we have examples of NT interpretation of OT history as being typical of NT events (Matt. 12:40; Luke 17:26; John 3:14; 1 Cor. 3:7ff.; 1 Cor. 15:22; Gal. 4:22ff.; Heb. chaps. 3-10). With such an extensive inspired use of typology it would be vain to deny its validity.

It is important to note that types are truly historical. They are not mythological occurrences that are adapted by the NT writers to signify a spiritual truth. Indeed, their spiritual significance depends upon their historical reality.

Great care must be taken in interpreting OT events typically in places where we do not have the inspired interpretation of the NT:

1. As in all interpretation, nothing contrary to the analogy of faith may be inferred from a supposed type *(see **Hermeneutics**; **Scriptures, Interpretation of**).*

2. A type may legitimately be used to corroborate a doctrine clearly laid down in the word of God, but not to establish a doctrine that may not otherwise be proved from Scripture.

3. The nature of a type (see the terms discussed above) means that it will not always contain a full exposition of the truth it portrays—e.g., the experience of Jonah typified the resurrection of Christ after three days under the power of death (Matt. 12:40), but may not be further used to furnish a detailed description of that event.

4. Types are part of the unfolding history of redemption, and may not therefore be used in a wild and fanciful way to set forth things which are not part of that history and to which the type has no relevance outside the fancy of the interpreter. C. H. Spurgeon's advice to his students is in order here: "I counsel you to employ spiritualizing within certain limits and boundaries....An allowable thing carried to excess is a vice, even as fire is a good servant in the grate, but a bad minister when raging in a burning house" (*Lectures to My Students*, "On Spiritualizing").

U

UBIQUITY

Omnipresence. Lutheran writers employ the term to convey their theory that Christ's humanity entered into the full exercise of all the divine perfections, which had been communicated to it at the incarnation,* and thus became omnipresent. This idea is developed in the Lutheran doctrine of consubstantiation,* the concept that the actual body and blood of Christ, being omnipresent, are locally present in the Lord's Supper.

See Communicato Idiomatum; Lutheranism.

ULTRAMONTANISM

A Roman Catholic movement in the 19th century which advocated the centralization of all power and authority in the Pope, so that the political, intellectual, and religious attitudes of Roman Catholics would be determined by Rome.

Ultramontanism was adopted by the Vatican Council of 1870 and although the second Vatican Council (1962-65) allegedly moved the Roman Catholic church toward decentralization, Ultramontanism is still predominant in Vatican thinking (though challenges by individual Roman Catholics to papal authority in many areas of their private lives are common).

UNDERSTANDING

One of the two basic powers of the soul, as taught by earlier theologians, the will* being the other.

"Understanding is the cognitive faculty of the soul" (Shedd). It is comprised of intellect and conscience. The intellect is the *perceptive* faculty and the conscience the *preceptive* faculty in the understanding. The Biblical usage of the word indicates that understanding denotes more than a mere mental apprehension of facts. It is a wise perception and reception of the significance of those facts as laid down by God. Thus, the understanding of the ungodly is said to be "darkened" (Eph. 4:18), for "the carnal mind is enmity against God: for it is not subject to the law of God, neither indeed can be" (Rom. 8:7). It needs to be "enlightened" (Eph. 1:18) and until it is, it will remain in the condition described in 1 Cor. 2:14.

See Analogy; Epistemology.

UNGODLINESS

The sinfulness and depravity of fallen human nature.

Romans 1:18 clearly distinguishes *ungodliness* from *unrighteousness.* The latter refers to the multitude of wicked fruits, while the former refers to the foul root which produces such fruits. The order of the words in Rom. 1:18 is important, a fact also seen in Titus 2:12, where Paul teaches that the grace of God first deals with ungodliness and only then with unrighteousness.

UNIFICATION CHURCH

This cult* was started by Sun Myung Moon, who was born in Korea in 1920. When he was 16 years old Moon had his first vision, at which time he claims he was commissioned to save the world. In 1957 Moon published *Divine Principles,* which is not only supposed to be inspired but which is also given precedence over the NT. The book denies the doctrine of the Trinity,* holding that God has been trying to form a Trinity. God formed a *spiritual* trinity when Christ was perfected, and God is now attempting to form a *physical* trinity. While teaching that Christ is not God, the Unification church says that He became a form of deity. They also reject the resurrection of Christ's physical body and teach that He failed to accomplish the redemption of His people. God has appointed Moon to complete this redemption as the newly-chosen Messiah, which is, to their church, a sort of Second Advent. Moon's authority permeates the movement even to the point of choosing a person's mate and then performing large ceremonies where thousands are married at one time.

The Unification church, popularly called the "Moonies," was officially established in 1954 and has had its greatest impact in Korea and Japan. The cult gained a foothold in the United States in the early 1920's, and Moon not only bought property in the United States, but also moved there. His movement controls the *Washington Times* newspaper and *Insight* magazine. Some would estimate the cult to have between one and two million followers worldwide.

UNION OF TWO NATURES IN CHRIST
See Hypostatic Union.

UNION WITH CHRIST
See Mystical Union.

UNIPERSONALITY
The truth that "the two natures in Christ, the Divine and the human, constitute only one Person" (Shedd).

By the incarnation, a divine person took into union with Himself a human nature, not a human person. Thus, the theanthropic person* of Christ is a *single* person.

A striking proof of the unipersonality of Christ is found in those Scriptures which ascribe human attributes to Christ when He is designated by a divine title, and those which ascribe divine attributes to Him when He is designated by a human title (Acts 20:28; Rom. 8:32; 1 Cor. 2:8; Col. 1:13,

14; Matt. 1:23; Luke 1:31, 32; John 3:13; 6:62; Rom. 9:5; Rev. 5:12). "From these Biblical representations, therefore, it follows that both human and divine qualities and acts may be attributed to the God-Man under any of His names" (Shedd).

UNITARIANISM
Antitrinitarianism. Rooted in the ancient heresies of Monarchianism,* Arianism,* and Sabellianism,* Unitarianism gained great impetus in 16th-century Hungary and especially in Poland, where Faustus Socinus became its leader *(see Socinianism).*

In England, the founder of Unitarianism was John Biddle (1615-62). At first, unitarian views were confined to scattered individuals, but in the rationalistic atmosphere of the 18th century many Presbyterian and Baptist churches fell prey to the heresy. Indeed, by the second half of the century both had become mainly Unitarian denominations. The first self-styled Unitarian church was opened in 1773 when Theophilus Lindsey left the Church of England and opened his Essex Chapel in London.

In the United States, Unitarianism was introduced to New England as early as 1710, and by 1750 it had largely infected the Congregational churches of the area.

In Ireland, Unitarianism caused havoc in the Presbyterian church. Unitarians dominated the Presbytery of Antrim and found many sympathizers throughout the denomination. Only the heroic stand of Henry Cooke finally (1828) forced them out of the Presbyterian church in Ireland, to form the Non-Subscribing Presbyterian church.

Unitarianism became more and more rationalistic and openly anti-scriptural as it proceeded, repudiating all vestiges of the supernaturalism of Socinus and his followers. It thus became increasingly humanistic and antichristian. It rejects not only the doctrines of the Trinity,* the deity of Christ,* and the deity and personality of the Holy Spirit,* but it also repudiates the Bible as the word of God, with particular reference to the doctrines of creation and the fall, the blood atonement and resurrection of Christ, and salvation by grace through faith in Christ. It is universalist in its outlook *(see Universalism)* and rejects every idea of endless punishment. In a word, Unitarianism is man setting up himself as the supreme authority, making a god on the basis of that authority, and thereby worshipping himself in the god he has created.

UNITY OF GOD

Theologians usually consider this divine attribute in two ways:

1. *Unitas singularitatis,* the unity of singularity, stresses the fact that there is but one living and true God.

2. *Unitas simplicitatis,* the unity of simplicity, stresses the fact that the divine essence is indivisible. God is not composed of Father, Son, and Holy Ghost, each of whom has a fragment of the divine essence. Infinity is indivisible, and the Persons of the Trinity, each possessing all the divine essence, "are one God, the same in substance, equal in power and glory" *(Shorter Catechism,* Q. 6).

UNIVERSAL ATONEMENT

The theory that Christ died equally and indiscriminately for all men without exception, and not uniquely for His church, His elect. In this view, not only was the blood of Christ sufficient to atone for all of the sins of all men, but He shed it with that aim. On this basis it is difficult to escape the force of the argument that Christ failed to a large degree in His work. This does not correspond with the representation of Isa. 53:11 that He is "satisfied" with the results of His atoning work.

Another trenchant argument against the theory is that it compromises the justice of God by teaching that He receives a double payment for sin, first from Christ and then from sinners who bear His wrath in hell.

See Arminianism; Atonement; Calvinism; Universal Terms; Universalism.

UNIVERSAL TERMS

The general, or indefinite, terms which are frequently used in Scripture in connection with Christ's atonement,* and the invitation of the gospel. Such expressions as the *world,* the *whole world, all,* and *all men* are often urged against the Calvinistic view of the extent of the atonement, as if the bare use of such terms proved universal atonement. But John Owen *(Death of Death,* p. 191) said: "I hope we shall very easily make it appear that the general terms that are used in this business will indeed give no colour to any argument for universal redemption, whether absolute or conditionate."

Each text must be examined and interpreted in its context and with regard to the argument of the passage. The mere presence of general terms does not invalidate the truth of particular redemption.* For example, Owen showed how *world* is used in five distinct senses in Scripture:

1. The *world containing,* either for the heavens and the earth and all they contain (Job 34:13; Acts 17:24; Eph. 1:4), or for the heavens (Ps. 90:2), or the habitable earth (Ps. 24:1; 98:7; Matt. 13:38; John 1:9, etc.).

2. The *world contained,* i.e., it is used to mean men in the world. At times it is used to mean literally everyone (Rom. 3:6, 19; 5:12). It is also used to refer to men generally without distinction (John 7:4; Isa. 13:11). At other times it means many, and this is the most usual use of the word (Matt. 18:7; John 4:42; 12:19; 16:8; 17:21; 1 Cor. 4:9; Rev. 13:3). Again it can mean a great part of the world (Rom. 1:8; Matt. 24:14; 26:13; Rom. 10:18). Then it may refer to the inhabitants of the Roman empire (Luke 2:1). Finally, it may be used to denote God's people, believers (Ps. 22:27; John 3:16; 6:33, 51; Rom. 4:13; 11:12, 15; 2 Cor. 5:19; Col. 1:6; 1 John 2:2); or the wicked (Isa. 13:11; John 7:7; 14:17, 22; 15:19; 17:25; 1 Cor. 6:2; 11:32; Heb. 11:38, etc.).

3. The world *corrupted* (Gal. 1:4; 6:14; Eph. 2:2; James 1:27; 4:4; 1 John 2:15-17; 1 Cor.

7:31, 33; Col. 2:8; 2 Tim. 4:10, etc.).

4. The *world carnal* (Ps. 73:12; Luke 16:8; John 18:36; 1 John 4:5, etc.).

5. The *world cursed,* as under Satan's power (John 7:7; 14:30; 16:11, 33; 1 Cor. 2:12; 2 Cor. 4:4; Eph. 6:12).

Since the word *world* has such a varied usage in Scripture, it is foolish to think that its mere presence in a gospel text proves universal atonement. For example, in John 1:10 it has three distinct senses and thus emphasizes the need for sound Biblical interpretation in ascertaining its force in any given text.

The same is true of *all* and other general terms. *All* may mean "all of a particular sort" (1 Cor. 15:22; Eph. 4:6; Rom. 5:18) or "some of all sorts" (Heb. 8:11; John 12:32; 1 Tim. 2:4).

When texts with universal terms are examined in detail, with regard to context and argument, their testimony will favour the truth of particular redemption.*

As to the use of universal terms in the presentation of the gospel, we should always remember that it is every creature's responsibility to obey God and trust His Son. General calls and invitations reflect this; they do not intimate the purpose of God to bring all, without distinction, to salvation.

UNIVERSALISM

This term is used to denote two things:

1. The Arminian view that Christ died for all men indiscriminately *(see **Universal Atonement**).* John Owen in his *Death of Death in the Death of Christ* showed that if the scriptural significance of the death of Christ is maintained, the Arminian view leads naturally to the conclusion that all men will be saved—a conclusion which evangelical Arminians repudiate, though somewhat illogically.

2. The heresy of the ultimate salvation of every man. Some universalists have held that at death all are perfectly restored to God, while others have held that such restoration follows a period of future purgatorial punishment. Universalism uses Acts 3:21 and Col. 1:20 to teach that God's purpose is to restore all things to their original created purity through Christ (Rom. 5:18; Heb. 2:9), so that ultimately every soul will be brought into union with God (1 Cor. 15:24-28). Such an interpretation of these texts is arbitrary and clearly at variance with the rest of Scripture. All men who are savingly united to Christ, not all men indiscriminately, will be eternally saved. The Bible teaches that the wicked perish eternally (Ps. 9:17; Matt. 25:46; Luke 16:19-31; Rev. 20:10-15), and this effectively demolishes universalism. Unitarianism has long been universalist, and in 1959 formally merged in the United States with the Universalists, now going under the name of Unitarian Universalists.

UNPARDONABLE SIN

Blasphemy against the Holy Spirit is the sin that will never be pardoned (Matt. 12:31, 32). According to Matthew 12 this blasphemy is the deliberate attribution to Satan of the Holy Spirit's work in Christ (vv. 22-28). It is not a sin which can be committed by justified people and is, therefore, to be carefully distinguished from "the sin unto death" (1 John 5:16), which Christians may commit. This latter leads to physical death, and is a divine chastisement, the end of which is the escape of the believer from condemnation with the wicked (1 Cor. 11:30-32).

UNRIGHTEOUSNESS
See *Ungodliness*.

V

VARIANT READINGS

The variations of content, wording, or spelling observable in the manuscript copies of Scripture that have come down to us. *See **Textual Criticism.***

VATICAN COUNCIL

The name given to two councils of the Roman Catholic church.

The first was convened by Pope Pius IX and lasted from 1869 until 1870. At this council, after a period of decline in papal power in Europe, Ultramontanism* asserted itself and the dogma of papal infallibility was promulgated. The Second Vatican Council (1962-65) was set up by Pope John XXIII and while it left every Roman Catholic dogma unchanged, it fostered the ecumenical spirit with apostate Protestantism.

VENIAL SIN

According to the Roman Catholic church, a small, pardonable offence against God or our neighbour.

"Mortal sin destroys charity in the heart of man by a grave violation of God's law; it turns man away from God, who is his ultimate end and his beatitude, by preferring an inferior good to him. Venial sin allows charity to subsist, even though it offends and wounds it" (*Catechism of the Catholic Church,* ¶1855).

Rome takes the fact that all sins are not equally heinous to mean that not all sins are mortal. But that is unscriptural and false. All sin is mortal (Gal. 3:10; James 2:10).

*See **Mortal Sin**.*

VERACITY OF GOD
*See **Truth of God**.*

VIATICUM

Latin, meaning "on the way with you," it denotes a preparation for a journey, particularly the journey from this world to the next. In Roman Catholicism it has had two uses: first, broadly to describe the sacraments of baptism and the eucharist, both of which are reckoned necessary to conduct souls safely to heaven; second, and more properly, the final reception of the eucharistic sacrament before death.

The *Catechism of the Catholic Church* says, "As the sacrament of Christ's Passover the Eucharist should always be the last sacrament of the earthly journey the 'viaticum' for 'passing over' to eternal life" (¶1517). "Communion in the body and blood of Christ, received at the moment of 'passing over' to the Father, has a particular significance and importance. It is the seed of eternal life and the power of resurrection, according to the words of the Lord: 'He who eats my flesh and drinks my blood has eternal life, and I will raise him up at the last day.' The sacrament of Christ once dead and now risen, the Eucharist is here the sacrament of passing over from death to life, from this world to the Father" (¶1524). The proof text for this last statement is given as John 13:1, though there is not even the slightest suggestion of such teaching in that text. The amazing thing is that after all this talk of "passing over to the Father" and of "passing over from death to life," Rome really means that the journey is from the sufferings of death to the incalculably worse sufferings of Purgatory* for an indeterminate (but very long) time.

VICARIOUS ATONEMENT
*See **Atonement**.*

VICARIOUS REPENTANCE THEORY OF THE ATONEMENT

Also known as the Theory of Sympathy and Identification; we may summarize it under the following points:

1. The only atonement necessary for sin is a perfect repentance.

2. Such a repentance from man would have been sufficient for salvation, had he been able to offer it.

3. Christ offered a perfect repentance on behalf of man and so procured forgiveness.

4. The death of Christ was merely a sympathetic entering into the Father's condemnation of sin, and as such showed the wickedness of sin and condemned it.

The theory is objectionable on various grounds:

1. It fails to see that sin makes the sinner liable to punishment.

2. It denies any objective quality in the atonement.

3. It is a contradiction in terms—repentance is a purely subjective thing and cannot be valid unless it is personal. That Christ felt and sorrowed over the sins He vicariously bore for His people is certain (Ps. 40:12), but it was impossible for Him to turn *back* to God from committed sin, for—even in bearing our sins—He had never turned *away* from Him.

4. There is not a fragment of scriptural support for it.

VIRGIN BIRTH OF CHRIST

The word of God, in setting forth the doctrine of the incarnation,* emphasizes the fact that the humanity of Christ was produced in the womb of the Virgin Mary by the supernatural activity of the Holy Spirit.

Thus, Jesus was born without a human father. Not only so, "but no coitus of any kind, natural or supernatural, took place. The virgin birth was a special miracle wrought by the Third Person of the Trinity, whereby the Second Person of the Trinity, the eternal Son of God, took to Himself a genuine and complete human nature, and

was born as a man, without surrendering in any way His complete divine nature" *(Baker's Dictionary of Theology).*

Textual Proofs of Virgin Birth

The scripture proof of this doctrine is full and final.

Genesis 3:15: "I will put enmity between thee and the woman, and between thy seed and her seed; it shall bruise thy head, and thou shalt bruise his heel."

This verse records God's curse on the serpent (Satan, Rev. 12:9; 20:2) and most commentators acknowledge it as the *protevangelium,** the first intimation of the gospel after the fall,* though some rationalists have insisted that it speaks of nothing more than man's aversion to snakes! In this first gospel promise, God speaks of one who would crush the serpent's—that is, Satan's—head. He calls that one the "seed of the woman." Thus conservative scholars generally see Gen. 3:15 either as a direct prophecy of Christ the virgin-born redeemer, or as a prophecy that has its full and final meaning in Christ.

Henry Cooke, one of Irish Presbyterianism's most famous sons, wrote, "The principal part of Satan's curse lay in the ruin brought on him by Jesus Christ, the eminent 'seed of the woman,' in his redemption of mankind. Jesus Christ is called the 'seed of the woman,' not only to import the reality of his manhood…but chiefly to signify that he was none of Adam's natural posterity represented in the covenant of works, and that he would be born of a virgin" *(Interpreter's Bible).*

The LXX* clearly identifies the seed of the woman as a single person. It uses the masculine pronoun *autos* rather than a neuter, although grammatical agreement with *sperma,* "seed," would require a neuter. It would appear that the LXX translator chose to be grammatically incorrect in order to emphasize the individual identity of the promised seed.

Some expositors object to seeing the *seed of the woman* as a reference to Christ, at least in a primary sense. H. C. Leupold argues that since "the seed of the serpent" must mean the children of the evil one—that is, a number or class of wicked people (John 8:44)— "the seed of the woman" must refer to another number or class of people who oppose them. The weakness in this exegesis is that those who are called the seed of the serpent are as much the seed of the woman as those who oppose them. And Leupold himself shows that God speaks of the seed of the woman as *he,* clearly a reference to an individual.

It could be just as cogently argued that since the seed of the woman is certainly an individual, the seed of the serpent must refer to another, antagonistic, individual. Paul identified one who is preeminently "the man of sin"* (2 Thess. 2:3), and John spoke of "the beast," empowered by Satan (Rev. 13:2). There is no insuperable difficulty in seeing *the seed of the woman* as Christ the virgin-born Saviour, whether we identify the seed of the serpent as sinners who are of their father the devil, or as the antichrist.*

Another objection to identifying *the seed of the woman* as a prophecy of Christ's virgin birth arises from the fact that in Gen. 24:60, Rebekah's family refer to the children they expect her to bear as "thy seed." In a similar construction in Gen. 16:10 the angel of the Lord promises Hagar, "I will multiply thy seed exceedingly." Obviously there is no hint of a virgin birth in such references. J. Barton Payne strongly makes the point that this prohibits us seeing the "seed of the woman" in Gen. 3:15 as a reference to the virgin birth.

In fact Payne's argument misses the point. The question is not whether the word *seed,* when described as a woman's must always mean a virgin birth. Clearly that is not the case. The real question is what it means in the context of God's curse on the serpent. In the other texts there is no intention to teach anything but that in Hagar and Rebekah seed

from a man will produce children. In either case the seed is not really theirs at all, except in the sense that they receive it. But is that the case in Gen. 3:15? Here *seed* appears practically as a personal identification. The promised deliverer, or redeemer who would crush Satan's head at the cost of personal suffering, bears the title, "the seed of the woman." That denotes something unique about his birth. As the seed of the woman, he is, in Paul's phrase, "made of a woman" (Gal. 4:4). He is not the product of any sexual union between his mother and a man, or the product of the Holy Spirit's* implantation of a divine seed in the womb of his mother. The *seed* from which his humanity arises belongs to his mother. That is the import of this first gospel promise.

Isaiah 7:14: "The Lord himself shall give you a sign; behold, a virgin shall conceive, and bear a son, and shall call his name Immanuel."

According to Matt. 1:23, this is a prophecy of a virgin birth that received its fulfilment in the virgin birth of Christ. However, rationalistic scholars deny that Isaiah makes any reference to Christ or His virgin birth here. They hold that Matthew simply accommodated Isaiah's statement to his own purpose. They support their contention with two arguments:

The Meaning of Virgin *in Isaiah 7:14.* Rationalists' first argument is based on the Hebrew word translated "virgin." It is *'almah,* not *bethulah,* the word they claim to be the technical term for virgin. They argue that *'almah* merely denotes a young woman, not necessarily a virgin. Thus, Isaiah's statement is that a young woman would bear a son conceived in a perfectly natural and normal way.

There are strong arguments against this view—arguments which show that *'almah,* not *bethulah,* is the technical term for virgin. The following points will demonstrate that it is, at least, the only word that without any qualification means "virgin."

First, *'almah* is never used in Scripture of a young woman who is married or of one who is demonstrably not a virgin.

Second, *'almah* never needs any explanatory statement to denote virginity. "Damsel," *na'arah,* may need to have *bethulah* alongside to leave no doubt that it is describing a virgin. This is never so of *'almah.* In Gen. 24, all three words are used of Rebekah (*bethulah,* v. 16; *'almah,* v. 43; *na'arah,* v. 16, 57). However *bethulah* and *'almah* are not placed in apposition: unlike *na'arah, 'almah* does not need *bethulah* to prove it refers to a virgin, whereas *na'arah* may. A *na'arah* may or may not be a virgin (Deut. 22:20, 23) but there is not the slightest suspicion in Scripture that an *'almah* is anything other than a virgin.

Third, in Gen. 24:16 *bethulah* is followed by the explanation, "neither had any man known her." If *bethulah* is the technical term for virgin, this is tautology. Of course, tautology may be used to emphasize the point of Rebekah's virgin purity but it is just as possible that since both *na'arah* and *bethulah* (both of which appear in the verse) may sometimes be used of one who is married, or no longer a virgin, the explanatory clause is necessary to establish Rebekah's virginity.

Fourth, while commentators routinely claim that a *bethulah* is always a virgin, Joel 1:8 uses it of a young woman who had lost "the husband of her youth." It may be argued, but not proved, that this refers to an espoused wife who had not begun to cohabit with her husband. The fact remains that *bethulah* is here a description of a married woman and that fact alone is sufficient reason for not using it in Isa. 7:14. If opponents of the virgin birth have mounted such an attack on the word *'almah,* which is never associated with one in the married state, what would they not have said if *bethulah* had been used? Joel 1:8 would undoubtedly have appeared as a proof text that nothing more than a young married woman was intended!

On the use of *'almah,* J. A. Alexander said, "A virgin or unmarried woman is designated here as distinctly as she could be by a single word....That the word means simply a *young woman,* whether married or unmarried, a virgin or a mother, is a subterfuge invented by the later Greek translators" *(Commentary on Isaiah).*

Scope of the Prophecy. Rationalists' second line of argument concerns the scope of the text in its context. They hold that vv. 15 and 16 show that the child spoken of in v. 14 was to be a sign to Ahaz and that he would grow up in a time of privation and affliction in Judah. Before he would "know to refuse the evil, and choose the good," Israel and Syria, Judah's enemies, would be forsaken. The sole meaning of the promise, therefore, is that a young woman in Judah who was then pregnant would soon give birth, and before her son had reached the age of accountability, Judah would have relief from her foes.

However, insuperable difficulties surround this interpretation of the text.

1. A natural birth could not be a *sign* in the sense of the Hebrew *'oth,* which the context leads us to expect. Both Alexander and J. Barton Payne *(The Theology of the Older Testament)* rightly stress this point. The *sign* here is a *supernatural* sign. "This presumption is strengthened by the solemnity with which the Prophet speaks of the predicted birth, not as a usual and natural event, but as something that excites his own astonishment, as he beholds it in prophetic vision" (Alexander).

2. Parallel passages in Isaiah indicate that 7:14 does not speak of a merely natural birth. The terms of Isa. 8: 8; 9:6 point to a supernatural birth.

3. The combination of the idea of virginity in *'almah* with that of childbearing implies a miraculous birth.

4. "The name *Immanuel,* although it might be used to signify God's providential presence merely (Ps. 46:8, 12; 89:25; Josh. 1:5;

Jer. 1:8; Isa. 43:2), has a latitude and pregnancy of meaning which can scarcely be fortuitous, and which, combined with all the rest, makes the conclusion almost unavoidable, that it was here intended to express a *personal* as well as a *providential* presence. If to this we add the early promise of the *seed of the woman* (Gen. 3:15), rendered more definite by later revelations, and that remarkable expression of Isaiah's contemporary prophet Micah (5:2), *until the time that she which travaileth hath brought forth,* immediately following the promise of a *ruler,* to be born in Bethlehem, but whose *goings forth have been of old, from everlasting–* the balance of probabilities, as furnished by the Old Testament exclusively, preponderates decidedly in favour of the supposition, that Isaiah's words had reference to a miraculous conception and nativity" (Alexander).

5. The NT use of the text is not a mere accommodation of Isaiah's language to a use the prophet had not intended. Matthew 1:23 is a strict quotation that gives the full native force of Isaiah's words.

How was the Virgin Birth a Sign to Ahaz? Orthodox scholars have suggested various ways in which a promise of the virgin birth of Christ could have been a sign to Ahaz. Calvin and others have supposed that the Isaiah passage speaks of two distinct births and two distinct children, usually identified as Isaiah's son Shearjashub and Christ. According to this view, v. 14 teaches that Christ would be born of a virgin, while vv. 15, 16 refer to Shearjashub and promise that before he became old enough to distinguish good from evil Judah would be delivered. This approach appears to be a very contrived and artificial exegesis. As Alexander remarked, "Nothing but extreme exegetical necessity could justify the reference of verses 15, 16 to any person not referred to in v. 14."

Others, such as Albert Barnes in his *Notes,* see a double sense in the prophecy, one referring to a natural birth in Isaiah's day and

the other to the supernatural virgin birth of Christ. Proponents believe they have scriptural warrant for their view because the context in Isaiah speaks of a deliverance during the early years of a child born in the reign of Ahaz, while Matthew assures us that Isaiah's ultimate meaning was that Christ, the real deliverer of His people, would be born of a virgin. The problem with this view is that it makes the same words describe both a perfectly natural birth and a supernatural birth. This double sense is improbable and, without clear scriptural authority, unjustifiable.

Others refer Isaiah's prophecy entirely to Christ's birth. Matthew's quotation favours this approach. It recognizes only one child in the prophecy, the Messiah. Critics of this view pose two questions: how could something so remote in time as the birth of Christ be a sign to Ahaz, and how can v. 16, which predicts the fall of the kings of Syria and Israel during the infancy of the promised child, refer to one born 700 years later?

The first of these questions poses no great difficulty. In Scripture, events that are yet in the more or less remote future are set forth as signs. Exodus 3:12 makes the promise that Israel would worship God at Sinai, a sign to Moses of their deliverance from Egypt. Isa. 37:30 makes the future tillage of the ground a sign to Hezekiah of Sennacherib's imminent removal from Judah. At the second coming of Christ "the sign of the Son of man" appears in the heavens (Matt. 24:30) and this coming has always been a spur to holiness to saints (1 John 3:2, 3) and a warning to sinners (Acts 17:31). Similarly, the promised birth of Christ, of the line of David, could well have served as a sign to Ahaz that his two foes would not succeed in destroying his kingdom.

The second question—how v. 16 relates to the birth of Christ—is much more difficult. Vitringa (1669-1722) suggested that Isaiah was speaking hypothetically: if Messiah were to be born now, before He could grow to an age when He could discern good from evil, Judah's enemies would fall. Hengstenberg took a similar line, only he understood Isaiah to be speaking in ideal terms: all the blessings of God's people were bestowed through Christ and so the prophet ascribed this deliverance to His birth, which he saw in prophetic vision, as if it were already happening. These are ingenious suggestions but there is nothing at all to indicate that Isaiah was speaking either hypothetically or ideally.

Other solutions rest on the fact that when Ahaz refused to ask for a sign, the Lord gave one not only to him, but to the whole house of David. There is a significant change from the singular *thee* to the plural *you*. The Lord directs Ahaz, "Ask *thee* a sign" (v. 11). When he refused, the Lord addressed His promise to the house of David: "The Lord Himself will give *you* [plural] a sign." Thus, He gave a sign that would both speak to Ahaz and be capable of fulfilment only by the virgin birth of Christ. It was so worded that Ahaz could receive it and adjust his life in the light of it. In fact, its fulfilment lay far in the future under circumstances Ahaz could not have foreseen.

Liberals object that the deliverance of Judah from the kings of Israel and Syria was to take place during the infancy of the child Isaiah described. Thus, the promise could not have been intended as a prophecy of Christ, for He was not born for some 700 years. Conservatives usually respond that the text prophesies that Judah's deliverance would occur *"before* the child shall know to refuse the evil, and choose the good." Though Ahaz was not to know it, the predicted event was centuries away. The kings of Israel and Syria had certainly perished before that.

Perhaps a better way of understanding Isaiah's meaning is by noting his use of the grammatical form known as *futurum instans*. The particle *hinneh,* "behold," is used with a participle—a grammatical device employed

in prophecy to denote the imminency of the prophesied event. The force of the words of Isa. 7:14 therefore is, "A virgin is already pregnant and is about to bear a son." Looking on the birth of Immanuel as imminent, Isaiah announces the time of Judah's deliverance: it will take place within the time span of His growing to the age of discernment. In just such a time (two or three years, 734-732 B.C.) Judah was indeed delivered of her two great foes. Thus, the *length of time the child would take to reach the age of discernment* was the part of the prophecy that directly related to Ahaz, not His *actual birth.* On the other hand, the virgin-born child was the sign, not to Ahaz, but to the house of Judah.

However orthodox scholars differ on how to relate the prophecy to Ahaz's circumstances, they all see Isaiah's great prophecy as a prediction of the miraculous virgin birth of Christ.

Matthew 1:23: "Behold, a virgin shall be with child, and shall bring forth a son, and they shall call his name Emmanuel, which being interpreted is, God with us."

This NT quotation of Isa. 7:14 not only validates the view that Isaiah prophesied the virgin birth of Christ but also establishes the historical fact of it as the basis of the gospel. According to Matthew's record Mary was a *parthenos,* "virgin," when she gave birth to Jesus. In the case of *parthenos,* its sole meaning is indisputably "virgin." Before Mary and her espoused husband Joseph came together, she "was found with child of the Holy Ghost" (v. 18). The angel of the Lord assured Joseph, "That which is conceived in her is of the Holy Ghost" (v. 20). This is the basis of the assertion that this birth fulfils the prophecy of Isaiah 7:14.

Luke 1:27-35: The angelic announcement to the Virgin Mary that she would bear a son left her perplexed for she had not known a man (v. 34). "And the angel answered and said unto her, The Holy Ghost shall come upon thee, and the power of the

Highest shall overshadow thee: therefore also that holy thing which shall be born of thee shall be called the Son of God" (v. 35). That the text here intends to teach a virgin birth is beyond question.

That does not stop rationalistic scholars and a certain class of textual critics from seeking to weaken the force of the testimony of Matthew and Luke. For example, the *Revised Standard Version* in a footnote to Matt. 1:16a states: "Other ancient authorities read *Joseph, to whom was betrothed the Virgin Mary, was the father of Jesus who is called Christ.*" Moffat's translation adopts this reading, but the truth of the matter is, as even the translators of the *New English Bible* admit in their footnote, that there is only a single Greek manuscript in which this reading is found. The integrity of the text of Matt. 1, with its attestation of the virgin birth, is unimpeachable.

A more serious attack has been made on the integrity of Luke 1:5-2:52. This passage is crucial. Deniers have maintained that the idea of the virgin birth was derived from pagan sources, but J. Gresham Machen conclusively showed that the passage in question "is strikingly Jewish and Palestinian both in form and content."

The question deniers of the virgin birth must face is: How could such a pagan idea have found its way into "the most strikingly Jewish and Palestinian narrative in the whole New Testament"? The rationalist answer is that though the passage is of Palestinian origin, the attestation to the virgin birth is a later interpolation into Luke's text. Machen disposed of this theory in his work *The Virgin Birth of Christ* (chapter 6, "The Integrity of the Lucan Narrative") and showed that there is no ground, other than rationalistic prejudice, to question the right of Luke 1:34, 35 to its place in the original text of Luke's gospel.

Galatians 4:4: "When the fulness of the time was come, God sent forth his Son, made of a woman, made under the law."

The force of the verb *exapostello* is that God *commissioned* His Son to go out from Him to redeem His people. This is the equivalent of the statements of John 1:1, 14, the Son "was with God," "was God," and "was made flesh." Paul explains how He was made flesh: "He was made of a woman." The verb here is *ginomai,* and it means "became," or "got to be" (Lenski). Lexicons and theological dictionaries routinely give "be born" as a primary meaning and cite Gal. 4:4 as proof. Most modern English translations (NEB, RSV, NASB, NIV, GNB, Amplified) translate *genomenon ek gunaikos* "born of a woman." But this is a clear mistranslation. Had that been Paul's statement he would have used *gennethenta,* not *genomenon.* The Greek text means that the Son whom God commissioned to go out from Him "became out of a woman" in executing His mission.

Lenski defends the interpretation that takes "made of a woman" as a description of Christ's virgin birth: "The phrase [*of a woman*] denotes more than the separation from the womb, it includes the entire human nature of the Son as this was derived from his human mother. The word *genomenon* is exactly the proper word to express this thought, even the tense is very accurate. The Son's going out from God on his mission is seen in his becoming man. He did not cease to be the Son of God when he became man. He did not drop his deity, which is an impossible thought. He remained what he was and added what he had not had, namely a human nature, derived out of a woman, a human mother. He became the God-man."

1 Timothy 3:16: "Without controversy great is the mystery of godliness: God was manifest in the flesh, justified in the Spirit, seen of angels, preached unto the Gentiles, believed on in the world, received up into glory."

While Paul does not here discuss the virgin birth as such, he states the mystery and miracle of the incarnation in terms that are certainly consonant with it and incompatible with any notion that Christ was born by natural generation. (For a discussion of the text of this verse *see* **Textual Criticism of the New Testament**.)

Hebrews 10:5: "When he cometh into the world, he saith, Sacrifice and offering thou wouldest not, but a body hast thou prepared me."

Prepared is the verb *katartizo,* which has the idea "to frame" (Heb. 11:3), "to fit," (Rom. 9:22), or "to perfect," (1 Thess. 3:10; Heb. 13:21). In the NT this *preparing a body* is unique to the body of Christ. It describes the direct action of God to frame that body in the womb of the virgin Mary. While it is true that every man should praise God that his body is the result of divine skill and work (Ps. 139:15), the special, direct action to which Heb. 10:5 refers, sets the birth of Christ apart from all others. His body was not the result of an ovum fertilized by any man's seed. It was made by God of the substance of Mary alone. That is a virgin birth.

"Made of a Woman"

It is vitally important to remember that Christ's humanity was made of the substance of the Virgin Mary. The Nicene Creed says that He was incarnate by the Holy Ghost *of* the Virgin Mary. The *Westminster Confession of Faith* says that He was conceived "by the power of the Holy Ghost, in the womb of the virgin Mary, *of her substance."* It is essential to maintain this if we are to hold unimpaired the cardinal doctrine of Christ's real humanity. He came of the lineage of Abraham and of the seed of David (Rom. 9:5; 1:3). Since He had no human father this could be true only if His humanity was made of the substance of Mary.

Some evangelicals have imagined a kind of heavenly humanity for Christ. Some describe the virgin birth in terms that make the Holy Spirit "the father of Christ's humanity." There is nothing of this in Scripture. The Holy Spirit did not supply the place of a man

to impregnate Mary. That is a heathen, not a Christian, idea.

In an attempt to protect the truth of the sinlessness of Christ, some teach that Mary contributed nothing to the body and blood of the babe developing in her womb. They view Mary nothing more than a channel God used to bring into the world the human body and soul He had created independently of her substance. These are dangerous views. They contradict the plain statements of Scripture. They effectively deny the true humanity of Christ by making his human nature some new species. Thus they imperil the entire Biblical scheme of salvation in which our Saviour and Substitute is one with us in our humanity, though not in our depravity.

The scriptural doctrine of Christ's humanity being made from the substance of Mary by the supernatural action of the Holy Ghost in no way legitimizes the use of the title *Mother of God* for Mary, nor does it support the notion of her immaculate conception.*

Protestant theologians used to speak of the *sanctification* of the human nature of Christ in the womb of the virgin. This language appears a little dubious, or ambiguous. It carries the unintended suggestion that there was a period, however brief, when Christ's human nature, which never existed for an instant except in union with His divine nature, was less than sinless. That is an utterly unacceptable suggestion, however unintended it may be. Not for an instant was the human nature of Christ anything but impeccably sinless.

Luke 1:35 seems to suggest that the Holy Ghost so acted upon Mary's substance that what was born of her was sinless and absolutely pure. Thus it was *her substance* that was sanctified, not the humanity of Christ. We do not know the exact nature of the miracle performed on the substance of the Virgin Mary, but it was sufficient to produce the supernatural result, a virgin-born Saviour (Luke 1:35).

VOLUNTARISM

1. In the discussion of the relation of morality to the authority of God, it is the doctrine that a principle derives its moral imperative from the fact that God wills it, not from the fact that it reflects His moral nature. This has serious implications in the doctrine of the atonement.*

Samuel Rutherford expressed his voluntarist view that God could have pardoned sin without an atonement had He so willed. This is scholastic trifling because God cannot will contrary to His moral nature, for to *will* sin is to be as guilty of sin as *committing* the act willed (Matt. 5:27, 28). The divine will that establishes moral good necessarily expresses God's moral perfection.

2. In soteriology,* it is the doctrine of the free will* understood in Arminian terms; or the notion that saving faith is "a personal encounter," or a personal trust, without reference to the Biblical content of the faith. In other words, it is a form of subjectivism and irrationalism* in which faith is the exercise of the will to reach out to God without the engagement of the understanding to grasp and receive the truths of the gospel set forth in Scripture.

VOLUNTARYISM

The belief that church membership is a free association of like-minded Christians in churches that are free from all state control. It is the opposite principle to that of the folk church* and contends for individual liberty to form churches and worship according to the dictates of conscience.

VULGATE

The translation of the Bible into Latin, attributed to Jerome (*circa* A.D. 342-420).

WALDENSES

According to most standard histories, the followers of Peter Waldo (G. P. Fisher, *The Reformation,* p. 56; Will Durant, *The Reformation,* p. 505; Tim Dowley, editor, *The History of the Christian Church,* p. 315). This view traces the origin of the Waldenses to France in the late 12th century. Certainly they were evident in France at that time, and Peter Waldo was a notable leader of the Poor Men of Lyon (so called because they repudiated the effete luxury of the clergy and exemplified the virtues of poverty). However, there is convincing evidence that the Waldenses represent, not a late 12th-century revolt against Rome, but a very ancient Christian witness to the purity of the gospel.

In his *History of Protestantism,* J. A. Wylie says, "The Waldenses stand apart and alone in the Christian world. Their place on the surface of Europe is unique; their position in history is not less unique; and the end appointed them to fulfil is one which has been assigned to them alone, no other people being permitted to share it with them.

"The Waldenses bear a twofold testimony. Like the snow-clad peaks amid which their dwelling is placed, which look down upon the plains of Italy on the one side, and the provinces of France on the other, this people stand equally related to primitive ages and modern times, and give by no means equivocal testimony respecting Rome and the Reformation. If they are old, then Rome is new; if they are pure, then Rome is corrupt; and if they have retained the faith of the apostles, it follows incontestably that Rome has departed from it. That the Waldensian faith and worship existed many centuries before Protestantism arose is undeniable; the proofs and monuments of this fact lie scattered over all the histories and all the lands of mediæval Europe; but the antiquity of the Waldenses is the antiquity of Protestantism. The Church of the Reformation was in the loins of the Waldensian Church ages before the birth of Luther" (Book 16, chap. 1).

For just how many centuries the Waldensian church existed before the Reformation is not clear, but there is good reason to believe that its history goes back to at least the eighth or ninth century. Indeed it may represent the unbroken continuation of Biblical Christianity that maintained the purity of the gospel in an age when Rome increasingly departed from the truth. Wylie dates the Waldensian *Nobla Leyçon* to the year 1100, though others suggest 1200 or even 1400 (see Philip Schaff, *The Creeds of Christendom,* 1:571). Wylie contends that this poem is a confession of faith which exhibits a deep knowledge of the doctrines of the gospel in opposition to the errors of Rome. If Wylie's dating is accurate, the *Nobla Leyçon* argues strongly for the antiquity of the Waldensian church, for it would be incredible that this church should come into existence in the 12th century with such a systematic statement of pure theology already in place. Wylie gives further reason to believe that the Waldensian history stretches back before the ninth century:

"Their greatest enemies, Claude Seyssel of Turin (1517), and Reynerius the Inquisitor (1250), have admitted their antiquity, and stigmatized them as 'the most dangerous of all heretics, because the most ancient.' Rorenco, Prior of St. Roch, Turin (1640), was employed to investigate the origin and antiquity of the Waldenses, and of course had access to all the Waldensian documents in the ducal archives, and being their bitter enemy he may be presumed to have made his report no more favourable than he could help. Yet he states that 'they were not a new sect in the ninth and tenth centuries, and that Clause of Turin must have detached them from the church in the ninth century'" (Book 1, chap. 6).

Rome branded the Waldenses schismatics and Manicheans* and launched against them the most prolonged and bloody persecution in which she ever engaged. Philip Schaff summarized the sufferings of what he termed *the Israel of the Alps:* "In 1209, Otto IV issued an edict of banishment and in 1220 Thomas, count of Savoy, threatened with fines all showing them hospitality. But their hardy industry made them valuable subjects and for a hundred years there was no persecution in the valleys unto death. The first victim at the stake perished, 1312.

"Innocent VIII, notorious for his official recognition of witchcraft, was the first papal persecutor to resort to rigorous measures. In 1487, he announced a crusade, and called upon Charles VIII of France and the duke of Savoy to execute the decree. Everything the Waldenses had endured before, as Leger says, was as 'roses and flowers' compared with what they were now called upon to suffer. Innocent furnished an army of eighteen thousand. The Piedmontese Waldenses were forced to crouch up higher into the valleys, and were subject to almost incredible hardship. The most bitter sufferings of this Israel of the Alps were reserved for the sixteenth and seventeenth centuries, after they had accepted the Reformation. It was of the atrocious massacres perpetrated at that time that Milton exclaimed: 'Avenge, O Lord, thy slaughtered saints, Whose bones lie scattered on the Alpine mountains cold.'" (*History of the Christian Church*, 5:212).

The primitive Waldensian creed is preserved in the *Nobla Leyçon*. Wylie says that Waldensian theology "was drawn from the Bible. The atoning death and justifying righteousness of Christ was its cardinal truth. This, the *Nobla Leyçon* and other ancient documents abundantly testify. The *Nobla Leyçon* sets forth with tolerable clearness the doctrine of the Trinity, the fall of man, the incarnation of the Son, the perpetual authority of the Decalogue as given by God, the need of Divine grace in order to [do] good works, the necessity of holiness, the institution of the ministry, the resurrection of the body, and the eternal bliss of heaven.…They held substantially what the apostles before their day and the Reformers after it, taught" (Book 1, chap. 7).

The Waldenses were a Bible people. There is evidence that they possessed the NT in the vernacular. It was most probably Peter Waldo who financed and superintended the earliest complete and literal translation of the NT not later than 1180. The Waldenses transcribed and spread this translation of the Scriptures far and wide.

When they heard of the Reformation in Germany and Switzerland the Waldenses were elated. They sent deputies to the Reformers in both places. In 1530 they met with Ecolampadius in Basel and presented him with a document in Latin detailing their doctrine and church order. They requested his judgment on the scripturalness of their positions and asked for a specific statement of the nature and extent of anything defective in them. They did the same on meeting Martin Bucer in Strasbourg, Germany. The Reformers welcomed the Waldensian pastors but warned them of a compromising softness that had appeared in their dealings with Rome. In 1532 the Waldenses and the Reformed churches of Switzerland met and produced a *Short Confession of Faith*, thereby marking the unity of the ancient witness of the Waldensian church with the new witness of the Reformation.

The union brought new life and vigour to the Waldenses. It also brought ever increasing persecution. By 1686, persecution had all but eradicated all traces of Waldensian life and witness. After indescribable butchery, the prisoners who remained in Piedmontese gaols were released and sent into exile. In the dead of an Alpine winter they made their way to Geneva where the first of them arrived on Christmas Day 1686. Many had perished on the journey. Only 3,000 remained as a remnant of the ancient Waldensian church. Geneva welcomed them, but soon they longed to return to their beloved valleys. Despite opposition from their Protestant hosts and the might of French arms, they fought their way back to their ancient homeland where, because of a grand league of Britain, Germany, Spain, and Holland against France, by 1690 they were finally and peacefully settled.

WELTANSCHAUUNG

German, meaning "worldview."*

WESLEYANISM

The Methodist Arminianism* espoused by John Wesley and adopted by the Methodist churches that followed his leadership.

WESTMINSTER STANDARDS

The productions of the Westminster Assembly of Divines which met in Westminster Abbey from 1643 to 1648. The *Westminster Confession of Faith,* with the *Larger* and *Shorter Catechisms,* has ever since formed the confessional standards of Presbyterianism* and, with some modification in areas of church government, of the Congregational churches. It was also the basis on which the *Baptist Confession* of 1689 was constructed. In other words, it is the essential statement of faith of the Protestant dissenters, whatever their differences on non-essentials.

The *Westminster Standards* are remarkable for their conciseness, lucidity, and strict adherence to Scripture. The first answer in the *Shorter Catechism* expresses the fundamental outlook of the Westminster divines:

"Man's chief end is to glorify God, and to enjoy him for ever." It develops this theme in two main sections. We may loosely term them *doctrinal* and *practical,* though in truth they are theological throughout. In the first 38 entries the *Catechism* gives succinct Scriptural answers to questions about God, the divine decree, creation, providence, man, the covenant of works, the fall, and the covenant of grace. This last subject leads to an exposition of the person, offices, and work of Christ the sole Redeemer and Mediator, including the fruits of that work in the salvation of all His believing people.

The second main division of the *Catechism* expounds the law* of God, shows its curse upon sinful man, explains the only way of salvation by grace through faith in Christ, and finally sets forth the means of grace. In this last section it carefully establishes the evangelical Calvinist view of the sacraments and ends with an examination of the Lord's Prayer.

The first chapter in the *Confession of Faith* sets out the basis for every other adopted in the *Westminster Standards.* This chapter, "Of the Holy Scripture," is the classic statement of the Protestant view of Scripture.

The *Confession* takes a strict view of the inspiration and authority of the Bible. Scripture is "immediately inspired by God" (sec. 8). Its authority *rests on the basis of this fact* (sec. 4), though "our full persuasion and assurance of the infallible truth, and divine authority thereof, is from the inward work of the Holy Spirit, bearing witness by and with the Word in our hearts" (sec. 5).

Section six emphasizes the Protestant doctrine of the completeness of Scripture: "The whole counsel of God, concerning all things necessary for his own glory, man's salvation, faith, and life, is either expressly set down in Scripture, or by good and necessary consequence may be deduced from Scripture: unto which nothing at any time is to be added, whether by new revelations of the Spirit, or traditions of men." The *Confession* stresses that

437

the inward work of the Spirit is necessary for the saving understanding of the Scripture and that God's word does not address every detail of personal or church life. In such cases we must be guided "by light of nature and Christian prudence, according to the general rules of the Word" *(see Regulative Principle)*.

This section is as vital today as when it was first written. Truth is challenged from many sides. Two prominent challengers are tradition and fanaticism. Rome still maintains tradition as the equal of Scripture while Charismatics and Pentecostalists inject new "revelations" as authoritative guides to Christian living.

Section seven maintains the doctrine of the perspicuity of Scripture: "All things in Scripture are not alike plain in themselves nor alike clear unto all; yet all those things which are necessary to be known, believed, and observed, for salvation, are so clearly propounded and opened in some place of Scripture or other, that not only the learned, but the unlearned, in a due use of the ordinary means, may attain unto a sufficient understanding of them."

The *Confession* adopts the position that God has "by his singular care and providence" preserved the authentic Hebrew and Greek text of His word and that it is to the Scripture in its original language, not in any translation, that we must appeal as the final court of judgment in any matter" (sec. 8).

With the basis for all theological discussion carefully laid, the *Confession* proceeds to set forth eminently scriptural statements of the great doctrines of historic Christianity. It starts with a beautifully constructed statement of the doctrine of the Trinity. This view of God colours everything that follows as the discussion moves to the doctrines of God's decree, creation, providence, the fall of man, the covenant of grace, and the mediation of Christ with all its fruitful results. Each chapter is admirable but the statements on God's eternal decree (chap. 3) and on Christ the Mediator (chap. 8) are particularly excellent. The careful adherence to Scripture's own *ordo salutis* is clear in the treatment of the application of redemption (chap. 9-18).

The balance of the *Confession* in dealing with many difficult subjects is constantly evident. Its framers were consistent in their refusal to go beyond Scripture. They did not indulge in needless speculation or in a party spirit.

The fulness of the *Confession* is in vivid contrast to the almost meaningless brevity that marks the statements of faith produced by churches and para-church organizations today. Because of its eminently full and scriptural treatment of the important subjects it covers, it provides a good basis on which to judge ecumenical attempts to bridge the gulf between Protestantism and Romanism. All too often these proceed on the basis of a deliberate ambiguity of language or a recognized difference of understanding of terms. This is not agreement but a deliberate masking of differences under equivocal language. The *Westminster Standards,* the quintessence of Protestant theology, furnishes a safeguard against all such ecumenical duplicity.

John Murray mentions another reason for maintaining the place of the *Confession* in the modern church: "The flabby sentimentality so widespread is not hospitable to the rigour and vigour of a document like the Confession. Its system of truth and way of life do not comport with current patterns of thought and behaviour. This is the reason for the collapse of the religious and moral standards which our Christian faith represents. It is folly to think that we can retain or reclaim Christian culture on any lower level than that which the Westminster Assembly defined. Christian thought may never be stagnant. When it ceases to be progressive, it declines. But we do not make progress by discarding our heritage. We build upon it or, more accurately, we grow from it.

"Oftentimes it is pleaded that the Christian message must be adapted to the modern man. It is true that the message must be proclaimed to modern man, and to modern man in the context in which he lives and in language he can understand. But it is much more true and important that modern man must be adapted to the gospel. It is not true that the doctrine of the Confession is irrelevant to the modern man. It is indeed meaningless to him until he listens to it. But when a man today becomes earnest about the Christian faith, when he gives heed to the Scriptures as the Word of God, when he faces up to the challenge of unbelieving ways of thought and life and demands the answer which Christianity provides, he cannot rest with anything less than the consistency and vigour which the Confession exemplifies. Unbelief is potent and subtle, and the believer requires the truth of God in its fullest expression if he is to be furnished to faithful witness and confession" (*Collected Works,* 1: 321, 322).

It is "the truth of God in its fullest expression" that the *Westminster Standards* seek to set forth. To an incomparable degree, they have succeeded.

WILL

One of the two basic powers of the soul, the other being the understanding.

Definition

"The will is that faculty or mode of the soul which self-determines, inclines, desires and chooses in reference to moral and religious objects and ends. These objects and ends are all centered and summed up in God....Speaking generally the voluntary and moral desires relate to God. They are either inclined or averse to Him; they are either love or hatred" (W. G. T. Shedd, *Dogmatic Theology,* 2:119). Shedd's definition rejects the idea of later psychology, that the powers of the soul are intellect, sensibility, and will. This latter analysis is defective because it fails to recognize that sensibility (i.e., moral affections and desires) belongs

to the will. It makes the mistake of limiting the activity of the will to volitional acts. Shedd's definition, on the other hand, rightly sees that inclination is voluntary, i.e., it belongs to the power of the will.

Scripture Terms

The Scripture's use of terms supports this view of the will. The NT employs three terms to denote the activity of the will: *kardia,* "heart," *thelema,* "will," and *boule,* "will" or "counsel."

Kardia: The NT includes inclination as part of the will (Rom. 1:24; 2:5; 10:9, 10; Luke 1:17). "The heart in scripture is the practical principle in the soul, and so includes the will also. It is the actual compliance of the will and affections with the mind and understanding, with respect to the objects proposed by them" (John Owen, *On the Spirit,* 3:iii).

Thelema: This denotes inclination as distinct from volition (Matt. 6:10; 7:21; Eph. 1:5; 2:3). "In these passages, the 'will' is the will of desire and delight" (Shedd, 2:129).

Boule, boulema: These denote volition, as distinct from inclination, a particular decision as distinct from the continuing disposition of the will (Luke 23:51; Acts 18:15 "will be" = "decide to be"; 19:30; 25:22; 2 Cor. 1:15).

The NT uses all these terms as definitive descriptions of the will, thereby establishing the definition with which we commenced.

Thus the will is more than the mere power of volition. It includes the desire or inclination behind the volition, for as Jonathan Edwards long ago pointed out (*Will,* 1:i), a man never wills anything contrary to his will, i.e., he does not *decide* contrary to the prevailing *inclination* of his will. Only natural or instinctive desires are involuntary; all other desire is voluntary and belongs to the power of the will.

Voluntary Inclinations

The importance of this definition is great, for it emphasizes that not only fallen man's inclinations, but his volitions as well, are sinful and culpable. Some modern psychologists think of the will not as a faculty but as an expression of the entire personality. This view, while lacking the clarity and consistency of Shedd's definition, may serve to emphasize that the entire expression of the total personality (which must include inclination as well as volition) is sinful and culpable.

In saying this we make man responsible for his inclination as well as for his volition. Sin does not consist merely in acts. We also recognize the enormity of the guilt of the great change in the human will at the fall.* Adam's sin brought about a radical and total change of inclination in the human will, disposing it toward self and away from God. That was a voluntary act, one in which we all participated (Rom. 5:12).

The selfish inclination of the fallen will of man is something in which every man naturally delights, and for which God holds him accountable. Every volition, or choice, flows from this wicked bias of the will. This bias is the *ungodliness* which produces the *unrighteousness* of Rom. 1:18. Fallen man is powerless to originate a new inclination of will. He is "free" only in the sense that he chooses according to the inclination of his will *(see **Free Will**, **Self-Determination**, **Inability**),* and a wicked inclination cannot produce godly volitions.

Thus, if a man is to be saved, God must create a new inclination or disposition. "The new man...after God is created in righteousness and true holiness (Eph. 4:24). Summarizing, we note:

1. When God first created man, He created him in righteousness and holiness. That is, He placed a positive bias toward God in his will. He did not create man sinless and then leave his will in a state of balance between good and evil.

2. The fall wrecked this bias of the will and substituted a bias toward self and sin.

3. Salvation can be experienced only when God "creates" a "new man," imparting a new disposition of will. Thus, all godly volitions, such as repentance, faith, and evangelical obedience, are the results of a sovereign, gracious work of God renewing the will—for godly volitions can never be the responses of the unregenerate will (Rom. 8:7).

WILL WORSHIP

In Col. 2:23 Paul uses a word, *ethelothreskeia,* which is unique. *Ethelo-* may imply "would-be" and denotes pretence. Paul's argument is against heretics whose parody of Christian obedience allegedly initiated devotees into higher mysteries. H. C. G. Moule (*Colossians,* pp. 115, 116) says: "The Greek compound noun denotes a self-chosen, self-imposed, service (in the religious sense); a round of supererogatory observance; a parody on the genuine reverence and obedience of the Gospel—The element in the compound represented by 'worship' is the noun used, James 1:27 (and see 26), and rendered 'religion' in our Versions."

Will-worship is now used to denote worship according to human innovation without divine authority, and by some Calvinists to denote Arminian emphasis upon the role of man's will in salvation.

WISDOM OF GOD

"That attribute of God whereby He produces the best possible results with the best possible means" (H. B. Smith).

A. A. Hodge described the divine wisdom as follows: "Knowledge is a simple act of the understanding, apprehending that a thing is, and comprehending its nature and relations, or how it is.

"Wisdom presupposes knowledge, and is the practical use which the understanding, determined by the will, makes of the material of knowledge. God's wisdom is infinite and eternal. It is conceived of by us as selecting the highest possible end, the manifestation of His own glory; and then in selecting and directing, in every department of His operations, the best possible means to secure that end. This wisdom is gloriously manifested to us in the great theatres of creation, providence, and grace."

WORD OF GOD
See *Logos*; *Scriptures*.

WORD OF GOD AS A MEANS OF GRACE

In contrast to Rome's position that the church is the all-sufficient channel of grace for sinners, Reformed theology holds that the word of God, the fountainhead of all theological knowledge, is the means employed by the Holy Spirit to bring souls to Christ and then build them up in Him. The *Shorter Catechism* (Q. 89) sums up the Reformed doctrine: "The Spirit of God maketh the reading, but especially the preaching of the Word, an effectual means of convincing and converting sinners, and of building them up in holiness and comfort, through faith, unto salvation." (Ps. 19:7; 1 Thess. 1:6; Rom. 1:16).

WORLD COUNCIL OF CHURCHES

The WCC was formed in Amsterdam, on 23rd August, 1948. In its original constitution it claimed to be "a fellowship of churches which accept our Lord Jesus Christ as God and Saviour." It later expanded this by adding the words, "according to the Scriptures and therefore seek to fulfil together their common calling, to the glory of one God, Father, Son and Holy Spirit."

Background to WCC

The WCC grew out of three organizations:

The Faith and Order Movement. In 1910 a World Missionary Conference was held in Edinburgh, one of the results of which was the formation of the Faith and Order Movement (F&O). The American Episcopal Church was the prime instigator of this movement. That is an important point, because in 1908 that church refused to have any

part in a federation of churches. It sought something more radical than mere federation. It sought "one visible Church of Christ on earth."

The vision of F&O was church union and the creation of an ecumenical vehicle for the achievement of full oneness in matters of faith and order. When its 1927 conference convened in Lausanne, Archbishop Nathan Söderblom included a paragraph in the final report that caused intense opposition. Söderblom recalled an encyclical letter issued in 1920 by the Patriarchate of Constantinople proposing a "*koinonia ton ekklesion,* a league of churches for practical purposes" (W. A. Visser 't Hooft, *The Genesis and Formation of the World Council of Churches,* p. 22). This fell short of the organic union sought by many in the F&O. Though this description remained in the report, it was seen as a possible solution to the pressing problem of interchurch relations, not as a replacement of the F&O aim of church union in matters of doctrine and discipline.

However, the emphasis on cooperative action as a means of ecumenical expression became increasingly popular in F&O and made the movement receptive to a plan to seek the formation of a new ecumenical council in conjunction with other strands of the ecumenical movement.

The Life and Work Movement. Immediately after World War I, Söderblom proposed the formation of an ecumenical organization. Visser 't Hooft, later the General Secretary of the WCC, explained his thinking: "As soon as the war was over, Söderblom began to prepare the way for a world conference of churches. In his thinking, however, this conference was not to be an end in itself, but should lead to the establishment of a permanent body, which he called 'an Ecumenical Council of Churches.' He explained the plan in an article which appeared in *The Contemporary Review* in England and in *Die Eiche* in Germany. He puts the plan in a wide context. Now that the war is over and a new period in history begun, it is time to think about the world task of Christianity. That task is first of all to manifest the universal character of the Church itself. It is furthermore to work for reconciliation, unity and peace in the relations between nations. The League of Nations will only be an empty shell unless it is filled with the Christian spirit.

"We need an evangelical catholicity which will not demand uniformity but serve and strengthen the cause of spiritual unity. A common organization must be formed, capable of representing Christendom. 'What I propose is an ecumenical council, representing the whole of Christendom, and so constructed that it can speak on behalf of Christendom.'

"For the time being, he went on to say, we cannot expect that Rome will be ready to participate. There remain two ancient offices which have special qualifications to have a place in the council, namely the Patriarchate of Constantinople and the Archbishopric of Canterbury....The time has come when we may venture to believe in the unity of Christianity and take definite measures to express the same" (*Genesis and Formation,* pp. 12, 13).

In the summer of 1920, Söderblom, the Swiss Federation, and the Federal Council of Churches in the United States combined their efforts to plan a preparatory meeting in Geneva for The Universal Christian Conference on Life and Work (L&W). While some envisaged this as a pan-Protestant conference, Söderblom was determined that it would not be so restricted. The Church of England agreed; it had no intention of joining an exclusively Protestant council. Thus L&W from the beginning included the Eastern Orthodox churches.

The emphasis of L&W was on cooperative action. The churches should act *as if* they were one. When L&W convened for the first time in Stockholm in 1925 it faced serious divisions on the plan to establish a permanent ecumenical council of churches.

The Church of England, for example, was unwilling to create a council in which the Roman Catholic church would not participate. Thus, L&W was forced to take the road of practical cooperative ecumenical activity, rather than pursue the goal of organizational unity. It sought to deal mainly with social problems and to develop united Christian activity to meet these problems.

During the early 1930's F&O became more "practical," while L&W became more "theological." Thus, the way was being paved for a union of their organization and efforts. Representatives from both movements met at Westfield College in London, July 8-10, 1937. "The first general discussion showed that there was a readiness to take two radical decisions: to bring together Life and Work and Faith and Order and to set up a fully representative assembly of the churches" ('t Hooft, pp. 39, 40).

Later in 1937, the L&W met at Oxford and the F&O at Edinburgh. Both accepted the "radical decisions" of their joint representatives: the formation of the World Council of Churches was underway. Its constitution was discussed and decided in Utrecht in 1938, and invitations to take part in establishing the WCC were sent to the 196 churches that had been invited to participate in the Oxford and Edinburgh conferences.

World War II interrupted the progress of F&O and L&W toward the establishment of the WCC. It would be another ten years before that was finally accomplished, though the "Provisional Committee for the World Council (in Process of Formation)" continued the ecumenical tasks of the two organizations that had united to form it.

The International Missionary Council. The International Missionary Council grew out of the 1910 conference in Edinburgh. It first met in 1921. It is remarkable that much of the impetus for ecumenical activity has come from the mission field. In 1927 the Anglican Bishop of Dornakal (India) told the IMC,

"Divided Christendom is a source of weakness in the West. In non-Christian lands it is a sin and a stumbling-block. If the non-Christian world is to be won for Christ our message must be one. If our message is to be one, we must be one." The bishop was stating the ecumenical movement's conviction that unity is necessary in order to present a united message to the world. That means that ecumenical churchmen must come together to discuss and formulate what they consider to be the united message of their churches. The bishop's statement was an important admission for it indicated the initial absence of agreement on the Bible's message among those who launched the ecumenical movement. The programme of ecumenism is not the unity of people who believe in the same message. It is rather the unity of people who have abandoned the message of the Bible and are trying to formulate another message.

Proof of this was furnished by a statement at an IMC meeting in Jerusalem in 1928. "The comparative science of religion has very diligently studied the non-Christian religions and made their main ideas known. Confronted by these facts many Christians dare not any longer maintain that Jesus is unique. Even missionaries have said: 'We should no longer come to the so-called heathen with the conviction that we have something better to give them. Instead of that we should place ourselves side by side with the adherents of other religions and together learn from each other.' "

When F&O and L&W were uniting, IMC stood aloof, unwilling to surrender its independence as a council whose constituents were, in many cases, missionary societies who did not wish to come under the control of the churches. Still, IMC maintained a very close relationship with the embryonic WCC.

Constitution of WCC, 1948

In Amsterdam, 1948, 147 churches from 44 countries met to form the WCC.

"All confessional families except the Roman Catholics were represented. A number of Roman Catholics had been invited to attend as observers, but they could not accept the invitation because in June the Holy Office had issued a *Monitum* to the effect that no Roman Catholic would receive permission to attend" ('t Hooft, p. 63). Visser 't Hooft told the assembly that the new council was not seeking to become a super-church, or to pursue political ends. He claimed that its purpose was to pursue the goal of "the manifestation of the One Holy Church." He continued:

"The functions of the Council follow from this situation. We are a fellowship in which the churches after a long period of ignoring each other come to know each other. We are a fellowship in which the churches enter into serious and dynamic conversation with each other about their differences in faith, in message, in order. We are a fellowship in which Christian solidarity is practised, so that churches aid their weak or needy sister churches. We are a fellowship in which common witness is rendered to the Lordship of Christ, in all matters on which a common word for the churches and for the world is given to us. We are above all a fellowship which seeks to express that unity in Christ already given to us and to prepare the way for a much fuller and much deeper expression of that unity" (p. 67).

The WCC's report of the Amsterdam meeting summarized its aims and claims:

"Christ has made us his own and he is not divided. In seeking him we find one another. Here at Amsterdam we have committed ourselves afresh to him, and have covenanted with one another in constituting this World Council of Churches. We intend to stay together. We call upon Christian congregations everywhere to endorse and fulfil this covenant in their relations one with another. In thankfulness to God, we commit the future to him."

The WCC in Action

Amsterdam's euphoria made it appear that the WCC was a fundamentally Christian organization. Visser 't Hooft's statement of the WCC's aims and functions cloaked its real design. In the years to follow, it demonstrated its lack of commitment to anything resembling evangelical Protestantism as it pursued union with Rome, became embroiled in supporting various Marxist revolutionary groups around the world, promoted radical political and feminist theology conferences, and engaged in syncretistic dialogues with heathen religions.

Pursuing Church Union. The WCC, in conjunction with the Roman Catholic Paulist Press, has published *Growth in Agreement,* a detailed report of the various agreements and approaches to agreement the WCC has sponsored among various churches. Wherever there has been agreement, it has been at the expense of Biblical, Protestant orthodoxy.

In the *Moscow Statement 1976,* the Anglicans agree with the Eastern Orthodox that "we know, receive, and interpret Scripture through the Church and in the Church" (*Growth in Agreement,* p. 41). They agree that "Holy Tradition completes Holy Scripture" and that Holy Tradition is "the entire life of the Church in the Holy Spirit. This tradition expresses itself in dogmatic teaching, in liturgical worship, in canonical discipline, and in spiritual life" (p. 42). In the *Llandaff Statement 1980,* the Anglicans further agreed with prayers for the dead, even those in hell, for "God's wrath is none other than his love" (p. 58). They also agreed that "the Blessed Virgin Mary possesses a unique place in the economy of salvation by virtue of the fact that she was chosen to be Mother of Christ our God" (p. 58).

In their conversations with the Roman Catholic church the Anglicans strove to allow some sense in which the eucharist may be accepted as a sacrifice, and accepted that failure to venerate the bread and wine contradicts the true doctrine of the eucharist (p. 69-76). They agreed that though "the New Testament contains no explicit record of a transmission of Peter's leadership...it is possible to think that a primacy of the bishop of Rome is not contrary to the New Testament and is part of God's purpose regarding the Church's unity and catholicity" (pp. 107, 108). They went even further: "We nevertheless agree that a universal primacy will be needed in a reunited Church and should appropriately be the primacy of the bishop of Rome" (p. 108).

Similar agreements have been reached between the Lutherans and Rome (to the extent of reaching a "fundamental consensus" on justification, *Ecumenical Documents 4: Building Unity* p. 274), the Methodists and Rome, and to some extent, the Reformed and Rome.

F&O has sought to accelerate the pace of ecumenical agreement. It has a strong Roman Catholic representation in its membership, for though Rome is still not a member of the WCC she cooperates with it and allows full participation in F&O. In 1982, F&O issued its Lima report on *Baptism, Eucharist, and Ministry* (BEM), which in many ways is the essence of the various ecumenical dialogues between Rome and other churches.

Ecumenism at Parish Level. In recent years the WCC has backed away somewhat from its global approach to ecumenism and its grand design of organizational unity, and has been laying a lot more emphasis on smaller, more local events. It has been paying more attention to encouraging ecumenism at parish level through its agreement on liturgy, in the belief that people who worship together will be more likely to seek ultimate union.

Approaches to Other Religions. The WCC has a vision of a unity that includes even non-Christian religions. In its sixth assembly in Vancouver, 1983, it welcomed participation by representatives of Buddhism, Hinduism, Islam, and Judaism. *Gathered for Life,* the official report of the Vancouver assembly, gives details of "a native arbour, 'a sacred meditative area among the trees.'…A sacred flame burned nearby for the duration of the assembly. Appropriately it was lighted by an elder of the Musqueam tribe.… A 15-metre high totem pole, carved by Native inmates of Agassiz Mountain Prison to symbolize humanity's spiritual quest through the ages, was raised on the campus during the Assembly. It will find a permanent home in Geneva [WCC headquarters]" (p. 15). WCC delegates participated in a worship service at the "sacred flame" each morning, thereby validating native animism and ancestor worship as authentic spirituality.

In Nairobi in 1975, at the fifth assembly, the moderator of the Central Committee asked, "Should we not make greater efforts to discern how Christ is at work in other faiths, generally in their traditional patterns and more particularly in their renewal movements which have felt the impact of Jesus Christ?" (*Breaking Barriers: Nairobi 1975*, p. 236). He even went so far as to call for cooperation with secular humanists "for a secular human culture and community, and even for a secular humanism open to insights from all religions and ideologies, evaluated in the light of and informed by the true manhood of Jesus Christ" (p. 236).

Radical Theological, Political, and Social Action. From its inception, the WCC has been deeply involved in political, social, and even revolutionary action. In his *Report of the Moderator of the Central Committee* to the fifth assembly of the WCC in Nairobi, 1975, M. M. Thomas said, "There can be no authentic theology except within responsible encounter with the contemporary world in the name of the dignity of humanity" (*Breaking Barriers: Nairobi 1975*, p. 237). This is what ecumenists mean by "doing theology," rather than "knowing theology." He advocated that "socio-analytical and ideological political criteria now become an integral part of ecclesiology" (p. 239). In plain language this means, "We have come to recognize the need for changing existing power structures" (p. 239).

The most public way in which the WCC put this socio-political theory into practice was its Programme to Combat Racism. Nothing the WCC ever did excited as much criticism as this programme. Politicians, pressmen, and even many ecumenical churches denounced it for its financial support of so-called liberation armies or groups, even some operating in the United States. The flow of WCC money to Marxist revolutionary groups finally compelled some churches, including the Presbyterian Church in Ireland, to withdraw their membership.

The WCC has also sought to include radical theological movements in its vision of church union. It has continued to sponsor conferences on feminist concerns (see *Feminist Theology*) and on a wide variety of "social justice" issues. The WCC solutions to the social and economic problems of the world were, and remain, uniformly socialist.

Challenge of WCC to Evangelicals

At first, there was little evangelical involvement in the WCC. Evangelicals correctly saw the WCC as antagonistic to the purity of the gospel. However, many evangelicals remained in membership in churches that were in the WCC, and this created both tension and compromise. After its fourth assembly in Uppsala, 1968, the WCC began an attempt to meet evangelical criticism and at times made encouraging noises about Christian evangelism and mission. When the IMC became fully integrated in the WCC it became The Commission for World Mission and Evangelism (CWME). At a CWME conference in Bankok in 1973, the theme was "Salvation Today." Its agenda was so liberal that Peter Beyerhaus, a critic of evangelical involvement in the WCC, castigated the "pan-religious and humanistic-ideological interpretation of salvation" in the conference's preparatory documents (*The Ecumenical Review*, 40:463).

After the 1974 International Congress on World Evangelization in Lausanne, there was a distinct change in the evangelical mood. The evangelicals concerned would be better termed *new-evangelical,** for they increasingly turned away from the traditional evangelical approach to what many of them had previously identified as the apostasy of the WCC. As a result, evangelicals and Roman Catholics can now proclaim a fundamentally common faith, even discovering a form of words to conceal the deep differences between evangelicalism and Romanism on justification (see *Evangelicals and Catholics Together: The Christian Mission in the Third Millennium,* a 26-page document whose evangelical signatories include Bill Bright, Os Guinness, J. I. Packer, and Pat Robertson).

Evangelicals who remain true to the Scripture on the fundamental doctrines of salvation, without compromise with the Romish perversions of those doctrines, cannot take the road of ecumenical involvement. It is impossible to be faithful to the principles of the gospel and the Protestant Reformation, and participate in the WCC either directly or indirectly through continued membership in a church affiliated with it. While many Christians seek to avoid the issue, the teaching of the word of God is too clear to be misunderstood. There can be no excuse for any Christian remaining in such a fellowship (Rom. 16:17; 2 Cor. 6:14-18; Eph. 5:11; 1 Tim. 6:3-5; 2 John 10, 11; Rev. 18:4).

WORLDVIEW

The philosophical or theological spectacles through which we view the world and all reality; the framework within which we interpret the data of the world and of life.

A Christian worldview uses the Biblical revelation* as the foundation for a proper understanding of the nature and purpose of our existence. That revelation establishes divine truth about God, man, sin,* salvation,* purpose, and our destiny. Thus both our belief and our behaviour are governed, not by changeable theories, but by God's immutable truth.

WORSHIP

The OT term *chawah* and the NT term *proskuneo* indicate "prostration" and "obeisance." In a relative sense obeisance may be offered to human dignitaries, but in a religious sense it belongs to the triune God alone (Matt. 4:10). The fact that it should be offered to Christ (Heb. 1:6; John 5:23) is a striking proof of His Deity. In a broad sense, worship describes the honour paid to the Lord in the service of His house (1 Sam. 1:3). In the narrow usage of the word, it indicates pure adoration of God, in which the worshipper is taken up with the glory of what the Lord is. "Matthew distinguishes between the presentation of gifts by the Magi to the Christ child, and their worship of Him; Matthew 2:11" *(Baker's Dictionary of Theology).*

True worship, whether in the broad or narrow sense, should be "in spirit and in truth" (John 4:24), i.e., it should be both sincere (as distinct from legalistic ritual) and scriptural, for God can be worshipped only as He has directed in His Word *(see **Regulative Principle).** The beauty of true worship is not in any aesthetically pleasing surroundings, but in holiness (Ps. 96:9).

WRATH OF GOD

"The wrath of God" is a scriptural phrase (Rom. 1:18) that describes the settled opposition of God's nature against evil, His holy displeasure against sinners, and the punishment He justly metes out to them on account of their sins.

Paul calls this punishment "the wrath to come" (1 Thess. 1:10) and describes the time of its execution as "the day of wrath" (Rom. 2:5). This punishment is denominated "endless punishment" by the Lord Jesus Christ (Matt. 25:31-33, 41, 46), in a place of "hell fire where their worm dieth not, and the fire is not quenched" (Mark 9:47, 48). There the wicked endure endless, conscious suffering (cf. Luke 16:19-31).

In view of the fact that the cults and the liberals deny the reality of such wrath in God, it is interesting to note the conclusions of A. B. Davidson, a rationalist, who on philosophical grounds rejected the idea of God's wrath inflicting endless punishment:

"If a specific sense be attached to words, never-ending misery is enunciated in the Bible. On the presumption that one doctrine is taught, it is the eternity of hell torments. Bad exegesis may attempt to banish it from the New Testament Scriptures, but it is still there, and expositors who wish to get rid of it, as Canon Farrar does, injure the cause they have in view by misrepresentation. It must be allowed that the New Testament record not only makes Christ assert everlasting punishment, but Paul and John."

Martyn Lloyd-Jones noted (*Studies in Romans,* 1:74) that in the OT alone there are more than 20 words to describe the wrath of God and these words are used in their various forms a total of 580 times. Only by rejecting the clear testimony of the Scriptures can anyone deny the awful reality of the wrath of God. It surpasses all description and imagination. "Who knoweth the power of thine anger?" (Ps. 90:11). From this text we learn that the full power of the wrath of God has never yet been manifested on earth—not in the deluge, or in the destruction of Sodom, or in any other judgment. The full fury of God's anger will be seen when "the great day of his wrath is come" and the ungodly feel the indescribable torment of "the wrath of the Lamb" (Rev. 6:16, 17).

See *Gehenna*; *Hades*; *Justice of God.*

X

XIMENES

Cardinal Ximenes, who was the head of the Spanish Inquisition,* produced a six-volume edition of the Bible in the early 16th century, known as the *Complutensian Polyglot*. He exhibited the Hebrew text of the OT, with the Latin and Greek translations, and the Greek text of the NT with the Latin translation.

XYLOLATERS

"Wood Worshippers," a term used of Eastern Orthodox believers who were given to the use of images and icons in their worship.

Y

YAHWEH

The vocalization of the tetragrammaton,[*] the divine name *JHWH,* favoured by most modern scholars in preference to *Jehovah.*

In the Hebrew consonantal text, the letters are *Yod, He, Waw, He,* which are usually transliterated *J* (or *Y*) *H V* (or *W*) *H.* When the later Jews came to read this divine name, they refused to pronounce it, because of a mistaken interpretation of Lev. 24:16. Usually they substituted the word *Adonai,* "Lord," in their reading, and when *Adonai* and *JHWH* appeared side by side they read *Elohim,* "GOD," for the latter. Most modern scholars accept the idea that the vowel points placed with *JHWH* are those of *Adonai* and do not therefore give any idea of the original pronunciation of the Name. Thus they reject *Jehovah* as the proper vocalization of *JHWH,* preferring *Yahweh.* However, O. T. Allis, who at times favours *Yahweh* admitted, "The correct pronunciation of the Name may be Yahweh. But this is not certain; and Yahweh has a decidedly strange and unnatural sound" (*The Five Books of Moses,* p. xii).

The tetragram is derived, according to Davidson (*Hebrew and Chaldee Lexicon*) and Gesenius (*Hebrew and Chaldee Lexicon*) from the verb *hawah* (or *havah*), "to be." G. L. Archer (*A Survey of Old Testament Introduction,* p. 123) holds that *hawah* is merely the original form of the verb *hayah* found in Exod. 3:14, "I AM THAT I AM." He infers that therefore the Hebrew in this text would originally have read *'aweh asher 'aweh,* instead of the *'ehyeh asher 'ehyeh* now in the text. Thus, if Moses had gone to Egypt to declare of the Lord "HE IS," he would have said, "Yahweh." This is the most convincing argument that is produced for *Yahweh* in preference to *Jehovah.* It should be said that *Yahweh* is a form that is never found in any Hebrew literature; the only evidence produced in its favour is conjecture.

It has been argued that *Jehovah* is "an impossible form" in Hebrew, but this is not so. It is unusual, but not unique, as the forms *howeh* (Ecc. 2:22) and *howah* (Ezek. 7:26) show; in both words the *waw* doubles as a consonant and a vowel, as in *Jehovah.*

There is solid evidence that *Jehovah* represents the original pronunciation, that its vowel points retain the original vocalization of the word, and that they are not the vowel points of *adonai* appended to *JHWH.*

1. The vowel points for *JHWH* and *Adonai* are not exactly the same: *Adonai* carries a composite shewa under the initial letter, *JHWH* carries a simple shewa.

2. The Masoretes did place a composite shewa under the initial *Yod* in *JHWH* when *Elohim* was to be read, for *Elohim* carried one. This indicates that though the vowel points of *JHWH* and *Adonai* are very similar, those of *Adonai* are not carried over to *JHWH.*

3. The etymology of *JHWH.* It is from the verb *hawah,* "to be." The *Jeho* of *Jehovah* comes from the future of the verb and the *vah* is an elided form of the preterite. Thus the verb *hawah* appears twice in the word, just as the cognate verb *hayah* appears twice in Exod. 3:14, with the same meaning.

4. The frequent use of *Jeho* or *Jo* as a prefix in Hebrew names (e.g., Jehoshaphat, Jehoram, etc.) indicates that *Jehovah* is the original vocalization of the divine name. In these Hebrew names, it is undoubtedly a reference to the Lord and is utterly incompatible with *Yahweh*. Both Davidson and S. P. Tregelles (commenting in his edition of Gesenius) indicate that this argument goes a long way to prove the originality of the vowel points given to *JHWH* by the Masoretes, thus establishing the vocalization *Jehovah*.

Some modern liberal scholars refer to *Yahweh* as a tribal deity, and some even name Him as a Kenite deity or the fire god of Sinai, introduced to Israel by Moses. Such blatant infidelity has not been much inhibited by the utter want of evidence to support it.

Jehovah expresses the thought of Exod. 3:14 (cf. 6:3). It has in it the idea of the Lord's self-existence. Archer denies this, holding that the verb *hayah* in Exod. 3:14 always means "to happen, become, enter into a new condition or state or relationship." Thus it is the Lord's covenant relationship which is noted, not His self-existence. Though the idea of covenant relationship is certainly included—even preeminent—self-existence, absoluteness, and immutability must also be included. In Mal. 3:6 immutability and covenant relationship are combined in the majestic statement, "I am Jehovah, I change not; therefore ye sons of Jacob are not consumed."

YEAR-DAY THEORY

In expounding prophetic Scripture, a method of interpreting time, which originated at the end of the 14th century with Walter Brute. It holds that a day means a year in some prophetic portions, and has been used by various cults to calculate (always wrongly) the date of Christ's return.

In support of the theory, advocates cite Num. 14:34, but this verse does not address the point at issue. Indeed, in saying that for every day they searched the land, the children of Israel would spend a year in the wilderness, Moses laid down a prophecy in which *years* mean *years*. On the year-day theory, Israel would still be in the wilderness and would remain there for all of 14,400 years!

Another "proof text" is Ezek. 4:4-6. S. P. Tregelles points out: "This is not a symbolic prophecy at all, but simply a symbolic action, which was commanded by God; and unless there had been the express statement we never could have known that what Ezekiel did, for so many days, really represented the actions of the same number of years. It is true that this is an instance in which a day symbolically represents a year, but the way in which this is done is wholly different from any such ground being taken as though in prophetic language the one were used for the other.

"If in this passage day meant year, or if it were to be interpreted by year, what should we find?—that Ezekiel was commanded to lie on his left side three hundred and ninety years, and on his right side forty years" (*Daniel*, p. 116).

Another passage often cited is Dan. 9:24-27. In reality it has no bearing on the question. Indeed, *week* is not a proper interpretation of the Hebrew *shabua*, which indicates merely something divided into seven parts, a *heptad* or *hebdomad*. There is no suggestion of days in it and therefore it has no bearing on the year-day theory.

Some have used Luke 13:31, 32 in support of the year-day theory. This is altogether a fanciful use of a Scripture which simply states that after three days the Lord would arrive at Jerusalem.

In every passage cited, years are years and days are days.

Having established their theory on such evidence, year-day advocates apply it as the proper interpretation of the prophecies in Dan. 7:25; 12:7; Rev. 12:14 ("time, times, and a half"); Dan. 8:14 (2,300 days); Dan. 12:11 (1, 290 days); Dan. 12:12 (1,335 days); Rev. 9:5, 10 (five months); Rev. 9:15 (one hour, day, month and year); Rev. 11:9, 11 (three and a half days); Rev. 11:2; 13:5 (42 months); Rev. 11:3; 12:6 (1,260 days).

The year-day theory is an arbitrary invention, without warrant in Scripture. It also flies directly in the face of the most careful use of language, designed to avoid any mistake about the literal nature of the expressions quoted above from the Revelation. Here the same period of time is described in three distinct ways: 1,260 days; a time, times, and a half; and 42 months. If this threefold designation of time cannot be taken to mean what it says, the task of understanding the plainest of statements becomes hopeless. Any theory that so opposes the plain statements of God's word is objectionable and dangerous.

Z

ZWICKAU PROPHETS

An Anabaptist* group, led by Thomas Müntzer, which aimed at complete social revolution as well as spiritual reform. Besides being revolutionary, the Zwickau Prophets were spiritualistic—i.e., they claimed immediate inspiration from the Holy Spirit, instead of submitting to the final authority of Scripture. They settled in Saxony and finally moved to Wittenberg, the centre of Luther's activities, though they bitterly opposed the German reformer. In 1525 Müntzer took a leading part in the ill-fated Peasants' Revolt, at the end of which he was executed.

See **Anabaptists**.

ZWINGLI, ZWINGLIANISM

Ulrich Zwingli (1484-1531) led the cause of the Reformation* in Zurich and had a powerful influence throughout German-speaking Switzerland. He opposed the sacramentalism of Rome and thus rejected Luther's view of consubstantiation.* *Zwinglianism* is usually employed to denote Zwingli's belief that Christ is spiritually present at the Lord's Supper, the celebration of which is solely a commemoration of Christ's death. *(See **Sacramentarian**.)*

Berkhof remarks that Zwingli changed his views somewhat, and while at times he spoke of the Lord's Supper as a mere sign or symbol, he also contemplated it as a seal or pledge of what God does for the believer in the sacrament. At any rate, Zwinglianism is the rejection of mysticism* and all notions of a real, or local, presence of Christ in the sacrament.

Zwingli died at the battle of Kappel, 1531, acting as chaplain to the army of Zurich, which had been attacked by the five Roman Catholic Forest Cantons of Switzerland. His death abruptly halted the progress of the Reformation in the German-speaking part of Switzerland.